JOHN E. ALSUP

THE POST-RESURRECTION APPEARANCE STORIES OF THE GOSPEL TRADITION

A history-of-tradition analysis
With Text-Synopsis

Wipf & Stock
PUBLISHERS
Eugene, Oregon

Wipf and Stock Publishers
199 W 8th Ave, Suite 3
Eugene, OR 97401

The Post-Resurrection Appearance Stories of the Gospel-Tradition
A History-of-Tradition Analysis
By Alsup, John E.

ISBN 13: 978-1-59752-970-9
ISBN: 1-59752-970-2
Publication date 9/20/2006
Previously published by Calwer Verlag, 1975

TO MY FATHER AND MOTHER
FOR A LIFETIME OF LOVING SUPPORT

PREFACE

This study wishes to exceed the boundaries of the contemporary discussion of the Resurrection by examining the post-resurrection appearance stories of the gospels with the goal of discovering their traditional origins. After consideration of the far-reaching neglect of these texts in their own right revealed in the history of research and weighing the degree and kinds of relationships between them and other resurrection traditions, the primary goal of the analysis presents itself in the separation of their redactional from traditional layers and the determination of the latter's literary *Gattung* through a history-of-religion comparison. By establishing the integrity of the *Gattung* as a particular theological statement and by advancing the form-question to the brink of suggestive implications for the matter of ultimate historicity behind the tradition, it could be—as the author hopes—that the present state of research will find provocative stimulation for critical re-examination of an inherited prejudice and skepticism. It is perhaps debatable whether or not a more direct and extensive confrontation with the question of historicity than occurs in the final chapter is of necessity implied in a history-of-tradition analysis of these stories, but it appeared prudent in the light of the clearly defined scope of this present work and the necessity for additional (systematic) considerations of methodology on the question to postpone this endeavor until such time as it can be done properly.

The investigation was accepted as doctoral dissertation by the Protestant Theological Faculty of the Ludwig Maximilian University of Munich in the summer semester of 1973. While the manuscript was revised for publication to enhance readability, it has undergone no essential alteration of content. A concerted effort was made to correct inadvertent mistakes in the text and apparatus of the original, to include the secondary literature which has appeared since the conclusion of research and to supply English equivalents for German expressions (outside of quotations) where these are not known as standard theological termini. In the latter regard the three most troublesome terms were *Sache, sachlich* and *Grundbestand;* for better or for worse the equivalents decided upon were *subject matter, essential* and *traditional matrix.* Publication of the manuscript was made possible through the generous financial assistance of the scholarship agencies of the Lutheran Church of Bavaria and the Ludwig Maximilian University of Munich.

This project was suggested and guided from its inception in 1967 by the insight and spirit of my teacher and "doctor father," Prof. D. Leonhard Goppelt, who died unexpectedly on December 21, 1973. Without his generosity and tireless encouragement this investigation would never have been completed. To him and his family for their constant demonstration of friendship and love my family and I owe a great debt of gratitude. A special word of thanks is also due Prof. Dr. Harald Hegermann, who so generously accepted me as his assistant in 1969 and to the present has granted me the time and freedom to complete my work. My thanks also to the theological faculties of Hamburg and Munich for an atmosphere of critical stimulation and the Calwer Verlag for publishing my manuscript in the series *Calwer Theologische Monographien*. Certainly it is an indication of its ecumenism and international vision that an English language dissertation from an American Presbyterian was approved by its editorial board. In this context a word of thanks also to Prof. D. Georg Kretschmar, who in accord with the wish of the publisher so kindly assumed the role of adviser in the preparation of the manuscript in the absence of Prof. Goppelt. Finally I wish to acknowledge my indebtedness to the following persons, who helped so indefatigably during the completion of the dissertation: my wife Carole and my good friends Allan Selander and Jan Schimpf, all of whom cheerfully extended themselves to the very limits of endurance; and Rosemarie Wipfler, Hans Bald, Hermann Patsch, Maria Kohlert, Paul Kübel, David Livingston and Monika Kemmler. The revised manuscript was IBM composer-set with great skill and care by Jan Schimpf, my wife Carole and Rosemary Rennicke; the indices were compiled by Friedrich Iohn. My sincere thanks. It would be impossible to mention the names of that large number of persons and institutions having assisted and encouraged me during my residence in Germany. They know who they are and here I ask them to accept this inadequate expression of my gratitude.

Easter 1974
Munich, W. Germany

John E. Alsup

CONTENTS

N.B.: For the reader's convenience all *loc. cit.* references have been replaced by *op. cit.* and page(s) or by a shortened form of the title in question with page(s) wherever more than one work by the same person appears in the bibliography.

ABBREVIATIONS

ABR	Australian Biblical Review
AFAW	Annalen der finnischen Akademie der Wissenschaft
AJPhil	American Journal of Philology
AJTh	American Journal of Theology
AnBibl	Analecta Biblica
Anchor	Anchor Bible
ARW	Archiv für Religionswissenschaft
ASNU	Acta Seminarii Neotestamentici Upsaliensis
ASTI	Annual of the Swedish Theological Institute
ATD	Altes Testament Deutsch
ATh	Arbeiten zur Theologie
AThANT	Abhandlungen zur Theologie des Alten und Neuen Testaments
Bb	Biblica
BBB	Bonner Biblische Beiträge
BeO	Biblica et Orientalia
BEvTh	Beiträge zur Evangelischen Theologie
BFChTh	Beiträge zur Förderung christlicher Theologie
BHB	Biblische Handbibliothek
BGU	Berliner Griechische Urkunden
BhEvTh	Beihefte zur Evangelischen Theologie
BHTh	Beiträge zur historischen Theologie
BNTC	Black's New Testament Commentaries
BS	Bibliotheca Sacra
BSt	Biblische Studien
BU	Biblische Untersuchungen
BuK	Bibel und Kirche
BuL	Bibel und Leben
BWANT	Beiträge zur Wissenschaft vom Alten und Neuen Testament
BZ	Biblische Zeitschrift
BZAW	Beihefte zur Zeitschrift für die alttestamentliche Wissenschaft
cf.	confer
CBQ	Catholic Biblical Quarterly
CIL	Corpus Inscriptionum Latinarum
CLEp.	Carmina Latina Epigraphica
Col. Mech.	Collectanea Mechliniensia

col(s)	column(s)
Conc	Concilium
CThM	Calwer Theologische Monographien
Diss.	Dissertation
Düss.	Düsseldorf
ed(s)	editor(s) or edition
e.g.	*exempli gratia*
EGF	Epicorum Graecorum Fragmenta
EHS	Europäische Hochschulschriften
EKD	Evangelische Kirche in Deutschland
EKK	Evangelisch-Katholischer Kommentar zum Neuen Testament
Eng.	English
ErgBd	Ergänzungsband
et al.	*et alii*
EThL	Ephemerides Theologicae Lovanienses
EThS	Erfurter Theologische Studien
EuA	Erbe und Auftrag
EvTh	Evangelische Theologie
ET	Expository Times
f(f); F.	following (plural); Folge
Fasc.	fascicle
FB	Forschungen zur Bibel
FHG	Fragmenta historicorum Graecorum
FRLANT	Forschungen zur Religion und Literatur des Alten und Neuen Testaments
Fst.	Festschrift
FThL	Forum Theologiae Linguisticae
Ga.	Georgia (USA)
Ger.	German
Ges. Aufs.	Gesammelte Aufsätze
GHkAT	Göttinger Handkommentar zum Alten Testament
Gött.	Göttingen
GP	Gospel of Peter
Greg	Gregorianum
HAW	Handbuch der Altertumswissenschaft
HDSB	Harvard Divinity School Bulletin
HNT	Handbuch zum Neuen Testament
HThR	Harvard Theological Review

HThSt	Harvard Theological Studies
HUCA	Hebrew Union College Annual
ICC	International Critical Commentary
IG	Inscriptiones Graecae
Int	Interpretation
JbAC	Jahrbuch für Antike und Christentum
JBL	Journal of Biblical Literature
JRel	Journal of Religion
JQR	Jewish Quarterly Review
JThS	Journal of Theological Studies
KBANT	Kommentare und Beiträge zum Alten und Neuen Testament
KlT	Kleine Texte für theologische und philologische Vorlesungen und Übungen
KNT	Kommentar zum Neuen Testament
KuD(Bh)	Kerygma und Dogma (Beiheft)
LA	Los Angeles (California, USA)
LB	Linguistica Biblica
LCL	Loeb Classical Library
LXX	Septuaginta
Methuen	Methuen's History of the Greek and Roman World
Meyer	Kritisch-exegetischer Kommentar über das Neue Testament
Mich.	Michigan (USA)
Moffatt	Moffatt New Testament Commentary
ms(s).	Manuscript(s)
Mü.	München
n(s).	footnote(s)
n.d.	no date
(NF)	Neue Folge
NICNT	New International Commentary on the New Testament
NovTest	Novum Testamentum (Supplement)
(n.s.)	New Series
NT	New Testament
NTA	Neutestamentliche Abhandlungen
NTD	Neues Testament Deutsch
NTS	New Testament Studies
NTTS	New Testament Tools and Studies
N.Y.	New York (USA)

OCD	Oxford Classical Dictionary
OCT	Oxford Classical Texts
OT	Old Testament
p.(p.)	page(s)
Pa.	Pennsylvania (USA)
part.	participle
passim	throughout; in various parts
Phil.	Philadelphia (Pa., USA)
Pitt.	Pittsburgh (Pa., USA)
PTS	Patristische Texte und Studien
PW	Pauly-Wissowa, Real-Encyklopädie der klassischen Altertumswissenschaft
RAC	Reallexikon für Antike und Christentum
RB	Revue Biblique
re:	regarding
rec.	recension
REL	Revue Ecclésiastique de Liège
rev.	review
RHPhR	Revue d'Histoire et de Philosophie Religieuses
RHR	Revue de l'Histoire des Religions
RNT	Regensburger Neues Testament
RSR	Recherches de Science Religieuse
RThPh	Revue de Théologie et de Philosophie
RVV	Religionsgeschichtliche Versuche und Vorarbeiten
SAH	Sitzungsberichte der Heidelberger Akademie der Wissenschaft, philosophisch-historische Klasse
SBL	Society of Biblical Literature
SCHNT	Studia ad Corpus Hellenisticum Novi Testamenti
SJTh	Scottish Journal of Theology
SNTSMS	Studiorum Novi Testamenti Societas Monograph Series
SO	Symbolae Osloenses
StANT	Studien zum Alten und Neuen Testament
StBSt	Stuttgarter Bibelstudien
StBTh	Studies in Biblical Theology
StEv	Studia Evangelica
StNT	Studien zum Neuen Testament
StTh	Studia Theologica
Stutt.	Stuttgart
StZ	Stimmen der Zeit
Syll.	Syllographi Graeci=Corpusculum poesis epicae Graecae ludibundae, vol. II

TAPhS	Transactions of the American Philosophical Society
Th	Theology. A Monthly Journal of Historic Christianity
ThB	Theologische Bücherei
ThBl	Theologische Blätter
ThF	Theologische Forschung
ThGl	Theologie und Glaube
ThHK	Theologischer Handkommentar zum Neuen Testament
ThLZ	Theologische Literaturzeitung
ThR	Theologische Rundschau
ThViat	Theologia Viatorum
ThW	Theologisches Wörterbuch zum Neuen Testament
ThZ	Theologische Zeitschrift (Basel)
trans.	translated (translation/translator)
TSt	Texts and Studies
TT	Texts and Translations
TTh	Themen der Theologie
TU	Texte und Untersuchungen zur Geschichte der altkirchlichen Literatur
Tüb.	Tübingen
UNT	Untersuchungen zum Neuen Testament
Va.	Virginia (USA)
VF	Verkündigung und Forschung
vol(s)	volumn(s)
VT	Vetus Testamentum (Supplement)
VTh	Vox Theologica
WB	Wissenschaftliche Buchgesellschaft
WMANT	Wissenschaftliche Monographien zum Alten und Neuen Testament
Württ.	Württemberg
WUNT	Wissenschaftliche Untersuchungen zum Neuen Testament
WZKM	Wiener Zeitschrift für die Kunde des Morgenlandes
WZKMU	Wissenschaftliche Zeitschrift der Karl Marx Universität, (Gesellschafts- und sprachwissenschaftliche Reihe)
ZAW (Bh)	Zeitschrift für die alttestamentliche Wissenschaft (Beiheft)
ZKG	Zeitschrift für Kirchengeschichte
ZKTh	Zeitschrift für katholische Theologie
ZNW	Zeitschrift für die neutestamentliche Wissenschaft und die Kunde der älteren Kirche
ZThK	Zeitschrift für Theologie und Kirche

I. Introduction: Problem, Method and Overview of Research

The following investigation of New Testament research focuses upon an aspect of the resurrection question. It is a history-of-tradition analysis of the post-resurrection appearance *stories* of the gospel tradition. This delimitation of perspective and subject matter implies several distinctions in comparison to other possible approaches. The topic under discussion, for example, is not the Easter event itself; that topic has been subjected to critical scrutiny from every quarter over the centuries and especially in recent times. The degree and quantity of research on this question is an indication, on the one hand, of the timely nature and importance of the general thematic which constitutes the overall theological locus of this investigation; on the other hand, it is also an indication of the necessity for a clear differentiation between related lines of questioning and our own; failure to heed this necessity for precision would have been a serious handicap, as anyone familiar with this problem area can well attest. This investigation, therefore, is not the product of a research project on contemporary theological literature with the theme of questions on the Resurrection;[1] *rather it concentrates upon the Easter appearance stories of the gospels and seeks through an analysis of their form and structure to answer the question of their pre-redactional origin and intention as Gattung.* In a word, our investigation pursues a line of questioning which seeks to start with the Easter appearance stories at the redactional level and then to work back to their origins as far as an analysis of their form will allow us to go. It may be that suggestive possibilities may emerge from this study with regard to the question of ultimate historicity, but while recognizing the importance of this question it, nevertheless, places itself primarily before the goal of *Gattung* determination. This means that it will be necessary to differentiate between distinct forms within the spectrum of resurrection traditions. The earliest witness to the resurrection appearances literarily is contained in

1 For an overview of the recent discussion on the Easter event and the hermeneutic and systematic problems behind a theology of the Resurrection cf. the collected essays in B. Klappert (ed.), *Diskussion um Kreuz und Auferstehung* (Wuppertal, 1967) and W. Marxsen, U. Wilckens, G. Delling, H.G. Geyer, *Die Bedeutung der Auferstehungsbotschaft für den Glauben an Jesus Christus* (Gütersloh, 1968, 7th ed. [='66]); the analysis of R. Niebuhr, *Resurrection and Historical Reason* (N.Y., 1957), B. Klappert, *Die Auferweckung des Gekreuzigten. Der Ansatz der Christologie K. Barths im Zusammenhang der Christologie der Gegenwart* (Neukirchen, 1971), A. Geense, *Auferstehung und Offenbarung. Über den Ort der Frage nach der Auferstehung Jesu Christi in der heutigen deutschen evangelischen Theologie* (Gött., 1971) and the systematic monographs of W. Künneth, *Theologie der Auferstehung* (Mü., 1951, 4th ed.)–also the recent debate (1964) E. Fuchs/W. Künneth, *Die Auferstehung Jesu Christi von den Toten. Dokumentation eines Streitgesprächs*, ed. Chr. Möller (Neukirchen, 1973)–, F. Mußner, *Die Auferstehung Jesu* (Mü., 1969), W. Pannenberg, *Grundzüge der Christologie* (Gütersloh, 1964), pp. 47ff., his "Dogmatische Erwägungen zur Auferstehung Jesu," *KuD*, 14 (1968), pp. 105-118, G. Koch, *Die Auferstehung Jesu Christi* (Tüb., 1959), A. Kassing, *Auferstanden für Uns* (Mainz, 1969), N. Clark, *Interpreting the Resurrection* (London, 1967), A.M. Ramsey, *The Resurrection of Christ* (London, 1961), S.H. Hooke, *The Resurrection of Christ as History and Experience* (London, 1967), L. Geering, *Resurrection: A Symbol of Hope* (London, 1971), D.P. Fuller, *Easter Faith and History* (Grand Rapids, Mich., 1965), J.C. O'Neill, "On the Resurrection as an Historical

the kerygma tradition of I Cor. 15:5ff., but we are interested in this tradition only in terms of its relationship to the gospel appearance stories, since we are asking within our line of questioning, for example, if the latter is in any sense dependent upon the former or if the *story Gattung* goes back to a traditional existence independent of the kerygma tradition. Furthermore, this focus implies that the empty tomb tradition—generally recognized as a tradition distinct from that of the appearances among the resurrection narratives of the gospels—and the summary statements of Acts, etc., are also of importance only in terms of their relationship to the appearance story *Gattung.*

With this delimitation of perspective and subject matter comes also the question of method. The method applied here to get at our lead question is a *history-of-tradition analysis* which as an exegetical approach utilizes such aspects of historical-critical investigation as literary-, form- and redaction-criticism and history-of-religion comparison. The usefulness of the method becomes clear when one asks what other methods have been used in the investigation of the gospel appearance stories over the years. An inquiry into methodologies, moreover, is more instructive than rehearsing the broad spectrum of views on individual questions in the history of research not only because the latter would require a volume in itself but also because an understanding and critique of the various methods provides the key for developing an independent alternative.

The most widely applied method and that with the longest history as well is that of taking the texts at face value as eye-witness reports and building upon the displayed content anything from devotional homily to scathing rebuttle. The latter stemming largely from without the Church finds its classical representation in the attack on Christianity by the late second century A.D. platonist, Celsus, in his work Ἀληθὴς Λόγος (extant in the quotations of Origen's mid-third century A.D. work

Question," *Christ Faith and History: Cambridge Studies in Christology*, eds. S.W. Sykes and J.P. Clayton (Oxford, 1972), G. Schille, *Osterglaube*, ATh, 51 (Stutt., 1973) and P. Stuhlmacher, "Das Bekenntnis zur Auferweckung Jesu von den Toten und die Biblische Theologie," *ZThK*, 70 (1973), pp. 365ff. An independent approach to the narrative sections of the gospels in general under the designation *Linguistic* has not been included in our investigation as a separate voice in the methods discussion. The contributions of certain individuals on specific questions within our line of questioning have been taken into consideration, but one must wait and see what conclusions the method as such is going to offer on our problem. A volume has been announced, in any case, for publication in 1974/75 in which individual narratives are to be analyzed, among them hopefully the appearance stories: *Theorie des Evangeliums. Studien zur Semiotik der Evangelienerzählung* (FThL 6), eds. E. Güttgemanns and P.H. Lai. With regard to the systematic/hermeneutic discussion, cf. E. Güttgemanns, " 'Text' und 'Geschichte' als Grundkategorien der Generativen Poetik. These zur aktuellen Diskussion um die 'Wirklichkeit' der Auferstehungstexte," pp. 38-55 and J. van der Veken, "Theologische Sprachlogik der Auferstehungsverkündigung," pp. 176-189 both in: *"Linguistische" Theologie. Biblische Texte, christliche Verkündigung und theologische Sprachtheorie*, eds. U. Gerber and E. Güttgemanns, FThL, 3 (Bonn, 1972) and in general the critique of K. Koch, "Reichen die formgeschichtlichen Methoden für die Gegenwartsaufgaben der Bibelwissenschaft zu?," *ThLZ*, 98 (1973), cols. 801-814, W. Schenk, "Die Aufgaben der Exegese und die Mittel der Linguistik," *ThLZ*, 98 (1973), cols. 881-894 and his "U. Gerber und E. Güttgemanns (eds.), *"Linguistische" Theologie* (Review)," *ThLZ*, 98 (1973), cols. 904-906.

ΚΑΤΑ ΚΕΛΣΟΥ).[2] He says, "But we must examine this question whether anyone who really died ever rose again with the same body. Or do you think that the stories of these others [references here to Demeter, Orpheus, Heracles *et al.*] really are the legends [*τῶν ἄλλων μύθους εἶναι*], which they appear to be, and yet that the ending of your tragedy is to be regarded as noble and convincing. . .While he was alive he did not help himself, but after death he rose again and showed the marks of his punishment and how his hands had been pierced. But who saw this? A hysterical female [*γυνὴ πάροιστρος*], as you say, and perhaps some other one [*εἴ τις ἄλλος*] of those who were deluded by the same sorcery [*ἐκ τῆς αὐτῆς γοητείας*], who either dreamt in a certain state of mind [*κατά τινα διάθεσιν ὀνειρώξας*] and through wishful thinking had a hallucination due to some mistaken notion [*κατὰ τὴν αὐτοῦ βούλησιν δόξῃ πεπλανημένῃ φαντασιωθείς*]–an experience which has happened to thousands –or, which is more likely, wanted to impress the others by telling this fantastic tale [*ἐκπλῆξαι τοὺς λοιποὺς τῇ τερατείᾳ ταύτῃ θελήσας*], and so by this cock-and-bull story to provide a chance for other beggars [*διὰ τοῦ τοιούτου ψεύσματος ἀφορμὴν ἄλλοις ἀγύρταις παρασχεῖν*, II:55]." Without attempting a Celsus interpretation in general it is clear that his principal objections directed at the appearance stories are 1) their absurdity–people do not come back from the dead like this! 2) a history-of-religion comparison demonstrates them to have their closest analogy in contemporary "*μύθοι*" and 3) those who claim to have participated in such appearances are hysterical, hallucinatory or given to equivocation. Elsewhere Celsus objects further that one cannot base proofs upon the statements of believers, since they are not objective witnesses (II:67). The motivation behind Celsus' argumentation, therefore, is to raise the question of historical veracity of the post-resurrection appearances and to disclaim it. The method used to answer the question is to take the stories as ostensible reports, to discredit them as such and then label them instead as legends. It is astonishing to note the degree to which this approach has repeated itself in one form or another through the centuries down to the present.

This more or less naive eyewitness report method, yet with a more positive, constructive motivation (including the retorts of second century apologists,) enjoyed pre-eminence in the Church with a relative lack of resistance for centuries. With the rise of rationalism in the Enlightenment and the tradition of classical humanism inherited from the Renaissance, however, came renewed criticism. This time critical statements arose not only without, but also within the Church itself. Early attempts at *literary criticism* in this era made much of the contradictions between the various appearance stories which created apparently insurmountable difficulties for the eyewitness report method and finally led to its coup-de-grâce. Hermann Samuel Reimarus, for example, in his "Apologie oder Schutzschrift für die vernünftigen Verehrer Gottes" (published posthumously as anonymous fragments by Lessing in 1777)

2 The Greek text reproduced here is that of *Origenes Werke: Bd. I, Gegen Celsus*, ed. by P. Koetschau (Leipzig, 1899), pp. 178f. and the English translation is that of H. Chadwick, *Origen. Contra Celsum* (Cambridge, 1965), p. 109. Cf. hereto H. Chadwick, "Origen, Celsus, and the Resurrection of the Body," *HThR*, 41 (1948), pp. 83-102.

drew up a list of these contradictions and concluded that the only viable explanation for them is that the disciples contrived a hoax.[3] In this approach the method has been altered somewhat in that a critical comparison has been made, but the actual line of questioning already seen in the Celsus-attack has remained basically the same: the historical question has been raised and rebutted because the texts are seen to be summarily unreliable. David Friedrich Strauß in his *Leben Jesu*[4] some two generations later opposed Reimarus' explanation of the contradictions as being historically unjustifiable and proceeded, moreover, to criticize the whole approach of naturalistic solutions which provided the undercurrent of rationalism.[5] His mythological alternative focused on the reflective powers of the soul, the *Gemüthsleben* of the disciples, which brought forth the resurrection appearances. That the body of Jesus was stolen or resuscitated by the disciples is an impossibility for Strauß; the body remained in the grave.[6] Mythological schemata accrue then to the gospel stories as they move from the earliest visionary experiences of the disciples to a series of accounts stressing objectivity and concreteness.[7] Strauß' approach distinguishes itself from that of Reimarus and others in this period, but like them the historical question has been raised and rebutted in a shift from natural explanations to that of the *psychological* in an earnest attempt to interpret the accounts' significance. It was not until around the turn of the 20th century that the positions expressed in the Enlightenment began to take on programmatic dimensions and became more and more refined. The liberal theologian Johannes Weiß, for example, in his *Das Urchristentum* of 1917 pursued the historical question of the Easter event and came to the conclusion that the personality of Jesus in his life had been so strong that the disciples came to *believe* that their Master was raised and the appearances were visions emerging out of that faith. In his words, the Easter appearances are "nicht wie es (den Jüngern) damals schien, der Grund, sondern eine Wirkung ihres Glaubens."[8]

3 G.E. Lessing (ed.), *Von dem Zwecke Jesu und seiner Jünger. Noch ein Fragment des Wolfenbüttelschen Ungenannten*, 1778. (cf. also *Ein Mehreres aus den Papieren des Ungenannten*, Fünftes Fragment - "Über die Auferstehungsgeschichte"), *Lessings Werke*, eds. J. Peterson and W. von Olshausen Teil 22/vol. 18 (Hildesheim, 1970=['25]), pp. 207-326 (pp. 152-186). Hereto the interesting data of H.K. McArthur, *The Quest Through the Centuries* (Phil., 1966), pp. 102ff., also W.G. Kümmel, *Das Neue Testament. Geschichte der Erforschung seiner Probleme* (Freiburg, 1970[2]), p. 105 and A. Schweitzer, *The Quest of the Historical Jesus* (N.Y., 1962), p. 21.

4 First published 1835/36 in 2 vols. with successive editions to 1840. In 1864 he published his *Volks-Ausgabe*, a trend of the period which produced other popular "Lives." By this time the discussion around his earlier editions had reached a focal point and his references, for example, to Schleiermacher and Baur, etc., make this edition, in spite of justified critique (cf. A. Schweitzer, *op. cit.*, pp. 193ff.), very useful.

5 D.F. Strauß, *Das Leben Jesu. Volks-Ausgabe* (Bonn, 1904, 14th ed.), I, pp. 148ff. esp. 152f. Cf. also his *H.S. Reimarus und seine Schutzschrift für die vernünftigen Verehrer Gottes* (Leipzig, 1862), reprinted in his *Ges. Schriften*, (Bonn, 1876), V, pp. 229ff. and A. Schweitzer, *op. cit.*, pp. 43ff., 60, 64f., 68ff. and 78ff.

6 Strauß, *Leben Jesu*, I, pp. 157ff.

7 *Ibid.* and II, pp. 148ff.

8 J. Weiß, *Das Urchristentum* (Gött., 1917), p. 22.

Over against the earlier positions of Reimarus, *et al.*, Weiß followed up an interest in the historical question, but—not unlike Strauß—found little source for stumbling in the contradictions of the appearance stories, since they were for him visions *after the fact*. Moreover, vision as category is not to be understood, according to Weiß, as a picture which corresponds to an outward object.[9] Accordingly then, the gospel appearance stories are treated once again by a method that has placed the historical veracity question at its center and then has been forced to look elsewhere for a criterion to determine their worth. A representative of the *history-of-religion school*, Wilhelm Bousset, showed greater interest in the form of the appearance stories and concluded that they expressed in their christological development simply contemporary forms of the disciples' *Umwelt* as symbols of this same impression of Jesus' personality upon his followers.[10] It was indeed an important methodological step to compare these texts with possible analogies in the contemporary religious world, but this marriage, as it were, between liberal theology and the history-of-religion school in the question of the historical causes behind the form, namely the overwhelming impression of Jesus' personality upon the disciples, led to a short circuit of the method. The hermeneutic principle in both cases was that of historicism which as in the natural sciences was determined to see all history in the context of imminent causation.

The first truly significant breakthrough in the treatment of the appearance stories of the gospels in New Testament research came about with the emergence of the *form-critical* method after WW I. It provides an important, indeed indispensable, methodological key for our line of questioning and becomes, therefore, a most important perspective for review, because it has by no means exhausted its potential in this area. This method following the suggestive strides of Old Testament scholars, e.g., Hermann Gunkel,[11] is represented, for example, in the publications of Martin Dibelius, above all his *Die Formgeschichte des Evangeliums,* 1919, which sought to analyze the various forms in which New Testament traditions are capsuled, to establish a *Sitz im Leben* for them in the believing community and to determine relation-

9 *Ibid.*, p. 20, n. 3.

10 W. Bousset, *Kyrios Christos* (Gött., 1967, 6th ed. [='21, 2nd ed.]), says for example, "Man ist auf kritischer Seite darin weithin einverstanden, daß es sich hier um einen rein geistigen Vorgang in den Seelen der Jünger handle. . ." and "Der treibende Faktor war der mit nichts zu vergleichende, gewaltige und unzerstörbare Eindruck, den Jesu Persönlichkeit in den Seelen der Jünger hinterlassen hatte. . ." (p. 17), and "Dann aber ist es weiter von ungeheurer Wichtigkeit gewesen, daß in der zeitgenössischen Apokalyptik ein fertiges Messiasbild geschaffen war, das nun für das ganze unheimliche Rätsel, das die Jünger erlebt hatten, das lösende Wort zu enthalten schien. . .Sie warfen ihrem Meister den fertigen Königsmantel um, setzten ihm die höchste ihnen erreichbare Krone auf das Haupt und bekannten sich zu Jesus dem Menschensohn, der durch Leiden und Tod zur Herrlichkeit eingegangen sei" (p. 18).

11 Most noteworthy in this regard his Genesis and Psalms commentaries. Cf. below Gunkel's contribution to the discussion on the Emmaus story and the *Gattung* problem, pp. 239f. and n. 617, and the Hamburg dissertation cf. W. Klatt, *Hermann Gunkel. Zu seiner Theologie der Religionsgeschichte und zur Entstehung der formgeschichtlichen Methode*, FRLANT, 100 (Gött., 1966).

ships between such traditions in their origins, growth and development.[12] For Dibelius on the matter of the resurrection traditions the key factor was the missionary preaching activity of the primitive church. In this connection he concludes that the earliest witness to that preaching is the kerygmatic formula of I Cor. 15: 3bff., where the cross, the Resurrection and post-resurrection appearances were affirmed as the core of missionary propaganda/proclamation. To the question of the origin of the appearance *stories* of the gospels, he contended that they were paradigms or illustrations to the kerygma which arose by and by in that missionary context as visual aids, as it were, to enable traveling preachers to give graphic imagery to their kerygmatic statements.[13] This approach then follows two basic presuppositions: 1) the beginning point is the kerygma which existed as traditional entity by itself and 2) to understand the appearance stories one must see them from the perspective of that kerygma tradition because a) they are dependent upon it for their origin and b) they served it as illustrations in the missionary environment. Although the form-critical method has found wide acceptance in the investigation of the appearance stories with an ongoing refinement and multiplication of detailed analysis, this basic thesis of Dibelius on the origin of those stories as dependent upon the kerygma has gone by and large unchallenged.[14] A primary focus of our investigation is to do precisely that: is it correct to assume that the gospel tradition here is dependent upon the kerygma tradition for its origin? This must be taken up below where we raise the question of the relationship of the two complexes to one another, but first it is important to note several other form-critical contributions to see what has been done subsequently with the method and to determine its possibilities and limitations.

R. Bultmann in subsequent editions of his *Geschichte der synoptischen Tradition*, 1921, acknowledges considerable dependence in his views on the appearance stories upon two scholars writing in the early 1920's: Martin Albertz, "Zur Formgeschichte der Auferstehungsberichte," *ZNW* 21 [1922], pp. 259-269 and Lyder Brun, *Die Auferstehung Christi in der urchristlichen Überlieferung* [Oslo, 1925].[15]

12 Dibelius himself wanted to distinguish between an "analytical" (Bultmann, *et al.*) and his own "constructive" application of the method, with the latter seeking "Lebensbedingungen und Lebensfunktionen der ersten christlichen Gemeinden zu erschließen. Wenn man auf diese Arbeit verzichtet, so stehen die von der Analyse erhobenen Quellen und kleinen Einheiten im leeren Raum, ohne daß ihre soziologische Beziehung, ihr 'Sitz im Leben' deutlich wird." *Die Formgeschichte des Evangeliums* (Tüb., 1961, 4th ed.), p. 9.

13 *Ibid.*, pp. 15ff. and in general the chapters on "Paradigma" (pp. 34ff.), "Legende" (pp. 101ff.), "Leidensgeschichte" (pp. 178ff.) and above all "Form, Geschichte, Theologie" (pp. 287ff.). In his "Die alttestamentlichen Motive in der Leidensgeschichte des Petrus- und des Johannes-Evangeliums," *Fst. W.W. Baudissin* (Gießen, 1918), p. 150, he writes, ". . .vor allem Schrifttum war die Predigt; geschichtliche Überlieferung und erbauliche Betrachtung haben dort ihren Ausgangspunkt, und ihr Werden und Wachsen kann nur von dort aus verstanden werden."

14 General critique of the "constructive" approach of Dibelius has been widely exercised, cf. G. Iber's *Nachtrag* to the 4th edition, 1961, pp. 302-312 and most recently E. Güttgemanns, *Offene Fragen zur Formgeschichte des Evangeliums* (Mü., 1970), pp. 82ff., but the particular issue of the origin of the Easter appearance stories has gone in the main untouched.

15 R. Bultmann, *Geschichte der synoptischen Tradition* (Gött., 1970, 8th ed.), p.311.

Bultmann does go beyond them in developing his perspective on the tradition's legendary character (referring thereby to H. Gunkel and M. Dibelius, for example),[16] but his (systematic) theological presuppositions prohibit further interest in the stories.[17] We may, therefore, understand the following remarks on Albertz and Brun as having validity in the main for Bultmann as well, if not in all their implications. The fundamental strength of the way in which these two scholars apply the form-critical method is that they attempt a frontal confrontation with the gospel appearance stories without direct recourse to Dibelius' thesis. They appear, in fact, to be disinterested in challenging it, since their assumption that the two complexes are basically harmonious and that the one brings to a variety of expression what was present in the other as a fundamental notion in the terminus ὤφϑη presumably led them to a tacit affirmation of it.[18] Be that as it may, they give the stories a hearing unprejudiced by the weight of theories favoring the absolute priority of I Cor. 15 and proceed to perform a thoroughgoing dissection by classifying them according to like groups, fixing attention upon particular recurrent motifs within them and postulating the significance of the groups and their motifs for life in the early Christian community. This is really the first time in the history of research that such a task was undertaken.

Another strength in their application of the method was a deliberate waiving of the historical question: did the appearances actually take place and if so was it like the stories tell it? They do not treat the accounts primarily as eyewitness reports but as stories with the intention of expressing a theological statement and, therefore, they are not forced into the either/or alternative of earlier investigations. They recognize, of course, that the accounts bear the stamp of witness, but treat them against the backdrop of ecclesiastical situations and apologetic currents. Says Brun, for example:

"Überhaupt mischen sich nicht ganz selten geschichtliche Urteile etwas verfrüht in die traditionsgeschichtliche Betrachtung ein, während es doch zunächst darauf ankommen dürfte,

16 *Ibid.*, pp. 308ff. and esp. p. 310, n. 1.

17 R. Bultmann, "Das Verhältnis der urchristlichen Christusbotschaft zum historischen Jesus," *Exegetica* (Tüb., 1967), p. 469, "Mehrfach und meist als Kritik wird gesagt, daß nach meiner Interpretation des Kerygmas Jesus ins Kerygma auferstanden sei. Ich akzeptiere diesen Satz. Er ist völlig richtig, vorausgesetzt, daß er richtig verstanden wird. Er setzt voraus, daß das Kerygma selbst eschatologisches Geschehen ist; und er besagt, daß Jesus im Kerygma wirklich gegenwärtig ist, daß es *sein* Wort ist, das den Hörer im Kerygma trifft. Ist das der Fall, so werden alle Spekulationen über die Seinsweise des Auferstandenen, alle Erzählungen vom leeren Grabe und alle Osterlegenden, welche Momente an historischen Fakten sie auch enthalten mögen, und so wahr sie in ihrem symbolischen Gehalt sein mögen, gleichgültig. An den im Kerygma präsenten Christus glauben, ist der Sinn des Osterglaubens." Written in reaction to the widely accepted historical skepticism of the Bultmann school was among others G. Stählin (trans. W.P. Todd), " 'On the Third Day.' The Easter Traditions of the Primitive Church," *Int*, 10 (1956), pp. 282ff., esp. 289ff.

18 L. Brun, *Die Auferstehung Christi in der urchristlichen Überlieferung* (Oslo, 1925), pp. 42 and 64: M. Albertz, "Zur Formgeschichte der Auferstehungsberichte," *ZNW*, 21 (1922), pp. 264ff.

die vorhandenen Überlieferungen von traditionsgeschichtlichem Gesichtspunkt aus genau durchzuarbeiten, wobei die Frage nach den geschichtlichen Ergebnissen vorläufig zurückgestellt sein mag."19

With their conclusions emerges for the first time under full critical recognition of diversity in the accounts a picture of similarities and theologically motivated forms of expression in contrast to the former critical lists of contradictions alone. For Albertz a form-critical analysis demonstrates that for the primitive church the representation of an appearance of the resurrected One before the group of assembled disciples alone was constitutive and that other appearance stories were only of relative importance in accord with a great variety of particular interests. For Brun, on the other hand, the conclusion of such a study is a recognition of the integrated importance of all accounts in the formation of a unified front of witnesses to the "that" of the Resurrection. He does construct a scheme of literary dependence for the traditions, but his primary interest is clearly in showing that those traditions in their variety corresponded to the diverse requirements of mission and congregational life and that subordinating one to the other oversimplifies the historical givens of Christian beginnings. Brun is moving in his use of the form-critical method very close to the rebound of redaction-criticism which made itself felt in the 1950's and thereafter.

These early attempts at analyzing the gospel appearance stories made application of the form-critical method correctly without dependence on the historical question of former methods and that with an interest in the theological thought processes evident there, but were guided, nevertheless, by a distinct theological-sociological picture of early Christianity. This picture was in part that of the history-of-religion school, on the one hand, in which the primitive church was hardly distinguishable from other currents of thought in a seething brew of syncretism, and on the other hand, that of the determined struggle of that community to establish the distinctiveness of its proclamation. This led Dibelius, as we have seen, to postulate missionary origins for the gospel appearance stories, but (Bultmann) Brun and Albertz are also very much influenced by this picture. For them this led to the conclusion that individual motifs in the stories as well as their groupings can be traced back to specific early Christian needs, problems and factional strife. This is the natural product perhaps of a method that focuses singularly on isolated elements and seeks to find a *Sitz im Leben* for each. With the projected understanding of the historical situation of life in the earliest community, motifs and themes appearing in the stories are lined up, as it were, with developments presumed to have given rise to such in the first place. In doing so the authors did not differentiate clearly enough between the distinctions of earlier and later periods in the life of the community. Of course, in hindsight the *redaction-critical* method has provided new criteria through which may be determined which motifs and themes in those stories reflect the historical situations and theological interests of the individual evangelists and those

19 Brun, *Auferstehung*, p. 8.

which antedate them—a methodological asset which was not at their disposal. Thus going beyond these form critics requires a keener awareness of and a more accurate picture about the differences between the traditions passed on to the evangelists and their adoption and alterations of them. Moreover, it is necessary to ask the question of the nature of the pre-redactional tradition as a whole and not only of individual themes and motifs thereof as fragmentary reflections of some apologetic aspect of early Christian life and thought.

Roughly thirty years after Albertz and Brun a very interesting attempt to go beyond the form-critics of this earlier period was made by C.H. Dodd in his article "The Appearances of the Risen Christ: An Essay in the Form-Criticism of the Gospels," *Studies in the Gospels, Essays In Memory of R.H. Lightfoot* (ed. D.E. Nineham), 1957. Dodd like his earlier two counterparts also thinks that grouping the appearance stories is useful, but rather than following the single or group appearance categories Dodd is more interested in showing that it is possible to type these appearance accounts according to *formal categories* just as one does in other layers of the gospel tradition. His starting point is their compositional form and with this perspective he concludes that they can all be divided into "concise" or "circumstantial" narrative categories or perhaps a combination of the two, the "intermediate" type. This step of seeing here a pattern where the particulars make sense only in the total form of which they are a part, is indeed something truly new in attempting to analyze the gospel appearance stories. Dodd tries to deal with tradition and not redaction (although the brevity of the article made it very difficult to go into detail on the many and complex problems here) and his treatment of particular motifs and themes as contributing elements to a definite unified form enabled him to avoid, in the main, the pitfalls of his predecessors who never really got beyond the trees to the forest, so to speak. His concise category, therefore, is a story which is expressed in economical, "concise" language which limits its scope to a statement about what is purported to have happened and to have been said. The circumstantial category, on the other hand, calls upon details to round out a more fully developed picture in the "art and craft of the story-teller"[20] and to kindle the imagination of the listener. These can be called in terms of the science of literature according to Dodd "Novellen" or tales typical of folklore—a designation which is by no means original to Dodd but is rather current terminology for the form-critical school in general. The concise type is rather fresco-like, i.e., could be passed on as a familiar story; such actually stood alone without any particular context because of polished brevity. Comparing such stories to "apophthegms" and miracle stories, for example, which are drawn from oral tradition Dodd sees them as embedded in the "corporate memory" of the Church, deeply cherished and constantly repeated because of their central importance to the primitive community.[21] The "tales," on the other hand, allow more room for personal taste and creative initiative and were,

20 C.H. Dodd, "The Appearances of the Risen Christ: An Essay in Form-Criticism of the Gospels," *Studies in the Gospels, Essays in Memory of R.H. Lightfoot,* ed. by D.E. Nineham (Oxford, 1957), p. 9.
21 *Ibid.*, pp. 9f.

therefore, more subject to alteration and "improvement." Nevertheless, they are not to be reduced to a place of secondary value as later developments (cf., e.g., Mt. 8: 18-34 and 9:18-26 to Mk. 5:1-20, 21-43).

Taking as examples Mt. 28:8-10, 16-20 and Jn. 20:19-21, he notes the following themes as basic to all three pericopae: 1) Christ's followers are bereft of their Lord 2) the Lord appears 3) he greets them 4) they recognize him and 5) he gives the word of command (commission) and then concludes that this means that a basic center or kernel is common to all and that the adding of detail has not altered a concise resurrection pericope form.[22] Examples of the circumstantial type would be the Emmaus story and John 21. These do not represent a common (oral) traditional source, but reflect a private source and the creative initiative of the writer.[23] The intermediate type is reflected according to Dodd in "Mk." 16:14-15, Lk. 24:36-49 and Jn. 20:11-17, 26-29, but the traits deviating from a "common pattern" are by and large redactional enlargements and, therefore, in type these are close relatives of the concise accounts, Jn. 20:11-17 for Dodd excepted, which is truly circumstantial.[24] Separate and distinct from these types of appearance stories for Dodd, moreover, are the traditions in the Book of Revelation, the appearance to Paul on the road to Damascus (Acts 9, 22, 26), the Ascension, the apocryphal materials, I Cor. 15 and the summaries in Acts,[25] but in terms of the relationship question Dodd fully accepts Dibelius' thesis that the gospel appearance stories, especially the concise type, served to *illustrate* the statements of the kerygma in the early Christian mission.[26] Thus, in summary, Dodd concludes that the concise type reflects a corporate oral tradition which focused attention on the entire apostolic body as a block witness, I Cor. 15 particularized those witnesses and the circumstantial type included individuals but only for enrichment of the story and not to adduce a specific witness to fill the credibility gap. The latter is typical of the legend style and is distinguishable from the purpose of naming individuals in I Cor. 15.[27] Dodd offers then the following chronological breakdown: the earliest form of the appearance tradition is the kerygma, equally as old are the summary statements of Acts and then come respectively concise and circumstantial types (the intermediate type is merely a variant). He resists, however, any devaluation of one form over against the other as "secondary" since each displays its own integrity. He is fighting, as it were, on two fronts: 1) to see lines of development in the outgrowth of traditions and 2) to counter demeaning prejudice against the integrity of the gospel appearance traditions.

Dodd has seen correctly that it is necessary to approach the gospel appearance texts literarily, to analyze them as category and to differentiate them from other forms of resurrection appearance traditions. Yet, he does too little with his "com-

22 *Ibid.*, pp. 17f.
23 *Ibid.*
24 *Ibid.*, pp. 16ff.
25 *Ibid.*, pp. 21ff., 26, n.*, 26ff. and 34, n. *, etc.
26 *Ibid.*, pp. 26f.
27 *Ibid.*, pp. 29ff.

mon pattern," for although he makes on occasion passing but suggestive observations about Greek literary forms (ἀναγνώρισις in Greek drama,[28] and the categories of Aristotle in *De Art. Poet.* I, 1 and *Anal. Pr.* XXVII, 70b.2[29]), it is never clear just why this pattern should have shown such tenacity in the oral tradition other than perhaps ostensibly to have preserved succinctly and most accurately the "facts" of appearance encounters. This is probably too little. When one inquires further on this point Dodd answers that the form was most useful to early Christian missionaries–following Dibelius–as sermon illustrations, because they outlined briefly the key aspects of the appearances which were to be retold.[30] This and his entire chronological breakdown are all very hypothetical and depend upon the substantiality of Dibelius' view of dependence which must be tested. Dodd's method of comparison in search of a common center and structure at the pre-redactional level needs to be extended to all of the stories together. His breakdown of concise, circumstantial and intermediate types, moreover, is too formal and keeps him from achieving a truly integrated picture of the stories as a complex unto themselves. Here a more thoroughgoing use of redaction-criticism will help to break up the confinements and rigidity of the categories he has imposed upon the accounts by differentiating more clearly between redactional concern and traditional form.

The methodological alternatives characterized up to this point represent the major options which have been followed in approaching the gospel appearance stories. We have mentioned redaction-criticism from time to time as an aspect of the history-of-tradition method and although the movement to establish the pre-eminence of redactional considerations as a reaction to the classical form-critical school has found widespread acceptance,[31] this approach remains for this investigation an integrated part of the entire history-of-tradition analysis. The end-point in the development of the gospel appearance tradition constitutes the opposite end of the spectrum to the focus of our reflections; *redactional considerations are important only in as much as they provide criteria for the separation of later from earlier elements in the development of traditional processes.* A host of articles, monographs and especially commentaries have been written since the inception of the redaction-critical method which have made it into an absolute for our texts. Their concern is clearly not with the traditional matrix, its form and function, and, therefore, they fall outside the immediate scope of our methods discussion, although some appear below on particular questions.

A significant number of monographs have been written since WW II, however, which lay claim in part at least, to the form-critical method and have had a decided influence on the *status of the contemporary critical discussion* in New Testament research. To these we now turn our attention again with primary focus upon the

28 *Ibid.*, p. 18, n. †.
29 *Ibid.*, pp. 26f., n. †, etc.
30 Cf. in general also the role of the summaries in Acts here and his view of the sermons in Acts and their relationship to the kerygma in his *The Apostolic Preaching and Its Developments* (N.Y., 1962), delivered as lectures in 1935.
31 Cf. J. Rohde, *Die redaktionsgeschichtliche Methode* (Hamburg, 1966).

methodological approaches each applies in order to gain perspective on the immediate exegetical context of our investigation and to see if they have been able to bring the discussion beyond the classical form-critics.

One of the most widely read and influential monographs on the appearances of the resurrected One to appear during the 1940's was W. Michaelis', *Die Erscheinungen des Auferstandenen*, 1944. The author, professor in Bern, Switzerland, wrote this book with the intention of countering the earlier work of E. Hirsch, *Die Auferstehungsgeschichten und der christliche Glaube*, 1940, thereby joining forces, as it were, with P. Althaus, who did much the same in his *Die Wahrheit des kirchlichen Osterglaubens*, 1940 (1941 [2]). Michaelis' presentation offers a step for step rebuttal of the position of Hirsch. His own statements are motivated by a quest for the historical kernel behind the stories and are supported by a pervading optimism that such is indeed there. The crux of the debate comes in his chapter on "Erscheinungen und Visionen,"[32] for here he fights tooth and nail against Hirsch's assumption that the original form of the appearances is to be seen in the "vision" of Paul and that this form retreated in the gospels due to apologetic interests. [33] Since Paul, according to Michaelis, places his own appearance on the same level as those in the gospels, the whole complex originates in the same sort of experience; moreover, since Paul's appearance (as expressed in the terminus ὤφθη) is not at all like the visionary experience recorded in II Cor. 12:1, for example, but is entirely different, [34] one must conclude that neither for Paul nor for the gospels are categories like *ekstatische Schauungen, enthusiastische Schauungen* or *visionäre Schau* valid. [35] Satisfied that he has found sufficient support by further consultation with texts like I Cor. 9:1; Acts 9, 22 and 26; Gal. 1:15f.and I Cor. 15:5ff.as well as by deliberation over the meaning of ὤφθη as an expression of visionary seeing neither for Paul nor for its LXX background, but rather, as an expression of the activity of the appearing One as subject [36]—opposing, moreover, any analogy between Paul's Damascus experience and that of Stephen in Acts 7:55f.[37]—he comes to the conclusion for his entire work:

"Hirsch irrt sich auf der ganzen Linie. Die Quellen bezeugen deutlich. . ., daß Paulus und die sonstige Überlieferung darin übereinstimmen, daß die Erscheinungen *keine Visionen* im Sinne der ihnen sonst bekannten Visionen waren, sondern daß sie sich, obschon sie nicht ohne weiteres mit den gewöhnlichen Sinnen wahrgenommen werden konnten, *im nicht visionären Bereich* abgespielt haben, wobei die Frage nach der Art der Wahrnehmung auf eine nicht zu übersehende Weise als unwichtig behandelt wird gegenüber dem Eindruck, daß es sich in den Erscheinungen um Vorgänge handelt, die in die Kategorie des Offenbarungsgeschehens gehören."[38]

32 W. Michaelis, *Die Erscheinungen des Auferstandenen* (Basel, 1944), pp. 97ff.
33 *Ibid.*, pp. 97.
34 *Ibid.*, pp. 99ff. and 117.
35 *Ibid.*, p. 100.
36 *Ibid.*, pp. 103ff. Cf. also W. Michaelis, "ὁράω, εἶδον, βλέπω," *ThW*, V, pp. 315-381, esp. pp. 355ff.
37 Michaelis, *Erscheinungen*, pp. 114ff.
38 *Ibid.*, p. 121. Contemporaneous but far more general in scope were the two volumes of A.T. Nikolainen, *Der Auferstehungsglaube in der Bibel und ihrer Umwelt*, I/II (Helsinki, 1944/46).

As this reference makes clear, Michaelis is involved primarily in the controversy over the historical factuality of the appearances and their revelational significance which was the status of the discussion for his time and especially for his chosen debate-partner. He poses the question of a historical kernel throughout his investigation of the gospel texts and analyzes the content of such chiefly in terms of the redactional form without making any particular differentiation between this form and the tradition antedating it. This general approach prohibited Michaelis from making greater use of the more literarily oriented approaches of the classical form-critics and his determination, moreover, to bring Paul and the gospels together (in opposition to Hirsch) led him to efface the evident formal differences between the two and to overlook their consequences for the *Gattung* question, although his point with regard to ἐν πνεύματι appearances was well taken.

Approximately a decade later K.H. Rengstorf wrote his *Die Auferstehung Jesu. Form, Art und Sinn der urchristlichen Osterbotschaft*, which was first published from his lecture manuscripts at Münster in 1952, then enlarged in 1954², reprinted in 1955³ in East Berlin, and reworked in 1960⁴. It was the stated intention of the author [39] to publish a fifth edition which would be more than a revision of the first four, but in 1967⁵ it became, nevertheless, necessary to publish a slightly revised reprint of the fourth edition and although the author pledged the intended new edition it has never appeared. Rengstorf's approach to the gospel appearance stories differed from that of Michaelis in several ways. For one thing, his theme, as is seen in part in the title itself, is the Resurrection, its proclamation in primitive Christianity and its theological relevance in general for the origins of Christian faith. His starting point, therefore, is I Cor. 15 and the kerygma tradition and the place of the gospel appearance stories receives only marginal treatment. He says, "In diesem Buch geht es nicht um die Osterberichte und um das Ostergeschehen als solches, sondern um die urchristliche Osterverkündigung als Kerygma."[40] Rengstorf has correctly seen methodologically that it is also an important contribution to analyze Easter traditions formally as traditions without immediate and constant recourse to the question of historical veracity, but his particular focus is of little assistance to us because it concerns itself with the *kerygma* and *its* development. Where he does deal with the gospel tradition it has somewhat the function of an excursus, e.g., relating to the problems posed by the use of ὤφθη in the kerygma and a (principally redactional) thematic emphasis on the bodily nature of the appearing One as Jesus in the gospels, [41] or to the matter of displaced appearance stories in the traditions of Jesus' earthly ministry.[42] Accordingly, Rengstorf's book has figured prominently in the discussion of the kerygma tradition but not directly of the gospel tradition.

Of particular importance with regard to the history of research, the question of the relationship between the gospel appearance stories and the kerygma tradition

39 K.H. Rengstorf, *Die Auferstehung Jesu. Form, Art und Sinn der urchristlichen Osterbotschaft* (Witten/Ruhr, 1967, 5th ed.), p. 7.

40 *Ibid.*, p. 17.

41 *Ibid.*, pp. 57ff. and 74ff.

42 *Ibid.*, pp. 146ff.

and particularly the matter of method and approach, is the book of the Marburg systematician Hans Graß, *Ostergeschehen und Osterberichte*. As an indication of the book's widespread influence and popularity are its two editions and two reprintings between 1956 and 1970[4] and its frequent appearance in the footnotes of literally all of the major works on the question of resurrection traditions and resurrection faith since the first edition. This book has had such acclaim because it is one of the few monographs of any proportion which truly focuses upon the appearance narratives of the gospels as a document of New Testament research. While many other volumes have been available which devote attention to I Cor. 15 and/or to the whole spectrum of problems connected with the Resurrection in general from both the perspective of New Testament research and systematic theology, no other work has been so widely used or of such singular importance for the interpretation of the gospel accounts–and that includes the pastor's study–as Graß' "Easter Event and Easter Reports." For this reason a critical evaluation of this book and especially of its methodology is imperative.

As the title itself suggests Graß proposes to let two questions confront one another in terms of a comparison: 1) what happened in the Easter event and 2) do the appearance stories of the gospels investigated from the standpoint of historical objectivity give an answer to the lead question? With these two questions the direction and methodological approach has been cast: the author asks the historical question "what happened" and proposes to apply the "historical-critical" method of investigation to the texts purporting to report what happened. From his perspective the method is necessary "weil heute nicht nur in der kirchlichen Praxis, sondern z.T. auch in der Theologie Tendenzen vorhanden sind, die historischen Fragen beiseite zu schieben und, ohne durch sie hindurchzugehen, eine Theologie der Auferstehung zu entwickeln."[43] Our impression of the present state of research is that the reverse has been true, namely that the historical question "did they happen or not" has so dominated the treatment of the resurrection appearance stories that they have not been granted a fair hearing in their own right. Thereby the question poses itself: what does one mean by historical investigation?

Graß understands historical investigation primarily from the standpoint of contemporary historical research on events of the past and what can be said about their veracity. His motivation is the establishment or discrediting of historical documents in their ability to communicate a reliable, acceptable picture of what actually took place "back then" for the inquirer "today,"[44] With this goal he can come to his "radical conclusion"[45] and say that the gospel appearance stories are so "legendary" in character that they are unreliable sources for his primary interest in answering the question of what happened in the appearances. He says for example,

43 H. Graß, *Ostergeschehen und Osterberichte* (Gött., 1970, 4th ed.), p. 14: p. 14, n. 4 refers to M. Barth, *Der Augenzeuge* (Zürich, 1946), Künneth, *op. cit.* and Rengstorf, *Auferstehung*.

44 He says, for example, *ibid.*, p. 260, "Wir haben uns bei unserer historischen Untersuchung der Osterberichte immer von der Frage leiten lassen: was ist ursprünglich geschehen, wie haben sie es erlebt und gesehen? "

45 His advice to preachers at the end (*ibid.*, pp. 281f.) acknowledges that his investigation

"Sämtliche Berichte [of the gospels] tragen einen stark legendären Charakter. Das gilt von den Geschichten, wie sie in den Evangelien literarisch fixiert vorliegen, wie auch/von den diesen Geschichten zugrundeliegenden Quellenstücken und Traditionselementen. Der historische Ertrag für die Osterereignisse ist mager und fragwürdig."46

and again

"Was bleibt nun als historischer Kern der legendären, von mannigfaltigen Motiven gestalteten Ostergeschichten der Evangelien? . . .Nichts Sicheres kann den Berichten mehr entnommen werden über die Art und Weise der Erscheinungen."47

The historical-critical method as an exegetical approach is, of course, also applied in comparing the various texts in question, but a clear use of and differentiation between the lines of questioning in New Testament research of traditional and redactional analysis are wanting (as becomes especially clear in the second half of the book) because of an overriding skepticism that such holds any promise anyway.[48] As stated above, the historical question is important, but it is to be asked if this skepticism over against a history-of-tradition analysis of these stories and a preconception of the only alternative remaining has not led Graß 1) to overlook important aspects of an application of the method and 2) to abandon the tradition that may in the end prove to be a very important locus for answering in part the issue of historicity itself. With regard to the latter it remains to be seen. We turn now, therefore, to a review of his use of the exegetical methods.

Of key importance to his exegetical presuppositions, for example, is his refusal to differentiate between the so-called *Lichterscheinung* or *Lichtglanz* (heavenly radiance) type of appearance story (e.g., Paul's Damascus Road experience) [49]and the appearance in human form type of the gospels. His reasoning runs as follows: in trying to get at what actually happened in an appearance *qua* appearance it is impossible to think of it in the gospel form because they are late, materialistic expressions of resurrection theology so that one must seek to get behind them to the earliest and their more original form, which is the heavenly radiance type. In his own words,

"Die Tatsache, daß die evangelischen Osterberichte durchweg nur einen realistischen Umgang mit dem Auferstandenen kennen, besagt nun aber nicht, daß die Begegnungen mit dem Auf-/erstandenen wirklich so realistisch geschehen sind, sondern daß alle Berichte einer Entwicklungs-

has led to radical conclusions about the gospel appearance stories as legends without historical content, but that does not mean one cannot preach any longer about them. In this vein he urges 1) no one should be compelled to preach about them 2) no one should have to defend the historicity of the stories and 3) the realism here is *Symbol- und Zeichensprache* and as such should enable one to utilize it for visual aids but concentration ought to be upon the kerygmatic content alone.

46 *Ibid.*, p. 85f.

47 *Ibid.*, p. 93. Cf. also p. 107, "Die evangelischen Berichte sind. . .stark legendär und geben kein echtes Bild mehr von den Vorgängen," and p. 220.

48 *Ibid.*, p. 11, where he says, "Auch sind die Ostergeschichten besonders bruchstückhaft, denn selbst wenn es gelänge, alle legendären Bildungen und Wucherungen abzuziehen, so würde sich doch kein Kern herausschälen lassen, von dem gesagt werden könnte, er spiegle die ursprünglichen Ereignisse. . .eindeutig und einleuchtend wider."

49 *Ibid.*, pp. 218ff. and 221f.

stufe des Osterglaubens angehören, in der man sich die Erscheinungen des Herrn nicht mehr anders vorstellen konnte. Die folgende Analyse. . .muß versuchen, ob man hinter diese Entwicklungsstufe noch zurückkommen kann."[50]

"Aber der älteste Osterglaube war noch weit von diesen materialisierenden Vorstellungen entfernt."[51]

"Daß die Erscheinungen des Auferstandenen. . .mit dem Kreis dieser Phänomene (Visionen, Offenbarungen, himmlische Weisungen, ekstatische Vorgänge) zusammengehören, kann von einer nüchternen historischen Betrachtung schwerlich bestritten werden."[52]

If, however, the primary focus of investigation is not what happened and, therefore, the texts need not be discredited as legendary, unreliable accounts under that rubric, then the differentiation between the forms as literary types can stand next to each other as thoroughly distinct–a fact which Graß does not dispute as such. Since his insistence that the heavenly radiance type stands behind the other is predicated upon the impossibility of the material realism of that latter form as an acceptable answer to the "what happened" question, it is to be asked if this step is not unnecessary and literarily without foundation. That is to say, is it legitimate to assume that the heavenly radiance type is constitutive for the appearances in general? Graß superimposes this criterion over the gospel appearance accounts and judges them by their conformity or divergence from it. His argumentation on this point is circular: he points out that ecstatic, visionary enthusiasm is not only attested in the letters of Paul, but also in the gospels so that one can speak of a general atmosphere current in New Testament times both within and without the immediate context of the primitive church and that a direct analogy between this kind of experience and the appearances of the resurrected One exists–therefore, the gospel appearance stories must have been such too. [53] Furthermore, Paul appears to make no distinction in I Cor. 15. Two major objections must be raised here: 1) if it may be granted that the gospel appearance stories are not pure eyewitness accounts of a biographical nature, but are theological statements of intense complexity this does not mean that they must give place to a supposed earlier, more authentic form on the grounds that such was known elsewhere in the "experience" of the participants and therefore becomes the only logical alternative, and 2) that Paul sees his own appearance as a substantial parallel to those of the other apostles does not necessarily mean that originally they were all parallel in form as well. The distinction and integrity of the two forms must be maintained without prejudicing one over against the other because of a search for historically trustworthy information.

To those observations must be added a word on the accuracy of the term *Lichterscheinung* as a designation for the actual experience of the disciples and Paul at all. Graß opts for this designation because he wishes to emphasize the "from above"

50 *Ibid.*, pp. 89f.
51 *Ibid.*, p. 206.
52 *Ibid.*, p. 207. Cf. also then the development of this thesis on pp. 226ff.
53 *Ibid.* Michaelis' objection to the inclusion of ἐν πνεύματι appearances here is correct, Graß, p. 222, notwithstanding.

dimension and to place the reality of a resurrection appearance experience on the level of vision, both of which seem to be amenable to it. With regard to the former it would appear dubious to assume 1) that sufficient clarity with regard to the term in the history-of-religion backgrounds allows the designation to carry exclusive weight for this concept desired, and 2) that the accounts subsumed under that term in the New Testament by Graß and others are in fact representations of the type presumed. The latter aspect is certainly key for Graß' entire argumentation, but it is equally as troublesome as the other. He says,

"Die Christophanie des Paulus ist als ein Vorgang zu verstehen. . .Dann ist die Folgerung unausweichlich, daß es sich um eine wirkliche Vision des Paulus gehandelt hat. . ."[54]

"Es besteht aber keine Notwendigkeit und für eine historische Betrachtung auch keine Möglichkeit, um der Sonderstellung der Ostererscheinungen willen ihren visionären Charakter zu bestreiten."[55]

Others have used the category vision for the appearances and have laid the emphasis thereby on the subjective experience of the participants. Graß maintains that the majority of opposition to this category comes from those who resist reducing the content of subject matter to the subjective personal level, since, after all, this opens the door to fabrication and self-deception. He agrees with this objection, but adds that vision does not necessarily mean *subjective vision*. He sees no way out of retaining the vision category itself and qualifies it by insisting on the term *objective vision*, i.e., God actively initiates the appearance and not the "seer" and activates thereby the visionary receptive capacity of the individual(s).[56] As we shall see later the attempts often made to differentiate between dream visions and visions in a waking state, etc., in the spectrum of history-of-religion comparative materials are fraught with difficulties, but it should be mentioned here that Graß is not really heading in either direction since his concern is to differentiate between what can be said about the "visions" from the perspective of an objective historian and from that of *theologischer Betrachtung*.[57] It must be said that the concern behind Graß' statements here is correct, but selection of the term vision is in any event unfortunate for the entire spectrum of the resurrection appearances, because it obliterates the distinction between these and communications "in the Spirit" which not only Luke but also Paul himself makes.[58] The relationship between the so-called heavenly radiance type and visions as categories of representation needs to be the subject of further research, but to bring vision—even "objective vision"—and gospel appearance stories together is inadmissible.

Finally then it must be said in summary that our confrontation with Graß on methodological issues and their consequences has led to the necessity for reviewing

54 *Ibid.*, p. 222.
55 *Ibid.*, p. 232. Cf. also p. 226.
56 *Ibid.*, pp. 244ff.
57 *Ibid.*, pp. 242ff.
58 Cf. n. 53.

the way in and the place at which the historical question should be posed. If that question precedes and so dominates the exercise of historical investigation that separate and distinct literary types are brought together and the one considered to be primary is used to discredit the other as secondary, then it must be asked if the placement of the question in relationship to exegetical preparation for it has not been reversed. In this respect Graß represents a continuation methodologically of the last century.[59] To reverse the order of approach by seeking after and finding in the gospel stories only "Easter theology" and "kerygmatic significance" without pursuing the additional questions of form specifics and origins, and in the heavenly radiance type both theological significance and *Ostergeschichte* via *theologische Betrachtung*[60] is problematical in view of the need for an unprejudiced history-of-tradition analysis of the gospel appearance stories themselves. *Gattung* determination along with the probe of possible history-of-religion backgrounds for the anthropomorphic type of appearance story is for Graß as good as non-existent and such is an indispensable aspect of the inquiry at hand. In this regard a testing of the adequacy of history-of-religion terminology in general–not only *Lichtglanz* but also such widely accepted designations as "Christophany," "Angelophany," etc.–must be made. Moreover, other terms like "Legend," "Report," "History," "Story" must all constitute aspects of an alternate approach in an analysis of this traditional complex, even if observations in this regard can only make suggestive strides in a direction that must be filled out in a systematic direction.

Demonstrating a keen interest in the relationship of the various resurrection traditions to one another is U. Wilckens in his many publications on the topic from 1961 to the present. His early statements on methodology appeared in his article "Das Offenbarungsverständnis in der Geschichte des Urchristentums" in *Offenbarung als Geschichte* (ed. W. Pannenberg), 1961, and was developed further with regard to the gospel appearance stories in his articles "Der Ursprung der Überlieferung der Erscheinungen des Auferstandenen" in *Dogma und Denkstrukturen* (ed. W. Joest and W. Pannenberg), 1963, "Jesusüberlieferung und Christuskerygma - Zwei Wege urchristlicher Überlieferungsgeschichte" in *Theologia Viatorum* (ed. U. Wilckens), 1966, "Die Überlieferungsgeschichte der Auferstehung Jesu" in *Die Bedeutung der Auferstehungsbotschaft* (ed. F. Viering), 1966, and finally in his book *Auferstehung. Das biblische Auferstehungszeugnis historisch untersucht und erklärt* (Themen der Theologie Vol. 4), 1970.[61] As in the case of Graß so too Wilckens not only begins with I Cor. 15 because it is the earliest form but also ascribes to it primary importance because it alone is ostensibly constitutive for the earliest Christian understanding of the appearances. In contrast to Graß, however, Wilckens is not chiefly interested in the question of historical veracity but in the origins and formation of the traditions within the developing theological reflections of an expanding

59 *Ibid.*, p. 14, but also pp. 233ff. and our remarks above pp. 21ff.

60 *Ibid.*, p. 253.

61 The last named work is apparently the "wissenschaftliche Begründung" announced as forthcoming in U. Wilckens, "Die Überlieferungsgeschichte der Auferstehung Jesu," *Die Bedeutung der Auferstehungsbotschaft*, ed. by F. Viering (Gütersloh, 1966), p. 46, n.2. Now as paperback, Gütersloh, 1974.

church. Wilckens does not wish to make light of the historical question (over against von Campenhausen),[62] but he is convinced that the method of a history-of-tradition analysis must work backwards through the processes of a *Vorstellungsgeschichte.*[63] His goal is 1) to determine what role the various levels of tradition played in the original setting of the church and 2) to come to grips with the concepts resident in the language forms of those traditions: "Die Verbindung schließlich dieser zweiten mit jener ersten Frage führt zu einer detaillierten Erkenntnis der Überlieferungsgeschichte; und erst diese ist der allgemeine Rahmen der historischen Frage nach den Ostereereignissen selbst."[64] The manner in which Wilckens achieves this proposed goal is crucial: a history-of-tradition analysis includes a *vorstellungshistorische Betrachtungsweise,*[65] which means for him the reconstruction of the probable thought-historical context for the expressions of the various traditions. He begins with the eschatological preaching of the earliest missionaries (cf., I Thess. 1: 9f) and concludes that the chief point preached was that God raised Jesus from the dead and exalted him to Lord in the heights of glory and power.[66] The context for this preaching was that, exalted, the Lord is the guarantor of salvation for those believing in him and that the destiny of those is locked up in their expectation of being raised just as he in fact had been raised, but in the (near) eschatological future.[67] The hope of such a resurrection is that of early Jewish apocalyptic and a wedding of this hope and the conviction of its new foundation in the reality of Christ's Resurrection localizes the center of early resurrection traditions. The appearance stories of the gospels, however, do not belong in this earliest period nor in Palestinian environs at all—he claims, for instance, that Mark did not even know such stories at the time he composed his gospel[68]—but arise as a later Hellenistic outgrowth: they do not belong to "dem judenchristlich-urgemeindlichen und auch nicht dem Bereich der paulinischen Mission, sondern dem der hellenistischen Gemeinden im nördlich angrenzenden palästinisch-syrischen Gebiet". . ."Aus Jesus, dem eschatologisch vollmächtigen Rabbi, wurde Jesus, der epiphane Gottessohn, der einzigartige θεῖος ἀνήρ und σωτήρ.[69] No, "In diese Anfänge gehören die evangelischen Erscheinungsgeschichten nicht hinein."[70] The hermeneutic principle behind this decision is clear: with the kerygma as the criterion for the earliest form all other forms are then

62 The work in reference here is H. von Campenhausen, *Der Ablauf der Ostereereignisse und das leere Grab* (Heidelberg, 1966, 3rd ed.), whose focus is the aspect of historical veracity resident in a kernel, at least, related to the events in and around the empty tomb tradition. He appears below in our next chapter under the appropriate section and from time to time elsewhere as well.

63 Wilckens, "Der Ursprung der Überlieferung der Erscheinungen des Auferstandenen," *Dogma und Denkstrukturen, Fst. E. Schlink,* ed. by W. Joest and W. Pannenberg (Gött., 1963), pp. 56f. Cf. also his "Die Perikope vom leeren Grab Jesu in der nachmarkinischen Traditionsgeschichte," *Fst. F. Smend* (Berlin, 1963), p. 30.

64 Wilckens, "Ursprung," p. 57.

65 *Ibid.*, p. 58.

66 *Ibid.*, p. 59.

67 *Ibid.*, pp. 60f.

68 Wilckens, *Auferstehung*, p. 50.

69 Wilckens, "Ursprung," p. 94.

70 *Ibid.*

measured and the degree of their departure places them according to the nature of variance at a corresponding distance from the primary origins of the resurrection traditions. Regarding the beginnings of appearance traditions he says:

"Hier werden die Erscheinungen als Legitimation der Gemeindeführer angeführt. Dem entspricht die Formung der Überlieferung. Es handelte sich um geraffte Formeln sakralrechtlichen Charakters, die darauf abzielten, die bloße Tatsache der Auferweckung und Erscheinungen Jesu vor den dadurch zur Führung berufenen und legitimierten Christen zu nennen. Denn in dem Ereignetsein der Erscheinungen gründete der Führungsanspruch. In der Mission wurden diese Legitimationsformeln dann jedoch zur zusammenfassenden katechetischen Überlieferung gebraucht, in der die Erscheinungen des Auferstandenen die Funktion von Erweisungen seiner ereigneten Auferstehung gewannen."[71]

Thus Wilckens like Graß in the end cannot offer, therefore, a history-of-tradition analysis of the gospel appearance stories either in the strictest sense of the word because he opts for the kerygma and it alone receives then close analytical scrutiny.[72] Moreover, Wilckens shows here his general agreement with Dibelius' thesis as well that it was the Christian mission which gave rise to a shift from the formula tradition to reports: "Aus Formeln thetischen Charakters werden Legenden."[73]

Finally, a similarity to Graß' approach can also be seen in his inquiry into the nature of the appearances as *Widerfahrnis* (occurrence, "a befalling") in view of the terminus ὤφθη. Following his own understanding of *Vorstellungsgeschichte* he asks about its meaning in the Old Testament[74] and sees the immediate conceptual horizon for Paul as that of Jewish apocalyptic.[75] He does qualify the apocalyptic designation by pointing out that no future plans and secrets are revealed here by the resurrected One[76] so that only those texts which speak apocalyptically about the resurrection as event yet to occur constitute that apocalyptic thought-background. Even though Paul sees in his calling the now already raised Jesus[77] and thereby the eschatological raising of the dead as completed,[78] the fundamentally Jewish character of this concept in the primitive Christian message is also supplemented by Paul with Hellenistic traditions.[79] Fundamental to the original pre-pauline concept, moreover, was the exaltation of Jesus who is resident in the heavens with glory and who then appears from there in heavenly splendor.[80] This is as true for the gospels

71 *Ibid.*, p. 81.

72 *Ibid.*, pp. 63-94.

73 *Ibid.*, p. 76. Cf. also U. Wilckens, "Jesusüberlieferung und Christuskerygma–Zwei Wege urchristlicher Überlieferungsgeschichte," *ThViat*, 10 ('65/'66), pp. 328f. Also opting for the formula tradition and in other respects reflecting views similar to Wilckens' is A. Vögtle, "Wie kam es zur Artikulierung des Osterglaubens? ," *BuL*, 14/4 (1973), pp. 231ff.

74 He follows by and large the emphasis there on the singular activity of God, expressed by R. Rendtorff, "Die Offenbarungsvorstellungen im Alten Israel," *Offenbarung als Geschichte*, ed. by W. Pannenberg (Gött., 1961), pp. 21ff., esp. 23ff.

75 Wilckens, "Ursprung," p. 84 and *Auferstehung*, pp. 111ff. and 128ff.

76 Wilckens, "Ursprung," p. 86.

77 *Ibid.*, pp. 87f.

78 *vollzogen, ibid.*, p. 88.

79 *Ibid.*, pp. 89ff.

80 Wilckens, *Auferstehung*, pp. 89ff. Cf. below n. 181.

as for Paul and/or John the Seer in the Book of Revelation: "So macht es keinen grundlegenden Unterschied. . ." [81] We shall see below that it does, however, make a very big difference when it comes to the issue of dependence and especially of Hellenistic ϑεῖος ἀνήρ backgrounds for the gospel stories. [82] Raising in this context then the question of historical explication for the emergence of early Christian resurrection preaching Wilckens says:

> "Zunächst ist nach den *Osterereignissen* zu fragen, die der ältesten Osterüberlieferung zugrunde liegen. Nach den Untersuchungen. . .kommen hier von vornherein nur zwei Texte in Betracht: 1. die Ostergeschichte Mark. 16, 1-8 in ihrer ältesten Gestalt und 2. die Formelreihe I Kor. 15, 5ff., in der die Erscheinungen des Auferstandenen aufgezählt werden. . .[unanimity exists], daß es sich jedenfalls bei der Ersterscheinung vor Petrus I Kor. 15,5 um ein wirkliches Erlebnis handelt, das Petrus wahrscheinlich in Galiläa widerfahren ist. . .Dort ist ihm. . .eine *Vision* [italics mine] nach Art der von Paulus Gal. 1,15 beschriebenen 'Offenbarung' widerfahren. . ."[83]

This term "vision" recurs frequently thereafter without direct recourse to the "objective" qualification of Graß, but in content and means of arriving at this designation the two are for all intents and purposes inseparable. The kerygma has again become constitutive for an understanding of the gospel stories [84] and the latter have come up short.

In general, publications in catholic quarters of New Testament research on our question since the second Vatican Council display on the one hand an openness to and energetic involvement in the critical questions and methods of contemporary historical investigation, and on the other hand misgivings over against the extremes found in certain protestant quarters and a readily apparent concern for the exigencies of practical "constructive" interpretation. This leads more often than not to a combining of the two sides in the development of the investigation itself. A good example is to be seen in the work of the professor for Biblical Theology in the Aachen Priesterseminar, J. Kremer, *Die Osterbotschaft der vier Evangelien*, 1969³ (originally 1968; cf. also his. . *.denn sie werden leben. Sechs Kapitel über Tod, Auferstehung, Neues Leben*, 1972, and *Das älteste Zeugnis von der Auferstehung Christi*, 1970³ [originally 1966]). After the success of his first work on the resurrection (I Cor. 15)–*Das älteste Zeugnis*–he was asked by many friends and colleagues to address himself to the gospel narratives in order–as becomes clear throughout the work–to bring a word of clarity and balance to an inflammatory, controversial area. He states that the critical methods and conclusions of modern biblical research have made many uneasy about the reliability of the gospel accounts [85] and, therefore, his goal in following what he understands the task of scientific research of these texts to be is to interpret the Easter message of the gospels in an understandable and believable way and also so "daß auch der kritisch eingestellte Leser unserer Tage sie

81 *Ibid.*, p. 91.
82 Cf. below pp. 231ff.
83 *Ibid.*, p. 145.
84 Cf. also *ibid.*, p. 71.
85 J. Kremer, *Die Osterbotschaft der vier Evangelien* (Stutt., 1969, 3rd ed.), p. 5. Cf. also his evaluation of the current state of research in "Ist Jesus wirklich von den Toten auferstanden? ," *StZ*, 183 (1969), pp. 310ff.

als eine ihn angehende, glaubwürdige Botschaft verstehen kann."[86] This means for Kremer in the development of his analysis a recurrent asking of the question of historical reliability, rejection of the "legend" category as inadequate and confusing and–although often examining texts on their traditional merits–primary interest in their redactional form coupled with the question what this witness means "for us" today. By and large Kremer shows a great deal of reserve in attributing historical fact to the accounts choosing rather to stress that the forms of expression here are to be understood in the ancient context (especially Old Testament Jewish, but also Hellenistic on occasion). Yet, he is equally reserved over against the skepticism which denies historical backgrounds saying that the sources do not offer historical reports in the way that we understand the historian's work today, but that does not mean that these forms of expression are any less true. In fact, in view of the quandary faced by the evangelists to express the inexpressible, the "mythological" or "legendary" forms–understood in their strictest sense–are more adequate expressions of truth than report. Kremer too then–as many others–starts from the point of the contemporary state of research and develops an apologetic, as it were, in connection with one aspect of that discussion, namely historical skepticism. His solution to the problem is: 1) not to deny directly the difficulties here but to underscore the integrity of the question itself by declaring that the forms of antiquity do not necessarily militate against historical truth, and 2) to maintain focus on redaction criticism so that the "what does this mean" question may be primary and may become the needed link to his practical theological interests, the "for us today" question. In terms of method then *Traditionsgeschichte* does find its place in his work but only in terms of part one of his solution which is dominated by the problem of historicity and although he can occasionally speak of relationships between the traditional levels under the rubric of literary dependence (or lack of same), motifs and themes, such is sporadic and not directed at the possibility that at this level the sources may share a common form and purpose. His goal has been a general attempt at interpretation and that he has done admirably; one can sympathize with his concerns which are manifest throughout and still opt for an even more rigorous application of the historical-critical method without abandoning the hope that the conclusions may lead to the "building up of the saints." In light of his remarks[87] it is to be assumed that Kremer himself welcomes such efforts.

The focus of P. Seidensticker, *Die Auferstehung Jesu in der Botschaft der Evangelien*, 1967, is in spite of its title not primarily the gospel appearance narratives, but rather their place in the developing Easter proclamation of primitive Christianity. The author's goal is to determine the earliest form of this proclamation and then to trace its development throughout the texts bearing witness to both. His methodological approach thereby is not as much a history-of-tradition analysis of the gospel texts as it is a more abstract "thought historical" analysis, i.e., into the living situation of earliest Christianity which had a virgin assurance of the reality of the Resurrection itself he projects the question: how was this event conceived and proclaimed

86 Kremer, *Osterbotschaft*, p. 12.
87 Cf. *ibid.*, p. 5.

to the world? The *Resurrection* itself is the fundamental given and to it the church responds with its *proclamation* of it. Having this base for working further he turns quite naturally to the sermons in Acts for support of this base and then focuses attention upon the kerygmatic formula of I Cor. 15 as our earliest literary witness to the Resurrection event. He concludes here that older and younger elements have been combined and that the oldest form of the kerygma contained only the statement: "he appeared to more than five hundred at one time" (he translates "once and for all")! Seeking a correspondence to this form then in the gospels he concludes that the "galilaean appearance" of Mt. 28:16-20 is this very appearance referred to in the kerygma calling it the "apocalyptic type." The two other group appearances of Lk. and Jn. also originate in this type and were re-formed or "translated" [88] to meet the theological interests of those two evangelists. Jn. 21 is ruled out as an appearance at all in the strictest sense–it is a reworking of the earthly ministry tradition found in Lk. 5 for a later situation [89]–and the Emmaus story and the Mary Magdalene (and Peter) pericope are later legendary accounts of no constitutive value for the establishment of the church since they arise rather out of the pious memory of individuals (*Erlebnisberichte privater Art*); [90] moreover, the latter adopt an entirely different thought-form from the original type, namely the real, physical appearance concept which finds its origin in the Jewish dogma of the resurrection of the body. Jn. 20 then shows a return to the original "apocalyptic" type where the key interest is not in the demonstration of bodily reality but the communion and fellowship between the resurrected Lord and his Church. [91]

It is imperative that we examine the presuppositions operating behind the methodological decisions and final conclusions of this original and interesting attempt at solving the complex issues. Important for understanding Seidensticker's interpretation is his particular concept of early Christianity which presupposes a sophisticated degree of theological reflection. But in addition to this he sees the church involved in missionary proclamation and above all discussion and dialogue with Judaism. This latter aspect is in fact normative for the development of the tradition: the church formulates its statements of resurrection proclamation in such a way as to be understood by Jewish hearers, especially theologically trained Jewish hearers. This has the following consequences for him: the pre-synoptic Easter proclamation had two interpretive categories at its disposal in its Jewish context, 1) the terms "be raised" or "arise" which came from the early Jewish teaching of the eschatological resurrection of the dead and 2) the teaching which was also acute in *Frühjudentum* of the suffering and then the later glorification of the righteous One "die sowohl beim einzelnen Frommen wie auch kollektiv beim ganzen Volke Israel angewendet

88 P. Seidensticker, *Die Auferstehung Jesu in der Botschaft der Evangelisten*, StBSt, 26 (Stutt., 1967), p. 79. Cf. also P. Seidensticker, "Das Antiochenische Glaubensbekenntnis I Kor. 15, 3-7 im Lichte seiner Traditionsgeschichte," *ThGl*, 57 (1967), pp. 286-323.

89 Seidensticker, *Auferstehung*, p. 65.

90 *Ibid.*, p. 75. Cf. also p. 105.

91 *Ibid.*, pp. 129ff and 147.

wurde und sogar bis in die eschatologischen Verdichtungen dieses Motivs in messianischen Gestalten (Gottesknecht, Menschensohn) wirksam ist."[92] The latter was chosen as the more appropriate to the original understanding of the church on the resurrection question. Bound up with this concept was also that of the apocalyptic translation of the prophets Enoch, Elijah and other righteous Ones.[93] These concepts were then taken over and applied to Jesus, as the sermons of Acts as well as other texts, e.g., Phil. 2:6-11, I Tim. 3:16, etc., ostensibly demonstrate.[94] Additional witness to this decision for the second interpretive category is to be found, according to the author, in the oldest form of the antiochaean formula of faith, the appearance to 500 (I Cor. 15:6)[95] which is reproduced in the gospels in Mt. 28:16-20 (also the Mk. 16:7 reference).[96] That is to say, the original "proclamation of Christ" outside the sermons of Acts spoke of only one single Easter appearance.[97]

Before tracing further developments he attempts to anchor the solidarity of witness to the initial interpretive category of the church by investigating the content of this second group of witnesses. Beginning with the terminus ὤφθη he concludes that it is in and of itself nebulous, that the other gospel accounts make their statements without its help and that, therefore, only Paul himself (I Cor. 15:8) in the Damascus Road experience can be of help in determining the nature of that single appearance under question.[98] Regarding Paul's experience then he concludes that Paul, knowing himself related to the classical prophets of the Old Testament, represented his experience in the same expression as they, i.e., he used the form of Old Testament *Epiphanie-Berichte*—the *Lichtglanz* visionary type.[99] Out of this then he draws the following conclusions for the content of the pre-synoptic appearance type of I Cor. 15:6 and Mt. 28:16-20: the same *Epiphanie-Bericht* representation is behind them. In quest of more light on the revelation aspect of this type he then investigates the Old Testament theophanies of the visionary δόξα—*Herrlichkeit* sort,[100] which he characterizes as "apocalyptic," secret-picture symbolic (Isa. 6:1, Ez. 1:4-3:16 and Ex. 19:16-19)[101] and applies to it the designation *Osterberichte apokalyptischen Stils.*[102] Inextricably bound up with this "style" was the concept of the messianic regent which was applied to the Easter lordship of Jesus (*Thronmotiv*).[103] He sees this reflected, as it were, in the Son of Man christology:[104] "Jesus erscheint in der Gestalt und Macht des 'Menschensohnes',"[105] (cf. also Acts 7:55f. and Mk.

92 *Ibid.*, p. 17.
93 *Ibid.*, p. 18.
94 *Ibid.*, pp. 17ff.
95 *Ibid.*, pp. 26ff.
96 *Ibid.*, p. 28.
97 *Ibid.*, p. 29.
98 *Ibid.*, pp. 31ff.
99 *Ibid.*, pp. 36ff.
100 *Ibid.*, pp. 40ff.
101 *Ibid.*, p. 42.
102 *Ibid.*, p. 43.
103 *Ibid.*, pp. 44f.
104 *Ibid.*, p. 45.
105 *Ibid.*, p. 46.

9:2-8).[106] In connection then with II Pet. 1:16-19 he draws the remaining threads imaginatively together by claiming historical recollection for the author of II Pet. 1:18 about the "holy mountain" whose experience is grounded in the Mount of Transfiguration (Mk. 9:2), the same mountain as Mt. 28:16, which stands in a *heilsgeschichtlich* relationship to Mount Sinai: "Insbesondere stellt der Berg Sinai als Ort der Begegnung Israels mit seinem Gott, die zur Gründung des Gottesvolkes und des ewigen Bundes führte (Ex. 19-24), auch den Berg in Galiläa in sein Licht, wo die konstituierende Begegnung der Jüngergemeinde mit dem österlichen Herrn geschah."[107] He concludes then sweepingly,

". . .daß in der Frühzeit der Urgemeinde die österliche Offenbarung des Auferstandenen mit den Stilmitteln der Apokalyptik als Parusie, als 'Kommen des Menschensohnes' dargestellt und als die Machtübertragung und Präsentation des Messias-Menschensohnes verstanden wurde, so wird auch verständlich, *warum die Kirche sich mit einer einzigen Ostererscheinung zufrieden gab: Das 'Kommen' des Menschensohnes ist einmalig und erfolgt 'ein für allemal'* [italics mine] (1 Kor 15, 6)."[108]

and

". . .so können wir als Ergebnis registrieren, daß es vor unseren Evangelien einen Typ von Osterüberlieferungen gegeben hat, der die Erscheinung des Herrn im apokalyptischen Stil als das von Jesus selbst verheißene Kommen des Menschensohnes in Macht und Herrlichkeit, als Parusiegeschehen verstanden und verkündet hat (2 Pet 1, 16ff.)."[109]

He returns then to his investigation of further developments of the Easter traditions and offers the following explanation for the retreat of the original "apocalyptic" type: this type was not "close enough to reality" so that it stood in danger of being misunderstood and misrepresented in the discussion on the proclaimed Easter event as unreal,[110] "discussion" meaning here confrontation with Judaism. The Pharisees did not have any understanding for apocalyptic, but believed in the resurrection of the body and, therefore, the church switched to the other option at its disposal for representing the character of the Easter event, although it was less adequate, i.e., poorer theologically: "Die Kirche aber ist realistisch genug, auf ungeeignete [here the apocalyptic] Darstellungsweisen in ihrer Verkündigung zu verzichten, wenn es die Notwendigkeiten ihrer Predigt nach innen und außen erfordern"[111] and, "Damit ist gleichzeitig die neue Situation angezeigt, die zur Entstehung der Evangelien überhaupt geführt hat. Die Kirche beginnt, ihren Auftrag in dieser Welt klar zu erfassen und zu normieren."[112] Of particular interest is Seidensticker's understanding of the historical situation responsible for the emergence of the so-called

106 *Ibid.*, pp. 47f.
107 *Ibid.*, p. 53.
108 *Ibid.*, p. 54.
109 *Ibid.*, p. 55.
110 *Ibid.*, p. 56.
111 *Ibid.*, p. 57.
112 *Ibid.*, p. 58.

"resurrection body"/"Jerusalem-type" representations. He says,

> "Das Anwachsen der *pharisäischen Geistesrichtung* innerhalb der Urgemeinde in Jerusalem, der die Welt der Apokalyptik fernliegt, wird schon sehr früh einen Wechsel im darstellersichen Motiv des Osterereignisses veranlaßt haben, zumal die auftretende Diskussion um die Osterbotschaft der Kirche eine gemeinsame Plattform mit den Diskussionsteilnehmern erforderte."[113]

> "Die im vorsynoptischen Stadium verbreitete Form einer im apokalyptischen Stil vorgetragenen Osterverkündigung wird zurückgedrängt, weil die missionarischen Notwendigkeiten eine Akkomodierung der Verkündigung verlangte [sic]. Die Kirche 'übersetzt' ihre apokalyptische Aussage von der österlichen Parusie des Menschensohnes in die realistische Stilform der Deutungskategorie 'Leibliche Auferweckung von den Toten.' Diese Transponierung ist notwendig geworden, weil die Diskussion mit dem Judentum (Sadduzäismus, Pharisäismus) auf breiter Front begonnen hatte und selbst in der Kirche sich der Zweifel am richtigen Verständnis der Osterbotschaft zu Worte meldete (Mt 28, 17b)."[114]

> "Ein Überblick über die Entwicklung der Osterpredigt in der apostolischen Zeit zeigt, daß die Kirche in jenem ersten Jahrhundert eine enorme geistige, theologische Leistung vollbrachte, um das Ostergeschehen in seiner Bedeutung zu verstehen, glaubwürdig zu verkünden und zu sichern."[115]

In spite of the energetic and imaginative nature of this solution it must be asked if it is not a construct which creates conditions without actual historical foundation. It sounds as though the rise and dissemination of resurrection traditions took place among 20th century theologians rather than believers in the ancient context. Moreover, a debate with Judaism in the way and to the degree assumed here as the motivation for a major transition of thought is equally dubious; that missionary outreach —and especially mission as theological debate with pharisaic Judaism—is the catalyst behind the process forming the gospel stories outside the proposed "galilaean type" is conjecture.

One could question the exegesis leading to the author's conclusions about I Cor. 15:6 and the derivation of types from the two options, as it were, at the "disposal" of early Christianity as well, but more significant for our purposes is what consequences the supposed "apocalyptic type" has for treatment of the gospel appearance stories themselves: [116] these do not require a careful history-of-tradition, history-of-religion investigation because they were not constitutive for the early church and reflect trends of less theological weight than the "earlier" one; they are private experiences allowing for their separation from the only genuine appearance story, namely the group appearance of the "galilaean type" found in Mt. 28, Lk. 24 and Jn. 20. This reduction and neglect of the full complement is the product of the method, not unlike that of Graß, which judges it by a separate traditional strata, the kerygma.

Somewhat more concealed but nevertheless a fully operative presupposition is also the historical question here: the author asks the "what happened" question

113 *Ibid.*, p. 71.
114 *Ibid.*, p. 104.
115 *Ibid.*, p. 150.
116 *Ibid.*, pp. 76 and 79.

throughout and although he does not allege that we can know what it was through these texts he chooses rather to affirm the historicity matter on the basis that 1) it grounds and establishes itself[117] and 2) it is witnessed to by the Church's testimony in all of its variety and is worthy of belief on the basis of the integrity of that testimony. A particular understanding of the Church is at work in the background here, and the Resurrection event and appearance stories have been separated conveniently as sectors a) for belief and b) for subjection to the historical question. [118] In this way, as noted in other works as well, the historicity question is indeed a hindrance to the independent, careful treatment of the gospel accounts which they deserve.

Two books of recent vintage on our theme have been written at the University of Regensburg, the one coming from F. Mußner, *Die Auferstehung Jesu*, 1969, who is professor for Biblical Theology (NT) there, and the other from his assistants, F. Schnider and W. Stenger, *Die Ostergeschichten der Evangelien*, 1970. Mußner's excellent contribution falls outside the realm of our immediate attention, however, because it foregoes an exact analysis of the gospel appearance stories and chooses rather to refer on this matter to the books of Seidensticker, Kremer and above all Schnider/Stenger. The latter then provides the most recent analysis of our question from catholic exegesis, [119] in which Mußner himself writes the forward and credits the book as *Ergänzung* to his. Moreover, the preface points out that the primary goal is to offer: "Hilfe für Prediger und Katecheten" and a "positive Formgeschichte, die zur Vertiefung der Glaubenseinsicht zu führen vermag." [120] The direction of these two statements is, indeed, repeated in the book itself. It must be said that the work is very limited in scope and that it does not offer a history-of-tradition analysis in the strictest sense, but rather a form- and redaction-critical overview as something of a handbook for interested laymen.

One of the most recent publications on the formation of the gospel appearance

117 *Ibid.*, pp. 82 and 145.

118 *Ibid.*, p. 74.

119 Also deserving of mention, however, among the most recent Roman Catholic works is E.L. Bode, *The First Easter Morning. The Gospel Accounts of the Women's Visit to the Tomb of Jesus*, AnBibl, 45 (Rome, 1970), but since the author's primary interest is the tomb tradition his contribution, like that of von Campenhausen, will appear below (ch. II) in the appropriate section. Although G. Lohfink has focused his attention on the ascension and the pauline appearance questions (cf. below ns. 437 and 181) he has also offered a contribution to the question of the gospel appearance stories in his "Die Auferstehung Jesu und die historische Kritik," *BuL*, 9 (1968), pp. 37-53. He points out, for example, that an analysis of their literary *Gattung* is badly needed. He makes many suggestive distinctions in the article and then says, "Wenn man versucht, die literarische Gattung dieser Erzählungen zu bestimmen, könnte man am ehesten von *Verkündigungserzählungen* sprechen. Sie dienen der Verkündigung, daß Jesus wirklich von den Toten auferstanden ist" (p. 43). We have already met this basic orientation in Dibelius and Dodd and it would appear that further pursuance of the *Gattung* question beyond Lohfink's categories here is necessary. Moreover, he opts for an analysis of I Cor. 15 under the question of historicity–not unlike Graß–and leaves thereby many questions unanswered regarding the gospel stories themselves (pp. 46ff.).

120 F. Schnider and W. Stenger, *Die Ostergeschichten der Evangelien*, Schriften zur Katechetik, 13, ed. by P. Neuenzeit (Mü., 1970), p. 7.

narratives in the English language is R.H. Fuller's, *The Formation of the Resurrection Narratives* (first published in the USA in 1971 and then in England in 1972), which began as lectures at Union Theological Seminary, New York, in the summer session of 1967, was expanded and rewritten and in part delivered orally in 1969 during a sabbatical in Europe. In his introduction Fuller says,

". . .it is the task of the systematic theologian to wrestle with the scientific, philosophical, and theological problems posed by the New Testament message of Christ's resurrection, but it is the task of the New Testament scholar to probe the historical basis of this proclamation. . .It is this task which the present work has set itself–a critical study of the resurrection narratives."[121]

Such has not been attempted in English for over a generation, he maintains, and then he points to the works of K. Lake[122] and P. Gardner-Smith[123] as earlier works which used only the method of source-criticism.[124] Now we have better methods and the time is ripe for a fresh attempt using the new methods.[125] In terms of secondary literature he says that M. Goguel is valuable but outdated and then he mentions the essays by W. Marxsen, *et al.* and H. Graß.[126] He announces that he will follow his own independent line on certain major issues, e.g., the tomb tradition, but in the main he acknowledges indebtedness to the aforementioned essays and Graß.[127] His plan is to work from I Cor. 15 to the gospels:

"In doing so our purpose will be to reconstruct the history of the tradition from its earliest recoverable form in allegedly factual reports (beyond this the historian cannot go) through its successive developments in the preliterary and literary stages. In the process we shall seek to lay bare the motivations behind the developments and shaping of the narratives into their final form."[128]

He is not trying to smooth away discrepancies or to iron out inconsistencies but to discover the reasons for them and the secret why they could stand side by side in the New Testament.[129] He shows keen interest in the meaning of the appearances as revelation from the other world when he says,

"These are disclosures not of something which is visible or discernible within this world or age by ordinary sight or insight: they are disclosures that come from 'heaven above' to this world, or (as takes place with increasing emphasis in Jewish apocalyptic) from the eschatological future to the present. Such disclosures often include a preview of the end. . .They designate not necessarily physical seeing, not necessarily visions in a subjective sense (involving, for example, ecstasy or dreams), but a revelatory self-disclosure or disclosure by God of the eschatologically resurrected Christos."[130]

121 R.H. Fuller, *The Formation of the Resurrection Narratives* (London, 1972), p. 6.
122 K. Lake, *The Historical Evidence for the Resurrection of Jesus Christ* (N.Y., 1907).
123 P. Gardner-Smith, *The Narratives of the Resurrection* (London, 1926).
124 R.H. Fuller, *op. cit.*, p. 6.
125 *Ibid.*, pp. 6f.
126 *Ibid.*
127 *Ibid.*
128 *Ibid.*, p. 7.
129 *Ibid.*, pp. 7f.
130 *Ibid.*, p. 31.

He, like Graß, then appeals to Paul, I Cor. 9:1, the Damascus Road experience, Gal. 1:16, etc., and says that arguing this eschatological meaning for the *gospels* as well as for *Paul* is legitimate "since he [Paul] arranges them in a continuous series," [131] In his section, "The Nature of the Appearances," [132] which comes before the actual historical-critical analysis, he objects, however, to the term (objective) "vision" since all strata (except for Acts 26:18) avoid this term; the real problem is "that there are no categories available for the unprecedented disclosure of the eschatological within history," [133] he says, "The farthest we can get perhaps is to say that the *events through which* the Easter revelations were conveyed were visionary, but to describe them as visions, even as 'objective visions,' is not entirely felicitous." [134] This observation is an important corrective to the use of a term which has found more or less indiscriminate application on more than one occasion in works reviewed up to this point. Yet, the retention of the category at all creates additional hindrances for an analysis of the gospel stories because of its prejudicial weight. This raises then the question of the relationship of the various appearance traditions to one another in Fuller's view of the subject matter and forms.

It is somewhat difficult to arrive at a clear answer to this question because of the way that he jumps somewhat sporadically back and forth between I Cor. 15 and the gospels. He concentrates, moreover, on individual aspects of relationship in a way reminiscent of the approaches used by Albertz and Brun. It is clear, however, that like Graß, *et al.*, Paul's experience becomes the measure of the gospel stories. He says:

"What we know of Paul's appearances (enlarged by his other references to it [sic]) can be applied. . .to the interpretation of the earlier appearances."[135]

"Such appearances, we may conclude, involved visionary experiences of light, combined with a communication of meaning. They were not in their innermost essence incidents open to neutral observance or verification, but revelatory events in which the eschatological and christological significance of Jesus was disclosed, and in which the recipient was called to a particular function in salvation history."[136]

"Their outward, historically definable form is a vision (perhaps a vision of 'light'), accompanied by an audition (i.e., a communication of meaning)."[137]

Like Wilckens, moreover, Fuller assumes that Mk ended at 16:8 intentionally

131 *Ibid.*, p. 32.
132 *Ibid.*, pp. 32ff.
133 *Ibid.*, p. 33.
134 *Ibid.* On p. 202, n. 48, he quotes E.G. Selwyn, "The Resurrection," *Essays Catholic and Critical*, ed. by E.G. Selwyn (London, 1938), pp. 281-319, esp. pp. 296-299 and Graß as the chief exponents of "objective vision" although Selwyn preferred "veridical visions" (p. 310). Fuller claims that the objective vision hypothesis is to be traced back to T. Keim and his 'telegram from heaven' theory of the appearances.
135 *Ibid.*, p. 43.
136 *Ibid.*, p. 48.
137 *Ibid.*, p. 49.

because he did not know of any appearance *stories*; he knew only of the kerygma and to that Mk suggestively refers in the angel's words. [138] Mk reflects, therefore, a time of traditional development roughly equivalent to I Cor. 15 and is in any case earlier than the gospel narratives of the appearances. [139] The appearance before the women in Mt., moreover, is important, among other reasons, because this is the first instance of materialization of the appearances; as lists they had retained a spiritual character, but:

". . .they could be narrated as external events only by modeling them on the stories of encounters with Jesus during his earthly ministry. It is particularly significant that it is precisely those later traits in the narrative tradition of the earthly Jesus' ministry which represent him as a 'divine man' (theios anēr) and are taken into the resurrection narratives. Thus the women 'touch' his feet (cf., Mk. 5:22) and they 'worship' him (cf., Mk. 5:6). This is the strongest argument against the primitive character of the appearance *narratives*."[140]

Taking Mt. further as a representative in the question of relationship to the kerygma, Fuller, sounding again much like Wilckens, says:

"This history of the tradition runs from I Cor. 15:5 through Mk. 16:7 to Mt. 28:16, not from the source of Mt. 28:16 to I Cor. 15:51."[141]

and in regard to the origins of a motif like doubt:

"Since there is no / evidence prior to Matthew's Gospel for the existence of appearance *narratives,* we surmise too that a reference to doubts may have occurred in some lists of appearances. . ."[142]

". . .it is possible that Matthew knew of a list of appearances which, unlike Paul's list, located the primary appearances *on a mountain* in Galilee."[143]

Positing Syrian origins for the narratives in Lk. and also for the gospels in general, he says:

"It was here [Syria], in circles which loved to tell stories and which operated with a theios anēr (divine man) interpretation of the earthly Jesus, that the late resurrection narratives may well have originated. In them the Risen One is portrayed on the one hand precisely as if he were still the earthly Jesus. . .All these data are reproduced from the tradition of the earthly Jesus in the Gospels. Yet on the other hand he is a mysterious 'divine man', who appears and disappears at will."[144]

A further characteristic of his approach is seen in the following statement on the Emmaus story:

138 *Ibid.*, pp. 66f.
139 *Ibid.*, p. 66.
140 *Ibid.*, p. 79.
141 *Ibid.*, p. 80.
142 *Ibid.*, pp. 8lf.
143 *Ibid.*, p. 81.
144 *Ibid.*, p. 106.

"It may contain a basic nucleus of historical fact, if it can be identified with one of the appearances included among the appearances 'to all the apostles' and especially if the name Clopas warrants some connection with James. A primitive *statement* of such an appearance, if it is historical, was later thrown into the form of a *narrative* with the kind of legendary elements one might expect in such an environment as Syria—still fairly Semitic in outlook, but with overtones of the theios anēr (divine man) Christology."[145]

Further examples could be multiplied but the forgoing is sufficient to demonstrate that Fuller to a far-reaching degree has produced a synthesis of current European views for the English reader. His format is basically like that of Graß (including the preacher's guide at the end), with the exception that he does not begin with the narratives themselves. Rather, I Cor. 15 is seen as the earliest form of resurrection traditions and then chronologically via date of redactional composition he moves on to Mk., Mt., Lk. and Jn., taking up all resurrection traditions including burial, tomb, appearances and ascension. Moreover, in general his views are largely those of Graß, though he does not allow the vision category to go without further qualification and focuses thereby upon the message of the church which is embedded here. What was said earlier about the problem of positing θεῖος ἀνήρ backgrounds for the gospel stories need not be repeated here.

A more or less contemporaneous publication in English to Fuller (the latter's preface, 1970, indicates that the book in question had not yet appeared at the completion of his own manuscript) on the subject of the Resurrection was C.F. Evans' *Resurrection and the New Testament*, 1970. In order to understand the author's approach one must really begin with his appendix: "The Resurrection: Theology and History."[146] Otherwise it appears that the goal is to probe the question "what happened" in the Easter event, but it becomes clear in that appendix that this line of questioning is really not his own but that of the majority of recent works on the Resurrection. It is no coincidence that the works reviewed there are by systematicians—Ramsey, Künneth, Hooke, Niebuhr, Pannenberg, etc.—for whom the question of historical reality in the Resurrection is central. Here Evans seeks to demonstrate the impossibility of their undertaking. Thus the "what happened" question is for Evans really a rhetorical one! "Preoccupation with the problem of historicity in the resurrection tradition is apparent in much of the best modern writing on the subject."[147] He is writing himself, therefore, primarily from the standpoint of systematic theology with an eye not on the question "what happened" but what do the sources convey about the meaning of the Resurrection and resurrection faith, *since* the sources do not deliver historical information about the event itself! That is the conclusion of his historical-critical evaluation earlier in the book as much as for Paul as for the gospel narratives. The author approaches his New Testament texts by asking first about the idea of resurrection in the milieu of primitive Christianity and while acknowledging that the apocryphal and pseudepigraphical materials do indeed

145 *Ibid.*, p. 113.
146 C.F. Evans, *Resurrection and the New Testament*, StBTh, 12 (London, 1970), pp. 170ff.
147 *Ibid.*, p. 170. Cf. also p. 131.

represent this concept in a variety of forms, this very variety makes it impossible to see a direct link between them and the New Testament resurrection traditions. Moreover, Jesus himself does not seem to make much use of them, so that Evans concludes that the New Testament traditions must have their source in the actual Resurrection of Jesus and says.

". . .if the doctrine of resurrection was not firmly fixed in Judaism, and if it is largely absent from the teaching of Jesus, then / particular attention is focused on the actual resurrection of Jesus. It may be suggested that only this event, whatever it may have been, could have brought it about that there emerged in Christianity a precise, confident and articulate faith in which resurrection has moved from the circumference to the centre."[148]

From this point then he turns to the New Testament resurrection traditions beginning with I Cor. 15. He notes that the list here and the gospels cannot be harmonized; they are distinct from one another [149] and that in regard to Paul's own experience here and statements elsewhere a fundamental distinction must be made as to form. [150] Moreover, Paul's own statements are not distinct enough to state what he considered the appearance to have been: "Thus the pauline evidence hardly provides a fixed point from which the rest of the resurrection tradition may be assessed."[151]

He then turns to the gospels and asks as form-critic about the function and purpose of a resurrection story, what it should say and do. [152] He stresses the original singularity and complete detachment from context prior to redactional work [153] and then says such had one function only, i.e., to say that the Lord is risen or that Jesus is the Lord. [154] One such well-attested story would plainly have been enough then. [155] He lauds Dodd's article, [156] but says among other things that his schematization fails to account for the fact that "some of the stories at least may be more determined in their shape by the significant sayings to which they lead than by a common pattern." [157] This is a key point in Evans' treatment of the gospels because he is wont to stress singularity and ignore patterns of any kind: his primary thesis is that we have here floating traditions and fragments of traditions. He sees the difference between narrative form here in comparison with other gospel material as follows:

". . .their intention cannot be to add to an already existing stock of information about the

148 *Ibid.*, pp. 39f.
149 *Ibid.*, p. 52.
150 *Ibid.*, pp. 55, 66, 105 and 140.
151 *Ibid.*, p. 56.
152 *Ibid.*
153 *Ibid.*
154 *Ibid.*, p. 57.
155 *Ibid.*, p. 58.
156 *Ibid.*, p. 59.
157 *Ibid.*, p. 61.

earthly Jesus. . .What they have to say is directed to all that has / been said, about the earthly Jesus between birth and death, and are intended to place it in a totally new dimension."[158]

"But how could truth of this kind be expressed in the form of a narrative, since narrative of event is related to history, and history can know of no event of such a kind as to stand outside the series of events? The truth is expressed in fact by stories of the man Jesus alive after death making himself known to his friends. . .It could thus be possible for independent stories which originally belonged to the post-resurrection period to wander into the main body of the gospel tradition for lack of any clear indication in the story itself that it was the risen Christ and not the earthly Jesus who was speaking or acting."[159]

"He appeared," as in the kerygmatic formula, is hardly enough to convey a meaning like "he came out of the sphere of eternity and invisibility and was made manifest by God."[160] Here again, we see a suggestion of Evans' antipathy toward forms as themselves capable of speaking and bearing clear indications that a resurrection story is intended. He goes on to deal with the terms around ὤφθη, e.g., "coming into presence," "drawing near," etc., but he does not stumble, as it were, onto a pattern.[161] Interestingly enough he refers to C.F.D. Moule, "The Ascension –Acts 1,9," *Exp. T.* 68 ('56/'57), p. 206, n. 1, where a "linguistic" parallel is drawn to Tobit 12:16-22, but he misses much of the potential of such by stressing the claim of Raphael that this was a mere vision because it seemed he had eaten something;[162] nor does he follow up his brief reference to the history-of-religion backgrounds to the Emmaus story.[163] He goes on then to argue that the gospel stories do not say "he appeared" but that "seeing" here is a kind of confessional metaphor with the christological goal of stating that this One is the Lord and must mean that

". . .something of what was to belong to that 'seeing' which was to take place at the parousia (cf. Mark 14.62) is transferred to the resurrection appearances. This may have been reproduced by Matthew in an appearance in which the risen Jesus is worshipped as the universal Lord (Matt. 28.9, 17ff)."[164]

This inference goes far afield of what otherwise may be won from a historical-critical analysis of the materials. He does distinguish correctly between the Transfiguration and a "seeing-in-glory" and these stories, but in saying that the kerygmatic formula expressed sightings only, while the gospels predominantly express audition comes probably from a misunderstanding of the subject matter behind the terminus, ὤφθη, for the whole tradition.[165] In the gospels "sight" is secondary to what is "heard," he thinks, and there existed no need for attestation of the appearance (in contrast to the kerygma) but only the need to express "various truths which the Lord has to utter."[166] This again raises the question if Evans has not

158 *Ibid*., pp. 61f.
159 *Ibid*., p. 62.
160 *Ibid*.
161 *Ibid*., pp. 62ff.
162 *Ibid*., p. 63, n. 34.
163 *Ibid*., p. 105, n. 107.
164 *Ibid*., p. 65.
165 Cf. *ibid*., p. 66.
166 *Ibid*.

underestimated thereby visual aspects throughout the narratives in opting for what this tradition is "saying." [167] It is, for instance, a matthaean Lord, lukan Lord, johannine Lord who speaks and catches the attention of Evans; it is never the same Lord speaking the same thing. [168] That is to say, Evans' observation points primarily to the redactional level and not to the traditional!

He then considers the four gospels one at a time [169] focusing on a number of diverse problems, many of which are strictly redactional, and is in his overall evaluation quite harsh, e.g.,

"It is plain that Matthew's final chapter furnishes neither reliable historical information nor early Christian tradition about the resurrection, but only an example of later christological belief as it had developed in one area of the church, and of the apologetic which had been conducted in that area in the face of Jewish attacks."[170]

His observations are by no means bereft of traditional considerations, but he admits that his analysis could have been more detailed; nevertheless, his skepticism—not altogether unlike that expressed earlier by Graß—finds expression as follows:

". . .it is likely that however detailed an analysis, it would not diminish the impression that it is not simply difficult to harmonize these traditions, but quite impossible."[171]

"Each of these [expressions of the Easter faith] is complete in itself; each has developed along its own line so as to serve in the end as a proper conclusion for an evangelist of his own particular version of the gospel. . .Each evangelist gives his own version as a total version, which was not intended to stand up only if it stood alongside another, or was supplemented by another.[172]

And with regard to the historical question of the Resurrection itself in connection with the traditions giving witness to it he says,

"Whatever the Easter event was, it must be supposed to be of such a kind as to be responsible for the production of these traditions as its deposit at whatever remove. The events themselves, however, both the resurrection appearances and the empty tomb, lie so deeply concealed within the traditions that they can be glimpsed only very indirectly, so that the principal difficulty here is not to believe, but to know what it is which offers itself for belief."[173]

"There is a marked contrast between the centrality of the Easter faith in the New Testament, and the almost fortuitous character of the traditions which now support it; and between the events on the one hand, which remain so shadowy because the narratives. . .are so casual about the risen Lord's state and condition, and their interpretation / on the other hand, which is expressed so eloquently through the mouth of the risen Lord speaking in Matthaean, Lukan and Johannine tones respectively. The reader of the gospels or preacher of the gospel is likely to be able to appreciate and use this eloquence to the extent that he is not over-preoccupied with historical considerations."[174]

167 *Ibid.*, *et passim.*
168 *Ibid.*, p. 67.
169 *Ibid.*, pp. 67ff.
170 *Ibid.*, p. 85.
171 *Ibid.*, p. 128.
172 *Ibid.*
173 *Ibid.*, p. 130.
174 *Ibid.*, pp. 130ff.

With that we have Evans' manifesto against both Biblicists and all others who would look for history in the resurrection accounts and are not *primarily* listening to the redactional frequency, as it were, of *words*. All the rest is a hindrance! The narratives are already themselves the reflection of a conviction about a "central Christian truth–the exaltation of Jesus to universal status and authority, the effusion of the spirit, the apostolic mission of the Church to the world, and the understanding of the gospel in the light of scripture." [175] He then proceeds to develop a theology of the Resurrection in terms of a so-called "re-active" concept, whereby the action of God is stressed as a response to a human condition or activity. [176] At this point he concludes:

". . .whatever it [the Resurrection] may have been as an event it is now seen to be the *fons et origo* of Christian faith in the lordship of Jesus. However little we may be able from the nature of the sources, to reconstruct what happened at the resurrection, it must be presupposed to be of such a kind as to impart to the earthly ministry and death of Jesus the eschatological import which was deemed proper to them. It made both him and his work new. How far, and in what way, he may himself have contemplated this it is hardly possible to say, since our sources seldom, if ever, ascribe faith to him, but only certain knowledge in advance."[177]

Evans' evaluation of these gospel sources has led to the conclusion that one should dispense with using them for the historical question and concentrate rather on listening to what meaning is coming through *the word* found there. [178] In this he and Graß, for example, are in perfect agreement. While one cannot object, on the one hand, to a rejection of the naive reading of these sources as accounts of strictly historical recollection, one must ask if the conclusion that the sources are so contradictory, irreconcilably diverse and so fortuitous that all forms of "harmonization" are doomed from the outset–even if the motivation is not primarily to anchor historical veracity–is sufficiently grounded exegetically. This poses then for Evans the methodological question: has the historical-critical discipline been applied adequately or has it been itself significantly influenced by this distinctive anti-historical polemic? It would appear that Evans has adopted in reality the same *line of questioning* as those he wishes to confound (in all due respect) and fails thereby to pursue a thoroughgoing historical-critical evaluation of the texts with the requisite–even if preliminary–neutrality on the historical question. This built in blind spot, as it were, prohibits him from accomplishing a consistent development of issues raised in the historical-critical section of his work and its otherwise incisive presentation. Aside from his own over-preoccupation with the "what happened" *line of questioning*–if not the historical question itself–the book does in fact represent one of the best works available in English on the need for and use of historical-critical methods in approaching the resurrection narratives. All in all, his clear statements, basic avoidance of speculation, good characterization of problem areas and broad use of the current secondary literature make Evans' book very useful.

175 *Ibid.*, p. 132.
176 *Ibid.*, pp. 132ff.
177 *Ibid.*, p. 148.
178 Cf. *ibid.*, pp. 41, n. 1, 131 *et passim.*

At the beginning of our methodological considerations we stated that our goal was not to investigate the nature of the Easter event itself, but rather within the promising directives of form-critical research to analyze the pre-redactional form and content of the gospel appearance stories as *Gattung* and to probe its origin. It has become sufficiently evident, one would think, from our critical dialogue with the history of research on methodologies that the widespread failure to differentiate clearly enough between these two disparate lines of questioning has led to a kind of impasse in the present state of research. In this respect the contemporary spectrum of research on the gospel resurrection appearances displays a proclivity to the last century (and Celsus of the second century) in large measure under the influence of Graß' approach. In a sense the gospel stories appear to be something of an embarrassment; their "realism" is offensive. What few independent voices are being heard and are applying historical-critical methods almost *in toto* have absolutized one aspect of the methods available and come up, therefore, with a correspondingly limited view of these stories.

It must not be misconstrued, however, so as to assume that we are placing the historicity of the Resurrection of Jesus itself into doubt. Rather we have drawn a distinction between that line of questioning and our own in order to free the latter from the unfortunate mixture of the two which has been the cause for prejudice and/or neglect of the appearance stories of the gospels as a distinct traditional layer among the other resurrection traditions. Pursuing our line of questioning while waiving the other for the time being may, indeed, result in conclusions which shed some light on that one as well.

Finally it must be stressed that while this introductory overview of the ways in which the gospel stories have been approached, has drawn attention to and recognized the valuable insights of others, it has also led through critical dialogue to the necessity for an alternative approach. The particular direction of the analysis below is by and large without parallel—the article of C.H. Dodd being the only partial exception—and one may conclude that in the strictest sense of the word a history-of-tradition analysis of the gospel tradition here does not exist! Therefore, two consequences are inevitable: 1) the questions deemed central by research to the present are going to appear in comparison to have been dealt with too marginally, and 2) the actual analysis of the gospel stories will not be able to enjoy the extensive support of dialogue from the secondary literature. So that it will become clear, however, that we have not thereby discounted the weight of arguments which see the gospel appearance stories in another light, in particular as having some kind of dependence upon the kerygma and other traditions, we shall turn now to a preliminary chapter on the spectrum of alternatives before we proceed to an analysis of the gospel tradition itself. The goal of that chapter is to raise the question of the distinctions resident in the various resurrection traditions and their relationship to one another.

II. Resurrection Traditions: Distinctions and Relationships

A. The Kerygma Tradition: I Cor. 15:3b-5, 6-7, 8

As stated in our introduction the kerygma tradition is recognized throughout the critical discussion as the oldest of the resurrection traditions, not only because it appears in a document written before the composition of the gospels, but also because as formula tradition it goes back to pre-pauline, Palestinian origins.[179] We have seen as well that many have assumed, therefore, that the gospel appearance stories grew out of this formula tradition as conceptual accommodation to later church needs, especially those of the primitive Christian mission. It is not our purpose here to add one more history-of-tradition analysis of I Cor. 15 to an already thoroughly plowed field (in contrast to the gospel stories).[180] Nor do we intend here to gather together the many secondary sources which work from I Cor. 15 to the gospels in a chronological development and then test each approach one by one. Rather we are interested here only in the essential relationship of the one to the other and approach the problem, therefore, from the *gospels* as point of departure and ask as lead question how the kerygma tradition is related to them and *not* vice versa. With this perspective a considerable number of problems accruing to the origin and development of the kerygma itself in oral and written form fall outside the scope of our attention and receive no mention. Moreover, we have already registered our reasons for objecting to the identification of the so-called heavenly radiance type of appearance form with the gospel accounts at the ostensibly earliest point of their development; this

179 K. Lehmann, *Auferweckt am dritten Tage nach der Schrift. Früheste Christologie, Bekenntnisbildung und Schriftauslegung im Lichte von I Kor. 15,3-5*, Quaestiones Disputatae, 38, ed. by K. Rahner and H. Schlier (Freiburg, 1968), pp. 68ff. and 87ff.

180 Cf. hereto the most recent analyses of Lehmann, *op. cit.*, H. Conzelmann, "Zur Analyse der Bekenntnisformel I Kor 15,3-5," *EvTh*, 25 (1965), pp. 1-11, J. Kremer, *Das älteste Zeugnis von der Auferstehung Christi*, StBSt, 17 (Stutt., 1970, 3rd ed., originally 1966), P. Trummer, *Anastasis. Ein Beitrag zur Auslegung und Auslegungsgeschichte von I Kor. 15*, Diss. (Graz, 1966), J. Charlot, *The Construction of the Formula in I Corinthians 15, 3-5*, Diss. (Mü., 1968), J. Blank, *Paulus und Jesus. Eine theologische Grundlegung*, StANT, 18 (Mü., 1968), pp. 133ff., H.-F. Richter, *Auferstehung und Wirklichkeit. Eine exegetische, hermeneutische und ontologische Untersuchung zu I Korinther 15, 1/11* (Berlin, 1969), G. Kegel, *Auferstehung Jesu – Auferstehung der Toten. Eine traditionsgeschichtliche Untersuchung zum Neuen Testament* (Gütersloh, 1970, which conducts in part a debate with K.H. Rengstorf, cf. above, p. 31), B. Spörlein, *Die Leugnung der Auferstehung. Eine historisch-kritische Untersuchung zu I Kor. 15*, BU, 7, ed. by O. Kuß (Regensburg, 1972, 3rd ed., originally 1971), (P. Siber, *Mit Christus leben. Eine Studie zur paulinischen Auferstehungshoffnung*, AThANT, 61 (Zürich, 1972), whose chief interest is the history-of-tradition of the Easter kerygma outside I Cor. 15 and its consequences for Paul), M. Kwiran, *The Resurrection of the Dead. Exegesis of I Cor. 15 in German Protestant Theology from F.C. Baur to W. Künneth*, Th. Diss., 8, ed. by Bo Reicke (Basel, 1972), L. Goppelt, "Die Auferstehung Jesu: Ihre Wirklichkeit und ihre Wirkung nach I Kor. 15," *Der auferstandene Christus und das Heil der Welt* (Witten, 1972), pp. 98-111 and P. von der Osten-Sacken, "Die Apologie des paulinischen Apostolats in 1 Kor 15, 1-11," *ZNW* 64 (1973), pp. 245-262.

identification has been motivated by the historicity question and the selection of Paul's Damascus Road experience as conceptual model for all others because I Cor. 15 builds a list of seemingly parallel appearance references. We repeat our earlier judgment: the identification of these two groups--heavenly radiance and anthropomorphic appearance types–in terms of subject matter is at the moment an open question which is in need of further research, but in the *form* they are distinct and require strict separation.[181] Our inquiry into the relationship of gospels to kerygma, therefore, is not weighted additionally by the question of the relationship of Paul to the kerygma itself, since I Cor. 15:8ff., clearly reflects a pauline addition to the original kerygmatic formula taken over by the apostle in the composition of chapter 15.[182] In following the particular question of *relationship* the key issue is to test the thesis of Dibelius that the gospel stories owe their origin to the need for sermon illustrations of the kerygma in the primitive mission.

When one asks what points of contact could indicate a direct relationship of any kind between the gospels and the kerygmatic formula the following possibilities offer themselves:

181 G. Lohfink in his *Paulus vor Damaskus*, StBSt, 4 (Stutt., 1967, 3rd ed.), says: "Es ist einfach undenkbar, daß es dort [Lk. 24 and Acts 1] von den Aposteln geheißen hätte: 'Sie sahen ein Licht und hörten eine / Stimme.' Nicht einmal von einem Lichtglanz über der Gestalt Christi ist dort die Rede. Die Apostel verkehren ganz unmittelbar mit dem Auferstandenen. . .Diese Darstellung, die sich so scharf von der des Damaskusereignisses abhebt, paßt nun genau in den Tatbestand, daß nach Lukas die Auferstehungserscheinungen nur vierzig Tage dauern und dann grundsätzlich durch die Himmelfahrt Christi abgeschlossen werden. . .Für Lukas gehört die Erscheinung vor Damaskus nicht mehr zu den Ostererscheinungen" (pp. 22f.). He goes on in part III, esp. pp. 53ff. to analyze the "conversation" aspect of the *Lichtglanz* type in Acts 9, 22 and 26 and to make a suggestive comparison of the style of Gen. 31:46 and Ex. 3 and other apocryphal and pseudepigraphal texts. An expansion of the *Darstellungsform* needs to include a history-of-tradition analysis of the entire heavenly radiance type of *Gattung* which could then test his conclusion (p. 59) that Lk and not a traditional source is behind the references in Acts. Cf. also his "Auferstehung," pp. 37-53, and above all his "Eine alttestamentliche Darstellungsform für Gotteserscheinungen in den Damaskusberichten (Apg. 9; 22; 26)," *BZ*,9 (1965), pp. 246-257. Albertz, *op. cit.*, pp. 28ff., failed to distinguish clearly enough on this difference and subsumed even the gospel stories under the term δόξα as type. Perhaps on certain aspects of subject matter correct but on the form mistaken is K. Gatzweiler, "La Résurrection de Jésus, Ses Répercussions dans L'Histoire," *REL*, 53 (1967), p. 277. Similar is G. Haufe, "Jesu persönliche Zukunftserwartung" (Referat to Diss.), *ThLZ*, 85 (1960), col 468, who says that the appearances "trugen nur den Charakter der Damaskus-Vision." J. Jeremias, *Neutestamentliche Theologie*, I (Gütersloh, 1971), p. 292, also sees "in der Schau des Lichtglanzes" of the Damascus Road encounter "den pneumatischen Charakter der Christophanien; sie darf als typisch für alle gelten." Cf. further the older but related position in general of W. Weber, *Christusmystik. Eine religionsgeschichtliche Darstellung der paulinischen Christusfrömmigkeit* (Leipzig, 1924), pp. 32f.

182 Not only the way that the consecutive δέ interrupts the pattern established in the structure of the whole, but also Paul's use of the term ἔκτρωμα introduces a new element. The significance of the term is a problem for pauline interpretation. Cf. Kremer, *Osterbotschaft*, pp. 97ff., also J. Munck, "Paulus Tanquam Abortivus (I Cor. 15:8)," *NT Essays in Memory of T. W. Manson* (Manchester, 1959), pp. 180ff., von Campenhausen, *Ablauf*, pp. 19f., n. 64, T. Boman, *Die Jesus-Überlieferung im Lichte der neueren Volkskunde* (Gött., 1967), pp. 236-240, N. Huffman in an address before the SBL in Toronto, Nov. 18, 1969, entitled, "The Translation and Significance of hōsperei tō 'ektrōmati (I Cor. 15:8)," stressed the autobiographical nature of the term which reflected ". . .memories of his persecuting days. . .a confession that he was the lowest of all" (p. 9, cf. bibliography).

1) the naming of particular participants in the appearances.
2) the burial of the crucified Jesus as presupposition for both.
3) the Resurrection of the crucified Jesus as presupposition for both.
4) the qualification of time for the Resurrection: τῇ ἡμέρᾳ τῇ τρίτῃ
5) the scripture motif: κατὰ τὰς γραφάς
6) the terminus: ὤφθη

An examination of these six possibilities gives rise to the following observations: except for a single reference (Lk. 24:34), which must be investigated separately below (pp. 61ff.) not one single reference to the appearance participants, not even the designation for the appearing One himself (the gospels read normally κύριος instead of the χριστός of the kerygma), shows a direct overlap. [183] The kerygma references to the "twelve" or to "all the apostles" are perhaps suggestive of the group appearances represented in the gospels, but clear identification is tenuous. [184] In any case, the reference to an appearance before "five hundred brothers at once" is quite singular, [185] as are those to Peter [186] and James, [187] and in spite of many energetic

183 Cf. below, pp. 149ff., for the question of the identity of the appearing One and the other participants involved. In any case Hooke, *op. cit.*, p. 46, is quite right when he says, "it is, however, difficult, if not impossible, to identify any of the appearances in the Pauline list [I Cor. 15] with any of those in the Synoptic traditions." Contra is F. Cornelius, *Die Glaubwürdigkeit der Evangelien* (Mü., 1969), p. 13. E.L. Allen, "The Lost Kerygma," *NTS*, 3 (1957), pp. 349ff. raises the question why those mentioned in I Cor. 15 do not appear in the gospel accounts with any degree of certainty and concludes that the two traditions emerge from different *Sitze im Leben* and are controlled, therefore, by a different set of needs; his observations underline the breach of continuity in the traditions.

184 At best we have here two references to a traditional witness regarding the group appearances, but the fact that two distinct groups are apparently implied and exactly what origins are behind the two, whether merely a terminological difference or factional groupings are intended, makes the clear identification of these references with the gospel group appearance stories very difficult. Cf. M.H. Shepherd, Jr., "Paul and the Double Resurrection Tradition," *JBL*, 64 (1945), pp. 227-240. H. Mosbech, "Apostolos in the New Testament," *StTh*, 2 (Lund, 1948), p. 190, conjectures that the second group is equivalent to "all the missionaries" and was an "apparition" which took place as the community in Jerusalem was about to send out missionaries. Von Campenhausen, *Ablauf*, pp. 17ff., conjectures the setting of the Lord's Supper for the "12" and missionary backgrounds for the other. The latter see correctly a fundamental element for both kerygmatic formula and gospel traditions that here resurrection appearance witnesses are the apostles. Cf. L. Goppelt, *Die apostolische und nachapostolische Zeit* (Gött., 1966), pp. 13f. and P. Schubert, "The Structure and Significance of Luke 24," *Neutestamentliche Studien für Rudolf Bultmann* (Berlin, 1954), pp. 169f.

185 Cf. above pp. 40ff., for the contra thesis of Seidensticker. The most commonly proposed solution to the impasse is to identify this appearance reference with Pentecost (cf. Acts 2). So S.M. Gilmour, "The Christophany To More Than Five Hundred Brethren," *JBL*, 80 (1961), pp. 248ff. and also his, "Easter and Pentecost," *JBL*, 81 (1962), pp. 62ff. and esp. p. 66, W. Grundmann, "Das Problem des hellenistischen Christentums innerhalb der Jerusalemer Urgemeinde," *ZNW*, 38 (1939), pp. 48ff., Cornelius, *op. cit.*, pp. 10f. and J. Jeremias, *Theologie*, pp. 292 and 286, n. 4. Contra are, e.g., Goppelt, *Zeit*, pp. 12 and 14ff., E. Lohse, "Die Bedeutung des Pfingstberichtes im Rahmen des lukanischen Geschichtswerkes," *EvTh*, 13 (1953), pp. 435f., H.-W. Bartsch, "Die Argumentation des Paulus in I Kor. 15,3-11," *ZNW*, 55 (1964), p. 264 and von Campenhausen, *Ablauf*, p. 18, n. 58, also pp. 10ff. Cf. also Wilckens, *Auferstehung*, pp. 28f.

186 and 187 (next page)

but forced attempts at parallelization the participants in appearances for the gospels are to be distinguished from those in the kerygmatic formula. Attempts have also been made to show internal parallels in the scheme of grouping, namely that of appearances to individuals and then to groups; [188] this too is dubious because any hint of such a grouping is to be found only at the level of redactional reworking in the gospels and not in the pre-redactional story *Gattung* itself, as will become clear below in chapter III. An overview of the redactional picture in cross section, moreover, shows that such a schematization is followed by no means consistently even at that level. Any dependence, as it were, on grouping appearance stories with an eye toward the kerygma is then a loose, indirect one here as well.

The question whether or not the empty tomb tradition tacitly stands behind the ἐτάφη has been hotly disputed in the history of research, [189] but from the perspective of the gospel tradition it is evident, as we shall see below, that appearance stories and tomb tradition existed independent of one another traditionally and were joined for the first time at the redactional level. Thus, any contact here could hardly be more for both complexes than the general background of the passion story and the hard reality of Jesus' expiration. The same must be said about the Resurrection itself, since the gospel *appearance* stories in their traditional form are precisely that and *not resurrection* stories as such: no one sees the Resurrection event itself but rather the (obviously) resurrected Lord appears. The reference to the "third day" after the Crucifixion is also a problem that has been much discussed in the history of research with conclusions ranging from the one extreme, here we have a reference to a historical fact imbedded in the memory of those who were there and passed on accordingly, [190] to the other, this is a legendary motif with broad parallels in many history-of-religion analogies. [191] Whether or not one view is to be preferred over the

186 The question of the petrine appearance is discussed below pp. 61ff. in connection with the Lk. 24:34 reference.

187 The only story material connected with an appearance before James is found in the Gospel of the Hebrews and is discussed below in this chapter, section "D", pp. 127f. A. von Harnack, *Die Apostelgeschichte* (Leipzig, 1908), pp. 126f., saw here a reference to a legend that emerged after the death of James in the Jerusalem community of the second generation. Similar are Cornelius, *op. cit.*, pp. 10f. and E.P. Sanders, *The Tendencies of the Synoptic Tradition* (Cambridge, 1969), p. 60.

188 Cf. above, pp. 24ff., on the approaches of Albertz and Brun, and Kremer, *Zeugnis*,p. 69, n. 20.

189 The problem takes its focus in the fact that the empty tomb is not expressly mentioned here and whether or not this may be taken as an indication that at this early time the tradition did not exist or was unknown to Paul. Cf., e.g., von Campenhausen, *Ablauf*, pp. 20f., Kremer, *Zeugnis*, pp. 36ff., Rengstorf, *Auferstehung*, pp. 51ff. and Bode, *op. cit.*, p. 98.

190 E.g., Künneth, *op. cit.*, p. 52, n. 81, and in connection with the discovery of the empty tomb as at least a live option von Campenhausen, *Ablauf*, pp. 11f. and Kremer, *Zeugnis*, pp. 47ff. Cf. further J. Jeremias, *Theologie*, pp. 288ff. and N. Walker, "After Three Days," *NovTest*, 4 (1960), pp. 261f.

191 E.g., J. Leipoldt, "Zu den Auferstehungs-Geschichten," *ThLZ*, 73 (1948), pp. 738f., F. Nötscher, "Zur Auferstehung nach drei Tagen," *Vom Alten zum Neuen Testament. Ges. Aufs.*, BBB, 17, ed. by F. Nötscher and K. Th. Schäfer (Bonn, 1962), pp. 231ff. and F.J. Dölger, *Ichthys, II: Der Heilige Fisch in den antiken Religionen und im Christentum* (Münster, 1922), p. 566.

other, or whether a combination–which is more likely [192]–is closer to the actual origins of the reference is of little significance because the gospel tradition knows of this reference only in the empty tomb tradition and at the redactional level of the appearance stories. That a tendency of the gospel appearance story tradition existed very early to place them in the vicinity of the tomb, a tendency which the evangelists themselves follow throughout, and, therefore, to bring those appearances under the control function of the time reference, cannot be disputed. Nevertheless, the tendency itself appears to be motivated primarily by the importance of the grave locale and only indirectly by the time factor. Greater concern seems to have been aroused at the other end of the time frame spectrum, concluding redactionally with Luke's forty-day scheme and the much longer periods of the extra-canonical sources. In any case, any direct relationship between a reference to the "third day" and the gospel appearance accounts does not exist. Therefore, for both the gospel and kerygma traditions this time reference belongs primarily to the assumed Resurrection event as background and not to a witness of resurrection appearances.

No less problematical is the *κατὰ τὰς γραφάς* reference, since for the kerygmatic formula it is unclear if the reference is supposed to bear meaning for both Resurrection *and* appearances. The latter is at first glance doubtful; it is difficult enough to find direct Old Testament references for the former. [193] This has led many scholars to broaden the field of reference for "scripture" to include, for example, a broader spectrum of early Jewish literature. [194] Be that as it may, it will become clear below that this helps very little for the gospel appearance stories and that the only direct references to general Old Testament backgrounds as well for them can be established with any degree of certainty in later redaction alone; yet, an intense dialogue with the Old Testament was apparently one of the social-religious givens of primitive Christianity in general at its inception. Thus the possibility that such backgrounds are at work in the formation of the traditional form of the gospel stories

192 Cf. B.M. Metzger, "A Suggestion Concerning the Meaning of I Cor. XV.4b," *JThS* (ns), 8 (1957), p. 123 and above all the compendious work of Lehmann, *op. cit., passim* where this motif receives its widest treatment. Says Lehmann, " 'Auferweckt am dritten Tag nach der Schrift' markiert also zunächst nicht die Entdeckung des leeren Grabes oder die ersten Erscheinungen, sondern bezieht sich–ganz nach dem Wortlaut *aller* neutestamentlichen Aussagen über den 'dritten Tag'–auf diese Tat Gottes selbst. 'Drei Tage' bedeutet in diesem Zusammenhang die aus aller Aussichtslosigkeit des erfolgten Todes geschehende Rettung. . .Die 'drei Tage' gewinnen hier eine strikt eschatologisch-transzendente Bedeutung," (p. 337). B. Lindars, *New Testament Apologetic. The Doctrinal Significance of the Old Testament Quotations* (London, 1961), pp. 59ff. sees here a reference to Jesus' temple word and Hos. 6:2. Cf. also Bode, *op. cit.*, pp. 105ff. and F. Mildenberger, "Auferstanden am dritten Tage nach der Schrift," *EvTh*, 23 (1963), pp. 267f.

193 Lehmann, *op. cit.*, pp. 205-261. H.K. McArthur in an address before the annual SBL meeting in Toronto on Nov. 18, 1969, entitled, "On the Third Day (I Cor. 15:4)," argued in favor of the Hos. 6:2 passage as the origin for the 3rd day reference by showing that rabbinic interpretation of the passage would suggest an understanding current in NT times which made it amenable to such use, pp. 3ff. Now published: " 'On the Third Day'," *NTS*, 18 ('71/'72),pp. 81-86.

194 Lehmann, *op. cit.*, 262-290. Cf. also J. Leipoldt and S. Morenz, *Heilige Schriften* (Leipzig, 1953), pp. 37ff.

cannot be excluded prematurely. If such were the case, the statement in the kerygmatic formula would more likely be another witness to the reflection level of the primitive church than the immediate source for the formation of the gospels themselves.

The above observation finds a degree of support in the final point of possible contact, namely the terminus ὤφθη with its broad ramifications in the LXX accounts of Jahweh's self-disclosure.[195] This connection has been noted by many scholars and while our overview of the history of research above has shown that many wish to bind the terminus to a particular content, namely, the heavenly radiance type of appearance *Gattung*, its diversity of application in the LXX would seem rather to necessitate ascribing to it more of a titular function, i.e., it stands more as a superscription over a variety of stories that then follow using a variety of distinct forms. In regard to the relationship question this would mean that for both the gospel and kerygmatic formula traditions the terminus points to appearances *qua* appearance and that the latter tradition displayed no interest in filling out the content in a descriptive way.[196] The gospel tradition, on the other hand, did this by calling upon a particular (anthropomorphic *Gattung*) form, while the heavenly radiance type posed another alternative form. This hypothesis must, of course, be tested, especially since outside of the kerygmatic reference in Lk. 24:34 the terminus appears nowhere in the gospel texts. It will be necessary to examine the field of ex-

195 Cf. Michaelis, "ὁράω," pp. 324ff., Rengstorf, *Auferstehung*, pp. 117-127, L. Goppelt, "Das Osterkerygma heute," *Christologie und Ethik. Ges. Aufs.* (Gött. 1968), p. 91, R.H. Fuller, *op. cit.*, pp. 30ff. and X. Léon-Dufour, "Apparitions du ressuscité et herméneutique," *La Résurrection du Christ et l'Exégèse Moderne*, Lectio Divina, 50 (Paris, 1969), pp. 167f. Cf. further the discussion in Bode, *op. cit.*, pp. 93ff.

196 This corresponds, of course, to the very nature and purpose of the two traditions. The kerygma, on the one hand, proclaims the event which grounds Easter faith not in the words Jesus is arisen–as found in the confessional responses to the kerygma, e.g., Rom. 1:3f., 10:9 or I Thess. 4:14–, but in the words he has been raised–i.e., God raised him–(on the third day according to scripture) and has appeared to Cephas (and then to the twelve), a contrast to the view which sees in the witness of the kerygma an expression of Easter faith itself. As an explicating witness to an encounter as the source of resurrection faith the appearances are put forth and interpreted as witness to the Resurrection in the form of credo proclamation. Goppelt, "Osterkerygma," p. 87, points to the *Urcredo* of Deut. 26:5-11, as its *nächste Entsprechung*, i.e., like it the kerygma gives witness in faith to the great acts of God. As such it gives witness in accord with its form and intention not by reiterating a report but as a kerygmatic statement of proclamation. The appearance stories, on the other hand, while giving witness to the same event which grounds Easter faith goes a step further and presents that witness in a form that itself owes its origin to a particular understanding of Easter faith, i.e., the stories presuppose a high degree of interpretive activity. How this activity took place and out of what backgrounds it was motivated and for what reasons is a problem for further study below. In any case, the milieu in which the stories speak and their place in the *gospel tradition* as a whole must be carefully considered. Cf. also J. Schmitt, "Urkerygma and Evangelienberichte. Bestand und Wandel der neutestamentlichen Auferstehungstradition," *BuK*, 22 (1967), pp. 14-18, who stresses the continuity of subject matter here, but in ascribing the appearance stories to a stage of development "zu jung und zu verschieden" to allow for "Rückschlüsse über die frühere Entwicklung" (p. 16) and stating the relationship question as the kerygma of I Cor. 15 being sermon points, "welche der jeweilige Missionar oder Katechet an Hand des parallel tradierten Beweis- und Erzählungsstoffes auszuführen hatte" (p. 15), he leaves open the decisive question of origin and could be interpreted in the categories of Dibelius.

pression which may allow for synonymous substitutes, but one thing is clear: to take the triad, ὤφθη—Paul's personal reference (15:8)—the ostensible heavenly radiance of Acts 9, 22, 26, etc., as a compelling measure for judging the gospel tradition and its form of expression is unfounded. One cannot say more than the following: ὤφθη reflects Old Testament (LXX) terminology by which an encounter of theophanic dimension is intended and further information about the descriptive nature of that encounter cannot be won from the terminus alone but must be arrived at through an analysis of the form following the superscription.

These remarks then have considerable consequences for the Dibelius thesis. We have seen that a comparison of the gospel appearance stories with the kerygma shows first of all that they do not cover one another in the participants purported to have been involved in the appearances. Moreover, the other possible points of contact show either a loose, indirect relationship at the redactional level or a common background here and there on specific points such as the general importance of the passion story and the Old Testament/Jewish thought world. A direct relationship, especially the dependence of the *stories* upon the kerygma tradition for their origin is impossible on formal grounds. How then is a relationship of dependence to be established? We noted above that the approach of Dibelius and others reflects a particular understanding of primitive Christianity and above all its missionary activity. The final arbiter then in the question must be: if the gospel appearance stories emerged indeed as sermon illustrations to the kerygma their content must be shown to have been able to speak in that environment. We saw above already in the introduction how such stories were received outside the believing community in the reaction of Celsus. One could object to Celsus as characteristic of the primitive Christian milieu, since he is a platonist with nothing but ridicule for such a physical representation, but it is doubtful that Celsus is really so exceptional here. Certain streams of Jewish thought at this time were, indeed, thinking of physical resurrection, yet this was to be first in the end time; an acceptance of the gospel stories as illustrations can hardly be thought of as convincing for any sector of Christian mission in this earliest period. What is expressed here, as it were, in the particularity of these stories is fully singular and thoroughly absurd for the world of New Testament times. Some other origin for these stories must be found that more adequately provides a believable *Sitz im Leben* where their complex and specific theological content is not neglected. The relationship of the one to the other, therefore, is not to be seen as a subordinate but a complementary one. They both give witness in accord with their particular direction of statement to the same foundation, are independent of one another as two streams flowing side by side and were, of course, brought together from time to time (as is seen in Lk. for example) as mutual enlargements upon the common theme of the unprecedented, "absurd" Resurrection of Jesus.

Excursus: Lk. 24:34

Since Lk does, as we have noted, provide the one direct connection between appearance *stories* and the kerygma in his gospel (24:34), we must inquire into the nature and function of this reference in connection with the so-called "protophany" question before probing the relationship question of the summary statements in Acts. The protophany question and the appearance to Peter poses itself as a problem for the relationship of the gospel tradition to the kerygma because outside of the lukan reference (cf. I Cor. 15:5) we do not find any other such reference elsewhere and what is more disconcerting, there is no extant petrine appearance *story*. We noted this fact above in general with reference to the disparity between the participants in the two complexes so that the absence of a petrine story could be taken as in no way astonishing at all. When, however, both the kerygma and Lk by way of the kerygma emphasize that the first appearance involved the person of Peter and when one considers, moreover, the place of Peter in the gospel traditions in general, the failure of the gospel appearance stories to record such for Peter raises the question how this could be. Furthermore, according to outer criteria both Jn and Mt oppose, as it were, such a petrine appearance, since the "women" at the tomb receive the first appearance. This remains true in considering Mt at other levels as well—as is seen in the alteration of his markan source in vs. 7, etc.—but it has been argued by some that in Jn. we do in fact have tacit acknowledgement of the petrine appearance if one were not to apply the "later addition"-category to Jn. 21 too harshly. Although Jn. 21:14 indicates that the galilaean appearance here is called the "third" it is clearly evident—so it is argued—that this appearance was originally described *first* in the gospel of John ahead of the Magdalene story. Although others are pictured as present along with Peter at this appearance, in its original form it was ostensibly the petrine appearance; thus is found the long sought after narration of this appearance and indeed in all likelihood the actual original ending to the gospel of Mark.[197] Ingenious as the solution is we are left to conclude by virtue of the many questions the solution leaves unanswered—as will be noted below in our investigation of Jn. 21—that we have no narrated form of the petrine appearance in our canonical sources.

The ramifications of this problem for the extra canonical sources are yet to be considered (pp. 124ff.) but at this point we must ask methodologically as others have done if the scope can be broadened within canonical sources which fall outside of the "recognized" appearance stories. In the vast amount of literature on the role of Peter in the early church this absence of a narrative of the petrine appearance is judged in basically two ways: 1) it is one of the major riddles of the New Testament that an appearance to such an important man in the early church can go untold in our sources, but it is simply a fact that it is not, and 2) this is more than a riddle, it is both embarrassing and impossible and, therefore, the narrative *must* have been inadvertently buried in or otherwise woven into other traditions which have to do with the petrine call to discipleship stories, or apostolic commission. The major proposals are: Jn. 21:15ff, Lk. 5:1-11 and other so-called "displaced" appearance stories, where Peter is pictured as having played a major role, and the "rock of the church"—saying in Mt. 16:17ff.[198] As we shall see later in this chapter (cf. pp. 139ff.) each of these possibilities faces the insurmountable difficulty that these ac-

197 Cf. below, n. 200 and p.203, ns. 585f. and pp. 86ff., n. 266(a2) and Bultmann, *Tradition*, pp. 277f. and p. 314, n. 1, his *Theologie des Neuen Testaments* (Tüb., 1968, 6th ed.), pp. 47f., and more remote his "Die Erforschung der synoptischen Evangelien," *Glauben u. Verstehen*, IV (Tüb., 1965), p. 33, and O. Cullmann, *Petrus: Jünger, Apostel, Märtyrer* (Mü., 1967), pp. 66ff. and 202ff. Quite singular is the fantastic proposal of Cornelius, *op. cit.*, pp. 11f. who claims that the Emmaus story is the petrine appearance. He must explain the change of the name from Kephas to Kleopas through unlikely accidence and postulate the entry of another person into the story because of the *anschließende Feier des Brotbrechens* in the process as well as assume that this was contained in the lost ending of Mk. For identification of Kleopas with Alpheus *et al.* in the literature, cf. V. Taylor, *The Gospel According to St. Mark* (N.Y., 1966), p. 233 and E. Hirsch, *Frühgeschichte des Evangeliums* (Tüb., 1941), claims Lk "hat sie [a first appearance to Peter] gekannt (Lk 24,34) and dennoch nicht brauchen mögen. Es ist nichts Unverständliches daran, daß ein Evangelienschluß [Mk.], der sie als erste enthielt, kurzerhand weggeschnitten wurde" (pp. 181f.). His reconstruction of that appearance, however, comes not only from Jn.21, but also Mk. 6, Mt. 14 and Lk. 5 and then concludes that he would consider it "einen streng wahrhaftigen Erlebnisbericht" (p. 186). For Schmithals' proposal cf. below, n. 429.

198 Cf., e.g., Kremer, *Zeugnis*, pp. 68f., Cullmann, *Petrus*, pp. 66ff. and 202ff. and F. Gils, "Pierre et la foi au Christ Ressuscité," *EThL*, 38 (1962), pp. 5ff.

counts are firmly embedded in their non-resurrection context prior to the redactional composition of the whole or show no substantial indication that they existed prior to the redactional work of the evangelists in question and, therefore, in their form-critical analysis resist incorporation into our search for the pre-redactional appearance *Gattung*. Methodologically, this second alternative to the "riddle" leaves us in something of a vacuum and we must conclude that as solution it is motivated more often than not by dogmatic necessity.[199]

Perhaps one further possibility should be considered before drawing our conclusions on the petrine appearance. In looking ahead for a moment to another aspect of the relationships within the entire complex of resurrection traditions, namely the tomb and appearance traditions, we note that one of the chief questions of our study here is: does the geographical tomb locale play any role in the layers of appearance stories? In this connection one must ask: is it mere coincidence that Peter is mentioned throughout the empty tomb texts (Mt. excepted)? The women are linked with both the tomb and appearance traditions and then through the rearrangement of motifs and emphasis a coherent seam between the two stories is achieved for those evangelists who are interested in the seam at all (cf. below pp. 107ff.). In both categories we are dealing with story narration. For Lk and Jn, Peter is also present in both categories, but they go separate ways on the degree of narration. For Lk, Peter has no narrational significance in either the tomb story or the appearances, while for Jn the opposite is true (if we may take at least the inclusion of Peter in Jn. 21:1-14 as a suggestive possibility for johannine sources in general in contrast to Lk.). For the appearance in Jn. 21:1-14, however, Peter has no express "first appearance" significance nor does the grave nor its vicinity play any role. In the "race story" of Jn. 20:3ff., to the contrary, Peter does have central significance and the tomb has a direct bearing. Narrationally, then, anything resembling a petrine appearance in the vicinity of the tomb is missing in Jn., while the tomb and Peter are joined organically in the "race story" (cf. below pp. 95ff.). For Lk, Peter is associated with both, but not directly in story form. For the only other reference, Mk. 16:7, the name Peter appears within the tomb story, but has no apparent relationship to it and has only speculative value for the appearance stories, since, in contrast to Lk. 24:34, it is predictive and not a statement of affirmation. There have been attempts to link the petrine appearance to the tomb story, but in the light of the above it appears to be an impossibility—not to mention, as noted earlier, the problems connected with the role of the tomb in I Cor. 15! The conclusion is unavoidable: the declarative affirmation of Lk. 24:34 "the Lord has appeared to Peter" comes directly from the kerygma and nothing of a petrine appearance story was passed on to and/or was utilized by the evangelists.

Why such was the case with the petrine appearance is a matter that has led to far-reaching speculation. Reasonable enough is the suggestion: a first appearance to Peter or any other individual never was a matter of gravity and consequence for the gospel tradition. Yet, the contrary has been argued as well: such an appearance was critical in the beginning, because groups with competing interests in the early church rallied around individuals who had a claim to this distinction.[200] In I Cor. 15, for example, it is argued that two such rival groups gathered around Peter

199 For a consideration of the problems within petrine studies in general cf. W. Dietrich, *Das Petrusbild der lukanischen Schriften*, BWANT, 5.F. 14, ed. by K.H. Rengstorf and L. Rost (Stutt., 1972), F. Obrist, *Echtheitsfragen und Deutung der Primatsstelle Mt. 16,18f. in der Deutschen Protestantischen Theologie der letzten dreissig Jahre*, NTA, 21 (Münster, 1961), R. Pesch, "Die Stellung und Bedeutung Petri in der Kirche des Neuen Testaments. Zur Situation der Forschung." *Conc*, 7 (1971), pp. 240ff. and R.E. Brown *et al.* (ed.), *Peter in the New Testament. A Collaborative Assessment by Protestant and Roman Catholic Scholars* (N.Y., 1973), *passim*.

200 J. Jeremias, *Theologie*, p. 291, proposes the deliberate activity of group interests against the petrine tradition. For him, the fact that a petrine story is missing "kann unmöglich Zufall sein" and that Mt strikes the reference to Peter in his markan source of the tomb story points to a peculiar uncertainty. Seeing traces of a rival tradition in the Gospel of the Hebrews and the Syriac Didaskalia he concludes, "Keine Frage, es sind die radikalen Kreise des palästinischen Judenchristentums, die sich an dem Universalismus des Petrus stießen (Gal. 2,12b; Apg. 11,2) und die ihn darum aus der Rolle des Empfängers der Ersterscheinung verdrängt haben." Similar views of some form of blatant excision of this appearance from the

and James—both claimed by their respective groups to have been the recipient of the first appearance—and that Paul not wishing to take sides in the dispute just included them both as traditional lists in vss. 5 and 7.[201] Further this same rivalry is supposed to have been behind the gradual but thorough reduction and/or elimination of the first appearance stories in the canonical gospels. We shall see below what happened to the tradition in the apocryphal accounts and what other "individual" appearances are added. The rivalry-hypothesis is without doubt a possibility, but we just do not know enough about this particular kind of tension in the early church in spite of glimpses into apostolic ecclesiastical life as are found in I Cor., Acts, etc., and what effect they may have had upon the formation of the gospel appearance stories. More probable is the former explanation that the naming of individuals and especially the singling out of one individual to stand at the head of the list had a theologically functional significance for the kerygma tradition and did not for the gospel tradition. Lk's reasons for incorporating this reference from the kerygma are to be sought at the redactional level in the theological motivations behind his composition and not in the sources of the story tradition themselves. The degree to which the Jewish maxim of "two or more witnesses" may have played a role here and/or the increasing need to anchor the resurrection testimony in the combined witness of the apostolic circle of the "Twelve" is uncertain, but we must at least for our line of questioning distinguish methodologically between the story form and the single kerygmatic statement in the gospel appearance materials. That means further as reply to the question posed earlier, we are *not* to broaden the scope of our investigation to include the speculative solutions directed at the supposed impasse of Lk. 24:34.

B. The Summaries of Acts

In turning from the kerygmatic formula tradition to the *summaries* of Acts we find that the latter bear structural and internal characteristics which are in many respects similar to the former. Such would be the case, for example, in the expres-

"lost" ending of Mk. out of early group rivalries are found in Cornelius, *op. cit.*, p. 11f., H.R. Balz, "Furcht vor Gott? ," *EvTh*, 29 (1969), pp. 631 and 633f., n. 16, Cullmann, *Petrus*, p. 64, Brun, *Auferstehung*, pp. 50ff., Albertz, *op. cit.*, p. 267. Contra is von Campenhausen, *Ablauf*, pp. 10f., n. 12 and 15ff. A. Strobel, *Kerygma und Apokalyptik* (Gött., 1967), p. 173, sees a conflict between the tradition of an appearance before the women and that of Peter; cf. M. Hengel, "Maria Magdalena und die Frauen als Zeugen," *Abraham unser Vater, Fst. O. Michel* (Leiden, 1963), *passim* and esp. p. 256 and his, "Die Ursprünge der christlichen Mission," *NTS*, 18 ('71/'72), p. 33, where he emphasizes the centrality of the petrine appearance without particular reference to a rivalry. Regarding the failure of the women to appear in I Cor. 15 because they were not *zeugnisberechtigt*, cf. J. Jeremias, *Theologie*, p. 286, n. 4. Interesting, even if not convincing, is the view of Wilckens, *Auferstehung*, p. 146, that since visions usually came to individuals in Jewish tradition the petrine appearance is the substance behind the claim of a group appearance; one ought to suppose, "daß sie die ersten waren, die Petrus auf die ihm zuteilgewordene Vision hin zusammenrief, und sie die Neukonstituierung ihrer Gruppe durch die Petrus widerfahrene Erscheinung begründet ansahen." Dibelius, *Formgeschichte,* pp. 190f., simply has Mk himself substituting the petrine appearance with the empty tomb story. J.A. Bailey, *The Traditions Common to the Gospels of Luke and John*, Suppl, NovTest, 7 (Leiden, 1963), pp. 88f., assumes that 24:34 is original and not a lukan addition to the Emmaus story. Also, P. Winter, "The Treatment of His Sources by the Third Evangelist in Luke XXI-XXIV," *Studia Theologia*, 8 (1954), p. 168. In all, the conclusion of J. Héring, *La Première Epitre de Saint Paul aux Corinthiens* (Neuchâtel, 1959), p. 136, regarding the conflict over the petrine appearance is to be preferred: "nous ignorons pourquoi les Synoptiques ne lui attachent pas plus d' importance." Cf. further Evans, *Resurrection*, pp. 53 and 106f., Brun, *Auferstehung*, pp. 35ff. and E. Haenchen, "Petrus-Probleme," *NTS*, 7 ('60/'61), p. 188; also below n. 580.

201 Cf. above, n. 188, regarding Albertz and Brun, and also Bartsch, *Argumentation*, pp. 263f.

sions of the kerygma in the sermons of chapters 2, 3, 5, 10 and 13. Approaching roughly a similarity in overall form to the gospel appearance stories are both the résumé of chapter one and, at least as narrative *per se*, the accounts of the appearance to Paul in chapters 9, 22 and 26. Other accounts differing in degree of narrative and potentially bordering on a similarity of form are found in chapters 7 (Stephen's vision) and 8 (Philip and the Ethiopian eunuch). These many examples raise the question: can traditional forms be postulated here or are we to ascribe these statements and accounts in their *summary* style exclusively to redactional composition of the author of Acts? In short, the relationship between *both* the kerygma and the gospel appearance stories to these summaries should be clarified. Our line of questioning prohibits any detailed treatment of the one and necessitates concentration upon the gospel tradition alone.[202] In considering points of contact we find ourselves in the midst of a thorny problem, namely the question of the sources and composition of Lk/Acts as a whole. It is not our purpose here, however, to rehearse the many-sided conflict on a variety of these issues, but to focus on the relationship question.[203]

202 It should be pointed out, however, that the close similarities between statement and form in the summaries and I Cor. 15:3-5, have their source in a common origin. They constitute a two-sided direction of statement for the Easter witness, the one (the kerygmatic formula of I Cor. 15:3-5) directed inward with a catechetical summary function, while the other (the summary sermons of Acts) is directed outward with a missionary call-to-repentance function among Jewish contemporaries. Cf. Goppelt, "Osterkerygma," pp. 85-89.

203 A representative sampling of the basic contours of the discussion over Acts is, nevertheless, worth noting for our textual considerations; they have been concerned traditionally with two major problems. For many years the debate centered upon the ostensible Aramaic sources behind Acts. The chief exponent of this position was C.C. Torrey, *The Composition and Date of Acts*, HThSt, 1 (Cambridge, 1916), (cf. bibliography for this and all succeeding references), whose opinion was that the first fifteen chapters of Acts represent an Aramaic source, which Lk found in Rome, translated and then added the address to Theophilus (pp. 5 and 59). Acts in relation to the gospel was quite an afterthought (p. 68). As he put it: "The Book of Acts was not a work of research, nor of any considerable labor. It was merely the translation of a single document–a lucky find–supplemented by a very brief outline of Paul's missionary labors, enlivened by miscellaneous personal reminiscences" (p. 68, n. 1). In subsequent years nearly all scholars of Acts rejected this extreme position of Torrey's by pointing out that his understanding of semitic influences upon Greek was much too restrictive and his argumentation for Lk as a semiticist and for certain obvious "mistranslations," e.g., Acts 2:47, were quite indecisive (cf. J.H. Moulton and W.F. Howard, *A Grammar of New Testament Greek*, II [Edinburgh, 1929], p. 483). The other extreme in the discussion is best represented by H.F.D. Sparks, "The Semitisms of the Acts," *JThS* (n.s.), 1 (1950), who rejects the Torrey view and concludes that the key to understanding semitisms in Acts is Lk's "deliberately devised and cunningly conceived" use of the LXX (p. 27). In somewhat stilted language he says: "The Mystery and the Bible were for the Christian inseparably linked. What more appropriate language therefore than the language of the Bible could anyone possibly choose as the main medium through which to present the manifestation of the Mystery" (p. 27). More recent treatment of the question has shown a greater balance and a verification of the observation of Dibelius: "Semitismus" ist kein eindeutiger wissenschaftlicher Begriff" (*Formgeschichte*, p. 33). C.S.C. Williams, for example, in his *A Commentary on the Acts of the Apostles*, BNTC (London, 1964), makes a useful distinction between the written and oral source possibilities, even if his two-draft hypothesis falls of its own weight (pp. 12f.). A most sensitive and differentiating treatment of the question is to be found in the work of Matthew Black's student,

A very brief recapitulation of views tying kerygma, summaries and stories together is in order at this point to provide a backdrop for our inquiry in this section.

M. Wilcox, *The Semitisms of Acts* (Oxford, 1965), cf. also Black's own book, *An Aramaic Approach to the Gospels* (Oxford, 1967, 3rd ed.) and the appendix to this question in Moulton and Howard, *op. cit.*, pp. 413-485, esp. summary on pp. 477ff. Wilcox draws upon such sources as Qumran and the Targumim in broadening the research spectrum and concludes that Semitisms are present in varying degrees of recognizability, some most likely already in Lk's Greek sources. These "protruding Semitisms" (p. 184) give weight to the conclusion that the material here is very ancient. Though he rejects the double-edition hypothesis for Acts he does lean heavily upon the "D" variant readings as a store of semitisms (p. 185; cf. also re: Codex "D" F.J. Foakes-Jackson, *The Acts of the Apostles*, Moffatt [London, 1931], pp. xixf.). The historical survey on pp. 1-19 is also most useful. Another standard work on this side of the Acts controversy is the article of J. Jeremias, "Untersuchungen zum Quellenproblem der Apostelgeschichte," *ZNW*, 36 (1937), which is quite firm in its rejection of Torrey's conclusions, but then proposes to demonstrate the importance of Jewish *Strafprozeßordnung* (p. 212) in understanding lukan sources and that Lk is using essentially a single (antiochaean) source which he combines with insertions as well as with parts of his own composition; the first is more prominent in chapters 1-15 and the second in chapters 16-28 (*passim*). It was this latter article which served as a major stimulus among others for a shift in concept for treating Acts (for the contributions of others in this period especially the work of M. Dibelius, cf. E. Haenchen, *Die Apostelgeschichte*, Meyer [Gött., 1968, 15th ed.], pp. 32ff. and U. Wilckens, "Interpreting Luke-Acts in a Period of Existentialist Theology," *Studies in Luke-Acts. Essays presented in honor of Paul Schubert*, ed. by L.E. Keck and J.L. Martyn [London, 1968], pp. 60ff.). The article itself remained within the basic contours of the source school, being occupied with the same questions, but a *Festschrift* for its author provided the occasion for a significant article in critique of this school by E. Haenchen. The article has to do with a specific problem text but the scope of "Quellenanalyse und Kompositionsanalyse in Acts 15," *Judentum Urchristentum Kirche, Fst. J. Jeremias*, ed. by W. Eltester (Berlin, 1968), pp. 153-164, as a new alternative is of much greater significance for the whole question of Acts. Haenchen points out that source research has all too often neglected the aspects of the compositional integrity and theological goals of the author himself. That is to say, many problems which the source school chooses to solve by reference to sources—written or oral—could more satisfactorily be solved by recourse to the author himself (*passim*). He respects, of course, the certainty of *Überlieferung* behind the efforts of the evangelist (p. 155; cf. also his *Apostelgeschichte*, pp. 72ff. and 77ff.), but rejects the old concept of block sources and speaks rather of tradition, which he supports by a comparison with Lk's sophistication in using Mk. as a source in the gospel ("Quellenanalyse," p. 156). In dealing with Acts 15, he challenges the positions of Bousset and Bultmann (p. 157) and maintains that Lk's theology and view of history are really central in understanding the apostolic council and the subsequent place of Paul in the narrative (p. 160). The appearance of the council's decision three times in the narrative of Acts (15:20, 29 and 21:25) in varying forms shows "daß Lukas hier einer Tradition folgt, nicht einem uralten Dokument, das er irgendwo aufgestöbert hat" (p. 163). Haenchen's linguistic argumentation is often inconclusive, but this new emphasis on the importance of Lk himself in the composition of Acts was a most valuable step forward, especially since he avoided the temptation to underestimate the role of tradition at the same time. This has not always been the case in other works of this persuasion and general redactional interest. An example of excessive weight on the redactional side may be seen, in our opinion, in the article by Schubert, "Structure." In spite of his useful treatment of the history of the Lk /Acts question (pp. 165f.) and his praise of the form-critical discipline his working method appears to function by and large independent of either. Another work which highlights the initiative and genius of Lk is R. Morgenthaler, *Die lukanische Geschichtsschreibung als Zeugnis*, 2 vols. (Zürich, 1948), which as the title indicates concerns itself with proving a conscious effort on the part of Lk to write both reliable history and a trustworthy theological witness. As with Schubert, who is the chief proponent of the scripture-proof motif as the guiding principle for Lk's composition (Schubert, "Structure," p. 173, n. 20 and for the speeches of Acts his "The Final Cycle of Speeches in the Book of Acts,"*JBL*, 87

As noted in the introduction a widely held thesis about the relationship existing here contains the notion that the shorter accounts of the kerygmatic formula and the sermon sketches of Acts represent the original form of the tradition and that the accounts of the gospels are the product of later development within this tradition, which came about chiefly because of the needs 1) of missionary preaching and 2) of the church for a more sophisticated bulwark of witness in its own right. C.H. Dodd, for instance, groups both the Acts summaries and the formula of I Cor. 15 together as a related type of resurrection appearance tradition and then in describing the relation of the former to the gospel of Luke says: "The summary is a literary composition by an author who looks back to what he has himself written in the first volume of his work (Luke 24)." [204] With regard to chapters 2, 3, 5, 10 and 13 of Acts, and their relationship to the gospels he says:

"If these forms of kerygma in Acts may be accepted as representing with reasonable fidelity the

[1968], pp. 1-16; cf. also H.J. Cadbury, *The Making of Luke-Acts* [London, 1958], pp. 302ff.), Morgenthaler is also trying to prove that Lk has recorded both history and witness in a non-contradictory form. They are both fully secular notions and rest upon a "ganz profanes und banales historisches Ereignis. . .die Auferstehung" (*Geschichtsschreibung*, II, p. 96). He rejects the notion that Lk thinks at all in terms of *Heils-*, *Ur-*, or *Übergeschichte* in his understanding of history (p. 97) and in comparing the work to that of Thucydides, Plutarch and Caesar (cf. also Foakes-Jackson, *op. cit.*, pp. xvf.) he writes: "Wenn der Satz 'Das Wort ward Fleisch' wahr ist, wenn es wahr ist, was Lk. etwa in den Kindheitsgeschichten so plastisch schildert: die banale Wirklichkeit dieser Geburt–bis auf die Windeln!–, wenn es wahr ist, was Lk. in den Auferstehungsberichten auch so plastisch schildert: die banale Wirklichkeit dieser Auferstehung–bis auf das 'Fleisch und Knochen' und das Essen von 'gebratenem Fisch'–, wenn das wahr sein soll, dann ist es nicht möglich, daß die evangelische Geschichte andere Geschichte ist als Profangeschichte, dann ist es aber auch nicht anders möglich, als daß das Zeugnis von dieser Geschichte ganz banale Geschicht [sic] schreibung ist" (pp. 97f.). In spite of the useful observation that Lk is consistently concerned with the weight of a double-witness motif in the light of Jewish *Prozeßrecht* (pp. 7-10 and 96; cf. also Jeremias above) the naivete in the author's view of both history and theological witness makes it necessary to reject his position most sharply. One of the more recent works to date in terms of a good overview of the strengths and weaknesses of the major works treating the Lk./Acts problem in modern scholarship is U. Wilckens, *Die Missionsreden der Apostelgeschichte* (Neukirchen, 1963), cf. esp. pp. 7-31. As the title indicates the author is concerned chiefly with the preaching texts of Acts, but his discussion over the heritage and worth of current literature in the field is extensive and useful. Though we are obliged to take issue with Wilckens' general thesis that the preaching texts themselves owe their form to lukan creation and do not go back to tradition, its survey value must be mentioned here. In the Acts literature since Wilckens the key issue still undecided for the entire complex of the lukan double work is the exact relationship between Lk's theological interests and his use of sources. For the most recent contributions to the discussion cf. J. Dupont, *The Sources of Acts–The Present Position*, trans. by K. Pond (London, 1964), E.F. Harrison, "The Resurrection of Jesus Christ in the Book of Acts and in Early Christian Literature," *Understanding the Sacred Text, Fst. M.S. Enslin*, ed. by J. Reumann (Valley Forge, Pa., 1972), pp. 217-231, W.-G. Kümmel, "Lukas in der Anklage der heutigen Theologie," *ZNW*, 63 (1972), pp. 149-165, the collected essays *Studies in Luke-Acts. Essays presented in honor of P. Schubert*, ed. by L.E. Keck and J.L. Martyn (London, 1968) and the second edition of H. Conzelmann, *Die Apostelgeschichte*, HNT, 7 (Tüb., 1972). The many problems connected with this issue of source and redaction for lukan studies do not need to concern us directly, but the implications thereof do most certainly, since they play a decisive role in evaluating the relationship question for the summaries and the appearance stories.

204 Dodd, "Appearances," p. 27.

general type of early preaching, as I believe they may, then the Gospel narratives which we have been examining would readily serve the purpose of exemplifying or illustrating the statements made in general terms in the kerygma. The 'concise' narratives would be precisely (in Dibelius' sense of the term) 'paradigms' for the use of the preacher."[205]

The second alternative has often been inferred from the development of the resurrection terminology in Acts. We find this principle of interpretation expressed, for example, in the article of Herbert Braun, "Zur Terminologie der Acta von der Auferstehung Jesu," *ThLZ*, 77 ('52), cols. 533-536. He sees a basic chronological split in Acts between the resurrection terminology and the witness terminology surrounding the former, which, in its definition of "apostolic" for those who are witnesses to the Resurrection, appeared later on the scene and served the interests of the "early catholic" period of the church. This tendency toward "Sicherungen, die den Frühkatholizismus einleiten" [206] is the "new" scope within which the older tradition rests [207] and the interest of the gospel accounts in the bodily character of the resurrected One, especially Lk's, makes them by implication part of this later development.[208]

With these two clarifications the matter is apparently and simply explained. The kerygma was the oldest form of the tradition and then the tradition found appropriate enlargement in the preaching of missionaries and in the ecclesiastical struggles of the church. The question remains, nevertheless: are these adequate categories with which to interpret the gospel texts in the light of their particularities? The assumption that statement, summary, story constitute a direct chronological line of development has never been demonstrated adequately. We are asking, therefore, because of the nature of the gospel materials if perhaps the appearance stories in their pre-redactional form existed independently alongside the kerygmatic formula and summaries of Acts in their own right. At least in terms of the contemporary picture of theological variety in early Christianity it is hardly justifiable to assume without question that the kerygma/preaching pattern is responsible for the gospel tradition of the appearance stories. If the Easter witness in its kerygmatic interpretation existed at least in a double-sided variety [209] from the earliest times then a linear view of origins for the gospel stories themselves is also highly questionable. We must ask: what is the express form and central address of both types? The theological function of the statement, summary and story forms of the tradition must be stated more clearly. What are they saying? In establishing any relationship to one another this must be answered; so much depends on clarity over this point because it will lead us to the most probable source of origin. Braun's remarks about the later needs of the "early catholic" period provide a very interesting point from which to em-

205 *Ibid.*

206 H. Braun, "Zur Terminologie der Acta von der Auferstehung Jesu," *ThLZ*, 77 (1952), col. 535.

207 *Ibid.*, cols. 533f.

208 Cf. the comment of Braun without special reference to the gospels in col. 536.

209 Cf. above, n. 202.

bark, because it raises the question: what were the needs of the community(ies) prior to that period *in respect to* the older tradition which was amalgamated into the new environment? One notes, for example, that certain motifs, e.g., extreme bodily proofs, are redactional and we would, therefore, agree with Braun in this respect that later influences are at work, but are we to assume that the acknowledged older Palestinian material is merely synonymous with the kerygmatic statements of the non-gospel material and that prior to the gospel composition it had no independent (traditional) form?

The texts in Acts then comprise three basic categories: 1) the sermon summaries of chapters 2, 3, 5, 10 and 13, 2) the narrative résumés of chapters 7, 8, 9, 22 and 26 and 3) the overview summary introducing the whole work in chapter one. Only the latter and a couple of brief statements from the sermon summaries provide any direct reference to the gospel appearance stories and comprise, therefore, the focus of our attention. It will be possible to devote only brief attention to the second category, and in particular the appearance to Paul, at the end of this section, because it poses for Lk himself a separate and distinct genre and deserves, therefore, much fuller treatment under the topic of the heavenly radiance appearance type than is possible within the limits of our investigation.

Acts 1: (1-3) 4-5

In the first chapter of this the second half of the lukan double work we have another account or a repetition of a/the group appearance. In vss. 1-3 we have the introductory remarks, noteworthy because of their summary style in addressing Theophilus, and a statement on the nature and duration of the resurrection appearances on the whole. This latter factor is important as a new element because it was not mentioned in the gospel that anything like a period of forty days circumscribed the length of time for the appearances. On the other hand, a close continuity with the earthly ministry is maintained much in the same way as the gospel. In the latter this is done primarily through the physical signs offered by the crucified/risen One. Here this is achieved through a statement about the nature of the continuity itself: "all that Jesus began to do and to teach until the day in which he was taken up into heaven." The continuity, however, does not exist separate from the role of the disciples; indeed, the foundation of the apostolate is carefully laid and supported in the words: "he gave specific instructions through the Holy Spirit to the apostles whom he chose." Then, as a careful transition, follows a statement to link the earthly days with a forty-day resurrection appearance period: "to whom he also showed himself alive after his passion with many convincing proofs, through a forty day period allowing himself to be seen by them and speaking to them about the kingdom of God."

We have here then a complete and reflected statement about the entire period of Jesus' encounter set within the contours of a specific time sequence. Jesus acted, taught and chose disciples from the "beginning" and then broke the continuity only at the Ascension. Is this time sequence based on the assumption that Lk's gospel was before the reader's mind's eye and that it was, therefore, only necessary to summarize the appearances prior to the more elaborate account of the Ascension itself? I.e., does the *summary* refer back to the redactional close of Lk's own gospel?

Time, however, is not the only striking element of this prologue account in general. The matter of the nature of the Jesus-encounter, both before and after the Passion, is also of primary importance. We see, for example, that in vs. 2 Jesus a) chose the disciples, b) gave them specific instructions and c) did the latter through the Holy Spirit. These three features are selected from the earthly ministry as the basic elements for a meaningful encounter and commission and they are carefully set within a period after the Passion and before the Ascension. The life of cult and mission are based upon and nourished through the initiative of Christ, the commission to go into the world and his abiding presence through the Holy Spirit. Then in vs. 3 the focus is strictly upon the forty-day period. Here we find (again in summary fashion) a description of the nature of the encounter after the Resurrection in general, i.e., proofs of his reality! These "many infallible proofs" fall into two categories which are very much like those in the gospel: 1) there is a visual revelation and 2) words of commission are uttered, i.e., here in the form of words about the kingdom of God (itself a pointer to the future in the light of what follows in Acts).

Interestingly enough, the emphasis on the many proofs as such (the element that won the disciples over to faith—seeing him alive) is here de-emphasized, although one would expect just the opposite in the light of the strength of *παρέστησεν ἑαυτὸν ζῶντα, πολλοῖς τεκμηρίοις* and *ὀπτανόμενος αὐτοῖς*. The summary statement about the kingdom of God, on the other hand, receives the stress in the following account of a group appearance. This raises two questions: 1) do we have here in fact a later tradition which is really non-lukan? And if not 2) what is the doing/teaching, showing/speaking relationship of this introduction to the gospel? Put another way, why does Lk recap his gospel in this way and then go on to picture a group appearance and Ascension as we find it here? It would appear that the solution to these questions is to be found in the relation of the factors of theme to composition as a whole.

In vs. 4 we have an appearance, or more correctly, an occasion in which the risen One is present with them before the Ascension and which corresponds to Lk. 24:49, i.e., judging from the content of the opening command not to leave Jerusalem before receiving the gift of the Father. Yet, the features of suddenness, standing in their midst and overcoming their doubts through demonstrations of his Crucifixion are missing. Such may have been unnecessary if the group appearance in the gospel was taken for granted, especially in the light of the "many infallible proofs" of vs. 3. In any case the theme of a word-revelation or commission is certainly primary. The outer circumstances and conditions, which provide such fertile soil for redactional enlargement in the gospel accounts in general are here reduced to one (important) participle, *συναλιζόμενος*. The concentration is upon the words spoken by the risen One. The command not to leave Jerusalem is reiterated with its promise. The promise is enlarged from the description in the gospel by the clarification that John baptized with water, but (strong *δέ* adversative) they were going to be baptized with the Holy Spirit not many days hence. This is the second time that the Holy Spirit has received special emphasis in the opening verses of Acts. The gospel account leaves the "promise of the Father" rather ill-defined, but here not only the Holy Spirit is specifically designated, but also another strong point of contact with the early days is expressed (cf. vs. 2). In the johannine account this same continuity is drawn in the affirmation that as the Father had sent Jesus so he was sending them—"receive the Holy Spirit" (20:21-22). It is of redactional significance to ask, of course, why Lk has waited until the second half of his work to specify the promise of the Father. Since the commission and Ascension are present in the gospel it seems tenuous to maintain simply that the Spirit does not play a dominant role in the first work. We do have here positive pointers to Pentecost, which is just around the corner in Acts, but it could be questioned if Lk really points any less to this event in the gospel itself (especially in the light of vs. 5 as an enlargement of the promise common to both accounts). The question is then: is Lk working with tradition here or is it his free composition which simply expands the commission motif? [210]

The summary in this chapter has caused considerable unrest among scholars for years because of the apparent theological and compositional discrepancies between it and the final chapter of the Gospel of Luke. Although it makes the task easier simply to say that the situation in Acts is so radically different that a comparison between the two is really quite impossible, [211] it does not enhance the illumination of the problematic of Acts. It is certainly not incorrect to emphasize the uniqueness of Acts, but it is to reject any parallels between the two as a basis for comparison. That is to say, compositionally and theologically the criteria for determining redaction and special source by Lk will remain the same.

Some scholars have maintained that Lk/Acts was originally one work which was first separated at the time of acceptance into the canon and that because of this arbitrary separation it became necessary to add an ending to the gospel and a beginning to Acts. [212] Others are equally convinced of the late character of the first chapter either in its entirety or in part without insisting on the separation through acceptance into the canon. [213] With regard to the former position Haenchen says:

> "Wenn man sich diese Haltung des frühchristlichen Schriftstellers Lukas vergegenwärtigt, hat man nicht mehr nötig, angesichts des Actaproömiums Alarm zu schlagen und Hypothesen über das zu entwerfen, was bei der 'Aufnahme in den Kanon' geschehen ist."[214]

210 Although the words of vss. 6-8 bear an integral relation to the promise of vss. 4-5 and thereby tie the Ascension to this account, it will be observed that they really belong to the ascension scene itself. Support for this can be seen in the participle *συνελθόντες* which implies that we have not the same but another "coming together," and that the Ascension of the risen One into the cloud follows directly on the heels of what here proves to be a repetition of the promise of the Spirit.

211 Cf. Haenchen, *Apostelgeschichte*, p. 72.

212 *Ibid.*, p. 113.

213 E. Norden, *Agnostos Theos* (Darmstadt, 1971, 5th ed.[='12]), pp. 311-313, E. Meyer, *Ursprung und Anfänge des Christentums*, I (Stutt., 1929), pp. 35ff., H. Braun, "Terminologie," col. 534, n. 8, Shepherd, *op. cit.*, p. 236 and M. Goguel, *Introduction au Nouveau Testament, Le Livre des Actes*, III (Paris, 1922), p. 174.

214 Haenchen, *Apostelgeschichte*, p. 115.

With regard to the second position an equal number of scholars are convinced that a separation of this chapter from the rest of the book is purely arbitrary and totally unfounded.[215] Whether or not Lk/Acts entered the canon together is both beyond the problematic of our inquiry and also a matter of conjecture as well. The matter of lukan authorship, however, does concern us.

The first question to engage us on the matter of authorship is the absent δέ clause. One would expect such to follow the *μέν* in Lk's classical style and because of its absence many reject lukan authorship of at least these opening verses–vs. 1 often excepted.[216] It is, however, a dubious argument to see here a non-lukan characteristic[217] and especially to build upon it a source hypothesis.[218] Whether or not this is a true anacoluthon due to the magnitude of the author's own engagement in his story to the extent of forgetting his first sentence[219] is an open question, but, in any case, that the construction is not so terribly unusual and that the reader's recollection of the gospel account can be presumed are strong arguments in favor of the originality of the text in spite of the absence of δέ.

We ask next about other philological characteristics which can be determined by terminological considerations, e.g., word statistic. We note the following:

1. Theophilus–mentioned only here and in Lk. 1:3.

2. *ἄχρι ἧς ἡμέρας*–in the gospels only found in Mt. and Lk.: Mt. (13:30–with some text-critical questions) 24:38 and Lk. 1:20; 17:27. In Acts we find the use of the article and the demonstrative instead of the relative pronoun (1:2; 2:29; 23:1; 26:22 and ἕως in 1:22). In the letters only with the anarthrous form II Cor. 3:44 and Phil. 1:5,6.

3. ἐντέλλομαι–frequent enough in all of the gospels, but it occurs in Lk. only once and that as an OT Psalm quote. It is used most frequently as an aorist (cf. also Acts 13:47 for perfect) and the only part. use in NT is to be found here in Acts 1:2 out of a total of 16 references.

4. ἐκλέγομαι–out of 21 NT locations 11 are in Lk/Acts. In the gospels: 4 out of 9 are in Lk. It is not to be found in Mt. at all, but the reference in Mk. 13:20 is very similar to this one. Jn uses all aorists (one inf.) while the general preference in NT is imperfect and part. forms (one future).

5. ἀναλαμβάνω–found in "Mk." 16:19 but otherwise only found in Acts 1:2,11,22; 7:43; 10:16; 20:13,14;23:31 and Eph. 6:13,16; I Tim. 3:16; II Tim. 4:11. In the meaning here only the other Acts 1 references, 10:16 and I Tim. 3:16 (and of course, "Mk." 16) are to be counted.

6. *παρίστημι*–this verb does not appear in the Easter texts. It, like the *φανερόω* of "Mk." 16, bears a peculiar summary quality not present in the other accounts. We do find the non-compounded ἵστημι and intransitive forms elsewhere in the Easter accounts. The descriptive verbs for the appearance texts are to be compared below.[220] Interestingly enough, the only other

215 *Ibid.*, pp. 113ff. and W. Knox, *The Acts of the Apostles* (Cambridge, 1948), pp. 18f. and F. Dornseiff, "Lukas der Schriftsteller," *ZNW*, 35 (1936), pp. 134ff. *et. al.*

216 Shepherd, *op. cit.*, p. 236.

217 Cf. A.T. Robertson, *A Grammar of the Greek New Testament in the Light of Historical Research* (Nashville, 1934), pp. 440 and 1150ff. and Dornseiff, *op. cit.*, p. 135.

218 Cf. Haenchen, *Apostelgeschichte*, p. 73.

219 Dornseiff, *op. cit.*, p., 135.

220 Cf. Text-Synopsis.

sense-parallel in the NT occurs in the story of Peter's raising of Dorcas, Acts 9:36-43 (esp. 39 and 41). We have a certain similarity in Romans 6:13-19, but the concentration upon the notion of "life's devotion" creates an inevitable distance. The notion of "manifest" is also to be found in Eph. 5:27 and Col. 1:22 and 28.[221]

7. *μετὰ τὸ παθεῖν*—although the usage is *hapax* for the NT (cf. however the *πρὸ τοῦ με παθεῖν* of Lk. 22:15 and Phil. 1:29 without the prep.) the articular infinitive is not uncommon. In fact, the construction is very common for Lk and Paul[222] and with the prep. *μετά* the articular infinitive occurs fifteen times in the NT and over half of them are lukan (predominantly Acts.)[223]

8. *πολλοῖς τεκμηρίοις*—This phrase is *hapax* for the NT. We do have parallels in non-biblical materials: *Diod. S.* 17, 513 *τεκμήρια τῆς ἐκ τοῦ θεοῦ γενέσεως*. Dit. *Syll.* 3 867, 37 *μέγιστον τεκμήριον* written around A.D. 160 in relation to *σεβασμός* for which a month is named after the goddess Artemis. We also find in this ephesian inscription *Syll.* 3 685, 84 written around 139 B.C. *μέγιστον καὶ ἰσχυρότατον τεκμήριον*. Also *P Tor* I, 1, IV. 11 written ca. 116 B.C. *μέγα τι συμβάλλεσθαι τεκμήριον* (also in 1, VIII. 32). In *P Gieß* I, 39, 9, the ptolemaic P, we find *τεκμήριον* standing beside *ὅρκος* being written ca. 204-181 B.C. Also Josephus *Ant.* 5, 39 and in 17, 128 it stands with *παραστῆσαι*.[224]

9. *δι' ἡμερῶν τεσσαράκοντα*—the notion of forty days is found in the *Dicaearch*, fragment 35b W., of Pythagoras *ἀποθανεῖν τετταράκοντα ἡμέρας ἀσιτήσαντα*, and also in Mt. 4:2 in conjunction with forty nights (cf. also Mk. 1:13 and Lk. 4:2; *Ps. Callisth.* 3,26,7 p. 127,3). The influence of the OT can be seen in Ex. 34:28 (cf. also I Cl. 53:2 and Barn. 4:7;14:2).[225]

10. *ὀπτανόμενος*—from the late present form of the passive *ὤφθην*—*ὀπτάνομαι* taking the dative instead of *ὑπό*.[226] The verb is *hapax* for the NT, but we find non-biblical usage: *P Oxy.* XIII, p.4; *P Par* 49,33 (164-158 B.C.): *εἰ δὲ δι' ἄλλο τι οὐκ ὀπτάνεταί μοι*[227] and *P Tebt.* I,24,5 (117 B.C.): *καὶ μηδαμῶς ὀπτανομένων ὑπ*...In A.D. 300 we find the magical papyrus *Par* 574, 3033 *ὁρκίζω σε τὸν ὀπτανθέντα τῷ* 'O(=I)*σραὴλ ἐν στύλω φωτινῷ καὶ νεφέλῃ ἡμερινῇ* an interesting reference to Ex. 13:21.[228]

11. *τὰ περὶ τῆς βασιλείας τοῦ θεοῦ*—commensurate with lukan usage (cf. Lk. 9:11 and Acts 8:12 and 19:8).

12. *συναλίζομαι*—*hapax* for the NT.[229]

13. *χωρίζω*—occurs only twice in the gospels (Mt. 19:6 and Mk. 10:9) and not at all in Lk. or Jn. Three occurrences in Acts (1:4; 18:1,2), twice in Rom., three times in I Cor. and one each for Phil. and Heb.

14. *παραγγέλλω*—although the number of occurrences is predominantly lukan (four in Lk.

221 Cf. W. Bauer, *Wörterbuch zum Neuen Testament* (Berlin, 1958, 5th ed.), cols 1244f.
222 Robertson, *op. cit.*, pp. 1064f.
223 *Ibid.*, p. 1074.
224 Cf. G.H. Liddell and R. Scott, *Greek-English Lexicon* (Oxford, 1958, 9th ed. [='40]), s.v., J.H. Moulton and G. Milligan, *The Vocabulary of the Greek Testament* (London, 1957 [='30]), p. 628 and Bauer, *op. cit.*, col. 1599.
225 For monographs on the number forty cf. Bauer, *op. cit.*, cols. 1608f. and H. Balz, "*τεσσεράκοντα*," *ThW*, VIII, pp. 134-139.
226 Bauer, *op. cit.*, col. 1142, and F. Blass and A. Debrunner, *Grammatik des neutestamentlichen Griechisch* (Gött., 1954, 9th ed.) para. 191,1; 313 and 101.
227 Cf. A. Deissmann, *Licht vom Osten* (Tüb., 1923, 4th ed.), p. 65, Moulton and Milligan, *op.cit.*, p. 454.
228 Cf. Deissmann, *op. cit.*, p. 252, and also the LXX references in I Kings 8:8 and Tobit 12:19 (B,A) and Bauer, *op. cit.*, col. 1142.
229 Quite late in usage and rare, cf. H.J. Cadbury, "Lexical Notes on Luke-Acts, III, Luke's Interest in Lodging," *JBL*, 45 (1926), p. 311.

and eleven in Acts) and pauline (two in I Cor., one in I Thess., four in II Thess., and five in I Tim.) we also find two occurrences each in Mt. and Mk. None in Jn. There is also nothing unusual about the construction here.

15. *περιμένω*—*hapax* for the NT (Acts 10:24 is a "D" interpolation). We do have some interesting LXX examples such as Gen. 49:18: *τὴν σωτηρίαν περιμένω κυρίου*; and also non-biblical examples, e.g., *P Gieß* I, 73,4 from the time of Hadrian: *ἐκομισάμην σου τὴν ἐπιστολὴν ἡδέως καὶ περιμένω σε* and *P Oxy*. XIV, 1762,10 from the second or third century A.D.: *οὔπω μέντοι εἰς διαλλαγὰς ἐλθεῖν ἠθέλησεν...σὲ περιμένων*, and *BGU* II, 388, II, 39 also from the second or third century A.D.: *ἐ(ν) ᾗ πλαστυγραφίᾳ περιμ(ενο)ν ἐστιν τὸ ὄνομα*. Also Jos. *Ant*. 12,193; 1,219; 2,69; 6,176.[230]

16. *μετὰ πολλὰς ταύτας ἡμέρας*—not unusual as lukan expression of time duration.

From this statistical breakdown, therefore, we see that the terminology is on the whole either quite common or *hapax legomena*. Since the terms common to the NT also find their place in characteristic lukan constructions and, therefore, present no problem to stylistic, redactional considerations, we shall concentrate upon the *hapax* references to determine if they too are redactional or come from a non-lukan source. Interestingly enough, they come by and large together in vss. 3 and 4, i.e., *παρίστημι*, *πολλοῖς τεκμηρίοις*, (*δι' ἡμερῶν τεσσαράκοντα*), *ὀπτανόμενος*,*συναλίζομαι*, (*χωρίζω*) and *περιμένω*.

We have already seen above in the verb *παρίστημι*, that it 1) does not appear in the other appearance texts and 2) has its closest sense-parallels in the story of the raising of Dorcas, Acts 9:36-43 and also Eph. 5:27 and Col. 1:22,28. This is not without significance because it both serves as a characteristic, late summary form of the appearance event and as such includes the entire tradition and not just one particular account and also expresses a central motif of the appearances, i.e., that Jesus did not just appear as an apparition, but that he presented himself alive as the One who alone could restore the broken fellowship with his disciples. As Goppelt has put it, "Sie haben ihn verlassen und aufgegeben, er gewährt ihnen erneut die Gemeinschaft." [231] It would be an oversimplification to say that the verb in this context bears this theological weight exclusively. We shall see below under the "many infallible proofs" motif that at least one of the major aspects of the verb here is a continuation of anti-docetic polemic as well as an apt description for the whole appearance tradition.

The notion of "many infallible proofs" is the fundamental indicator in this text of the summary form. We find the same kind of remark in Jn. 20:30, Πολλὰ *μέν οὖν καὶ ἄλλα σημεῖα ἐποίησεν ὁ Ἰησοῦς ἐνώπιον τῶν μαθητῶν αὐτοῦ ἃ οὐκ ἔστιν γεγραμμένα ἐν τῷ βιβλίῳ τούτῳ* and in Jn. 21:25, *Ἔστιν δὲ καὶ ἄλλα πολλὰ ἃ ἐποίησεν ὁ Ἰησοῦς*, and even though both of these references occur at the end of an appearance narrative, the Acts reference is just as much a summary and has most probably the gospel narrative in mind as well. The mention of *σημεῖα* in Jn. 20:30 is most interesting because the scope of this term for Jn is in all probability the

230 Moulton and Miligan, *op. cit*., p. 506.
231 Goppelt, "Osterkerygma," p. 93. Questioned by Wilckens, *Auferstehung*, pp. 157f.

entire Gospel of John and has little if anything to do with the resurrection appearances themselves,[232] while this very strong substantive τεκμήριον in Acts has clearly to do with post-resurrection events; indeed, within a "forty day" period. Although Jn. 21 allows for a more direct reference to the appearance sequence and/or the appendix chapter itself it is likely that the entire book as "the witness of the beloved disciple" is intended. We see, therefore, that in terms of the summary form Acts 1 stands quite alone. The question is, therefore: who is responsible? A conclusive answer is difficult, but in the light of Lk's concern for bodily proofs, which will be seen to be clearly redactional in the gospel, we may well conclude that he alone is responsible here as well, if we may assume that the reader was free to reflect on that gospel narrative to which this summary guided him.[233] Further support could be suggested if one may assume that Lk had gained access to further stories in his research, was unable to measure their credibility and in this way could make indirect reference not wishing to discredit and fully eliminate them. As a man of faith he may have incorporated, in fact, as many of the motifs present in these stories as he could in the last chapter of his gospel, and then as historian was forced to circumscribe the rest in this "many infallible proofs" reference in Acts. Most instructive, however, is perhaps the question: what kind of a summary tradition could have existed with this statement? Alone it could have had no value at all. In its context flanked by "presenting himself alive" on one side and the "being seen by them" on the other, we can see that the reference serves little else than the anti-docetic polemic which can be seen in the gospel.

In conjunction with Jesus' presenting himself alive after his Resurrection with many infallible proofs we find a second form of descriptive verb stressing the visual encounter and then the verbal encounter for a period of forty days. This visual aspect, ὀπτανόμενος, is of primary concern, as we have already seen in the word statistic, because it offers both an alternative to the descriptive verbs in the gospels and a point of contact with the kerygmatic ὤφθη, being an alternate form of the latter.[234] The visual stress for the summary here is very important, because it forgoes any attempt to describe or narrate and chooses rather to accentuate "visuality" plain and simple. Cadbury is quite right when he develops the meaning of this verb primarily in terms of Lk's own vocabulary (cf. Lk. 24:23 and Acts 16:19) and rejects the thesis of Krenkel that this verb is to be attributed to Josephus.[235] In drawing upon what appear to him to be parallels, (e.g., Tobit 12:19, πάσας τὰς ἡμέρας

232 Cf. K.H. Rengstorf, "σημεῖον," *ThW*, VII, pp. 241-257, esp. p. 253f. and most recently R.T. Fortna, *The Gospel of Signs* (Cambridge, 1970), *passim* and esp. pp. 197ff.

233 Braun, "Terminologie," col. 535, n. 1, ascribes this proof notion to a later insertion in keeping with his working method: everything which smacks of *Sicherungen* must be early catholic and not original. Here is thus another indication of the basic gap between resurrection terminology and μάρτυρες structure.

234 Cf. *ibid.*, col. 534, n. 8, where Braun maintains that the whole ὤφθη notion for the resurrection tradition was no longer of importance to the author of Acts, claiming that it appears only in 10:40 and 13:31. He rejects along with Norden, *Agnostos*, pp. 311-313 and Meyer, *op. cit.*, pp. 35ff. any claim of originality for Acts 1:3ff.

235 H.J. Cadbury, "Lexical Notes on Luke-Acts. I," *JBL*, 44 (1925), pp. 218ff.

ὠπτανόμην, ὑμῖν, καὶ οὐκ ἔφαγον οὐδε ἔπιον ἀλλὰ ὅρασιν ὑμεῖς ἐθεωρεῖτε; I Kings 8:8 *et al.*) Cadbury leans toward a translation of "to be visible" and goes on to say:

> "Acts 1,3, then, means not merely that Jesus was seen but that he was to be seen. . .Its opposite is the idiomatic *ἄφαντος γενέσθαι* of Lk. 24:31. . .The English 'being visible' may sound strange in Acts 1,3, but it probably is a better translation than 'appearing,' which suggests distinct occasions and appearances at the initiative of Jesus. . .The author of Acts may have thought of Jesus as becoming visible from time to time during the forty days. . .[leaving the gospels and I Cor. out of our minds Acts would most naturally be understood as] continuous visibility for forty days [concluded by a definite ascension, followed by] later visions [to Stephen and Paul]."236

He further feels that there is nothing here to stress the degree of reality in the appearance and it does not show, in relation to Lk. 24:37ff., whether they saw a spirit or not.[237] This is most certainly the case since this summary is to be understood in light of the gospel and not the reverse.[238] In any case, we see that the author has quite effectively summarized the visual side of the appearance tradition with this one participle.

The oral aspect of the appearance will appear below under our considerations of the meaning of the whole summary since it has no claim to extraordinary, perhaps non-lukan terminology. We find ourselves rather up against one of the most thorny terminological problems of the text in the verb *συναλίζομαι*. It has been suggested that we have here a clear reference to a common meal between Jesus and his followers after the Resurrection.[239] The only other group appearance text which suggests the meal motif is "Mk." 16:14 *ἀνακειμένοις*, but there the risen One is not a participant.[240] The "meal" interpretation, however, is not without its difficulties,[241] nor is that of the other two major proposals, "coming together"[242] and

236 *Ibid.*

237 *Ibid.*

238 A.N. Wilder, "Variant Traditions of the Resurrection in Acts," *JBL*, 62 (1943), p. 312, notwithstanding.

239 Cf. under the reflections of Bauer, *op. cit.*, col. 1552, and Cadbury, "Lexical Notes III," pp. 310ff.

240 Cf. below, pp. 119ff. and 196ff.

241 "eating together"–here the root of the word is the best indicator of meaning. All of the Latin, Syriac and Coptic translations took it as such. E. Gill postulates the idea of "salt covenant." (Cf. Bauer, *op. cit.*, col. 1552). Similarly Torrey chose to render it "have table-companionship with" taking it to be derived from the Aramaic ithpa'al מתמלח (Torrey, *op. cit.*, pp. 23f.). Another early advocate of this position was Th. Zahn. (Th. Zahn, *Die Apostelgeschichte des Lucas* [Leipzig, 1922, 3rd ed.], pp. 23ff.) He assumes that the basic meaning is "to eat salt" and adds that this image was quite common in the ancient world from the time of Plutarch on as an expression of hospitality which "den Sinn freundlicher Tischgemeinschaft angenommen hat." (*ibid.*, p. 24.) He cites Origen's *Contra Celsum*, II, 21: *κοινωνεῖν ἁλῶν καὶ τραπέζης* (*ibid.*), and concludes that this is a typical lukan scene of eating indoors (Lk. 24:30, 42 and Acts 10:41) while referring to the "Clemensroman" recension which talks of the Eucharist with bread and salt without wine (*ibid.*, p. 26). The most recent advocate of this position is Max Wilcox (*op. cit.*, *passim*). He supports Torrey in his recourse to an Aramaic original here (cf. IV Ezra 1:4) and even suggests that it may have a Syriac origin ܐܬܡܠܚ since Lk could have been a Syrian of Antioch (*ibid.*, p. 107). He also sees no reason why it might not stem directly from the Hebrew אלחם as in Psa. 140 (*ibid.*, pp. 108f. F. Delitzsch,

"being present with" [243] This last solution to the *crux interpretum* seems very attractive because it does not require the addition of a motif not present in the gospel group appearances and continues the practice of the text up to this point to summarize: Jesus was with them (cf. the manner in which the church fathers linked this with vs. 3 and often inserted it after *ὀπτανόμενος*).[244] On the other hand, the notion of a common meal is not to be discarded lightly because the form of the verb and its connection with a meal are explainable without recourse to an orthographic change in spite of the *lectio difficilior* of some of the minuscule witnesses. We know,

Hebrew New Testament (London, 1960[='89]), p. 213, translated ... ובאכלו לחם עמהם.

242 "coming together"–this meaning in both the active and passive voices can be found in Herodotus, Josephus and others. Many have taken this interpretation in opposition to the common meal notion. F. Field, for example, takes the verb in its ordinary sense of *congregari* or *convenire* and stresses the present part. coming up with "as he was assembling with them, as he was on the way to meet them (some of them being in the same company with them) he gave them this charge" (F. Field, *Notes on the Translation of the New Testament* [Cambridge, 1899], pp. 110f.). Field is supported by J.H. Moulton (Moulton, *Grammar of New Testament Greek. I, Prolegomena* [Edinburgh, 1908, 3rd ed.], p. 47). The singular form of the part. has been of some trouble to interpreters and led to the proposal that the preferable reading is a dative plural. The present tense followed by an imperfect is also a difficulty for this position.

243 "being present with"–the context would suggest that the part. is really an alternative spelling for *συναυλίζομαι*. This alternative is in fact offered by some of the minuscule witnesses. The deponent *συναυλίζομαι* actually means "lying together or sleeping together" in the majority of cases, but the more general meaning of "to be with" is also admissible. Thus the strain of the singular number and the present tense is mitigated. The chief advocate of this orthographic change is H.J. Cadbury. He rejects the two former alternatives and proposes the translation "to spend the night together in the open" (Cadbury, "Lexical Notes III," pp. 312f.). He argues that it is not a textual error but another spelling for *αυ* which is to be found in other contemporary documents (cf. *ibid.*, p. 313, n. 18 and p. 314, n. 21). Most severe in his criticism of Zahn, Cadbury maintains that it is hardly insignificant that Lk would wish to mention Jesus' lodging with his own (*ibid.*, p. 315). This also eliminates in his opinion the difficulty of Lk. 24:40ff. because they are not in Jerusalem at all but are "bivouacking in the neighborhood" and experience the Ascension at night because it takes place after the evening meal (*ibid.*, p. 316). Cadbury is supported by many. Moulton and Milligan also stress the orthographic change in the Koine and cite the following illustrations: *BGU* III, 713,42 (A.D. 41-42): Τιβερίου Κρατίου = Κλαυδίου, and IV, 1079,25 (A.D. 41): *βλέπε σατὸν* (=*σεαυτὸν*) *ἀπὸ τῶν Ἰουδαίων* and P Lond 1912,94 (the letter of Claudius to the Alexandrians A.D. 41): *ἀπολάοντας* (Moulton and Milligan, *op. cit.*, pp. 601f.). One of the most recent supporters of this position has been C.F.D. Moule who favors the translation "spending festival lodging with," i.e., temporal lodging in Jerusalem (C.F.D. Moule, "The Post-Resurrection Appearances in the Light of Festival Pilgrimages," *NTS*, 4 ['57/'58], p. 60). Finally we find that Liddell and Scott give the *αυ* reading as the *varia lectio* for Acts (Liddell and Scott, *op. cit.*, p. 1694). It is not as though this position was not without opposition, however. Moulton and Howard point out that although this shift from *αυ* to *α* is known it is nevertheless among the less educated papyri fragments (Moulton and Howard, *op. cit.*, p. 87). As in Moulton's *Prolegomena* the stress is on the limited usage and not its frequency (Moulton, *op. cit.*, p. 47). We may have orthographic parallels in II Pet. 1:19 and 2:14 (Moulton and Howard, *op. cit.*, p. 87), but the objection of Zahn that *συναυλίζομαι* would "einen ganz bedeutungslosen Nebenumstand in unverständlicher Weise hervorheben" (Zahn, *op. cit.*, p. 25, n. 38) is a contextual consideration that offers some real difficulties to be reckoned with, Cadbury notwithstanding. Also of interest is the fact that the Clementine homilies preserve the *α* reading (cf. *ibid.*, p. 25, and Cadbury, "Lexical Notes III," p. 312, n. 14).

244 Cadbury, "Lexical Notes III," p. 312, n. 15.

for instance, that a fairly well attested reading of Psalm 140 (141):4 in the *Hexaplorum Origenis* renders the Hebrew ובל-אלחם במנעמיהם with *μὴ συναλισθῶ ἐν ταῖς τερπνότησιν αὐτῶν* (with the alternative of *μηδὲ συμφάγοιμι* in Symmachus). We also find that Chrysostom reads a "meal" text.[245]

It would seem that a certain resolution of this impasse is wanting. With Lk.24:41ff.and the Emmaus meal incident in mind it would appear, nevertheless, fair to assume that Lk could have intended to mention such an incident here. Jesus' eating in the presence of the disciples does not relate to the eucharist thematic in Lk.24:41ff., as we shall see, but was the *quod erat demonstrandum* of the bodily proofs thematic and in Emmaus the meal motif is hardly a secondary matter, but is rather the key to recognition for the blinded disciples. Even if we were dealing here with a pre-lukan text it would appear improbable, however, judging from lukan literary and theological tendencies that he could have left this theme to an ambiguous participle without a more exact reference and most of all that he could have allowed such to stand in this particular location in the development of the summary. On the other hand, Lk could have intended here simply to *allude* to the theme that Jesus ate in their presence. This could explain the singular person and would be but a summary of what was indeed present in his gospel account. The notion of "coming together" raises the following question: if Lk meant this notion pure and simple why does he use this verb here and in vs. 6 the more common expression *συνέρχομαι*?[246] Even if the singular form can be settled through an assumed "with them" (in spite of the syntactical strain), this matter of vocabulary is still most serious. Because of its *hapax* character the only apparent alternatives are 1) we have here a non-lukan source or 2) this is a translation which though perhaps not directly from Lk was the current equivalent for a semitic notion. The difficulty with the latter is that we do not find support for the notion that *συναλίζομαι* reproduced a Hebrew verb of "coming together" in the LXX or subsequent literature steming from such a bilingual community. Moreover, recourse to a non-lukan source at this point throws up too many uncertainties. If both vss. 4 and 6 mean the same thing, *convenire*, it is hard to understand why Lk would have left the redundancy where he is trying to avoid such through a summary. It would appear that the fact of no redundancy, i.e., different meanings, would be much more logical as a basis for retaining the *hapax* term of vs. 4. We shall see, on the other hand, that the motif of "coming to and being present with them" is very much a part of the group appearance motifs and if the participle were meant to be a summary pointer to this aspect as prelude to the commission and promise of the Holy Spirit then it seems very appropriate. We would thus conclude on literary and theological grounds that the rendering of a "meal" translation is highly suspect (in spite of the argumentation of Wilcox and others), that a "coming together" translation also has serious obstacles and that "being together" as the sense intended is perhaps to be preferred. The *αυ* to *α*

245 Chysostom, *Opera Omnia*, III, 89a. 767e and IX, 7c.
246 The verb occurs 17x in Acts, 2x in Lk's gospel, 1x in Mt., 3x in Mk. and 7x in I Cor.

orthographic change may indeed have some weight since it does not rest upon the necessity of a scribal error but rests upon the existence of a legitimate form.

Last among the unusual and *hapax* terms are two of the verbs in the charge of Jesus *μὴ χωρίζεσθαι, ἀλλὰ περιμένειν τὴν ἐπαγγελίαν τοῦ πατρός*. Of course, *χωρίζω* is itself nothing unusual, but the fact that Lk never uses it except here and in 18:1f. (the latter occuring in a travel log and as a summary of the policy of Claudius regarding the Jews in Rome) makes it very interesting. The fact that the command "not to leave" stands here in the charge is arresting for two reasons: 1) it is coupled with a positive expression, i.e., "wait for the promise of the Father" and 2) in comparison with the charge of the gospel account (24:49) it is the only negative present. There it is *καθίσατε ἐν τῇ πόλει* (the journey of vs. 50 is no contradiction since Bethany was a suburb of Jerusalem).[247] This is interesting because of the former's relatedness to the summary style. The positive form fits the direct discourse better, while the negative form gives the substance of the charge sharp and clear in indirect, summary form. We would be inclined, therefore, to see the *χωρίζω* form in a dependent relationship to *καθίζω*.

The second half of the charge, however, presents greater difficulties. It is fully *hapax* for the NT and does not stand as the negative expression of a positive one in the gospel. In the latter we find an entirely different idea: *ἕως οὗ ἐνδύσεσθε ἐξ ὕψους δύναμιν*. Does a relationship possibly exist between them? Curiously enough we find this aspect of the question in Acts expanded rather than telescoped in relation to the gospel. Perhaps that is not surprising at all since this second work of Lk begins with and is based upon the encounter of the followers of Jesus with the Holy Spirit–his on-going presence with them. That *is* Lk's theological thematic at this point and we see three levels of development: 1) vs. 4 is called the promise of the Father, then 2) vs. 5 is called baptism in the Holy Spirit and finally 3) vs. 8 is the pointer to an encounter with *δύναμιν* when the Spirit has come upon them. Herewith the stage is set for Pentecost and the knot is tied with the announcement of *ἐξ ὕψους δύναμιν* in the gospel account. The literary hand and the theological plan of Lk are unmistakable here and in one sense at least we may say that as the negative expression of "do not leave" was related dependently to "remain in the city" so too here a dependent relationship with intentional expansion is an unavoidable conclusion. This, as we shall see below, tells us a great deal about the character of the whole summary section and the purpose of Lk in including this introduction at all. One problem remains however: *περιμένω* is not a lukan term. Moulton and Milligan have shown that this word was by no means unknown with this meaning in the first few centuries A.D.[248] Unfortunately, most of their examples are later than Lk/Acts, but Josephus *Antiquities* 12,193; 1,219; 2,69 and 6,176 are of some interest as is the LXX of Gen. 49:18: *τὴν σωτηρίαν περιμένω κυρίου*. With such expressions current it is perhaps not at all surprising that Lk may have chosen this

247 Cf. Acts 1:12.
248 Moulton and Milligan, *op. cit*., p. 506.

term especially if we glance back once more to the gospel account. There we found the term "remain" with regard to a place and that was then summarized with a corresponding notion put in the negative. With the charge not to leave, the second and decisive aspect is added, i.e., being clothed with power from on high or more precisely here in Acts "waiting for the promise of the Father," a notion which, as pointed out above, is expanded and enriched in three descriptive stages. This would appear to be an instance where mere word statistic is certainly rendered insufficient by literary and theological considerations.

We come now to a summary of the whole. How are we to judge this material in relation to the group appearance of Lk's gospel? When we look at a cross-section view of the material we see that there are reasons for and against attributing this appearance account to Lk's creative hand–in this case, his summary style. We have seen, for example, that there is some reason for attributing vss. 3 and 4 to a prelukan source, which was then incorporated by Lk into the framework of the whole. Yet, the recognition of such a source is a very difficult matter, because of the brevity of the summary and also because lukan characteristics of style and thought are unmistakably present where terminological supports are wanting. For this reason we would also object to the "later addition" hypothesis of Braun, Norden, Meyer, *et al.* We note further that with one minor exception there are no *hapax* or specifically late terms in the rest of this chapter through the Ascension and address of the "two men" (vs. 11, cf. also the "two men" at the tomb in Lk. 24:4). There is thus no justification in the light of vocabulary and theological considerations for reducing this chapter to a later, non-lukan classification. [249] We see, for example, that the latter part of vs. 4 after the charge not to leave and to await the promise of the Father shifts to the first person, namely the direct address of Jesus. Does such bespeak the presence of an independent source? Such would seem an unsubstantiated conclusion since the direct discourse continues in vs. 5 and is clearly a literary development of vs. 4. Moreover, in the light of the first person precedent already found in the gospel a literary kinship seems quite clear.

Another solution seems more cogent: Lk is the author behind this first chapter group appearance scene in its entirety. [250] His plan is to summarize the motifs already known to him in the group appearance as he recorded and developed them in

249 Cf. also E.F. Harrison, *op. cit.*, pp. 217ff., esp. p. 231, who concludes that Lk's failure to deviate on matters regarding resurrection terminology as found in later patristic sources speaks for the unity of the work, its distance from those sources and its close proximity to the resurrection traditions themselves.

250 Grundmann, "Problem," p. 47, assumes that this is a tradition which comes from Jewish-Christian circles in Jerusalem, but that this is a tradition at all is problematic to say the least. He fails to give sufficient weight to the lukan composition here. Knox, *op. cit.*, pp. 18f., also favors a semitic source behind this first chapter (following Torrey's view through 5:16) because of 1) the alleged semitic style in vs. 1 and 2) the contradiction of the ascension scene in respect to the gospel account. For the rest of Acts he concludes oral sources for Lk (*passim* and p. 39). We have already discussed the futility of the early source school approach and the need for a more equitable approach today.

his gospel account.[251] The purpose of the summary was not simply to reconstruct that scene via abbreviation, but was the dramatic moment needed from which to embark on the thematic of the second volume: the promise and fulfillment of Jesus' abiding presence with his community in world mission through the coming of the Holy Spirit. We have already seen that this aspect of the appearance—the word aspect in general and the promise of the Father—is enlarged rather than telescoped and the implications are clear: the summary as a whole has been developed within the concern of the commission. Peculiar to lukan theology, the commission is linked most directly and convincingly with the presence of the Holy Spirit. Lk grasps, as it were, the heart of the post-resurrection encounter and through his summary combines 1) the disciples' personal encounter with the Lord and 2) the personal nature of their commission as mission under the Holy Spirit.

Acts 2, 3, 5, 10 and 13

The sermon summaries distinguish themselves in the context of our investigation over against other such summaries in Acts either because they make direct reference to the appearance of the resurrected One or refer to the Resurrection with the remark that the purported speaker or the apostolic body is "witness" to it, a tacit reference in all probability to appearances. The latter is the case for 2:32; 3:15 (cf. 4:10 and 33); and 5:30 and 32. The nature of these references makes it impossible to establish any connection between them and the appearance stories of the gospel tradition. They are rather kerygmatic in tone finding their closest parallel in the formula tradition and taking in all probability their origin there.[252] More relevant for our relationship question are the references of the first type mentioned above where direct reference to the appearances is made.

Such is the case in 10:40f. and 13:30f. In the first we have the reference to the Resurrection [*τοῦτον ὁ θεὸς ἤγειρεν*] along with the third-day qualification, both of which call to mind the formulation of the kerygma in I Cor. 15. Thereafter comes the rather unusual expression: *καὶ ἔδωκεν αὐτὸν ἐμφανῆ γενέσθαι, οὐ παντὶ τῷ λαῷ, ἀλλὰ μάρτυσιν τοῖς προκεχειροτονημένοις ὑπὸ τοῦ θεοῦ, ἡμῖν*. . .(vss. 40b-41a). The reference to the appearances is self-evident, the question is whether it is a summary of the gospel stories or an independent formulation of the kerygma. As we saw above, the appearance terminus for the kerygma is *ὤφθη* which is then bound to a list of witnesses. A sober appraisal of Acts 10:40f. suggests that the same neutrality with regard to appearance forms as such is present here. It would appear further that the same emphasis on divine initiative inherent in the passive form *ὤφθη*

251 Among the many lukan characteristics of style, Robertson, *op. cit.*, p. 123, says that Lk "accumulates participles especially in Acts, but not without stylistic refinement." This refinement here in any case also corresponds to a theological and literary goal.

252 Cf. n. 202. For the kerygmatic scheme behind the sermons in Acts cf. Goppelt, "Osterkerygma," pp. 86ff. *et al.* Contra Wilckens, *Missionsreden*, pp. 188 *et passim*.

comes to expression in this construction.[253] These observations lend support to the conclusion that the author of Acts is responsible here for this formulation and that without any direct connection with the appearance stories but rather with the kerygmatic formula tradition. The only difficulty with this proposal is vs. 41b. It is here, namely, that the quite singular claim is added: *οἵτινες συνεφάγομεν καὶ συνεπίομεν αὐτῷ μετὰ τὸ ἀναστῆναι αὐτὸν ἐκ νεκρῶν*. As we saw above, the *συναλιζόμενος* reference in 1:4 is fraught with too many difficulties to allow it to stand as a clear indication that a meal with the resurrected One is intended and, as we shall see below in chapter III, none of the gospel appearance stories in their pre-redactional form allow this either, so that 10:41b becomes the only reference to such in the entire appearance tradition. Since this reference is not covered, so to speak, by the appearance accounts in Lk's own gospel this could be taken as an indication that behind the statement stands an independent non-lukan tradition.[254] This perspective does not appear compelling, however, in the light of the following considerations: it has been maintained frequently in studies on Lk's theology that he intends at least indirectly in his redactional use of the Emmaus story and perhaps the group appearance to point to the Eucharist as the focal point for the continued communion between the resurrected, glorified Lord and the Church.[255] It is certainly possible that whereas too direct a reference was difficult in his gospel appearances because of the prescriptions of the tradition, here a greater freedom was possible. That both eating and drinking are singled out here would seem to add support to the proposal that the elements of the Eucharist are intended. Of course, it could be objected that such a reference could have little function in this missionary context, but even this objection is insufficient, since it can indeed find contextual justification in the light of the whole Cornelius episode.[256] Nor is it at all clear why this statement should not find an adequate place in the general "proofs" and "witness" themes found elsewhere in the summaries of Acts. This would mean, therefore, that Lk has formulated his summary statement here in 10:40f. out of a two-sided coupling with traditions familiar to his readers: he reaches back to the kerygma in vss. 40b-41a and to the appearance stories–with an eye toward his own redactional achievement–in vs. 41b.

In the second reference, 13:30f.,we have the same reference to the Resurrection that we saw in 10:40a. In 13:31 we read: *ὃς ὤφθη ἐπὶ ἡμέρας πλείους τοῖς συναναβᾶσιν αὐτῷ ἀπὸ Γαλιλαίας εἰς Ἰερουσαλήμ, οἵτινες [νῦν] εἰσιν μάρτυρες αὐτοῦ πρὸς τὸν λαόν*. The key features of this summary are the terminus *ὤφθη*, the

253 Cf. p. 60 and n. 196. Contra, Kegel, *op. cit.*, p. 93, in debate with Rengstorf that this is a *sinngemäße* interpretation of the terminus.

254 So, for example, among others J. Roloff, *Das Kerygma und der irdische Jesus* (Gött., 1970), p. 255. Cf. also Wilckens, *Missionsreden*, p. 144.

255. Cf. below, ns. 564ff. and 597.

256 That the story flows into the conclusion that Cornelius and household embrace Christianity gives it a distinctively different cast than say, for example, the Mars' Hill address of Paul in Acts 17. Both are missionary sermon summaries, as it were, but the eucharistic motif would hardly be appropriate in the latter.

reference to "many days," the delineation of appearance participants as "those who had gone up with him from Galilee to Jerusalem" and the statement, as in the other sermons noted above: we are "witnesses." These features all point to lukan redactional construction out of the kerygma and whereas it could be maintained that the Jerusalem locale could point back to Lk's intentions in his representation of appearance stories, it could be argued just as convincingly that his Jerusalem-outwards mission schematization in Acts itself is at work here. Moreover, the "many days" here and the "forty days" discussed above for chapter one stand much closer together than would be the case by positing a reference to the time factor in his gospel account which is decidedly different. It would be exceedingly precarious to insist on a traditional source here, therefore, which could remove the necessity for seeing the redactional hand of the author composing this summary out of the givens of the kerygmatic formula tradition.

Acts 7, 8, 9, 22 and 26

The narrative résumés in these chapters have no direct but only indirect relevance for the relationship question under investigation. Chapter 7:55ff.records the stoning of Stephen which includes a post-resurrection appearance of sorts, i.e., Stephen is granted a vision of the glorified Jesus at the right hand of God: *ὑπάρχων δὲ πλήρης πνεύματος ἁγίου ἀτενίσας εἰς τὸν οὐρανὸν εἶδεν δόξαν θεοῦ καὶ* Ἰησοῦν *ἑστῶτα ἐκ δεξιῶν τοῦ θεοῦ, καὶ εἶπεν· ἰδοὺ θεωρῶ τοὺς οὐρανοὺς διηνοιγμένους καὶ τὸν υἱὸν τοῦ ἀνθρώπου ἐκ δεξιῶν ἑστῶτα τοῦ θεοῦ·* For Lk, of course, the resurrection appearances as such have come to a close and the Lord has ascended so that an appearance form anything like those contained in his gospel would have been impossible. It is generally recognized, however, that Lk himself is not alone responsible for this account, but that he is reworking a Stephen-tradition in which was already embedded this account of his martyrdom with its vision.[257] Aspects of that "sighting" may indeed have been made more concrete by Lk's hand, e.g., the clear identification of Jesus with the Son of Man, etc., but the basic form of the "appearance" in its pre-redactional state is probably intact. Whether or not this assumption is true does not affect in the final analysis the main point, namely, that we are here confronted with an entirely different *Gattung* than what we shall find in the gospel stories. It is an *ἐν πνεύματι* representation perhaps influenced by the heavenly radiance type with characteristic mention of light–in this case the *δόξα θεοῦ*–the opened heavens and the sighting of the heavenly figure above in the presence of God.[258] An adequate understanding of this type then would require separate attention under an investigation in search of the origins of this *Gattung*.

257 Cf. R. Pesch, *Die Vision des Stephanus*, StBSt, 12 (Stutt., 1966), pp. 26ff. and lit. Also the discussion in Haenchen, *Apostelgeschichte*, pp. 227ff., and esp. pp. 246ff., H. Conzelmann, *Apostelgeschichte*, pp. 58f. Graß, *op. cit.*, pp. 221f. and G. Schille, *Anfänge der Kirche. Erwägungen zur apostolischen Frühgeschichte*, BEvTh, 43 (Mü., 1966), pp. 143ff.

258 Cf. above, n. 181.

It is enough here to point out the distinctions and to differentiate between this type and the one found in the gospels.

In chapter eight we find the account of Philip's encounter with the Ethiopian eunuch and although the complete absence of an appearance of the resurrected/glorified One would make any relevant comparison of it with the gospels under the relationship question seem impossible, other more formal considerations bring it perhaps into very close proximity to them. The story demonstrates a rather complex pre-redactional history of transmission.[259] Both the angel of the Lord [*Ἄγγελος κυρίου* vs. 26] and the spirit [*πνεῦμα* vs. 29 and *πνεῦμα κυρίου* vs. 39] are the divine agents or messengers and both speak particular instructions: "rise and go" and "approach and join!" Philip follows instructions and serves the eunuch as interpreter of Isaiah 53, preacher of the gospel of Christ and agent of the eunuch's Christian baptism. When they come up from the water Philip is taken away by the Spirit and the eunuch sees him no more: *πνεῦμα κυρίου ἥρπασεν τὸν φίλιππον, καὶ οὐκ εἶδεν αὐτὸν οὐκέτι ὁ εὐνοῦχος* (vs. 39); thereto is added that the eunuch went his way rejoicing and Philip "found himself" [*εὑρέθη εἰς*] in Azotos. Of course, even on formal grounds the points of comparison here with the gospel accounts are sparse. Yet, the travel motif and those of the conversation and disappearance do call to mind a certain similarity with the Emmaus story, etc. If one may consider the references to the angel of the Lord and the Spirit of the Lord and the motifs of being carried away and disappearing as reflecting an Old Testament story *Gattung*, e.g., that found in I Kings 18:12, which was then adapted for an expression of Christian theology, it may indeed be possible to posit some kind of relationship of an indirect sort, providing, of course, that such backgrounds can be demonstrated as plausible for the gospel accounts. This question will be dealt with below in chapter IV.

Chapters 9, 22 and 26 contain accounts of the appearance to Paul on the road to Damascus. The three stories demonstrate certain internal tensions so that one may posit without difficulty that variant accounts existed at a pre-redactional level. Significant for our investigation, however, is the observation that although we do indeed find here the story form more or less as résumé, its type as *Gattung* is that of the heavenly radiance appearance, not unlike Acts 7 noted above, and as such is to be held separate from the gospel type. The questions of the relationship of this type to the kerygma and Paul's autobiographical addition in I Cor. 15:8ff. have been touched upon earlier.[260] The differences in concept and form existing be-

259 Cf. Haenchen, *Apostelgeschichte*, pp. 263ff.

260 Cf. above, n. 181. The most recent study of these accounts in Acts is by K. Löning, *Die Saulustradition in der Apostelgeschichte*, NTA (NF) (Münster, 1973). Put briefly his thesis runs as follows: ch. 9 alone is of interest in recovering the original Saulus tradition (p. 18). Pursuit of the origins' question leads to the form-critical recognition that two levels of tradition have been combined with a high degree of theological sophistication to formulate the conversion of Paul: the *Gattung* of the temple-theft legend (cf., e.g., Heliodor in II Makk. 3) and contemporary Jewish propaganda literature (cf., e.g., Joseph and Aseneth) with its *metanoia* motif (pp. 63ff. and 70ff.). The *Sitz im Leben* of the tradition is to be sought in the missionary acti-

tween this type and that of the gospels are so categorical that two distinct traditional origins are undoubtedly to be sought. As noted earlier, the fundamental conviction of faith in the earliest community that the Lord appeared (ὤφθη) after his Resurrection, stands behind them both, but in their development two separate thought-horizons are at work in spite of the probable common basis of subject matter. Apostolic commission is at stake and it would appear that Paul's use of ἐκτρώματι in I Cor. 15:8 is, among other things, a tacit recognition of the apparent divergence in form.[261] It is in any case a premature judgment to relegate the gospel form–at least at its pre-redactional level–to a subordinate position of dependence on the basis of a theory that "bodily encounter," as it were, reflects later conditions in an ecclesiastical climate that thought originally in "spiritualistic categories." The gospel stories were formulated within the special context of the gospel genre, the heavenly radiance type by and large was not; possible exceptions, e.g., the transfiguration story, will be discussed below.[262]

In conclusion then the following must be said about the *summaries* in Acts: where there is a clear indication of a relationship between them and the gospel tradition they stem from the deliberate theological interest of Lk to direct the reader's attention back to the appearances in his gospel *in the redactional form he has given them.* Where it appears that traditions are at work behind the summaries the source appears to be either the kerygmatic formula tradition itself or possibly a combination of this with story accounts no longer extant or a separate branch of a story form that is independent of the gospel tradition. The summaries then build a distinct complex of witness to the resurrection appearances and are related as far as can be determined with any degree of certainty only indirectly to the pre-redactional form of the gospel stories.

C. The Empty Tomb Tradition

In the introduction we affirmed the consensus of opinion in New Testament research regarding the empty tomb and appearance traditions, namely, that the two are to be differentiated and regarded–in terms of the history-of-tradition–as origi-

vity of the primitive church under the sphere of influence of Hellenistic Judaism (particularly in Damascus, pp. 70ff. and 77). For the *Gattung* the divine appearance motif had the protective function of hurling the persecutor to the ground, blinding and driving him away from a Holy Place (pp. 63ff.), a function which is altered to a revelation experience by Luke (in ch. 9 and especially in 22 and 26). Says Löning, "Sicher sekundär ist die Formulierung Ἰησοῦς ὁ ὀφθείς σοι ἐν τῇ ὁδῷ ᾗ ἤρχου; denn damit wird die Christusbegegnung vor Damaskus im Unterschied und Gegensatz zum ursprünglichen Sinn der Darstellung im Rückblick als Offenbarungsgeschehen–ὀφθείς ist term. techn.–interpretiert. Die Lichterscheinung hat ursprünglich in ihrer niederschmetternden und blendenden Wirkung primär die / Funktion, den Frevler zu bannen; das kann schwerlich mit ὀφθῆναι ausgedrückt werden" (pp. 86f.). If Löning is correct this may offer a plausible explanation why the form was more suited for the missionary literature of the NT and if at all only indirectly for the gospels!

261 Cf. above, n. 184.

262 Cf. below, pp. 141ff.

nating and existing independent of one another in the oral tradition of the primitive church. Yet, a certain group of resurrection appearances are very closely tied—indirectly or directly—to the discovery of the empty tomb and, therefore, this affirmation of the *opinio communis* does not mean that at least certain aspects of the tomb tradition cannot be useful for our line of questioning. To the contrary, it is imperative that we try to make precise the point at which the two are brought together and to clarify the nature of that relationship. That is to say, were post-resurrection appearance stories at the tomb anchored in the earliest tradition or were such constructed only secondarily to achieve a union of two originally independent traditions? To arrive at a satisfactory solution to this question we must of necessity follow an approach which begins with a brief analysis of the complex compositional relationships in the empty tomb tradition itself and then moves to the appearance stories linked to it. The reason for this is clear: only by first isolating the traditional from the redactional elements of the tomb stories can we hope to gain access to criteria for determining the origins of the appearance stories so closely connected with them. The following analysis then must give answer to three questions:

1) what is the traditional matrix of the tomb story in contrast to its redactional enlargement and prior to its incorporation into the larger tomb/appearance complex?
2) what setting and function did the traditional matrix originally have in relationship to appearance stories?
3) what kind of "seams" unite this tradition with the appearance tradition and how has the former influenced the latter?

1. The Empty Tomb: Its Traditional Matrix

A comparison of Mk. 16:1-8 and parallels in Mt. 28:1-8 and Lk. 24:1-12 with Jn. 20:1-13 demonstrates that we have two forms of the tomb tradition to clarify before we can probe the relationship-question *vis-à-vis* the appearances: a) the synoptic tradition where Mt and Lk make use of Mk's gospel but go beyond it and b) the johannine tradition which suggests the possibility of an independent source; in this latter connection Lk. 24:12 and 22-24 must be compared.

a. Synoptic Tradition

It has long been disputed whether or not the Gospel of Mark originally could have ended with the empty tomb story and the words *ἐφοβοῦντο γάρ* as its Easter conclusion.[263] Although it has been argued recently that Mk did close his gospel

263 Cf. below, "Mk." 16:9-20, pp. 117ff. and n. 340 for a brief cross section view of the literature.

with appearance stories and that these were not then subsequently lost or excised but are to be found embedded in the so-called "inauthentic ending" at vss. 15-20, [264] and although others would like to see an indication of appearance stories in

264 Most recently argued by E. Linnemann, "Der (wiedergefundene) Markusschluß," *ZThK*, 66 (1969), pp. 255-287. She concludes that although Mk. 16:9-14 does indeed contain a summary of the appearances found in the other gospels and may, therefore, be considered a subsequent addition to Mk., the same cannot be said about the verses 15-20 (pp. 258f.). She sees in these latter verses "verschiedene Überlieferungsstücke redaktionell miteinander verbunden," which were not originally a unit but could have been joined sometime in the oral tradition (p. 259, n. 11). 'Die Geistestätigkeit, die für V. 15-20 vorausgesetzt werden muß, ist demnach die gleiche, wie sie Markus bei der Abfassung seines Evangeliums ausgeübt hat" (p. 259). That is to say, for Linnemann Mk. originally ended with vss. 15-20 after the empty tomb story, but a later redactor–striving for completeness–summarized the stories of the other gospels known to him, inserted the summary between the tomb and appearance stories and altered both of these slightly in order to achieve a smooth literary transition; for this latter reason one must speculate what words were altered in the original to make the coupling between vss. 8 and 15 successful (pp. 259 and 269f.). She claims that both Mt and Lk must have known this original ending (pp. 260ff., 270ff. and esp. 278). She argues her case on three fronts: a) the text-critical problem is not insurmountable since the codices "B" and "א" can be defective, and both Justin Martyr and Iraneus seem to have known the vss. 15-20 as the original ending of Mk. (pp. 261f.), b) she takes R. Morgenthaler (*Statistik des neutestamentlichen Wortschatzes* [Frankfurt, 1958]) to task by showing the methodological weakness behind a strictly statistical approach to solving the authenticity question (pp. 262ff.) and c) she differs with both E. Lohmeyer (*Das Evangelium des Markus,* Meyer [Gött., 1967, 17th ed.], pp. 358ff.), who sees no original unity in the entire section, and E. Helzle (*Der Schluß des Markusevangeliums (Mk 16,9-20) und das Freer-Logion (Mk 16, 14W), Ihre Tendenzen und ihr gegenseitiges Verhältnis. Eine wortexegetische Untersuchung*, Diss. [Tüb., 1959], p. 204), who sees an original unity in the whole, but as a non-markan composition and a subsequent addition, in order to affirm a unity and markan origin behind vss. 15-20 alone (pp. 264ff.). Further, where Taylor (*op. cit.*, pp. 610ff.) calls the imagery and language second century and non-markan she objects: "Taylors Beweisführung vermag uns nicht zu überzeugen" (p. 282), and then goes on to affirm the capacity of this ending to round out the entire gospel organically so that it can no longer be called a mere torso (p. 287). Linnemann intended to show that her conclusions are possible if not necessary; she has succeeded in doing that, but it would seem that her criticism of Taylor is valid for Linnemann herself. She has made too light of the problems connected with the text (cf. thereto K. Aland, "Der wiedergefundene Markusschluß? Eine methodologische Bemerkung zur textkritischen Arbeit," *ZThK*, 67 [1970], pp. 3-13), language and style (on all three counts cf. also, J.K. Elliot, "The Text and Language of the Endings to Mark's Gospel," *ThZ*, 27 [1971], pp. 255ff.). One would also have to draw a question mark methodologically over her attempts to reconstruct the missing link between Mk. 16:8 and 15 via the other gospels, especially Mt., since she presupposes that Mt and Lk had, indeed, read "Mk." 16:15ff. as the original ending and that Mt. 28:16-20, for example, was an intentional reworking of it, and then proceeds to work in reverse by finding the proposed and necessary missing link in the reworked remnants of the original and–in part–missing conclusion. Such a method is questionable at best. Finally, however, her rejection of Helzle's thesis (*op. cit.*, pp. 204 *et passim*) that a unity exists in the entire section vss. 9-20 in the words: "Daß Themengleichheit und thematische Verwandschaft kein Indiz für literarische Einheit abgeben" (p. 266) overlooks the elements throughout the section which do in fact overlap and form a literary unit in spite of the methodological weaknesses of the *Wortexegese* pursued by Helzle. It is to be granted that the switch to direct discourse in vs. 15 offers a marked contrast to the style of the preceding summary, but the conclusions drawn therefrom by Linnemann seem unwarranted and excessive; summary can exist in both direct and indirect discourse. W. Schmithals, "Der Markusschluß, die Verklärungsgeschichte und die Aussendung der Zwölf," *ZThK*, 69 (1972), pp. 379ff., esp. 403ff., while following Aland's critique in general makes use of Linnemann's argumentation on Mk. 16:15-20 in his own attempt to reconstruct a pre-markan Easter narrative source (hereto, cf. below n. 429).

an original—but now lost—ending of the gospel by way of synoptic comparison suggesting that the other evangelists read such in their markan source,[265] it must be concluded that all such attempts are exegetically top-heavy and problematic. The creative—yet often fanciful—attempts at reconstruction are indeed imaginative, but less compelling than the position: the empty tomb story (Mk. 16:1-8) is the intended conclusion of this gospel. What Mk for his part intended to say about the Resurrection with these last eight verses is variously interpreted in New Testament research,[266] but there is general agreement that the key is to be found in the

265 Cf. E. Schweizer, *Das Evangelium nach Markus*, NTD 1, (Gött., 1968), p. 212, regarding the supposed markan source for Mt. 28:9f., also B. Lindars, "The Composition of John XX," *NTS*, 7 ('60/'61), p. 142, and A. Richardson, *An Introduction to the Theology of the New Testament* (N.Y., 1958), pp. 193f. For other themes in Mt. and Lk. which are supposed to be dependent on the lost ending of Mk. cf. A. Strobel, "Der Berg der Offenbarung. . .," *Verborum Veritatis, Fst. G. Stählin*, ed. by O. Böcher and K. Haacker (Wuppertal, 1970), pp. 133ff., 140 *et passim*, and Linnemann, *op. cit.*, p. 273: "Nach allem wird man. . .annehmen dürfen, daß Mt 28,18-20 eine kritische Bearbeitung von Mk 16,15-20 durch den Verfasser des ersten Evangeliums ist. Sollten dann aber nicht auch die Verse Mt 28,16f. auf den bislang vermißten Markusschluß zurückgehen. . .? " Thereto cf. B. Steinseifer, "Der Ort der Erscheinungen des Auferstandenen," *ZNW*, 62 (1971), p. 258. W.C. Allen, *A Critical and Exegetical Commentary on the Gospel According to St. Matthew* (Edinburgh, 1912, 3rd ed.), p. 303, would also like to see the influence of the lost ending in Mt., but note the critique of G. Barth, "Das Gesetzesverständnis des Evangelisten Matthäus," *Überlieferung und Auslegung im Matthäusevangelium* (Neukirchen, 1961, 2nd ed.), p. 123, n. 2. For further opposition in general to this approach, cf. F. Neirynck, "Les femmes au tombeau: 'Etude de la rédaction Matthéenne (Matt. XXVIII. 1-10)," *NTS*, 15 ('68/'69), pp. 170ff., and Wilckens, "Perikope," p. 33. Also P. Stuhlmacher, *Das paulinische Evangelium I. Vorgeschichte*, FRLANT, 95, ed. by E. Käsemann and E. Würthwein (Gött., 1963), p. 254ff., would like to see "Mk." 16:9-20 as in part terminologically older than Mt. with the latter countering certain enthusiastic tendencies in the former but he is careful to make his claim on the basis of analogous streams of tradition behind the text and not upon the entire text itself. He focuses his attention, however, upon the term "gospel" and its origins in mission and not upon the appearances themselves. G.W. Trompf, "The First Resurrection Appearance and the Ending of Mark's Gospel," *NTS*, 18 ('71/'72), pp. 308-330 also proposes an original ending with an appearance to the women, in particular the mother of Jesus, reflected esp. in Mt. 28:9-10.

266 The colorful and varied spectrum of interpretation among those basically considering the tomb story to be both the original ending of Mk. and a separate tradition from that of the appearances can be divided basically into two groups: **a**) those who see here for Mk. some kind of direct relationship to the appearance tradition and b) those who would see only an indirect relationship or none at all. For the first category the following may serve to illustrate the variety:

a,1) the tomb story was itself actually once an appearance story which was then altered because of the inadequacy of the witness of the women in a Jewish community. Thus: Ch. Masson, "Le Tombeau Vide," *RThPh* (ns), 32 (1944), pp. 164ff., 170, n. 2 and 171ff.—the 3rd-day reference is an indication that Mk has made an angelophany out of an original christophany with the goal of achieving a kerygmatic message similar to I Cor. 15 and a rebuttal to those who would place the resurrection message entirely at the feet of the women. Similar is Albertz, *op. cit.*, pp. 267f. *et passim*. This scheme is seen as an oversimplification by Brun, *Auferstehung*, pp. 7ff. Most recently it has been argued on the basis of a christological, baptism-symbolic significance for the "angel" that "empty tomb" story is a misnomer and that it is actually a "resurrection-announcement" story, i.e., the figure is no angel at all, but rather Jesus himself, R. Scroggs and K.I. Groff, "Baptism in Mark: Dying and Rising with Christ," *JBL*, 92 (1973), pp. 534ff.

a,2) the tomb story replaced an appearance story (probably the "protophany" to Peter) which

n. 266 con't.
originally stood at this place, but had to be suppressed for one reason or another due to the internal struggles of the church. Thus Dibelius, *Formgeschichte*, pp. 190ff. Variations to this view: G. Hebert, "The Resurrection-Narrative in St. Mark's Gospel," *SJTh*, 15 (1962), pp. 66ff. (cf. critique thereto in H. Anderson, "The Easter Witness of the Evangelists," *The New Testament in Historical and Contemporary Perspective. Fst. G.H.C. MacGregor*, ed. by H. Anderson and W. Barclay [Oxford, 1965], pp. 42f.) and elsewhere (e.g., H.W. Bartsch who is dealt with below, n. 310, because he does not consider this Mk.'s original ending).
a,3) the tomb story does not directly replace the appearance stories, but merely points to them; for theological reasons the latter are not narrated. Thus: E. Haenchen, *Der Weg Jesu* (Berlin, 1968, 2nd ed.), p. 546; R.R. Bater, "Towards a More Biblical View of the Resurrection," *Int.*, 23 (1969), pp. 61ff. (going on then to interpret the appearances intended here and indeed the whole appearance tradition as "resurrection-ascension" appearances). A variation to this position can be seen in Wilckens, "Perikope," p. 41 and *Auferstehung*, pp. 50ff. and 54f.–Mk refers to the fact of the appearances here but not to the stories themselves because such did not exist at this time; Mk makes then redactional references to this tradition and the disciples so that the latter and not the women become the heralds of the Resurrection, an aspect formerly missing from the tomb story. In critique of Wilckens is, e.g., Schmithals, *op. cit.*, p. 582.
a,4) the tomb story does not directly oppose the appearance stories, but in the light of the concept of history behind the composition of Mk. a narration of such would have been impossible. Thus: J. Roloff, "Das Markusevangelium als Geschichtsdarstellung," *EvTh*, 29 (1969), p. 92: "was am Ostermorgen folgt, läßt sich nicht mehr in gleicher Weise als vergangene Geschichte darstellen."
For the second category the following illustrate the above mentioned variety:
b,1) the tomb story is to be understood as a translation (*Entrückungs-*) story. Thus: N.Q. Hamilton, "Resurrection Tradition and the Composition of Mark," *JBL*, 84 (1965), pp. 418ff.–this is Mk.'s equivalent of the kerygma in I Cor. 15 and is to be understood as a translation aretalogy; it may, indeed, be called an "antiresurrection story" (p. 420). Also, M. Goguel, *La Foi à la résurrection de Jésus dans le christianisme primitif* (Paris, 1933), pp. 175f. and 182ff.; H. Anderson, "Easter Witness," pp. 42ff.–this story is to be interpreted in the light of Mk.'s transfiguration story in chapter 9 and means: "the day appointed by God for the salvation of the world has come" (p. 44); E. Bickermann, "Das leere Grab," *ZNW*, 23 (1924), pp. 281ff. (similar: J.S. Ruef, "The Resurrection Appearances: Theme and Variations," paper read at the annual meeting of the SBL in 1965 [cf. *JBL*, 86 (1967), p. 126] the main points of which were reconstructed for the author by Prof. Ruef in a letter dated August 31, 1967). Contra, Lohfink, "Auferstehung," p. 50.
b,2) the tomb story points not to the appearances but rather to the parousia in Galilee. Thus: E. Lohmeyer, *Evangelium*, pp. 358ff., W. Marxsen, *Der Evangelist Markus*, FRLANT, 49 (Gött., 1959, 2nd ed.), pp. 54, 142 *et passim*; as part of the concept of Anderson, "Easter Witness," pp. 42f., though differing in part with Lohmeyer and A.M. Ramsey, *The Glory of God and the Transfiguration of Christ* (London, 1949), pp. 118f. and the latter's *Resurrection*, pp. 39ff. and 77f.; also part of the view of N.Q. Hamilton, *op. cit.*, pp. 418ff.
b,3) the tomb story points not to the appearances but rather to the presence of the Lord in Galilee and his/the church's mission there. Thus: L. Schenke, *Auferstehungsverkündigung und leeres Grab*, StBSt, 33 (Stutt., 1968), pp. 49ff. and n. 71, with the added element of a distinct anti-Jerusalem polemic; M. Karnetzki, "Die galiläische Redaktion im Markusevangelium," *ZNW*, 52 (1961), pp. 249ff. concluding this concern not only for Mk. but also for the post-markan redaction: "Galiläa ist nicht das Land der eschatologischen Sammlung unmittelbar vor der Parusie, sondern das Land der Verkündigung und Sammlung der Gemeinde und zugleich der Ausgangspunkt der Mission unter den Heiden" (p. 256); M. Wichelhaus, "Am ersten Tage der Woche," *NovTest*, 11 (1969), pp. 60ff., "Und der positive Hinweis auf Galiläa will nicht die Ostererscheinungen orten. Wenn die Deutung Galiläas das Verständnis des Markus getroffen hat, scheidet der Markus-Evangelist als Gewährsmann für die Entscheidung über Erscheinungen Jesu in Jerusalem oder in Galiläa überhaupt aus. Markus lehrt, wo Jesus zu finden ist: er ist in der Mission unter den Heiden zu finden" (p. 63); cf. N.Q. Hamilton, *op. cit.*, p. 421.
b,4) the tomb story is essentially motivated by polemic against anti-Christian accusations or heretical claims. Thus: Bode, *op. cit.*, pp. 25ff.; von Campenhausen, *Ablauf*, pp. 35ff. and 40ff.; Cornelius, *op. cit.*, p. 13; contra: Richardson, *op. cit.*, p. 196; J. Delorme, "Résurrection et Tombeau de Jésus: Marc 16, 1-8 dans la tradition évangélique," *La Résurrection du Christ et L'Exégèse Moderne* (Paris, 1969), pp. 142, 145ff. *et passim.*

angelus interpres, the person and message of the νεανίσκος.[267] For purposes of investigating the relationship between the tomb and appearance traditions–keeping in mind the history-of-tradition differentiation here–this is indeed the critical juncture for our synoptic comparison because whether or not Mk himself actually makes reference here to appearances before the "disciples and Peter" (vs. 7) when the messenger says, *προάγει ὑμᾶς εἰς τὴν Γαλιλαίαν* at least for both Mt and Lk this is the crucial link for further and independent development, i.e., the inclusion of the appearances after they have followed Mk. up to this point rather judiciously.

It has been argued that Mk himself is responsible for the creation of the tomb story,[268] but internal evidence would suggest to the contrary, that Mk has here passed on a rather complete, intact tradition and has joined it with the passion narrative; he is apparently undisturbed by the contextual difficulties (e.g., motivation of the women) and stylistic incongruence which arise over the "seam" linking the two, something which is then corrected later by Mt and Lk.[269] The major question

267 This terminus is used here in a broader sense than is often the case in the literature (cf. Graß, *op. cit.*, p. 21 and n. 1) to include the element of the message. Even where a general consensus may be assumed here regarding Mk. once again the interpretation is characterized by variety. It has been argued, for example, that the νεανίσκος is identical with the νεανίσκος in Mk. 14:51 and/or Mk himself. Thus: J.H. McIndoe, "The Young Man at the Tomb," *ET*, 80 (1969), p. 125: "Mark records only what he personally witnessed with regard to the resurrection, namely, the empty tomb and his own encounter with the women, and left it at that. Such an interpretation would tend to confirm the trustworthiness of Mark's historiography" (*ibid.*). Such a proposal is very unlikely. The identity with Mk. 14:51, however, is possible. Thus: A.M. Ferrar, *A Study in St. Mark* (London, 1951), pp. 141, 174 and 334; Delorme, "Resurrection," pp. 142, 145 *et passim*; H. Waetjen, "The Ending of Mark and the Gospel's Shift in Eschatology," *ASTI*, 4 (1965), pp. 117ff., 119 and n. 26–in Mk. 14:51f. we have the interpretive key for Mk. 16:5f. in which an OT *νεανίσκος-Gattung* (e.g., Joseph and others) has been used by Mk as an example of steadfast witness under persecution; this is a fulfillment of Amos 2:16; there may have even been an order of the νεανίσκοι in the early church; similar but with Elijah as the prototype is N.Q. Hamilton, *op. cit.*, pp. 417ff. That Mk is intended here is also the view of J. Finegan in his latest publication, a historical fiction on Mk entitled *Mark of the Taw* (Richmond,Va. 1972) although here Mk is not a Christian but becomes one after further contact with the disciples. Trompf, *op. cit.*, p. 320, makes fetching mention of this "strange νεανίσκος (a 'body snatcher'?). . ." Scroggs and Groff, *op. cit.*, pp. 534ff. argue for a double symbolic function of this figure whereby Jesus is pictured in the resurrection mode of existence announcing his own triumph over death and at the same time the baptismal initiate stands in Jesus' place wearing a new garment to announce the Resurrection and Christian participation.

268 Proposing a markan creation are N.Q. Hamilton, *op. cit.*, pp. 416ff., who sees it as a markan translation story (thereto cf. Bode, *op. cit.*, pp. 154 and 164; also in general opposition to the idea of an *Entrückung* in the early church is Lohfink, "Auferstehung," p. 50). Similar to Hamilton are Ruef, *op. cit.*, cf. n. 266 and Bickermann, *op. cit.*, pp. 281ff.

269 A major index on internal evidence is the matter of context. Beginning with vs. 1 of chapter 16 we have a definite break with the preceding passion narrative which concludes with the burial of Jesus. The repetition of the women's names is superfluous in light of 15:40, 47, and is an indication of a seam not present in the former tradition. Moreover, the passion narrative is greatly influenced by the scripture-quote motif while it is entirely missing in the tomb story. In addition to these factors the absence of later levels of theological reflection and christological motifs and the recognizable points at which markan redaction focuses the story in the direction of the author's particular interest all bespeak the traditional existence of the story. So, for example, W. Nauck, "Die Bedeutung des leeren Grabes für den Glauben an den

arises over the authenticity of the vss. 5b, 6 and 7: did the angel and his message to the women originally belong to the story or is this element a markan interpretive addition? The *angelus interpres* has been considered either *in toto* or *in partem* markan redaction because of the obvious connection between vs. 7 and ch. 14:28. The problem has then two aspects: 1) how are 14:28 and 16:7 related to one another and 2) is the answer to 1) determinative for vss. 5b and 6 as well, i.e., does the originality of the angel motif stand or fall on the originality of vs. 7? To the first question it must be said that, as noted above, the passion narrative and the empty tomb tradition originally were circulated independently and that their union was achieved by Mk. [270] The context of 14:28 makes evident that the original continuation of vs. 27 was vs. 29 and not vs. 28. The latter markan insertion is an attempt to point beyond the scandal of the cross to the re-assembling of the sheep

Auferstandenen," *ZNW*, 47 (1956), pp. 249ff.; Schenke, *op. cit.*, pp. 30ff.; Bode, *op. cit.*, pp. 5ff.; Delorme, "Résurrection," pp. 121f.; G. Hartmann, "Die Vorlage der Osterberichte in Joh 20," *ZNW*, 55 (1964), p. 218; I. Broer, *Die Urgemeinde und das Grab Jesu: Eine Analyse der Grablegungsgeschichte im Neuen Testament*, StANT, 31 (Mü., 1972), p. 283 and his "Zur heutigen Diskussion der Grabesgeschichte," *BuL*, 10 (1969), pp. 50f. Seeing a pre-markan story but originally connected to the passion narrative are, for example, Wilckens, *Auferstehung*, pp. 51ff.; Strobel, *Kerygma*, pp. 175ff.; E. Gutwenger, "Zur Geschichtlichkeit der Auferstehung Jesu," *ZKTh*, 88 (1966), pp. 262ff. and 273ff. and J. Jeremias, *Theologie*, p. 285. That the story's original ending differed from that preserved in vs. 8 and is now for us no longer discernible is the thesis of von Campenhausen, *Ablauf*, pp. 36f., esp. n. 147 (questioned by Graß, *op. cit.*, pp. 17ff., esp. p. 21, n. 3). Regarding the source/dependence question between Mt/Lk and Mk cf. C.H. Talbert and E.V. McKnight, "Can the Griesbach Hypothesis be Falsified? ," *JBL*, 91 (1972), pp. 339-344.

270 Wilckens, *Auferstehung*, pp. 51ff. and Gutwenger, *op. cit.*, pp. 262ff. and 273ff. (cf. n. 269) both contend that the incongruence of the women's names is evidence of a later addition (Gutwenger: to motivate their visit at all, pp. 273f.) and not of an original separation of the two traditions. Wilckens maintains that the grave story was originally an Easter conclusion to the passion narrative and that as such it was not interested in the proclamation of the Easter event but rather in information about the resurrection (*Osterp r e d i g t* versus *Auferstehungsk u n d e*, pp. 54f.). He bases his view on a dramatic understanding of the passion narrative with the OT motif of the Holy One of God in the hands of sinful men as the core of the suspenseful narration. "Die große Zahl derartiger Anspielungen auf die alttestamentlichen Leidenspsalmen zeigt deutlich, daß die Passionsgeschichte Jesu streckenweise völlig aus dem Alten Testament erzählt ist. Die Christen, die diesen Bericht gestalteten, haben offenbar im Leidensweg ihres Herrn das Geschick des paradigmatischen Gerechten aus den Psalmen erkannt" (p. 60). The grave story then answers the question of Jesus' abandonment by God–Psalms 22–with a clear "no"; at last the cry of Israel for justice has been answered in the triumph of Jesus in the Resurrection (pp. 61ff.). Similar but connecting the tomb story theologically with Acts 4:10 instead of the passion narrative *per se* is Delorme, "Résurrection," pp. 121f. But as Nauck, *op. cit.*, pp. 249ff., has pointed out the reference to the OT is entirely missing in the grave story, a thorny problem for Wilckens' thesis. Strobel, *Kerygma*, pp. 175ff., does not argue for the original unity so much on the basis of textual observations as "von inneren Gründen her. . .Für die nächsten Angehörigen bestand die religiöse Verpflichtung zur Beklagung des Toten. Die ersten drei Tage spielten dabei eine besondere Rolle" (p. 176), so also P. Gaechter, "Die Engelerscheinungen in den Auferstehungsberichten," *ZKTh*, 89 (1967), pp. 191-202. Without doubt this practice is verified in contemporary Jewish literature. Yet, the questions of the relationship between the literary *Gattung* gospel and the *Vita Jesu* and the specific goals and character of the passion narrative and the tomb story tradition–not to mention the contextual and literary incongruities noted above–make the insistence upon traditional unity of the pericope on the basis of this form of argumentation rather tenuous.

with the Shepherd.[271] This same theme of the scandal and call to discipleship implicit for Mk. in the cross is then taken up in the final words of the angel (vs. 7); the flight of the women and the response of Mk's readers constitute the intended conclusion of this theme which has now reached its climax. In short, both 14:28 and 16:7 are redactional and provide for Mk the essential theological seam between the passion narrative and the empty tomb story. To the second question it must be noted that the story attains its kerygmatic pinnacle in vs. 6 and that without it the story remains mute and open to various interpretations. The angel motif itself begins, of course, in 5b, but the address of the *νεανίσκος* comes in vs. 6; without vs. 6 the fright of the women at the appearance of the heavenly messenger is central and the story loses its capacity to communicate a specific reference to the Resurrection.[272] Strict insistence upon actual human recollection as the historical kernel

271 The chief difficulty in the passage is the meaning of the term *προάξω*. Cf. Taylor, *op. cit.*, p. 549; Haenchen, *Weg*, p. 488; Schenke, *op. cit.*, pp. 44ff.; O. Michel, "Der Abschluß des Matthäusevangeliums," *EvTh*, 10 ('50/'51), p. 17; J. Rohde, *op. cit.*, pp. 101ff. Several attempts have been made to unravel the tradition/redaction relationship. In 1923 Sir Edwyn Hoskyns concluded that vss. 27 and 28 comprise a "mysterious and oracular saying" of Jesus having symbolic significance in connection with Mk. 10:32 ("Adversaria Exegetica," *Th*, 7 [1923], p. 148). Mk then places the saying in the mouth of the angel in 16:7 and thereby alters its meaning to refer to appearances of Jesus when actually a world-wide gentile mission was intended (pp. 150f.). Expressly carrying the position of Hoskyns further is then C.F. Evans, "I Will Go Before You Into Galilee," *JThS*(ns), 5 (1954), pp. 3-18, who claims that Galilaean appearances in Mt. 28 and Jn. 21 are constructed from this saying in Mk. 14:28 and 16:7 and do not actually presuppose a tradition rivaling that of Jerusalem appearances (p. 12). Cf. von Campenhausen, *Ablauf*, p. 24, n. 83. Wilckens, *Auferstehung*, on the other hand, concludes that 14:28 does refer to appearances, but could only be offered in the form of the reference in 16:7 since "Markus hat eine ausgeführte *Erzählung* über diese Erscheinung noch gar nicht gekannt" (p.50). He knew no more than Paul in I Cor. 15, and since the original tomb story did not have references to the disciples he constructed such via the redactional seams of 14:28 and 16:7 (p. 51). This enabled Mk to go beyond the *Tatsache*-character of the Easter story and to make of the disciples witnesses (in contrast to the women. . .thus their silence in 16:8, pp. 51ff.). Karnetzki, *op. cit.*, pp. 238-272, agrees that these verses are not original but also non-markan; rather we see here a Galilaean redaction. "Ich halte im Gegenteil Mc 16,7 par. für eine tendenziöse Bearbeitung des ursprünglichen Schlusses der Geschichtsquelle (= Lc 24,6b-9)" (p. 252). Graß, *op. cit.*, p. 21, n. 3, points out that vs. 7 is not a postmarkan *Einschub* and could reflect an old tradition along with 14:28 which Mk then "umgeformt und dem Engel in den Mund gelegt hat," Cf. Hoskyns! Goguel, *La Foi*, pp. 175f. thinks that vss. 5-7 and 14:28 are all post-markan additions. Cf. also Neirynck, "Les Femmes," pp. 175f. re: the redactional character of vs. 7. Steinseifer, *op. cit.*, pp. 232-265, in large measure agrees with Schenke when he says: "Über den redaktionellen Charakter von Mk 14,28 *und* 16,7 *und* über die ausdrückliche und beabsichtigte Zuordnung beider Verse ist kein sinnvoller Zweifel möglich" (p. 253). As traditional elements behind these verses used by Mk redactionally he sees not a Jesus-Logion but a *Reminiszenz* and not one standing as an appearance tradition at all (pp. 253f.). Mk. 16:8b is also redaction in direct relation to vs. 7 and focuses the whole on Jerusalem (pp. 254f.). As mentioned above in n. 266 the spectrum of interpretation on Mk's redactional intention is extremely varied. The weight of critical evidence in any case would seem to shift the balances for the redactional origin of 14:28 and 16:7 even if the exact intention itself remains an open question.

272 Cf. Schenke, *op. cit.*, pp. 80f., 94f. and 110ff. where he maintains that the original form of the story was not a proof of the Resurrection, but a proclamation through the angel, the heavenly messenger, probably indicating its origin in the ancient cultic practice of primitive Christian *Anamnese* in Jerusalem where pilgrims celebrated yearly at the grave of Jesus. "In dieser Verkündigung ereignete sich das berichtete Geschehen in der nun feiernden Gemeinde

prior to theological interpretation is a possibility one should not scoff at, but in any case it is as impossible to think of this story circulating without the important interpretive element of the angel and his declaration for the oral tradition as it would be for Mk himself.[273] Since the ability of this story to speak as a resurrection witness depends entirely on vss. 5b and 6, and since the assumption that Mk is himself responsible for the angel motif implies that the story could circulate in one form or another–but in any case without the angel–presupposes a kind of interest in uninterpreted reporting unfamiliar to the gospel sources or an interest in polemic against anti-Christian accusations which is apparently first virulent in a time subsequent to the writing of Mk's gospel, we must conclude that the place of the angel motif was already established in the tradition taken over by Mk.

In summary then, we may say that Mk has taken over and passed on an account of the empty tomb in relative completeness, enlarging upon the message of the angel in vs. 7. As noted earlier, it is probable that Mk was familiar with the appearance tradition, but deliberately avoids making narrational use of it; he is content to make reference to it in vs. 7, presupposing the kerygmatic formula tradition as

neu" (p. 91). He then seeks to buttress his hypothesis with historically oriented observations (pp. 92-103). Similar is the suggestion of Nauck, *op. cit.*, pp. 260ff. Also Delorme, "Résurrection," pp. 122f., 142, n. 112 *et passim*. On the matter of origin and *Sitz im Leben*, cf. below, pp. 105ff.!

273 Stressing recollection are, for example, von Campenhausen, *Ablauf*, pp. 38ff., P. Benoit, "Marie-Magdeleine et les Disciples au Tombeau selon Joh. 1-18," *Judentum Urchristentum Kirche, Fst. Jeremias* (Berlin, 1964), p. 150, Nauck, *op. cit.*, pp. 264f., A. Oepke, "Wie entsteht nach den Schriften des Neuen Testaments der Glaube an die Auferstehung Jesu? ," *WZKMU*, 3 ('53/'54), p. 80 and R. Fuller, *op. cit.*, pp. 69f. Opposing the latter is H.M. Teeple, "The Historical Beginnings of the Resurrection Faith," *Studies in New Testament and Early Christian Literature, Fst. A.P. Wikgren*, ed. D.A. Aune (Leiden, 1972), p. 110 and n. 2. Commenting on the angel motif as a necessary history-of-religion element for such a story is von Harnack, *Apostelgeschichte*, p. 129, n. 1. Similarly supporting a traditional role for this motif with parallels from history-of-religion analogies is Hebert, *op. cit.*, pp. 66f. Also Wilckens, "Perikope," p. 32 and Schenke, *op. cit.*, pp. 69ff. insist on the pre-markan role of the angel here. In this connection Schenke also sees the reasonableness of the women's reaction: "Furchtreaktionen gehören zum Stil legendarischer Angelophanien (p. 84). . .Solche Schilderung der entsetzten Reaktion des Menschen vor dem erfahrenen Hereinbrechen der Botschaft und des Handelns Gottes in diese Welt findet sich als festes Stilmittel der Theophanieerzählungen aller Art sowohl im Alten als auch im Neuen Testament" (p. 85). Finally, Schenke maintains that although the category of legend–here the tomb story is to be understood as an *ätiologische Kultlegende* (p. 88)–is not synonymous with anti-historical or *reiner Erfindung* (p. 65, n. 25), nevertheless, the attempts to reconstruct a historical picture of the Easter events (von Campenhausen, Vögtle, Gutwenger *et al.*) are fully *gescheitert* (pp. 94f.). Von Campenhausen, *Ablauf*, p. 24, wishes to separate the angel motif as legendary in contrast to other historical elements in the story. So also A. Legault, "Christophanies et Angelophanies," *Science et esprit*, 21 (1969), pp. 455ff. Sceptical on the matter of history is Graß, *op. cit.*, pp. 20f. Gaechter, "Engelerscheinungen," p. 201, concludes quite simply in contrast, that angel encounters are to be understood as "eine persönlich erlebte, sinnhafte Wahrnehmung von Engeln. . .Es war nicht so, daß es zuerst nur eine Überlieferung über das leere Grab ohne die Erwähnung von Engeln gegeben hätte und die Engelerscheinungen späteren und legendären Ursprungs wären. . . Die Berichte der Frauen sind so unreflektiert, daß sie uns unmittelbar zum tatsächlichen Geschehen und Geschauten führen, m.a.W., daß sie geschichtlich glaubwürdig sind." Greater caution on the matter of historicity and motif elements in the tomb story is necessary than appears in the position represented by Gaechter!

familiar to the reader. This would mean that for Mk the empty tomb story sufficed as a declaration of the Easter message and was considered by him to be an appropriate conclusion to this gospel.[274]

Assuming then that the original form of the tomb story received by Mk contained at least the vss. 1-6, 8—vs. 7 and certain transitional hinges being redactional[275]—the natural question is: what was the setting and function of the story for the earliest Christian community? This matter must be settled before we can ask about the nature of its relationship to the appearance tradition. Yet, to get at this question we must determine if Mk does indeed offer the earliest available account of the tomb story. We have already noted the dependence of Mt and Lk in large measure on Mk for the tomb story, but also noted a significant departure in Lk.

274 Similar are the conclusions of O. Lindton, "Der vermißte Markusschluß," *ThBl*, 8 (1929), cols. 229-234. Also W. Grundmann, *Das Evangelium nach Markus*, ThHK, II (Berlin-Ost., 1971, 5th ed.), p. 324 and Schenke, *op. cit.*, pp. 49ff., n. 41.

275 Word-Statistic alone is not a completely satisfactory method for determining markan redaction since as Delorme, "Résurrection," pp. 111f., points out only a few terms have a possible claim to specific markan origin. διαγίνεσθαι (vs. 1) is *hapax* for Mk. and appears only two other times in the whole NT—both times in Acts (25:13 and 27:9). μνῆμα (vs. 2) is equally tenuous since not only does the term appear elsewhere in the NT (5x Lk /Acts, 1x Rev.) alongside the four occurrences in Mk., but also to be considered is the difficult text-critical problem; μνημεῖον is also well substantiated in the ms. tradition, not to mention its occurrence in vss. 3, 5, and 8! When one notes that the latter appears 7x in Mk. as well as frequently elsewhere in the gospel tradition it becomes exceedingly difficult to refer to statistical analysis for any kind of a witness on the tradition/redaction question. If one were to decide in favor of the former via *lectio difficilior* one could possibly consider vs. 2 *partem* markan redaction since vss. 1 and 3 are not impossible without vs. 2. Yet, since the two terms can be used synonymously—just as the designations "tomb" and "grave" story in English—by the same author, and since the content of vs. 2 is preserved in all four synoptic and johannine accounts, to decide for the absence of this verse from the pre-markan form of the story seems an unnecessary conclusion. ἐκθαμβεῖσθαι (vss. 5 and 6) is clearly markan as it appears only four times in the entire NT and that in Mk. (9:15, 14:33 and here). Once again, however, to conclude that Mk introduced this element when the fear/awe motif is so deeply embedded in the entire tradition of the appearances of heavenly messengers, of Jesus' miracles and of the Resurrection would certainly be a short circuit. The statistical findings do not preclude the possibility of traditional terminology; at best one could perhaps suggest markan stylization, but even that would remain conjecture. τρόμος and ἔκστασις (vs. 8) are further examples of the difficulties connected with the exclusive use of the statistical approach. The former is *hapax* for Mk. and the other gospels but by no means for the entire NT. The latter finds wide distribution in Lk /Acts as well as the two occurrences in Mk. (5:42 and here). In addition to the above it must be said that while other terms in the pericope cannot be called—strictly speaking—non-markan the possibility of further markan *Retouche* cannot be excluded. The inability to differentiate more precisely on the basis of terminological analysis is simply an indication of the weakness and problematic nature of the method. It can deliver no more than probability categories. The recent article of E. Güttgemanns appears to promise a solution to this problem according to its title, "Linguistische Analyse von Mk 16,1-8," *LB*, Heft 2, 11/12 (1972), pp. 13-53 on the basis of new insights via *Generative Poetik*, but it is more concerned with describing the linguistic function of the text in its entirety according to the technical terminology of linguistic research, i.e., Mk. 16:1-8 serves as an illustrative example for a program of methodology, and with opposing certain representatives of *traditioneller Exegese* in their inaccurate usage of linguistic categories and/or false (=*intuitive*) exegetical assumptions than with deciphering the traditional matrix of the tomb story. On the basis of his categories the question is indeed superfluous. Cf. pp. 47f. *et passim*.

This departure provides a striking parallel to the Gospel of John and we must now turn our attention to this latter account of the tomb story: b.1. Johannine Tradition b.2. Luke.

b. Johannine Tradition

It has long been assumed that Mk offers us the earliest version of the tomb story[276] and that Jn is dependent by and large on the synoptic tradition for his account.[277] A comparative perusal of Jn. 20:1-13 offers some striking variations to the synoptic account of the tomb story and its key departures are noteworthy. For one thing, the other women mentioned in Mk. 16:1; Mt. 28:1 and Lk. 23:55 and 24:10 are missing and Mary Magdalene comes to the tomb alone. Then, and most importantly, the angel motif does not stand at its synoptic location but follows the so-called "race story" in which Peter and the Beloved Disciple verify Mary's report that the tomb is empty. Further, the angel motif itself appears to be little more than decoration to the story in comparison with the synoptics: the two angels of the story merely ask Mary why she is crying. They are not the bearers of the resurrection message in any verbal sense, only perhaps in a symbolic one. There is, in fact, no need for the former since as in Mt. an encounter with the resurrected One follows immediately at the grave, pre-empting the need for the announcement. This aspect is a striking contrast to the lukan version where the angel's message is restricted to this announcement and is void of any reference to future appearances. The appearance itself will be investigated below, but here we must ask if we are confronted with a radical johannine redaction of the synoptic tradition or is Jn relying on an independent source?

No one would deny that varied levels of expressly johannine redactional traits are evident throughout this account;[278] yet, it has been argued recently that behind Jn is a source older and more reliable than Mk. and to be understood as a variant to it.[279] In noting differences and similarities between the two, the singular role of

276 For example, Nauck, *op. cit.*, p. 251.

277 On the relationship question, cf., e.g., O. Michel, "Ein johanneischer Osterbericht," *Studien zum NT und zur Patristik, Fst. E. Klostermann* (Berlin, 1961), pp. 35ff. and 42, n. 1.

278 Similar to the redactional traits found in Jn. 21 is the observation of R. Schnackenburg, "Der Jünger, den Jesus liebte," *EKK*, 2 (1970), p. 115.

279 The source/redaction question and Jn.'s relationship to the synoptics is a controversial subject spanning, in general, many years with distinct stages of development and broad fronts. It is not our purpose here to rehearse this discussion in its many contours. For this purpose may be recommended: Fortna, *op. cit.* (cf. review by D.M. Smith, Jr., in *JBL*, 89 [1970], p. 501), F.L. Cribbs, "St. Luke and the Johannine Tradition," *JBL*, 90 (1971), pp. 422-450, J.M. Robinson, "The Johannine Trajectory," *Trajectories Through Early Christianity*, Essays by J.M. Robinson and H. Koester (Phil., 1971), pp. 232-268 and J. Blinzler, *Johannes und die Synoptiker. Ein Forschungsbericht*, StBSt, 5 (Stutt., 1965). Expressing something of a consensus in present johannine studies Cribbs says: "Thus, even though the evidence that has been accumulated during recent years has not resolved the issue of John's relationship to the Synoptics, clearly the hypothesis that John used the Synoptics can no longer be assumed" ("St. Luke," p. 426; contra, Blinzler, *op. cit.*, p. 58 for example). The exact nature of the pre-johannine sour-

Mary Magdalene, while possibly bearing special redactional significance for Jn, does not constitute an essential incongruence since Mary retains the same function ascribed to the women in the synoptics.[280] Here as there, inner criteria support the supposition that the tomb story and the passion narrative were not originally an organic unity.[281] The first major problem arises over the question of the "race story" and the so-called "angelophany." Since the role of the two disciples in the entire narrative has taken on central significance the question is whether or not a redactional enlargement has taken place within the tradition of the empty tomb at some stage of on-going development; or was the place and significance of the disciples already established in the tradition available to Jn? The same sequence of questions needs to be asked of the angel motif not because of its centrality, however, but because of its relative insignificance and possible redactional reduction in

ce is disputed since the history of this gospel's transmission appears to have been complex indeed and, therefore, the deciphering of actual source(s) from various levels of redactional development in the gospel's history of transmission is very difficult, but a not insignificant number of scholarly voices contend today that a related or parallel but independent source to that of the synoptic tradition is clearly discernible behind Jn. Cf. Cribbs, "St. Luke," pp. 422ff., 427, ns. 21 and 22, p. 449, n. 66 and p. 450, n. 67; also Cribbs, "A Reassessment of the Date of Origin and the Destination of the Gospel of John," *JBL*, 89 (1970), pp. 38-55 and Fortna, *op. cit.*, pp. 221-236, esp. pp. 226-228.

Supporting the independence and antiquity of Jn's tomb story is further J. Jeremias, *Theologie,* p. 289, who alludes to *einem bahnbrechenden Aufsatz* from Benoit, "Marie-Magdeleine," and asserts that Mk's account actually belongs to *einem späten Stadium der Osterüberlieferung* while Jn. offers the older form of the story (for particulars of Benoit's argumentation cf. below n. 289). Exactly how one conceives of the "source" here is the key issue. Fortna admits that a source-critical analysis here is difficult since "the *Vorlage* itself (apparently a combination of traditions) is more complex here than elsewhere, and / John has redacted it in a more complex way" (*op. cit.*, pp. 134f.), but agrees, nonetheless, with the analysis of Hartmann, *op. cit.*, "that the whole passage exhibits a pre-johannine literary continuity" (p. 135). Thus, while Fortna acknowledges that a variety of traditional influences have been combined here his interest is primarily in the proposed pre-johannine literary source: an early gospel of signs and other narrational material written "as a textbook for potential Jewish converts. . .to prove one thing, and one thing only: that Jesus was the Messiah in whom men should believe" (p. 234) to which the tomb story including both Mary and Peter together already belonged (pp. 135ff. and 143f.). (Contra Fortna here that the passion and resurrection narrative was originally in the miracle source is Robinson, "Johannine Trajectory," pp. 247ff.) Be that as it may, our interest here is not in the redactional combination of traditions but in the origin of those traditions themselves prior to redactional union. Cf. in this connection R.E. Brown, *The Gospel According to John*, II, Anchor (London, 1971), pp. 995ff.

280 It has also been argued that the "we"-form *οἴδαμεν* in vs. 2 is an indication that the plural number of participants in the synoptics and not the singular in Jn. is original to both accounts. So Hartmann, *op. cit.*, p. 199, leaving open the question of who made the alteration. Fortna, *op. cit.*, credits the pre-johannine *Vorlage* with the change. J. Jeremias, *Theologie*, p. 289, n. 20, argues, however, for the possibility of a Galilean-Aramaic idiom having influenced this *erste Person Pluralis* (cf. G. Dalman, *Grammatik des jüdisch-palästinischen Aramäisch und aramäische Dialektproben* [WB, Darmstadt, 1960(='05, 2nd ed.), p. 265]). Cf. also H. Windisch, *Johannes und die Synoptiker*, UNT, ed. by H. Windisch, 12 (Leipzig, 1926), p. 87.

281 Hartmann, *op. cit.*, pp. 218f., in opposition to Benoit, "Marie-Magdeleine," pp. 147f. (cf. below, n. 289 thereto). The former leaves open the question when they were united, but is convinced that it was not original (p. 219, n. 55). Also seeing the passion narrative as *abgeschlossen* in itself is R. Bultmann, *Das Evangelium des Johannes*, Meyer (Gött., 1968, 19th ed.), pp. 516ff. and 529; Brown, *op. cit.*, p. 958 (also differing with Benoit).

comparison with the synoptics. As in Jn. 21 so too here among the participants of the "race story" and the visit to the tomb the figure of the Beloved Disciple–here addressed by Mary Magdalene along with Peter [πρὸς τὸν ἄλλον μαθητὴν ὃν ἐφίλει ὁ Ἰησοῦς vs. 2]–may be excluded from the traditional matrix as a characteristic johannine addition.[282] This observation would suggest, moreover, that the entire competition aspect is to be seen as johannine redaction and that the story is to be analyzed solely on the basis of a pericope about Mary as messenger and then Peter at the grave, unless a traditional but unnamed disciple (cf. the Emmaus story) is to be presupposed in a competition story that Jn then specified through τὸν. . .ὃν ἐφίλει ὁ Ἰησοῦς.[283] For the former speak internal grounds since the elements of competition and the structure of the whole reflect both johannine terminology and the ecclesiastical concerns (e.g., the qualified place of Peter) characteristic of the community(ies) in which the johannine writings originated and were circulated.[284] Of primary interest in this regard is the redactional nature of the dénouement "seeing and believing" in vs. 8b.[285] Yet, the above cannot in and of itself preclude the possibility of a pre-redactional form of the "race story," further grounds are needed. The chief elements of Jn's tomb story for investigation under the question of a traditional or redactional origin of the race motif are: 1) Mary Magdalene and her report to Peter (and the other disciple) vss. 1 and 2, 2) the visit to the tomb of Peter (and the other disciple) vss. 3-6a, 3) the grave garments and their significance vss. 6b-9 and 4) his (their) return to the other disciples vs. 10. The transition to vss. 11ff. demands close scrutiny as well.

The complexity of motif-interrelatedness in not only the "race story," but, indeed, also in the entire sequence of the narration of events at the tomb and among

282 So, Schnackenburg, "Jünger," pp. 102f., T. Lorenzen, *Johannes 21. Eine traditionsgeschichtliche Analyse; zugleich ein Beitrag zur Lieblingsjüngerfrage*, Diss. (Zürich, 1970), para. 32-38; Fortna, *op. cit.*, pp. 92 and 135; Hartmann, *op. cit.*, pp. 199f.; Brown, *op. cit.*, pp. 1000-1002, 1004-1008; A. Kragerud, *Der Lieblingsjünger im Johannesevangelium* (Hamburg, 1959), *passim*; J. Roloff, "Der johanneische 'Lieblingsjünger' und der Lehrer der Gerechtigkeit," *NTS*, 15 ('68/'69), *passim*; Benoit, "Marie-Magdeleine," pp. 148f. Contested by R. Pesch for Jn. 21, *Der Reiche Fischfang, Lk 5, 1-11 Jo 21, 1-14*, KBANT (Düss., 1969), p. 132 and S.S. Smalley, "The Sign in John XXI," *NTS*, 20 ('73/'74), p. 286, n. 4. Unsure is Bailey, *op. cit.*, p. 91.

283 Such is the suggestion of A.R.C. Leaney, "The Resurrection Narratives in Luke (XXIV, 12-53)," *NTS*, 2 ('55/'56), p. 114, when he asks if the two could not perhaps be identified with the same two subjects of the Emmaus story. He concludes himself, however: "But speculation has perhaps gone far enough." Also suggesting a traditional, unnamed companion of Peter is Brown, *op. cit.*, pp. 1000-1002. Hartmann, *op. cit.*, pp. 197ff. and 220, n. 57, thinks Mary and Peter were originally the subjects of the story in the *Vorlage* to which were then added vss. 4, 6, 12 and 13 among others by the final redaction. Cf. Fortna, above n. 279.

284 Michel, "Osterbericht," emphasizes the importance of Jewish backgrounds here for understanding the elements of two witnesses, the rivalry motif and the grave garments indicating a characteristic johannine interest in historicizing the passion and Easter narratives (pp. 35ff.). Also Fortna, *op. cit.*, pp. 136f.

285 Most recently stressed by F. Hahn, "Sehen und Glauben im Johannesevangelium," *Neues Testament und Geschichte, Fst. O. Cullmann* (Zürich, 1972), pp. 125-141, esp. pp. 129f. Also Schnackenburg, "Jünger," p. 105.

the gathered disciples for Jn makes the task of deciphering tradition from redaction extremely difficult. One must reckon at nearly every juncture with the possibility that Jn is not himself responsible for these motifs in all cases but that he has rather developed in his own style motifs that were suggested to him already in his source(s).[286] Nevertheless, with a certain degree of caution one may single out the following elements which contribute to a clearer differentiation between tradition and redaction: 1) even though it can be argued that a union of the participant motif producing a consistent account of Mary's visit within the "race story" took place prior to the actual johannine redaction it is clear that no organic relationship originally existed between the visit of Mary and the "race story." Rather we are confronted with two separate traditions here which have been edited in vss. 1 and 2 to achieve a motivated transition to the vss. 3-10. In the one account Mary comes and returns to the disciples—as in the synoptics—and in the other she is suddenly standing outside the tomb, vs. 11—a tension in the present text which can only be resolved by the unlikely suggestion that the original form of the "race story" did not contain a reference to Peter and the Beloved Disciple, but rather Peter and Mary.[287] A further matter is 2) the problem of ascertaining the nature of the relationship of the two accounts to one another, i.e., do vss. 3-10 constitute an insert into the former account whereby the opening verses of the Magdalene pericope were separated from vss. 11ff. or has one or the other been constructed from elements within the more original one? The latter is unlikely since the two are in content and purpose entirely independent of one another in spite of the elaborate efforts of very early redaction to achieve a unity.[288] Removed from the present johannine context vss. 2-10 are motivated only by an assumed reaction of the disciples to the message of the empty tomb via the prior discovery of the women/Mary. Its original concern is quite singularly an affirmation of apostolic witness at the grave itself whereby the absence of the body of Jesus and the implicit resurrection nature of the event (vs. 8) and its explicit diction (vs. 9) are interpretively underscored.

When one asks what these observations suggest for the tradition/redaction question the obvious conclusion seems to be: even if Jn himself is responsible for neither the composition of the "race story" in vss. 3-10 nor the first redactional union of the two tomb story accounts, but has taken over a tradition which he has then refined further,[289] it is clear that the two separate and disparate stories which have

286 So Fortna, *op. cit.*, pp. 134ff.

287 So Fortna following Hartmann cf. above, n. 283.

288 Bultmann, *Johannes*, pp. 528f., supports the original distinction of the two stories, but asks if it is not possible that vss. 3-10 contained borrowed motifs from the Mary story, in particular that which Peter sees in the tomb (vss. 6f.).

289 On the question of source/redaction here in vss. 3-10, the most recent advocate of a source is Benoit, "Marie-Magdeleine," (cf. n. 273). His concern is to show that the Magdalene-oriented story has basic affinities to the synoptic tradition and that the Peter-oriented story has at its base "un récit primitif plus simple où Pierre figurait seul, constatait le tombeau vide, avec les linges rangés et s'en retournait perplexe" (p. 144). To understand the construction of the whole (vss. 1-18) he thinks that the burial account (vss. 31-42 of chap. 19) affords a close parallel and appeals to its parts to illuminate the traditional/redactional elements of the johan-

been woven together are also chronologically discrete; the disciple-oriented version represents, namely, in structure and content interests which are both distinct from and subsequent to the Mary-oriented form. [290] In short, the "race story" affords a later broadening to the spectrum of witness to the empty tomb by adding the redactional, secondary support of apostolic authority. The addition has, moreover, now shifted the weight of emphasis in the johannine tomb story from the older form to the later, to the witness of the disciples and their powers of observation

nine tomb account. He maintains that for the former vss. 31-37 and 39-42 constitute two johannine traditions divided by Jn then by the insert of vs. 38 which is a synoptic tradition tailored by Jn for his purposes here. Similarly then, reasons Benoit, the Peter-oriented tomb story and the appearance of Jesus to Mary Magdalene in vss. 11a and 14b-18 constitute johannine source material which are then divided by the insertion of synoptic material, namely the Mary-oriented tomb story also in a tailored form (p. 147). He asserts further that the primitive account behind Jn. 20:1-10 (and Lk. 24:12 as well) is very ancient, soberly written and void of the miraculous (p. 148). The material borrowed from Mk. 16:1-8 has undergone theological development: we have a kerygmatic stylization with close parallels to Acts 4:10; 13:30 and I Cor. 15:4, etc. (p. 149). Viewing both forms of the tomb story he concludes: "Historiquement, le fait du tombeau trouvé vide en ressort plus solidement attesté: s'il existait dans la tradition littéraire antérieurement à son interprétation par le message angélique, c'est donc qu'il n'a pas été inventé pour introduire ce message et prouver la Résurrection, mais que, d'abord reconté pour lui-même, il a été ensuite utilisé comme un des appuis de la foi. Il apparaît comme donnée archaïque, objective et solide" (p. 150). Similar is the conclusion of Bailey, *op. cit.*, p. 102. Benoit's analysis is called *scharfsinnig*, but rejected by Hartmann, *op. cit.*, since in his opinion "Weder die Maria-Geschichte noch die Erzählung vom Wettlauf können isoliert voneinander bestanden haben. Daraus folgt, daß ein ursprünglich einheitlicher Bericht beiden Erzählungen zugrunde liegt" (p. 198, also n. 6; cf. also above Fortna, n. 279; Brown agrees that Benoit glosses over many difficulties, but also finds Hartmann's proposal to be "attractive" yet inadequate, *op. cit.*, p. 998). In contrast to the somewhat unusual method of Hartmann, but basically agreeing with Benoit via an analysis of Lk. 24 is Leaney, "Resurrection Narratives," p. 111, also Leaney, "Jesus and Peter: the Call and the Postresurrection Appearance (Lk V. 1-11 and XXIV.34)," *ET*, 65 (1954), pp. 381-382. Cf. also J.N. Sanders, "Those Whom Jesus Loved," *NTS*, 1 ('54/'55), pp. 29-41. Seeing vss. 3-10 as a free johannine composition, on the other hand, is Dibelius, "Motive," pp. 125-150, esp. p. 136; Lindars, "Composition," makes direct reply to the proposals of Leaney and concludes that the terminology here "renders the possibility of *other* sources unlikely" (p. 147) in comparison with the synoptics, and specifically on vss. 3-10: "It thus becomes possible to regard the episode as a fabrication based on the kind of hint in Luke XXIV.24" (p. 146). Thus, according to Lindars, Jn's work here consists of taking over the same traditions as the synoptics have at their disposal, all of which existed in a variety of forms, and in rewriting them for his own purposes in a free development (p. 147).

290 Michel, "Osterbericht," also maintains a distinction between the two stories since "das Motiv des leeren Grabes erscheint in der Marienperikope als höchst beunruhigende Entdeckung, in der Erzählung vom Wettlauf der beiden Jünger dagegen als Grundlage einer neuen Ostergewißheit. Die Ratlosigkeit der Frau (V.2.15) erinnert an den synoptischen Typus, die Rivalität der beiden Jünger und ihre Entdeckung dürften johanneische Eigenart verraten" (p. 35). Further, "Das leere Grab is nun nicht mehr Anfechtung und Not, sondern Bestätigung und Rückhalt für die Verkündigung des Auferstandenen" (p. 42). On the matter of source/redaction for Jn. in relationship to the synoptics he merely remarks that the issue is unsettled (p. 42, n. 1). Contra is Benoit, "Marie-Magdeleine," (cf. n. 289) who fails, however, to recognize that even if a traditional base be granted, vss. 3-10 contain an orientation which cannot pre-date the other form. The thesis of Hartmann, *op. cit.*, mentioned in ns. 283 and 289 that a unified Mary-Peter source is to be reckoned with here is untenable on form-critical grounds. Not two different traditions but "two different forms of the same one" is the view of Bailey, *op. cit.*, p. 91.

and reflection,[291] whereby the former now becomes a mere prelude to an appearance of Jesus at the grave.

What can be said then about the rest of the johannine tomb story and in particular about the angel motif? As noted above, vss. 1, (2) and 11ff. lay claim to an independent existence outside of vss. 3-10. Vss. 1 and 2 cannot, however, be joined directly to vs. 11 [292] because of redactional alterations intended to achieve the transition to the "race story" insert. Without difficulty the particulars of vs. 1 remain intact. While vs. 2, however, does present an element contained both in the johannine (cf. vs. 18) and synoptic tomb events, namely, the report to the disciples, its function here is to be seen as a repetition intended to supply motivation for the insert and as such is then redactional at this point. Vs. 11 then picks up the train of thought interrupted by the insert and characterizes Mary's distraught condition over her discovery that the stone has been rolled away from the entrance to the tomb and the (traditional) assumption–later developing into the anti-theft polemic–that the body of Jesus is not present/has been stolen or removed. Of critical interest is the question of the originality of vss. 11b-13 and their relationship to the appearance story to which they are so directly attached. It is namely at this point that the angel motif finds its place. In contrast to vss. 3-10 where the grave garments [293] are observed, Mary sees here two angels described a) in the characteristic style of heavenly revelations and b) as sitting at the head and foot of the place where the body [τὸ σῶμα] of Jesus lay. Although Mary is not expressly described as reacting in the customary manner at such an appearance, i.e., with fear, a characteristic element of angel appearances is, nevertheless, retained: they take the initiative, break the silence and address her.[294] Yet, it must be granted that we have here a

291 The "reflection" of vs. 9 is considered by some to be a later gloss, e.g., Bultmann, *Johannes*, pp. 530f. and Kegel, *op. cit.*, p. 117. That it belongs rather organically to the situation of Mary in vs. 11 is the view of Hartmann, *op. cit.*, pp. 201f. Yet, its place within the interest of the whole of vss. 3-10 as a traditional element is plausible. So, Hahn, "Sehen und Glauben," p. 129, n. 17.

292 An almost universally recognized difficulty in the literature. Cf., for example, Benoit, "Marie-Magdeleine," pp. 141f., W. Wilkens, *Die Entstehung des vierten Evangeliums* (Zollikon, 1958), p. 87, Dibelius, "Motive," p. 136 and Lindars, "Composition," p. 143, etc. Brown, *op. cit.*, pp. 999f. presents the alternatives: 1) vss. 1-2 and vss. 11-13 constitute two separate versions of the women's visit, or 2) these verses constitute a single version of that tradition which was edited by a separation of vss. 1-2 from vss. 11ff. and the insertion of vss. 3-10; Brown favors the former over the latter alternative since he finds it difficult why the "awkward 'we' in vs. 2" should have been retained "if this [verse] is a free composition of the editor, created for transitional purposes" (p. 1000). He does not, however, suppose that his two-story hypothesis is without difficulty and, in fact, grants that there may have been a desire on the part of the editor to keep the Magdalene visit close to the appearance sequence in vss. 14ff., if one were to accept the insertion view (p. 1000).

293 Benoit, "Marie-Magdeleine," p. 149, considers the grave-garment motif to be characteristic johannine apologetic. Hartmann, *op. cit.*, p. 200, n. 10, disputes the point and goes on to assert its originality in the context of the anti-theft polemic (p. 202).

294 Since the fear motif is missing here some have considered the entire motif of the angels to reflect a later redactional stage of borrowing from the appearance motif in vss. 14ff. So, for example, Hartmann, *op. cit.*, pp. 206f. Yet, it would appear that just the opposite could be true as well. The matter can be settled only by a careful evaluation of the relation-

striking contrast to the "message" of the synoptic accounts; we have instead a question which supplies the opportunity for articulating the reason for Mary's weeping.

Exactly what layers of tradition and forces are at work here in vss. 11b-13 is a question which places us before one of the most difficult problems of our inquiry into the traditional matrix of the johannine tomb story. It is evident that the present redactional form has achieved a high degree of balance and perspicuity in relationship to the whole chapter. Probing behind the redactional wall must begin with the question: 1) has the angel motif been significantly altered either by Jn or by a hand prior to Jn in the light of the insert vss. 3-10? The option appears, indeed, to be a live one since not only the witness of Mary, but also the angels' proclamation of the empty tomb is absent in that insert and instead we have a report here based on the observation and reflection of apostolic authority. Unanswered by such a proposal, however, is the question why the disciples themselves do not encounter the (an/some) angel(s) if this insert has significantly altered the other form. Did their "insight" now pre-empt such, i.e., do we have here in fact an index for the later date of the insert? In any case, the question can be answered with two observations: a) nowhere in the resurrection tradition of the canonical gospels are angel appearances associated with the disciples, only with the women and that at the tomb; b) a redactional alteration of the angel motif through the insert of vss. 3-10 could only be suggested if it could be demonstrated that the latter in terms of form and content reflected an interest in such, and precisely that is not the case; instead we have an *addition*. We may thus conclude that the insert itself constitutes an answer to a different set of problems connected with the empty tomb than the other form, and that a direct influence on the angel motif would be a dubious conjecture. Further then we ask 2) if the appearance context in vss.14ff. supplanted the need for the message of the angels and thus is the source for a possible reduction, i.e., is the reply to the question "where is he" indeed superfluous since the appearance of the "Lord" himself gives the clearest answer? Or 3) is the angel motif in reality itself a later addition, i.e., secondary to the primary appearance-of-the-Lord motif, added as it were as a literary device and dependent upon the latter entirely? Both of these questions demonstrate the undeniably close relationship between the two stages of the narrative. The exact nature of that relationship is the question to be raised below, but here it may be said with caution that while an influence is almost certain it cannot be maintained that the angel motif itself owes its origin to the appearance of the "Lord" as a free literary construction; the existence of this element is traditional and it has been at best adapted for transitional purposes and not reduced. As noted above, the report of Mary has been moved to vss. 2 and 18, for example, to achieve a similar transitional adaption. The mode of expression and emphasis of the motif belongs rather quite naturally to the kind of narrative here. It is a traditional alternate to the synoptics, a different way

ship between the two traditional complexes as a whole (cf. below, pp. 105ff.). Of course, a tendency toward historization could be proposed quite legitimately, but equally as cogent is the proposal that the motif has been left unembellished.

of expressing the seeming imponderables connected with the question mark of the tomb tradition. The particulars of the narrated scenery are themselves an equivalent expression to the synoptic "he is not here."

One question remains to be considered: is this account or form older than the synoptics? Strictly speaking, both a yes and a no may be replied. If the criterion is the absence of secondary additions from a redactional hand, i.e., is disposed to focus on Mary as an "eyewitness," then no. The reduction afterall from a plural number to Mary Magdalene alone *in the tomb visit* itself is a redactional accommodation to achieve harmony with the Magdalene appearance account. But measured by the degree of theological reflection and manner of narration, then perhaps yes. The modesty and reservation characterizing the narrative and especially the angel motif could indeed be an index for the age of the text. On the basis of Jn. 21 we know, for example, that johannine sources can reach back to the earliest forms of the resurrection tradition without relying on the synoptic sources directly. Such a possibility for this form of the tomb story must also be taken seriously. To claim that we have here the pure reminiscence and detailed recollection of eyewitnesses would be, of course, absurd since a variety of traditional influences are clearly at work here, but it is not only possible, but also very likely that we do have here a very old form of the tomb story in terms of the history of its tradition, perhaps not too remote from some kind of personal recollection.[295]

In conclusion then we may summarize as follows: the traditional matrix of the tomb story in Jn. is composed of two distinct segments, an earlier and a later form of the tradition, which were then secondarily brought into a unity. Internal evidence would suggest that their union was accomplished before the final johannine redaction and that the transitions and theological unity were then reworked once again by Jn. The earliest form–the women-oriented one–is similar to the synoptics, but bears significant features of distinction the likes of which betray either an earlier form or an alternate source to them. The relatively small kernel of the story contains a reference to the women, their visit to the tomb, an implied remorse at not finding the body of Jesus and an encounter with the angels there in its place and, finally, their return to the disciples with the news. The insert of vss. 3-10 reflects a subsequent development by placing Peter (and the other disciple) at the grave and making him (them) the voice of apostolic authority. This insert is by its very nature an addition, an augment to the former and is as such a complementary development.

Luke 24:12, 22-24

As noted above, we have an additional witness to the content of the johannine

295 Though a differentiation regarding the content of Jn. 20:1ff. is necessary the general affirmation of J. Jeremias, *Theologie*, p. 289, can be considered valid: "wie nicht ganz selten, hat also der literarisch späteste Text die älteste Gestalt der Überlieferung aufbehalten." Reservation over against the explanation of Gaechter, "Engelerscheinungen," is in order, however,

tradition in the significant departures from the synoptic accounts found in Lk. 24:12 and 22-24.[296] The text-critical worth of vs. 12 has long been questioned, but recent studies have demonstrated the arguments for its inclusion in the original text of Lk. 24 outweigh those against.[297] Vss. 22-24, on the other hand, are text-

when he says that the whole johannine account contained too much personal experience and aspects unforgettable for the participants and too little general interest for broad acceptance in the synoptics (p. 197).

296 A somewhat unusual thesis in this regard is the proposal of W. Grundmann, *Das Evangelium nach Lukas*, ThHK, 3 (Berlin, 1971, 6th ed.). He takes issue with the contention that Lk is by and large following his markan source for the tomb story and that vs. 12 is the only major departure. He sees rather a distinctly lukan source here, into which he then introduced markan elements here and there. This special source had many similarities to Jn. all of which lead him to conclude: "Diese Berührungen verstärken nicht nur den Eindruck einer gemeinsamen lukanisch-johanneischen Passions- und Ostertradition gegenüber der markinisch-matthäischen, sondern schaffen auch für V. 12 eine wichtige Ausgangsposition" (p. 439). The points of contact outside of vs. 12, however, do little to support his thesis that the order of Lk's use of Mk. and a special source are to be reversed. Not too distant from this thesis is also the view of Hartmann, *op. cit.* After isolating what he thinks to be the *Vorlage* of Jn. for the Easter events–stated in conclusion on p. 220 as vss. 1-3, 5, 7-11, 14-27 (19=26), 20, 28, 21-23–Hartmann proposes that this corresponds to the lukan *Vorlage* as well, the Emmaus story excepted. The basic format common to both was a) experience of the women b) doubt of the disciples at the report of the women and c) an appearance of Jesus before all of the disciples. "Das kann aber nur heißen, daß beide aus der gleichen mündlichen Tradition schöpfen. Es kann nicht angenommen werden, daß Johannes und Lukas gemeinsam eine schon fixierte Quelle benutzen" (p. 218). Favoring vs. 12 as a witness to this early tradition–even if its literary fixation came about via a detour and "...ist zu einem Zeitpunkt geschehen, an dem der Text des Lc im Westen schon selbständig überliefert wurde" (p. 204, n. 18)–he says: "Die von Johannes benutzte Vorlage stellt gegenüber dem hinter Lc 24 stehenden Traditionsgut deutlich eine schon weiterentwickelte Form der Überlieferung dar. Die vorjohanneische Form hat dann ihrerseits in Lc 24, 12 nach der schriftlichen Fixierung des Lukastextes einen Niederschlag gefunden" (p. 218, n. 52). Thus Hartmann accepts the interpolation theory, but is, nevertheless, convinced of the antiquity and reliability of the source. While Grundmann tends to oversimplify the nature of the "similarities" by concluding that a source is responsible for the overlap, Hartmann's efforts to bridge the text-critical difficulty are unnecessary and his assumptions regarding a *Vorlage*-format supposedly common to both Jn. and Lk. are too general and do not account for the far-reaching dissimilarities; for both it must be said that an attempt to harmonize the varied aspects by way of a block-source leaves too many questions unanswered and neglects the complex weave in the fabric of many traditional strands. It is possible, for example, to speak of a traditional matrix of the tomb story, but highly questionable if such were ever the case for an uninterrupted sequence of Easter events in the oral tradition; if that were not true it would be fair to assume that we would have a greater degree of unanimity between the gospels from the tomb story on.

297 For an overview of recent studies cf. Grundmann, *Lukas*, p. 439, n. 5; Schnackenburg, "Jünger," pp. 103f.; Bode, *op. cit.*, pp. 68f.; cf. also J. Jeremias, *The Eucharistic Words of Jesus* (N.Y., 1966), pp. 149-151 (=Ger. ed. '70, 3rd ed., pp. 143f.) and L. Brun, "Zur Kompositionstechnik des Lukasevangeliums," *SO*, 9 (1930), p. 50. Favoring the interpolation theory are, for example, Hartmann, *op. cit.* (cf. n. 296); von Campenhausen, *Ablauf*, p. 35, and Schubert, "Structure," p. 172, n. 18, who says, "It is a clumsy and unnecessary attempt to fill out the statement of vs. 24a." His presupposition for this judgment, however, is that the empty tomb story is of little importance for Lk at all. A third alternative–among others, Brown, *op. cit.*, pp. 969 and 1000–is that Lk. 24:12 is neither original to the lukan text nor is it an interpolation, but rather is an early redactor's addition probably borrowing from an early form of the johannine tradition. He thus concludes: "If this is true, Luke XXIV 12 does not constitute an independent witness to the story of the disciples' visit to the tomb" (p. 1000).

critically well established, but as we shall see are quite clearly a lukan summary introduced into the tradition of the Emmaus appearance.[298] The two references are, however, not without tensions in relation to one another, as well as in relation to the johannine account. For one thing, the summary in vss. 22-24 agrees with the synoptic tradition in the number of women at the tomb, namely the plural [*τίνες* vs. 22], but is at odds with the singular of Jn. The tension is, however, only apparent since the singular in Jn. is secondary. Then they disagree–and this is more serious–with the reference in vs. 12 on the number of disciples going to the grave reading *τίνες* again (vs. 24) while the former speaks only of Peter. Thus the summary agrees with the johannine account, if the reference to "the other disciple" be considered traditional. As noted above, the reference to the number of women at the grave is a variable in the tradition with the plural being the more original so that the key issue then is the question of the disciple (Peter)-oriented aspect of this lukan witness.

As in Jn. we note here in 24:12 that the disciple-oriented visit to the tomb is distinct and separate from the other form. Here as there it is motivated by the news of the empty tomb, but in contrast to Jn. there is no attempt to insert one into the other, but it is merely added on at the end. The basic elements of content remain the same, however, as is the case for vss. (22-)24 as well, and the question quite naturally arises: if the narrative is original to Lk's gospel and is not an interpolation from Jn. then where does the account come from? The cogent reply of recent studies is that both Jn and Lk are relying here upon a common source.[299] Two questions must be asked about this source in connection with Lk.: 1) is Peter indeed alone the subject originally and 2) is the age of and are the influences behind the source to be judged in the same way as in Jn.? The answer to 2) is probably to be an affirmative since the content of both vs. 12 and vss. 22-24 make this estimate unavoidable.[300] The answer to 1) is, to be sure, a difficult question not only because of the variables in both Lk. and Jn., but also because the entire question of the relationship of Peter to the resurrection tradition poses such a thorny problem. When, however, the motivation behind the source itself is taken into consideration the answer becomes quite apparent: apostolic confirmation of the empty tomb was necessary and all variants in this context are credible whether "Peter," "some of those with us" or "Peter and another disciple." As a secondary development to the original women/Mary-oriented form of the story even where Peter is singled out as

298 Brown, *op. cit.*, pp. 1000ff., grants that vs. 24 appears in a lukan context, but adds that "it is part of a summary of post-resurrection happenings that may have come to Luke partially formed" and draws the consequence that "24 must have been part of Luke XXIV before 12 was added. . .this verse constitutes an independent witness to the / story of a visit to the empty tomb by the disciples" (pp. 1000f.).

299 Cribbs, "St. Luke," esp. pp. 446ff. and Fortna, *op. cit., passim*. Also J. Schniewind, *Die Parallelperikopen bei Lukas und Johannes* (Hildesheim, 1958[='14]), pp. 88ff.

300 Brown, *op. cit.*, p. 1001, while opting for vs. 24 as the original lukan witness here over against vs. 12 observes that the account in both Jn. and Lk. from the standpoint of the history of tradition is "relatively late."

here in vs. 12, he is the representative of apostolic authority. In any case, we have an association of Peter with the empty tomb only in a secondary sense and we cannot say the primary role ascribed to him in other layers of the resurrection tradition and his role here at the tomb are identical. That a relationship between the two may exist is another matter and is to be investigated below under the question of the influence of the tomb tradition upon that of the appearances.

We may conclude then by saying that Lk as well as Jn preserves a tradition separate and distinct from, younger than and supplementary to the older form of the tomb story which does not contain references to Peter and/or the disciples. As a secondary accretion it reflects later interests than the former, but not necessarily competing ones.

c. Traditional Matrix of the Tomb Story: Conclusions

In asking what the traditional matrix of the tomb story was prior to its redactional enlargement within the processes of literary fixation and prior to its incorporation into the larger tomb/appearance complex for the synoptics and Jn. we must distinguish between three layers of development: 1) the johannine and oldest form of the women/Mary-oriented account in Jn. 20:1, (2) and 11-13 characterized by brevity of style and minimal theological sophistication, 2) the synoptic form of this same account in Mk. 16:1-6, 8 and parr. characterized by a literary structure and theological reflection level which indicate a somewhat later stage of interpretation and transmission than the corresponding johannine account and 3) the Peter/disciple-oriented account in Jn. 20:3-10 and Lk. 24:12 added later to the older form as an insert in Jn. and as an appendage in Lk. and reflecting a distinctly separate and supplementary development to the tradition as a whole, a development arising out of the further process of reflection of the tradition upon itself. It must be stressed, however, that in all three cases we are dealing with traditional developments in the oral tradition which antedate in all probability their literary fixation in the gospels. We have designated 3) as "secondary" not in the sense of the summary of Lk. 24: 22-24, but in the sense of an ancillary outgrowth–indeed early–to the initial form ascribing the discovery of the tomb to the women/Mary without the support of the disciples' witness. We must ask now what setting and function supplies the background for the tomb story and then probe the "seams"-question to determine how and when in the traditional processes of development union with the appearance tradition was achieved and what influence the former had upon the latter.

2. Original Setting and Function of the Traditional Matrix

From the very outset it must be reiterated that our reason for posing this question at all is to get at the tomb tradition's relationship to the appearance tradition. Implicit, therefore, is the recognition that many other questions deserve attention, but cannot here be considered since they have no direct bearing on our line of questioning.[301] We must limit ourselves to the following scope: the fundamental theological problem posed by the tomb tradition from its inception was its uncertain meaning in the interpretive context of Jesus' death and Resurrection. In a word, its content produced bewilderment, fears and consternation, but not faith. The questions directing our investigation at this point are: a) why has such a tradition been preserved and b) how was it able to retain its independence and integrity? Put in this way the question affords us entrance into the historical and theological dimension where the relationship to other traditional currents can be found.

In essence this tradition had to be preserved because it is in its origin historically reliable. In spite of the weak position of the female witness in a Jewish-Christian community it could not be displaced, only modified. This tendency toward modification included both the authority of the angel motif and of apostolic witness. That is to say, at the earliest point where the element of some sort of personal recollection was united with the formulation of a traditional account of the discovery of the empty tomb the first modification took place: the presence of angels was included—functionally in its simplest form in Jn. 20:12—though the singular number here could be more original. The presence of such is a statement on the divine nature of the event. That is, to be sure, not an apologetic but rather an inner-Christian development.[302] This is already the first aspect of a reply to the question how the tradition could be retained. The angel motif allows the tradition to speak an initial word of clarification. Of course, this motif leaves many questions unanswered as well, as the consternation at the tomb in Jn. and in the synoptics demonstrates. A subsequent development in the tradition moves to make further clarification both in an inner-Christian and in an apologetic direction, namely the confirmation of the report through apostolic authority. This step buttresses the witness of the women/Mary within the primitive church and counters Jewish polemic as well. This stage of development demonstrates the broad fronts of reflection at a very early date. Yet, here too fear and consternation are not overcome. This latter problem is remedied

301 Questions like the following: does the tomb story reflect the concern of the early church to mark and honor the grave of Jesus, or the worship of that community at the grave where the worshiper experienced the message of the Resurrection for himself anew as *Anamnese* while the story was retold, or a very early pilgrim practice, fall outside the scope of our concern here. For an overview of the methodological difficulties on such questions, cf. the recent work of Broer, *Urgemeinde* (also his literature).

302 It has been thought that a relationship between the tomb tradition and a primitive Christian catechism—the former upon the latter—could be demonstrated, albeit in accord with the formula: died, buried, risen, appeared, when one compares I Cor. 15 to the synoptic gospels. So, E. Dhanis, "L'ensevelissement de Jésus et la visite au tombeau dans l'évangile de saint Marc (Mc. XV,40-XVI,8)," *Greg*, 39 (1958), pp. 367-410, esp. pp. 395f. and 401. But it has been objected that this approach oversimplifies matters by neglecting 1) the layers of tradition apparent in the variety of elements which are combined in the tomb story and 2) the question of the appearances in the pattern for Mk. So, Delorme, "Résurrection," pp. 118f. Moreover, aside from the hypothetical nature of the catechetical source proposed by Dhanis it is more likely on the matter of relationship between I Cor. 15 and the gospels that it is one complementary in nature and not dependent. I.e., they are not to be seen as a linear development at all. So, Delorme, "Résurrection," pp. 119ff. Contra, Dhanis, *op. cit.*, pp. 395f. and

only through the formulation of the whole in the *context* of the appearance tradition; out of the two separate and distinct traditions a narrated whole is finally woven together.[303] Mk. is, of course, an exception in one sense, but only in as much as no narrational unity is achieved; the "seam" is, nevertheless, there by virtue of the reference in 16:7. As noted earlier 16:7 is, to be sure, a markan redactional element in its present context, but it must be asked if Mk does not indeed betray his familiarity with the movement of the tradition by his very reference and does not indeed at the same time, show his independence *vis-à-vis* this movement by omitting the narrational accounts otherwise becoming the natural accruement via currents directing the formation of the whole. This tendency, in a word, is the imperative so widely felt for removing all internal ambiguities by linking the tomb story to the traditional narratives which alone made clear the place where Easter faith begins and answers once and for all the question: where is the Lord if he is not in the tomb; enter: the stories about the appearance encounters. With this movement toward confirmation and final solution to ambiguity we have before us the problem now of clarifying the "seams" which the other evangelists in accord with this tendency employ in order to hold the complex interweaving of the traditions together.

3. The "Seams" Uniting the Tomb/Appearance Traditions and the Influence of the Former upon the Latter

In light of the foregoing analysis of a traditional matrix to the tomb story we must differentiate between the context and seams within Mt. in his relationship to his markan source and Lk./Jn. and their double source. That is to say, Mt does not know or does not make use of the secondary development which places Peter and/or disciples in general at the tomb; his tomb story does enlarge upon Mk. via the grave guard account, but a designation of this pericope as coming from a pre-matthaean

410, Dibelius (cf. n. 13), Taylor, *op. cit.*, pp. 658f. and J. Schmitt, "La résurrection du Christ: des formules kerygmatiques aux récits évangéliques," *Parole de Dieu et sacerdoce* (Paris, 1962), pp. 93-105. Cf., e.g., Schenke, *op. cit.*, pp. 72ff., 79 and 86ff. who speaks of the contemporaneous development of *Botschaft* and *Bekenntnis* in the worshipping community. For him this means: "die kultische Begehung der Auferstehung Jesu muß selbstverständlich jünger sein als der Glaube an den Auferstandenen selbst. In diesem Sinne ist die Tradition hinter Mk 16,1-8 eine späte, dem Auferstehungsglauben und -kerygma zeitlich nachzuordnende / Tradition. Trotzdem muß ihre Bildung in die frühste Zeit der christlichen Kirche eingeordnet werden" (pp. 109f.). The question to be asked, however, is whether or not both the origins and the development of the tradition are indeed to be sought within the cultic life of the early church. Schenke means by cult "pilgrimages" and *Anamnese*–not unlike Moule (cf. n. 242)–(pp. 82f., and 88ff. esp. n. 96) centering on the tomb as a place for gathering. Understood in the broader sense of the church in faith and reflection the category "cultic life" would be useful–at least for the origin of certain motifs, but not for the kernel. Schenke himself says as much where he opposes the attempts to reconstruct that historical kernel. We share the concern here at least for the matrix of the *tradition* alone.

303 Cf. H. Thielicke, "The Resurrection Kerygma," *The Easter Message Today* (N.Y., 1964), p. 79. The exact chronological development of this tendency to unite the traditions remains an open question. The nature of that development itself, however, and its directing motifs can be deciphered by an analysis of the seams achieving the unity.

source is fraught with insurmountable difficulties. Raising the question then of what the tendency to unite tomb and appearance accounts has meant for all three and what influence this tendency had upon the latter in connection with the former implies certain important methodological considerations: 1) we must probe above all the *Gattung* designation "appearance" in connection with the appearance accounts at the grave and compare them with "appearances" elsewhere and then give an answer to the question of subject matter: do the former really deserve this designation over against the latter? and 2) we must then turn to the matter of the importance of locale in general for these "tomb-centered appearances," i.e., is the phenomenon of appearances at the tomb entirely or only partially explicable on the basis of the observable tendency to unite the tomb and appearance traditions? The solution to both sides of the problem resides in the task of separating redaction from tradition and in the relationship of the one to the other in the history of their development.[304] The natural place to begin in the light of the differentiation above is with Mt.

Matthew 28:1-8 and 9, 10
The Empty Tomb and the Appearance to the Women

Outside of several basic editorial alterations whereby the names of the women and their motivation for visiting the tomb in vs. 1 is changed (now *Μαριὰμ ἡ Μαγδαληνὴ καὶ ἡ ἄλλη* Μαρία and then not *ἵνα ἐλθοῦσαι ἀλείψωσιν αὐτόν* as in Mk., but *θεωρῆσαι τὸν τάφον*),[305] the accent on drama is heightened (earthquake, descent of the angel of the Lord and his triumphant mounting of the stone now rolled from the entrance of the tomb and the union with the first part of the grave

304 Wilckens, "Perikope," pp. 31ff., draws attention to this methodological distinction when he points out that although one can quite correctly speak about a redactional tendency to mold the individual traditions into a unified *Szenarium* and "eine dort sich abspielende Ereignisfolge" (p. 31), yet "die Überlieferungsgeschichte ist unbeschadet dieses allgemeinen Trends auf Konzentration vielschichtig" (p. 31). He proposes thus not to ask about the relationship of the tomb events to the appearances, but rather to ask "nach dem Verhältnis der markinischen Grabes*perikope* zu den Erscheinungen im nachmarkinischen Überlieferungsstadium. . ." (p. 31). Wilckens does see Lk using an additional source to Mk.; Lk. 24:12 is original (i.e., *Parallelüberlieferung*; pp. 33ff.). Wilckens' basic thesis is that in each case it is the evangelist himself who is responsible for the union of the two traditions (*passim*) and that in the post-markan handling of the tomb story the tendency is not "die Grabesszene als solche mit den Jüngererscheinungen näher und wesentlicher zu verknüpfen," but rather "die Grabesszene durch eine Erscheinung des Auferstandenen selbst sozusagen zu vervollständigen und darum auch schon die Frauen zu Zeugen des Auferstandenen zu machen" (p. 40). While we can affirm the former, as the evangelists–Mk excepted–follow the internal necessity inherent in the growth of the traditions, we must reserve judgment on the latter until we have determined whether or not one may speak of a traditional base to the appearances at the grave.

305 Cf. Wilckens, "Perikope," pp. 31ff., Kremer, *Osterbotschaft*, p. 36, von Campenhausen, *Ablauf*, pp. 28f. and n. 107, and Schnider and Stenger, *Ostergeschichten*, pp. 30ff. and R. Fuller, *op. cit.*, pp. 76f. Some assume that Mt. preserves here the more original motivation for their visit, cf. Neirynck, "Les femmes," p. 169 and P. Benoit, *The Passion and Resurrection of Jesus Christ*, trans. by B. Weatherhead (N.Y., 1966), pp. 256ff.

guard account 27:62-66, 28:4,11-15)[306] and the reference to Peter in the angel's message (vs. 6 cf. Mk. 16:7) is deleted,[307] Mt follows Mk. most judiciously up to vs. 8 where he then alters the response of the women from *τρόμος καὶ ἔκστασις* to *μετὰ φόβου καὶ χαρᾶς μεγάλης* and the enigmatic conclusion of Mk to *ἔδραμον ἀπαγγεῖλαι τοῖς μαθηταῖς αὐτοῦ*. And then in vss. 9-10 the redactional seam is sewn between the tomb and appearance traditions with the women encountering the resurrected One as they depart. The question here is: has Mt linked a traditional appearance story to the tomb story or has he created one in his fundamental desire to unite the two larger complexes? Put differently, does the seam consist solely in the act of union or in composition as well?

A statistical analysis of the vocabulary and style of these two verses does not yield singularly conclusive evidence one way or the other.[308] A closer look at the content, however, in comparison with the message of the angel in the preceding verses leads one to an astonishing observation: vss. 9-10 offer merely a repetition and re-emphasis of that message as preparation for a galilaean group appearance! Moreover, motifs which may be called in part characteristic of the appearance *Gattung*–the greeting, the recognition (and worship) motif, the charge to deliver a message (here to "brothers" and not "disciples")–are, in fact, present in abbreviated form, but their function in the episode is so minor in comparison with the emphasis on the drama of the tomb story that one must ask if we do not have here indeed either 1) a story constructed by Mt out of motifs borrowed from the tomb and other appearance stories[309] or 2) a shortened form of a traditional story in accord with Mt's theological intention.[310]

306 Cf. below, pp. 116f.

307 The reasons for the omission are unclear. Whether or not it was due to an anti-petrine polemic in Mt. as the result of a factional preference in his community (cf. above, n. 200) or perhaps to a desire to place the sole weight of his resurrection witness on the group encounter (cf., e.g., Wilckens, "Perikope," p. 33 and Neirynck, "Les femmes," p. 182) is a question to be decided in the context of matthaean redactional studies.

308 The vocabulary as such here is found on a somewhat even distribution throughout the gospels with a slight tendency towards matthaean dominance of usage. Cf. W.F. Moulton and A.S. Geden, *A Concordance of the Greek Testament* (Edinburgh, 1957), s.v. and Morgenthaler, *Statistik*, s.v. That the worship motif is a favorite of Mt is clear, cf., e.g., Mt. 14:33, parr. and H.J. Held, "Matthäus als Interpret der Wundergeschichten," *Überlieferung und Auslegung im Matthäusevangelium* (Neukirchen, 1961, 2nd ed.), p. 252, G. Strecker, *Der Weg der Gerechtigkeit–Untersuchung zur Theologie des Matthäus* (Gött., 1971, 3rd ed.), pp. 123ff. and J. Rohde, *op. cit.*, p. 63. Seeing clearly matthaean terminology here Neirynck, "Les femmes," p. 178, n. 1 and his "La rédaction matthéenne et la structure du premier évangile," *EThL*, 43 (1967), pp. 41-73, esp. pp. 49f. regarding, e.g., *προσέρχομαι*.

309 Bode, *op. cit.*, p. 56, Graß, *op. cit.*, pp. 27ff. and p. 90, Evans, *Resurrection*, p. 83, Lohfink, "Auferstehung," p. 41, F.W. Beare, "Sayings of the Risen Jesus in the Synoptic Tradition: an inquiry into their origin and significance," *Christian History and Interpretation. Studies Presented to John Knox*, ed. by W.R. Farmer (Cambridge, 1967), pp. 161-181, and most recently, N. Walter, "Eine vormatthäische Schilderung der Auferstehung Jesu," *NTS*, 19 (July, 1973), pp. 415f. Neirynck, "Les femmes," pp. 176ff. sees a combination of elements out of the tomb story with a traditional "epiphany" account (cf. hereto the critique of Delorme, "Résurrection," p. 137, n. 96), as does R. Fuller, *op. cit.*, pp. 77f.

310 Trompf, *op. cit.*, p. 318, Hengel, "Frauen," p. 255, Wilckens, "Perikope," p. 33, but less certain in his *Auferstehung*, p. 68. Delorme, "Résurrection," p. 137, finds it difficult to

This brevity and the essential reproduction of the angel's address in this new context suggests the conclusion that this "appearance" is secondary, a matthaean construct. One does well, however, to exercise caution and to take other factors into consideration before passing judgment. The role of the women as witnesses in one form or another persists stubbornly in many layers of the apostolic and post-apostolic resurrection traditions in spite of the relative weight of their testimony as females in the semitic culture of their day. It has been proposed, in fact, that the group of women stood alongside the group of apostles as witnesses of equal worth[311]—in the early Christian community at least—and although this extreme claim hardly can be borne out by a close scrutiny of the canonical sources before us here, it must, nevertheless, be granted that the women do occupy a solid place in the tomb tradition and in the seams so that the possibility of traditional sources standing behind Mt. must be weighed carefully. There have been a number of solutions offered in the history of matthaean research to explain the impasse. Among the most noteworthy was the claim that the so-called "angelophany" of the tomb story was originally a "christophany," i.e., that the resurrected One was in fact not at all preceded by an angel appearance for the earliest tradition, but that he announced his own Resurrection in the first appearance to the women at the grave. Then—so it is argued—in the passage of time it became increasingly difficult to let the latter stand as a primary witness under the duress of anti-Christian polemic. For this reason then the "christophanies" to the women were reduced to the rank of "angelophanies" so that the weight of credibility would rest rather on the "two or more" male witnesses of the community in keeping with the Jewish standard. This

imagine a strict construct here; similar is A. Descamps, "La structure des récits évangéliques de la résurrection," *Bb*, 40 (1959), p. 731, W. Grundmann, *Das Evangelium nach Matthäus*, ThHK, 1 (Berlin, 1971, 2nd ed.), pp. 567f. and Masson, *op. cit.*, p. 170. Presupposing an appearance tradition here of the following sort is H.-W. Bartsch, *Das Auferstehungszeugnis. Sein historisches und sein theologisches Problem*, ThF, 41 (Hamburg-Bergstedt, 1965): behind it all is "ein Bericht über eine Erscheinung des Menschensohn-Herrn. Von daher ist dann ebenfalls zu erklären, daß Matthäus die Grabeslegende mit einer Erscheinung des Auferstandenen vor den Frauen verbindet. Er hatte jedenfalls einen Erscheinungsbericht vorliegen. . ." (p. 12). He reconstructs that appearance as follows: "Und siehe, es geschah ein großes Erdbeben; denn der Menschensohn-Herr stieg herab vom Himmel, und sein Anblick war wie ein Blitz und sein Gewand wie Schnee. Aus Furcht vor ihm aber erbebte ich, Petrus, und fiel zu seinen Füßen, wie ein Toter. Der Herr aber trat herzu und sagte: Fürchte dich nicht" (p. 12). He proposes further that all of the original appearance stories were reports about the coming of the Son of Man as fulfillment of apocalyptic expectation (pp. 13f.). They were *getilgt* since they could be understood as parousia stories and the view that the parousia was yet *in unmittelbarer Nähe* had early replaced the former (p. 15). Cf. also his, "Die Passions- und Ostergeschichten bei Matthäus," *Entmythologisierende Auslegung. Ges. Auf.* (Hamburg-Bergstedt, 1962), pp. 88f. In his latest publication on this question, "Der Schluß des Markusevangeliums. Ein Überlieferungsgeschichtliches Problem," *ThZ*, 27 (1971), pp. 241ff., esp. 252f., Bartsch reiterates his position but with greater reserve on the matter of a reconstruction of the appearance story. For critique of Bartsch, cf. below, n. 339.

311 Cf. above, n. 200 and Trompf, *op. cit.*, pp. 308ff. and esp. pp. 325ff. Trompf wishes to see in "the other Mary" a reference to the mother of Jesus (p. 309) upon which he then postulates that this "Mary" and the "family" of Jesus were motifs that the Peter and James groups were suppressing (pp. 312ff.). Cf. also Wilckens, "Perikope," p. 40, Michel, "Abschluß," p. 16 and Strobel, *Kerygma*, p. 174.

ended then with the full weight being carried of necessity by the combined apostolic witness through the group appearance.[312] As fascinating as the proposal sounds it has not found much acceptance because of two considerations: 1) at no point can it be said that the two traditions–tomb story and its angel appearance and the appearances–were so closely united as this position presupposes [313] and 2) as *Gattungen* the angel appearance and that of the resurrected One are to be distinguished categorically from one another; the appearance or visitation of heavenly messengers is to be observed throughout the gospel narratives and as such they are to be differentiated from the resurrection appearances even if one were to grant the so-called "displaced" appearance stories a place in the resurrection tradition.[314] In essence this view implies that the angel of the tomb story was in the final analysis a later construct from the appearance tradition and in a certain sense became the other's competitor. Support for this kind of origin and tendency within the tradition is simply not available. Does this automatically lead to the conclusion then that a traditional source stands behind Mt. 28:9-10? As stated above, the options seem to be clear: either it is a matthaean construct or it is a shortened form of a traditional story. For the latter we know of no other source for such other than perhaps an early form of the Magdalene pericope in Jn. Methodologically then it would appear essential to compare the two before deciding which option is more likely.

We shall see below in chapter III that the Magdalene pericope itself does not owe its origin to redactional composition to unite tomb and appearance traditions. Our question here is strictly that of Mt. 28:9-10 and its relationship to the Magdalene story. Although it is not too difficult to establish for Lk and Jn common traditional sources, not only throughout the resurrection, but also in other gospel materials, [315] the same for Mt and Jn is singularly difficult. Nevertheless, some agreement here seems apparent. The χαίρετε greeting of vs. 9 is arresting and while it does not appear here in the Magdalene story it is a fundamental element in the johannine group appearance of 20:19ff. (cf. also Lk. 24:36ff.). The Μαριάμ address might be con-

312 Generally the position of (Albertz) and Brun (cf. above pp. 24ff.). Also, e.g., Masson, *op. cit.*, pp. 171ff. and H. van Vliet, *No Single Testimony. A Study on the Adoption of the Law of Deut. 19,15 par. in the New Testament*, StTh, IV (Utrecht, 1958), pp. 88f. who assumes that from the very beginning double attestation was necessary. Contra, Graß, *op. cit.*, pp. 87ff.

313 Wilckens, "Perikope," p. 41, concludes a reverse of the "angel-/christophany" relationship by positing a replacement of the former and the whole tomb tradition by the latter.

314 It would be of considerable interest to make a comparison of the literary *Gattungen* behind the promise/birth narratives, the gospel appearance stories and the tomb tradition. Because of certain history-of-religion backgrounds proposed below for our texts (cf. pp. 239ff.) such a comparison promises to be most fruitful. Cf., e.g., Graß, *op. cit.*, p. 183, P.S. Minear, "Luke's Use of the Birth Stories," pp. 111-130, and N.A. Dahl, "The Story of Abraham in Luke-Acts," pp. 139-158, both in: *Studies in Luke-Acts. Essays in Honor of P. Schubert*, ed. by L.E. Keck and J.L. Martyn (London, 1968), and such Old Testament scholars as C. Westermann, "Arten der Erzählung in der Genesis," *Forschung am Alten Testament. Ges. Studien* (Mü., 1964), pp. 9-91, esp. pp. 11ff., and his, "Alttestamentliche Elemente in Lukas 2,1-20," *Tradition und Glaube. Fst. K.G. Kuhn* (Gött., 1971), pp. 317-327, and E. Kutsch, "Gideons Berufung und Altarbau," *ThLZ*, 81 (1956), col. 79, n. 25.

315 Cf. above, n. 279 and Bailey, *op. cit., passim.*

sidered a functional equivalent for Jn. here. Further, the *ἐκράτησαν αὐτοῦ τοὺς πόδας κ.τ.λ.* element in the same verse of Mt. might indeed, as has often been suggested, bear a structural relationship to the *μή μου ἅπτου* of Jn. 20:17.[316] The most frequently argued point of contact, however, is the reference to the words *τοῖς ἀδελφοῖς μου* or *πρὸς τοὺς ἀδελφούς μου*. The message that Mary is to deliver to these is fundamentally different, but this is after all—it is argued—the most natural point for the redactional hand to make theological alterations.[317] An essential motif element present in the Magdalene story, but missing in Mt., is the incognition/recognition aspect. Since, however, the key to the change from one story (the tomb) to the other (the appearances) comes at the address of Jesus in Jn., and since Mt. does include the *χαίρετε* greeting it could be argued that merely one half of the motif has been eliminated—an element which is softened considerably in the group appearance of Mt. 28:16ff. as well. This possibility receives further support in the structural development of the story following the word of address in Mt.; the matter being portrayed is very much like that of Jn. That is to say, when the specifically johannine redactional elements are set aside and the incognition side of the recognition motif is seen to be presupposed though not dwelt upon by Mt., the two stories demonstrate a certain similarity.

The question is obvious: do these similarities necessitate the conclusion that Mt is dependent on the tradition behind Jn's Magdalene pericope or must one rather speak of parallels emerging indirectly? That both develop specific interests regardless of the source question is clear. It could be argued that Jn, writing later, read Mt. and in his characteristic sense for dramatic representation and suspense-filled dialogues altered key points and embellished others to produce the story found there.[318] Nevertheless, we have learned to be more cautious in recent times in general with assumptions of johannine dependence on the synoptic tradition and radical alterations thereof from his theological bent. The possibility of Jn having independent sources at his disposal, which at least parallel if not directly compete with the synoptic sources, must be reckoned with throughout his gospel, so that direct dependence of Jn. on Mt., moreover, is no internal necessity and to postulate such would be without critical basis. Our question here though works the other direction: is Mt depending on Jn., i.e., the pre-johannine source for the Magdalene story? If this were the case the relationship would be one of an astonishing concentration on brevity, equally as problematical as Jn having arrived at his story out of the likes of Mt's two verses! The singularity of Mary Magdalene would have given way to the inclusion of the "other Mary" or would have been eliminated entirely since the sole indication of participants is found in the *αὐταῖς* of vs. 9. Further, there is no reason to suggest that Mt has made deliberate changes from Jn's source since his variations have the character of a distant relationship rather than a con-

316 Cf. below, pp. 206ff., ns. 604 and 602.

317 Cf., e.g., Neirynck, "Les femmes," pp. 176ff.

318 So, Haufe, *op. cit.*, p. 190. Cf., von Campenhausen, *Ablauf*, p. 28, similar also Dibelius, "Motive," p. 139.

scious rewriting, e.g., the response of the women after the address of Jesus and the message they are to deliver. The only two remotely difficult problems arise over the references "my brothers" and further removed the "johannine character" of Mt's *χαίρετε*-greeting. The latter while certainly not strictly matthaean vocabulary [319] cannot be called johannine either for that matter as it is the current Greek vernacular greeting, equally as thinkable for the Jewish-Christians as the semitic שלום. [320] As such there is no reason to insist on any dependence. The matter of the "brothers"-reference is indeed thorny, but not insoluble without recourse to matthaean dependence on Jn's source. In both Jn. and Mt. the narrative reference is to the disciples while the direct discourse reference is to the brothers and it is to be asked if it is not really the only possible reference in an appearance to the women/Mary whereby a differentiation is made between the "brothers" and "sisters" so to speak in the Christian community—the latter also being "disciples," broadly speaking. [321] One counter consideration is, of course, the question: why is the distinction not present in the tomb story and the message of the angel(s), also an "incident" involving only the women in the earliest stage? Since the reference to the "brothers" in Jn. is to be found in the redactional vs. 17 and that as an edited form of the tomb story's conclusion it can be argued that the differentiation is in fact a late tendency of the tradition and that Mt. is then simply an additional and independent witness to the tendency. This becomes all the more compelling when it is seen as an aspect of achieving the seam between the tomb and appearance traditions in general. That would mean that while Mt retains the basic wording of his markan source for the angel's message and has made the reference differentiation only in the subsequent appearance of vss. 9f., Jn, on the other hand, has taken the final step of altering the words of charge within his independent and early tomb story source or has retained the wording of a charge prior to his reception of that tradition, provided such a charge had taken place. The former is more likely than the latter since the nature of the total integration of johannine theology and compositional subordination of the earlier form of the tomb story in general reflects the redactional sophistication of the sequence's end product. [322]

319 The verb occurs 6x in Mt. and 3x as a form of greeting, here, in the betrayal scene (26:49) and at the crucifixion (27:29). In the latter it is from the markan source while in 26:49 it is a matthaean addition.

320 Trompf. *op. cit.*, pp. 320f. sees in the matthaean term an Aramaic original which was ostensibly present in the markan (lost) ending and Mt "unwittingly replaced it by a Greek greeting out of tune with usages in the rest of his Gospel" (p. 320); Mt has translated an Aramaic original with a Greek equivalent (p. 321). Suggesting the same possibility that the same Aramaic original may be behind this term and the "peace to you" of Jn. 20:19ff. is Dodd, "Appearances," p. 11.

321 Cf. Trompf, *op. cit.*, p. 322, who sees in the "brothers" reference the last part of a sequence—disciples/Peter/brothers—which he brings into contact with the kerygmatic formula tradition (esp. vs. 6, "500 brethren") and maintains that the pieces of the jigsaw puzzle of conflicting resurrection traditions are beginning to fit together. Hengel, "Frauen," p. 255, sees in the "brothers" reference an indication of a common source between Mt. and the Magdalene story. P. Gaechter, "Die 'Brüder' Jesu," *ZKTh*, 89 (1967), pp. 458f., rejects the idea of Jesus having had human brothers or sisters and translates "ihm nahestehende Menschen" (p. 459).

322 To be discussed below under chapter III, section A.4.

With these last observations the insistence upon a matthaean dependence on a pre-johannine form of the Magdalene pericope becomes unnecessary. The most reasonable explanation here would seem: Mt himself is responsible for the construction of vss. 9, 10, an appearance story which he has composed out of the elements of other appearance story motifs, but most directly out of the markan tomb story. He is not dependent on the Magdalene pericope in any sense. Contrarily Jn, as we shall see below, has taken over a genuine appearance story tradition located at the tomb and has then reworked it at certain fundamental junctures to achieve a harmonious sequence of "events" at the tomb. We thus conclude that in part one may indeed contend that the "appearance to the women" owes its origin to the redactional tendency to unite tomb and appearance traditions, but only in part since the Magdalene pericope owes its reworking to this tendency, but not its origin as such.

Luke 24:1-12, 22-24
The Empty Tomb without an Appearance Seam

As noted earlier we find Lk making use of two tomb traditions like Jn, but unlike Jn he does not 1) weave the two together and he does not 2) directly integrate them via a subordinate position to an appearance before the women. Moreover, in contrast to Jn. the markan source to the tomb account remains primary for him,in the narrational section vss. 1-12, while the summary of vss. 22-24 does demonstrate something of a more deliberate attempt to balance them. In respect to his markan tomb source Lk makes three radical changes: 1) instead of reproducing the *νεανίσκος* we read *ἄνδρες δύο*,[323] and 2) in 24:6 he alters the reference to Galilee for the promised appearance to the disciples making of it rather a reference for recollection from the days of Jesus' earthly ministry in Galilee, and then finally 3) in the response of the women and in the conclusion the fear motif is dropped entirely and they leave the tomb to report to the "eleven and all the rest": *καὶ ὑποστρέψασαι ἀπὸ τοῦ μνημείου ἀπήγγειλαν ταῦτα πάντα τοῖς ἕνδεκα καὶ πᾶσιν τοῖς λοιποῖς*.

The alteration to "two men" has led some to suggest that Lk is related to Jn here who also reads a plural form, but it is far more likely that Lk himself has interjected a stylistic change here to heighten this interpretive element within the markan source.[324] The other two changes tend in a similar direction; the words of the angels reinforce the kerygmatic statement, as it were, "he has been raised" and lose their predictive function, while the reference to the women underscores their credulity and the incredulity of the disciples, a subtle and preparatory play upon one of the leading motifs of the group appearance in Lk. (and elsewhere). Noteworthy also is the fact that along with the alteration at 24:6 the specific reference to Peter—as in Mt. 28:7 [325]—has been deleted. The consequences implied within these changes

323 Cf. the same two figures in the ascension scene of Acts 1:10ff. where they assume a predictive role.

324 Cf. Bultmann, *Tradition*, pp. 343ff. and R. Fuller, *op. cit.*, p. 96.

325 Cf. above, pp. 61ff. For Lk, however, the omission was apparently necessary in light of the re-formation of the statement altogether and not because of anti-petrine polemic (Lk. 24:34).

for the question of the relationship between tomb and appearance traditions for Lk are rather clear: on the one hand, he has deliberately moved away from the Galilaean predictive *dictum*, while, on the other hand, he has laid the ground work for a group appearance by stressing the disciples' incredulity. This latter motif receives then further stress in the Emmaus story.

What can be said about this tendency for Lk. in light of the summary woven into the Emmaus story vss. 22-24? First, with regard to structure Lk. has no appearance account of any sort prior to the Emmaus story to link the traditions;[326] the women are entirely restricted to the tomb tradition for him. Just as the Peter/disciple-oriented tomb story reference is added (vs. 12) without any obvious attempt to build a homogeneous unity with the earlier form so too Lk goes immediately in his narrative to the Emmaus appearance from the tomb traditions as a whole. That is to say quite simply, Lk is not concerned about weaving the two together in a narrational transition. He is content to let them stand–tomb and appearance traditions–side by side with the suggestive changes in vss. 1-11 and the somewhat retroactive summary in the Emmaus story, vss. 22-24. That summary, however, allows for an important observation: where the women are mentioned no appearance of the resurrected One is singled out; instead he says, "...λέγουσαι καὶ ὀπτασίαν ἀγγέλων ἑωρακέναι" (vs. 23b) and although testimony is confirmed "οἵ λέγουσιν αὐτὸν ζῆν" there is no indication that such is based on any other "experience" than the message of the angels. This means that if Lk was aware of any traditional appearance before the women forming–hypothetically–the background to Mt. 28:9f. he has refused to include it. In connection with Lk's stated concern to check out and include authentic traditions known at his time and within the scope of his knowledge–Lk. 1:1-4–one could argue that he doubted the integrity of such a tradition; since he knew the same tradition that Jn did about the disciple-oriented visit to the tomb, one could ask if he 1) knew about the Magdalene pericope and yet 2) also doubted its integrity. It would be unnecessary, however, to insist that in every case all johannine sources were known to him. If he had known of these traditions it seems otherwise likely that he would have included them one way or another since he above all others champions the cause of women elsewhere in his gospel. The line of questioning, however, leads to no certain conclusions because of its speculative nature. With caution, therefore, it would be better to leave the matter of prejudiced judgment about the integrity of the Magdalene pericope open and simply register the fact of its absence in Lk. and the restriction of the women to the tomb tradition. In any case, two points must be stressed in the relationship of Lk. to Jn. at the traditional level: 1) the tomb and appearance stories (the group appearance and some of the material embedded in Jn. 21/Lk. 5)[327] bespeak a knowledge of common sources, and 2) Lk makes very little of the tomb locale as such and the separate and distinct ways of uniting the traditions at this point and the dis-

326 Hartmann, *op. cit.*, p. 204, n. 18, claims that vss. 12 and 24 show evidence of being introduced later and that originally vss. 11 and 36 were joined as the transition between tomb and appearance stories–without the Emmaus story in between. Cf. above, n. 296.

327 To be taken up below in chapter III, sections A.1 and 3.

tribution of the weight of importance may very well have influenced the motivation for bringing the Emmaus story in the one case and the Magdalene pericope in the other. This is not to suggest that both had access to sources which resembled a collection of short stories and folk tales and which they, resembling essayists, could leaf through and select what was appropriate, but rather that other factors being equal both evangelists stood within streams of tradition which were developing out of common origins and along similar lines. The particulars of development at the point of redactional incorporation are of no interest to our line of questioning, while the origins of the appearance materials are indeed.

In summary to this section we may conclude: the differentiation between empty tomb and appearance traditions is fully justified. An early tendency to unite them existed at certain levels by motivating a use of the tomb locale for the redactional construction of an appearance story (Mt. 28:9-10) or for the composition of an adequate transition between the tomb story and a traditional account of an appearance at the tomb (Jn. 20:14-18). On the other hand, it was possible to let their disparity stand without any particular attempt at union (Lk. 24:1-12, 22-24).

Excursus: Mt. 24:62-66; 28:2-4,11-15: The Grave Guard Story

Before turning to the complex of gospel appearance stories itself, its relationship to one other closely associated stratum must be outlined briefly. Coming on the heels of our observations on the significance of the tomb story for Mt. 28:9-10, this stratum poses the question of a related aspect of it, namely: how is the so-called matthaean *grave guard story* related to the tomb and appearance traditions? It has been argued recently that this story is not only pre-matthaean in origin, but also was originally an appearance story. Such is the thesis, for example, of the 1965 Harvard Divinity School dissertation by B.A. Johnson, *The Empty Tomb in the Gospel of Peter Related to Mt. 28:1-7.* Johnson's argumentation runs as follows: Mt. 27:62-66; 28:2-4, 11-15 build a unit which as story in comparison to the Gospel of Peter 28-49 and the Ascension of Isaiah 3:14b-17 demonstrates key matthaean distortions of an earlier tradition.[328] The latter two are not dependent on Mt. and are separate witnesses to an original "resurrection authentication story."[329] Johnson claims that this story like the source of the transfiguration account was originally an eschatological epiphany story where Jesus is seen in the company of heavenly beings.[330] The presence of the *descensus ad inferos* motif is taken as being no clear indication of the story's lateness.[331] Thus, for Johnson, Mt. has substituted an emphasis on the tomb story and an appearance before the women for an original epiphany at the tomb and thereby reduces the proof-of-the-resurrection theme to polemic against Jewish slander contained in a grave robbery legend;[332] in the GP credence is given to the Resurrection in the epiphany by non-believers.[333] Constructing then what he believes to be the original form of this early epiphany story Johnson sees its original intention as serving to exonerate Pilate of blame for the Crucifixion and to place the proof of the Resurrection in the hands of neutral, non-believing witnesses, namely the Romans.[334] The GP does not go back to Mt. but rather both go back to a common empty tomb appearance tradition where women are not present.[335] John-

328 B.A. Johnson, *The Empty Tomb in the Gospel of Peter Related to Mt. 28,1-7,* Diss. (Harvard, 1966), pp. 50ff.

329 *Ibid.*, p. 57.

330 *Ibid.*, pp. 81ff.

331 *Ibid.*, p. 84, n. 35.

332 *Ibid.*, pp. 84f. and 102f.

333 *Ibid.*, p. 92.

334 *Ibid.*, pp. 115ff.

335 *Ibid.*, pp. 119ff.

son is certainly correct when he argues earlier[336] that the tomb story of the GP does not go back to Mk's account, but his case for an independent tomb/appearance tradition is problematical. One could perhaps agree that prejudice against the GP because of the label "apocryphal" is unfounded,[337] but the relationship between Mt. and GP in terms of subject matter on the grave guard problem has been clarified inadequately by recourse to earlier tradition. We shall have more to say about the GP appearance account below,[338] but it would appear impossible to ascribe the origin of a tradition, which expanded the scope of witnesses to the resurrection appearances to non-believers, to any other beginnings than Mt's redactional hand.[339] That neutral observers such as the Roman guards should carry out this function in the light of the anti-theft polemic so evident behind the formulations in Mt. lends further support to this objection. The way in which Mt allows the announcement of the angel in the tomb story to assume an important function for his tomb vicinity appearance would also suggest the most probable origin for the formal use of the angel motif in the grave guard story. The dramatization of the scene, moreover, bespeaks matthaean redactional characteristics and although one might be justified in assuming that Mt is following to some extent theological trends current in his community, the hypothesis that he is reworking an original appearance story needs more support than the kind of evidence the GP can muster. We must, therefore, conclude that on the basis of what material is presently available the grave guard story in Mt. 27 and 28 must be excluded from our investigation on the grounds that it is 1) redactional in origin and 2) no resurrection appearance story at all.

D. The Summaries of "Mk." 16:9-20 and the Extra-Canonical Sources

We move now from a consideration of the relationships between other resurrection traditions and the gospel appearance story tradition to the complex relationship between various strata of gospel appearance stories themselves. We come first to the question of such accounts outside of the immediate scope of Mt., Lk. and Jn. and begin by turning to "Mk." and the extra-canonical sources.

336 *Ibid.*, p. 17.

337 *Ibid.*, p. 123.

338 Cf. pp. 125f.

339 Cf. the remarks above on the Celsus polemic, pp. 20f., also von Campenhausen, *Ablauf*, pp. 28ff., Grundmann, *Matthäus*, pp. 565ff., R. Pesch, "Eine alttestamentliche Ausführungsformel," *BZ*, 10 (1966), pp. 91ff., Graß, *op. cit.*, pp. 23f. and 87, Hartmann, *op. cit.*, p. 198, n. 4, and Broer, *Urgemeinde*, pp. 60ff. and esp. p. 78, all or some of whom see these redactional origins in part as an apologetic reaction to Jewish polemic about a theft of Jesus' body or as a movement toward confirmation of the Resurrection through the testimony of objective witnesses, and, moreover, a development of this matthaean tendency in the Gospel of Peter. Cf. also Justin, *dial. c. Trypho*, 17, 234D and 108,1 and below among the extra-canonical sources, esp. the Gospel of Nicodemus, pp. 126f. and also n. 381. As noted above in n. 310, the most profiled exponent of the theory that Mt.'s grave story was originally an appearance story to Peter is Bartsch. Opposing his views are Gutwenger, *op. cit.*, p. 273, Seidensticker, *Auferstehung*, p. 55, n. 42, and most recently Walter, *op. cit.*, pp. 415-429. The latter's critique runs as follows: Bartsch sees in the descent and appearance of the angel in Mt. 28:2f. grounds for the reconstruction of a parousia appearance of the Son of Man before Peter, but it is *traditionsgeschichtlich* "unwahrscheinlich, daß aus einer ursprünglichen Christophanie im Laufe der Überlieferung bzw. durch Matthäus eine Angelophanie gemacht worden sein sollte" (p. 418). Moreover, Mt would not have given up an appearance story with Peter as the chief human character in the light of 16:17-19. The principal difficulty in Bartsch's view and with that of Seidensticker as well, according to Walter, is that they wish to see in vss. 2-4 an old type of Easter appearance story (pp. 418f.). Following the suggestion of Graß then he places vss. 2-4 in the larger context of 27:62ff. so that vss. 2-4 are the *Mittelstück* of an *Erzählfaden* that ends in vss. 11-15. In

We have already discussed the problems connected with the ending of Mk. above under the empty tomb tradition.[340] There we came to the conclusion that Mk intentionally ended his gospel at vs. 8 and that his account of resurrection events contained no stories of appearances. What we find in 16:9-20, therefore, must be designated "Mk." because it was added subsequently as appendix. The question is, of course, whether or not internal evidence allows one to trace this material back to traditional sources. In addition to an interest in the origins of this material we are also looking for subsequent trends of development which may help us to understand better the extra-canonical sources, as with Mt. and GP in the previous section, and then the relationship of the whole complex to the appearance story question in

search of an *Erzählungstyp* for this account he proposes that of a *Befreiungswundererzählung* (p. 419; cf. also, E. Schweizer, *Das Evangelium nach Matthäus*, NTD, 2 [Gött., 1973], pp. 340f.), because of the prominence of the guard motif. After examining possible history-of-religion analogies (pp. 419f.), he concludes that these verses give evidence for an original story taken over by Mt, which pictured the Resurrection itself. The angel originally descended to lead the deceased Jesus from the grave (as in Acts 12:7ff.). Thus, we have an Easter story, "die neben den Erzählungen von Ostererscheinungen und der Erzählung von der Auffindung des leeren Grabes einen dritten Typ, eben den einer Erzählung vom Auferstehungsvorgang selbst, belegt" (p. 421). Its origin is an "erzählerische Ausführung des Bekenntnissatzes 'Gott hat Jesus von den Toten auferweckt' (Röm. IV.24; VIII.11; X.9; I Kor. XV.15. . .)" (p. 421). Walter argues then that this same story type is to be found in GP and that it is not dependent on Mt. but both go back to a tradition independently (p. 422). Support for his claim he finds in the old Latin ms. k to Mk. 16:3 (cf. K. Aland, *Synopsis Quattuor Evangeliorum* [Stutt., 1964, 3rd ed.], p. 204), which though text-critically late, ostensibly goes back to this tradition independent of Mt. (p. 422). In contrast to these, however, Mt altered the source because the graphic portrayal of the Resurrection "sich theologisch nicht durchhalten läßt, weil das Ostergeschehen alle denkbaren Analogien irdischen Geschehens. . .überschreitet" (p. 423). Finally, Walter affirms that this story type is to be differentiated from the older appearance stories and that the former is an *Umsetzen in Erzählung* of the kerygma, but, nevertheless, "ist Matt. XXVIII.2-4 kein 'erster Schritt. . .in der Richtung auf die Schilderung der Auferstehung selbst hin,' dem dann im Pt. Ev. die weitere Durchführung folgte, sondern Ergebnis bewußter Reduktion eines solchen Verlangens frühchristlicher Legendenbildung" (p. 425). There follows then an *Anhang* on the GP (pp. 426ff.). We can follow Walter's reasoning fully up to the point of insisting on the traditional basis for the story. That the angel and guard motifs must indicate the reception of a *Befreiungstyp* story by Mt is not convincing in the light of the redactional drama about the Passion, e.g., 27:51ff. (cf. Goppelt, "Osterkerygma," p. 89, n. 27, Jörg Jeremias, *Theophanie. Die Geschichte einer alttestamentlichen Gattung*, WMANT, 10, ed. by G. Bornkamm and G. von Rad [Neukirchen, 1965], p. 164, Grundmann, *Matthäus*, pp. 561f. and Michel, "Abschluß," p. 16), and Mt's interest in countering Jewish polemic (28:15). We would agree in general, therefore, with Walter's critique of Bartsch, but have to maintain that matthaean redactional interest is nevertheless behind the inception of the grave guard story. In debate with Broer, *Urgemeinde*, the recent monograph of R. Kratz, *Auferweckung als Befreiung. Eine Studie zur Passions- und Auferstehungstheologie des Matthäus*, StBSt, 65 (Stutt., 1973), also develops the thesis that the literary *Befreiungswunder* type lies behind the matthaean account and although conceding considerable redactional elements in the present form extended subsequently by GP, he opts, nevertheless, for a traditional source in which apologetic and epiphanic strains were already present (pp. 72ff.).

340 pp. 86ff. Since a breakdown of the varying opinions on the relationship between Mk. and the appearance traditions is offered in n. 266 we restrict ourselves here to a brief cross section of the literature regarding the question of a "lost" ending and the problems connected with a text ending with γάρ. Hirsch, *op. cit.*, pp. 181ff., W.-G. Kümmel, *Einleitung in das NT* (Heidelberg, 1973, 17th ed.), pp. 70ff., Taylor, *op. cit.*, pp. 610ff., B.M. Metzger, "The Ending of the Gospel According to Mark in the Ethiopic Manuscripts," *Understanding The Sacred*

general. We saw above during our considerations of the positions of Albertz, Brun and Dodd in the introduction that the "extra biblical" sources play little or no role at all for them. They concerned themselves with the question of historicity and chronology (Albertz, also Bultmann and Graß) or a modified form of this question (Brun with his interest in theological motifs) and form-criticism (Dodd), but not with our line of questioning directly. We ask here about the specific *Gattung* relationship between these sources and the gospel appearance stories.

Because of its many-sidedness and unusual accents "Mk." is very interesting and worthy of intensive study in its own right, but we cannot do this here.[341] With regard to the group appearance (vss. 14-18) we find two major phases: 1) the reaction of the disciples to their encounter with the risen One, pictured in the immediate context of their constant doubt and disbelief at the reports of others, and 2) the commission motif which has been summarized in a) a command to preach and b) a statement on the consequences of belief and unbelief. It would appear that a veritable storehouse of material from both the other gospel appearance stories and additional themes have been borrowed and woven together into this account and we shall see from this example of the group appearance how this entire summary form came into being.[342]

The text begins with a temporal statement. It is not exact but simply states that "later," i.e., after the report of the Emmaus travelers to the "rest" and the disbelief of the latter, this group appearance occurred. The proper name "Jesus" or "Lord" does not appear anywhere in the sequence as subject although "he" is to be assumed from the passive verb forms. Only in the narrative of vss. 19-20 do we find the designation "Lord" and perhaps "Jesus." In the Freer Logion the unusual term for these texts is "Christ."[343] The term the "rest" seems to afford an echo from the lukan account of the women at the tomb and it would further suggest that at least for this writer the two travelers were disciples.[344] The transition supplied by the temporal adverb and the use of the group designation "the rest" point to a very im-

Text. Fst. M.S. Enslin, ed. by J. Reumann (Valley Forge, Pa., 1972), pp. 165-180 and his *The Text of the New Testament* (N.Y., 1964), pp. 226-229; J. Luzarraga, "Retraducción semitica de φοβέομαι en Mc 16,8," *Bb*, 50 (1969), pp. 497-510 (suggesting that the semitic *bhl* stood behind the "fear" meaning actually ἐθαμβοῦντο (p. 510 *et passim*), Bultmann, *Tradition*, pp. 102f. (-308ff.), Evans, *Resurrection*, pp. 67ff. and Helzle, *op. cit.*, pp. 204ff. *et passim* and his Referat thereto, *ThLZ*, 85 (1960), col. 470, Dodd, "Appearances," pp. 15f., Grundmann, *Markus*, pp. 324ff. and Nauck, *op. cit.*, pp. 251f. Cf. also H. Almquist, *Plutarch und das Neue Testament*, ASNU, 15, ed. by A. Fridrichsen (Uppsala, 1946), p. 59 for a parallel construction to Mk. and C.F.D. Moule, "St Mark 16:8 Once More," *NTS*, 2 (1955), pp. 58f., who reconstructs a conclusion by placing the fear clause in parenthesis and adds the delivery of the women's message to the disciples.

341 This has been done, for example, in the dissertation of Helzle (cf. n. 264), who while recognizing that the material here is "'altes' Gemeindegut des zweiten Jahrhunderts" (Referat, col. 470, cf. n. 340), insists, nevertheless, upon an analysis to determine its kerygmatic significance in its own right. Cf. also Beare, "Sayings," pp. 162ff.

342 Cf. G. Lohfink, *Die Himmelfahrt Jesu. Untersuchungen zu den Himmelfahrts- und Erhöhungstexten bei Lukas*, StANT, 24, ed. by V. Hamp and J. Schmid (Mü., 1971), pp. 119ff.

343 Cf. above for the kerygmatic formula tradition on this point.

344 Cf. below on the Emmaus story in Lk., pp. 190ff.

portant aspect of this story: the writer has with full deliberation joined the various appearances together with the notion of achieving a synthesis out of the other gospels and a sense of increasing suspense and movement toward culmination in the group appearance.

The centrality of the group appearance is not only a matter of its placement at the end of a sequence, but also the manner in which it is related to the others. We find that Mary Magdalene reports to the disciples, called here "companions," who were weeping and mourning, that he has been raised and appeared to her, but they do not believe her.[345] They simply do not believe that he lives and has appeared. It is important to note that an apparently slight but significant shift in terminology has taken place; the verb *θεάομαι* bears the weight of the appearance and for the first time the ***recipient*** of the appearance is stressed: *καὶ ἐθεάθη ὑπ' αὐτῆς*. The same is to be said of this verb in vs. 14. These are the only two instances of the verb in the appearance accounts.[346] Two of their number then experience him in another form (*ἐφανερώθη ἐν ἑτέρᾳ μορφῇ*) while traveling *εἰς ἀγρόν*. They too face a cool reception from the rest and the stage is set to rid them of doubt once and for all. This happens in the group appearance. Their number is in keeping with the earthly disciples of Jesus (minus Judas = 11) and the imagery of the table fellowship of that group (*ἀνακειμένοις*) is perhaps preserved. We noted above that the summaries of Acts (1:4[?] and 10:41) suggest a meal participation for the appearances. This reference here does indeed point to a fellowship meal for the disciples, but the resurrected One is not pictured as taking part. Not only can little more be said than that the disciples are pictured as eating—that the Eucharist is intended is unclear—but also the form of the meal motif as found, for example, in the Emmaus story is missing here. Of course, this might have been due to the summary nature of this account, but it would have been strategic for the author to tie the two events even more closely together by virtue of the common and important meal motif. We must, therefore, reserve judgment on the meal motif as an authentic part of the original tradition until we have considered its relation to the clearly redactional thematic elements in the gospel stories.

The description of the group appearance itself here is strikingly bereft of detail. The "appearance" is in reality the occasion for a verbal exchange between the disciples and the risen One and for the sending and commission of the former. The setting is really quite insignificant (much more so than for the summary of Acts 1); the verb *φανερόω* is simply used to describe the event. We note that both this and the Emmaus account contain this verb of appearing while the appearance to Mary has *ἐφάνη*.[347] Here it is worth noting that *φανερόω* as such is not in and of itself a

345 The summary nature is evident from a comparison with Jn. 20:11-18, cf. pp. 95ff. and 206ff. The emphasis on doubt at her report comes probably from Lk. 24:11 or from a general development on the theme.

346 Acts 1:11 is not within an appearance story; cf. above for the term *ὤφθη*, pp. 60ff.

347 The *ἐφάνη αὐτοῖς* in the shorter ending regarding the group is bereft of a textual claim to originality, Taylor, *op. cit.*, p. 614, notwithstanding.

late verb for "appearing" or "making evident," but the use of the term in the resurrection appearances is. The only other NT usage of this passive in the resurrection context is, also as summary, Jn. 21:14, *τοῦτο ἤδη τρίτον ἐφανερώθη Ἰησοῦς τοῖς μαθηταῖς ἐγερθεὶς ἐκ νεκρῶν.* In the Barnabas epistle we have a similar usage: "in which Jesus rose from the dead, appeared (*φανερωθεὶς*) and ascended into heaven."[348] The specialized terminology in the gospel texts for "appearing" uses a variety of expressions, but not once does *φανερόω* appear. It may be that this term tended to become more desirable for this summary approach to the narrative because of its integral significance for two other christological motifs, namely 1) the incarnation (appearing–generally–in the flesh),[349] and also 2) the parousia.[350] The term is also used in II Cor. 5:10 of the appearance of Christians before the judgment seat of Christ and it may very well be that this general weight of usage in central areas of early Christian thought as a less specialized term, and, therefore, one of greater flexibility or wider range of applicability, turned out to be in fact decisive for this aspect of description.

In terms of the other motifs which are characteristic for the group appearance we see that both the notion of the recognition of Jesus and his coming and standing in their midst are missing. As noted above, the author is not concerned with such details. Further there is no description of how he looked to them, nor does he show them proofs of his bodiliness. Indeed, in the light of the other texts where doubt and unbelief are not nearly so pronounced as here (the Thomas pericope excepted) the absence of "demonstrations" of his identity with the crucified One is quite striking and instructive. In place of the tendency to dispel doubts through proofs we have here a curt but effective verbal rebuke. This formulation has the author's community clearly in mind. It is often noted regarding the Thomas pericope that the writer focused upon the relating of the kerygma as a witness *to be believed* and that within the Christian community itself; Thomas was a symbol of unbelief.[351] Here too we have a verbal address in the same direction, but this time to the entire group or at least those outside of the women and the two Emmaus travelers. This means basically that the entire college of apostles has been tried for faith and has been found wanting. What is said of Thomas in Jn. is here in essence ascribed to all of them: they were unbelieving and resisting those who had borne witness to them of the Lord's Resurrection.

This shift from physical proofs to verbal rebuke, if it is indeed a shift, raises some questions which are of minor importance to the precursors or have been posed much differently by them. The central controversy seems to be one of authority and not merely one of witness as in Jn. The controversy is of importance for our investigation only in so far as it has influenced the placement of accent in the ap-

348 Barnabas 15:9.

349 Cf. I Tim. 3:16; Heb. 9:26; I Pet. 1:20; I Jn. 1:2a; Ign. *Eph.* 19:3 and Barn. 5:6, 6:7, 9,14 and 12:10.

350 Cf. Col. 3:4a; I Pet. 5:4 and I Jn. 2:28 and 3:2b.

351 Cf. below under the johannine group appearance, pp. 164 and 172ff.

pearance accounts and not in all of its ramifications for markan studies. We have already noted that the author has placed the doubt of the disciples at the points of transition as the link which gives all three of the accounts a coherent unity and their basic movement. The disciples clearly represent something to the reader since not one individual but the whole is involved in this central motif. In the other major accounts one sees that the word motif consisted of the commission to go into the world; here we see the new aspect of rebuke. This is not "new," of course, in the light of the "oh, you of little faith" in other gospel strata. In this broader context one could understand the rebuke here. Before Easter, doubts had their place because of misunderstanding but thereafter not. This creates problems, however, because their incredulity was only in reference to Christ and his Resurrection *indirectly*; the witness "he is alive" was the *direct* object of their disbelief. The problem becomes somewhat assuaged when one includes the "promise" of the earthly Jesus to go before them into Galilee where the scattered sheep, which had been scandalized in him, would be gathered again. This would seem to remove the indirectness. In any case, to the word of the risen One accrues the place of central importance. Significant, of course, in terms of the representative place of the disciples is that this word of rebuke has come to disperse all doubt over the Resurrection at the very heart of apostolic authority.

This second aspect of authority is in fact the fundamental reason for the group appearance here as the inherent structural progression in the stories of vss. 9-20 has shown. But with it another problem comes to the surface: the rebuke in vs. 14 has indeed become a source of embarrassment to the dignity of the apostolate. Jn avoided this impasse on authority by allowing Thomas to bear the unbelief of the disciples. While Mt. preserved "and some doubted" this account drew the full consequences and in making the disciples at least co-partners at center stage created a tension for succeeding generations. This tension could not go on unchallenged. In the Freer Logion, for example, we find that the narrative could simply not go on to vs. 15 without the disciples being given a chance to reply to this "defamation" of their character. There is no text-critical question really regarding this logion as a witness to the so-called original ending of Mk.,[352] but it is noteworthy for this study for the following reasons: 1) it is the first time that the disciples are pictured as trying to defend themselves before the risen One. They are not only not in awe of him particularly, but they also are disturbed by the "injustice" of his one-sided rebuke. 2) We find here the description of a dualistic battle between God and Satan. The rebuttal of the disciples is accepted as legitimate and a revelation about this cosmic struggle is imparted. In the other accounts there is nothing of the struggle of the powers of darkness against the purposes of God. 3) The reflections of a different language system are also present. Here we meet such terms as: "this age of

352 Cf. above, n. 340. N.B. the non-markan and *hapax* terminology. In discussing the positions of Helzle and Aland, K. Haacker, "Bemerkungen zum Freer-Logion," *ZNW*, 63 (1972), pp. 128f., considers it thoroughly possible that the longer ending originally contained the Freer-Logion.

lawlessness," "unclean (or evil) spirits,"[353] "the true power of God," "the limit of the years of Satan's authority," "the drawing near of other crises," "on behalf of the sinners. . .that they may sin no more,"[354] "the inheritance of the spiritual and incorruptible glory of righteousness in heaven," etc.

In vs. 15 another aspect of the address of the risen One is expressed. He has rebuked them for unbelief and then he proceeds to commission them for service. The closest parallel to this commission is perhaps Mt. except that the expression of transcendent power and its consequences for the Christian mission are added only indirectly later in vs. 20 after the ascension scene. The transition into the commission is clearly a forced one. Moreover, the brevity of the commission is also striking; it even surpasses the brevity of Jn.! For the latter it is a sending in "peace," while for Lk. it is linked to the role of the Spirit. This is not the case for "Mk." We do find in the shorter ending, however, the notion not unlike Mt. that Jesus himself continues to be responsible for the preaching mission: the holy and incorruptible kerygma of eternal salvation is sent out by Jesus from East to West through his messengers. The commission is then compounded in the longer ending with a curious list of signs and confessional statements (vss. 16ff.). In the narrative of vs. 20 the "Lord" is again behind the proclamation. Yet, the notion of cooperation is stressed (συνεργοῦντες) and "signs" buttress and verify the word of proclamation (cf. Acts 4:29ff.). Perhaps the ring of Jn. 3:16-17 is to be heard in the words: "He who believes and is baptized will be saved, but he who does not believe will perish." The statement is somewhat similar to the capsule form of the intention behind the Thomas story in Jn.: the right response to the witness is faith. The signs which follow believers–a notion foreign to the other accounts–described as: "In my name they will cast out demons, they will speak with new tongues, they will lift up serpents and if they drink anything poisonous it will not hurt them and they will lay hands on the sick and they will recover," would seem to have a strong literary affinity to the words of the narrator in the markan account of the sending of the disciples during the earthly ministry[355] and to motifs in Jn.,[356] but as Taylor has rightly pointed out ". . .once more the point of view is later."[357]

How is one to judge this material? Dodd takes a very positive approach and while he clearly recognizes that this whole longer ending was not part of the original Gospel of Mark, he nevertheless, accepts vss. 14 and 15 of the group appearance as worthy of equal weight with the canonical gospels when he says:

"Thus it is not improbable that we have, here again, a generalized trait in the current tradition finding independent expression in a particular formulation. In short, it appears reasonably likely that Mk. 16:14-15 is to be added to Class I, as another example of the formulation of

353 Cf. also Mk. 6:7.
354 Cf. in this connection Justin *apol.* 1,61,93D with reference to the conversional centrality of baptism.
355 Cf. Mk. 6:12,13.
356 Cf., e.g., Jn. 14:12.
357 Taylor, *op. cit.*, p. 612.

the tradition in a 'concise' narrative. In that sense it would be a 'genuine' record, in spite of its dubious credentials, since it adheres closely to the general traditional pattern without slavishly following any other written account known to us."[358]

Is this material really so independent of the other accounts? Dodd applies a very formal criterion ("general traditional pattern") in making his decision about this account. When a variation of theme appears in his pattern for the group appearance, the account is simply independent of the others and, therefore, to be accepted as a separate witness. It may be, of course, that certain elements are independent and, therefore, to be questioned as to their place in the history of tradition, but to deny literary dependence in this account on the group appearance is a mistake. Before drawing final conclusions we shall consider the extra-canonical texts to see if a pattern of development is beginning to take shape here in "Mk." that is then enlarged upon elsewhere as well. Yet, tentatively it may be said that this "markan" text shows both many points of contact with the other gospel texts *and* a distinct interest in questions which were first important to second and third generation Christians.[359] It is not only a summary of sorts, not unlike Acts 1 in this respect, but also independent of it in that themes absent from or in embryonic form in the earlier texts are incorporated into the heart of the narrative. This elaboration or addition of favorite themes established a very important precedent as we shall see below in the extra-canonical sources. The focal point of elaboration/reduction for "Mk." was the doubt motif; it stood in the place of the proof theme. Proofs are not needed where the word of the risen One dominates. Moreover, the relationship between the disciples and the appearing One has also reached a new level through the accentuation of doubt: anthropological interest has been underscored.[360] The scenery is basically the same, yet the lighting and speaking parts in this drama have been altered considerably. And what can be said about the cathartic effect of the new emphasis? Faith is lauded, baptism is required for salvation and Christians are followed by signs. These signs are not just characteristics of a relationship to the risen One, but specific acts and services performed by the early Christian community. Strangely enough, however, the signs could indeed be a theme in the johannine and lukan redactional strata in other clothing: the "proof" motif enters through another door, this time in respect to the bearers of the witness and not the risen One. In conclusion it would be fair to say that this "appearance" is handled in principle much like that of the Thomas story of Jn., i.e., it is the occasion for something else.

We turn now to the *extra-canonical sources* to determine the nature of developments in the appearance story tradition in the same way that we have dealt with "Mk." Our sources are 1) the Gospel of Peter 2) the Gospel of the Hebrews 3) the Epistula Apostolorum 4) the Syriac Didaskalia and 5) other accounts related to the

358 Dodd, "Appearances," p. 16.
359 Cf. Taylor, *op. cit.*, pp. 611f.
360 The Emmaus story of Codex Bezae pursues a similar tendency.

latter two in brief overview, e.g., the Straßburg Papyrus, the Gospel according to Nicodemus *et al.*

The Gospel of Peter

This document written in all probability at the end of the first century A.D. or the beginning of the second in Syria[361] offers considerable material for the topic of the empty tomb and the place of the women,[362] but the text appears at first glance to have no appearance account at all outside of the grave guard problem already discussed above.[363] In extant fragments, however, which are far from satisfactory in number and unity, the resurrected One *and* the Resurrection itself are *seen* but no encounter takes place. In connection with that grave guard question we have the following scene which builds the nucleus of the visual factors: there is the sounding of a heavenly voice [IX:35], the heavens open and two men [*δύο ἄνδρες* IX:36] descend, the stone before the tomb rolls away by itself [*ἀφ' ἑαυτοῦ κυλισθεὶς ὑπεχώρησε παρὰ μέρος* IX:37], the grave opens [*καὶ τάφος ἠνοίγη* IX:37], the men enter [this time they are called *οἱ νεανίσκοι* IX:37] and soon they emerge with another man and are seen by the guards [*πάλιν ὁρῶσιν ἐξελθόντας ἀπὸ τοῦ τάφου τρεῖς ἄνδρας* IX:39]. This third party is helped out of the grave under the support of the two others [*καὶ τοὺς δύο τὸν ἕνα ὑπορθοῦντας* IX:39].[364] A curious reference to a cross following them is added as the solemn procession emerges from the grave [*καὶ σταυρὸν ἀκολουθοῦντα αὐτοῖς* IX:39]. The risen One and the chief of the other two then ascend [*χωροῦσαν*] into heaven; the "one" is led by the hand by the other(s!) [*τοῦ δὲ χειραγωγουμένου ὑπ' αὐτῶν ὑπερβαίνουσαν* X:40] and then he, however, ascends even further towering above the heavens. To these visual aspects is added a word pronouncement, a kind of subjectless exchange. The risen One and the chief aide hear a voice out of the heavens calling, *Ἐκήρυξας τοῖς κοιμωμένοις*; [X:41] and the answer [*καὶ ὑπακοὴ ἠκούετο ἀπὸ τοῦ σταυροῦ*] comes from the cross, *Ναί* [X:42]! This description of the Resurrection suggests the artistic brushstrokes of an apologist filling out the canvass of tendencies begun in Mt.

361 Cf. the remarks of Eusebius *hist. ecc.* VI, 12 regarding Bishop Serapin of Antioch's decision to ban the use of a 'Gospel according to Peter' in the church of Rhossos ca. A.D. 200–also III, 3.25, and P. Gardner-Smith, "The Date of the Gospel of Peter," *JThS*, 27 (1926), pp. 404ff., also his, "The Gospel of Peter," *JThS*, 27 (1926), pp. 255-271, L. Goppelt, *Christentum und Judentum im ersten und zweiten Jahrhundert*, BFChTh, 55 ed. by P. Althaus, H. Dörries and J. Jeremias (Gütersloh, 1954), pp. 207f., and E. Hennecke and W. Schneemelcher, *Neutestamentliche Apokryphen*, I (Tüb., 1959, 3rd ed.), pp. 118ff., "The Gospel of Peter," trans. by D.R. Cartlidge, *Source Book of Texts for the Comparative Study of the Gospels*, ed. by D.R. Cartlidge and D.L. Dungan (Missoula, Mont., 1972, 2nd ed.), pp. 157-162, and E. Preuschen, *Antilegomena, die Reste der außerkanonischen Evangelien und urchristlichen Überlieferung* (Gieszen, 1905, 2nd. ed.), pp. 15ff. and 145ff. The Greek text is that of L. Vaganay, *L'évangile de Pierre* (Paris, 1930), pp. 202-338.

362 Cf. VIII:28-XI:49 and XII:50-57.

363 Cf. pp. 116f.

364 Considered not to be assistance but rather "einen antiken Gestus der Ehrerbietung," by Lohfink, *Himmelfahrt*, p. 127.

On the other hand, a group appearance probably followed this narrative. We find the following pointers: 1) the women have been told by the heavenly messenger, *ἀνέστη καὶ ἀπῆλθεν* and again, *ὅτι οὐκ ἔστιν, ἀνέστη γὰρ καὶ ἀπῆλθεν ἐκεῖ ὅθεν ἀπεστάλη* [XIII:56] and then they flee the tomb [*τότε αἱ γυναῖκες φοβηθεῖσαι ἔφυγον*, XIII:57]. Immediately thereafter follows an adversative *δὲ* in XIII:58 where 2) the alleged writer. "Simon Peter" carries the narrative further by adding his comments on the events after this as follows: it was the final day of the feast of unleavened bread [*τελευταία ἡμέρα τῶν ἀζύμων*] and the festival visitors were beginning to turn homewards [*πολλά τινες ἐξήρχοντο ὑποστρέφοντες εἰς τοὺς οἴκους αὐτῶν...*]. The twelve disciples [*ἡμεῖς δὲ οἱ δώδεκα μαθηταὶ τοῦ κυρίου*] in contrast did not leave immediately, but remained together. They had been suffering under the pangs of sorrow [*ἐκλαίομεν καὶ ἐλυπούμεθα* (cf. "Mk." 16:10: *πενθοῦσιν καὶ κλαίουσιν*)] and finally being saddened over what had happened each went home [*καὶ ἕκαστος λυπούμενος διὰ τὸ συμβὰν ἀπηλλάγη εἰς τὸν οἶκον αὐτοῦ*]. Why exactly they stayed longer than the others is not developed, but the notion that the group with one exception separated is certainly stressed. In vs. 60 three of their number remained together. Simon Peter, his brother Andrew and Levi, the son of Alphaeus whom the Lord. . .[had called from tax collecting? cf. Mk. 2:14] took their nets and went fishing.

At this point the text breaks off. If an appearance story followed, which seems likely, and bore similar traits to the kind of story preceding it or was closer to the Jn. 21 account, as some have supposed, is a moot question.[365] What value it might have for our investigation would be speculative and, therefore, we must forego any direct use at this point.

The Gospel of the Hebrews

Known to us only in fragments preserved in patristic quotations the Gospel of the Hebrews apparently closed with a Lord's Supper scene, a grave guard account in

365 While rejecting any literary dependence of GP upon Jn. 21, Gardner-Smith, "Gospel of Peter," p. 259, says, "all we can say is that 'Peter' and John both knew a tradition that some incident had occurred when Simon Peter and a few of his companions were engaged in fishing. How great was the degree of verbal similarity between the two versions of the common tradition we do not know, but judging from the few words of 'Peter' which survive it was not very great." In the light of what we have seen regarding the likely dependence of GP upon Mt. for the grave sequence with additional motifs corresponding to the writer's apologetic interests it would appear far more likely that the author is similarly working with a full knowledge of the canonical sources in the appearance account here. Cf. above n. 339, and in general also E. Sanders, *op. cit.*, pp. 67f., Dibelius, *Formgeschichte*, pp. 269f. and his, "Motive," pp. 148ff., Lohfink, *Himmelfahrt*, p. 128, von Campenhausen, *Ablauf*, pp. 30f., D. Völter, "Petrusevangelium oder Ägypterevangelium," *ZNW*, 6 (1905), pp. 368ff., J. Finegan, *Die Überlieferung der Leidens- und Auferstehungsgeschichte Jesu* (Gießen, 1934), pp. 97ff. and A. von Harnack, "Ein jüngst entdeckter Auferstehungsbericht," *Theologische Studien. Fst. B. Weiß* (Gött., 1897), pp. 1ff. With regard to those who seek the alleged lost ending of Mk. here, Shepherd, *op. cit.*, p. 228, remarks candidly, "One lost ending cannot be proved to be based upon another lost ending!"

which not only the Romans but also the Jews were represented and an appearance of the resurrected One before James. Only the last account is preserved in the reference of Jerome in his *de viris illustribus* 2, but the other two can be surmised on the basis of hints contained in the latter. The text reads:

"Now the Lord, when he had given the linen cloth unto the servant of the priest, went unto James and appeared to him (for James had sworn that he would not eat bread from that hour wherein he had drunk the Lord's cup until he should see him risen again from among them that sleep). . .Bring ye, saith the Lord, a table and bread. . .He took bread/and blessed and brake and gave it unto James the Just and said unto him: My brother, eat thy bread, for the Son of Man is risen from among them that sleep."366

Exact data on the place and time of composition are difficult to determine in this gospel because of its fragmentary nature, but a high degree of probability accompanies the date of around the early second century A.D. It is common knowledge that the mention of an appearance to James in the list(s) of I Cor. 15 has its only possible counterpart (however that may be specified is an open question) in "gospel" materials in the reference quoted above. This means that in terms of the relationship question none exists for all practical purposes with the canonical gospels at all, but possibly with the kerygmatic formula tradition. Indirectly it could be argued that a grave guard story with somewhat similar contours to GP was included in the text, but this is mere conjecture. All that is suggested in the one reference is that perhaps Jewish representatives were also present at the tomb and witnessed the Resurrection. If that be true our remarks on GP and its dependence on tendencies of the tradition set into motion by Mt's grave guard story and the possibility of non-Christian witnesses could be true here too. The meal motif is equally obscure here so that the focus of our attention concentrates on the appearance account. The fact that it is without parallel in the canonical gospels does not necessarily preclude a very old, reliable tradition, deserving of inclusion in our analysis. But other considerations make this improbable. The major problem is that in comparison to the stories of the other gospels we do not really have a story here. Indeed, it reads much more like a construct put together out of other motifs not unlike the method employed by Matthew in 28:9-10. That is to say, outside of the basic motif that an appearance before James takes place the rest of the account seems to revolve around themes foreign to appearance story traditions: James' oath not to partake in the eucharist meal until he had seen the resurrected One, the centrality of the Eucharist itself and the direct identification of the resurrected One with the Son of Man. These elements occur, as noted above, at the redactional level alone. These observations suggest that the James appearance account is indeed a redactional composition out of motifs familiar to the writer in canonical accounts and specific issues current in his local situation, e.g., the question of apostolic authority

366 The Latin text is quoted by von Campenhausen, *Ablauf*, p. 31, n. 121. The translation here is that of M.R. James, *The Apocryphal New Testament* (Oxford, 1953), pp. 3f.

and the person of James and the celebration of the Eucharist in some special way connected with it.[367]

The Epistula Apostolorum

In trying to weigh the value of this comparatively long document[368] one is faced from the outset with some basic procedural questions which make themselves felt all the more urgently in comparison with the preceding text because of *form.* The Gospel of Peter retains something of the basic form of the canonical gospels while giving way slowly to the demands of literary style current at the time of its composition. These demands led sometimes to the seemingly bizarre, but at least an attempt to retain the "family resemblance" is recognizable. This is not the case in the Epistula Apostolorum. All of the gospels share to one degree or another the post-Easter perspective, but this document presses the tendency to the extreme of placing the entire "gospel" into the setting of a post-resurrection appearance. Seen from the standpoint of sheer bulk, therefore, we have the most extensive group appearance in the extant literature; moreover, the existence of both the number "11" and the term "The Twelve" (cf. 2[13] and 19[30] the latter in the Ethiopian text) makes this text seemingly ideal for our study. Certain critical problems, however, stand in the path, namely, those of compositional structure and thought-world.

We have before us compositionally both thematic overlaps and direct echoes from the canonical gospels. Thematically, for example, demonstrations of the corporeality of Jesus, his revelations in word, explanations from the OT for the fate of the Messiah and the commission to serve in the world are all present in abundance. Such echoes as "cry no more" and "tell my brothers" (cf. 10[21] to Jn. 20:14ff. and Mt. 28:7ff.), "be not afraid," "he seemed like a ghost" and "some doubted" (cf. 11[22] to Mt. 28:10; Lk. 24:37,39 and Mt. 28:17) and "go and preach" (cf. 30[41] to Mt. 28:19) are also to be found. It is, however, the presence of the above in their bizarre forms and disproportionate quantities that makes the decision of relevance a particularly difficult one. In the canonical gospels reserve and modesty are by and large the rule; here they are not. Not only is the tendency to emphasize the human side of the appearance present, but also we find now that the disciples occupy center stage. We have already noted in "Mk." 16:14-18 in the Freer Logion that the disciples have been granted a retort at the rebuke of Jesus; here a full scale question and answer session takes place. Moreover, the objections

367 Cf. below, n. 389.

368 The text exists in Coptic and Ethiopic versions with one fifth century page of Latin. Cf. C. Schmidt, *Gespräche Jesu mit seinen Jüngern nach der Auferstehung* (Leipzig, 1919), pp. 21f., Hennecke-Schneemelcher, *op. cit.*, I, p. 132, James, *op. cit.*, pp. 485-503. The date and origin of this document and its relationship to the gnostic question are matters of dispute. Cf. C. Schmidt, *op. cit.*, pp. 367-402 and 198ff., Lohfink, *Himmelfahrt*, pp. 130ff. and Hennecke-Schneemelcher, *op. cit.*, pp. 126f. We follow here the latter's translation.

to scepticism and doubt that existed in the synoptics and Jn., some intense and some quite mild, are now rapidly fading. In fact, a premium is placed on the role of questioning. The disciples are pictured as probing, questioning and searching *because* of faith, i.e., to unite faith and understanding so that the future life and mission of the church might be firm and clear (cf. 23[34]). Mingled with Jesus' astonishment in the first half of their continued probing ["and yet you still doubt and question" *passim*] we find a fundamental change of attitude in the second half (cf. 22[33]). The theme of questioning comes to a crisis and then resolves itself in the acknowledgement of Jesus that their probing is worthy and no longer a short circuit in their relationship. Their questioning has indeed been "with their whole heart" (cf. 25[36]) and therein lies its merit. Revelations of one sort or another then unfold in even greater quantities.[369] The disciples find in these words the clarifications that secure for them the future (cf. also the prophecy of the conversion of Paul, 31[42f.]). The whole encounter is then concluded with an ascension described in the form of a violent storm, a dramatic opening of the heavens, an ascent into a cloud and the singing of angels. The last word of the ascending Christ is: "Go in peace!"

A comparison raises at least two major questions: 1) as a "gospel document" cast in the "appearance form" can it be maintained that the form itself is more than a construct? Put differently, does it preserve the tradition of the "appearance form" or does it simply utilize the form literarily in order to gain an audience? The distinction may seem arbitrary, but it is really quite decisive. The "appearance form" within the group motif is for the canonical gospels inseparably united with the rest of the gospel narrative as a whole. Here, however, the earthly days are for practical purposes eliminated (21[32] notwithstanding), and the entire "life of Jesus" is telescoped into this one form. This step is inconceivable for the canonical sources as their witness is not a witness to the events "after the Resurrection" alone, but rather to the whole ministry of Jesus. It might be objected that the "appearance tradition" itself did not represent anything more than just the appearances and that the Epistula Apostolorum is in this respect not at all dissonant. The point is, however, that this document claims for itself, if not from its title at least from its content, to be a gospel and thus its failure to relate to the earthly days while using the appearance form must be reckoned with. And 2) what about the use of specific motifs? We noted in GP that a direct relationship to the other gospels in general form assisted in the relevance question in spite of the relative paucity of comparative material. Here the quantity is overwhelming, but interestingly enough the references to themes, as pointed out above, are almost all direct quotes or very familiar echoes from the canonical gospels. The writer seems to have gathered themes at will from those accounts in order to create a composite

369 For further comments on the gnostic theme with regard to James the Just, John and Peter after the Resurrection, cf. Eusebius *hist. ecc.*, II, 1.4 (Clement of Alexandria, Bk. VII, *Hypotyposen*), where the *Kurios* gives τὴν γνῶσιν to them and they in *paradosis* succession to the apostles and then they to the ἑβδομήκοντα.

picture for his dialogue/revelational goals. We also note the presence of three themes in particular which are not part of the canonical sources nor of "Mk.": 1) the inclusion to the apostolic company of Paul 2) the *descensus ad inferos* (cf. 21[32] [370] and 3) the relation between the celebration of the Passah and a memorial to Christ's death. [371] All of these are of interest to a subsequent generation and with regard to form in general we see, in fact, that a new *Gattung* has come into being.

The Syriac Didaskalia

The statements about the appearances in general within the Syriac Didaskalia [372] are, as has been true on occasion above, cast in the form of a reduction of the style of the canonical gospels and the expansion of certain favorite themes. It shares on the whole with the Epistula Apostolorum the tendency to use the appearance motif to further its own didactic goals. It differs from the latter in that proportionally much less is ascribed to the lips of the risen One himself. The "apostolic" teaching itself enjoys here a preferred status and wide acclaim and does not need, apparently, the authoritative stamp of the "words of the Lord."

In chapter XXI we find that Mary and Mary Magdalene have come to the tomb at the dawn of the first day of the week. There occurs a great earthquake, an angel of the Lord descends and rolls away the stone from the entrance of the tomb. Then comes a curious reference to "again the sabbath day." This confusion of the time element is further complicated in the following verses. There we read that a sacred fulfillment of scripture has taken place "three hours of the night after the sabbath in which our Lord slept ("and rose" is added in parenthesis)." We are told that the saying was thus fulfilled (a marginal reference warns the reader here to "take heed!"): "It is required of the Son of Man that he should pass through the heart of the earth, three days and three nights" as it is written in the Gospel. That is not all however. The text goes on to enlarge the picture with the following:

> "Again it is written in David, 'Behold thou hast appointed my days by measure,' because therefore these three days and nights are made short. Thus it is written, 'In the night, therefore, as the first day of the week dawned, He was seen by Mary Magdalene, and by Mary the daughter of James; and in the night of the first day of the week He went in to Levi, and then He was seen also by us."

370 Cf. also I Pet. 2:9, Oden Solomos 21,3 and 42,16 and C. Schmidt, *op. cit.*, pp. 453-576.

371 Cf. C. Schmidt, *op. cit.*, pp. 368 and 577ff.

372 The text exists in Latin and Syriac translations of a no longer extant Greek original. Cf. H. Achelis and J. Flemming, *Syrische Didaskalia*, TU, 25 (Berlin, 1904), pp. 243f. (an English translation in M.D. Gibson, *The Didascalia Apostolorum* [London, 1903] and the Syriac text in P. de Lagarde, *Didaskalia Apostolorum Syricae* [Gött., 1911]). In all probability the text was composed in the 1st half of the 3rd century A.D. (cf. Achelius and Flemming, *op. cit.*, pp. 369-377) in Syria (cf. Goppelt, *Christentum*, p. 205). It shows a relationship to the Didache and Mt's gospel (cf. also the 4th century *Apos. Constitutions*) and demonstrates internally as much an interest in apologetic legal matters crucial for Jewish Christianity as in the questions of gnosticism. We follow the translation of Gibson, *op. cit.*, here.

From these references several observations regarding form surface immediately: 1) the other gospel accounts are assumed to be available to the reader or part of a (general) collective written tradition, 2) the third day theme is the central time element (whatever the meaning of the sabbath reference), 3) the prophetic element has now been introduced to serve a specific goal, namely, to clarify the meaning of the burial period. The question of Christ's activities in the interim between the cross and Resurrection, a question which does not concern the canonical texts of the gospels, has now become a key issue. [373] And regarding the participants in the group appearance itself we hear nothing more than that he was seen finally "by us," i.e., the apostles. [374] Jesus asks them if they will be fasting because of him "in these days" and if he needs them to afflict themselves. It is not certain that the reference is depicted as having occurred at the time of the group appearance (the introductory words, "But he said unto us when he was teaching us. . ." are somewhat obscure), but this seems most likely in the light of the context where an expansion of the meal and questioning themes exists. On the heels of this inquiry of Jesus we find a rather lengthy rehearsal of several OT references, allusions to the teaching of the earthly days and the ramifications of both for practices in the church.

In terms of the focus of the group appearance one notes that the motifs serving the needs of the writer are in many respects similar to those of the Epistula Apostolorum: their scope is that of teaching, their form is that of an appearance story. To resolve key difficulties the support of authentic words from Jesus complemented to a great extent by the interpretation of contemporary apostolic authority are called upon. The themes of scripture (OT proof texts) and fasts are most central, but the greatest single modification is the nature of the "we" to whom Jesus appears. They are pictured as men of great piety and remorse at the impiety of the nation Israel. The trend to de-emphasize the disciples' own doubts and lack of faith has now reached the point where the disciples are indeed faultless. Only the "others" are in need of prayer and forgiveness.

Other Accounts in Brief Overview

In treating the extra-canonical sources we want to consider briefly the formal characteristics of accounts related to the latter two. The principle of selection is their kinship of *Gattung* and/or use of references to other appearances or specifically to a group appearance with a designation of the "Eleven," the "Twelve," the "Disciples," the "Apostles" [375] or any combination thereof.

373 A further development of this theme of the *descensus* is found in the Gospel of Nicodemus, cf. Hennecke-Schneemelcher, *op. cit.*, I, pp. 348-353.

374 In chapter XV we read that the Twelve, the "chosen people," were sent out with a commission to teach the gentiles (cf. Justin *dial.* 53,273c, *apol.* 1,50.67b = Preuschen, *op. cit.*, p. 36; on Justin in general cf. Goppelt, *Christentum*, pp. 284-301), but the women with them were not sent out. Further related and significant references in Justin are: *dial.* 51 and 106, and *de resurr.* 9.

375 In Josephus we find a reference to the Passion, Resurrection and the appearances on

Straßburg Papyrus

A very fragmentary account of a conversation of Jesus with the "apostles" is to be found in the Straßburg papyrus.[376] The text seems to preserve in spite of its many gaps a prayer of Jesus, his promise of power and apostleship to the disciples and their viewing of his majestic splendor. The trouble with the text fragments, however, is that they are most reluctant to divulge positive indications that we have here indeed an appearance text. Some references seem to fit, e.g., the revelation of Christ's majesty, a demonstration of his power and the secret of the apostolate, the admonition not to fear in the world because of his overcoming power and a definite view toward the future, but others do not, e.g., the prayer of praise, which fits Jn. 17 better than the resurrection texts, the warning that the hour of Jesus' departure is near, which bears much more of a pre-passion tone than the words to Mary Magdalene in Jn. 20:10-17, and Jesus' request that the disciples stay awake, which sounds much like Mt. 26:38. One reference at the end of the dorso side mentions a "mountain" which could bear a relationship to one of the mountains mentioned in the texts above, but as is the case with the text as a whole, the reference is too fragmentary to take us beyond conjecture.[377]

The Gospel According to Nicodemus

In this text we have two indirect references to resurrection appearances.[378] The soldiers from the grave watch are pictured as discussing the events at the tomb with the Jewish authorities. In chapter XIII the soldiers are made responsible for confirmation of the Resurrection, the angels' report that Jesus was lingering in Galilee and for a rebuke directed at the Jews for constant disbelief. In the very next chapter the Jews are surprised by the report of three of their own number. Phines the Priest, Adas the Teacher and Angaeus the Levite return to Jerusalem by way of Galilee and report to the others that they have seen Jesus with his disciples on a mountain called Mamilch. They go on to report that he commanded the disciples to go into all the world and preach to all men. Then follows a list of signs and wonders that accompany the believers.[379] After an address of Jesus the Ascension is said to

the third day "alive again" in: Josephus, *Antiquities of the Jews* (cf. trans. by W. Whiston [Phil., 1957], XVIII, 3,3. Cf. Hennecke-Schneemelcher, *op. cit.*, I, p. 324). In addition to the objection that this witness lays no claim to originality, however, but is clearly a remark from early Christian preaching, it is far from certain that it is really from Josephus at all. As Bauer points out (cf. Hennecke-Schneemelcher, *op. cit.*, I, p. 325), the remark makes no sense except as the witness of faith. Perhaps we have here the work of a very early Christian revisionist, but any attempt to reconstruct the original text is hardly possible (p. 325). The elements of "appearance" (on the third) day, "prophecy" and "witness" are certainly there, but simply affirm that the risen One appeared "alive," that the ones called "Christians" after him have not died out (cf. I Cor. 15:6b), and that if doubt and unbelief were once important they have no place in this public announcement.

376 Coptic 5 and 6. Cf. Hennecke-Schneemelcher, *op. cit.*, I, p. 156.

377 For further comments on its place in the gnostic corpus cf. *ibid.*, pp. 155ff.

378 Chapters XIII and XIV. Cf. *ibid.*, pp. 342f.

379 Cf. "Mk." 16:16-18.

have taken place. Perhaps more than any other extra-canonical source this one discloses the creative imagination of the author in his handling of the canonical material. Writing sometime in the fourth century A.D.[380] the author leans almost exclusively on Mt. for his material at this point, and while he goes beyond Mt. by giving the mountain in Galilee (Mt. 28:16) a name, he follows the tendency noted for Mt. above[381] by allowing both the group appearance and the words of commission to be attested by non-Christian sources. The degree to which the themes of the group appearance are attributable to anti-Jewish polemic is manifest.

The Sophia of Jesus Christ

In this text we find several secret revelations which are typical of the gnostic gospels.[382] After the Resurrection the "twelve disciples" and seven women, who had followed Jesus as disciples, come to a mountain in Galilee, which is called "the place of maturity and joy," and which is indirectly associated a few lines later with the "Mount of Olives in Galilee(?)." The group has come to this place with a series of uncertainties and questions which need to be resolved. The "redeemer" [σωτήρ] appears to them, but not in his "original form" [μορφή]; rather in that of an invisible [ἀόρατον] spirit. His form was that of a great angel [ἄγγελος] of light, it is virtually indescribable for the author and yet, he manages to explain that the redeemer could not bear mortal flesh [σάρξ], but a pure [καθαρόν] and perfect [τέλειος] flesh [σάρξ]. He then likens what they saw to the experience on the Mount of Transfiguration.[383] The redeemer greets them with the words: "peace be with you," and explains that it is his peace that he is giving them. Their reaction is one of astonishment and fear, but he smiles and asks them why they are troubled and uncertain and what they are seeking. Then follow the answers to their questions which prove to be revealing to them.[384] This text is the first one up to this point which has not at least had some direct relationship to references in the canonical group appearance stories, but exists by and large independent of them. Its closest relative seems to be the Letter of Eugnostos.[385] Its value for our search

380 Cf. Hennecke-Schneemelcher, *op. cit.*, I, pp. 331f.

381 Cf. above p. 117 and n. 339. The so-called *Schatzhöhle* (cf. P. Rießler, *Altjüdisches Schrifttum außerhalb der Bibel* [WB, Darmstadt, 1966], pp. 942ff. and esp. 1012f.) has the resurrected Messiah coming out of the grave and appearing to Cephas and John (54,3), the former having conceived of a plan to get the grave guards drunk on wine and while they slept to open the grave and remove the body without breaking the seal *so that the Jews would not say that the disciples had stolen it!* Yet, as the guards eat and drink the Resurrection takes place and the Lord and Messiah appears to Cephas [who has believed all along], before he could get near the grave, then he appears openly to the grave guards and proceeds then to visit the group in the upper room, where Thomas touches him. The series continues until all of the canonical accounts have been retold, along with additions of themes, e.g., the baptism of Mary, the mother of Jesus, and John, by Cephas, etc.

382 Cf. Hennecke-Schneemelcher, *op. cit.*, I, pp. 168ff.

383 I.e., if the words "the Mt. of Olives in Galilee" is indeed a reference to that occasion.

384 References to those who raise the questions, Hennecke-Schneemelcher, *op. cit.*, I, p. 171.

385 *Ibid.*, pp. 168ff. and p. 271.

for traditional witnesses and the development of their motifs is minimal in spite of its many details since its origins and direction of statement are to be sought in the context of a *Gattung* both distinct from and subsequent to our canonical sources.

The Dialogue of the Redeemer

After the Sophia in the library of Nag Hamâdi came the Dialogue of the Redeemer.[386] Like its neighbor it is cast in the form of a question and answer period between Jesus and specific disciples (Judas and Matthew), or twice the "disciples" or "12" and the holy women (Mary, Mariam and "Marihammē"). Although there seem to be many echoes from the canonical gospels as well as from extra-canonical ones, the document's dialogue form and revelations on matters of cosmology and eschatology presuppose a *Gattung* that limits its value for our study in much the same way as the Sophia.

The Apocalypse of James

Of the gnostic texts found in the Nag Hamâdi library the third and fourth texts of the Codex VII bear the name of James and constitute an apocalypse of the brother of the Lord. There are no gnostic gospels extant under this name,[387] but various texts of another variety are known. The "Proto-Gospel of James" (a fantastic report on the virtues of the holy Mary and a sequence on the birth of Jesus) and coptic fragments over the Resurrection and the Emmaus disciples are among them.[388] In this latter group we do have an appearance of Jesus before the "12" and the granting of special revelations shortly before the Ascension, the esoteric character of which identifies it with the gnostic apocrypha.[389] Two points are particularly interesting. 1) The time span between the Resurrection and Ascension differs significantly from those references within the canonical gospels. Here it is set at 550 days.[390] 2) The place of James and Peter as the recipients of the "gnosis" is preserved in this tradition as well.[391] The redeemer answers their questions regarding the prospects of the future (persecution and prophecy), and then the two of them alone are granted the privilege of being present at the Ascension through the "chariot of the Spirit," in contrast to Acts 1:9. They receive a farewell by the ascending One and then they report back to the others. Shortly thereafter James distinguishes himself from the rest of the group by sending them to another place. If this represents a symbolic sending of the disciples into the world, then he

386 Cf. *ibid.*, pp. 173f.

387 Cf. *ibid.*, p. 245.

388 Cf. *ibid.*

389 For a discussion of the history and significance of the whole James tradition cf. *ibid.*, pp. 244ff.

390 Much like the eighteen months of the Valentinian and Ophite sources, cf. Irenaeus *adv. haer.* I,3,2 and I,30,14 and the 545 days of the Ascension of Isaish 9,16.

391 Cf. above n. 369.

is the leader of the group and not Peter, and he has, moreover, assumed the role of the Lord himself (in the light of Mt. 28:19). According to Lk. 24:52 and Acts 1:12 the whole group returns to Jerusalem, but here James alone returns, and the text closes with his wish that in accord with his commission to preach his address may be illumined and that he may find his place among the children of God.

The account is in many respects similar to chapters 42-51 of the Epistula Apostolorum and it also brings to mind the departure speech of Jesus (Jn. 16), the OT ascension of Elijah and the vision of Ezekiel; the possible influence of the triumphal processions of the caesars may also be a possibility.[392] In spite of the departures from the canonical gospels the document has been considered to be an outgrowth of early Christian literature which had not yet come into contact with Gnosticism.[393] Yet, it is to be asked if even with an early date of composition (ca. A.D. 125-150)[394] its vocabulary and content really differ substantially from what we have noticed in the strongly gnostic gospels? For our line of questioning its relevance is negligible since gnostic or not its formal adaption of the appearance representation is secondary.

The Pistis Sophia

Here we have a group of works within Codex Askewianus. These are analogous to the gnostic texts considered above and probably find their closest relative in the Letter of Eugnostos as well.[395] Its concern is to relate the esoteric teachings of the risen One to the combined group of his disciples and the holy women. Unlike similar such accounts, however, it maintains that twelve years were required after the Resurrection for the redeemer to fully initiate them into the mysteries that they had to know. The final day, the day of the Ascension, is set precisely at the 15th of the moon in the month of Tōbe (January).[396] The scene is perhaps the best example of this type of special revelation/ascension scene in the extra-canonical literature.[397] The elements of the scenery share something of the combination of motifs similar to Mt. 28:16-20, etc. The aspects of location (the Mount of Olives), the place of the women in the whole picture, the expansion of time and the centrality of the question theme are especially arresting. Although questions come from both the disciples and the women as groups they also come from individuals among them. Interestingly enough, of the forty-six questions asked thirty-nine of them are raised by Mary Magdalene.[398] These elements are then altered in the second text of Codex Askewianus. The time is changed to the day of the Resurrection ("the third

392 Cf. Hennecke-Schneemelcher, *op. cit.*, I, p. 249.
393 According to W.C. van Unnik. Cf. *ibid.*
394 *Ibid.*
395 *Ibid.*, pp. 174ff.
396 *Ibid.*, p. 177, for a reference to Clement of Alexandria who mentions a gnostic baptismal festival on this date.
397 *Ibid.*, pp. 177ff.
398 *Ibid.*, p. 180.

day") and the participants in the gathering become "his disciples."[399] The physical setting is also quite volatile. It changes from "the water of the ocean" to "a place in the air along the way of the middle" to "the mountain of Galilee" to "the Amente(?)."[400] The revelation of secrets remains the main concern, but the addition of secret word formulas on the order of incantations (the first of which resembles a word play on the Tetragrammaton) and a curious association with "treasures of light" make the scene most bizarre even by gnostic standards. The genus of these eccentricities is distinct from the appearance stories of the canonical gospels and provides a most interesting contrast to them.

The Two Books of Jeû

These texts are also in the gnostic family.[401] The address of the risen One is directed at his disciples in general, but specific terms are also used, e.g., "the Apostles," "the Twelve," "the Twelve Disciples" and "the women (disciples)." As in the Gospel of Thomas and in the Manichaean documents Jesus is designated as the "Living One" (the resurrected One) or "the One who brings to life" (cf. Rev. 1:18). The revelations of the "living One" are prompted, sometimes more sometimes less, by the questions of the hearers. There is no appearance form as such. The theme of the spoken word has completely reduced the other themes which are an essential part of the appearance stories of the canonical texts. Such telescoping has already been noted on occasion above.

The Gospel of the Twelve Disciples

We have here a group of documents that represent variously gospels of the "Twelve" or the "Twelve Disciples," "Twelve Apostles" or the "Seventy" or the "Memoria Apostolorum" all of which stem from the collection of gnostic gospels. The theme basic to all of them is the revelation of mysteries and secrets which correspond to the systems of the sect communities represented.[402] None of them give indication of preserving directly anything of the canonical appearance stories; yet, while they are almost all "conversations" of Jesus with the disciples before the Ascension, they offer precious little for comparison.

The Kerygma of Peter

According to Clement of Alexandria[403] we have here an address of Jesus to the "Twelve" whom he had chosen and whom he was now sending into the world after

399 *Ibid.*, p. 181.
400 *Ibid.*, p. 182.
401 *Ibid.*, pp. 183ff.
402 *Ibid.*, pp. 186ff.
403 Clement of Alexandria *Strom.* VI,6,48.

the Resurrection.[404] They were to preach to all men, so that they would confess one God and through faith in the Christ be open to the future which belongs to those who fear, believe and are saved. The rest who do not believe will, therefore, be without excuse since they will have heard the truth. Unfortunately one finds little comparative material in any direct sense, but it is clear that a group appearance of sorts is present. Once again, however, the word theme has become the controlling center for the whole.

The Acts of Paul

In the Acts of Paul 10 we have a word about the institution of the "Twelve."[405] Although there is no appearance scene as such, we do have a motif thereof, namely, the notion of the commission. These are the men whom Jesus has chosen (cf. Acts 1:5), whom he understood and has had faith in. Through them, moreover, he raises the dead, heals the sick, restores the unclean, gives back sight to the blind, makes straight the cripple and lame and brings relief to the possessed. The idea of the signs of the believers is here focused upon the disciples.[406]

The Ascension of Isaiah

In the Ascension of Isaiah we encounter the terms "the Twelve Disciples" or simply "the Twelve" to name the group around Jesus in the earthly days.[407] This same group is involved in an appearance. Several points of contact with the form of the group appearance stories should be mentioned. The grave is opened in this account on the third day by both the Holy Spirit and the archangel Michael. The "Beloved" comes forth from the tomb sitting on their shoulders (?) and from this position he sends the "Twelve Disciples" forth into the world to teach all peoples and tongues about the Resurrection of the "Beloved" for salvation to those who believe on his cross and on his Ascension into the seventh heaven. To those who believe is granted to speak in the power of the Spirit and signs and wonders shall follow them.[408] Then comes a reference to the end days shortly before his return ("when he is near").[409] At that time his disciples will leave the teaching of the "Twelve Apostles" (Didache?), the faith, their love and purity; moreover, strife will develop over his nearness. Much like Mk. 13 par., I Tim. 4, II Tim. 3 and Rev. 1-3 "signs of the times" are mirrored wherein the church goes a wayward path.

404 Cf. on this text Hennecke-Schneemelcher, *op. cit.*, II, p. 63 and Goppelt, ***Christentum***, pp. 220f., who sees its home as Egypt in ca. A.D. 130.

405 Cf. Hennecke-Schneemelcher, *op. cit.*, II, p. 264.

406 Cf. "Mk.," above pp. 121ff.

407 Ascension of Isaiah 3,13ff. Cf. Hennecke-Schneemelcher, *op. cit.*, II, pp. 457f. Regarding the text's relationship to Gnosticism, cf. A.K. Helmbold, "Gnostic Elements in the 'Ascension of Isaiah'," *NTS*, 18 ('71/'72), pp. 222ff.

408 Cf. n. 406.

409 Chapters 3,21 and 4,1.

From many the Spirit must withdraw himself. Although again there is no appearance scene as such we do hear some echoes: ". . .and I saw as he sent his twelve disciples and ascended."[410] The literary genre of the text is a prophetic vision with apocalyptic features and is distinct from the gospel appearance story *Gattung*.

The Revelation of Peter

In conjunction with the already mentioned Mount of Transfiguration theme elsewhere we have here a very similar text which does little more than to refer to "we, the twelve disciples" and to point to the mountain theme in the words: "Let us go up to the mountain and pray." [411] The setting, however, is even more uncertain than in the Ascension of Isaiah and free composition has played such a strong role that it has little to offer for a comparative study.

The Gospel According to Mary

Here we have a fragmentary gospel cast in the typical gnostic revelation form. [412] It is a conversation of the "redeemer" or "blessed One" [413] with his disciples. As in other formally related texts Jesus answers questions and divulges the contours of the future. He greets them with "Peace to you" and assures them that it is his peace that they are inheriting (cf. Jn. 14:27). He warns them against false teaching and tells them to follow the Son of Man, who is in their inner being. They are then ready to be commissioned and sent into the world to preach the kingdom of God. [414] After a statement on the giving of no further commandment other than what he had already given them, the disciples raise their questions. No answers, however, come from the "redeemer" because Mary[415] interrupts their questioning to comfort them. They take heart at her words and begin to discuss the meaning of the "redeemer's" words. Andrew and Peter, however, do not believe that Mary's words ring true (Andrew) and that it is impossible that the redeemer would speak openly to a woman and not to them (Peter). This sort of objection is not infrequent in this literature. [416] Mary is naturally saddened at their mistrust, but is quickly defended by Levi. [417] The essence of his rebuke is "whom the Lord makes worthy

410 Chapter 11,22.

411 Cf. Hennecke-Schneemelcher, *op. cit.*, II, pp. 468-483; Akhmim text 4 and 5.

412 *Ibid.*, I, pp. 252 and 255. Part of the text is a Coptic (Sahidic) translation of an original Greek composition and is found at the beginning of the fifth century papyrus Berolinensis 8502, cf. *ibid.*, pp. 251ff.

413 Cf. Irenaeus *adv. haer.* I,1,3.

414 Hennecke-Schneemelcher, *op. cit.*, I, p. 252.

415 Allegedly Mary Magdalene who is normally the person in this role for the gnostic literature.

416 Cf. a development of both in the Pistis Sophia, 100 (Andrew) and 36 and 72 (Peter); also the Gospel of Thomas, Logion 114 where Peter wants Mary to go away because she is a woman. Jesus, on the other hand, proposes to lead her and all women of faith into manhood!

417 Cf. GP XIII:60.

you ought not to call unworthy."[418] She has loved more than they, Levi maintains, and they should all be ashamed to put on completed manhood (?).[419] With that they send themselves (!) into the world to preach as they were commissioned. The place of Peter here has been considerably diminished.

In summary we may say that "Mk." 16:9-20 and the extra-canonical sources of this section provide an immensely interesting and equally as difficult collection of texts to evaluate under our line of questioning. They reveal an amazing breadth of development in the resurrection traditions pursuing unique theological questions and pressing apologetic and other ecclesiastical issues. In all we have seen some basic lines of continuity regarding themes and motifs present in the canonical gospel stories, especially in certain redactional tendencies, above all those of Mt and Lk. On the other hand, equally as apparent are the departures from those stories where extraneous and originally unrelated and/or other topics, e.g., the *descensus* question, are fused together. The question is to be asked throughout: at those points of contact with and radical departures from the canonical sources are late trends being reflected or are these matters which have a claim to a very early traditional basis? It is unwise to generalize in the formulation of a reply, since each text has its own specific merits, so to speak, but we can say perhaps that for the appearance stories themselves we found no examples–one possible exception in the Gospel of Peter where the actual appearance account is missing and we can only speculate unfortunately about its content–which may help illuminate their pre-redactional form and function. We have noted alterations in the gospel form in general and a constant recourse to the importance of appearances of the resurrected One, especially in the aspects of words of commission and the communication of secrets and their meaning for the church and her mission. In most cases these texts are following paths at this point independent of the canonical sources, independent even of the mere composite summary form out of the other accounts as we saw in "Mk." In many cases we are dealing with a new *Gattung*.[420] We conclude, therefore, that as interesting and instructive as these texts are for research into early church history, especially on the question of the place of appearance accounts in the developing resurrection traditions, they are only of relative importance for our investigation.

E. "Displaced" Appearance Stories

Since the inception of form-critical analysis it has been a widely held assumption that post-resurrection appearance stories are to be found elsewhere in the gospel

418 Cf. Acts 10:15.

419 Cf. Hennecke-Schneemelcher, *op. cit.*, I, p. 254.

420 We noted, for example, especially in the group of gnostic texts from the library in Nag Hamâdi that the variety of motifs characteristic of the traditional appearance story form has been by and large dispensed with to concentrate upon conversation and address; the result is that a new "story" form has been created which serves as the casing for a new and unrelated subject matter in comparison with its precursor, namely the communication of secret truths. Cf. our remarks on the Ascension of Isaiah above and also Lohfink, *Himmelfahrt*, pp. 98ff. and esp. pp. 129ff.

narratives, having become detached somehow from their original context. It is of great interest that all of these "displaced" appearance pericopae represent a group or a modified group of the disciples. We shall consider them here for purposes of comparison.

The most commonly cited texts are: Lk. 5:1-11; Mk. 6:45-52 parr., 9:2-8 parr. and somewhat more remotely 4:35-41 parr.

Lk. 5:1-11

This is the story of the miraculous catch of fishes and finds its closest parallel in Jn. 21:1-14 which will be considered below.[421] It should be noted briefly at this point, however, that its dissimilarities really outweigh those points of contact, and that its place in the development of the tradition must be solved by some other method than identity with the appearance tradition.

Mk. 6:45-52 parr.

These texts, Mk. 6:45-52, Jn. 6:16-21 and Mt. 14:22-33, are classic locations for the "displaced" appearance narratives. The tradition is that of Jesus walking on the water. From the outset it clearly contains all of the elements that *could* indeed make it an appearance of the risen One, especially the johannine version. All of the disciples are presumably present and the group has left the crowd after the miraculous feeding scene (the 5,000), and then Jesus leaves the disciples. While he goes on land to pray they remain in the boat. The separation on both counts is characteristic of the appearance stories. The presence of Judas in the group, which is at least to be assumed at this point in the narrative, constitutes an irregularity, but the earthly group stress is really all the weight that "disciples" needs to carry. The evening hour comes and the disciples continue to wait on Jesus in darkness. With the exception of Jn. 20:19 none of the appearances are designated as nighttime events.[422] but the hour of the day and the turbulent wind which separated them even further from Jesus may bear symbolic (redactional) significance in the passage. In any case Jesus finally comes to them in their perplexity and danger. They see him walking on the water and as he draws near they are afraid and troubled at the mysterious apparition before them. Mk. 6:49f. and Mt. 14:26 add: (*ἔδοξαν* - Mk., *λέγοντες* - Mt.) *ὅτι φάντασμά ἐστιν. . . .* These elements have their parallel to one degree or another, when one considers their form, in some of the gospel stories.[423] Jesus then addresses them immediately: "Take courage (Jn. excepted), it is I, be not afraid!" In none of the group appearances does Jesus address the disciples in this exact form,

421 Cf. below pp. 200ff.

422 The Jn. 21 tradition spoke only of the early hour of the morning.

423 Most clear are the parallels in Lk.'s group appearance story (24:36ff.) and the Galilaean appearance story (Jn. 21:1ff.). Cf., e.g., R. Fuller, *op. cit.*, pp. 162f. and Hirsch, *op. cit.*, pp. 180ff.

but he does assuage their fears in a somewhat similar way in Lk. 24:36ff. At this point the texts vary. Mt. includes the request of Peter to join him on the water "if it is really you," and the act of Jesus saving Peter as he goes down with doubts. Jesus says: "ὀλιγόπιστε, εἰς τί ἐδίστασας;" (cf. Mt. 28:17) and is then received into the boat as the wind ceases and the disciples worship him saying: "Truly you are the Son of God!" Mk too has Jesus enter the boat, the storm calms and the disciples are deeply astonished, but for Mk they have simply failed to grasp the meaning of his majesty. In Jn., however, we are not told if Jesus actually entered the boat or not. The disciples "want" him to, but the boat is suddenly at the shore and they disembark.[424]

It may very well be that at an early stage there was some kind of obscure contact between this story and the appearance tradition.[425] The fact that Jesus does not specifically enter the boat in Jn. would suggest that this version rather than Mk. and Mt. is the closest to the appearance tradition, and that the former may, therefore, actually represent an earlier form of the tradition.[426] The question is whether we have here an appearance pericope which was actually transplanted either intentionally or inadvertently into a different context, or whether it was a narrative which originally belonged to the Galilean ministry and simply was influenced by the appearance tradition. Since the context indicates that in all of the parallels to Mk. 6:45-52 the story is firmly fixed in the Galilean ministry the latter is perhaps more probable, but we shall come upon the question again in the context of the group appearance tradition and the possible reasons for the omission of this story in the earthly ministry context by Lk.[427]

Mk. 9:2-8 parr.

We have here the well-known scene on the Mount of Transfiguration, which appeared above in several of the extra-canonical sources and which R. Bultmann

424 Pursuing a naturalistic explanation, i.e., that Jesus actually walked on the shore and the disciples in a confused state thought he walked on water, and then appealing to a comparison of Jn. 21:1 is N. Micklem, *Behold the Man, A Study in the Fourth Gospel* (London, 1969), p. 96.

425 Cf. Dodd, "Appearances," p. 23 n.*; cf. also Wilckens, *Auferstehung*, pp. 77f. Drawing no direct parallel here, but stressing the general background of a *heidnischen* miracle story is R. Reitzenstein, *Hellenistische Wundererzählungen* (WB, Darmstadt, 1963, 2nd ed. [='06]), p. 125. Similar is H.D. Betz, *Lukian von Samosata und das Neue Testament*, TU, 76 (Berlin, 1961), pp. 166f. Cf. below, pp. 215ff. for the problematic of Hellenistic backgrounds to the appearance stories.

426 Cf. Dodd, "Appearances," p. 24.

427 A.R.C. Leaney, "Theophany, Resurrection and History," *StEv*, 5 (1968), p. 102, claims that Lk omitted it "no doubt just because it savoured too much of the marvels perpetrated by pagan miracle-workers." Leaney's thesis is that the transfiguration story is a true theophany story, the only complete one within the gospel tradition, with the exception perhaps of the ascension story (p. 105). Moreover, for him theophany backgrounds are not to be sought in the resurrection appearance stories and thus there is no need to posit original appearance story backgrounds for such "displaced accounts" as this one (p. 107). We shall deal directly with this question below on pp. 168ff.

says has long been recognized as an original Easter story.[428] In terms of the comparison up to this point one must ask if this is really so. As with the first of these "displaced" narratives we have here a modified group appearance, i.e., Peter, James and John are the only ones present. Yet, can we call this an "appearance" at all? At least on formal grounds it must be rejected.[429] In the group appearance stories

428 Bultmann, *Tradition*, pp. 278ff., cf. also the *Ergänzungsheft* (1971, 4th ed.), pp. 91ff. for a further discussion and more recent literature. Drawing an indirect connection between the transfiguration story and the resurrection traditions, in particular an understanding of Mk. 16:1-8, is Anderson, "Easter Witness," pp. 42f. (Contra Hebert, *op. cit.*, pp. 66ff.) He sees in II Pet. 1:16-18 and Eth. Apoc. of Baruch an interpretation of the Transfiguration as an appearance story which is probably Mk's intention too as he connects the Resurrection and parousia most closely (p. 44).

429 Cf. Dodd, "Appearances," p. 25. Identifying the Transfiguration directly as a "misplaced appearance story" is C.E. Carlston, "Transfiguration and Resurrection," *JBL*, 80 (1961), pp. 233, 235 *et passim*. Because of the method he uses to arrive at this conclusion and the degree to which his views have been followed in a not insignificant amount of literature on this story it is necessary to reconstruct in brief his approach. He assumes that the story fits poorly into the scheme of things in the earthly ministry, since 1) Peter's denial and the cowardice of all three disciples at the cross are, *a priori*, unlikely following an incident like this, and it is, *a posteriori*, evident that fears and doubts were dispelled only at the Resurrection, 2) the story is a confirmation of Peter's confession and Jesus' predictions of suffering which are "difficult (if not impossible)" to locate in such an environment (p. 233), and 3) nowhere else is a miracle performed *on* instead of *by* Jesus, i.e., it says nothing about what Jesus can do but rather something about who he is (p. 234). Accordingly, it follows: "It is consequently not form-critical pedantry to insist that in function and type this story fits with other resurrection appearances. It does not create its own category. To this general observation we may perhaps add that the law of parsimony requires us to adopt the simpler explanation–in this case, the rearranging of chronology rather than the creation of a category with just one representative–unless overwhelming objections prevent us from doing so" (p. 234). As not compelling at all for Carlston is the argument that the appearances of a revivified earthly Jesus over an extended period before the Ascension rule out the identification, since the "older" concept of the Resurrection is that Jesus went directly into God's presence and then appeared on occasion from above to those faithful on earth as we see in the case of a Stephen (Acts 7:55) or a Paul (Acts 26, 9, 22) (p. 234). He refers to I Cor. 15:5-8, for Paul in opposition to Lk and then says: "The tradition that Jesus was *seen* as exalted Lord is ineradicably early" (p. 234), and ". . .the 'misplaced resurrection account' can be disproved as the correct explanation of the Transfiguration only if objections to the more primitive form–appearance directly from heaven–can be shown that for the Stephen and Paul accounts, as for the Apocalypse of Peter as well, the δόξα is central and precisely this form of appearance is what is anticipated in the NT and the literature of late Judaism (cf. Sib. Or. 5,426-432; Bar. 5:9; En. 60,2, etc.); even the "concrete and realistic appearances" bear a certain "oblique testimony to this transcendental conception" [non-recognition, appearing and disappearing at will and using tangible means to prove corporeality] (p. 235). "Jesus is of course a figure of δόξα" (p. 236). He adds that the voice from heaven is a parallel to the Stephen and Paul accounts and the call to obedience in it he tries to bring into contact with the commission motif of the gospel stories (pp. 238ff.). His attempts to unite the transfiguration with the gospel type in general requires some very unlikely exegesis, while the former parallels may indeed have a degree of probability. We have objected above in our introduction and elsewhere in this chapter to the method that makes the heavenly radiance type of appearance story into a criterion for discrediting the gospel type. The option either/or appears to be an unnecessary and inappropriate stating of the alternatives. Here the transfiguration story might qualify as an appearance story of the heavenly radiance type–or as having been influenced by that form of representation–, but its disparity in relationship to the gospel type must be stated most emphatically and that without prejudicing in any sense against the age and merits of that type itself. Following Carlston in the main line of argumenta-

a mountain is found only in Mt. The *μετεμορφώθη* or *προσώπου αὐτοῦ ἕτερον* terminology is approached only by the inauthentic ending of "Mk." (16:12) and the description of brilliance is attributed not to Jesus but to the angels in the gospels and to Jesus only within the heavenly radiance type. Moreover, the risen One does not share his appearance with others in the canonical accounts, while here we find

tion in connection with a proposed *theios anēr* background to the story is Th. J. Weeden, *Mark–Traditions in Conflict* (Phil., 1971), pp. 118ff. In basic sympathy with Carlston's thesis are J.M. Robinson, "Kerygma and History in the New Testament," *Trajectories Through Early Christianity*, Essays by J.M. Robinson and H. Koester (Phil., 1971), pp. 48ff., also his "On the Gattung of Mark (and John)," *Jesus and Man's Hope. A Perspective Book*, I, ed. by D.G. Buttrick (Pitt., 1970), pp. 116ff., M.E. Thrall, "Elijah and Moses in Mark's Account of the Transfiguration," *NTS*, 16 (1970), pp. 305ff. and p. 310, n. 4 and most recently U.B. Müller, "Die christologische Absicht des Markusevangeliums und die Verklärungsgeschichte," *ZNW*, 64 (1973), pp. 187ff.; more remotely is also Hooke, *op. cit.*, pp. 117ff. A parallel is drawn to Dio Chrysostom, 36, 40f. by G. Mussies, *Dio Chrysostom and the New Testament*, SCHNT, 2, ed. by H.D. Betz, G. Delling and W.C. van Unnik (Leiden, 1972), p. 71. In a recent article Schmithals, *op. cit.*, pp. 379ff., has made a gallant effort to defend this thesis and to supply a solution to the question of the ending of Mk. His argumentation runs as follows: It is a consensus of NT research that Mk had a narrative source of the Passion and Resurrection before him. It went on after the tomb story to relate both petrine and group appearance accounts. Because of his allegiance to the theme of the messianic secret, however, he could not make use of them at this point, but substituting the pointers of 14:28 and 16:7 relocated them. The petrine appearance, which originally related a total transformation of Jesus (not only his clothes) as a presentation of his divinity and then his disappearance (translation), was converted into the transfiguration story–he finds support here in 9:9f.; II Pet. 1:16-18; Rev. of Peter 1-14 and synoptic comparison as well–and the group appearance found its way into the call of the disciples in Mk. 3:13-19. The latter account referred to the same mountain as Mt. 28:16-20 and the Transfiguration and reflected a messianic enthronement scene complete with world-wide commission of the Twelve as Easter witnesses (this closed group did not exist as such in the earthly ministry) and Ascension; this scene is exegetically derivable (following Linnemann) directly from Mt. 28:18-20–Mt knew and made use of the markan source (preserved as well by a later redactor in Mk. 16:15-20)–and indirectly from markan redaction elsewhere. Thus, the ending of the original markan source is found in Mk. 9:2ff., 3:13-19 and 16:15-20. This reconstruction is certainly imaginative, but whatever else must be said about the particulars of his exegesis two major points must be singled out which cast considerable doubt on the viability of the whole: 1) it is simply an error to maintain that the consensus of NT research agrees that Mk had a block source of Passion and Resurrection narratives at his disposal. The fulcrum of his argumentation is this assumption throughout. 2) Schmithals fails to raise the probability question in terms of a form-critical comparison of his proposed appearance accounts with the other accounts of the gospel tradition. He must make exegetical leaps of considerable proportions to arrive at his group appearance and his reconstruction of the petrine appearance as presentation/translation story is no less problematical, although at least the elements suggesting possible Easter backgrounds here in general are more readily available. Opposing resurrection appearance story backgrounds to the Transfiguration although laying exclusive emphasis upon the interpretive milieu of the apocalyptic thought-world of late Judaism is H.C. Kee, "The Transfiguration in Mark: Epiphany or Apocalyptic Vision? ," *Understanding the Sacred Text, Fst. M.S. Enslin*, ed. by J. Reumann (Valley Forge, Pa., 1972), pp. 140 *et passim*. He is also emphatic in his rejection of the *theios anēr* backgrounds proposed by Weeden and others (*ibid.*), and in general thereto, cf. his, "The Terminology of Mark's Exorcism Stories," *NTS*, 14 ('67/'68), pp. 232ff. and esp. pp. 240-246. Rejecting recourse to sundry story backgrounds and opting rather for a christologically motivated (midrashic) compilation of discrete motifs in the catechetical context of the primitive church is H. Nützel, *Die Verklärungserzählung im Markusevangelium. Eine redaktionsgeschichtliche Untersuchung* (Würzburg, 1973), pp. 177ff.

both Moses and Elijah appearing on the scene.[430] The cloud image is reminiscent of the Ascension in Acts, but the voice from the cloud and the message thereof are entirely new aspects.[431] It is true, of course, that the term *ὤφθη* occurs here,[432] but it is used of the two visitors and not of Jesus, a decisive point in comparison with the other stories. The conversation with Jesus, especially as it is developed in Lk., and the proposal of Peter to build *τρεῖς σκηνάς* are further difficulties for this story in relating it to the appearance tradition of the gospels. Whether or not a union of this account with the heavenly radiance type has been achieved is an open question; a reply must be sought under an investigation of that form.[433]

Mk. 4:35-41 parr.

It has been suggested that like other "water" miracles the Stilling of the Storm story originally went back to an Easter tradition.[434] As in the Mount of Transfiguration story we have here a group of disciples pictured in a dramatic episode. Formal criteria, however, make it singularly difficult to compare the story with the appearance accounts below.[435] It may be that this story did have some place in the Easter tradition, but its place is so firmly set within another context with corresponding structure here that conjecture alone is its only support.

In summary then the so-called "displaced" accounts do not assist us in our pursuit of the pre-redactional form of the gospel appearance stories. The one exception may be found perhaps in the story of Jesus' walking on the water (Mk. 6:45-52 parr.), which we shall consider below under the group appearance (pp. 168ff.).

F. The Gospel Appearance Stories

Mt.

In chapter 28:9-10 the first appearance takes place before the women as they hasten from the grave to report to the disciples. This account, as we have seen, is matthaean redaction and without traditional basis. Between this pointer to Galilee and the appearance there Mt has inserted the story of the grave guard report and the theme of Jewish polemic, also matthaean composition. Thus, the final scene of the assembled disciples on a mountain in Galilee (vss. 16-20) is the only matthaean witness in our line of questioning to a traditional (group) appearance.

430 On the motif, cf. Albertz, *op. cit.*, p. 263 and Kee, "Transfiguration," pp. 142ff. and as "theioi andres" in Thrall, *op. cit.*, pp. 314ff.

431 Regarding Carlston hereto, cf. above, n. 429.

432 Cf. vs. 4 and then in vs. 8 the two visitors have disappeared: *καὶ ἐξάπινα περιβλεψάμενοι οὐκέτι οὐδένα εἶδον...*

433 Cf. above, n. 429.

434 Bultmann, *Tradition*, p. 246.

435 Dodd, "Appearances," p. 26 and R. Fuller, *op. cit.*, p. 162.

Lk.

The first appearance story for Lk. is the encounter of the two travelers on the road to Emmaus (24:13-35), and on the heels of that story comes the gathering of the disciples and the appearance of the resurrected One in their midst (24:36-49). These two stories provide our lukan witness to the story tradition.

Excursus: Lk. 24:50-53 and Acts 1:9-11: The Ascension Story

A complex to be touched on here is the *ascension* question. As noted earlier in the summaries of Acts, Lk has created and committed himself to a period of forty days during which the appearances of the resurrected One allegedly took place. The official close to this period comes about for Lk at the representation of the Ascension. Although the time factor in Lk. 24 constitutes a problem, since it appears that all events described there take place on the same day, the schematization concluding with the Ascension remains the same. Thus in the contexts of Acts 1:9-11 and Lk. 24:50-53 ("Mk." 16:19-20 is not a separate witness here) the Ascension comes as the final appearance story, as it were. This context, however, is secondary owing its origin to lukan redaction. Internally, moreover, the ascension *Gattung* is to be differentiated from the appearances owing its origin—as G. Lohfink in his excellent history-of-tradition analysis, *Die Himmelfahrt Jesu*, 1971, has shown[436]—probably to a combination of factors the principal conceptual background of which builds the idea of translation in the religious milieu of New Testament times.[437] In form and conceptual background other origins are to be sought for the appearance stories[438] and, therefore, the ascension question falls outside the scope of our investigation.

Jn.

In chapter 20:14-18 Jn records an appearance before Mary Magdalene. Then the

436 Lohfink, *Himmelfahrt*, pp. 70ff., 112ff. and esp. pp. 147-151.

437 The picture is somewhat complicated by the fact that we owe the ascension story to Lk., but in all probability not the concept. Lohfink uses the term *Erhöhungskerygma* (*ibid.*, *passim* and esp. pp. 242ff.) which is for him the designation for a pre-lukan tradition which the evangelist then combined with the *Grundschema* of a translation (*Entrückung*) story type current in this period in order to create a visual representation of the exaltation. This *Erhöhungskerygma* is for him the earliest understanding of the Resurrection, namely that Jesus was immediately exalted in the Easter event to a place of glory with God. The appearances then were originally conceived of as coming from this heavenly locale and were not thought of as some kind of interim period between the Resurrection and Ascension with Jesus existing in some transformed but not yet glorified state as the lukan schematization might suggest. Yet, it is questionable that Lk was really aware of this suggestion in his scheme, since to the question, "Where was Jesus during the forty days? " he hardly would have answered anything else than "with God" (impossible would be "in a cave," etc. Cf. the naturalistic explanations of rationalism in Schweitzer, *op. cit.*, above, n. 5). In any case, the appearing One in the tradition behind the gospel stories is very much the risen/exalted Lord along with his identification with the crucified One, as we shall see, and not some nondescript. Cf. also Lohfink's "Auferstehung," pp. 38f. and more distantly R. Fuller, *op. cit.*, pp. 127ff., Evans, *Resurrection*, pp. 98ff. and 137ff., Anderson, "Easter Witness," pp. 49ff., J. Dupont, "ἀνελήμφθη (Acts I.2)," *NTS*, 8 ('61/'62), p. 156, C.H. Talbert, "An Anti-Gnostic Tendency in Lucan Christology," *NTS*, 14 ('67/'68), *passim*, K. Lake and H.J. Cadbury, *The Beginnings of Christianity, Part I: The Acts of the Apostles*, III, ed. by F.J. Foakes-Jackson and K. Lake (Grand Rapids, 1966), pp. 20f., Bater, *op. cit.*, pp. 61f., Wilckens, *Auferstehung*, pp. 38f. and S.G. Wilson, "The Ascension: A Critique and an Interpretation," *ZNW*, 59 (1968), pp. 269ff.

438 Cf. below, pp. 214ff.

group of disciples is assembled behind locked doors in the scene of Jesus' appearance before them (20:19-29). An appearance with the general setting of the sea of Tiberias in Galilee is recorded then in 21:1-14. These are then the johannine witnesses to the story tradition.

Having probed the distinctions and relationships within the varied and complex resurrection traditions we proceed now to a history-of-tradition analysis of these gospel appearance stories as a distinct *Gattung* in the remainder of our investigation. A visual representation of the place of this *Gattung* in relationship to others and at the same time the task yet ahead of us in tracing its origins is offered below.

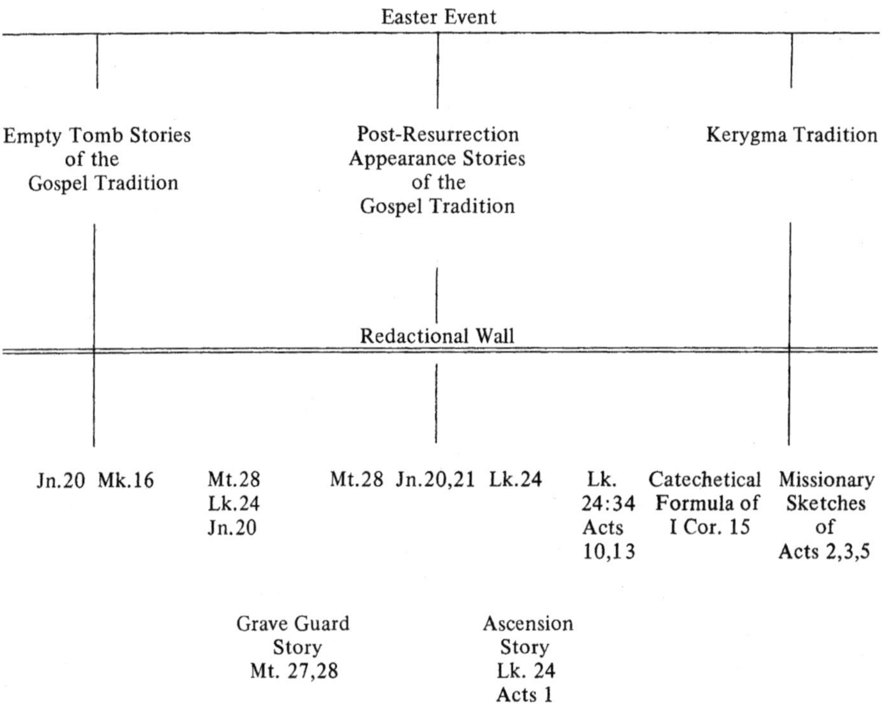

Uncertain is the exact placement of the so-called "displaced" stories, the heavenly radiance appearance type (Acts 9, 22, 26?) and appearances ἐν πνεύματι, while "Mk." 16:9-20 and the extra-canonical sources—perhaps with the exception of the GP and the Gospel of the Hebrews (?)—clearly presuppose the redactional wall itself. (Chronological relationship is not necessarily implied in all instances, but rather the emphasis lies on essential relationships).

III. The Post-Resurrection Appearance Stories of the Gospel Tradition: Traditional Matrix and *Gattung*

A. The Separation of Tradition from Redaction

As was expressed in the diagram to chapter II the appearance stories of the gospels confront us with a traditional stratum independent of both that of the kerygma and the empty tomb. Our goal in this chapter is to pursue an analysis of that stratum as far back into its traditional origins as formal categories will allow. Our first task, therefore, is to determine which elements of those stories can be attributed to redactional enlargement of an earlier source so that we may arrive at their original, pre-redactional matrix. The second step will be to compare the elements of structure, motifs and vocabulary of each traditional matrix to see if they share a common form sufficiently fixed to call it a *Gattung*. In the next chapter then we shall enlarge the scope of comparison to possible analogies in the primitive Christian surroundings. With the initial goal in mind of separating tradition from redaction the selection of text material with the greatest amount of cross section comparative potential would recommend itself. This would mean that we must begin with the group appearance stories in Mt. 28:16-20, Lk. 24:36-49 and Jn. 20:19-29. An additional advantage to starting here is that redactional tendencies, which are characteristic of these three evangelists, will have gained distinct profile and, therefore, be more easily identifiable in our analysis of subsequent stories (Mt. excepted). We shall begin with a brief characterization and disposition of the texts.

1. The Group Appearance

Mt. 28:16-20

Characteristic of the matthaean group appearance, as of the lukan and johannine as well, is that the disciples are gathered together. In contrast to the latter two, however, Mt's account is conspicuously terse. The focus of the account is clearly the address of the resurrected/appearing One and the sending. Vss. 16 and 17 supply the elements of context and the general description of the encounter and reaction. The transition from the conclusion to the grave guard story and Jewish polemic is a forced one and a strong indication that traditional material is being introduced. Vss. 18-20 then constitute the address itself. No reaction of the disciples to the address is mentioned, nor is any particular specification given to the nature of the appearing One's departure thereafter or his continuing presence. It must be said that the form of this concluding scene reflects a characteristically ancient near eastern form of expression.

Lk. 24:36-49

In the lukan narrative the picture is one of greater detail in several respects. First, it is more closely bound to the foregoing appearance than in the matthaean narrative. One does not know in Mt. whether or not the disciples heard the report of the women, but in Lk. there is no question: it appeared to them to be unbelievable. The same kind of clear progression is retained in relationship to the Emmaus story. In contrast to Mt., moreover, is the placement of the appearance: it is not Galilee but Jerusalem. Most striking, however, are the details of representation in comparison to Mt. An overview of the broad themes includes: 1) the sudden appearance of Jesus evokes a reaction of fear and consternation in the disciples, 2) recognizing this the appearing One attempts to restore them to faith through a) showing his hands and feet and speaking to them about the difference between himself and a spirit apparition, b) inviting them to touch him and c) asking for some food and eating fish before them, 3) after a pause presumably for the transition to faith, Jesus explains to them from scripture a) that the Christ had to suffer b) had to rise again on the third day and c) that repentance in his name for the forgiveness of sins is to be preached to the nations, 4) the disciples are witnesses of all these things and finally 5) they are to wait in the city for the promise of the Father, power from on high. The disposition of the lukan group appearance corresponds in the main to the development of these themes.

Jn. 20:19-23, 24-29

Much like Lk. this group appearance story in Jn. abounds in graphic detail. Similar also are by and large the sophisticated transitions and the placement of the appearance in Jerusalem. A general overlap of motifs is also to be noted between Lk. and Jn. here although the accents set upon them often differ distinctly. For example, in Jn. the disciples are not only in Jerusalem but also behind locked doors "for fear of the Jews," surprise and fear at the appearing One is practically nonexistent, proofs of his corporeality (in particular his Crucifixion) are given but are by and large unmotivated, a pronouncement of peace is repeated in vss. 19, 21 and 26 and then a sending coupled with a direct imparting of the Holy Spirit. The institutional form of the latter bears certain similarities to the sending in Mt. The greatest single difference between Jn. and the other two is the way in which not one but two group appearance stories are pictured, i.e., vss. 24-29 build ostensibly a second group encounter, but in actuality it is a thematic extension of the first in order to focus attention on the question of the proper, believing response to the resurrection message. The role of Thomas here is for him to stand as prototype of an inappropriate response to the apostolic witness. The disposition then of Jn. also corresponds to the placement and development of the aforementioned motifs with the vss. 24ff. assuming the place of an appendix under a separate and distinct question, namely, the Easter kerygma.

a. The Participants

As stated above, a distinguishing feature of these texts is that the entire group of disciples is the designated recipient of the appearance of the resurrected One, and in each of the gospels it comes compositionally at the end of other appearance sequences. These factors raise the question of the origin and significance of the participant motif here and its relationship to the same motif in the accounts connected with it. In terms of the variety of expression and complexity of relationships Lk's account is clearly the most difficult, then come Jn and Mt. We shall consider them now then in that order.

Lk.

He does not say that "Christ" or "Jesus" appeared. He says rather that "he" [*αὐτός*, 24:36] entered and stood in their midst. Who is the "he" and who are the "them" to whom he appeared? Neither term comes to illumination without considering the whole lukan passion narrative. This is necessary since in 24:36ff. we find nothing other than personal pronouns and 3rd person singular verb conjugations outside of direct address to represent the appearing One. It is clear, therefore, that the identity of this One is already clear from context. The same is true of the group to whom the risen One appears. The usage looks like the following:

He
vs. 15 *αὐτὸς Ἰησοῦς*
vs. 34 *κύριος*
vs. 36 *αὐτός*
vs. 39 *αὐτός*

They
vs. 9 *ἕνδεκα καὶ πᾶσιν τοῖς λοιποῖς*
vs. 10 *πρὸς τοὺς ἀποστόλους*
vs. 13 *δύο ἐξ αὐτῶν*
vs. 33 *ἕνδεκα καὶ τοὺς σὺν αὐτοῖς*
vss. 34f. *αὐτοί / αὐτοῖς*
vs. 36 *αὐτῶν*
vs. 40 *αὐτοῖς*
vs. 41 *αὐτῶν / αὐτοῖς*
vs. 43 *αὐτῶν*

The decisive verses are therefore located prior to the group appearance itself. The sequence factor is also key for Lk. The Resurrection is communicated to the women by two heavenly messengers and not through a direct appearance of the risen One. A very strong literary development of the group identity occurs in the following transitions:

vs. 11 *καὶ ἐφάνησαν ἐνώπιον αὐτῶν ὡσεὶ λῆρος τὰ ῥήματα ταῦτα καὶ ἠπίστουν αὐταῖς*
vs. 13 *καὶ ἰδοὺ δύο ἐξ αὐτῶν ἐν αὐτῇ τῇ ἡμέρᾳ...*
vs. 34 *λέγοντας ὅτι ὄντως ἠγέρθη ὁ κύριος καὶ ὤφθη Σίμωνι*

Thus Lk ties all of the elements of the resurrection story most convincingly together and by doing so points with particular emphasis to the group encounter. It is in this respect that we find that 24:34 is really a very central transition for the lukan narrative as a whole. As noted above, it is the only place in the whole gospel tradition where the same basic form of kerygmatic statement as in I Cor. 15 is preserved. We find that the Resurrection itself is mentioned [*ἠγέρθη*], that the appearance [*ὤφθη*] of the Lord before Peter is alluded to and that the drama is unfolded on the verge of the group appearance. Although the Emmaus story will receive special treatment below it is worth mentioning here that the story serves to tie the whole sequence of appearances uniquely together. Not only is the stage thereby set for the coming event of the group appearance, but also the foregoing announcement of the heavenly messengers is also drawn to the reader's recollection. Useful in this respect is the development of the passion narrative with its repeated concern for the identity question.[439] In all three accounts, i.e., the tomb story, the Emmaus story and in the group appearance, the significance of the plan of God in the suffering of the Messiah and his rising from the dead come repeatedly to the fore.[440] The compositional sophistication of the whole is really quite striking. We are justified, therefore, in identifying the members participating in the appearance with the pointers thereto found in the prior but coordinated narratives.

Jn.

In 20:19ff. we find a somewhat more simplified arrangement of the participants in comparison with Lk. The personal pronoun structure of the lukan account is contrasted herewith by a greater interest in and reliance upon more direct and immediate proper nouns. Nevertheless, the internal pointers of the preceding account, principally the Magdalene story (vss. 14-18), serve to accentuate the group appearance in much the same way as the Emmaus story for Lk. Whereas the heavenly messengers send the women to the disciples (lukan terminology notwithstanding at this point) in Lk., the risen One himself does this in vs. 17 and Mary obeys in vs. 18. Thus in this appearance immediately preceding the one before the whole group we find the following identity factors:

He
vss. 14,15,16,17 Ἰησοῦς

439 Cf. 23:35ff., 46ff. and 24:3ff., also E. Lohse, *Die Auferstehung Jesu Christi im Zeugnis des Lukasevangeliums*, BSt, 31, ed. by O. Weber, H. Gollwitzer and H.-J. Kraus (Neukirchen, 1961), p. 36.
440 Cf. also 9:21ff. and 18:31ff.

vss. 18,(15) *κύριος*
vs. 16 *ῥαββουνί* (*διδάσκαλε*)[441]

They
vs. 17 *ἀδελφοί μου*

In the group appearance we find all of the designations ı .he risen One as found in the Magdalene story (outside of the last), but a different term for the group. The designations are as follows:

He
vss. 19,21,24,26,29 *Ἰησοῦς*
vss. 20,25,28 *κύριος* (the latter united with the confession of the risen One as "my Lord and my God")

They
vss. 19,20,25,26,(30) *μαθηταί*[442]
vs. 24 *δώδεκα*

We thus see at a glance that with the exception of vs. 16 in the Magdalene story and vs. 24 of the group appearance the terms of identification are both consistent and uniform. What may be said of the two exceptions? The second, namely 20:24, appears at first glance to be the only location in the gospel tradition that directly seems to preserve the terminology of I Cor. 15 in the group appearance. A closer look, however, places this assumption under considerable doubt. We find that in the whole gospel, with the exception of two locations, the favorite term of Jn. for the followers of Jesus is *μαθηταί*. This is even true of the very important chapters 13-16, which play an immediate role in the formation of the resurrection narratives for Jn. The two exceptions are 1) the designation *φίλος* to describe the relationship between Jesus and his own,[443] the term *δώδεκα* in the confession of Peter.[444] Of primary concern here is the latter. In 6:67 "the twelve" are addressed by Jesus, in vs. 70 Jesus asks if he has not chosen them "the twelve" and then in vs. 71 the narrator adds that Judas, the betrayer, was "one of the twelve." It appears that vs. 71b as an editorial comment is superfluous in the light of vs. 70. In vss. 67 and 70, therefore, we find the only two locations in Jn. where the group is addressed as "the twelve." This in itself is of considerable interest since the confession of Peter in the synoptic tradition is not associated with the term "the twelve" at all, but rather *οἱ μαθηταί*,[445] but more than this we see that the confession is insolubly connected

441 Cf. 11:8.
442 Cf. 21:1,2,4,7,8,12,14 (20,23,24).
443 Cf. 15:13-15.
444 Cf. 6:67,70f.
445 Cf. Mk. 8:27ff. parr.

to the betrayal prophecy in Jn., i.e., the editorial comment of vs. 71 points to the fundamental reason for the use of "the twelve" here at all: the *betrayer* was one of them. Put another way, the term does not stand here independently. It exists rather in an epexegetical relationship to the betrayer. Is this true of 20:24? The person involved is Thomas instead of Judas, but the relationship does in fact seem to exist when we observe the development of the narrative. Prior to vs. 24 the group is quite clearly referred to as *οἱ μαθηταί*. In vs. 24 itself Thomas and not the group is the center of attention, and then in the following verses, when the attention is again shifted back to the group as a whole, the term "the twelve" quickly drops out and *μαθηταί* is again the accepted term. The conclusion seems obvious and persuasive. The term "the twelve" in 20:24 has its roots not in the group appearance tradition, but rather in the relationship of a single member of the group to the whole. It is true that this phrase *Θωμᾶς δὲ εἷς ἐκ τῶν δώδεκα* does not occur elsewhere in either the synoptic or johannine tradition, but we have already seen that it does occur with Judas as the subject in 6:71. The fact that the same phrase occurs of Judas in 12:4 with *μαθηταί* instead of *δώδεκα* and is associated with the designation "the twelve" in the synoptic tradition [446] may indicate that for both currents of tradition a very early relationship existed between the naming of individual members and the use of the term "the twelve" for that group. In any case such is almost certainly so with the betrayal tradition and that the influence of this formulation may have played a role in the formulation of 20:24 seems very probable in the light of the above. The significance of this relationship is an exegetical problem for Jn. and as such is not of primary interest to our investigation. That is to say that we have seen primary stress for Jn. on the term *μαθηταί* when the group itself is designated independent of particular members. This is especially clear in vs. 25 where we find: *οἱ ἄλλοι μαθηταί*.

The second exception to uniformity, namely vs. 17 *ἀδελφοί μου*, supplies a most interesting pointer to the group appearance. When we examine the term in its other johannine contexts we find ourselves confronted with the following question: does this term refer here to the disciples or to the family of Jesus? If the former is the case then a johannine reformation of the tradition may be assumed. If, on the other hand, the members of the family are intended then the appearance to the disciples would not here find a pointer, the Magdalene story would demonstrate a special independence and a new element unique in the gospel tradition would be introduced, namely, the family of Jesus is singled out for a special communication of the Resurrection. The former, however, has the benefit of context where the group appearance is the fulfillment of the promise to Mary and while the latter is a possibility since Jn. often makes a deliberate distinction between the two groups, i.e., the disciples and his brothers, it is—as with "the twelve" of vs. 24—an exegetical problem for Jn. [447]

446 Cf. Mt. 26:14, 47 par. Similar is Hartmann, *op. cit.*, pp.217f.
447 Cf. also 2:12; 7:3, 5 and 21:23.

Mt.

Unlike Lk and Jn, Mt presents the group appearance with references to the identity of both the group and the appearing One in such a way that it could exist independent of the rest of the resurrection narrative. The references are as follows:

He
vss. 16,18 ὁ Ἰησοῦς
vs. 17 αὐτόν

They
vs. 16 οἱ δὲ ἕνδεκα μαθηταί
vs. 16 αὐτοῖς
vs. 17 οἱ δέ

The simplicity of this scheme is consistent (one exception) with the verses preceding the group appearance. The one exception is, like Jn. 20:17 *ἀδελφοί μου*, to be found in the redactional 28:10. The women have been assured by the heavenly messenger that the "crucified Jesus" is alive and have been instructed to take this message to "his disciples" [*μαθηταί*]. They have been told to tell them that he is going before them [*προάγει*] into Galilee and that they will themselves have a visual encounter with him personally [*ἐκεῖ αὐτὸν ὄψεσθε*, vs. 7]. The women are then encountered by the risen One himself as they run from the tomb and the name of the risen One is simply ὁ Ἰησοῦς with the omission of the term "the Crucified." The only departure in the address itself is the redactional statement in vs. 10, *ἀδελφοί μου*.[448] The group here designated is almost certainly the disciples, as for Mt the group appearance in Galilee is the fulfillment of the promise made by the angel and the risen One. Although the term is associated with the Magdalene pericope, it does not recur in the group tradition. It is not "the brothers" that are gathered together, but rather "the eleven disciples." It is interesting to note that Mt mentions the group only once (the personal pronouns not included) in vss. 16ff., but with this addition of the number eleven. This is the only place in the NT where this combination occurs. Outside of this reference, moreover, the number eleven does not occur other than in four sparce references in Lk./Acts.[449] It seems clear then that as we observed Jn mentioning the relationship of one member to the group in 20:24, and in a way reminiscent of the betrayal tradition, so too we find Mt here specifying the nature of the group, i.e., they are the disciples, who in spite of the betrayal (27:3-10) and absence of Judas, remained together.[450]

Noteworthy is that for Mt. the term *κύριος* does not once appear for the risen One in the appearance tradition. It appears as an epexegetical genitive in 28:2 in

448 Cf. for the ἀδελφός-notion Mt. 12:46ff. and 25:40.
449 Lk. 24:9, 33 and Acts 1:26;2:14–"Mk." 16:14 is not included here.
450 Cf. Strecker, *op. cit.*, p. 208.

describing the heavenly messenger and the reference in 28:6 is text-critically an interpolation. For Mt the lordship motif is established in another way.[451]

We thus have before us the three principal sources for considering the participants in the group appearance. The question to be decided now is: do we find any element in the group motif among the above described factors that may be singled out as common to all sources and, therefore, to be recognized as early traditional material existing as a stratum prior to the redaction of the evangelists? We turn first to the identity of the risen One. He is:

Lk. 24	*Jn. 20*		*Mt. 28*
vs. 3 Lord Jesus	vss. 14,15,16,17	Jesus	vs. 5 Jesus (the Crucified)
vs. 15 Jesus	vss. 19,21,24,26,29	Jesus	vss. 9,10,16,18 Jesus
vs. 34 Lord	vss. (15),17	Lord	
	vss. 20,25,28	Lord ("...and my God" vs.28)	
	vs. 16,(11,8)	Rabbi	

We see at a glance, therefore, that the proper name "Jesus" is common to all and that for Lk. and Jn. "Lord" is also used as a specific term, while such fails for Mt. as a direct reference, but is, nevertheless, implied.

In considering the group itself we find the following:

Lk. 24	*Jn. 20*		*Mt. 28*	
vs. 9 eleven and all the rest	vss. 19,20,25,26	disciples	vss. 7,8	disciples
vs. 10 the apostles	vs. 24	the twelve	vs. 16	eleven disciples
vs. 13 two of them	vs. 17	my brothers	vs. 10	my brothers
vs. 33 eleven and those with them				

This group identity seems to have been more subject to redactional influences than the identity of the risen One. We find that for Lk. a direct parallel to Jn. or Mt. does not exist although it seems relatively clear that the pointers prior to the group appearance in content do parallel the other two. In Mt. and Jn. the most common term is "disciples" and the variations have been shown to be by and large redactional elements. The two references to "my brothers" (Jn. 20:17 and Mt. 28:10) are redactional peculiarities as well. We thus arrive at the following conclusions for the group texts themselves: the risen One is identified with the *Jesus* of the disciples' former experience, the crucified One,[452] and he is recognized directly (Lk. and Jn.)

451 Cf. the direct address of the commissioning words.

452 Marxsen, *Problem*, pp. 22ff. chooses to separate this recognition of Jesus from the

or indirectly (Mt.) as the *Lord*. The recipients of the encounter are the *disciples*, who have remained together after the betrayal of Judas, being, therefore, eleven in number. We find from this statistical breakdown that we are immediately confronted with two questions: 1) what christological significance did the identity of the risen One play in these accounts and 2) what relationship does the assembled group have to the rest of the thematic elements of the appearance?

The Jesus and/or Lord statements of these texts are to be understood in terms of their christological implications. The history and development of NT Christology is, of course, a theme in itself, [453] but aspects of the problem in connection with the Easter tradition need to be drawn into the scope of our questioning. While the identity of the appearing One in the gospel accounts is "Jesus" and/or "Lord" the term "Christ" does not appear at all; the latter, however, is the only designation of identity for the kerygma of I Cor. 15. The question is: why? To posit a Palestinian environment for the "Christ" terminology and a missionary one for the "Lord" terminology is an oversimplification of the issues involved. [454] It is recognized that the development of christological terminology had a complex history in which various streams of tradition interacted upon one another.[455] It is important, however, that we develop the question from the internal evidence of the texts before us and ask: what theological environment and what strata of tradition could be re-

entire notion of the "resurrected One" on the assumption that the latter is the product of later theological reflection and, therefore, not a viable category at all for the earliest tradition, i.e., it is *Interpretament vis-à-vis* Jewish apocalyptic. Cf. also Kegel, *op. cit.*, p. 20. As we have seen this distinction is questionable. In this regard cf. the critique of G. Friedrich, "Die Auferstehung Jesu, eine Tat Gottes oder ein Interpretament der Jünger? ," *KuD*, 17 (1971), pp. 153ff., esp. 179ff. and his "Die Bedeutung der Auferweckung Jesu nach Aussagen des Neuen Testaments," *ThZ*, 27 (1971), pp. 305ff. In a recent article entitled "Christian Origins and Resurrection Faith," *JRel*, 52 (1972), pp. 41ff., W.O. Walker, Jr., has advanced the thesis (as an extension to earlier reflections on Christian origins) that after the Crucifixion it was the experiences of "pneumatic phenomena" (not the Resurrection) comparable to those of Jesus' earthly ministry that proved decisive in convincing the earliest Christians that the delay of the parousia was only apparent and that Jesus had, in fact, assumed his eschatological kingly rule, and then only subsequently out of this eruption of enthusiasm via scriptural exegesis of Deut. 18,15-19 and Psa. 68,19a based on an analogy from current Jewish assumption stories about Moses and Elijah resurrection faith was born. As ingenious as this explanation is it becomes necessary to differ with Walker on 1) his overly simplified view of Jesus' relationship to his religious environment, 2) his approach to understanding Jesus' impression upon his disciples (reminiscent of the psychological approach discussed in our introduction, pp. 20f.), 3) his assumption that the ecclesiastical situation expressed in Acts and above all in the Corinthian correspondence is valid for the earliest Palestinian community and 4) his somewhat pat explanation for the relative scarcity of Psa. 68,19a references in our texts. Placing greater emphasis on the rational over against the exegetical and the psychological over against the pneumatic, but otherwise showing a significant number of similarities to the orientation of Walker is Teeple, *op. cit.*, pp. 107ff., esp. 117ff. Cf. further, K. Niederwimmer, *Jesus* (Gött., 1968), pp. 77ff., also below n. 590.

453 Cf. above all O. Cullmann, *Die Christologie des Neuen Testaments* (Tüb., 1957), F. Hahn, *Christologische Hoheitstitel* (Gött., 1966 [='63]), and W. Kramer, *Christos Kyrios Gottessohn* (Zürich, 1963). Cf. review of the latter by H. Hegermann in the *ThLZ*, 92 (1967), cols. 589-593.

454 Contra W. Foerster, "κύριος," *ThW*, III, p. 1093.

455 Cf. esp. Hahn, *Hoheitstitel, passim* and Kramer, *op. cit., passim.*

sponsible for the christological designations before us? We have already seen that the proper name "Jesus" is quite key to the identity of and continuity with the person of the earthly Jesus. This means, therefore, that the christological concern of these texts is in part represented by the terminus κύριος (the two exceptions– "my Lord and my God" Jn. 20:28, and "Rabbi" Jn. 20:16–correspond quite clearly to the redactional interests of the johannine gospel)[456] and in part by indications of honor and awe in the stories themselves. That is to say, the terminus alone is not the only index for christological significance. We saw for example, that Mt. does not use the title itself, but the scene and the expression "they worshipped him" suggest a view of the appearing One corresponding to an honorific title. In Lk. too where the terminus is used it does not stand alone but is filled out with the address of the resurrected One in vss. 44ff., in particular the confessional statement put in his mouth that the "Christ" had to suffer etc., and in Jn. the motifs of joy and reception of the Holy Spirit from the mouth of the resurrected One also lend important support to the presence of the terminus. Each of these categories has key significance for a redactional understanding of the texts and although we shall deal in part with these problems below where the motifs appear our central concern is not with this level. The christological significance for all at the pre-redactional level anchors itself in the sending theme common to all. This Jesus appears as the One who has been raised and, therefore, in eschatological power can send the disciples to preach. Whatever elements of distinct christological development accrue to this fundamental conviction, they share at their core an understanding of the Lord who lives and sends.

Excursus: ΚΥΡΙΟΣ ἸΗΣΟΥΣ

The terminus κύριος itself does, however, raise the question of its background and we must, therefore, sketch briefly the spectrum of problems.

The formula κύριος Ἰησοῦς (I Cor. 12:3) was clearly the central confession of the Hellenistic church and with it came to expression in that environment the notion of the risen One's exaltation to power and authority at the right hand of God, where he is the cosmological Lord of both the church and the world. If one posits a Hellenistic background for the gospel appearance stories on the whole,[457] then it is quite simple to accept this perspective as definitive for the meaning of "Lord" here. This solution is problematic, however, because it does not take into account the possibility of a) an earlier usage of the Lord terminology and, therefore, of b) another origin for the gospel appearance texts as a whole. In contrast to the confinement of the κύριος terminology to the Hellenistic world and its influence on the Christian community,[458] it has been demonstrated that the "Lord" terminology with reference to Jesus already had a place within the Palestinian environment of the early church before its missionary expansion

456 Hartmann, *op. cit.*, p. 216, thinks that Jn's use of κύριος may reflect an ancient confession as part of the *Vorlage* since he maintains that the evangelist himself displays no particular interest in reserving the title for the resurrected One.

457 E.g., among others, Wilckens, "Ursprung," p. 94.

458 Bousset, *op. cit.*, esp. pp. 77ff., W. Heitmüller, "Zum Problem Paulus und Jesus," *ZNW*, 13 (1912), pp. 333f. and his "Jesus und Paulus," *ZThK*, 25 (1915), pp. 176f., and Bultmann, *Theologie*, para. 7,5 and 12.

into the Hellensitic world; in fact, it is most probable that Jesus himself was addressed as "Lord" in his earthly ministry.[459] The decisive question, of course, is what this designation meant. Hahn traces the use of the term "Lord" through the relationship that Jesus had with his disciples contained in the aramaic terms רב and מר . He differentiates most radically, however, between the original address which took its meaning from profane usage and as such was the equivalent of a polite form of address[460] and that of later theological enlargement in which the divine lordship of Christ was made express and precise. Says Hahn:

"Schon auf Grund dieser sprachlichen Erwägungen ist damit zu rechnen, daß Jesus nicht nur mit רבי , sondern ebenso mit מרי angesprochen wurde. Unter keinen Umständen darf bei der Anrede מרי/*κύριε* eine auf Jesus übertragene Gottesbezeichnung angenommen werden. Es geht um einen ursprünglich profanen Sprachgebrauch, dem erst allmählich eine besondere christologische Bedeutung aufgeprägt wurde und der von der Herrenbezeichnung Gottes daher zunächst grundsätzlich unterschieden blieb."[461]

The question is: to what degree is this distinction justified? The answer to this question is bound up with the meaning of the old Palestinian eucharistic formula *μαρανα θά* and its relationship to the notion of the exaltation of Christ. That the transmission of this Aramaic liturgical formula was taken over into the Hellenistic, Greek-speaking church without translation is almost certain indication of the term's Palestinian origin and importance for that milieu's earliest christology.[462] The rejection of the linguistic evidence and the insistence by Schulz, ". . .die Einordnung des apokalyptischen Bittrufes Maranatha in die Herrenmahlsliturgie stammt erst sekundär aus dem hellenistisch-orientalischen Gemeindebereich"[463] is a mistake. His assumption that an identity would have existed between an *Adonai*-address and the Jesus-directed *Maranatha* leads him to conclude that such was only possible in Hellenistic Christianity because such would ostensibly have been blasphemy within the synagogue-oriented Palestinian church.[464] We shall see that this assumed identity is dubious. The philological considerations allow for two possible translations: 1) "Our Lord, come!" (imperative) or 2) "Our Lord has come"–and is here (indicative).[465] Although Hahn's insistence on the exclusive weight of the imperative[466] is not convincing, it is, nevertheless, in its focus on the parousia and expectation thereof and that in the light of the eucharistic situation (cf. I Cor. 11:26) probably the preferable translation. In support of the future is also Rev. 22:20 and perhaps Phil. 4:5 as well, but the problem is the nature of the future event itself and the relationship of the Eucharist-celebrating congregation to it. In Didache 10:6 the movement of the worship service[467] is from the common meal to the Eucharist as is the case with I Cor. 16:22, 11:26ff. and Rev. 22:20 and the accent in I Cor. 11:26ff. is "worthiness to eat" a warning of eschatological judgment, while for the Didache church discipline as such seems to occupy center stage. Hahn, on the other hand, maintains that the meal itself here is central as an anticipation of the fellowship meal in the eschaton and an expression of eschatological joy; it is alleged that only later did the meal become linked with the death of Jesus and its significance through the notions of vicarious sacrifice, the covenant and the remembrance motif.[468] The position is

459 Hahn, *Hoheitstitel*, pp. 74ff. in contrast to Foerster, *op. cit.*, p. 1093 and L. Goppelt, "Die Herrschaft Christi und die Welt," *Christologie und Ethik, Ges. Auf.* (Gött., 1968), p. 105 and n. 6.

460 Hahn, *Hoheitstitel*, pp. 81f.

461 *Ibid.*, p. 82

462 K.G. Kuhn, "*μαρανα θά*," *ThW*, IV, p. 474, Kramer, *op. cit.*, p. 96, Hahn, *Hoheitstitel*, pp. 100ff. Bultmann, *Theologie*, para. 7,5, maintains, however, that God and not Jesus was the object of the address. Contra, S. Schulz, "Maranatha und Kyrios Jesus," *ZNW*, 53 (1962), p. 126.

463 Schulz, *op. cit.*, p. 127.

464 *Ibid.*, pp. 138ff.

465 For the particulars cf. Kuhn, "*μαρανα θά*," *passim.*

466 Hahn, *Hoheitstitel*, pp. 103f.

467 Cf. Acts 20:7, 11.

468 Hahn, *Hoheitstitel*, p. 105.

attractive because it takes seriously the fact that Jesus and not God is the object of the address,[469] which is clearly the case in comparison with the tradition in the Didache, which independent of Paul goes back to the Palestinian church. Behind Hahn's position, however, is a church which was fashioned by its hope for an imminent return of the Lord and by its enthusiastic experiences of the Spirit. Thus the "later" development of theological reflection on the death and Resurrection of Jesus in this context is a necessary postulate to allow for the "delay" of the parousia. Is that the Palestinian church?

Cullmann[470] ascribes from the very beginning a comparable weight to the *Maranatha* formula in the cult of the Palestinian church as to the "*kyrios* Jesus" formula of the Hellenistic church, i.e., *göttlicher Herrscher*. He thereby stresses the second translation: the indicative, but we would tend to agree with Hahn's critique[471] that this neglects the difference between function and being in the thought of the primitive church and would ask if there be another approach to the question of the indicative. Schweizer has pointed out correctly that the notion of discipleship and the relationship of the Lord to the disciples is central to the question of what the future holds[472] and it is exactly this relationship—the self-offering of Jesus and his call to discipleship known to the disciples before the cross—that determines the meaning of the Eucharist. This perspective points to the centrality of the cross and Resurrection as that which gives meaning to both the present and future for his own and makes possible the "thy kingdom come" of the Lord's Prayer, because the Lord's kingdom comes with his coming! As Schweizer has put it:

"Wir sind davon ausgegangen, daß zunächst für die erste Gemeinde das Ostereignis die entscheidende Tatsache gebildet hat. Sie hat es als die Erhöhung Jesu zur Rechten Gottes verstanden."[473]

We would, therefore, agree with Kuhn[474] that it is correct to leave both sides open when it comes to the translation of the *Maranatha* formula. In both cases, however, the decisive question is how the exaltation concept in the primitive church differed from that of the Hellenistic church. Hahn's distinction between function and being in his critique of Cullmann is perhaps a good one in evaluating the exaltation concept of the two environments in question. We have already seen that the *Maranatha* prayer form is primarily an appeal for the parousia, i.e., the exaltation of Jesus is conceptualized as the "coming One."[475] A "being" or "position" as such remains at this early stage that of simply the "resurrected One," who has been established by God. In the synoptic tradition we see that this perspective of the exaltation of the Lord stands alongside the terms *Rabbi* and *Didascalos* which did not become terms of dignity in this respect. Another aspect is seen in the view of Jesus as the divine Helper.[476] Particularly instructive is the development of the absolute sense of "Lord" in connection with the notion: the Lord is the Master who calls to discipleship (Mt. 8:19-22) and provides the idea of the student/teacher, servant/master relationship (Mt. 10:24f. and Lk. 6:14). We see this absolute use of κύριος in Mk. 2:3 but primarily in Lk. and then in Paul as well.[477] This absolute use developed from the address form κύριε and is the form which we find chiefly in the Hellenistic church as well.

The question is: do overlapping lines of continuity and development exist here between the two environments? Kramer replies in the negative and maintains that the two are distinct and

469 In contrast to R. Bultmann, cf. n. 462.

470 Cullmann, *Christologie*, pp. 212f. and p. 219.

471 Hahn, *Hoheitstitel*, p. 106.

472 E. Schweizer, *Erniedrigung und Erhöhung bei Jesus und seinen Nachfolgern* (Zürich, 1962), p. 83.

473 *Ibid.*, p. 77.

474 Kuhn, "μαραναθά," p. 475.

475 Cf. Psa. 110.

476 Cf. the προσκυνέω-context in Mk. 7:28 and Mt. 8:6, 8 and 15:25, 27.

477 8x in Lk's redactional material and 7x in his special source material. Among the numerous pauline locations cf. Gal. 1:13 and I Cor. 9:5, thereto cf. Eusebius, *hist. ecc.*, I,7,14.

separate notions which grew up simultaneously and independent of one another.[478] This view has an element of truth in it in that the streams of tradition and their influence are here taken seriously, but it is too rigid and schematic in its form- and history-of-tradition criteria. *Kyrios* is by no means a mere translation of *Mari*, but the place of this Aramaic formula in the Greek-speaking, Hellenistic community is not fortuitous. To maintain that the Lord concept already existed in the Hellenistic church, perhaps even before the *Mari* formula, and that this was then simply absorbed as a complementary element is arbitrary because it fails to account for the fact that the *Kyrios* of the Hellenistic church is essentially an expansion and filling out of the content of the *Mari* formula. In this formula the parousia is central with a relative link to the present; for the *Kyrios* form the present reign of the exalted One is central with a relative link to a cosmological future. This latter had to be the case because the *Kosmokrator* in the world for the church was always the devil; the lordship of Jesus was a hidden lordship which became manifest through the preaching of the church, i.e., in faith.[479] The primitive church thought in terms of a durative history and the exalted One's relationship to it (the Church and the world) while the Hellenistic church thought in terms of the cosmological development of time and spheres of power over which the exalted One exercises his authority. The bridge between the two notions is a matter of how the addressee of the *Maranatha* plea is conceptualized. Schulz maintains that he is the Messiah of God, i.e., God's functionary and not the One appearing in God's place and the One whom the church asks to exercise his judgment office.[480] This view fails to take into account that the Messiah was never addressed in prayer within Judaism. Rather than "functionary" of God it would be preferable to understand the Messiah as representative of God, he who stands in God's place and to whom the church could pray. *Maranatha* does not stand for *Adonai* here,[481] but it comes very near to God in content.[482] This placement of equality between the Messiah and the Lord is the link between *Maranatha* and the *Kyrios* notion in the two environments. This has occurred through the placing of the exalted One to the right hand of God, i.e., in the place of God. This occurs finally for the Hellenistic church in the consummation where he is ultimately Lord. We see here how the *Maranatha* formula has been extended and filled out within the linguistic and conceptual world of Hellenism.[483] Thus, for both communities the enthronement of this exalted One existed in the tension of the "already" and "not yet" dialectic.[484]

We see, therefore, that the christological statements of the pre-redactional level of tradition as well as those of the redactional played a central role in the interpretation of the identity aspect for all of the group appearance stories. For this and other reasons one must object to the distinction between the "return to the existence of the disciples by Jesus" and the "Resurrection of Jesus, the Lord" as later *Interpretament*;[485] Jesus is at this inception of the appearance tradition not merely the One who is alive again, but it is the Lord who in eschatological power confronts and sends the disciples. The localization of the identity aspect placed the appearances in a particular christological light from the very beginning.

The importance, however, of the disciples present in relation to the matter of other thematic elements in the stories is yet to be clarified. Is it significant that in these accounts *all* of the disciples (with the exception of Judas) are present? We

478 Kramer, *op. cit.*, pp. 99ff.
479 Cf. Goppelt, "Herrschaft," pp. 109, 117 *et passim.*
480 Schulz, *op. cit.*, pp. 138ff.
481 Contra, Cullmann, *Christologie*, pp. 199ff. (Eng. ed.).
482 Cf. Acts 2:34-36 and Lk. 12:35-37.
483 Cf. I Cor. 8:5f., where the monotheism notion is bound to that of the Christ as the representative of God.
484 Cf. Phil. 2:10f. and Isaiah 45.
485 Marxsen, *Problem*, pp. 19f. (cf. above, n. 452).

have already seen that the importance of the term "the twelve" comes up only once and that in specific relationship to the redactional interests of the evangelist Jn, but in comparison to all of the other accounts this factor of the assembled disciples here constitutes a distinctive element in the overall structure. As we shall see below each of the appearance complexes is made up of constitutive factors and it is far from arbitrary that this appearance consists of the whole group. The fact of their assemblage is of key importance and their activities are quite secondary; the emphasis is on their simply "being together." This constitutes, as we shall see below, one of the greatest single differences between this complex and the appearance at the sea of Tiberias. Whether or not this aspect suggests that the question is really one of apostolic authority[486] and, therefore, that the motif itself is actually secondary to the *Gattung* cannot be judged prematurely and must wait until the matter of the participants in general for all has received due consideration.

b. The Encounter

With the group context assumed by our primary texts we find that the entry of Jesus into their midst comes at a moment of surprise. For Lk. we find the following usage of this theme:

> 24:36 *ταῦτα δὲ αὐτῶν λαλούντων αὐτὸς ἔστη ἐν μέσῳ αὐτῶν*...(38) *καὶ εἶπεν αὐτοῖς*...

For Jn. the following is to be observed:

> 20:19 ...*ἦλθεν ὁ Ἰησοῦς καὶ ἔστη εἰς τὸ μέσον καὶ λέγει αὐτοῖς*...

And for Mt. the following:

> 28:18 *καὶ προσελθὼν ὁ Ἰησοῦς ἐλάλησεν αὐτοῖς*...

486 Cf., e.g., Albertz and Brun above in the introduction, pp. 24ff., and the first appearance problem, pp. 61ff. It is not our purpose to rehearse the many-sided problem of the relationship of the circle of disciples of the earthly ministry to the institution of the apostolate. Cf. Hennecke-Schneemelcher, *op. cit.*, II, pp. 3-52, Goppelt, *Zeit*, pp. 121ff., G. Klein, *Die Zwölf Apostel. Ursprung und Gehalt einer Idee*, FRLANT, 77 (Gött., 1961), pp. 13f., 204f. *et passim* and J. Roloff, *Apostolat–Verkündigung–Kirche* (Gütersloh, 1965), pp. 159ff., 232ff. *et passim*. As we noted earlier the designations used for the group appear to have been far more subject to redactional alteration than was the case for the identity of the appearing One. Moreover, we noted that only Lk refers to them expressly as the "apostles" and that common to them all is either the numerical designation the "eleven" or its approximation or the term the "disciples." It is of central interest for the earliest form of the designation of the participants, therefore, to anchor the appearance to this particular group, the one that had been chosen by Jesus in the earthly ministry, for thereby the continuity with the past is re-established after the cross. The degree to which one may posit for the group motif here a relationship in the other direction, namely the grounding of the apostolate, in the earliest period is uncertain. In part an answer is tied up with the commission motif to be considered below.

We notice immediately that we are confronted by what appear to be the words of the narrator as he sets the scene for what is to follow. The question is, however, which narrator? The statements are too similar to be mere coincidence. We note that the degree of variation is really quite negligible and that those which are present seem to serve basically the stylistic interests of the writer.[487] The placement of the entry of Jesus upon the scene varies according to the evangelist's preference—it takes place immediately for Lk., but follows very important redactional statements in both Jn. and Mt.—but the element of his coming itself is basic to all: Jesus comes and encounters the disciples. Prior to his initiative here he has been absent from them. According to the representations he comes from outside of their experience into a present reality. How is this pictured by the evangelists?

For Lk. and Jn. the setting is Jerusalem and he comes *ἐν* [*εἰς τὸ*] *μέσῳ αὐτῶν*, while for Mt. it is Galilee and the encounter is simply *προσελθών*. The question is, of course, which of the forms is original? That is, have Lk and Jn incorporated the *ἐν μέσῳ* forms in order to comply with their setting (indoors?) in Jerusalem or has Mt dropped the *ἐν μέσῳ* form in order to make better sense out of his mountain top encounter? From what we know of the redactional importance of the mountain in general for Mt [488] and the structural importance of the apostolic witness in Jerusalem for Lk and the significance of the inner gathering for Jn [489] one might well attribute all of the statements of location themselves to the evangelist's own interests and theological goals rather than his source. That is to say, it is highly questionable if the group appearance tradition preserved and transmitted a firmly anchored statement on the specifics of location in connection with the appearance at all. The texts indicate that it did not.[490] The matter of his *coming into their midst*, however, would appear to be independent of redactional influence as an extension of the idea of coming itself; Mt. is not even really an exception apparently as he allows the verbal prefix to function in the same way. Similar considerations will recur with regard to other aspects of the appearance representation as we deal with fields of expression rather than rigid insistence upon specific verbal overlap to get at pre-redactional strata. This is a reminder that in all motifs to follow we are con-

487 Cf. for example the shift from parataxis to hypotaxis in Mt.

488 Cf., e.g., Strecker, *op. cit.*, pp. 98 and 208 and G. Bornkamm, "Der Auferstandene und der Irdische. Mt 28,16-20," *Zeit und Geschichte, Fst. R. Bultmann*, ed. by E. Dinkler (Tüb., 1964), p. 171. A. Strobel, "Berg," pp. 135ff. and 144f. proceeds on the assumption that *Offenbarungsstätten* are behind this notion and that it is just as important as tradition behind Lk (ascension) as for Mt, and that the location of Galilee was a key location with which all of the evangelists had to wrestle. Cf. also the literature in n. 490 below.

489 Cf. Jn. 13-16.

490 Correctly Brun, *op. cit.*, pp. 85ff., cf. above in introduction, pp. 24ff. Also Strecker, *op. cit.*, pp. 98 and 108, with regard to Mt. The question of Galilee or Jerusalem as locale for the appearances in general has long been disputed. Cases have been made for both possibilities. Cf. H.W. Bartsch, "Parusieerwartung und Osterbotschaft," *Entmythologisierende Auslegung, Ges. Aufs.*, Theol. Beiträge, 26 (Hamburg-Bergstedt, 1962), pp. 61ff., his "Zum Problem der Parusieverzögerung bei den Synoptikern," *Ges. Aufs.*, pp. 69ff. and his "Die Passions- und Ostergeschichten bei Matthäus," *Ges. Aufs.*, pp. 80ff. (cf. n. 310), E. Lohmeyer, *Galiläa und Jerusalem*, 1936, *passim*, Marxsen, *Markus*, pp. 33ff., Anderson, "Easter Witness," pp. 39f. and

fronted with the controlling question: Can one establish in a gospel complex, which compared to other gospel materials has no parallel—outside perhaps of the birth narratives[491]—in terms of its fluid character and wide-ranging variety, a transmitted traditional kernel behind and relatively unaffected by the redactional themes which are otherwise so dominant and can one identify that kernel with a formal, delineated *Gattung*?

c. The Disciples' Reaction and the Address of the Appearing One

We come upon the implications of this question immediately in the texts. Insolubly united with Jesus' entry into their presence is his immediate coming to expression. He *comes* and *speaks*. The question is: how? Is there a particular form of address that leads us to a common base for all? The question is not an easy one to answer because it is specifically at this point that the accounts begin to depart rapidly from one another through redactional peculiarities. Without specific regard at this point for placement within the stories we can see that there are certain elements that are common and basic to all three accounts. We shall consider them in terms of the influence that they have had upon the nature of Jesus' address.

Because of the brevity and the strong redactional lines in the account we turn first to Mt. We see that the coming of Jesus and his speaking are without a single interruption connected to the words of commission.[492] All authority is given to him and the church is, therefore, to be engaged in the work of evangelization

his *Jesus and Christian Origins* (N.Y., 1964), pp. 195ff., Karnetzki, *op. cit.*, pp. 255f., W. Thüsing, "Erhöhungsvorstellung und Parusieerwartung in der ältesten nachösterlichen Christologie," *BZ*, 11 (1967), pp. 219f., E. Schweizer, *Gemeinde und Gemeindeordnung im Neuen Testament*, AThANT, 35 (Zürich, 1962, 2nd ed.), pp. 30f., n. 100, Descamps, *op. cit.*, pp. 735ff., Grundmann, "Problem," pp. 45ff., W. Rordorf, *Der Sonntag. Geschichte des Ruhe- und Gottesdiensttages im ältesten Christentum*, AThANT, 43 (Zürich, 1962), pp. 227f., J. Rohde, *op. cit.*, pp. 33f., von Campenhausen, *Ablauf*, pp. 12ff., 20, and 44ff., Cribbs, "St. Luke," pp. 450 *et passim*, Evans, *Resurrection*, p. 88, and most recently Steinseifer, *op. cit.*, pp. 232ff. (cf. the reply to the latter of T. Lorenzen, "Ist der Auferstandene in Galiläa erschienen? Bemerkungen zu einem Aufsatz von B. Steinseifer," *ZNW*, 64 (1973), pp. 209ff., who sees correctly that the flight of the disciples after the Crucifixion is a matter of historical probability not to be taken lightly. He argues then chiefly for the Galilaean nature of the Jn. 21 account, but what consequences his focus may have for the geographical localization of the group appearance tradition remains dubious.) In the group appearance stories, at least, Brun's proposal still appears to be the best one: the matter of location is redactionally motivated. The other appearance story traditions may, however, be more firmly anchored in particular locations, as we shall see below.

491 Cf. above, n. 314.

492 The construction itself is clearly matthaean redaction as we shall see below, but it is to be asked if the coming and speaking of Jesus as motif is to be classified as redactional (cf. Strecker, *op. cit.*, p. 209), because of the mere frequency of *προσελθών* and *ἐλάλησεν αὐτοῖς λέγων* in other matthaean redactional material. For J. Zumstein, "Matthieu 28:16-20," *RThPh*, 22 (1972), p. 18, the entire group appearance is to be understood as the redactional composition of Mt out of traditionally independent motifs (not unlike Nützel on the Transfiguration, cf. n. 429).

[μαϑητεύσατε].[493] The question is, however, does the original form of the group appearance consist then, as here according to Mt., chiefly of his *coming* and *speaking* the words of commission? The question finds illumination in a comparison with Lk. and Jn. There we find that a great deal takes place before either of them arrives at the commissioning words. For Jn. a unique aspect of the address takes place immediately and then is repeated, namely the statement: "Peace be with you." The words are to be found in some mss. for Lk. 24:36 but they are to be considered text-critically later interpolation.[494] In the light of the significance of these words for the particularly johannine theological perspective[495] we may assume that the words here have to do not with an independent source but rather with the johannine formation of the address. That is to say, as the Jesus of their former experience had promised them peace in the world through the "comforter," so too here the promise becomes a reality as the Spirit brings peace to them through the mediation of that gift in the risen Lord. In typical johannine hypotaxis another aspect is joined directly to the address, namely the showing of the crucifixion scars. To this is then added the narrator's comment: "Therefore, seeing the Lord the disciples rejoiced." It is only after this sequence that we come to the commissioning words. The sequence for Jn. looks like the following:

1. The disciples are together
2. Jesus comes and enters their presence
3. and says to them, "Peace be with you"
4. and then he shows his scars.
5. *Therefore* the disciples rejoice seeing the Lord.

This scheme is basically duplicated in Lk. The first two points are all but identical and then the next two are reproduced (with the exception of the "Peace" termi-

493 Strecker (*op. cit.*, p. 209) considers the ἐξουσία motif to be non-matthaean, but in the light of the entire form of the group encounter here, which Mt appears to have in mind and which is a variant to the other two texts, it would seem that the term and the form belong together as a special matthaean understanding of the whole encounter. We have already seen, for example, that the lordship of Jesus is established by Mt not in the use of the designation "Lord" but rather in terms of an acclamation; this becomes evident especially in the words of commission, as we shall see. P.H. Lai, "Production du sens par la foi. Autorités religieuses contestées/fondées. Analyse structurale de Matthieu 27,57-28,20," *RSR*, 61 (1973), pp. 65ff., in applying linguistic criteria is not interested in the separation of tradition from redaction and focuses rather upon this element to demonstrate that in context Mt is not offering an apology for the Resurrection, but rather is dealing with the abandonment of religious authority and its reestablishment in Jesus (p. 95).

494 So, e.g., Bailey, *op. cit.*, p. 68, n. 2. Contra is A. George, "Les récits d'apparitions aux onze à partir de Luc 24,36-53," *La Résurrection du Christ et l'Exégèse Moderne* (Paris, 1969), p. 77 and Leaney, "Narratives," p. 112, who dismisses the "it is I, be not afraid" as redactional reminiscence of Mk. 6:50 (cf. also Jn. 20:19), but considers the "Peace" statement not unusual and perhaps a reflection of a common tradition.

495 Cf. Jn. 14:27; 16:33 and here in 20:19, 21 and 26. J. Jeremias, *Theologie*, p. 286, sees such single vocatives as Soul, Mary or Peace as the original forms of address in the tradition which were later extended into speech and dialogues.

nology itself) but in far greater detail. It is interesting to note that for Jn. the "peace" command has nothing to do with the doubt and uncertainty motif in the way that the direct address does for Lk. It is rather fulfillment of chapters 14 and 16 with a glance to the future. The Thomas story serves for Jn. by and large the function of the address in Lk. 24:38ff., i.e., the overcoming of doubts and apprehensions but with the issue of the Easter kerygma at stake.

Before we return, however, to the question of the function of the address of Jesus in direct relationship to the coming theme, i.e., the "going" of Jesus and therefore the commission,[496] we must first establish the meaning of the other aspects of address for Lk. as well as the multiplication of the signs motif. As already seen in the participants question Lk. presents a manifestly complex picture and requires special attention.

We have already seen that for Jn. the words prior to the commission reflect not an independent source, but the theological concern of the evangelist. How does this stand for Lk.? The words of commission do not occur for Lk. until the direct statement of vs. 48 (related, of course, to the OT rehearsal prior to it). It is instructive to note the relation of the words of Jesus to the sign motif which is woven far more convincingly than in Jn. In Jn. the showing of the crucifixion scars is really without literary occasion. By removing the doubt theme from the group of disciples directly so as to focus upon it in the Thomas story Jn has removed the basis for the sign motif, i.e., other than to say that the joy of the disciples was the result of seeing the Lord, the *crucified One.*[497] This is not the case for Lk. The problem of doubts and fears is addressed from the very beginning in word and action. Is this a redactional feature of Lk. or does it bespeak a source? We begin by looking for distinctive lukan traits at key junctures.

The Three Phases of Luke: Part I

The first part of the lukan group appearance can be broken into three basic phases. 1) A genitive absolute construction in vs. 36, clearly a lukan transition in context,[498] links this appearance with the discussion of the disciples over the Emmaus appearance. In this same verse the appearance itself occurs. The expression for the appearance, i.e., the coming of Jesus into their midst, is not terminologically identical with the expression of the kerygma, i.e., ὤφθη, but in content the two

496 We would object, however, to the categories and conclusions applied at this point by Marxsen, *Problem*, pp. 23f. and 33f. when he speaks about the furtherance of the *Sache Jesu,* although he correctly sees that the commission is indeed a focal point of this tradition.

497 Bailey, *op. cit.*, p. 95, even goes to the extreme of suggesting that not Jn but Lk is really responsible for the Thomas story, i.e., Jn was "so impressed by the Lucan passage that he used it as the basis of not one but two parallel incidents in his gospel." Seeing in the Thomas story rather the work of Jn in focusing the doubt motif at that point are, e.g., Dodd, "Appearances," p. 20 and Bater, *op. cit.*, pp. 59f. Cf. also Leaney, "Narratives," pp. 113f. Seeing in part a Thomas tradition here is Hartmann, *op. cit.*, p. 211 (cf. also below, n. 505).

498 That the *genitivum absolutum* is used in all three synoptic gospels is clear, but Lk is especially fond of such. Cf. Bultmann, *Tradition*, pp. 364, 376 and 385.

stand quite parallel in this opening stage. In the following two stages, however, we meet elements that are basic to the lukan description of the appearance. 2) The reaction of the disciples, being introduced with a participial construction, is pictured as that of fear and uncertainty. The risen One undertakes at once to assuage their doubts through reason and demonstration of his crucified corporeality. 3) As with the first phase this one begins with a genitive absolute. The disciples are still perplexed and unbelieving, but this time not from fear of seeing a ghost; instead, their very joy restrains them. It was all too good to believe. The risen One, therefore, asks for, receives and eats a portion of baked fish before them to dispel the last hindrance to their faith.

In addition to this structural development we see several other points of interest within the story itself. First, we find distinctive lukan terminology or constructions in phase 2 as follows:

1. πτοέομαι–Lk. 21:9 and here in vs. 37 only.

2. ἔμφοβος–outside of Rev. 11:13 only to be found here in vs. 37 and in Acts 10:4 and 24:25 and Lk. 24:5.

3. πνεῦμα–only here do we find a usage which is a synonym for "ghost" [φάντασμα]. The term stands in the NT primarily for the "Holy Spirit," the "Spirit of God" etc., or with other genitives, e.g., unclean or evil spirits. Outside of the gospels, especially in Paul, we find an antithetical relationship often between spirit and flesh.

4. θεωρέω–as a term for "seeing" in the appearance texts of the gospels this verb occurs only here and vs. 39 and in Jn. 20:14. Mt. 28:1 refers to the desire of the women "to see" the grave and it does not recur in the appearances themselves.

5. ταράσσω–outside of Mt. 2:3 and [Lk. 1:12] this verb only occurs within the markan tradition of Jesus walking on the water (Mk. 6:45-52 parr.) and here in vs. 38.

6. διαλογισμοί–the phrase in the gospels, "but Jesus perceiving their thoughts. . . ." with the use of the substantive is typical Lk. (cf. Lk. 5:22; 6:8; 9:47 and here). Yet, the verbal construction is used by all three synoptics (cf. Mt. 16:5-12; Mk. 8:14-21 and Lk. 12:1,17 etc.). In connection with the phrase ἐν τῇ καρδίᾳ ὑμῶν all three are quite united (cf. below).

7. ἐν τῇ καρδία ὑμῶν–in combination with the prep. ἐν and the verb ἀναβαίνω this phrase is *hapax* for the gospels. For other combinations cf. Mt. 21:5; Mk. 2:6,8; 9:33; 11:31 and [Lk. 1:29]; 3:15; 5:21f.; [12:17] and 20:14.

8. ἀναβαίνω–this location is the only place in the gospels where the notion of an idea coming to the mind is used. In Acts the usage occurs, but with other preps. The most common are ἐπί and εἰς (cf. Acts 7:23 and 10:41). For the former compare also the OT reference in I Cor. 2:9. Most of the NT, nevertheless, has persons as the subject of the verb. The major exception is Rev. where the imagery exists in a great variety.

9. ἴδετε–this plural form of the imperative is somewhat rare in the NT. We find it used once in Mt., once in Mk., three times in Lk., once in Acts (quote from Hab. 1:5) and then once in Jn. (although the latter has the singular form four times; cf. also Rom. 11:22; Gal. 6:11; I Jn. 3:1). Interestingly enough the Mt. location is within the resurrection narrative, but is put in the mouth of an angel instead of the mouth of the risen One as is the case in two of the three lukan locations and one of the johannine (singular, 20:27) locations. The markan location (6:38) is used with another imperative to mean: "go and find out." The other lukan reference

(21:29) seems to mean not only "take into your visual perspective," but also "consider" or "reflect about." Acts 13:41 is also to be translated in the visual/reflection sense. The johannine references are combined with the verb "come" (*ἔρχομαι* 1:46; 11:34 or *δεῦτε* as adverbial combination in 4:29) to mean "come and see" or stands alone with the meaning of "take note of and recognize" (11:34; 20:27 and I Jn. 3:1). The two pauline references are to be taken in this latter sense as well, i.e., "consider." We note, therefore, that outside of the markan reference all of thc gospel texts as well as the three outside thereof are in agreement over the combination of the visual image and reflection thereover. In Mt. it falls within the complex of Jesus' encounter with his disciples. For Lk. in particular it appears in vs. 39 and then is repeated in vs. 39b. The desired result in the first is: *ἐγώ εἰμι* and in the second it is: "I have *σάρκα καὶ ὀστέα* which no ghost could have." This combination of "flesh and bone" is here *hapax* for the NT. Both appear elsewhere alone. "Flesh" occurs in combination with "spirit" and "blood" in other locations, the latter bearing a special antithetical relationship to spirit and its soteriological implication (cf. Mt. 16:17; I Cor. 15:50 and Heb. 2:14).

10. *ψηλαφάω*–here *hapax* for the gospels. The only other locations are: Acts 17:27; Heb. 12:18 and I Jn. 1:1.

11. *δοκέω*–this is a common enough verb in the NT. It is also not unusual for the verb to occur along with *γίνομαι*. Interestingly enough, however, the most common usages do not parallel what we find here. The question: "what do you *think*? " is the most common form and is often somewhat rhetorical (cf. Mt. 18:12; 24:44; [Lk. 10:36]; 12:40,51 and [13:2,4] etc.).The idea "it seemed best to someone" is also quite common in the NT (cf. [Lk. 1:3]) as well as classical Greek (cf. also Acts 15:25). On several occasions, however, we have usages which parallel what we find here in vs. 37. In Jn. 20:15, for example, Mary Magdalene has *mistaken* the risen One for the gardner. Acts 12:9 provides another interesting parallel. The most illustrative example, however, is the miracle of Jesus walking on the water in Mk. 6:49-50 parr.:

"*οἱ δὲ ἰδόντες αὐτὸν ἐπὶ τῆς θαλάσσης περιπατοῦντα ἔδοξαν ὅτι φάντασμά ἐστιν καὶ ἀνέκραξαν· πάντες γὰρ αὐτὸν εἶδαν καὶ ἐταράχθησαν. ὁ δὲ εὐθὺς ἐλάλησεν μετ' αὐτῶν καὶ λέγει αὐτοῖς· θαρσεῖτε, ἐγώ εἰμι· μὴ φοβεῖσθε.*"

and for phase 3 we note the following:

1. *ἀπιστέω*–the only locations in the gospels are to be found here in vs. 41 and Lk. 24:11 (cf. Acts 28:24 and "Mk." 16:11,16). Outside of this complex this verbal form is to be found only in Rom. 3:3; II Tim. 2:13 and II Pet. 2:7; The substantive does not occur in Lk./Acts at all, but does in Mt. (13:58) and Mk. (6:6; 9:24; (16:14)) and elsewhere outside of the gospels. The adjective is to be found in the gospels only as follows: Mk. 9:19 (Mt. 17:17; Lk. 9:41) and Lk. 12:46 (Acts 26:8) and Jn. 20:17.

2. *χαρᾶς καὶ θαυμαζόντων*–in combination with the foregoing it occurs here *hapax*. Other combinations are to be found, e.g., in Mt. 28:8; Lk. 8:25 and 24:12 (Acts 2:7).

3. *βρώσιμον*–*hapax* for the NT. The term *βρῶμα* is much more common and is found in Lk. as well (cf. Mt. 14:15; Mk. 7:19; [Lk. 3:11]; 9:13 and Jn. 4:34 as well as *passim* outside of the gospels).

4. *ἐνθάδε*–outside of Jn. 4:15,16 this prep. is only to be found in Acts and then in this one location in the lukan gospel.

5. *ἐπιδίδωμι*–outside of Mt. 4:9,10 this verb is only to be found in Lk./Acts (Lk. 4:17; 11:11, 12; [24:30] and here in vs. 42; Acts 15:30 and 27:15).

6. *ἰχθύος ὀπτοῦ μέρος*–*hapax* for the NT.

7. ἐνώπιον αὐτῶν ἔφαγεν–Lk is very fond of this prep.[499] and outside of Jn. 20:30 it occurs only in Lk./Acts and in non-gospel material, especially in Rev. Parallels to this eating before someone are to be found only in Lk. 13:26 and Acts 27:35.

Lk and His Sources

We proceed now to the analysis of this statistical breakdown of the first half of the lukan group appearance so as to answer the question: where is his creative initiative to be found? In evaluating the above we notice several points of interest. Some terms and phrases within the narrative are by no means restricted to lukan parallels either in the gospel tradition or without. Others find wide usage in the rest of the NT, but have no parallels within the gospel tradition. Still others are either entirely restricted to Lk./Acts, perhaps with one or two exceptions, or are entirely *hapax legomena* for the entire NT. We shall, therefore, group together parallels which we know to occur only in lukan special source complexes (designated above with [ ]) and then those which occur within lukan redactional locations (underlined). In this way we shall attempt to look behind the growth of tradition which is here responsible for this first half of the lukan group appearance. In making this evaluation we shall divide the terminology into the following categories:

Those terms which occur nowhere else in the NT are: βρώσιμον and ἰχθὺς ὀπτός.
That which is *hapax* in the meaning found in this narrative is: πνεῦμα.
Those phrases which occur nowhere else or are very seldom to be found in the NT are: ἐδόκουν..., διαλογισμοὶ ἀναβαίνουσιν ἐν τῇ καρδίᾳ ὑμῶν, ἴδετε...ψηλαφήσατέ με καὶ ἴδετε...ἐγώ εἰμι...σάρκα καὶ ὀστέα, ἀπιστούντων αὐτῶν ἀπὸ τῆς χαρᾶς καὶ θαυμαζόντων and ἐνώπιον αὐτῶν ἔφαγεν.
That term which occurs only in special Lk. *if* it appears in Lk. at all (although it may also appear outside of Lk./Acts is: ταράσσω (once in Mt. and once in Mk. parr.).
Those terms which are exclusively or predominantly to be found in Lk. or Lk./Acts, but do not restrict themselves to special Lk. are: πτοέομαι, ἔμφοβος (one exception), ἐνθάδε (one exception) and ἐπιδίδωμι (one exception).
That which is common to all of the NT is: θεωρέω (although as a term for "seeing" in the appearance narratives it is found only here and in Jn. 20:14).

It would be much too mechanical to sketch the place of this section in the history of tradition from the terminology given for comparison in the above table alone. The breakdown does give us, however, an indication of possibilities. It is of interest to note that the subject matter of phase 3 is supported by two terms which have no parallel in the NT. Lk himself normally uses other terms (or other forms thereof) for both of these words and it would seem tentatively that the request of Jesus for βρώσιμον and his reception of ἰχθύος ὀπτοῦ μέρος corresponds to a special, prelukan source and that the point of the story, ἐνώπιον αὐτῶν ἔφαγεν, is not in

499 Robertson, *op. cit.*, p. 122. Cf. also George, *op. cit.*, p. 79.

conflict with this assumption since it too occurs rarely in the NT and bears the probable stamp of Lk's redactional conclusion to phase 3 in the light of his literary point in phase 2, i.e., "here is the proof!"

The rest of the material looks at first glance to be very indecisive. Nevertheless, upon closer examination and comparison with other NT complexes in which similar terminology occurs an interesting pattern begins to emerge. Under the parallel material cited for *δοκέω* we mentioned the miraculous walk of Jesus upon the water. It has long been suggested that this story was originally an Easter appearance story, and even Dodd who is normally very skeptical of the so-called "displaced" Easter stories on the basis of form-critical principles is quite prepared to grant this story a feasible place within the Easter tradition. The suggestion is of particular interest to us at this point because 1) Lk is the only evangelist who does not have the story in parallel form with the others and 2) our statistical comparison shows no other NT complex with more direct or indirect parallels to this story than what we have here. Is this mere coincidence? Perhaps, but the possibility that this miracle story which is embedded in the Galilean tradition for the other evangelists here makes its appearance in the lukan tradition at least to some extent remains a very live option. We note the following parallels from our terminological study:

1. This usage of the term *πνεῦμα* stands alone here in the NT and is a synonym for the term *φάντασμα* which is used in two of the three Walking on the Water miracle stories.

2. The description of the disciples' reason for consternation through the use of a *δοκέω*-construction is very similar:

Mk. *ἔδοξαν ὅτι φάντασμά ἐστιν...*
Lk. *ἐδόκουν πνεῦμα θεωρεῖν.*

As noted above, this use of *δοκέω* is not common for the NT and the construction variation here could represent simply an alternative form for expressing indirect discourse for Lk.

3. Fear and terror strike their hearts in both accounts, but the only parallel term is the occasion of *ταράσσω* in various forms which as a verb within Lk's gospel occurs only in one of Lk's special source complexes. In Mt. and Mk. the Walking on the Water miracle is the only occasion of the verb for them as well (with one exception in Mt.). In the one exception for Mt. it is also a special source section. Moreover, it is as in Lk. within the birth narrative complex. The subject is Herod the king in Mt. while for Lk. it is the priest Zachariah, the latter being startled by the appearance of an angel: *ὤφθη δὲ αὐτῷ ἄγγελος κυρίου ἑστὼς...εἶπεν...μὴ φοβοῦ.* Any connection between the two, however, seems very remote as their only common element is the general placement in the opening verses of their gospels. That we are dealing with Lk's special source for the only parallel in his gospel and that it is an "appearance" story as well is certainly of great consequence. In the fear motif we find a term which corresponds not to Lk's mode of expression but to that of his received source. And yet, in combination with *ταράσσω* for Mt. in the miracle story we find the terms *ἀνακράζω* and *κράζω*. For Lk., on the other hand, we find *πτοέομαι* and *ἔμφοβος* both of which are to be found exclusively in Lk./Acts parallels. As these parallels are all redactional in Lk., his stylistic initiative in handling his source may very well be at work. Interestingly enough, however, Mt. includes the phrase *ἀπὸ τοῦ φόβου* and all three accounts of the miracle include the command of Jesus (as the angel to Zachariah) *μὴ φοβεῖσθε* so that the fear side of their consternation is by no means a gap in the continuity. Lk's use of *ἔμφοβος* and *γίνομαι* as a parallel construction for Mt's *ἀπὸ δὲ τοῦ φόβου* may be seen in Lk. 24:5 and Mt. 28:4 (the latter including the words of the angel: *μὴ φοβεῖσθε*).

4. Certainly the role of what the disciples saw or thought they saw is of central importance to the theme of fear. For Lk. in vss. 37 and 39 the term θεωρέω comes to the fore while Mt. and Mk. use the participle ἰδόντες. Interestingly enough, however, the johannine account, considered by Dodd to be the most original form of the account preserves the present indicative θεωροῦσιν. This factor is certainly a support for the relatedness of the two accounts. Moreover, we find upon examining the uses of this verb in the latter chapters of Mt. and Mk. that Lk. is quite reluctant to use it even where it is apparently offered by his source.

Mt. 27:55 and Mk. 15:40–Lk. 23:49 ὁράω
Mk. 15:47–Mt. 27:61 καθήμεναι and Lk. 23:55 ἐθεάσαντο
Mt. 28:1–(Mk. 16:4), (Lk. 24:2 εὗρον), (Jn. 20:1 βλέπει)
Lk. 24:37,39 without parallel

This may be offered as further evidence that Lk is here working with a source and that this source may indeed be closely related to the Walking on the Water miracle.

If we may depart from our consideration of Lk. momentarily to trace another factor in relation to the appearance of θεωρέω in the johannine miracle story and its appearance once again in the johannine Easter story we may find an interesting support for the original close connection of the two traditions. We note that the only major difference in the form of the three miracle accounts is that the disciples' failure to recognize Jesus is absent in Jn. It would appear that in Jn. the disciples recognize him from the beginning but are nevertheless afraid. Jesus' walking on water then becomes the cause for their fear and not their mistaken notion that he was a spirit. Yet, in the Magdalene story of the johannine Easter complex we find the only occasion in the accounts of Jn. that the risen One upon appearance was not recognized (even if Jn. 21 is here included the failure of the disciples to recognize him was apparently caused more by the distance between Jesus and the boat and by the time of day than a specific identity problem). Both this text and Jn. 21 will be discussed below but suffice it here to ask: is it purely coincidence that the missing element in the miracle story should turn up in his Easter complex and that in conjunction with the only use of θεωρέω in the johannine Easter narrative? It is certainly to be granted that the thematic variations are more pronounced than is the case when Lk. is compared with the miracle story, but the additional support of the phrase ἐκείνη δοκοῦσα ὅτι ὁ κηπουρός ἐστιν lends its voice to Jn. as well. The reasons for the lack of recognition falling upon Mary Magdalene instead of the apostles is both a matter of Jn's chronological placement in the gospel tradition and of the whole notion of forgiveness and love in Jn. which finds its focus to a large extent in the person of the Magdalene.

In any case the above consideration for Jn at least strengthens the possibility of an early relatedness in the two complexes for the history of tradition and gives further reason for pursuing the connections in Lk.

5. Jesus addresses them in their fears in both accounts. In the Walking on the Water story Jesus assuages their fears immediately with his command while in the lukan narrative we find him questioning and reasoning with them. Between the two the only terminological parallel is the use of the phrase ἐγώ εἰμι. For both the recognition of his person is to be the decisive factor for their restoration to peace. At this point something must be said about the textual apparatus. There we find that many ancient mss. contain an imperative remark from the risen One almost identical with that of the miracle story: "Be not afraid, it is I (peace to you)!" The textual tradition at this point is certainly dubious and most text-critics relegate these words to a place of unequal worth because of their similarity to either the miracle story or the address of Jesus in Jn. It seems, however, that the textual supports are strong enough that in spite of the ring of similarity one must leave the possibility open that the original text contained these words or at least a combination thereof. Interestingly enough, the one codex that normally has additional readings or "explanatory clarifications," namely Codex Bezae, omits this reading but has φάντασμα for πνεῦμα. The exact history of this text, therefore, is uncertain, but the possibility exists that the connection between the imperative of the miracle story and the address of the risen One was closer than the present format would indicate. In any case, the place for reason

and "proofs" in expanded form are much more understandable in terms of the lukan redactional goals here (anti-Docetism) than for such in the miracle story.

We may here then sketch the essential points of overlap. With the removal of the water motif from the miracle story and the contextual anchor in the group appearance, i.e., the crucifixion scar motif, the two stories read very much alike. This may be seen in the following:

a) Jesus comes to his disciples.
b) The disciples are struck with fear thinking that they are viewing a spirit apparition (the latter excepted in Jn.).
c) Jesus dispels their fears by assuring them that it is he himself who has encountered them.

In spite of the apparent similarities the incongruities of content and location constitute, nevertheless, a very thorny problem in trying to estimate the nature of the relationship. Assuming that the similarities are not merely coincidental the chief difficulty becomes the matter of tracing satisfactorily the route by which the miracle story ended up in Lk. 24. As noted above, it is of considerable interest that Lk does not include the miracle story in his portrayal of the Galilaean ministry and that this particular story, so often counted among the so-called "displaced" appearance stories, should turn up—at least in certain major themes—in the lukan appearance complex. It would certainly be too pat an explanation and without exegetical foundation simply to claim that in Lk's copy of Mk. the miracle story was not present and/or was recognizable as an appearance story elsewhere, perhaps in a "lost" ending. Thus, the chief options for explaining the path of development encompass either a traditional source or radical redactional activity or perhaps a combination of the two, i.e., the appearance story came to Lk through a source independent of Mk., building as it were a duplicate pericope of sorts, or Lk encountered the miracle story in Mk., just like Mt, and then deliberately relocated and altered it in the context of his group appearance, perhaps in keeping with his theological goal of pointing to Jerusalem rather than Galilee as the *heilsgeschichtlich* center of his gospel. Although the latter alternative could find some justification in the redactional interests of the evangelist as evidenced, for example, in the alteration of 24:6, it is improbable that such a thoroughgoing change as the incongruities indicated above demonstrate would have been undertaken by Lk to make the miracle story "fit" his purpose. The degree of probability would speak rather for the traditional origin of the account itself. It might be that the double form as it were of the account had something to do with the omission of the miracle story in Lk's account of the Galilaean ministry,[500] but for our purposes it is sufficient to point up the distinctions between the two accounts and the improbability that the one owes its origin

500 One could argue here, for instance, in terms of the thesis of H. Schürmann, "Die Dublettenvermeidungen im Lukasevangelium. Ein Beitrag zur Verdeutlichung des lukanischen Redaktionsverfahrens," *Traditionsgeschichtliche Untersuchungen zu den synoptischen Evangelien, Ges. Aufs.* (Düss., 1968), pp. 280f., that Lk wanted to avoid *Dubletten* at all costs and that he, therefore, omitted this pericope within the "großen Auslassung" of Mk. 6:45-8:26 because of its essential re-occurrence in his group appearance. Cf. also below, n. 566.

directly from the other through redactional rigors. This would suggest that the stories enjoyed a very fluid place within the earliest tradition and that they had, in effect, a common origin while finding their way into two traditional complexes without situational alterations by the evangelists themselves. As the oral tradition began to solidify, the Walking on the Water miracle found independent expression in the markan framework, the appearance story form did not. The latter then came to Lk later through channels independent of his markan source, but the identity of content if not total structure remained unmistakable.

In the third phase another motif arises in which the proof of Jesus' bodiliness comes to a conclusion, namely Jesus eats fish before them. No direct source for comparison seems to be available to us on this point. And yet, it may be of some consequence to follow up our observations above. The sequence of material for the gospel synopsis is quite interesting at this point. First, for all four evangelists is the Feeding of the 5,000. On its heels comes the Walking on the Water story (Lk. excepted). Then come the healings at Gennesaret, parallels to which do exist for Lk. but in chapters 6 and 11. The question of the Syrophoenician woman comes next again with parallel in Lk. 7:10 and then follows the encounter with a great crowd: Jesus heals their sick and feeds them all (4,000). Neither aspect is paralleled in Lk. It may in fact be speculation, but one is forced nevertheless to ask: has an aspect of the Feeding of the 4,000 found its way into the third phase of Lk's group appearance? There are, of course, certain fundamental differences and it is here in no way suggested that the *stories* as such are in any way related. Not only is bread entirely missing in the group appearance, but also and more importantly it is Jesus who is the receiver and not the people, not even the disciples. Moreover, the occasion is not Jesus' compassion on the hungering, but his desire to assuage their doubts. On the other hand, the question remains: is it entirely coincidental that Lk should come up with "eating" (fish) as a means of proof and that this should be the element that fails so soon after the miracle walk in Lk.? We can be certain that the Feeding of the 4,000 was not originally an appearance story, but the theme of "eating" is of importance to at least two more of the appearance stories and the possible if slight influence of the miraculous feeding must be taken into view.[501] In any case, we do not have the extensive terminological parallels that we had in phase 2. Rather we have basically a *hapax* section. This would lead us to the tentative conclusion that Lk is here relying on his special source if not an aspect of the miraculous feeding. As the crucifixion scar motif in phase 2 corresponds to the apologetic interests of Lk and are, therefore, almost certainly the redactional formation of the appearance it would be fitting to classify this phase similarly because of its focus of this whole "proof" motif. That is to say, in spite of the failure of phase 2 terminology to stand in lukan redactional parallels, the content and goal is probably redactional. The "eating motif" will receive wider attention below under

501 Regarding the fish aspect here, cf. below under the meal motif, pp. (198f.) and 205f., esp. n. 597.

the Emmaus story and Jn. 21; we can only caution at this point against the premature exclusion of this aspect from the search for the traditional matrix as merely and certainly a redactional element.

Conclusions Regarding Luke

This first half of the lukan group appearance certainly presents us with a picture of complexity in terms of the history of tradition and although it would be convenient to eliminate those sections which depart from Mt. and Jn. as strictly lukan creation we have seen above that this is not possible on the whole because of the special source nature of the text.[502] The lack of comparative material in a similar (appearance) context makes it very difficult to judge, but our word study and glance to comparable locations in the synoptic tradition have pointed out that the tradition behind this section antedates Lk himself. If it is not purely lukan creation then, what role does this material play in arriving at the traditional matrix? First of all these observations suggest that at the traditional level the appearance stories were in part probably very fluid. Here Lk has received a story which in the oral tradition may indeed have had its roots both in the Galilean and Easter traditions or a story which at a very early date was adapted to one or the other. In the third phase as well we see that Lk has enlarged on the theme of convincing the disciples of Jesus' identity and bodiliness through the use of an independent source which at the same time served his chief redactional goal of setting himself against Docetism. The contours of this group appearance which we have already seen in Mt. are not here altered, but they are sketched with greater detail, in part from Lk's use of the crucifixion scar motif and in part from his source. Jesus comes to them. The human reaction of the disciples, this time doubt on all sides, is recorded and then Jesus sets about to convince them that it is really the Jesus of their former experience.

Conclusions: Jesus Addresses the Disciples' Reaction

We now see from cross section perspective that the lukan account is far more complex than Jn. A higher degree of literary sophistication is packed into Lk's narrative, the Magdalene and Thomas stories notwithstanding. That is to say, the differences in Jn. in comparison to Lk. are to be found on the whole in one or both of these two other accounts for Jn. For example, the lack of recognition of Jesus by Mary is quite central in the Magdalene story and the touching theme is central for the Thomas story. Outside of the fear motif and that of the eating of fish Lk does not stand alone in the development of this story. This raises, however, the source question. Does Jn owe his material to Lk. or does he have an independent source?

502 Positing a relatively high percentage of sources here for Lk in general and a rigorous fidelity to them are Lohse, *Auferstehung*, pp. 10 and 34, and Winter, "Sources," pp. 168ff. Cf. also F. Rehkopf, *Die Lukanische Sonderquelle*, WUNT, 5 (Tüb., 1959), p. 90.

From the outset a possible development in the tradition must be recognized at least tentatively as follows: Intentionally or not the earliest of the three has the shortest account of the group appearance. In doing so Mt places the weight of importance chiefly on the words of commission. Lk, writing either contemporaneously or slightly later, developed the group appearance with great imagination and detail, and in smooth literary transition unites it with two others: the Emmaus travelers and the appearance before Peter. Jn, writing at least twenty years later, shares much of the same material as the other two have, with the possible exception of the Magdalene story (and most certainly the sea of Tiberias story in Ch. 21) and could be dependent upon them. That is certainly possible, but it is most probable that Jn developed the group appearance material available to him through a source comparable to and not identical with the synoptic tradition and that into at least two and possibly three separate stories. When one considers the nature of the parallels between Jn. and Lk. and weighs the theological occasion for the differences for Jn. the probability and significance of dependence upon a common source seems to appear quite clear and convincing. It should be mentioned that the almost certain dependence of Jn. 21 and Lk. 5:1-11 upon identical sources supplies another support for this general conclusion.[503]

This alternative, of course, means that Jn. is using an independent but corresponding source. When one isolates and removes those elements key to johannine theology and recognizes those locations which bear the unavoidable marks of either the special johannine personal creativity or the natural enlargement of a good story, i.e., both theologically significant for the early community and particularly well suited for dramatic retelling, there is, of course, little left for the analysis of the independent source. The Thomas story, for example, can hardly be anything else than a deliberate development of the doubt and touching themes in a time when on the one hand, the reputation of the disciples as a whole had to stand above reproach, and yet on the other hand, the inappropriateness of doubt or at least of "unbelief" in view of the disciples' witness had to be addressed. That is to say, Jn is both the channel of the tradition's forward movement and is evangelist. This is the reason for the omission or softening of the fear and proof motifs as well, in comparison with the lukan form of these motifs. Fear as such may exist for Jn as the latent cause for the "peace" pronouncement, which occurs for him outside of the commissioning words both in the group appearance during Thomas' absence and again in his presence. The stress on proofs may have been for Jn unnecessary be-

503 Cf. below, pp. 200ff. Regarding the dependence of Jn directly on Lk, Bailey, *op. cit.*, p. 92 is quite clear: "Luke is, in fact, John's source here." Leaney, "Narratives," pp. 112ff., however, concludes that Lk and Jn go back to a fixed traditional account of the "Upper Room Appearance" (p. 113). In critique of Leaney are Hartmann, *op. cit.*, p. 218, who stresses an oral tradition behind them, and Lindars, "Composition," pp. 142ff., who simply concludes that Jn avails himself here of a tradition behind the synoptics (for his "fundamental pattern" common to all, cf. p. 143). Disavowing Jn's alleged dependence on Lk. is also Wilckens, *Auferstehung*, pp. 71ff.

cause of the stress on the "finger test" of Thomas or because of other redactional goals.[504]

In terms of this group appearance then it is difficult to take Jn. beyond Mt. and Lk. We shall see exceptions on the profile of the source perhaps later, but at this point it seems difficult to say much about Jn's source other than it resembled theirs very closely.[505]

In retrospect then we find some important implications for Mt. We have already noted that he preserves a group appearance with the immediate address of the risen One. We do find, however, comments of a suggestive nature, which as an editorial observation about the reaction of the disciples comes immediately prior to the address itself, namely the disciples "worshipped" but some "doubted."[506] We have seen that both Lk and Jn make a great deal of this latter theme and it must, therefore, be asked: is the statement here and the development there related to a common source? The fact that Mt comments here upon this reaction but is silent as to its development because of his more pressing goals[507] suggests that this aspect

504 E.g., the stress on "belief" as motif in the post-resurrection sequence as in the conclusion to the Thomas story or the role of the Beloved Disciple as believer. Cf. further, Proto-Gospel of James 19:3, Ignatius *Smyrneans* 3,1f.; in Epistula Apostolorum 11(22) and 12(23) Peter, Thomas and Andrew all have special invitations to make the test.

505 Hartmann, *op. cit.*, p. 211, can affirm that "den Versen 19-29 ein ursprünglich einheitlicher Bericht zugrunde liegt, der erst später auseinandergerissen wurde," and regarding part of the Thomas story he says, "daß in V. 24-26 nichts erhalten ist, was nicht als eine Bildung im Anschluß an V. 19ff. oder aber als johanneisches Interpretament zu erkennen ist." Vs. 25, however, is for Hartmann at least in part traditional and takes up vss. 1-18 (p. 212). Then vs. 26 represents a doublet to vs. 19 the latter being traditional with the exception of *διὰ τὸν φόβον τῶν*...(p. 212, cf. also Bultmann, *Johannes*, p. 535, n. 5). The *Angebot* of Jesus in vs. 27 in correspondence to vs. 20 Hartmann considers traditional although he admits that reconstructing the original wording is very difficult (p. 212). The mention of the side of the crucified One is seen as probably redactional and possibly it was originally the feet as in Lk. 24:39 (p. 212 and n. 37); vs. 27b is also *frei gebildet* (p. 213), while vs. 27c is difficult to assess, but it does seem to bear a closer affinity to redactional interests than traditional ones (p. 213). Hartmann then jumps back to vss. 21ff. for the continuation of the originally unified story which concluded with the imparting of the Spirit, although the confession of Thomas (originally the disciples), vs. 28, may have been original too (pp. 213f.). Moreover, the understanding of the Spirit here is seen as non-johannine, and, therefore, an ostensible tension is seen in vss. 21 and 23. The understanding here is also distinguishable from that of Lk (pp. 215f.). He says, "Demnach ist v. 21b von Johannes hier eingefügt, die Vorlage schloß mit v. 21a, 22f" (p. 215, contra is Bultmann, *Johannes*, pp. 534f.). He counters thereby the view that chapters 14-16 are behind this reference to the Spirit (cf. also p. 215, n. 45). The Ordination of vs. 22 he sees as "sachlich eine Parallele zur Aussendung Mt 28 16ff., auch Lc 24 47" (p. 215). His reconstruction then of this originally unified story consists of the progression vss. 19(=26), 27, 20, 28, 21, 22, 23 (p. 220).

506 Cf. the apparent borrowing of this "worship" motif in 28:10.

507 Cf. below under the words of commission. I.P. Ellis, "But Some Doubted," *NTS*, 14 ('67/'68) suggests that Mt's intention here is "being uncertain" or "hesitating". . ."they believed having first doubted" (p. 577). Similar, "alle zweifeln," is Grundmann, *Matthäus* (p. 576). Moreover, the point of the reference, according to Ellis, is not actually doubt focused upon the participants in a resurrection appearance, but the occasion for Mt to address an authoritative word of Jesus to the church on discipleship (p. 580). He shows, however, little interest in the question of tradition behind the motif. Similar is Graß, *op. cit.*, pp. 28ff. Cf. also Michel, "Abschluß," p. 22 and Bornkamm, "Der Auferstandene," p. 172, who says that the motif ". . .aus der Problematik der späteren Gemeinde verstanden werden will." He acknowledges, however, that the motif plays a role in all of the accounts.

of the disciples' reaction was basic to the whole group context[508] and that he and the others were free to develop the idea in a way that best suited their own goals. This seems to be substantiated by the way in which the reaction as "positive/negative" received different degrees of stress in the three. The positive is major for Mt. The negative is minor. For Lk. and Jn. there is an interplay between joy or faith/unbelief or doubt each having either a reverse of emphasis or difference of stress to one another and to Mt. We may thus conclude that the common elements prior to the words of commission are:

1. He comes (and speaks) to them.
2. The disciples' reaction is recorded: partially acceptance, partially scepticism
3. The risen One is recognized as Jesus the Lord by the disciples.

d. The Words of Commission

We have noted above that basic to all three accounts is that Jesus comes *and* speaks. For Jn. and especially for Lk. the address of the risen One upon arrival is not a communication of the words of commission, but is a dialogue with perplexity. This is not the case for Mt. The question is then: did the tradition originally preserve the coming *and* speaking together without the intervention of the disciples' reaction? In a word, is Mt. or Lk. here the more reliable? For Mt. the reaction of the disciples is based upon their "seeing" and not his "coming." Vs. 18 follows their two-sided reaction in the following order: 1) coming to them 2) he spoke to them 3) saying. That is, the sequence is uninterrupted. The same order is preserved in Lk. when one supplies the "seeing" element as the ground for the disciples' reaction, i.e., they are talking, Jesus comes into their midst (they are troubled at what they see), and he says (why are you troubled?). The same scheme is basically true for Jn. as well. It appears then that the content of the address depended in part on whether or not the evangelist felt himself called upon to retain and/or comment directly upon the doubt motif which the tradition had preserved as a basic element of the story.

Regardless of how the doubt problem was addressed there is no doubt about the most important aspect of the address itself. The literary development of the gospels and the content of the group appearance itself before the words of commission all constitute a unified pointer in the direction of these all-important words.

508 Contra Strecker, *op. cit.*, p. 208. Cf. also von Campenhausen, *Ablauf*, p. 39, n. 152. Seeing the motif as traditional and as a strong indication that the disciples' faith cannot supply the origin for the Resurrection is Kassing, *op. cit.*, pp. 147f. Further, cf. P. Billerbeck and L. Strack, *Kommentar zum Neuen Testament aus Talmud und Midrasch*, II (Mü., 1924), pp. 299f., regarding Lk. 24:38.

The Transition Problem

We begin with Jn. because of the unusual transition to the words in comparison with Mt. and Lk. Jesus comes, speaks and shows his scars and, therefore [οὖν], the disciples rejoice. Then comes the second therefore [οὖν] followed by another pronouncement of "peace." What then is the origin and intention behind this construction? If Jesus speaks "peace" into the disciples' assumed perplexity at the beginning of the appearance, does this mean that he must speak "peace" into their joy for Jn? Is the intention to show that Jesus brings peace into both sides of human reaction? The relationship between this second "peace" and the words which follow it is of central importance in answering these questions. In these words, namely, we find that Jesus' earlier promise of joy in the world where they would otherwise know tribulation now receives the certification of resurrection fulfillment. When we read these words with a glance fixed upon chapters 13-16 at the same time (especially 14: 15-31 and 16:33) this fulfillment relationship is readily recognizable. Yet, the forward glance to peace in the world is only one half of the transition. The second οὖν has a much more immediate backward glance. It is bound to the positive reaction of the disciples, which is not only joy but also recognition of the Lord who was standing before them. The disciples are (principally for the reader's assurance) fully prepared to receive the commission of their Lord. In this way the second half of the johannine group appearance [509] is literally bound to the first with convincing smoothness.

Lk. in comparison lacks this sort of transition. The last apparent element of the first half of this appearance is Jesus' eating of fish before the disciples. After this act (vs. 43) we find something of a silence because we are never told that this finally did win the disciples over from the doubts of vs. 41 and yet in vs. 44 we find the risen One addressing them with the words that culminate in their commission. For Lk. this discourse begins with the words εἶπεν δέ [510] and Jn. with εἶπεν οὖν. [511] It would thus appear that what for Lk. is an assumption in the silence, i.e., the disciples' coming to faith, is specific and emphasized in Jn. Jn's οὖν in view of his ἐχάρησαν and ἰδόντες τὸν κύριον is literarily much stronger than the lukan δέ. We see here another support for the close proximity of source for Jn. and Lk.

Mt. and Lk. are quite in agreement at this point in the transition to the words. Mt mentions doubts, but does not discuss the transition to faith. We hear only that the majority worshipped at first sight. Nevertheless, a certain dissonance is apparent between ἐδίστασαν and προσελθὼν. . .ἐλάλησεν. Lk as well builds the case for belief, but then like Mt draws back from telling plainly that doubt was actually overcome. Only Jn is precise on the issue with his ἐχάρησαν [512] and Thomas story.

509 The commentary of Jn on the doubt motif by way of the Thomas story is literarily, if not *traditionsgeschichtlich* a separate story.

510 J.M. Robinson, "Logoi Sophon," *Trajectories*, p. 88, sees here a quotation formula suggesting that Lk was aware of a collection of sayings of the resurrected One. As a lukan construction, cf. George, *op. cit.*, p. 79. Contra is Rehkopf, *op. cit.*, p. 93.

511 Cf. as "transitional particle" for Jn., Robertson, *op. cit.*, pp. 1191f.

512 Cf. Jn. 14:28.

The Commission Focus

Jn.

For Jn. the heart of the commission is a specific "sending." The decisive element of interpretation is the meaning of *καθώς* in vs. 21. The two possibilities are: 1) "to fulfill that for which. . . ." or 2) simply "as," i.e., those who are sent go in the power and at the direction of the Sender. Judging from the usual johannine stress on the relationship of the disciples to Jesus,[513] the latter is the most obvious choice, but it is not to be assumed to the exclusion of the former. To the contrary, it is the very essence of the sending that representation should transpire in the world to which they are sent and it is in the interest of theological specification that Jn supplies in vss. 22 and 23, the fulfillment to chapter 14: the reception of the Holy Spirit and the role of the church in the forgiveness question. It is interesting to note that while Jn is very conscientious about the transition at the beginning of the commission he has sacrificed smoothness between vss. 23 and 24. The "first" group appearance has no special literary ending before we pass into the next which ostensibly took place eight days later. In spite of the time interval, however, it is apparent that Jn intends the whole Thomas story to constitute the ending of the first story; it is, as it were, the immediate inactment of the sending whereby the Easter kerygma is witnessed to: *ἑωράκαμεν τὸν κύριον*.

The basic johannine sequence for the commission then has the following primary elements:

1. *καθὼς ἀπέσταλκέν με ὁ πατήρ, κἀγὼ πέμπω ὑμᾶς*
2. *λάβετε πνεῦμα ἅγιον*
3. *ἄν τινων ἀφῆτε τὰς ἁμαρτίας...ἄν τινων κρατῆτε*

Mt.

Again the consecutive particle *οὖν* is to play an important role. In the matthaean construction, however, it occurs in a different location than for Jn. For Mt. the particle occupies a strategic location between Jesus' declaration of his authority and the sending of the disciples. What in this construction is uniquely matthaean and what could Mt have taken over from an earlier tradition? The declaration itself: *ἐδόθη μοι πᾶσα ἐξουσία ἐν οὐρανῷ καὶ ἐπὶ* [*τῆς*] *γῆς*, has clearly no parallel in the other group appearance texts and although Strecker attempts to demonstrate, as we have seen,[514] that this is a non-matthaean declaration on the basis of a word statistic and the assumption that Mt has taken over the three-part *Offenbarungswort*[515] of an early Christian prophet, it remains very difficult to assume a pre-

513 Cf. Jn. 15:5.
514 Cf. above, n. 493.
515 Strecker, *op. cit.*, p. 210.

matthaean source at this point.[516] To the contrary, the representation of this sequence is not to be understood at all outside of the rest of Mt's gospel and vice versa. In this respect Michel is fully correct when he says:

"Nur unter dieser theologischen Voraussetzung von Mt. 28,18-20 ist das ganze Evangelium geschrieben worden [cf. 28:19 to 10:5ff and 15:24; 28:20 to 1:23 and 3:1]. Ja, der Abschluß kehrt in gewisser Weise zum Anfang zurück und lehrt das ganze Evangelium, die Geschichte Jesu 'von hinten her' verstehen. Mt. 28,18-20 ist der Schlüssel zum Verständnis des ganzen Buches."[517]

Moreover, indirect dependence of the declaration 18b upon Dan. 7:14 is probable and also quite in keeping with what is known about Mt and his use of the OT.[518] Another bone of contention at this point which we must consider in brief in spite of its place within the interpretation of Mt. is the place of this sequence under form-critical considerations. Some exegetes maintain that we have here an enthronement scene based on the analogy of the king's assuming power in the ancient Orient and especially in Israel [519] basing the assumption essentially on an alleged continuity between this text and the early Christian christological hymns of I Tim. 3:16, Phil. 2:9-11 and Heb. 1:5-14. Although this does not necessarily exclude the vital connection to the commission,[520] the emphasis is on the christological implications of the exaltation of Jesus.[521] On the other hand, this sequence has

516 W. Trilling, *Das Wahre Israel–Studien zur Theologie des Matthäus-Evangeliums*, StANT (Mü., 1964, 3rd ed.), pp. 24f., demonstrates that "authority" and "heaven/earth" are key concepts for Mt–in contrast to Strecker–throughout the content of his gospel. Cf. Evans, *Resurrection*, pp. 84f., who overstates the case. Also R. Fuller, *op. cit.*, pp. 79ff. (cf. above p. 48). As we saw earlier (n. 310), Bartsch develops an interpretation of Mt's grave guard story as an "epiphany" appearance story involving Peter and basing this interpretation on the concept of the parousia. With this concept falling out of vogue the grave story could ostensibly make its entry *and* provide the place for a Galilaean appearance too since it offered the possibility of a period in which the disciples could return home. The matthaean group appearance becomes for him then a compensation by which Mt can represent the enthronement of the Lord and at the same time place the completed parousia in the future. Cf. "Passions- und Ostergeschichten," pp. 91f., and above ns. 310 and 339. Bornkamm, "Der Auferstandene," pp. 175ff. speaks of Mt. taking up here ". . .dieses vorgegebene Motiv der Völkermission. . . ."

517 Michel, "Abschluß," p. 21.

518 So, e.g., *ibid.*, p. 22. Contra is Trilling, *Israel*, pp. 21ff. Cf. also Bornkamm, "Der Auferstandene," p. 174 and the recent statement of B.J. Malina, "Structure and Form of Matt. XXVIII.16-20," *NTS*, 17 ('70/'71), pp. 88f. The question of the Hebrew or LXX background here is an exegetical question for the interpretation of Mt. and does not concern us directly. In regard to Mt's understanding of scripture in this context, cf. J. Rohde, *op. cit.*, pp. 92f.

519 E.g., C.H. Dodd, "Matthew and Paul," *New Testament Studies* (Manchester, 1953), p. 56, Hahn, *Hoheitstitel*, pp. 126 and 130f., J. Jeremias, *Jesu Verheissung für die Völker* (Stutt., 1959, 2nd ed.), p. 33, Michel, "Abschluß," pp. 21f., E. Norden, *Die Geburt des Kindes* (Darmstadt, 1969 [='24]), pp. 116ff. (and *Agnostos*, pp. 254ff.), Trilling, *Israel*, p. 46, n. 153, K.H. Rengstorf, "Old and New Testament Traces of a Formula of the Judean Royal Ritual," *NovTest*, 5 (1962), pp. 229ff., Dodd, "Appearances," p. 21 and Evans, *Resurrection*, pp. 83ff. Cf. in general hereto also Kee, "Transfiguration," pp. 147f. S.E. Johnson, "The Davidic-Royal Motif in the Gospels," *JBL*, 87 (1968), pp. 136ff. does not make mention of Mt. 28:16ff. as being an enthronement scene in his article. Critical of the view is, among others, Grundmann, *Matthäus*, pp. 572ff.

520 J. Jeremias, *Verheißung*, p. 33.

521 Cf. also Trilling, *Israel*, pp. 21f. and 46. Bartsch, "Passions- und Ostergeschichten," p. 81, sees here an *Epiphanie des Menschensohnes*.

been recognized by others in its intimate relationship to the sending texts of the synoptic tradition (Mt. 10; Mk. 6 and Lk. 9 [10:3]) and thereby places primary emphasis upon the transitional and connective force of *οὖν*. Says Strecker, for example, "Aus der universalen Vollmacht des Erhöhten folgt die erneute Aussendung, die nun nicht mehr auf das empirische Israel beschränkt (10,6), sondern sich auf 'alle Völker' richtet."[522] Because of the fundamental distance in the form and content of this sequence in comparison with the christological hymns of the NT [523] and because of the basic importance of the sending to the group appearance the latter alternative is probably primary, even if the other constitutes a part of the formal background. In this affirmation of power bestowed on Jesus [524] the latter directs the words of commission to the disciples. This is, as noted above, the transitional weight carried by the *οὖν*. We note immediately that this idea is not unlike that of the *καθὼς* in Jn. When we remove the reference to the Spirit from the johannine account as directed at the promise of chapter 14 we have two basic notions left in Jn. regarding the commission: 1) I am sending you as the Father has sent me, and 2) you are to be integrally connected with the retention and forgiveness of sins. Do these notions find their parallel in Mt.?

The matthaean construction is based upon one imperative, three participles and one present indicative. They are as follows:

1. *πορευθέντες*
2. *μαθητεύσατε*
3. *βαπτίζοντες*
4. *διδάσκοντες τηρεῖν*
5. *καὶ ἰδοὺ ἐγὼ μεθ' ὑμῶν εἰμι πάσας τὰς ἡμέρας ἕως τῆς συντελείας τοῦ αἰῶνος*

The first notion, i.e., being sent in the power of the Sender, is certainly paralleled by Mt. We find this implicit in the *οὖν* and as an assumption based on the aorist participle *πορευθέντες*. The second part of the johannine commission finds no direct terminological parallel in Mt. because the johannine terms represent a different level of the early church's development. And yet the aorist participle bears a fundamental relationship to the imperative and the two other participles and as such lay great stress upon the content of the commission rather than the going itself. This is an implied element in the johannine *καθὼς...κἀγὼ πέμπω* as noted above and we must, therefore, ask: is the matthaean notion as a sequel to the participle *πορευθέντες* parallel–in Mt's own terminology of course–to that of the notion in Jn.? Put another way, are "retain and forgive sins" and "make disciples,

522 Strecker, *op. cit.*, p. 212. Cf. also Goppelt, *Zeit*, p. 123 and Bornkamm, "Der Auferstandene," pp. 181f.

523 Cf. Strecker, *op. cit.*, p. 210, n. 3 and Trilling, *Israel*, p. 47.

524 The passive *ἐδόθη* is certainly pregnant with meaning here especially in connection with vs. 20b. Cf. Malina, *op. cit.*, pp. 89ff.

baptizing and teaching them" parallel notions? Certainly "make disciples" is a special exegetical question for interpreting Mt.,[525] but just as with Jn. it bespeaks fundamentally a concept of the Church. For Jn the commission is to go and represent the risen One in the Holy Spirit to the world and that as a redemptive institution. For Mt that is also true in a qualified sense. That is to say, Mt very much thinks in terms of his ecclesiastical environment, but his concern in this sequence seems to be one of the very fundamentals for Christian existence. There is here an unmistakable emphasis on the continuity of the pre- and post-Easter situations. This is not only the literary continuity to his gospel as a whole, but also the definition of what for Mt is the Christian life: fellowship with the ever-present Jesus. We see this in the two participles baptizing and teaching. This terminology suggests an understanding of the sequence based upon the structure of the gospel itself, i.e., the great speech complexes (esp. the Sermon on the Mount in 5-7) and the miracles and healings of Jesus' ministry (8-9). The one line of continuity then is that of the teaching of Jesus under which the disciples themselves were instructed, the other is that of acceptance into the fellowship of God and union with Jesus, which is clearly the intention and meaning of 8-9, here through baptism. Both aspects are for Mt the basis for continued fellowship with Jesus after Easter. The implications of both terms for matthaean theology are manifold, but this is not our intention; they are clearly matthaean formulations and do not represent an earlier tradition.[526] The promise of vs. 20b then in connection with the sending motif is the final aspect of the complex to be considered.

The words of promise, based on the present indicative, form the very basic theological and literary conclusion for Mt., i.e., as God in the OT is present with his people so Jesus remains with his own.[527] The disciples' future work has meaning because the exalted One is *present.* Is this promise then in both form and content strictly the creation of Mt? To answer this question we must first examine the other two.

In spite of the truncated form of the johannine account we do see the same sort of parallel as noted above between the matthaean and johannine material. The form

525 Outside of Acts 14:21 the verb occurs exclusively in Mt. Cf. also 13:52 and 27:57. It is the central thesis of Malina, *op. cit., passim,* that "making disciples" here subordinates all other motives in the passage. I.e., ". . .for this evangelist the ideal Christian is by definition the ideal disciple. . .discipleship includes making others into disciples" (p. 103). Cf. also Bornkamm, "Der Auferstandene," pp. 182ff., and more distantly, H.B. Green, "The Command to Baptize and Other Matthaean Interpolations," *StEv*, IV (1968), pp. 60ff.

526 Strecker, *op. cit.*, pp. 209ff., notwithstanding. Of course, a word-statistic itself is quite inconclusive–outside perhaps of μαϑητεύσατε–and the content of Mt. as a whole remains the only reliable guide. Cf. also Trilling, *Israel*, p. 36 and Lohfink, "Auferstehung," p. 43. Regarding the question of the trinitarian baptismal formula, cf. Graß, *op. cit.*, pp. 30f., Michel, "Abschluß," pp. 23f., J. Rohde, *op. cit.*, pp. 67ff. and 77f., O. Moe, "Hat Paulus den trinitarischen Taufbefehl Matth. 28,19 und ein trinitarisches Taufbekenntnis gekannt? ," *Zur Theorie des Christentums, Fst. R. Seeberg* I, ed. by W. Koepp (Leipzig, 1929), pp. 179ff. and Green, "Command," *passim.*

527 Cf. Josh. 1:5 and Jer. 1:7f.

of this promise retains those features strictly representative of the two writers, but a basic theological and structural similarity is nevertheless discernible. In Jn. the compositional parallel extends back to the promise of chapter 14:16-24 with its theological fulfillment in the giving and reception of the Spirit in 20:21ff. In 14:16 Jesus promises to ask the Father to send the disciples another *παράκλητος* so that *μεθ' ὑμῶν εἰς τὸν αἰῶνα ᾖ*. He goes on to assure them in vs. 18 that he shall not leave them as *ὀρφανοί*, but *ἔρχομαι πρὸς ὑμᾶς*. He then makes reference to the words which he has taught them (especially vss. 23-26). From these parallels it would appear that either Jn and Mt are relying upon a common source or that Jn is basically following Mt. and has formed the material in accord with his own theological interests and the needs of his ecclesiastical environment, i.e., the emphasis on the Spirit as the *mode* of Jesus' presence and activity, an element which Mt expresses as the presence of Jesus himself. In light of what we have thus far noticed of Jn's handling of the group appearance the first alternative seems to be the most likely choice. We have seen that the matthaean commission with its promise of Jesus' abiding presence is thoroughly bound up with matthaean theology, but before deciding on the question of originality we must turn to our third source, Lk.

The Three Phases of Luke: Part II

We notice immediately that the whole structure of the lukan address differs considerably from that of the other two. We expect to find, of course, many rich and distinctive details in keeping with the tendencies noted in Lk. up to this point, but the number and character of these differences at this point in the narrative exceed all that has preceded. As with the first half of the group appearance we see three distinct phases in the second half as well. Phase 1 concerns itself with a very detailed interpretation of the OT pointers to the meaning of the Messiah's life and death, namely, so that forgiveness might be proclaimed in all the world. Those proclaiming this begin in Jerusalem itself.[528] The second phase is to be found in the key words of direct address in vs. 48: *ὑμεῖς μάρτυρες τούτων*.[529] The third phase is almost as short and contains the promise of the Holy Spirit. We do see, however, some similarities in structure between Lk. and Mt. Lk. begins with a statement in the indicative in phase one, then comes to the direct application of the foregoing words to the listeners (without the *οὖν* of Mt. and Jn., however) and then lastly comes to a promise. This latter aspect like Mt. begins with the expression *καὶ ἰδού*, but instead of the use of a "futuristic" present we find a simple future: *ἐξαποστέλλω*. The only imperative in the entire address, which like the *λάβετε* of Jn. or the *μαθητεύσατε* of Mt., is directly related to the Spirit question in Jn. and in-

528 There are some punctuation difficulties at this point, but the majority of reliable mss. connect the phrase *ἀρξάμενοι ἀπὸ Ἰερουσαλήμ* with the preceding OT clarification as an anacoluthon, although the nominative plural form of the participle could bear a syntactical relationship to the following direct application of this OT clarification. Cf. Robertson, *op. cit*., pp. 413, (435-445), 491, 946 and 1203.

529 Cf. Isa. 43:10-12 and 44:8.

directly to the imperative in Mt., while perhaps directly related to the promise of Mt. in the words: *καθίσατε...ἕως οὗ ἐνδύσησθε....*

In terms of the three phase structure of Lk., therefore, we do have specifically lukan characteristics, but it is to be asked if any aspects thereof correspond directly to either Mt. or Jn. seen from the perspective of content. As noted in the preceding paragraph we do find a compound cognate of the verb *ἀποστέλλω* in Lk., but interestingly enough it is not used in the same sense of the "sending/going" verbs of Mt. or Jn. The only real parallel to their *πέμπω* or *πορευθέντες μαθητεύσατε* is simply the lukan second phase, i.e., *ὑμεῖς μάρτυρες τούτων*. No less than in Mt. this statement is balanced literarily within the whole complex of the address (in contrast to Jn.), but the strong ties with the OT heritage represent a unique feature. Of course, we have noted above that the whole structure of the matthaean scene represents the OT heritage indirectly through Dan. 7 and the notion of the presence of God for vs. 20b, but the interest which he displays throughout his gospel in relating fulfillment passages has here faded. The question then arises: what is the place for the OT heritage question within the group appearance tradition?

Terminology

To answer this question and that of origins in general for Lk. we turn to a special analysis of the lukan narrative.

1. *ἔτι ὢν σὺν ὑμῖν*–this adverb of time with the verb "to be" is a common enough construction in the NT, but in conjunction with this prep. it is somewhat unusual. The largest number of uses occur in Lk./Acts and Rev. The most common construction is with the genitive absolute "while he was speaking. . ." cf. Mt. 27:63; [Lk. 14:32; 24]:6, [41]; Jn. 7:33; 13:33; 20:1; Rom. 5:8 and II Thess. 2:5.

2. *δεῖ πληρωθῆναι*–the verb with other complementary infinitives is common enough in the NT (largest number in Lk./Acts, however), but this combination is without parallel. Lk. 18:31 is very similar in respects other than this combination. It is most interesting to note the relationship between this fulfillment idea and the predictions of the Christ's sufferings (cf. Mk. 8:31ff.; 9:30ff.; 10:32ff. and parallels to each). In these prediction pericopae we find the following constructions:

> *δεῖ ἀπελθεῖν* (Mt.)
> *δεῖ πάσχειν*
> *δεῖ ἀποδοκιμασθῆναι* (missing in Mt.)
> *δεῖ ἀποκτανθῆναι*
> *δεῖ ἐγερθῆναι* (*ἀναστῆναι*) in Mk.

In the lukan parallel to the third prediction we find the first major addition (Lk. 18:31). Here the notion of the suffering of the Christ is specifically a matter of fulfillment (*τελεσθήσεται*, cf. also [Lk. 22:37]) to what was written in the scriptures. This adding of non-parallel material by Lk with regard to the suffering/fulfillment theme is also to be found in 17:25 and [24]:7, [26] and here in vs. [44]. Furthermore, outside of Jn. 20:9 the only parallel constructions to the *δεῖ* sections of Lk. are to be found in Acts (cf. 1:16 (9:16) and 17:3). Of main interest in the fulfillment aspect for it is here that Lk. differs from the markan tradition of the predicted sufferings. Certainly *πληρόω* occurs in Mt.'s fulfillment citations (*ἵνα πληρωθῇ τὸ ῥηθὲν διὰ προφήτου...*), but not only is the use of the verb with the term *γραφαί* unusual in the gospels (cf. Mt. 26:54, 56; Mk. 14:49; 15:28; Lk. 4:21; 7:1; 9:31; 21:24 and here in vs. [44]; Jn. 13:18;

15:25; 17:12; 19:24, 36 and cf. Acts 1:16), but also the ideas of "joy" or the more pauline νόμος (Gal. 5:14, also (Lk. 10:26) and James 2:23) are much more common as objects.

3. περὶ ἐμοῦ—this prep. is normally combined with the third person or second person personal pronouns, e.g., αὐτοῦ, αὐτῶν or σοῦ etc., but on occasion with the first person singular, i.e., as here μοῦ. In the synoptic tradition [Lk. 22:37] is the only other location, but in Jn. and in the epistle literature the construction is common enough. We find three references in Acts (22:18; 23:11 and 24:10). Although we do find περὶ αὐτοῦ in Mk. 14:21 and Mt. 26:24 (cf. [Lk. 24:27] also) the sequence "being written concerning me" is exclusively a Lk./Acts and Jn. construction. Although the johannine constructions often parallel those of Lk. the inclusion therewith of the neuter plural πάντα is nowhere to be found.

4. τῷ νόμῳ Μωϋσέως καὶ τοῖς προφήταις κ. ψαλμοῖς—is for the synoptic tradition only to be found here (cf. [Lk. 2:22] κατὰ τ. ν. Μ.) and in vs. [44] and Acts 13:38 (ἐν ν. Μ.); 15:5 (τ. ν. Μ.). The term "the law of Moses" occurs outside thereof in Jn. 7:23; I Cor. 9:9 and Heb. 9:19; 10:28. The term "Moses and the prophets" is also exclusively Lk./Acts (cf. [Lk. 16:29,31; 24:27] and Acts 28:23) outside of the one reference in Jn. 1:46. The combination "the law and the prophets" is to be found in the following variety of locations: Mt. 5:17; 7:12; 11:13; 22:40; Lk. 16:16; Acts 13:15; 24:14; 28:23; Jn. 1:45 and Rom. 3:21. Interestingly enough Lk./Acts is the only synoptic complex to use the term ψαλμός (cf. Lk. 20:42 and here in vs. [44] and Acts 9:20; 13:33 and the three epistle locations: I Cor. 14:26; Eph. 5:19 and Col. 3:16).

5. διανοίγω—outside of Mk. 7:34 this verb is only to be found in Lk./Acts (cf. [Lk. 2:23; 24:31,32] and here in vs. [45] and Acts 7:56; 16:14; 17:3). Interestingly, however, it is only in the references of [Lk. 24] and the last two of the Acts references where the meaning of "illumination" is meant. In the others and Mk. as well the verb is practically synonymous with its cognate ἀνοίγω cf. Mt. 7:7f.; 9:30; 20:33 and 27:52 and Lk. 11:9 etc. where the meaning is one of physical motion, (symbolic) promise or of healing.

6. νοῦς—for the gospels this reference is *hapax*. Elsewhere it occurs in the epistle literature and twice in Rev.

7. συνίημι—for the entire NT this is the only use of the verb as an articular infinitive.530 Moreover, this is the only location in which γραφή is the object. Nevertheless, wherever the verb itself is used in the NT it is chiefly in conjunction with OT references, e.g., Isa. 6:9,10; 10:9,10; 52:15 and Psa. 14:2: "hearing they do not hear nor understand. . ." etc. Of course, the term γραφή itself finds frequent enough usage in the NT alone. In the synoptic tradition, however, it is only to be found in the later chapters, i.e., after the Triumphal Entry into Jerusalem (cf. Mt. 21:42; 22:29; 26:54,56; Mk. 12:10,24; 14:49; 15:28; [Lk. 24:27,32] and here in vs. [45]). The one exception is Lk. 4:21. For Jn. it occurs throughout but only once in the resurrection narratives (20:9).

8. μετάνοια—as the subject of κηρύσσω also in Mk. 1:4; 6:12 and Lk. 3:3, but the construction is on the whole not very common. The term by itself is, of course, widely used in the NT.

9. πάντα τὰ ἔθνη—this combination is used throughout the NT (cf. Mt. 24:9,14; 25:32; 28:19; Mk. 11:17; 13:10; Lk. 21:24 and [here]; Acts 2:5; 10:35; 14:16; 17:26 and 21:21). Often the term πάντα is missing in Acts, but the idea of universality remains. This is also the case in other references (cf. Rom. 1:45; 4:17,18; 15:11; 16:26; Gal. 3:8; II Tim. 4:17 and Rev. 15:4; 14:8 and 18:3,23).

10. ἀρξάμενοι ἀπὸ Ἰερουσαλήμ—the verb used with a geographical location and the prep. ἀπό is used only in Lk. 23:5 and [here] and in Acts 1:4,8; 10:37. This is the only location where

530 As a favorite lukan construction. Cf. Robertson, *op. cit.*, p. 1065. Over one-third of all of the NT articular infinitives occur in Lk./Acts.

Jerusalem is the object of the prep. The spelling of Jerusalem is also of interest.[531] The spelling used here, i.e., with the dipthong ου, is the spelling most common to Lk. Outside of Mt. 23:37 the rest of the gospels use the shorter ο spelling. For Acts, however, the percentage is about 60-40 in favor of the ου spelling. Yet, both Lk. ([2:22]; 13:22; [23:7]; 19:28, the latter paralleled by all four gospels) and Acts (1:4 etc., cf. 1:8) have the ο spelling as well.

11. *μάρτυρ*—outside of special Mt. (18:16) and Mk. 14:63 (par. Mt. 26:65) the only locations in the gospel tradition are to be found in Lk. (cf. 11:48 and here in vs. [48]) and thirteen times in Acts, of which eight are especially interesting (cf. 1:8,22; 2:32; 3:15; 5:32; 10:39,41 and 13:31). These eight locations all seem to bear a direct relationship to this vs. [48] within the early apostolic preaching tradition. Most all of them end with their witness to the phrase (constitutive for Lk.): *καὶ ἡμεῖς μάρτυρες τούτων*.

12. *ἐξαποστέλλω*—outside of Gal. 4:4,6 this verb is to be found exclusively in Lk./Acts in the NT. We find seven in Acts and four in Lk. (cf. [Lk. 1:53]; 20:10,11; [24:49]).

13. *ἐπαγγελία*—this is the only occasion for this noun in the gospels although it occurs eight times in Acts and frequently in the rest of the NT, especially Paul and Hebrews.

14. *καθίζω*—in the gospels this reading is *hapax* in conjunction with the prep. *ἐν*. Elsewhere in the NT this verb and prep. appear in combination primarily with the meaning of "sitting at the right hand" or "employing" (cf. I Cor. 6:4; Eph. 1:20; Heb. 1:3; 8:1; 10:12; 12:2 and Rev. 3:21). Only here in vs. [49], however, do we find the meaning of "waiting in a place" (in a city).

15. *ὕψος*—only to be found in [Lk. 1:78] and here in vs. [49] in the gospels. It is found sparsely scattered in the rest of the NT (cf. Eph. 3:18; 4:8; James 1:9 and Rev. 21:16). Lk is quite fond of the cognates *ὕψιστος* and *ὑψόω*.

16. *δύναμις*—occurrences of this noun without an epexegetical genitive for clarification are quite rare in the NT, but especially in the gospels. Where it stands without this genitival clarification other compounds are to be found, e.g., "power and glory" or "powers and principalities." Interestingly, parallels are nevertheless to be found in: Mk. 14:62 (Mt. 26:64); Mk. 9:1, 39 and [Lk. 1:35]; 6:19; 8:46; 9:1 and Acts 1:8; 4:33 and 6:8.

Luke and His Sources

As with the first half of the lukan group appearance we consider here the second half in terms of the source/redactional problem. We have followed the same methodology in the statistical breakdown as noted above and see at a glance that the scattering of special Lk. and redactional parallels are roughly the same as the first half. Whereas the first half, however, was integrally related to a specific stratum of the synoptic tradition in a unique way, namely the Walking on the Water story, no such parallel serves here as the basic structural contour. What sort of material do we then have, and what is its relation to OT prophecy for Lk? The following categories supply a helpful directive:

Those terms which are entirely unique for the gospels (*hapax* readings for the entire NT do not exist in this complex) are:

νοῦς, *ἐπαγγελία*, *καθίζω...ἐν*, *δεῖ πληρωθῆναι*, i.e., as a combination.

531 Cf. the discussion of W.M. Ramsay, "Luke the Physician," *Luke the Physician and Other Studies in the History of Religion* (Grand Rapids, Mich., 1956[='08]), pp. 51ff., *et passim*.

Phrases which occur nowhere else or are very seldom to be found in the NT are:

τῷ νόμῳ Μωϋσέως κ. τοῖς προφήταις κ. ψαλμοῖς

Those terms which have parallels only in special Lk. if they appear elsewhere in Lk. at all (although they may be found outside of Lk./Acts) are:

διανοίγω (one exception, but not in this meaning), ὕψος

Those terms which restrict themselves to Lk./Acts but not necessarily to special Lk. are: ἀρξάμενοι ἀπὸ Ἰερουσαλήμ, μάρτυρες (two exceptions in the synoptic tradition), ἐξαποστέλλω

Those terms and phrases which are common to the rest of the NT, but may be of special importance in terms of their lukan construction are:

συνίημι (as articular infinitive with τὰς γραφάς a *hapax* reading, but a common lukan construction), ἔτι ὢν σὺν ὑμίν, περὶ ἐμοῦ, μετάνοια, πάντα τὰ ἔθνη, δύναμις

From the word statistic we note immediately that vs. 44 from the δεῖ construction to ψαλμοῖς is not particularly lukan whereas the adapting of the statement to the context is.[532] Vs. 45 is something of a question. The idea of making clear to their minds the meaning of scripture has on the one hand distinct lukan characteristics, e.g., the articular infinitive construction, and the use of διανοίγω. In this meaning the latter occurs only here and in the Emmaus story (vs. 32) for Lk. and Acts 16:4 and 17:3. In these cases we find a basic continuity of usage and even though they appear seldom so as to suspect a source rather than redaction, their place in the narrative and semi-narrative sections rather than direct discourse sections would indicate the work of lukan composition. On the other hand, the use of νοῦς as the object of the verb and the articular infinitive form of συνίημι as a final clause is certainly without parallel and that in spite of the fact that γραφή plays a central role for the διανοίγω locations cited above. So, it would appear that both vss. 44 and 45 are in essence non-lukan, but have been considerably reworked and placed within the context with literary polish.

In vss. 46ff. the issue becomes both more difficult and at the same time easier, i.e., more defined. In comparison to the matthaean and johannine texts this clear statement of prophetic fulfillment is unparalleled. Are we dealing, therefore, with a lukan creation or a pre-lukan source? The context may be of immediate assistance here. We find that the terminology itself is of no great consequence in terms of the word statistic because of the widespread usage in the entire NT. The possibility exists, therefore, as pointed out above, that the whole idea of suffering, dying and rising from the dead as a divine necessity was simply taken over by Lk from the markan tradition and here incorporated into the appearance narrative. On the other

532 Cf. the redactional change of Lk. 24:6 in comparison with parallels. Considering the δεῖ-construction to be typically lukan, however, are, e.g., Schubert, "Structure," p. 181 and Bode, *op. cit.*, pp. 64ff. For the relationship of the term to the predictions of suffering and the scripture motif in general for Lk., cf. J. Roloff, "Anfänge der soteriologischen Deutung des Todes Jesu (Mk. x.45 and Lk. xxii.27)," *NTS*, 19 (1972), pp. 38ff.

hand the construction itself indicates an element of inseparability between the prophetic necessity of the cross *and* Resurrection and the proclamation of repentance and forgiveness, the latter element representing common ground with the other texts in content, if not in form. The question is then: Are the elements of prophecy for the cross and Resurrection just as much reflections of early common tradition as the commission? The question cannot be answered perhaps with any degree of certainty because of the obvious early connection of the three within the reflection of the early church. We may, however, assume that we are not dealing strictly with a lukan creation because of several indicators. The form on the whole is that of an early kerygmatic statement placed here in the mouth of the risen One. Whereas vss. 44 and 45 have their focus in the first person singular, especially with regard to the *περὶ ἐμοῦ*, we find that vss. 46 and 47 revert to the third person singular (cf. especially the *ἐπὶ τῷ ὀνόματι αὐτοῦ* of vs. 47). If this was purely scripture quotation, as one would expect from the *ὅτι οὕτως γέγραπται* of vs. 46, the third person would be easy enough to explain. Such, however, is not the case. The significance of the Resurrection from the dead *τῇ τρίτῃ ἡμέρᾳ*, moreover, might be taken as general support for the source origin of the complex for although it is here lukan redaction the time notion itself had a very early place within the kerygma tradition in spite of the absence of OT scriptural proof for it.[533]

In vss. 47b and 48 we find parallels in lukan redactional sections almost exclusively. Not only is the *ἄρχω* and *ἀπό* construction with a temporal or geographical qualifier typical Lk, but also the whole theological perspective of his *heilsgeschichtlich* plan is here evident in the centrality of Jerusalem. Vs. 48 places the "witness" idea in the heart of the explanation of prophecy. It is for Lk the link that makes the intervening years between the event and the hearer of secondary importance and actualizes for him the meaning of tradition as a whole. Although this statement of the commission is a lukan formulation and, therefore, distinguishes itself from source material, the notion probably has its roots very early in the tradition.[534]

In vs. 49 we are confronted with some very difficult problems. The point of the prophetic narrative is reached in the commission of vs. 48 and with it the climax of the appearance, at least in terms of a comparison with Mt. What is the place then of

533 Cf. the *κατὰ τὰς γραφάς* of I Cor. 15:4, above pp. 59f.

534 Pointing out the significance of OT quotations in the growth of the synoptic tradition in general are, e.g., A. Suhl, *Die Funktion der alttestamentlichen Zitate und Anspielungen im Markus-Evangelium* (Gütersloh, 1965), *passim*, R.H. Gundry, *The Use of the Old Testament in St. Matthew's Gospel*, Suppl. NovTest (Leiden, 1967), *passim*, M. Rese, *Alttestamentliche Motive in der Christologie des Lukas* (Gütersloh, 1969), *passim*. Cf. also H.E. Tödt, *Der Menschensohn in der synoptischen Überlieferung* (Gütersloh, 1963[='59]), pp. 32f. *et passim*, Lindars, *Apologetic*, pp. 72ff. and 251-286, Dibelius, "Motive," pp. 126f., E.E. Ellis, "Midraschartige Züge in den Reden der Apostelgeschichte," *ZNW*, 62 (1971), pp. 94ff., Mildenberger, *op. cit.*, pp. 270f. and ns. 29 and 31, Kegel, *op. cit.*, p. 26, E. Sanders, *op. cit.*, pp. 200f. Stressing the lukan redactional origin of the scripture motif are Evans, *Resurrection*, pp. 96, 103 and 106, Lohse, *Auferstehung*, pp. 11f., Leaney, "Narratives," pp. 113f., Beare, "Sayings," pp. 169ff., and above all, Schubert, "Structure," pp. 173ff. and 176ff., who says, "we conclude that Luke's proof-from-prophecy theology is the heart of his concern in chapter 24" (p. 176). Cf. also Billerbeck, *op. cit.*, II, pp. 273-299.

the promise of the Father, power from above? It would appear that this verse has Acts in mind. The focus of the last two verses is overwhelming in content if not in sequence: repentance and forgiveness of sins *among all the nations*, beginning at *Jerusalem*, you are *witnesses* and I will send the *promise of the Father*, so *wait in the city* until you have been clothed with *power from above.* These categories summarize the first two chapters of Acts. Moreover, upon examination of the terminology we find that of the eleven parallels for *ἐξαποστέλλω* in Lk./Acts seven are in Acts; for *ἐπαγγελία* this is the only occasion for the gospels while it occurs eight times in Acts. On the other hand in vs. 49b we find terms which are not only not particularly lukan, but which are also without apparent linguistic relation to Acts at all. The expression *καθίζω...ἐν* is quite unique for the entire NT (the *παρήγγειλεν αὐτοῖς ἀπὸ Ἱεροσολύμων μὴ χωρίζεσθαι, ἀλλὰ περιμένειν τὴν ἐπαγγελίαν τοῦ πατρός* of Acts 1:4 notwithstanding). The only parallel occurrence of *ἐξ ὕψους* is special Lk. (1:78) as well. Even the cognates thereof are more frequently found in Lk. than they are in Acts. The idea, moreover, of being clothed with power (*ἐνδύσησθε δύναμιν*) is here *hapax* for the NT and outside of Paul this is the only location where garments of some kind are not meant. The use of a metaphor is really quite pauline. It would appear, therefore, that in vs. 49b we are dealing with a pre-lukan source and that vs. 49a is either a redactional adaption thereof in the light of Acts or corresponds itself to a source which then was incorporated by Lk. We discussed the summaries of Acts above, but it must be said here that the probability of the direct influence of Acts 1 upon this verse is linguistically relatively slight, since the terminology of that chapter is so different ("the promise of the Father" excepted). Moreover, the parallels in Acts to *ἐξαποστέλλω*, for example, do not even begin until the seventh chapter. But terminology offers only one of several criteria for determining lukan redaction and it would appear that theologically the lukan concept of *Heilsgeschichte* plays a significant role. Can one conclude that Lk is using a source at this point in the light of his theological goals? It would appear most probable that just as Jn mentions the promise of the Spirit in one place and then describes its fulfillment in his group appearance scene Lk too here is pointing quite consciously to that factor which is to prove the inception and heart of his second volume.

So, we have seen that certain elements within this second half of the lukan appearance reflect most probably a source and that secondary redaction occurs mainly at the compositional junctures of literary adaption and theological re-formation.

Commission and OT Prophecy

We come now to the cross section view of our sources with regard to this important and final element of the group appearance narratives. Of principal interest at this point is the question: If the sending of Jesus, i.e., the words of commission, were the focal element of the group appearance tradition, that element which served—expressed variously—as the basis upon which the Church was founded and the channel through which she was to come to her self-identity and carry forward the mission of her Lord, did the relating of these words to OT heritage and fulfillment constitute an original part of this tradition or was it a secondary addition? Do the texts offer any reasons to retain the fulfillment theme within the earliest structure of the whole tradition? We have seen up to this point that neither Mt nor Jn occupies himself with this question directly. Mt. does lean heavily upon Dan. 7 and the OT concept of the presence of God, but as we saw earlier there is no apparent possibility to take this construction beyond Mt himself as evangelist.

We have, therefore, only in Lk. the direct form of this statement. We shall see this later in the Emmaus story as well and must, therefore, ask: could this element have been a part of the general group appearance tradition, part of the contours of its earliest structure and still appear only in Lk.? We have already seen in our word statistic and context investigation of Lk. that the material here in part existed prior to lukan redaction and corresponds to a source. Was the source unknown to Mt and Jn? If so, then in the form found in Lk. the prophetic fulfillment aspect could not have been part of the general address form of the appearance. Two alternatives would then seem possible: 1) the uniting of the prophetic background of the Passion and the Resurrection and the great commission was a very early reflection in the primitive church as a specific aspect of the group appearance tradition, but was *not clearly formulated* within that tradition until Lk or his source had done so. The clear arrangement of chronological development, i.e., the overview of OT-NT continuity, was first the work of Lk following perhaps the direction of his source. For Mt the resurrection encounter is a monumental occasion, but more in terms of the present and future focus than the fusion of cross and Resurrection under the fulfillment motif. 2) The whole idea of prophetic fulfillment here was achieved by Lk through the markan material where it emphasized the prediction of the Christ's suffering. In this case the markan strata of the synoptic tradition would have played a direct role for Lk in the development of this aspect of his group appearance story. In the light of what we have already seen of Lk's compositions in Acts 10 and 13 the latter alternative has strong possibilities. A definite decision regarding the alternatives is, nevertheless, difficult and problematical. We simply do not know enough about the pre-lukan source to allow for certain elimination of the former. Earlier, we referred to this motif as an early kerygmatic statement of the church put into the mouth of the risen One, an expression of its understanding about who this One is. In this sense we could perhaps classify it as very early, i.e., part of an early expression of faith–not altogether unlike the Thomas story for Jn–, but not early as a part of the appearance tradition. That was first the work of theological reflection when the Easter narratives were literarily fixed. On the other hand, it is entirely possible that this union with prophecy grew up with the story and that the preexisting union was then put into the form of a statement by the lukan source. Both alternatives are possible, but it would appear that the alternative of lukan redaction has probability on its side when one considers the nature of his redactional work elsewhere in relationship to the kerygma and other traditions.

The Words of Commission–Conclusions

If certainty is wanting on the presence or absence of the fulfillment element in the commission for the earliest form of the tradition, does the cross section view of our three sources supply aspects which are unmistakably part of an identical tradition? With clarity and precision we find all of the texts laying great stress on those commissioned acting in the place of the departing Lord. Concretely, however, this clarity exists primarily at the redactional level, an indication that this element was the critical juncture for adaption by the evangelists. We saw this element in the matthaean and johannine transitions and use of *οὖν* and in the use of verbs of "going." The same was true in Lk's transitions through *ὑμεῖς μάρτυρες τούτων* and *ἀρξάμενοι ἀπὸ Ἰερουσαλήμ*. Thus, basic to the commission motif for all three is that the disciples were given a specific commission, albeit authority, from the risen One appearing in their midst, a commission of active representation in his coming absence. What sort of representation does this mean? For Jn. the content is one of the forgiveness and retention of sins. For Mt. it is the same, but is expressed as a mission of making disciples or evangelization and of baptizing and teaching. For both the church as institution is a fundamental assumption. Lk. too has the forgiveness motif as the central matter which is to be represented to the world, but the general emphasis on the institutionality of the church is replaced by the specific idea of the authority resident in the apostolic witness, i.e., in Lk's situation a further refinement of the notions "church" and "authority" was needed. In any case the two aspects of a message of forgiveness and the representative nature of the group of disciples are clearly part of the redactional form of this address. The question of the place of the Holy Spirit is not as obvious as these other elements. In the light of the johannine goals for this aspect, the distinct matthaean concept of Jesus' promise "to be with you" which follows the direct statement of commission and the lukan promise of Jesus "to send the promise of the Father" which also comes after the direct commission (vs. 49) it would appear that the evangelists introduced this element into the commission compositionally as a result of ongoing theological interests in the Christian community. Thus we must conclude that for the words of commission only the sending itself is original[535] and that the promise and/or reception of the Spirit were very early closely related to the commission.

The Group Appearance–Conclusions

Our analysis of the three group appearance stories has led to a rather clear differentiation between the motifs and themes characteristic of the evangelists in question and those which resist such classification. At some points redactional reworking has made the recognition of original motifs difficult, but in the main their reconstruction from aspects of the later form can be achieved without excessive

535 Seeing here the key to the group appearance and/or all of the appearances in general are, e.g., Strobel, *Kerygma*, p. 174, Leaney, "Theophany," p. 101, Wilckens, *Auferstehung*, pp. 76 and 88f., George, *op. cit.*, pp. 100f., Evans, *Resurrection*, p. 130.

speculation. Our primary concern, is, of course, with the traditional matrix and it is of key interest to note that at this pre-redactional level the stories share to a great extent major similarities. An attempt to identify that original form at this point is not necessary since we wish first to examine all of the appearance stories and then to compare the full complement under the *Gattung* question. It is sufficient here to note their basic similarities of motif, progression and overall structure.

1. The disciples are gathered together after the events of the Crucifixion
2. The appearing One comes and speaks to them
3. Their reaction is designated as partially acceptance and partially skepticism
4. He is recognized as indeed the crucified/resurrected Jesus
5. He, the Lord, commissions and sends them

Ancillary, but possibly with some claim to an early union are the additional elements:

6. The cross and Resurrection are the fulfillment of OT prophecy
7. The Holy Spirit brings the commission to living reality for the commissioned.

2. The Emmaus Story: Lk. 24:13-33,35

As in the group appearance so too in this and our other two stories we may presuppose a general familiarity with the text and, therefore, it will be necessary here only to draw attention to the major lines of dispositional development at the redactional level before moving to a separation of the traditional form from lukan redaction. The story is paced in stages or phases in much the same way as Lk.'s group appearance noted above. It begins somewhat abruptly but with a certain degree of continuity with the foregoing. We have *καὶ ἰδοὺ*, then the identification of the persons involved *δύο ἐξ αὐτῶν*, one of whom is identified in vs. 18 as *ὀνόματι* Κλεοπᾶς[536] and then the time reference *ἐν αὐτῇ τῇ ἡμέρᾳ* presumably a synonym here for the "third day." With these preliminaries then follows the first phase which is a travel scene in which the two "disciples" are on their way to Emmaus[537] dis-

536 We have already noted on occasion the problems caused by the names of the two travelers in the history of research, cf. above, n. 197 and below, n. 554 and also, e.g., Lohse, *Auferstehung*, pp. 24 and 26, Hennecke-Schneemelcher, *op. cit.*, II, pp. 257f. and R. Fuller, *op. cit.*, pp. 107ff. and above pp. 48f. R. Annand, "'He was seen of Cephas'. A Suggestion about the First Resurrection Appearances of Peter," *SJTh*, 11 (1958), pp. 180ff. proposes that Peter is the unnamed traveling companion of Cleopas.

537 The geographical location of the town has been of considerable interest to many and although there may be something to be said for the proposal that this story was in someway connected to a very early local Emmaus community tradition it is of no direct consequence for our line of questioning. Cf. Wilckens, *Auferstehung*, p. 79. Further, Billerbeck, *op. cit.*, II, pp. 269f., Lohse, *Auferstehung*, pp. 24f., A. de Guglielmo, "Emmaus," *CBQ*, 3 (1941), *passim*, E. Lipinski, "Les disciples d'Emmaüs," *REL*, 53 (1967), pp. 224ff., Cornelius, *op. cit.*, p. 15, n. 10, and G. Schille, *Anfänge*, pp. 167f.

cussing the events of the Passion[538] when suddenly Jesus draws near and joins them in their journey. They, however, do not recognize him. Then begins the second phase, a dialogue in which a conversation takes place between them on the nature of their dialogue prior to his entrance. In reply to Jesus' inquiry—only the hearer/reader is aware that it is an appearance story at all—Cleopas addresses him with a three point representation of those events: 1) a characterization of the ministry of Jesus up to and including his trial and Crucifixion, 2) a statement on the messianic hopes of those who had followed him from Galilee and 3) a report that the tomb had been found empty by both the women and some of the disciples and that although the women claimed to have seen an *ὀπτασίαν* of angels and were told that Jesus was alive the disciples had not seen him. The second part of this phase then contains the response of Jesus, which takes the form of a rebuke and a sermon on the prophecy/fulfillment character of the (his) Passion. At this point phase three begins with the arrival of the three at their destination and the appeal of the two for him to remain with them and his acceptance.[539] The climax of this phase and simultaneously for the whole story comes when he, the guest, assumes the role of housemaster host, breaks and blesses bread and passes it to them for it is at this moment that their eyes are opened and they recognize him; at that moment he disappears. They react with amazement at their blindness[540] and then begins the last phase as they rise and return to Jerusalem in spite of the late hour and relate to the eleven and those with them the events on the road and the moment of recognition.

In contrast to the often somewhat difficult decision in determining what is tradition over against redaction in the group appearance text in Lk. the same decision here is more readily attained because of the relative clear lines of demarcation within the story itself. Linguistic and theological considerations give the following picture: outside of the opening transition, and perhaps that transition's reference to the "same day" and the qualification of the distance of Emmaus from Jerusalem, vs. 13 contains nothing that may be ascribed to lukan redactional interest. Vs. 14 is somewhat more difficult because although the discourse motif is introduced by *ὁμιλεῖν*, a lukan term,[541] it is debatable whether or not the motif itself was originally present in the account and may have been restated then by Lk in his own words. The use of *συμβαίνω* in the same verse would suggest perhaps lukan composition alone,[542] but further observations must be made before a decision is made.

538 Pointing out that it was customary for Jews to busy themselves with thoughts and conversations of a religious nature while journeying together or if alone to reflect on the Torah is Billerbeck, *op. cit.*, II, p. 273; also Lohse, *Auferstehung*, p. 25 and A. Ehrhardt, "The Disciples of Emmaus," *NTS*, 10 ('63/'64), pp. 188f.

539 Seeing in the appeal an invitation form like that of Gen. 24:55; Jud. 19:9 and Tobit 10:8, etc., is H.-D. Betz, "Ursprung und Wesen christlichen Glaubens nach der Emmauslegende (Lk 24,13-32)," *ZThK*, 66 (1969), p. 12, n. 13.

540 H. Almquist, *op. cit.*, p. 71 compares to vs. 32 Plutarch *Mor.* 1059C, *De comm. not.* 1, Lucian *Calumnia* 14 etc., and says that it refers to "eine starke Empfindung des Unbehagens, die man 'löschen' möchte. . . ."

541 Found only here in vss. 14 and 15 and in Acts 20:11 and 24:26.

542 Occurs here, 3x in Acts, half the number of occurrences in the whole NT.

Vs. 15a sets the stage for the coming of Jesus upon the scene and is clearly a lukan redactional transition, while vs. 15b presents terminology that is also otherwise known in lukan special sources and may along with vs. 16 be ascribed to the Emmaus story source. Vss. 17ff. marks the inception of the dialogue between the travelers and Jesus and puts into focus the question of the originality of the discourse motif itself raised above in vs. 14. The verb *εἶπεν* occurs frequently in this phase of the story usually in connection with *πρὸς αὐτούς* (*αὐτόν*) but once (vs. 19) with *αὐτοῖς* (*αὐτῷ*). The latter occurs 65x out of 82x in lukan special source material, which raises the question if it is not possible that an aspect of the exchange–the question and reply–is pre-redactional. The question is critical because the content of the discourse in general in these verses seems to bear the stamp of lukan composition quite clearly. The summary of events, the expression of hope and final uncertainty addressed to Jesus and the latter's reply are almost entirely clothed in lukan terminology and theology.[543] Yet, the identification of one of the travelers as Cleopas and some of the (for Lk.) unusual grammatical constructions seem to offer an occasional flicker of a source behind the strong flow of lukan formulations. We noted above in our terminological analysis of the lukan group appearance specific lukan traits and they recur here with obvious frequency up to and including vs. 27. Yet, these verses also bespeak a rather complex interweaving of familiar traditional material–granted their expression in Lk's own words–so that it is summarily difficult to maintain that Lk is writing here entirely independent of sources. These factors suggest that the discourse motif was, in fact, originally present in the story in a form that did not suit Lk's theological goals here so that he then composed the present form out of traditions known to him–not unlike what we have seen regarding Lk on other occasions–, e.g., the tomb story(ies), the scripture motif in the kerygma and elsewhere, and especially his own compositional use of them in his total theological plan for the Resurrection and its implications for the church's mission. It cannot be said, therefore, what the original discourse was about unless it was basically a statement about the Passion (vss. 19f.) underscoring the contrast between the assumption of the travelers about Jesus' death while the resurrected One in fact walks and talks with them, a motif which Lk then expands and specifies. Admittedly, this proposal is based on the evidence of the *εἶπεν αὐτοῖς* (*αὐτῷ*)-form as non-lukan and, therefore, as support for a discourse motif at all, and the assumption that something like the content of vss. 19f. would fit most logically into the contrasts of such a story, but in view of what we saw in the group appearance story it is justified to contend that Lk, in contrast to Mt, customarily pursues his redac-

543 Vs. 25 does contain the phrase *ὦ ἀνόητοι καὶ βραδεῖς* which is *hapax* here for the gospels. The first term occurs 3x in Paul (cf. Gal. 3:1) and 2x in the Pastoral Epistles, while the second is found otherwise in Jas. 1:19 only. Regarding the former Betz, *Lukian*, p. 125, n. 4, calls it a *Schimpfwort* from ancient Greek comedy. If its origins are indeed classical it may perhaps be ascribed to lukan style here. Cf. also Moulton and Milligan, *op. cit.*, pp. 44f. and A. Plummer, *The Gospel According to Luke*, ICC (Edinburgh, 1960, 5th ed.[= '22]), p. 554 and Ehrhardt, "Disciples," p. 187.

tional alterations along already established lines of development within the tradition itself–24:6 the only exception.

In vss. 28ff., the third phase, we find in part another distinct shift away from lukan terminology suggesting that Lk has to some degree left this part of the story intact, though he apparently makes additions and rewrites at certain points. The term noted for the tradition in vs. 15b *ἐγγίζειν* in combination with *πορεύειν* [544] or cognate repeats itself here in vs. 28 and that along with the *εἰς κώμην* of vs. 13 as well. [545] The *καὶ αὐτός* noted in vs. 15 and above all in the participants question (pp. 148ff.) recurs here in vss. 28b and 31, a non-lukan designation really which Lk was, nevertheless, willing to leave as it was because of the clarity of identity in both the overall transition among all the stories and the specific content here achieved by his redactional efforts in the discourse preceding it. [546] Other non-lukan terms are: *προσποιέω* with the comparative adverb *πορρώτερον* (*hapax* for NT), *παραβιάζεσθαι* (1x in Acts and here for the whole NT), *πρὸς ἑσπέραν ἐστίν* (2x in Acts and here for the NT but in other constructions), and perhaps *εἰσῆλθεν τοῦ μεῖναι σὺν αὐτοῖς* and *διανοίγειν*. [547] Other than stylistic changes, however, the only major deviation would appear to be the lukan form which the words take on regarding the meal in vs. 30 to suggest most probably for the reader of the gospel his own eucharistic context. Yet, even here the motif is clearly original to the story for it is the key to the moment of recognition. Finally, the disappearance motif is non-lukan in its expression and forms the reversal to an assumed but not stated verb of seeing/appearing, e.g., *ὤφθη*. Whether or not the story originally ended here or continued in a way similar to vss. 32ff. is hard to say, since in these verses we have again the resumption of strong redactional composition. It could very well be that as in the discourse of vss. 17ff. a kernel of the original form is still retained (vss. 19f.), so too here expansion has taken place while the original, brief conclusion is retained (vs. 33a and perhaps vs. 35a) on the fringe of Lk's principal redactional modifications. Certainty is wanting, however, since the climax of the story is reached at the moment of recognition and it is doubtful that any sort of elaborate ending would have been added since it would have done little more than detract from this climax.

In summation we see from the analysis above that the Emmaus story is not a unity but is a composite made up of several constituent parts. It is not a lukan creation nor is it secondary [548] but rather came to Lk through his special source. [549]

544 This verb occurs 88x in Lk./Acts out of 150x for the whole NT.

545 Considered *lukanisches Sondergut* by Rehkopf, *op. cit.*, p. 93. Also *ἀπέχω* vs. 13 and *ἀφ' οὗ* vs. 21 (p. 92).

546 Ehrhardt, "Disciples," pp. 183f. in general affirms the non-lukan character of the whole section here, but he does consider the use of *αὐτός* typical of the LXX and not unusual for Lk.

547 F. Lentzen-Deis, "Das Motiv der Himmelsöffnung in verschiedenen Gattungen der Umweltliteratur des Neuen Testaments," *Bb*, 50 (1969), p. 313, n. 7, calls *διανοίγειν* Lk's *Nachahmung des LXX-Stils* comparing, e.g., Gen. 3:5, 7 and 24:45, etc., to vss. 31f.

548 H.-F. Richter, *op. cit.*, p. 73 notwithstanding, who sees it in the light of a presumed *Tendenz einer fortschreitenden Realitätsbetonung.* Moreover, he starts with I Cor. 15 as the standard and then compares the story to the "secondary" character of Jn. 20:26ff.

549 Says Betz, "Ursprung," p. 9, concerning the source: "Der ursprüngliche Erzähler ist uns unbekannt, muß aber ein theologischer Kopf von beträchtlichem Vermögen gewesen sein."

Lk then incorporated the story—perhaps the oldest of the resurrection stories [550]—into his accounts of the resurrection appearances making certain alterations for purposes of transition and certification.[551] These lukan redactional elements are the verses: (14), 15a, 17-27, 32 and the transitional elements of 33-35 (which contain the reference to the kerygma tradition and the petrine appearance). The pre-lukan elements of the story then are to be found in the verses: 13, 15b, 16 and 28-31.[552] Some exegetes wish to see several stages of growth to the story before it came to Lk, but the theory rests upon some very uncertain presuppositions.[553] We did note, however, that it is possible that the original story was both expanded and abbreviated by Lk to achieve a more satisfactory adherence to his general theological intentions, especially giving place of pre-eminence to the group appearance. It is most improbable, however, that this was the removal of certain personal names which were supported through the story as early church leaders in conflict with others.[554]

In the group appearance category we were able to compare the structure and motifs of the texts and our conclusions there on general contours had the advantage of relative certainty. Since "Mk." 16:12,13, the only other "Emmaus" text, represents a summary of the lukan account itself[555] (with the addition that the

Cf. also Ehrhardt, "Disciples," pp. 182f., 193f. and p. 194, n. 1, in opposition to H. von Campenhausen, *Tradition und Leben, Kräfte der Kirchengeschichte* (Tüb., 1963), p. 59. H. Dembowski, "Jesus Christus—Herr der Götter," *EvTh*, 29 (1969), pp. 579f., affirms the traditional source and calls it a paradigm to early Christian preaching as was seen in the Dibelius hypothesis. Winter, "Sources," p. 167, n. 1, says that the pericope vss. 13-21a, 25-35 probably existed in Aramaic "being one of the earliest written records of the Palestinian community of believers in Jesus' messiahship." Cf. further Lohse, *Auferstehung*, p. 15, K.H. Rengstorf, *Das Evangelium nach Lukas*, NTD, 3 (Gött., 1968, 13th ed.), pp. 281f., Shepherd, *op. cit.*, pp. 234f., J. Dupont, "The Meal of Emmaus," *The Eucharist in the New Testament*, trans. by E.M. Stewart (London, 1965), pp. 121ff.

550 Bultmann, *Tradition*, pp. 310ff., Dibelius, *Formgeschichte*, p. 191, and Roloff, *Kerygma*, p. 256. For both Dibelius and Bultmann the key descriptive term is "legend" (cf. below n. 617). Also Betz, "Ursprung," who says, "Beim Vorgang der Interpretation müssen wir also stets von dem methodischen Grundsatz ausgehen, daß wir es in dieser Legende mit theologischer Lehre und Verkündigung zu tun haben und nicht mit historischen Tatsachen im gewöhnlichen Sinne; anderenfalls nähmen wir uns von vornherein die Möglichkeit, diesen Text in adäquater Weise zu verstehen" (p. 8, cf. also pp. 13f.).

551 Winter, "Sources," pp. 171f., overstates a lukan fidelity to sources. Efforts to obtain the redaction-critical monograph of J. Wanke, *Die Emmauserzählung*, EThS, 31 (Erfurt, 1974), before completion of the manuscript were without success.

552 Cf. Schubert, "Structure," p. 174, and Roloff, *Kerygma*, p. 256, while Erhardt, "Disciples," pp. 182f. thinks vss. 13-32 are independent of Lk.

553 Winter, "Sources," pp. 167f., sees an ancient Palestinian credo source incorporated here along with a non-markan grave story all under the editorial efforts of Lk. In any case they are not part of the appearance story, as noted above pp. 114ff. and 192f. Similar to Winter is Betz, "Ursprung," pp. 8f.

554 Contra W.O. Walker, Jr., "Postcrucifixion Appearances and Christian Origins," *JBL*, 88 (1969), p. 165. Ehrhardt, "Disciples," pp. 182f., thinks that a certain Simon was the original traveling companion and that Lk omitted the reference to avoid confusion with Simon Peter in vs. 34. The whole question of group conflicts in the appearance stories is too uncertain.

555 So, Dodd, "Appearances," pp. 31f. Claiming a variant tradition is Annand, *op. cit.*, pp. 180ff.

others did not believe their report, vs. 13, which is the natural conclusion from the skepticism expressed in Lk. 24:36ff.)[556] we are without further recourse on the matter of the length of the pre-redactional story and must simply leave the question open.

The question of whether or not this story actually corresponds in general form and use of details to the anthropomorphic theophanies of the OT and/or the appearances of the dead in the Hellenistic literature, as has often been proposed, is not to be discussed here but below in the next chapter where we will consider the question of possible analogies for all of the texts. Our goal here is rather to ascertain which motifs and themes belonged to the original appearance account itself.

In the traditional form of the Emmaus story we see, therefore, the following motifs emerging: While the two travelers are enroute to their destination (vs. 15b) Jesus himself draws near [*ἐγγίσας*] and accompanies them [*συνεπορεύετο αὐτοῖς*]. Then follows the failure of the two to recognize him because of a mysterious force which prevents their eyes from grasping the identity of the One in their midst [*οἱ δὲ ὀφθαλμοὶ αὐτῶν ἐκρατοῦντο τοῦ μὴ ἐπιγνῶναι αὐτόν*, vs. 16]. At this point in the story comes the entire dialogue episode which, although in its present proportions was absent from the original story, may have existed in more modest ones.[557] With regard to the former it was certainly within the scope of Lk's theology to place this instruction from scripture in the mouth of the resurrected One as his response to the doubts of the two travelers, but we saw in the group appearance category that it is difficult to relegate this motif entirely to the influence of Lk's redactional hand. More probably Lk develops a theme which was a general and widespread given in the early Christian community. Be that as it may as a general observation regarding Lk and the background of this theme, it is improbable that it was as such a part of the original Emmaus story whose central theme is expressed in the recognition scene.[558]

556 Also an indication that the group appearance originally was a separate story for Lk and by no means a simple continuation of the Emmaus story, Lohse, *Auferstehung*, p. 34. To the contrary is Winter, "Sources," pp. 168f., who assumes that the entire group appearance is an elaboration of vs. 30, the meal motif of the Emmaus story (cf. below under meal motif discussion).

557 Cf. Roloff, *Kerygma*, p. 256, who holds the entire discourse for improbable.

558 Betz, "Ursprung," pp. 10ff. and esp. p. 11, n. 12 and p. 12, comes to the opposite conclusion. His remarks about *Wortgeschehen* are most interesting (cf. W. Marxsen, *Anfangsprobleme der Christologie* [Gütersloh, 1960], p. 35), but fail to recognize the form-critical lines of distinction which must be drawn here. Schubert, "Structure," pp. 176f., assumes that this motif woven into all of chapter 24 is clearly lukan redaction. Ehrhardt, "Disciples," pp. 185f. goes to great lengths to prove that the point of the story is singularly that of the resurrected One teaching from scripture and not the question of his identity and recognition in the meal. Of course, there is no dispute about the centrality of the "teaching" motif in the story as we find it in Lk., but the *crux* of the matter lies in its lukan origin for our concern with *Gattung* motifs (Rengstorf, *Lukas*, p. 284, makes the same mistake). Ehrhardt would like to assume that this motif already existed in "Q" and that Lk merely rearranges the material ("Disciples," p. 187, esp. n. 2). Be that as it may, he fails to see that this suggests nothing more than that the motif is lukan here (cf. p. 191). His further discussion about OT testimonia regarding the Messiah in the synagogue and the rise of specifically Christian OT testimonia is interesting but all too uncer-

After the editorial enlargement then of vss. 17-27 comes the climax of the story in vss. 28ff. This closing scene entails basically three motifs after the travelers take up their lodging for the evening: a) the inception of a meal, b) the mysterious opening of hitherto closed eyes and recognition of Jesus [559] and c) the latter's sudden disappearance. [560] Not only at the inception of the meal but also throughout the story up to this point the dominant motif has been the incognito presence of Jesus (without the added feature in "Mk." 16:12, *ἐν ἑτέρᾳ μορφῇ*). [561] The motif is without parallel actually when one fact is considered: the lack of recognition is not to be credited to human failure but rather to divine initiative! [562] That which the

tain to be adduced here as part of a pre-lukan Emmaus story (cf. pp. 188ff. and to the general testimonia theme, cf. H. Patsch, *Abendmahl und historischer Jesus*, CThM, 1 [Stutt., 1972], pp. 164f. and literature in notes; also, P. Grech, "The 'Testimonia' and Modern Hermeneutics," *NTS*, 19 [1972/'73], pp. 318ff.). Cf. the uniformity of usage on the scripture motif in vss. 27b, 32b and 45 of this and the group appearance story—a clear line of redactional expression. Hereto also Wilckens, *Auferstehung*, p. 80, and above n. 534.

559 Cf. Schubert, "Structure," pp. 172ff. That this is also a key motif in the Magdalene story of Jn. 20:11-18 will be discussed below. Cf. also Dupont, "Meal," p. 110 and Grundmann, *Lukas*, p. 442. F. Schnider and W. Stenger, "Beobachtungen zur Struktur der Emmausperikope (Lk 24,13-35)," *BZ*(NF), 16/1 (1972), pp. 94-114, make a linguistic analysis of the Emmaus story in accord with the methods of the contemporary science of literature which "ein literarisches Werk nicht aus seinen Beziehungen zu seiner Geschichte, seinem Autor, seiner Umwelt zu verstehen versucht, sondern es in einer werkimmanenten Analyse aus sich selbst erklären will" (p. 94). Their analysis of the structure and system of functions leads them to conclude that the original story (ending at vs. 31, following Schubert, "Structure"), its constitutive units (17 of them) making up a *Beziehungsbündel*, was a recognition story, which moves convincingly back and forth between the opposite poles: incognition/recognition, fellowship/nonfellowship (pp. 103ff.). The structural principle is that of opposites and the scheme is configurated ABABA with the chief subordinate theme to recognition being that of the meal.

560 In this latter aspect Dupont, "Meal," pp. 119f., points to the disappearance of Philip after the baptism of the Ethiopian eunuch for a striking parallel. Outside of this one formal element, however, the accounts have little else in common. Kremer, *Osterbotschaft*, p. 69, refers to both as *religiöse Unterweisung*. Schubert, "Structure," pp. 168f., emphasizes here that Jesus disappears and does not "depart" since it is a "direct and explicit transition" to Lk's second volume. He thinks then that vs. 51 bears the same meaning as vs. 31 here. Betz, *Lukian*, pp. 168f. links this element to Acts 8:39f. calling it an *Entrückungs- und Versetzungstopos* like that found in *de Syr. dea* 4 *et al.* He further links to the *Topos* the miraculous opening of doors implied (?) in Lk. 24:31, 36 and explicit (?) in Jn. 20:19, 26: "Dadurch soll seine Gestalt [Jesus] 'von vornherein als göttlich gekennzeichnet' werden" (p. 170). Also drawing Acts 8 and Emmaus together is G. Bouwman, *Das Dritte Evangelium. Einübung in die formgeschichtliche Methode* (Düss., 1968), p. 14, who adds, "Sollten wir nicht annehmen dürfen, Lukas habe den Bericht über die Emmausjünger deshalb ausgearbeitet, um anzudeuten, daß jeder, der einen Apostel aufnimmt, den Herrn selbst aufnimmt (Mt. 10,40; Jn. 13,20)? ," and J. Mouson, "Présence du Ressuscité. Les évangéliques d'apparition," *Col. Mech.*, 54 (1969), pp. 190ff., seeing here a typical scene under the scripture motif. Cf. also Ehrhardt, "Disciples," pp. 184f., who sees in vs. 31 the terminology of epiphanies in pagan religion. With more theological interest in the explicit use of this motif in the liturgical and catechetical practice of the church is Betz, "Ursprung," pp. 12f. For Mouson, *op. cit.*, p. 198, it is symbolic of the invisible presence of the Lord in his Church.

561 Ehrhardt, "Disciples," p. 184. Benoit, *Passion and Resurrection*, p. 274, is quite misleading in this respect.

562 Ehrhardt, "Disciples," pp. 183f. who also emphasizes ἐκρατοῦντο as a *passivum divinum* similar to the blindness of Jerusalem in Lk. 19:42 (cf. p. 184). It must also be asked to what degree this is the idea behind the parabolic teaching method of Jesus. In any case the

reader awaits is the healing of their blindness, the moment of ἀναγνώρισις or the recognition scene.[563] The occasion or vehicle of recognition is the meal, his sitting with them at the table, taking, blessing, breaking and giving the bread to them. Lk's transitional statement in vs. 35, "he was known to them in the breaking of bread" and his earlier formulations suggest to the reader what is already familiar to his own experience. The question is: how are we to understand the original recognition motif in the light of this meal setting? It is widely accepted in NT research that we have here, in fact, the eucharistic setting of the early church with all of the ramifications of the institution of the Lord's Supper on the night of Jesus' betrayal not only redactionally, but also traditionally.[564] This has been disputed recently by some, and rightly so, because the assumed lines of contact with the words of institution and the practice of the church in its eucharistic fellowship with the resurrected One are simply missing. Most difficult, of course, is the fact that at the moment we expect to find the clearest reference to the meal fellowship of Jesus with some of his disciples (a dubious inference!) after the Resurrection the chief character disappears and the two travelers return to Jerusalem to tell the good news–or so at least the lukan transition. To speculate that the disappearance motif replaced the original conclusion which had a fuller description of the meal in order to give it a mysterious quality fails to recognize the basic concurrence of the themes incognito/appearance, recognition/disappearance. This draws attention then to the basic structure of the story: the recognition motif is served by the meal and not vice versa.[565] This is an important observation because it means that if the meal was to become the primary goal of the story–namely a pointer to the Eucharist–it was going to have to *become* that through the hand of redactional influence.[566]

reference to magical deception in blindness of this type seen from the viewpoint of rabbinic Judaism (Billerbeck, *op. cit.*, II, p. 271) is hardly applicable.

563 Cf. Dodd, "Appearances," p. 14, who sees Greek drama in the background; also Schubert, "Structure," p. 174, Anderson, "Easter Witness," pp. 47f., who also calls the account in general "the most comprehensive 'philosophy of the Resurrection' in the New Testament," and Grundmann, *Lukas*, pp. 442ff. For other parallels cf. K. Kerényi, *Die Griechisch-Orientalische Romanliteratur in religionsgeschichtlicher Beleuchtung* (WB, Darmstadt, 1962, 2nd ed.), pp. 69ff. and the development of the motif below.

564 Cf., e.g., Betz, "Ursprung," p. 12, esp. n. 16 and p. 16. Also Lohse, *Auferstehung*, p. 30, Mouson, *op. cit.*, pp. 192f., Kassing, *op. cit.*, pp. 156f., H.-F. Richter, *op. cit.*, pp. 73f., Lipinski, *op. cit.*, pp. 222ff., Benoit, *Passion and Resurrection*, pp. 279ff., O. Cullmann, "The Breaking of Bread and the Resurrection Appearances," *Essays on the Lord's Supper*, ed. by O. Cullmann and F.J. Leenhardt, trans. by J.G. Davies (Richmond, 1958), pp. 8f. and in his *Urchristentum und Gottesdienst* (Zürich, 1950), pp. 18ff., he assumes the background of a eucharist meal in general for Lk. 24 and Jn. 21 via fish symbolic and calls it the *Vorwegnahme* of a messianic meal promised in the Lord's Supper. Contra, e.g., J Roloff, "Heil als Gemeinschaft. Kommunikative Faktoren im urchristlichen Herrenmahl," *Gottesdienst und Öffentlichkeit. Fst. H.-R. Müller-Schwefe,* ed. by P. Cornehl and H.-E. Bahr (Hamburg, 1970), pp. 94ff.

565 The "meal" serving the purpose of Jesus' corporeality in Lk. 24:36ff. is, therefore, similar in motif importance; the corporeality problem is incidentally absent here. Cf. Dupont, "Meal," p. 116

566 Cf., e.g., Dupont, "Meal," pp. 115ff. and Wilckens, *Auferstehung*, pp. 80f. Yet, even here there is some doubt as we shall see below. Lk could hardly have weighted the eucharist thematic by omitting it in the all-important group appearance. We have already noted the pro-

In our meal motif here the recognized Jesus does not participate beyond the inception.[567]

If then the meal motif is subordinate to the primary motif of recognition what in the meal is indeed the marvelous solution to their blindness? If the two did not suddenly remember the night of Jesus' betrayal and the way he instituted the supper on that occasion[568] where else is the key to be found? There seems to be only one practical solution: just as in the Magdalene story of Jn. 20:1-18 the address of the resurrected One "Mary" (vs. 16) is the trigger to recognition so here the act of the meal and Jesus' manner of conducting that meal provides the moment of recollection in their memories.[569] The question is: memory of what? One could suppose: their memory of his life with them in general and/or their meals together as the most significant expression of their fellowship. This is, of course, possible, but 1) we are not sure that these two were among the "12" at all and 2) we do not even know for sure that there were exclusive disciple meals with the explicit goal of the development and deepening of understanding and rapport between Jesus and his disciples.[570] When we consider carefully the terminology of vs. 30 we find, as

gression by which Lk points to the group appearance as the climax and to find even less "eucharistic" in the climax than in the Emmaus story must be something of a riddle to the eucharist position. Winter, "Sources," p. 168, in his insistence that vss. 36ff. grew out of vs. 30 is thus particularly problematical (Cullmann, "Breaking of Bread," pp. 8ff. also). Evans, *Resurrection*, p. 106, calls this motif a "powerful theme" in language recalling both the feeding of the 5,000 and the action of the Last Supper. It is beside the point to say that Jesus had a special way of breaking or blessing that made him recognizable (contra A.R.C. Leaney, *The Gospel According to Luke* [N.Y., 1958], p. 293). Rather the point is a typical lukan expression for a Christian common meal (Acts 2:42) and thus vs. 35b "would be a proper summary of his version of the last supper if the shorter text is to be read" (p. 106). "It is probably fortuitous that here and in the next incident [group appearance] there are possible parallels in wording to the markan story of the Walking on the Water, an incident omitted by Lk, such as the intention to go on further (Lk. 24:28; cf. Mk. 6:48), fear at seeing an apparition (Lk. 24:37; cf. Mk. 6:49) and the verb 'terrified' (*ταράσσεσθαι*, Lk. 24:38, cf. Mk. 6:50)" (p. 106).

567 The implications of this non-participation must be considered on the whole for Jn. 21 as well. As we saw in chapter II, Acts 10:41 is the only probable reference to participation of the resurrected One and, therefore, to possible eucharistic backgrounds.

568 Not only are the explicit points of contact missing, but also there is no way to justify assuming that these two travelers were even present on that night (an objection which Benoit, *Passion and Resurrection*, p. 279, fails to answer). As Roloff, *Kerygma*, p. 257, has pointed out we have no explicit parallels to unite 24:30 with 22:19 except the general participle *λαβών*. Rather there are the following differences: *εὐλογέω* instead of *εὐχαριστέω*, *κλάσας* instead of *ἔκλασεν*, *ἐπεδίδου* or *ἐδίδου* instead of the simple aorist and the absence of a statement of time in 22:19 and *passim* in Lk.

569 The modern psychological approach wishes to point to special characteristics in Jesus' manner of breaking the bread, etc., as the medium of recognition. This may be remotely admissible in the Magdalene story (cf. below pp. 206ff.) but here the point is the act itself and not the "how" (cf. Roloff, *Kerygma*, p. 257, Schnider/Stenger, "Struktur," p. 112, Evans, *Resurrection* [cf. n. 566 above], Benoit, *Passion and Resurrection*, p. 279; contra is Graß, *op. cit.*, p. 38).

570 Patsch, *op. cit.*, p. 37, makes reference to this whole question of *Jüngermahlzeiten*. He points out that exclusive meals were more the practice of the Dead Sea community than of Jesus. It is more meaningful to draw out the *Tischgemeinschaft mit den Sündern* and then concludes: "Aber da man von Jüngermahlzeiten nichts weiß, ist aus ihnen auch nichts zu folgern" (p. 37). The only exclusive meal we know about was the Last Supper and the connection to

noted above, that no direct suggestion was made to a correlation to the Eucharist in Lk. 22:19 and that the action of Jesus is not particularly unusual as he offers the customary opening prayer of a Jewish meal.[571] Where else do meals play a significant role in Jesus' ministry other than on the night of his betrayal? Besides the possibility of meals in various homes we think of another "meal" text, namely the Feeding of the 5,000: Lk. 9:10-17, parr., especially vs. 16.[572] The relationship between the two traditional strata is very suggestive and offers some interesting theological as well as philological possibilities. That is to say, the feeding traditions of the earthly ministry provide in retrospect a point of contact with a key dimension in understanding the initiative of Jesus' activity already established in the Jesus tradition in general. There he acts as provider and sustainer and speaks as teacher of truth and preacher of promise. The meal occasion itself signifies a profound moment of encounter between himself and those about him. That such would be extended as the heart of his ongoing fellowship and the moment of recognition–not to mention redactional suggestion then in Lk's use of the motif to the Eucharist–in this account would appear to be a live option. This would mean, in answer to our question: memory of what, that the recollection involved as motif looks back to the extensions of help and guarantee of fellowship characteristic of Jesus' ministry throughout, especially as this was manifest in the feeding traditions. In this context then, the recognition becomes understandable: their "sight" is restored through the initiative of the One who had granted his fellowship before. Since the recognition motif and not the meal motif itself is central here, however, a development of the latter at this point in the traditional account was unnecessary and impossible. Redactionally, on the other hand, it was since Lk was unwilling to let it retain its subordinate position.

Inseparably united with the recognition motif then follows that of the disappearance, the first clear indication in the story that this is in fact an appearance. The impression in its development that the story is about human travelers and their conversation with one another instantly proves itself to be a deception and its character as divine visitation is unveiled as the appearing One is suddenly gone from sight. Whether or not the story contained any further elements is unclear, as

that particular meal here is a dubious one. Typical is rather the sentence in Lk. 14:1: *καὶ ἐγένετο ἐν τῷ ἐλθεῖν αὐτὸν εἰς οἶκόν τινος τῶν ἀρχόντων τῶν φαρισαίων σαββάτῳ φαγεῖν ἄρτον*. . .and the reaction of the scribes and pharisees over his meals with others: *οὗτος ἁμαρτωλοὺς προσδέχεται καὶ συνεσθίει αὐτοῖς* (Lk. 15:2). That Jesus had private conversations with his disciples is recorded, but it would be incorrect to assume that this was the extent of their "fellowship" alone. The analogy of the Rabbi/student relationship may be an insufficient one, but as the establishment of a certain minimum we may perhaps read "between the lines" where nothing is recorded. Patsch's point is, however, well taken in that were these meals critical to understanding the Lord's Supper or the appearance stories they would be more readily available in the texts.

571 Unusual is the fact perhaps that the guest assumes the role of the head of the house (cf. Roloff, *Kerygma*, p. 256) but it is by no means certain that this was never the case when Jesus was the guest in other homes during the earthly ministry (cf. Mk. 1:29ff. parr., 2:15 parr., 6:41 parr., 14:3ff. parr., Lk. 13:26 and 19:5).

572 Cf. *ibid.*, pp. 257f.

was pointed out above, but the minimum of a reaction of some sort from the two travelers—if not in the redactional form here—seems likely. In any case, the reaction would have been motivated by the total impression of the sequence and not by any direct address before the disappearance of the appearing One. An overview of this traditional structure is drawn up below in the Text-Synopsis.

3. A Galilaean Appearance Story: Jn. 21:1-14

As in the foregoing appearance story, it is necessary here as well only to note disposition and major lines of motif development and progression before distinguishing between tradition and redaction. The transition is an extremely rough one through which the story is more or less tacked on to chapter 20, which has already closed the entire gospel, with a mere *μετὰ ταῦτα* and then a superscription that this is an appearance of Jesus to his disciples "once again" [*ἐφανέρωσεν ἑαυτὸν πάλιν 'Ιησοῦς τοῖς μαθηταῖς*]—vs. 14 has "the third time" after his Resurrection from the dead—at the sea of Tiberias (in Galilee).[573] Moreover, the lead statement "he appeared like this" immediately precedes the narrative. The participants, all but two of whom are named, follow the decision of Peter to go fishing and embark in their ship. The efforts to obtain a catch remain fruitless through the night and in the early morning hours Jesus is suddenly there standing on the shore unrecognized. The second phase of development ensues with a verbal exchange between them and him regarding their failure to secure a catch. Following his advice to cast their nets on the other side, they find their nets full and then the Beloved Disciple recognizes the stranger on the shore as the "Lord" and announces this to Peter. Following this moment of recognition Peter jumps overboard to swim to shore while the others follow in the boat with the catch of fishes. The third phase begins with the arrival of all and their discovery of a campfire upon which breakfast had been prepared. Jesus tells them to bring some of their catch, Peter responds by fetching the net full of fish, which in spite of the size of the catch—some 153—did not break, and Jesus invites them to eat. None of the disciples dare to ask him his identity, since they know it is the "Lord." The fourth and final phase sees Jesus draw near and distribute bread and fish to them.

As we noted above regarding verbs of seeing for the appearance traditions the

573 There have been attempts made to disprove the appendix character of this chapter, but they have been able to prove by and large nothing more than that the chapter bears certain linguistic affinities to the rest of Jn. That the tradition was known in circles preserving and transmitting johannine traditions is not disputed here, but that the story in vss. 1-14 was originally part of the gospel is. That the conversation in vss. 15ff. is distinct from these foregoing verses and is a redactional composition is generally recognized in johannine studies. Part of vss. 1-14 may have served to introduce vss. 15ff. Cf. for the history of research to Jn. 21, Lorenzen, *Joh. 21*, ch. I, and also W. Wilkens, *op. cit.*, pp. 158ff., E.D. Freed, "Variations in the Language and Thought of John," *ZNW*, 55 (1964), pp. 192ff., M.-E. Boismard, "Le chapître XXI de saint Jean. Essai de critique littéraire," *RB*, 54 (1947), pp. 473ff., B. Cassian, "John XXI," *NTS*, 3 ('56/'57), pp. 132ff. and R. Fuller, *op. cit.*, pp. 146ff.

term $\phi\alpha\nu\epsilon\rho\acute{o}\omega$ is only used in later redactional strata.[574] This along with the manner in which vs. 1 is introduced to follow chapter 20 and vs. 14 sums up the whole demonstrates that the appearance story is capsuled fore and aft with editorial seams.[575] The location at the sea of Tiberias was undoubtedly original in view of the whole account.[576] The names, moreover, in vs. 2 would appear to be a redactional insertion with Jn. 1:35ff. in view, although the fact that two go unnamed is somewhat problematical from this view; that a participant goes unnamed was also a feature in the Emmaus story. That the following verse focuses upon Simon Peter and the others–designations which repeat themselves throughout with the exception of the Beloved Disciple–would suggest that only part of vs. 2 is in any sense clearly formulated with Jn. 1 in mind. In any case, vs. 3 brings into focus the truly complex nature of this entire text because although its thematic setting–a fishing episode–is not redactional in the same sense we noted above for vss. 1 and 14, it does raise the question, in the light of frequently noted parallels to Lk. 5:1-11, of whether or not the elements not attributable to the same hand as vss. 1 and 14 all originally belonged together as an appearance story. It would appear that they did not and that the present form is a hybrid containing two distinct traditional strata woven together to form a unity. That is, the text contains strata which represent part of a Galilaean appearance story and united with it a marvelous-catch-of-fishes story which was firmly embedded in the Galilaean tradition of the disciples' call into service during Jesus' earthly ministry. This becomes evident on internal grounds for the story in its present form demonstrates tensions and contradictions that can be resolved only through such origins as those proposed here.[577] For example, the fishing episode in both detail and direction seems to show elements of opposition to the development of the same in the appearance story which takes its focus in the recognition and meal motifs. The meal in vss. 12 and 13 takes place according to vs. 5 because the disciples have been unsuccessful in their catch and as they come ashore (vs. 9) they find breakfast waiting for them; yet, in vs. 10 Jesus bids them fetch some of their catch, but his bidding turns out to serve only the count of fishes at 153 and the phenomenon that the net was not torn from the weight. Moreover, the place of Peter as the one who rises to the occasion in vs. 11 is tied very carefully to earlier mention of his person which in the development of the story is counter-

574 Cf. above pp. 120f. Further, the usage noted by E. Pax, ΕΠΙΦΑΝΕΙΑ. *Ein religionsgeschichtlicher Beitrag zur biblischen Theologie* (Mü., 1955), p. 214 and Helzle, *op. cit.*, p. 11, for the relationship to "Mk." 16:12,14.

575 Finegan, *Überlieferung*, p. 96, Kegel, *op. cit.*, p. 117, *et al.*

576 Whether or not this localization can in any sense be called local tradition is an open question, but in contrast to the geographical determiners of the group appearance stories this one would appear to be original. One could argue that this element belonged to the miraculous catch story and not to the appearance story, but while it could function for the former it is equally as important for the latter.

577 So, e.g., Roloff, *Kerygma*, pp. 258ff., Pesch, *Fischfang*, pp. 53, 154 *et passim*, L. Brun, "Die Berufung der ersten Jünger Jesu in der evangelischen Tradition," *SO*, 11 (1932), pp. 38 and 49f., Grundmann, *Lukas*, p. 127, Hirsch, *op. cit.*, II, p. 197, E. Schwartz, "Johannes und Kerinthos," *ZNW*, 15 (1914), p. 217 and R. Fuller, *op. cit.*, pp. 149ff.

balanced by the mention of the Beloved Disciple (vs. 7). Further, the recognition episode of vs. 7 is localized in the latter person redactionally (much like the race story where he sees and believes–20:8!)[578] so that the recognition motif *at this point* appears to be an insert achieved by final redaction and is not original to either of the two traditions being woven together.[579] The fact that the motivation for Peter's jump into the water with its comment and that it comes to no apparent goal in the story is further evidence that originally disparate elements were coupled and thereby aspects were left out which originally served to give the separate units their own continuity.[580] Terminologically there are other tensions such as the words for fish: vs. 5 mentions the term (*hapax* for the NT) *προσφάγιον* while vss. 6, 8, and 11 mention *ἰχθύς* and vss. 9, 10, and 13 *ὀψάριον*. The *ἰχθύς* references clearly belong to the units out of the miraculous-catch story, while the *ὀψάριον* references of vss. 9 and 13 belong to the appearance story and its meal motif (vs. 10 is apparently an accommodation of the term to the reference in vs. 9). The *προσφάγιον* of vs. 5 is more difficult since its location could serve the function of motivation for both. In view of the tension to vs. 10 noted above and the fact that their lack of success

578 Cf. above p. 97.

579 The figure of the Beloved Disciple plays such a key role in the gospel as a whole that its use here can hardly be ascribed to any origin other than final redaction. Cf. above p. 97 and n. 282 and also Brown, *op. cit.*, pp. 1071f. (and pp. 936f.), Finegan, *Überlieferung*, p. 96, Schwartz, *op. cit.*, pp. 217f., Schnackenburg, "Jünger," pp. 105f. and also his "On the Origin of the Fourth Gospel," *Jesus and Man's Hope. A Perspective Book* I, ed. by D.G. Buttrick (Pitt., 1970), pp. 233ff.

580 I.e., the place of the emphasis at this point on Peter probably functioned in some way for the catch story. As noted above, pp. 61ff., one of the most commonly suggested pericopae for the "lost" first appearance to Peter is Jn. 21:1-14 and 15ff. Quite often vss. 1-14 are then identified with Lk. 5:1-11 as identical or very closely related stories of that appearance. So, Leaney, "Theophany," p. 107, who says that Lk. 5 is the appearance story of Jn. 21 and that Lk "is shy of representing Peter as receiving his commission from the risen Christ because there were already those who looked askance at authority based on an appearance after the resurrection, anticipating those who later based some of their polemic against Paul on this very ground." Similar is his *Luke*, p. 56. Cf. also Wilckens, *Auferstehung*, p. 84, H.-F. Richter, *op. cit.*, p. 74, Cullmann, *Petrus*, pp. 64ff. and 202ff., H. Schürmann, "Die Verheißung an Simon Petrus. Auslegung von Lk 5,1-11," *Ursprung und Gestalt, Ges. Aufs.* (Düss., 1970), pp. 268ff., J. Delorme, "Luc V.1-11: Analyse Structurale et Histoire de la Rédaction," *NTS*, 18 ('71/'72), pp. 347ff., G. Klein, "Die Berufung des Petrus," *ZNW*, 58 (1967), pp. 19ff., 36ff. and 30ff., Smalley, *op. cit.*, pp. 285ff. and Lorenzen, "Galiläa," p. 217. Goguel, *La foi*, pp. 295ff., sees Jn. 21 as belonging to the Galilaean ministry after Jn. 2:11 and 4:54 as a "third manifestation." Cf. further Bailey, *op. cit.*, pp. 40ff., Obrist, *op. cit.*, pp. 48ff. and Kremer, *Botschaft*, pp. 128ff. More probable than these Easter origins for Lk. 5 in contrast to Jn. 21 is the proposal of Pesch, *Fischfang*, p. 111, "Die Fischfangerzählung setzt nicht die Ostersituation voraus, ist von Lukas also nicht vordatiert worden. Sie hat sich aber auch nicht zu einer Ostererzählung entwickelt, sondern ist in Jo 21,1-14 mit einem Erscheinungsbericht verbunden worden, der notwendig in die Ostersituation gehört." Similar is Brun, "Berufung," pp. 51f., especially regarding the petrine question. Cf. also C.H. Dodd, *Historical Tradition in the Fourth Gospel* (Cambridge, 1963), p. 144, and Benoit, *Passion and Resurrection*, p. 303. Somewhat undecided in general is Evans, *Resurrection*, pp. 126ff. It has been suggested regarding the reason for the disciples' remaining in the boat that they are already there while Peter must jump out to steady it as they come to shore (cf. Pesch, *Fischfang*, p. 100), but more probable is Bultmann, *Johannes*, pp. 544 (and 548). That the terms for boat vary also suggests the distinction between the two stories here combined (cf. again Pesch, *Fischfang*, p. 87). Cf. also Brown, *op. cit.*, pp. 1085ff.

has already been mentioned at the end of vs. 3 it would appear that this reference too belongs to the miraculous-catch sequence and not to the appearance story.[581]

These observations give the following picture regarding the traditional matrix: the original elements of the appearance story retained in this complex composition are to be found in the references to the sea of Tiberias in vs. 1, the participation of the disciples in vs. 2 and *passim* (redactionally then focused on Peter and the Beloved Disciple), the failure of the disciples to have caught anything in vs. 3c, Jesus stands on the shore early in the morning but is not recognized in vs. 4, the disciples disembark and find a campfire with fish and bread waiting for them in vs. 9, Jesus invites the disciples to eat and they refuse to ask who he is because they know it is the "Lord" in vs. 12 and Jesus comes and distributes bread and fish to them.

As we have seen, the general borders of the story and certain seams throughout are redactional; especially clear is the remark in vs. 14 that this was the third appearance when in reality the structure at no point gives the slightest hint that this was true, indeed shows quite the opposite.[582] Some scholars maintain that this was the original Galilean appearance,[583] the sole appearance to the "12,"[584] perhaps the tradition standing behind the appearance to Cephas[585] or perhaps even the "lost" ending to Mk. and maybe the compositional completion to the fragmentary "appearance" story at the end of the GP.[586] That the tradition is Galilaean[587] and that a comparison with the catch-of-fishes story in Lk. 5:1-11 is a necessary step in ascertaining the form and content of this appearance story is hardly disputable, but the danger of oversimplification evident in many of the conjectures mentioned above can be avoided only by a careful analysis of the traditional matrix, its struc-

581 Cf. below on the meal/fish motif question, n. 597.

582 Bultmann, *Johannes*, p. 543, finds it nothing short of astonishing that after the commissioning of the disciples in 20:22ff. they are then pictured here as going fishing and as experiencing another appearance. He says concerning the text then: "daß sie ursprünglich als erste Ostergeschichte erzählt worden war; und der redakt. V. 14 zeigt, daß sie nachträglich an den Platz gestellt ist, den sie jetzt einnimmt" (p. 543). That the second observation is true goes without saying, while the first is yet a question mark. (Cf. further *ibid.*, p. 546 and also Pesch, *Fischfang*, p. 147).

583 Cf. Roloff, *Kerygma*, pp. 260ff., Bultmann, *Johannes*, pp. 543f. and Graß, *op. cit.*, pp. 75ff. Contra, Pesch, *Fischfang*, p. 133, who argues against its age because of the presence of the Beloved Disciple and the competition motif.

584 Roloff, *Kerygma*, p. 260, and Bultmann, *Johannes*, pp. 546f. That this appearance is distinct from the group appearance stories is to be seen in the fact that they share only a rough approximation on the participants while showing telling differences on the specifics of motifs. That they share an overall form similarity with the other appearance stories can be seen in the Text-Synopsis.

585 Cf. Klein, "Berufung," p. 29 and Graß, *op. cit.*, p. 295 where the role of Peter in the appearance is emphasized; also n. 580 and Pesch, *Fischfang*, pp. 133 and 148, Roloff, "Lieblingsjünger," pp. 137f. and von Campenhausen, *Ablauf*, pp. 16f.

586 Cf. above p. 126. Any relationship to GP must remain at best suggestive and hypothetical. Moreover, our word statistic demonstrated no special markan terminology here. We simply know too little about the former and our analysis of the latter makes the "discovery" of the "lost" ending unnecessary. Cf. also Bultmann, *Johannes*, p. 546, n. 4.

587 That the Galilaean reference to "Tiberias" is not secondary can hardly be denied.

ture and motifs.[588] The job of unraveling the various motifs and motif chains is as difficult as it is crucial. As Bultmann puts it,". . .(vs. 13) schließt die Geschichte, die in der vorliegenden Form ein so merkwürdiges Durcheinander von Motiven bietet, daß man kaum sagen kann, worin ihre eigentliche Pointe liegt."[589] The discovery and analysis of the "point" is our goal.

On the basis of our text analysis we see immediately that the extant appearance story presents us with a rather small selection of motifs though it may be assumed perhaps that it has been tailored and that the original story contained other aspects not included here. After establishing the Galilaean location, the participants as the *μαθηταί*–a reference that by itself could qualify it as a kind of group appearance–and the unsuccessful fishing episode, the reference to Jesus' standing before them (on the shore) establishes his presence. As in the Emmaus story, he is not recognized and also similar to that account the recognition element comes at the end of the story; redactional is the preliminary stage where the Beloved Disciple recognizes the stranger. They all recognize him apparently at some moment prior to the meal (vss. 12f.), but no one dares to seek confirmation through a direct question. Their discovery of the campfire and the prepared meal as well as their reaction to the invitation to come and eat are cast in hues of doubt and uncertainty, i.e., instead of registering a motif of joy and gladness in their recognition before the meal there is a distinct tone of awe and perhaps fright: no one dares to ask![590] They are being invited (probably the intended moment of recognition)[591] to the meal by the

588 Dodd's skepticism that here is a problem "which our form-critical study of the post-resurrection appearances does not greatly help to solve" ("Appearances," p. 23) is overstated. Graß' failure to carry out a form-critical analysis is the chief weakness of his approach to Jn. 21 (*op. cit.*, pp. 78-81). Bultmann's text emendations are unnecessary (*Johannes*, pp. 544f.). Cf. Pesch, *Fischfang*, p. 98.

589 Bultmann, *Johannes*, p. 550.

590 *Ibid.*, p. 549, speaks about the *Scheidewand* done away with in the distribution of the bread and fish and contests the connection to Jn. 16:23. J. Jeremias, *Theologie*, p. 288, calls the *älteste Überlieferungsschicht* "die Erinnerung an das Überwältigende, Rätselhafte und Geheimnisvolle der Vorgänge" for the whole appearance tradition, where eyes are opened at the breaking of bread, there is a shining of heavenly light, a figure stands on the shore in the morning haze, an appearance behind supposedly closed doors occurs, a breaking forth of glossalic praise of God is heard, a sudden disappearance took place; "das sind Züge, in denen die älteste Überlieferung zu Wort kommt" (p. 288). The place of such motifs must be analyzed in terms of their function in the overall form and structure of these stories. Attempts to draw out their implications for a possible parapsychological interpretation of the events behind the stories have proved to be inconclusive and tend to neglect the theological function of such motifs in the story form as a whole (cf. below n. 622 and V: Summary and Conclusions). Compare in this regard, e.g., B. Schwank, "Die Ostererscheinungen des Johannesevangeliums und die Post-mortem-Erscheinungen der Parapsychologie," *EuA*, 44 (1968), pp. 36-53. Cf. the critique on such a method and further literature by Anderson, "Easter Witness," p. 36. J. Müller-Bardorff, *Jesu Erscheinungen auf dem See und die Topik der österlichen Erscheinungsberichte*, Diss. (Leipzig, 1941) apparently attempted an integration of the fear and other motifs of these stories with other accounts of the gospel tradition and of history-of-religion comparative material (according to Leipoldt, "Auferstehungs-Geschichten," col. 741), but all efforts to secure a copy of this work, including correspondence with the author himself, proved for this writer unsuccessful.

591 Cf. Roloff, *Kerygma*, p. 259.

"Lord," he comes and distributes to them as provider and from the disciples we hear nothing more.[592]

As in the meal motif of the Emmaus story the resurrected One is not pictured here as a direct participant.[593] As noted above the original ending is perhaps missing here and whether or not such contained a more complete account of the meal and/or the mysterious disappearance of Jesus is uncertain.[594] That could have been the case, however, similar to the Emmaus story. In any case the certainty of recognition in the context of the meal is the key here and important is that just as in the Emmaus story the meal stands on the spot which the word motif of the group category occupied.[595]

Dissimilar, however, upon closer investigation of the two meals is the following: here after once again stressing the disciples and their reaction of reverence which creates a distinct atmosphere Jesus then proceeds with the distribution of the meal elements. The emphasis on blessing the elements is missing,[596] moreover, and the

592 No reaction of the disciples is recorded, no sudden disappearance is mentioned, only the editor's capsule statement is added. Once again the key to interpreting the progression lies in the specific reference of the meal and recognition motifs. C.K. Barrett, *The Gospel According to St John* (London, 1960), p. 484, says, "The parallel acts recall also the distribution by Jesus of the bread and wine at the last supper. This meal was probably intended to call to the minds of the readers eucharistic associations. . .A fish occurs along with bread in some early representations of the eucharist; and fish-symbolism was very widespread in early Christianity." As in the Emmaus meal motif, however, it is to be asked here if these are adequate categories for understanding this reference or if the fish element is not another indicator that the meals in the synoptic tradition of Jesus' ministry are more immediate. Cf. especially below n. 597. Pesch, *Fischfang*, p. 133, advances the theory that perhaps the interpretation here does not necessarily hinge on the riddle of an abrupt ending, since vss. 15ff. can be taken as a sending as in Jn. 20. He says, "V. 15 würde nun gut anschließen, zumal alle Ostertraditionen in einen Auftrag des Auferstandenen münden; zwar käme der Erscheinungsbericht mit V. 13 zu einem Abschluß, doch die Osterberichte in Jo 20, die auch keinen deutlicher markierten Schluß haben, münden im Wort des Erscheinenden. Und sie dürfen zum Vergleich herangezogen werden, weil die Sprachform unseres Erscheinungsberichts ihn ja der johanneischen Tradition zuweist." These latter verses cannot, however, help to bridge the interpretive difficulty, since they do not stand on the same traditional footing as the others.

593 Cullmann, "Breaking of Bread," p. 11, assumes participation here even where the text is silent. Similar is J. Jeremias, *Abendmahlsworte*, p. 91. H.-F. Richter, *op. cit.*, p. 73, does not see the participation of Jesus here, but in Lk. 24:43, ". . .ißt er sogar selbst." Cf. also Bailey, *op. cit.*, p. 89 and Rordorf, *Sonntag*, pp. 221f., who assumes that in all of these meals bread and wine were distributed with the words of institution just as in the Last Supper. Hereto cf. Patsch, *op. cit.*, p. 37. Dodd, "Appearances," p. 15, says, "There is evidence in early Christian art that the meal of the seven disciples was treated, along with the Feeding of the Multitude, as a symbol of the Eucharist." Regarding eucharistic symbolism here in general cf. Brown, *op. cit.*, pp. 1093ff. More correct is the emphasis in this context on Acts 10:41, so Goppelt, "πίνω, etc.," *ThW*, VI, p. 142, Bultmann, *Johannes*, p. 549, n. 6. Cf. further Benoit, *Passion and Resurrection*, p. 301, Rengstorf, *Lukas*, p. 284 and Lohse, *Auferstehung*, pp. 29f.

594 Bultmann, *Johannes*, p. 545, assumes here with a degree of likelihood that during or after the meal Jesus talked to them, told them about their commission and, "Dann mag das wunderbare Verschwinden Jesu etwas wie Lk 24,31 erzählt worden sein."

595 Cf. above, pp. 212f., for the Emmaus story. Regarding the proposal of Pesch, *Fischfang*, cf. n. 592. Cf. also Hartmann, *op. cit.*, p. 211.

596 Roloff, *Kerygma*, p. 260, n. 208, assumes that "blessing" is included in "taking" the bread, etc. Be that as it may, the emphasis is missing.

inclusion of fish is an additional feature over against the Emmaus "meal."[597] Most important, however, is that the participants enter this meal from the very beginning knowing ὁ κύριός ἐστιν. Recognizing Jesus *in the distribution* of the elements is unnecessary here. Seeing this "stranger" and the meal he prepared and being invited was apparently sufficient. The contrast with the Emmaus failure to recognize Jesus is striking: here there is not the slightest hint that their "blindness" has a divine origin. Rather Jesus himself is there as a mysterious figure and the disciples simply fail as human beings to recognize him. Another contrast is that here the recognition motif is by no means predominant over against the meal in the same way as in the Emmaus story, but rather it exists alongside the latter and the aspect of the disciples' activities. A case could be made perhaps for the predominance of the meal whereby the other two factors contribute to the success of the meal provided the emphasis is placed on the identity of the One preparing and serving the meal because the recognition motif pointed to Jesus not merely as a strange and mysterious person but rather as the κύριος![598] An overview of the structural elements of this Galilaean appearance is also offered in the Text-Synopsis below.

4. The Mary Magdalene Appearance Story: Jn. 20:14-18

As noted in chapter II under the question of the tomb story and that of the originality of the appearance before the women in Mt. 28:9-10, the events at the

597 Outside of the use of ἰχθύος ὀπτοῦ μέρος in Lk. 24:42 the fish reference in vss. 9, (10) and 13 ὀψάριον are quite singular in the appearance tradition (in connection with προσφάγιον, cf. Pesch, *Fischfang*, pp. 88 and 95, Bultmann, *Johannes*, p. 548, n. 3). One asks quite naturally, where does this reference come from and what does it mean? With regard to the Lk. 24:42 reference Wilder, *op. cit.*, p. 313 sees here an indication that this material is Galilaean and not local to Jerusalem (cf. above, pp. 171f.). Bailey, *op. cit.*, p. 90 refers to fish in Jerusalem in Neh. 13:16 and 23:16 to counter the necessity for a Galilaean location. Many wish to see in the fish element a reference to early Christian symbolism where the Eucharist is supposed to have been celebrated exclusively or in part with the use of fish, or where the Eucharist was called the "fish" perhaps with reference to the abbreviation ΙΧΘΥΣ, Jesus Christ God's Son, Savior. Cf. Dölger, *op. cit.*, pp. 252ff., 452ff., 496, 502, 536ff., 542, 544ff., 549, 555, 568 and 573f. Schille, *Anfänge*, p. 106, speaks of a "Dankfeier der galiläischen Fischer bei Brot und Fischzukost." Roloff, *Kerygma*, pp. 239f. and n. 129, points out, however, that fish nowhere in the NT have eucharistic significance. That the inclusion of the fish is quite natural for a meal on the shores of the sea of Tiberias is hardly misleading, as is the recognition that fish were among the staples in normal Jewish meals (cf. Billerbeck, *op. cit.*, II, p. 586 and IV, 2, pp. 611-639). One can say little more about the fish in the context of Lk. 24:42 than that it probably owes its place in the appearance narrative to lukan redaction while the ὀψάριον of the appearance story in Jn. 21:9 and 13 was part of the original meal motif. Whether or not it has some special symbolic function and is not just simply part of the meal is *ungeklärt* (Patsch, *op. cit.*, p. 37). The fact, however, that the emphasis of the story as a whole depends upon the recognition of the Lord serving the meal prohibits an isolated preoccupation with its importance. In this context it would seem that the feedings of the earthly ministry as noted earlier for the Emmaus and lukan group appearance are a live option here as well. Cf. Roloff, *Kerygma*, pp. 260ff.

598 Cf. above on the participants question, pp. 150ff. and 154ff. Also Pesch, *Fischfang*, p. 97, Dodd, "Appearances," p. 15 and Roloff, *Kerygma*, p. 263.

tomb for Jn. 20 show a high degree of redactional alteration to bring the narrative into a unity. Nevertheless, this redactional vigor cannot disguise the fact that a source distinct from the foregoing has been incorporated. We shall begin as in the previous accounts with a consideration of disposition and internal development of the principal phases of the pericope.

Following on the heels of Mary's encounter with two angels and her verbal exchange with them (vss. 12 and 13) she turns back from the tomb's entrance and sees Jesus standing there before her (vs. 14). She does not recognize him. With this the stage is set and a second phase begins with a verbal exchange in which Jesus asks about her reason for weeping and the one whom she is seeking, to which she replies (assuming that he is the caretaker), that if he has removed the body of the crucified One would he please tell her where so that she may take it away (vs. 15). The third phase comes with the direct address *Μαριάμ* from Jesus and Mary's sudden recognition and reply *ῥαββουνί* (vs. 16). The fourth phase (vs. 17) follows this recognition with a two-fold address: 1) *μή μου ἅπτου* with the reason that he is ascending to the Father, and 2) go to "my brothers" with the message that I am ascending to "my Father and your Father, my God and your God." The final phase comes with Mary going and delivering the message *τοῖς μαθηταῖς* and saying that she had seen the Lord (vs. 18).

This story has Mary alone as the recipient of the appearance and its familiarity in the polemic of Celsus has already been mentioned in the introduction.[599] Some contemporary critical investigations have suggested that johannine redaction has singled out Mary as a representative of the women and/or of the Church much like Thomas has a symbolic role to play as the doubter in 20:24ff.[600] While this redactional tailoring is in fact probably the case in the reduction from a plural to the singular for 20:1-2, 11, 12, the Magdalene pericope on the other hand, demonstrates no internal reasons for such. Indeed, the opposite is more probable: the former itself was altered to accommodate to the latter so that a story could be reached which was contained in itself throughout.[601] So, the transition from the tomb

599 Cf. above p. 21. Also the strong allusion of E. Renan, *Vie de Jésus* (Eng. ed., N.Y., n.d.), p. 302 and ns. 25 and 26 to the hallucinatory capacity of Mary Magdalene and the origins of this appearance as, "Divine power of love! Sacred moments in which the passion of one possessed gave to the world a resuscitated God!" Hereto cf. Anderson, "Easter Witness," p. 35, further Lohfink, "Auferstehung," p. 49, and the psychological explanations and general backgrounds mentioned above, pp. 22ff. Hengel, "Frauen," p. 252 refers to the rabbinic designation for Mary as the *Frauenhaarflechterin* (cf. Billerbeck, *op. cit.*, I, p. 1047).

600 E.g., Evans, *Resurrection*, p. 122. Cf. also Anderson, "Easter Witness," pp. 51f. and Lindars, "Composition," p. 143.

601 Cf. above, pp. 95ff. Michel, "Osterbericht," pp. 35ff., also stresses the redactional transitions of originally independent sources. Dibelius, "Motive," pp. 136ff. sees in the Magdalene aspects of the entire sequence of Jn. 20 a pre-johannine epiphanic tradition (". . .in einem besonderen, in der Religionsgeschichte bekannten Sinn. . .nicht auf äußerer Verwandlung, sondern auf innerem Erleben begründet," p. 137) and fails to differentiate clearly enough between the independence of the tomb and group appearance strata and vss. 14-18. He concludes, "Das 20. Kapitel des Evangeliums weist also–die Kompositionen des Autors 20,3-10, 24-29 ausgenommen–zurück auf eine Darstellung, die Jesu Epiphanie vor Maria Magdalena erzählte, die

story–the verbal exchange with the angels–to the appearance story is deliberate but forced and although it has been argued as well that the two belong organically together, i.e., either johannine or pre-johannine redaction freely constructed the story out of the elements in the tomb story itself or some other strata, it seems more probable, as we shall see, that two separate traditions have been sewn together with a high degree of redactional deliberation.[602] The task of differentiating clearly between tradition and redaction is made difficult because the entire pericope is well-clothed in johannine style, vocabulary and theology.[603] The story's link with the tomb tradition–vss. 13 and 14–is also the product of redactional sophistication and yet in contrast to Mt. 28:9,10, the story itself has not been constructed to achieve the redactional seam between tomb and appearance traditions. Unlike the somewhat one-dimensional and colorless account of Mt. 28:9,10 this story has all the motif elements of a striking drama not unlike the qualities of the Emmaus and Galilaean appearance stories. A redaction-critical analysis of the account both facilitates and complicates a recognition of the various strata, i.e., certain elements are clearly on a par with late redactional elements comparable to motifs such as the Beloved Disciple, while other elements may have accrued to the story in a prior stage of editorial development before the final johannine hand, similar to what we

Erscheinung vor den Jüngern ankündigte und in die Aussendungsszene mündete. Dies war eine Erfüllung von Ps 21(22),23, aber die Beziehung auf das Alte Testament war nicht mehr die Hauptsache. Die Erscheinung vor den Frauen, ursprünglich nur Vorbereitung auf die Aussendungsszene (siehe Mt 28,9.10), war zur besonderen Geschichte verselbständigt und mit großer Feinheit unter Beschränkung der Zahl der Frauen auf eine novellisiert worden" (p. 139).

602 K.P.G. Curtis, "Three Points of Contact between Matthew and John in the Burial and Resurrection Narratives," *JThS*, 23 (1972), pp. 440ff. sees Mt. 28:9f. as redactional and the Magdalene story then being dependent upon it. Walter, "Schilderung," p. 416, speaks of a tendency in the tradition to let the women under the cross also have their part in the Easter *Widerfahrnissen*, as seen ostensibly in Mt. 28:9f., ". . .eine Tendenz, die sich in Joh. XX, wenn auch auf eine Frau eingeschränkt (Joh. XX.1 und 11-18), breiter entfaltet hat." Similar are Hartmann, *op. cit.*, p. 205, Bode, *op. cit.*, p. 83, and R. Fuller, *op. cit.*, pp. 136ff. (who also sees here as in most of the stories an anti-ϑεῖος ἀνήρ polemic). A variation to the Mt./Jn. relationship is Grundmann, *Matthäus*, p. 568, n. 4, "Die beiden Erzählungen sind nicht voneinander abhängig, sondern in ihnen gestaltet sich eine Maria-Magdalena-Tradition, aus deren Wurzel beide unabhängig voneinander gewachsen sind." Lohfink, "Auferstehung," p. 41, agrees that Mt. 28:9-10 is redactional and that Jn. 20:14-18 brings this "tendency" to its conclusion, and then adds skeptically, "Dieses Zusammenwachsen von Grabes- und Erscheinungserzählung kann uns zeigen, wie wenig wir in den Auferstehungsgeschichten der Evangelien eine exakt historische Wiedergabe des äußeren Ablaufes der Ereignisse erwarten dürfen. Eine große Zahl weiterer Widersprüche zeigt das in aller Deutlichkeit. . . ." Hengel, "Frauen," p. 255, is correct when he says, "Die Erscheinung des Auferstandenen vor Maria Magdalena ist von der Entdeckung des leeren Grabes traditionsgeschichtlich völlig zu trennen." He sees Mt. 28:9-10, moreover, as a reversal and shortened version of this tradition (p. 255). L. Marin, "Die Frauen am Grabe. Versuch einer Strukturanalyse an einem Text des Evangeliums," *Erzählende Semiotik nach Berichten der Bibel* (trans. K.H. Neufeld), ed. by C. Chabrol and L. Marin (Mü., 1973), pp. 67ff., has attempted a linguistic analysis of the grave complex, but because the approach does not work with the Greek text nor is interested in the question of a traditional matrix (cf. p. 10 of *Vorbemerkung*) it is of little assistance to us here.

603 Cf. W. Thüsing, *Die Erhöhung und Verherrlichung Jesu im Johannesevangelium*, NTA, 21, Heft 1./2. (Münster, Westfalen, 1960), pp. 263ff., Kremer, *Osterbotschaft*, pp. 98f. *et al.*

noted earlier about the two tomb traditions. The address in vs. 17, for example, is so strongly johannine in its theological concern that it is difficult to say much about an otherwise possible form in any kind of a pre-redactional matrix.[604] Moreover, its close connection with vs. 18 would suggest that the charge to go to the "brothers" is an editorial form of the original ending to the tomb story–oldest form–and vs. 18 itself is an expansion of that ending as well, altered to transport now the content of the appearance story. We have thus an indication in corroboration of earlier remarks that the oldest form of the tomb story has been broken up and placed in the service of the later form of the tomb story and this appearance account.[605] Thereby, the disciple-oriented story of 20:3-10 has become for all intents and purposes *the* tomb story for Jn. and the appearance account the crown of the immediate tomb related sequence. The tendency of the tomb/appearance traditions mentioned earlier in general has been fixed now in Jn. and the question thus becomes critical: does the rest of the Magdalene pericope stand on a traditional base outside of the catalyst of vss. 17 and 18? It is apparent that vss. 13 and 14a as well as the parenthetical insertion of vs. 16 are the work of Jn to achieve final redactional smoothness.[606] The elements of Mary's turning to see Jesus [vs. 14a *ἐστράφη*] and her turning in recognition of him [vs. 16b *στραφεῖσα*] raise the question if the one is a kind of redactional duplication of the other or if both are redactional in origin. The first instance of turning yields the kind of transition which carries the listener/reader from the one theme to the other in a deliberate movement towards dénouement. As such it is not essential to the context of the latter since its function is predominantly that of a bridge. One could speculate about an original beginning to the story which has here been replaced by the first transitional *ἐστράφη*, but be that as it may, little more is necessary than the context itself: Mary, while at the tomb, sees Jesus standing before her. In any case the second "turning" is original.[607] One could ask, however, if maybe the story has become dislodged from its

604 Cf. Lohfink, *Himmelfahrt*, pp. 115ff., Thüsing, *Verherrlichung*, pp. 268ff., W. Grundmann, "Zur Rede Jesu vom Vater im Johannes-Evangelium. Eine redaktions- und bekenntnisgeschichtliche Untersuchung zu Joh 20,17 und seiner Vorbereitung," *ZNW*, 52 (1961), pp. 213ff. Hartmann, *op. cit.*, p. 207, finds in vs. 17 a problem because it does not clearly reflect johannine theology. Lindars, "Composition," p. 145 would draw the "touch" of vs. 17 together with the "grasp" of Mt. 28:9. Cf. also Brown, *op. cit.*, pp. 989ff. and Barrett, *Jn.*, pp. 470f. Seeing vs. 17 in the context of a "spiritual" pointer to faith, the sacraments and communion in the new order of the Church via an allegorical interpretation of the Song of Songs 3:1-4 is A. Feuillet, "La Recherche du Christ dans la Nouvelle Alliance d'après la Christophanie de Jo. 20,11-18. Comparaison avec Cant. 3,1-4 l'épisode des Pélerins d'Emmaüs," *L'Homme Devant Dieu, Fst. H. de Lubac*, Exégèse et Patristique. Théologie 56 (Aubier, 1963), pp. 98ff.

605 Cf. above, pp. 95ff. Hengel, "Frauen," pp. 255f., on the other hand, concludes that vs. 18 is original when he says that the commission of Jesus retained in Jn. and Mt. is thus the original "Kern der Erscheinung/vor Maria Magdalena: Sie brachte den Jüngern als erste die Botschaft von der Auferstehung des Herrn, ohne jedoch auf Glauben zu stoßen." Hartmann, *op. cit.*, pp. 207ff. finds so many non-johannine motifs here that he reckons it–with some reservation nonetheless–to the *Vorlage*.

606 Hartmann, *op. cit.*, pp. 205 and 210, considers the angel episode to be by and large an *Einschub* constructed by the evangelist from the appearance story.

607 Cf., e.g., Fortna, *op. cit.*, pp. 139f. Bultmann, *Johannes*, p. 532, n. 1, removes the

original context and because of internal necessity to link this appearance as closely as possible to that stratum of resurrection tradition which was connected with the women anyway—the empty tomb tradition—has this link with the grave locale only secondarily. The possibility cannot perhaps be excluded since the element of locale is otherwise the place for secondary development elsewhere. Three observations, however, speak in favor of this context as original: 1) as an individual appearance it could have stood quite naturally at such a locale prior to a group appearance and while such does not necessarily tie it to the grave site it does place it generally within the sector of accounts where such would have been possible,[608] and 2) in its present place it chides against any other first appearance story and unless it had actually had this context originally it could hardly have come to it secondarily.[609] On the contrary, 3) the redactional embellishment of the setting in vs. 15, which is rich in johannine theology and style, is probably to be understood within the previously established context in the pre-johannine source.[610] This would suggest then that of a probably somewhat larger pre-redactional matrix the following has been retained: vss. 14bc, 15 (redactionally reworked) and 16 (omitting the parenthesis *ὃ λέγεται διδάσκαλε*), i.e., Jesus stands at the tomb before Mary unrecognized by her, talks with her and then upon hearing him address her *Μαριάμ*, she turns in recognition and cries out *ῥαββουνί*.[611]

In this story more than in any of the others we have such strong redactional reformation that it is extremely difficult to arrive at more of the original content than that which is expressed in these few verses or verse parts.[612] But as we noted in the

first "turning" along with vss. 12-14a in general and then understands the "turning" in vs. 16 as "die plötzliche und lebhafte Bewegung auf ihn hin. . . ."

608 Fanciful, however, is the reconstruction at the tomb by Trompf, *op. cit.*, pp. 322ff., who sees the original ending of Mk. as . . .*ἐφοβοῦντο γάρ, ἀλλὰ Ἰησοῦς ὑπήντησεν αὐταῖς λέγων, σαλώμ· μὴ φοβεῖσθε* [gap] *ὑπάγετε ἀπαγγείλατε τοῖς ἀδελφοῖς μου* [then either] *ἵνα ἀπέλθωσιν* [or] *ὅτι προάγω εἰς τὴν Γαλιλαίαν* and then has Jn dependent on this account for the tomb sequence altering the plural number of women which had included the mother of Jesus to the singular, Mary Magdalene, to counter the tradition because of 1) its placement of blessing upon the women before the disciples and 2) its association with the family of Jesus, since ecclesiastical struggles necessitated it (pp. 325ff.). The possibility of this locale depends neither upon an original lost ending of Mk. nor upon the empty tomb traditions at all.

609 Cf. above on the first appearance question, pp. 61ff. Also, e.g., Hartmann, *op. cit.*, p. 255.

610 Hartmann, *op. cit.*, maintains, of course, that the relationship between the two complexes as a whole is an inseparable one. "Weder die Maria-Geschichte noch die Erzählung vom Wettlauf können isoliert voneinander bestanden haben. Daraus folgt, daß ein ursprünglich einheitlicher Bericht beiden Erzählungen zugrunde liegt" (p. 198).

611 *Ibid.*, p. 206, maintains that the *Vorlage* picked up after vs. 11a in vss. 14b to 16 again. For Hartmann the central element of the story is the theme of the theft of Jesus' body. The address of Jesus must be part of the *Vorlage* because it does not correspond to normal johannine usage (p. 206). On the gardner question, cf. von Campenhausen, *Ablauf*, pp. 33f. and Dodd, "Appearances," pp. 18f. and regarding the address "Rabbouni" cf. A. Wikenhauser, *Das Evangelium nach Johannes*, RNT, 4 (Regensburg, 1961, 3rd ed.), p. 339.

612 Benoit, "Marie-Magdaleine," p. 151, says that vss. 14b-18 (Mt. 28:9-10 and "Mk." 16:9, which he holds to be a distinct voice, not unlike Dodd, and not dependent on the canonical gospels) rest on a *base sérieuse* and constitute *apparitions de reconnaissance*. He concludes,

group appearance especially for Lk. and Jn. redactional enlargements proceeded along already established lines of development and the same is probably true here. Yet, here the original form seems to have had two elements that made redactional reworking imperative: 1) it was an appearance to a woman and outside of the women and their place at the tomb such an appearance was not current elsewhere at this earliest period,[613] and 2) it was an encounter cast in a form very close to that of an eyewitness recollection, also unprecedented.[614] Nevertheless, it owed its tenacity as tradition—perhaps even in view of these two elements—to the theological expression assumed and communicated in its form, a form related to the other traditional stories. While it is necessary to speak, of course, about remnants of the original story probably with beginning and ending now altered for purposes of incorporation into the whole, it is, nevertheless, impossible to ascribe its origin—in response to the question posed above—*in toto* to redactional creation out of elements existing in other johannine resurrection traditions.

The structural elements for the Mary Magdalene appearance story are also offered in the visual overview in the Text-Synopsis below.

B. The Appearance Story *Gattung*

The Emmaus story, the Galilaean appearance story and the story of Mary Magdalene have shown in their traditional matrix certain basic similarities of structure and content. Without trying to press them into an identical mold we may note the following points of contact: 1) the participant(s) is(are) in a crisis situation as the result of Jesus' death, 2) into this situation Jesus comes unexpectedly, 3) he is seen but not recognized, 4) he addresses the recipient(s) of the appearance and a verbal exchange of some sort ensues and 5) recognition of him as the Lord, the Jesus of their former experience, is the focal point in some expression recalling the familiarity of that former experience. This element of recognition is, moreover, the point at which the stories' variance from one another is the strongest. Whether or not a disappearance of the appearing One as in the Emmaus story was also part of the

"la christophanie de M.-M. mérite donc d'être retenue. . .comme une donnée valable de la tradition primitive" (p. 152), but rather than dealing with particulars of the traditional matrix his chief interest is in showing that it is not dependent on the angel appearance of Mk. 16:1-8 or on Mt. 28:9-10, but is older than both of them.

613 In contrast to the increasing role of the women in the extra-canonical sources, cf. above pp. 124ff.

614 Referring to the eyewitness tone of the account (and the Emmaus story too) is Dupont, "Meal," pp. (106ff. and) 114. Albertz, *op. cit.*, p. 267 in differentiating between "Christophanies" and "Angelophanies" claims that Mary was the only bearer "des pneumatischen Erlebnisses," having been included in the former. Says Hengel, "Frauen," p. 252, "Selbstverständlich bleiben dies alles Vermutungen, andererseits muß, wer die Möglichkeit einer Ersterscheinung vor Maria Magdalena grundsätzlich verneinen will, versuchen, den bei Markus, Lukas und Johannes unabhängig voneinander sichtbar werdenden Rang dieser Jüngerin Jesu auf andere Weise befriedigend zu erklären." For an interesting statement on the tension between report and proclamation in the resurrection traditions, cf. H. Kahlefeld, "Die Oster-Evangelien. Bericht und Verkündigung," *Paschatis Sollemnia. Studien zu Osterfeier und Osterfrömmigkeit, Fst. J.A. Jungmann*, ed. by B. Fischer and J. Wagner (Basel, 1959), pp. 23ff.

original form for the other two is a tempting inference because of radical redactional alterations noted elsewhere in their present form, but for lack of specific indications of such we must leave the question open.

Calling to mind then our conclusions to the group appearance stories we see that this form of the three stories above constitutes a close parallel to the one concluded for them as well. They overlap one another in many aspects almost identically, e.g., the crisis situation, Jesus' coming into their presence, failing to be recognized—or as it is expressed there in the pre-eminence of the doubt motif—, his address and verbal exchange with them and the moment of recognition—or as it is found there in their coming to belief that it is the Lord in their presence. This recognition, moreover, while taking a variety of expressions in all of the accounts is more than a realization that he is no longer in the tomb as they had perhaps supposed, but is constitutive for a re-establishment of their fellowship with him. The break in continuity in the cross is bridged in the recognition motif. The elements of the Holy Spirit and scripture had a very early function apparently in the group appearance stories on this matter of the break in continuity, but their place in a primitive appearance story *Gattung* is uncertain.

The two chief differences between the two complexes are: 1) the commission motif and 2) the meal motif (the Magdalene pericope being the hybrid here since it knows of neither). The fluidity of the appearance traditions in general becomes most apparent here. As our analysis has shown at these two points we have the most concentrated redactional activity. In the one the movement toward the concluding words of commission is clearly the focal point of the whole. For the other complex recognition is key, of course, with the meal motif serving a subordinate role to this motif in the Emmaus story and sharing a place of equal weight with it in the Galilaean story; in the Magdalene story it is missing entirely. Yet, the direction of statement in the recognition motif and the meal motif in its two locations for the second complex, namely the restoration of fellowship after its interruption at the cross, is also characteristic of the group stories as noted above in the motif of coming to faith after overcoming doubts. That means essentially then that the only difference really between both complexes at the traditional level is the matter of the commission.

We saw earlier that the commissioning words of the resurrected One are cast entirely in the style, vocabulary and theological intention of the three evangelists in question: 1) the command to go into the gentile mission (Mt), 2) you are witnesses of all these things (Lk) and 3) you are forgiving and retaining sins (Jn). In each this is redactional interest and not traditional matrix. Can one conclude that this element was really original at all then? Several considerations allow for a reply in the affirmative. For one thing, even if some form of sending were resident in the second complex, which may indeed have been the case as we saw in the Emmaus story and its returning of the disciples to the others or more remotely the return of Mary Magdalene cast in the form of the report from the grave out of the tomb tradition, the logical place for such to find its emphasis and enlargement is in the complex where all disciples are present and structurally an end has been reached; thus its apparent absence in the second complex is not necessarily an argument against its originality in the first. For the same reason it would be erroneous to conclude that the whole first complex is secondary having emerged as a construct out of the second complex with the commission merely tacked on to round it off theologically. For another thing, the fact that all three expand on this element so radically independent of one another suggests strongly that a sending was in fact present in the source each has taken over. The strongest argument supporting its presence is, as we saw in chapter II, the existence of the kerygma itself which cannot be explained satisfactorily without the original sending. There we saw that both streams of tradition reach back at their core to common origins. Of course, it is very difficult to say very much about the development of the motif, i.e., whether or not it had its closest analogy in the sending accounts of the earthly ministry and/or stands in a direct history-of-tradition relationship to them. To go beyond this in any case and propose that as the historical Jesus probably did send his disciples out in the situation behind those accounts so too here the resurrected One did the same under the conditions of the new Easter situation *as expressed in these stories* is presumptuous in the light of what a history-of-tradition analysis can supply, and therefore, the question of the motifs' exact expression and form must be left open.

We must conclude, in view of the foregoing and the historical fact that the primitive community at the earliest stage of the traditions' development was conscious of having been sent and did not, in fact, become a closed community or sect retreating from the world into itself–acknowledging of course that exceptions did exist–, that the commission in the form of the sending motif was original to the basic form of the appearance *Gattung* for the first complex and perhaps remotely for the second as well.

We may, therefore, summarize the analysis of this section by saying that although the appearance stories of the gospel tradition show an almost unprecedented fluidity and proclivity to redactional freedom and variation a pre-redactional form with constants of motif and theme is discernible behind that fluidity, a form fixed enough in its aspects of development and general portrayal along with its basic direction of theological statement to call it a NT *Gattung*. We direct the reader's attention to the visual overview of the *Gattung* elements in the Text-Synopsis below for all the texts. We proceed then accordingly to ask the question of analogy to this *Gattung* and the specifics of its origin in the remainder of our investigation. In order to avoid forcing the particulars of each account into a preconceived mold in the aforementioned synopsis we shall note the variety by including the gaps as well as the overlap and present the whole in terms of fields of expression rather than a rigid scheme of individual terms that "must" necessarily appear–a schematization that often is used in such tables–for the recognition of such a *Gattung*. That is to say, it is important to remember that we are dealing with a dynamic complex, both in the texts analyzed up to this point and in those to follow, that resists reduction to a static minimum of words. The rich interplay of terms, concepts and clusters of expressions are essential to an adequate grasp of *Gattung* analysis. The question of *Sitz im Leben* which has been up to this point only of marginal significance in our investigation, will be considered in the following chapter, but especially in chapter V.

IV. History-of-Religion Background and the Analogy Question

We proceed now to expand the scope of investigation by placing the earliest discernible types of appearance stories of the gospel tradition into the realm of their larger historical context. This step represents a conscious and deliberate response to the history-of-religion imperative placed upon NT research as historical-theological discipline: are these stories related in any way to the general religious environment of the first century A.D. and if so how? The *method* to be used is one of *comparing* possible analogies and the *goal* is *to gain further clarity on the origin* of the structure and motifs of the *NT appearance Gattung* and *to ascertain the statement-intention* of that *Gattung* in context. Offering themselves for this comparison are such matters as: 1) terminology, 2) overall story form and 3) correspondence in the subject matter expressed.

It is of considerable interest to note the far-reaching neglect the appearance stories have received in the history of their treatment under this aspect of investigation. While such strata of the gospel tradition as the miracles of Jesus, his birth and baptism—as well as the implications of the latter for the baptismal practice of the early church—have been examined extensively from the history-of-religion perspective[615] such comparison to any degree of satisfaction for the appearance stories is conspicuously wanting.[616] What has been done on this question in this century stems by and large from the classical form-critical school and has suffered in the main from a one-sided emphasis upon the Emmaus pericope and a general

615 Examples of the monographs written on these and other aspects with a focus on the history-of-religion question can be found in Bultmann, *Tradition*, pp. 223ff. and in the *Ergänzungsheft*, pp. 77ff. Re: miracles cf. K. Kertelge, "Zur Interpretation der Wunder Jesu. Ein Literaturbericht," *BuL*, 9 (1968), pp. 140-153, his, *Die Wunder Jesu im Markusevangelium*, StANT, 23 (Mü., 1970), and G. Theißen, *Urchristliche Wundergeschichten. Ein Beitrag zur formgeschichtlichen Erforschung der synoptischen Evangelien*, StNT, 8 (Gütersloh, 1974). Also D.L. Tiede, *The Charismatic Figure as Miracle Worker*, SBL Diss. Series, 1 (Harvard Diss. 1970 under H. Koester; Missoula, Mont., 1972). History-of-religion backgrounds to the ascension question have been investigated most recently by Lohfink, *Himmelfahrt*, pp. 32-79 who concludes that a translation story scheme was utilized by Lk in converting an *Erhöhungskerygma* into narrative (*passim*). Regarding the appearance stories of the gospels he disowns connections with translation story schemes and says flatly, "Es gibt dazu keinerlei Parallelen oder gar Vorbilder aus der Religionsgeschichte" in "Auferstehung," p. 50. Further, cf. Friedrich, "Auferstehung," pp. 170ff.

616 Monographs on the topic of the appearance stories and their history-of-religion background are practically nonexistent. The articles of A. Ehrhardt, "Emmaus, Romulus und Apollonius," *Mullus. Fst. Th. Klauser* (Münster, 1964), pp. 93-99 and Schnider and Stenger, "Struktur," pp. 94-114 are two attempts under development of this line of questioning, which take seriously the specifics of form and expression. In contrast is the indiscriminate listing of many possibilities without precision on the decisive differences among the types by H. Braun, "Der Sinn der neutestamentlichen Christologie," *Gesammelte Studien zum NT und seiner Umwelt* (Tüb., 1962 [article pub. originally 1957]), pp. 258f., n. 46. Schnider and Stenger's *Ostergeschichten* only mentions the backgrounds question in connection with the Emmaus story (pp. 67ff.) and is not comparable in scope to their article. Further literature which touches more or less indirectly on this question is cited below at the appropriate location.

lack of thoroughgoing form-critical precision. It is, therefore, an obvious necessity that the scope of comparison for the gospel appearance stories be expanded, on the one hand, to include all of them in their pre-redactional form, and, on the other hand, that a more workable, clearly defined basis for drawing a comparison—as well as differentiating fundamentally between categories of formal similarity or correspondence within a *Gattung* and of essential identity—be found. The present state of research on the issues here must be considered wholly inadequate and be challenged to re-think and re-define its categories. "Analogies" have been claimed from time to time in a variety of sources without dealing at length with the problems connected with this designation and it is hoped that a delimitation of the broad spectrum of sources for comparison and a more differentiated classification of the analogy category will be a major contribution of this section. We are hereby focusing our attention upon "appearance story" as a traditional form with specific recognizable contours of motif and theme, and, therefore, it would be a mistake to exceed those contours and select a broad principle, e.g., the "concept" of epiphany or the "idea" of resurrection in the non-Christian world, as a basis for sifting through and comparing ancient texts. Such a broad approach would necessitate a comparison of practically all Greek, Graeco-Roman, Jewish, and Hellenistic-Jewish religious thought dealing with the question of diety(ies) and the problem of death and/or afterlife and thereby make our task unwieldy at best—if not quite impossible. That it would be interesting is no question, but it would allow the examiner an arbitrary and journalistic freedom to select whatever materials appeal to his own interpretive predilections. This would lame any control on historical and—in terms of the analogy question—essential accuracy. We noted above in chapter II that a high degree of differentiation among the various resurrection traditions themselves is to be reckoned with; reverting back to broader categories at this point would constitute a betrayal of our methodological procedure, since we would be forced to compare material paralleling a different current of the resurrection traditions than our defined focus here. We are not disposed, therefore, to ask if a general concept of resurrection or divine appearance existed in the immediate religious-philosophical milieu of primitive Christianity and/or if such ideas played a role in the theological reflection of that community. Rather we ask: 1) did a concurrent story *Gattung* exist that told of a divine appearance in human form and/or an appearance of the dead to those yet among the living *in a way comparable* to the gospel stories? and 2) if so, can both a formal and an essential relationship be determined between them?

A. The Hellenistic World

Where references have been made in the secondary literature from time to time to texts of Hellenistic origin in a comparison with the gospel appearance stories they have usually been of a general nature and often almost pejorative by bringing these and those together under the common rubric of "legend" and/or "myth."[617] These terms are too multi-dimensional and prismatic, as it were, to be useful here and they tend to do little more than prejudice and confuse.[618] A greater degree of

617 For both Bultmann and Dibelius the appearance stories come under the heading "legend" and therefore they are considered late in origin, Dibelius, *Formgeschichte*, pp. 101ff., 130ff. and 190ff., but on pp. 265ff. he urges caution with regard to the designation "myth" at all–at least for the synoptics–, although he offers no particular differentiation with regard to the appearance question (cf. on Bultmann below, n. 634. Eng. trans. of the above pages for Dibelius under the chapters on "Legends," "Analogies," "Passion Story" and "Mythology"). In connection with the Emmaus story Dibelius refers to parallels from the Homeric Demeter Hymn and the wanderer Asclepius healing at Epidauros, ("Motive," p. 137). H. Gunkel also saw a parallel to the Emmaus story in the wandering-god type in the *Umwelt* in particular of semitic origins (*Zum religionsgeschichtlichen Verständnis des Neuen Testaments*, FRLANT, 1 [Gött., 1910, 2nd ed.], p. 71; also his commentary, *Genesis* [Gött., 1910, 3rd ed.], pp. 193f., where he draws upon Gen. 16:7ff. and 18:1ff. and then his, *Das Märchen im Alten Testament* [Tüb., 1921], pp. 77ff.; cf. below ns. 676 and 705). Gunkel's categories and their implications for the myth question in the history of research on the appearances and the Emmaus story in particular have been the cause for fundamental critique not unlike the objections of Dibelius above (cf. above all Ehrhardt, "Romulus," pp. 93f.). Also W. Pannenberg, *Christentum und Mythos* (Gütersloh, 1972), pp. 13f. and n. 20. "Legend" as an element obscuring the origins of the Easter faith of the disciples is expressed by Bultmann: "Die Entscheidung für Jesu Sendung, die seine 'Jünger' einst durch ihre 'Nachfolge' gefällt hatten, mußte von neuem und radikal gefällt werden infolge der Kreuzigung Jesu. . .Die Gemeinde mußte das Ärgernis des Kreuzes überwinden und hat es getan im Osterglauben. Wie sich diese Entscheidungstat im einzelnen vollzog, wie der Osterglaube bei den einzelnen 'Jüngern' entstand, ist in der Überlieferung *durch die Legende verdunkelt worden* [italics mine] und ist sachlich von keiner Bedeutung" (*Theologie*, p. 47; Eng. trans., I, pp. 44f.). Cf. also his *Tradition* (pp. 308ff.; Eng. trans. pp. 284ff.). Bultmann relies by and large on the form-critical analyses of Albertz and Brun (cf. above, p. 24), but he goes beyond them in developing the analogy question when he designates all of the appearance stories and the empty tomb tradition, especially the Emmaus story, as "legend" and appears to be in basic agreement with the possible analogies offered by Dibelius and Gunkel (cf. below n. 677, where Bultmann's article, "Untersuchungen zum Johannesevangelium," *Exegetica* (Tüb., 1967), pp. 124-197 is key), but then adding two additional parallels of his own from Chinese traditions found in R. Wilhelm's, *Die Märchen der Weltliteratur* (Jena, 1917), pp. 55 and 73 (cf. *Tradition*, p. 310, n. 1; Eng. trans. p. 286, n. 1). Further, where the appearances make use of the *Sendungsmotif* they are "a quite late achievement of Hellenistic Christianity (if not also in part of Hellenistic Jewish-Christianity). . ./ Thus the original Easter happenings are almost as good as overlaid by legend" (Eng. trans., pp. 289f.; *Tradition*, pp. 313f.). For further problems connected with the category "epiphany" cf. below, n. 619.

618 Their "legendary" character often stamped the gospel stories as having "late" credentials and this led to a decline of interest in them in general for members of the Bultmann school, because these designations made them readily "explicable" as part of the dispensable "paraphernalia" of an ancient context which has nothing to do with the essential message; for us their function is to obscure (Bultmann: *verdunkeln*) the origins of Easter faith. As we saw above (n. 617), the "how" of emergence for Easter faith is uninteresting for Bultmann, since history as past phenomenon–and there the category of legend and its problems are localized–plays no significant role in faith and the Easter message. The consequences of this view–stated here admittedly in the form of rough approximation–for further research in the Bultmann school on the appearances in the gospels can be seen, for example, in the mere passing references to them in H. Conzelmann's, *Grundriß der Theologie des Neuen Testaments* (Mü., 1968, 2nd ed.), pp. 83ff. Cf. also for Vielhauer's student, D. Esser, *Formgeschichtliche Studien zur hellenistischen und zur frühchristlichen Literatur unter besonderer Berücksichtigung der vita Apollonii des Philostrat und der Evangelien*, Diss. (Bonn, 1969), e.g., pp. 149 and 156f. In any case, it would appear quite evident that the category "legend" has had a prejudicial affect upon NT research in general subsequent to the establishment of the form-critical method, not to mention its far-reaching implications for the process of elimination in Graß (cf. above, pp. 32ff.) and the need for four editions (1956-1970) in view of the dearth of analytical research on this subject matter.

differentiation in categories allows for a greater degree of precision in distinguishing between those story-types which are comparable and those which are not. To be excluded, for example, as exceeding the boundaries of our categories for formal comparison are the Greek and deutero-Greek epiphany stories,[619] e.g., the accounts

619 In addition to the problems connected with the application of epiphanic analogies of the form-critics mentioned above an examination of related works supports the assertion as well. A perusal of works written on "epiphany" by scholars of classical antiquities and others, for example, make the need for a higher degree of terminological precision readily apparent. Cf. the frequently cited ΕΠΙΦΑΝΕΙΑ (cf. n. 574), and the more recent article "Epiphanie," *RAC*, V (Stutt., 1962), cols. 832ff., by E. Pax where the breadth of definition allows for a grouping of otherwise distinct categories, e.g., *Theophanie, Christophanie, Angelophanie, Pneumaphanie, Staurophanie and Pyrophanie* (*RAC*, cols. 867ff.). As linguistic research of late has made clear the matter of context–for the appearance stories of the gospels the resurrected and appearing One in his identity with the crucified Jesus–dare not be overlooked. Inadequate consideration of context is also the primary weakness of R. Pfister's article, "Epiphaneia," *PW Suppl.*, IV (1963), cols. 277-323 (similar critique Michaelis, "ὁράω," p. 320, n. 35). Cf. in general the critique re: both Pax and Pfister by D. Lührmann, "Epiphaneia. Zur Bedeutungsgeschichte eines griechischen Wortes," *Tradition und Glaube. Das frühe Christentum in seiner Umwelt. Fst. K.G. Kuhn* (Gött., 1971), pp. 185-199, who maintains that the accepted definition of epiphany as "das plötzlich eintretende und ebenso rasch weichende Sichtbarwerden der Gottheit vor den Augen der Menschen unter gestalteten und ungestalteten Anschauungsformen, die natürlichen oder geheimnisvollen Charakter tragen" (e.g., Pax, ΕΠΙΦΑΝΕΙΑ, p. 20) is far–especially in texts of the Hellenistic period–from always intended in their context, and in fact even where this motif is present it is more often than not a subservient one; instead the emphasis is usually placed on *helfendes Eingreifen* of the deity (*passim* and esp. pp. 187f. and 191f.). Cf. also in connection with the identity question and the incarnation in general for the NT, Pannenberg, *Mythos*, pp. 64ff. (esp. pp. 68ff.). For an orientation into the exceedingly colorful and diverse picture of the wide-ranging beliefs and practices of religious personalities and organizations and the traditions about and made use of by them cf. in addition to the above the following: G. Haufe, "Hellenistische Volksfrömmigkeit," *Umwelt des Urchristentums* I (Berlin, 1967), pp. 68-100, and his, "Die Mysterien," *ibid.*, pp. 101-126, E. Lohse, *Grundrisse zum Neuen Testament: Umwelt des Neuen Testaments*, NTD (Erg. Heft, 1, pp. 163-206, U. Kahrstedt, *Kulturgeschichte der römischen Kaiserzeit* (Bern, 1958, 2nd ed.), pp. 305-417, E. Rohde, *Psyche, Seelencult und Unsterblichkeitsglaube der Griechen*, I (Tüb., 1925, 9th ed.) and II (Tüb., 1925, 10th ed.), *passim*, F. Taeger, *Charisma. Studien zur Geschichte des antiken Herrscherkultes*, I (Stutt., 1957) and II (Stutt., 1960), esp. II, pp. 542ff., S. Angus, *The Religious Quests of the Graeco-Roman World. A Study in the Historical Background of Early Christianity* (N.Y., 1967[= '29]), *passim*, N.P. Nilsson, *Die Geschichte der griechischen Religion*, II (Mü., 1950), pp. 175-294 (esp. pp. 214f.), and pp. 498-546 and his, *Griechischer Glaube* (Mü., 1950), pp. 155-168, K. Prümm, *Religionsgeschichtliches Handbuch für den Raum der altchristlichen Umwelt. Hellenistisch-römische Geistesströmungen und Kulte mit Beachtung des Eigenlebens der Provinzen* (Rome, 1954), pp. 357-534, J. Geffcken, *Der Ausgang des griechisch-römischen Heidentums* (WB-Darmstadt, 1972[='29]), *passim*, P. Wendland, *Die hellenistisch-römische Kultur (in ihren Beziehungen zu Judentum und Christentum)*, HNT (Tüb., 1972, 4th ed.[='12]), *passim*, Goppelt, *Zeit*, pp. 55ff., C. Schneider, *Kulturgeschichte des Hellenismus*, II (Mü., 1969), pp. 765ff., F.C. Grant, "Hellenismus," *RGG*3, III, cols. 209-212, and his *Hellenistic Religions* (N.Y., 1953), *passim*, M. Cary, *A History of the Greek World 323-146 B.C.*, Methuen, III, ed. by M. Cary (N.Y., 1932), *passim*, F. Cumont, *The Oriental Religions in Roman Paganism* (N.Y., 1956[= '11]), *passim*. We in no way intend to deny at this point that this broad picture of beliefs and especially belief in epiphanic phenomena in the Hellenistic period formed the general background to the NT accounts. Indeed, the latter were also at home at the level of the common man where the currents of popular religion and philosophy thrived. Our objection, however, is directed at the notion of the derivation of a specific *Gattung* from a diverse conglomerate of *Gattungen* as being too imprecise a generalization.

of the dying and rising of cult deities in the mystery religions with their often close association with primitive concepts about the vegetation cycle and rhythm of the seasons or the primeval struggles of the gods, the underworld and human fate,[620] the dream [κατ' ὄναρ] and visionary [καθ' ὕπαρ] encounters of the *homo religiosus* within and without the immediate confines of cultic experience (the Asclepius devotee *et al.*)[621] and the apparitions of parapsychology, a realm teeming with communications with the dead and encounters with violent spirits, ghosts, phantoms, spooks and the like that had to be dealt with through magic, amulets, incantations,

620 It was popular for some time to place the resurrection traditions into the context of the myths of dying and rising gods of the ancient world and in particular those of the gods known to us through the phenomenon of the mystery religions, e.g., Demeter and Chore, Isis and Osiris, Adonis and Attis, Tammuz and Marduk *et al.* While there may be cause for a certain (qualified) amount of credence for this view in terms of the empty tomb tradition and perhaps the baptismal practices of the early church, it has become clear that such backgrounds as a possible analogy to the gospel appearance stories lose their attraction very quickly when one scrutinizes the particulars of their primitive concepts. Cf. Leipoldt, "Auferstehungs-Geschichten," cols. 737-742, esp. col. 738; also Haufe, "Mysterien," pp. 101-126, and G. Wagner, *Das religionsgeschichtliche Problem von Römer 6,1-11*, AThANT, 39 (Zürich, 1969), pp. 69-269, esp. pp. 96f. and 120ff. (critique Haufe, "Mysterien," p. 103, n. 2), in contrast to R. Reitzenstein, *Die hellenistischen Mysterienreligionen nach ihren Grundgedanken und Wirkungen* (WB-Darmstadt, 1966[='27]), *passim, et al.* To be mentioned is also the older work of J. Leipoldt, *Sterbende und auferstehende Götter* (Leipzig, 1923), esp. pp. 51-80, although its chief interest is for the debate around the turn of the century with A. Drews, *Die Christusmythe* I/II (Jena, 1909/'10) in which others, e.g., P. Fiebig, *Jüdische Wundergeschichten des neutestamentlichen Zeitalters unter besonderer Berücksichtigung ihres Verhältnisses zum Neuen Testament. Ein Beitrag zum Streit um die "Christusmythe"* (Tüb., 1911) and his *Der Erzählungsstil der Evangelien im Lichte des rabbinischen Erzählungsstils untersucht, zugleich ein Beitrag zum Streit um die "Christusmythe,"* UNT, 11, ed. by H. Windisch (Leipzig, 1925) and Johannes Jeremias, *Wissen wir etwas Sicheres über Jesus?* (Leipzig, 1912), etc., also took part.

621 Here we refer to appearance stories recorded in connection with the practices of cult organizations, e.g., Asclepius. Here the Asclepius supplicant, for example, seeking a cure goes to the temple, spends the night in specially equipped rooms for such (the so-called *Incubation*, cf. L. Deubner, *De incubatione* [Leipzig, 1900], *passim*, and M. Hamilton, *Incubation or the Cure of Disease in Pagan Temples and Christian Churches* [London, 1906], pp. 49ff.), expecting an appearance through which the god diagnoses the ailment and prescribes the cure–if not instantaneous–to be carried out by the priests thereafter (cf. typical descriptions by Philostratus, *Life of Apollonius of Tyana*, trans. by R.C. Conybeare, LCL [London, 1969(='12)], I, 7-12; III,44; IV,11.18; also O. Weinreich, *Antike Heilungswunder*, RVV, 8 [Gießen, 1909], pp. 76ff. and R. Pfister, *op. cit.*, col. 295). Typical for the cults of Isis and Osiris are the vision descriptions of Apuleius, *Metamorphoses*, trans. by W. Adlington (rev. by S. Gaselee), LCL (London, 1971[='15]), XI,1ff. Hereto also Wagner, *op. cit.*, pp. 120ff. In addition to the locus of cultic practice other forms existed as well in the period of *Vorgeschichte*–categorized by R. Pfister (*op. cit.*, col. 295) as epic, mythical and fable epiphanies–whereby appearances, i.e., encounters with the deity in visible yet altered form, were part of every day life. Such appearances have a long history reaching back to the Homeric hymns and extending into the late Hellenistic period. Chronologically speaking, therefore, they could be considered an option for comparison especially since for Pfister they are in part carried over in the legend form which is the critical step along the way towards Hellenistic aretalogies (cols. 293ff., but cf. critique above, n. 619). Again it is important to give adequate consideration to form. Pfister contends that his analysis is of sources which are neither dream nor hallucinatory encounters but rather visions and experiences in a waking state [οὔτ' ὄναρ οὐθ' ὕπνος, col. 278] because he wishes to avoid prejudicing the question of historical occurrence (cols. 316f.). The problems connected with the categories of "subjective" and "objective" visions have been discussed above, e.g., pp.

exorcism and sorcery, etc.[622] These categories may or may not be of significance elsewhere in the NT, but here they play no direct role in the question of backgrounds and origins. In contrast to these accounts an identifiable group of formally comparable story types is to be found in the *aretalogies*[623] of the Hellenistic period in which certain individuals were singled out for their noteworthy virtue, wisdom and power. They were considered so exceptional that they were venerated as more

35f. and it is doubtful that the presence or absence of the termini κατ' ὄναρ and καθ' ὕπαρ makes much difference where the overlap of motifs is so thorough. In terms of externals only two of Pfister's examples under legend epiphanies come into something of an approximate formal vicinity of the gospel accounts: 1) the woman of Epidauros who leaves the temple disappointed at having not seen the god Asclepius in a dream and having not been cured, but who is met along the way home by an εὐπρεπὴς ἀνήρ and is healed (cf. *IG* 952, 26ff.=*Syll.*2 803, R. Pfister, *op. cit.*, col. 295 and Weinreich, *Heilungswunder*, pp. 172ff.) and 2) the account of the deliverance of the poet Simonides: he is having a meal as houseguest of the Scopads in Krannon of Thessaly when he is informed that two youths wish to speak with him outside, he goes out sees no one but in the same instant the house collapses; the interpretation: he has been warned of the impending disaster by the Dioskuren, the sons of Zeus, Castor and Pollux (R. Pfister, *op. cit.*, col. 296 and lit., also C.M. Bowra, "Simonides," *OCD* [London, 1949], p. 840; moreover, cf. here the pericope of Paul and Barnabas at Lystra in Acts 14). Yet even formal considerations make a differentiation here imperative for they are far too few and general in character to make such accounts any more than part of the broad conceptual background mentioned above (cf. n. 619). In this respect even Pfister's *typische Züge* of epiphany representations (*op. cit.*, cols. 314ff.) form a generalization related to the "illegitimate identity transfer" mentioned in the lexicography debate by J. Barr, *The Semantics of Biblical Language* (Oxford, 1961), pp. 206ff., and outside of a few rough equivalents ("amazement," "silence," "joy," etc.) several of the motifs singled out for the gospel appearance stories are either absent from his list of *Züge* or can be considered in part as militating against them (*das Übermenschliche, Gröse, Schönheit*–cf. in contrast also the angel(s) in the empty tomb tradition). Important, however, is Pfister's point that a fundamental shift was taking place in a major concept of the several epiphany traditions: it was becoming a question in Hellenistic times–even if a nucleus of the idea was already given in budding form via the hero cults–whether or not the more or less brief, episode type of godly appearance–even where human form was utilized as a disguise–was the most adequate way of conceiving of divine activity; was it not more accurate–in view of growing skepticism towards the pantheon–to think of outstanding men in terms of their true divine identity: enter the concept θεῖος ἀνήρ (cols. 306ff.). In this altered form we are coming closer in terms of form and age to the gospel accounts.

622 The ancient world thrived on such and especially the Hellenistic world of the first century and thereafter (for an especially colorful account of such cf. Lucian's, *The Lover of Lies (Philopseudes)*, trans. by A.M. Harmon, LCL [London, 1960(='21)], pp. 13ff.; also among others, O. Böcher, *Dämonenfurcht und Dämonenabwehr. Ein Beitrag zur Vorgeschichte der christlichen Taufe*, BWANT, 90 [Stutt., 1970], *passim*, and his *Christus Exorcista. Dämonismus und Taufe im NT*, BWANT, 96 [Stutt., 1972], *passim*, and L. Collison-Morley, Greek and Roman Ghost Stories [Chicago, 1967(='12)], *passim*). Somewhat uncertain but probably belonging to this apparition type around a grave is the *P. Oxyr.* 1368 (*EGF*, pap. 34) reference to a youth appearing at night along the way to Glauketes who then leads him back to his grave (cited by Kerényi, *op. cit.*, p. 34).

623 Cf. here the historical overview of literature and problems connected with this approach in the article of M. Smith, "Prolegomena to a Discussion of Aretalogies, Divine Men, the Gospels and Jesus," *JBL*, 90 (1971), pp. 174ff. and Esser, *op. cit.*, pp. 98ff.; T.L. Budesheim, *Aretalogie und Evangelium*, Diss. (Heidelberg, cf. Robinson, "Joh. Trajectories," p. 267, n. 59). Boman, *op. cit., passim*, C. Schneider, *Geistesgeschichte des antiken Christentums*, II (Mü., 1954), pp. 53ff. is too undifferentiated on chronology, etc. For the question of "aretalogy" and the empty tomb cf. above n. 266(b,1).

than mortal, they were divine men, *theioi andres*.[624] Among the many other characteristics of excellence reported about them were also the unique events associated

624 As M. Smith, "Prolegomena," pp. 174ff., has shown with more than ample clarity this line of questioning has a long history behind it. The standard work for many years and still of interest is L. Bieler, ΘΕΙΟΣ ΑΝΗΡ. *Das Bild des "göttlichen Menschen" in Spätantike und Frühchristentum*, I (Wien, 1935), II (Wien, 1936); also R. Reitzenstein, *Wundererzählungen, passim*, and his *Mysterienreligionen*, pp. 25f. and 236-240. The more recent literature though not always directly connected with any particular group–e.g., E. Schweizer, "Zur Frage des Messiasgeheimnisses bei Markus," *ZNW*, 56 (1965), pp. 1ff., esp. p. 8 and now: *Beiträge zur Theologie des Neuen Testaments* (Zürich, 1970), pp. 11-20, J. Schreiber, "Die Christologie des Markusevangeliums," *ZThK*, 58 (1961), pp. 154-183, esp. 157ff. and S. Schulz, *Die Stunde der Botschaft* (Hamburg, 1970, 2nd ed.), pp. 64-79, and his *"Q." Die Spruchquelle der Evangelisten* (Zürich, 1972), pp. 47ff., 182ff. and 483, *et al.*–focuses its attention for gospel research by and large on the Gospel of Mark, its literary *Gattung*, the function of the miracle stories in that *Gattung* and the question of ("audience criticism") backgrounds; cf. M. Smith, "Prolegomena," pp. 195ff., L. Keck, "Mark 3:7-12 and Mark's Christology," *JBL*, 84 (1965), pp. 341-351, N. Perrin, "Towards an Interpretation of the Gospel of Mark," *Christology. Fst. N. Perrin* (Claremont, Calif., 1971), pp. 1-78, esp. pp. 47 and 51ff. (in prep. *Gospel of Mark*, Hermeneia Series), T.J. Weeden, *Mark*, and his "The Heresy that Necessitated Mark's Gospel," *ZNW*, 59 (1968), pp. 145-158, P. J. Achtemeier, "Toward the Isolation of Pre-Markan Miracle Catenae," *JBL*, 89 (1970), pp. 265-291, his "The Origin and Function of the Pre-Markan Miracle Catenae," *JBL*, 91 (1972), pp. 198-221, and his "Gospel Miracle Tradition and the Divine Man," *Int*, 26 (1972), pp. 174-197, and the recent critique of E. Schweizer, "Neuere Markus-Forschung in USA," *EvTh*, 33/5 (1973), pp. 533ff. Further, H.D. Betz, *Nachfolge und Nachahmung Jesu Christi im Neuen Testament*, BHTh, 37, ed. by G. Ebeling (Tüb., 1967), p. 179, his "Christus-Aretalogie bei Paulus (2 Kor 12,7-10)," *ZThK*, 66 (1969), pp. 300ff., his "Jesus as Divine Man," *Jesus and the Historian. Essays in honor of E.C. Colwell* (Phil., 1968), pp. 114-133, his *Lukian*, pp. 100-179, esp. pp. 116-(124ff.)130, Robinson, "Joh. Traj.," pp. 235, 251f. and 266ff. (etc.), and H. Koester, "One Jesus and Four Primitive Gospels," pp. 186ff., and, "The Structure and Criteria of Early Christian Beliefs," pp. 216ff., both in *Trajectories Through Early Christianity*, Essays by J.M. Robinson and H. Koester (Phil., 1971). Of special interest in this context is the question of the transfiguration story, Mk. 9 parr. (for discussion and literature cf. above "Displaced" App. Texts, pp. 141ff.). For johannine backgrounds similar *theios anēr* thinking is presupposed, for example, by Koester, "One Jesus," pp. 186f., Betz, "Divine Man," pp. 116f. and Achtemeier, "Origin," p. 199. Judging from the widespread dependence of this literature upon D. Georgi's, *Die Gegner des Paulus im 2. Korintherbrief. Studien zur religiösen Propaganda in der Spätantike*, Diss. (Heidelberg, 1958), now, WMANT, 11 (Neukirchen, 1964), and his thesis on *theios anēr* christology in primitive Christianity (pp. 145ff. and 192ff. and 282ff.) it may be said that Georgi is in large measure responsible for the "renaissance" of *theios anēr* studies in NT research. Cf. furthermore, the older work of H. Windisch, *Paulus und Jesus. Ein biblisch-religionsgeschichtlicher Vergleich*, UNT, 24, ed. by H. Windisch (Leipzig, 1934), pp. 115ff., who does not include, however, our texts under consideration of the divine man theme. Whatever else may be said about the viability or lack of same for the application of *theios anēr* backgrounds to particular questions of other gospel traditions (cf. among others, the qualifying objections of Roloff, *Kerygma*, pp. 111ff., T.A. Burkill, "Mark 3,7-12 and the Alleged Dualism in the Evangelist's Miracle Material," *JBL*, 87 [1968], pp. 409-417, H.C. Kee, "Terminology," pp. 232-246, esp. 240ff., his "Aretalogy and Gospel," *JBL*, 92 [1973], pp. 402ff., D.L. Tiede, *Charismatic Figure, passim* and pp. 286ff. and O. Betz, "The Concept of the so-called 'Divine Man' in Mark's Christology," *Studies in New Testament and Early Christian Literature. Fst. A.P. Wikgren*, ed. D.E. Aune [Leiden, 1972], pp. 229ff.), it is to be regretted that none of the above cited works deal at any length with the appearance stories outside of the "displaced" account of the Transfiguration. In any case, the extension of implications drawn from the ostensible *theios anēr* background for the miracle tradition to the gospel appearance stories without a critical investigation of the particulars of the latter must be considered an inappropriate methodology.

with their deaths–if they should have died at all–and mysterious accounts of *translations*, deification (*apotheosis*) and *appearances* after death.[625] Such proved, as it were, their ongoing existence from corporeality to divine incorporeality and/or served to communicate further benevolences to those left behind. This element of sequential treatment of the *post-mortem* perspective with all of the problems connected with applying the death dimension to the *theios anēr* at all was a frequently used motif–regardless of the difficulties–in the *theios anēr Gattung*; perhaps in making use of and enlarging upon a theme provided by the heroic epics of old such events accrued quite naturally to the closing sections of their *Vitae*.[626] These accounts then constitute the Hellenistic locus of our search for parallels to the gospel appearance stories. We begin, therefore, with a collection of primary sources which may be regarded as typical of the Hellenistic type.

1. Sources

Apollonius of Tyana

The most frequently cited "classical" example of the Hellenistic *theios anēr* adduced to parallel the gospel appearances is the neopythagorean mystic and wandering teacher of truth the first century *Apollonius of Tyana*.[627] The only com-

625 The most notable type of *apotheosis* was that of the Roman Caesars at the peak of its development. Although the concept is related to the "translation" and "appearance" *Gattungen* it is separate and distinct from them. After death and, therefore, without the aid of "translation" and even of "appearance" concepts in any direct sense it was thoroughly possible, for example, in the cult of the ruler for *apotheosis* to flourish. A confirming appearance in the form of statement under oath was, however, common (e.g., Suetonius, *Augustus*, 100). As a dogma in this period it was taken for granted that the Caesars were divine and, therefore, they had to exit in this fashion, so much so that some Caesars protested for one reason or another, but to little avail. Cf., e.g., Kahrstedt, *op. cit.*, pp. 15f., re: Augustus, Tiberius, *et al.*, and below pp. 224ff. and 232ff. for the Romulus story to which certain aspects of the cult of the ruler from Alexander on most certainly owe their origin, also S. Lösch, *Deitas Jesu und antike Apotheose. Ein Beitrag zur Exegese und Religionsgeschichte* (Rottenburg a.N., 1933), pp. 2ff., 129ff. and esp. texts demonstrating resistance to the concept, pp. 47-67 and also his literature, S. Eitrem, "Zur Apotheose," *SO*, 10 (1932), pp. 31-56, 11 (1932), pp. 11-34, 15/16 (1936), pp. 111-137, G. Hansen, "Herrscherkult und Friedensidee," *Umwelt des Urchristentums*, I (1967), pp. 127-142, Taeger, *op. cit., passim*, E. Rohde, *Psyche*, II, pp. 374ff., L.R. Farnell, *Greek Hero Cults and Ideas of Immortality* (Oxford, 1970[='21]), pp. 396ff. and 402, Nilsson, *Gr. Glaube*, pp. 153ff., Kahrstedt, *op. cit.*, pp. 7-18 and 340ff., Haufe, *Zukunftserwartung*, p. 251, n. 105a.

626 Cf. Kerényi, *op. cit.*, pp. 24ff. and 91ff., C. Robert, *Die griechische Heldensage*, Griechische Mythologie, II (Berlin, 1966, 5th ed.[='20[4]]), pp. 1ff., Bieler, *op. cit.*, I, pp. 44-49, Haufe, "Volksfrömmigkeit," pp. 97ff., E. Rohde, *Psyche*, I, pp. 178ff. and II, pp. 365ff., esp. p. 378, Taeger, *op. cit.*, II, p. 665 and more distantly E. Rohde, *Der griechische Roman und seine Vorläufer* (Hildesheim, 1960, 4th ed.[='14, 3rd ed.]), *passim* and O. Weinreich, *Fabel, Aretalogie, Novelle. Beiträge zu Phädrus, Petron, Martial und Apuleius*, SAH, 7 (Heidelberg, 1931), *passim*, H.D. Betz, *Lukian*, pp. 116-130, Koester, "Structure and Criteria," pp. 116ff., and Esser, *op. cit.*, pp. 112f.

627 The most recent studies on the traditions about Apollonius of Tyana and the literary achievements of Philostratus are by G. Petzke, *Die Traditionen über Apollonius von Tyana und*

plete account of his life extant was written by Philostratus († ca. A.D. 249) whose account goes back ostensibly to the earlier memoirs and travelog of an Apollonius disciple-companion named Damis, and although the reliability and existence of this source remains an open question,[628] it is rather certain that Philostratus is working with traditions dating back to a period roughly contemporaneous with the period of NT beginnings.[629] The comparison is, therefore, in terms of chronology legitimate. The question of what materials come into question for comparison is not an easy one. At the conclusion of his *Vita Apollonii* Philostratus offers several accounts apparently current and gathered by the author regarding the departure of Apollonius from this life.[630] They contain a miraculous translation and a vision-type appearance to a follower who cannot accept the teacher's instruction on the immortality of the soul; the latter account is in form at least often compared with the experience of Paul on the road to Damascus since the others present in the room cannot see or hear Apollonius and must rely on the interpreter function of the one. Philostratus wishes to give guarded credence to the accounts because 1) he often stresses that death is but a transition to another sphere and is a matter to which Apollonius is particularly immune because of his divine nature, and 2) he affirms that no grave could ever be located for the man: *ergo* they must be true.[631] On form-critical grounds one must say that the translation and appearance while having perhaps some structural similarities to the Ascension of Jesus and the Damascus experience of Paul have no likeness whatsoever to the appearance stories of the gospel tradition, and that they partake in terms of literary form of an entirely different *Gattung*. One other reference could prove, however, of greater importance, namely the account of his disappearance from the trial before the Emperor Domitian and reappearance shortly thereafter in the nymph grotto of Dicaearchia (Puteoli) before Damis and Demetrius.[632] This "appearance" had been prophesied as it were to Damis prior to the trial: he and Demetrius should go to the sea by the island of Calypso "for there you shall see me appear to you" [*ἐπιφανέντα γάρ με ἐκεῖ ὄψει*, VII, 41]. To this prediction Damis asks: "alive" [*ζῶντα*] "or how" [*ἤ τί;*] and Apollonius replies smiling: "As I myself believe, alive, but as you will believe, risen from the dead" [*γελάσας δὲ ὁ 'Απολλώνιος, ὡς μὲν ἐγὼ οἶμαι, ζῶντα, εἶπεν, ὡς δὲ σὺ οἰέι ἀναβεβιωκότα, ibid.*]. Damis obeys, but in great despair for he

das Neue Testament, SCHNT, 1 (Leiden, 1970; rev. by D.L. Tiede, *JBL*, 92 [1973], pp. 465-467) and Esser, *op. cit*. Cf. on affinities between the *Vita Apollonii* and the gospels/apocrypha, Petzke, *op. cit*., pp. 61f.; also his literature and discussion of the older works on Apollonius, e.g., F. Chr. Baur and E. Meyer, *et al.* Cf. the earlier remarks of K.L. Schmidt on the life of Apollonius studies, "Die Stellung der Evangelien in der allgemeinen Literaturgeschichte," ΕΥΧΑΡΙΣΤΗΡΙΟΝ. *Fst. H. Gunkel*, II (Gött., 1923), pp. 81-83, and below pp. 230ff. and esp. ns. 653 and 654.

628 Petzke, *op. cit*., pp. 67-72, N. Walter, *ThLZ*, 97 (1972), col. 29, Ehrhardt, "Romulus," p. 96, n. 12, H.J. Rose, "Apollonius," *OCD*, p. 72 and Philostratus, *op. cit*., I, pp. viiff.

629 Petzke, *op. cit*., pp. 147ff.

630 Philostratus, *op. cit*., VIII, 29ff.

631 *Ibid.*

632 *Ibid.*, VII, 41ff.

does not believe that Apollonius will escape death, and three days later he is in Dicaearchia with Demetrius. Philostratus sets the scene for the appearance by blending in at this point the events of the trial climaxing in Apollonius' challenge to the Emperor to take his body since no one could touch his soul and his claim that he cannot even have that much: "Nay, you cannot take even my body" (followed by the quotation from Homer's *Iliad* 22,13): "'For thou shalt not slay me, since I tell thee I am not mortal'" [*μᾶλλον δὲ οὐδ' ἂν τὸ σῶμα τοὐμὸν λάβοις, οὐ γάρ με κτενέεις, ἐπεὶ οὔτοι μόρσιμός εἰμι*, VIII,5]. After the insertion of a written defense document ostensibly prepared by Apollonius himself Philostratus returns to pick up the thread of the narrative of the disappearance of Apollonius from the trial which occurs immediately after the *Iliad* quotation, [*καὶ εἰπὼν ταῦτα ἠφανίσθη τοῦ δικαστηρίου*, *ibid.*], and then he proceeds to relate the appearance itself. The sudden departure from the trial took place at ca. noon and the appearance to Damis and Demetrius at dusk the same day in Dicaearchia (VIII,10). The two disciples are walking along the shore mentioned in the *μυθεύματα* about Calypso:

"for they were almost in despair of their master coming to them, because the tyrant's hand was so hard upon all; yet out of respect for Apollonius' character they obeyed his instructions. Discouraged, then, they sat down in the chamber of the nymphs, where there is the cistern of white marble, which contains a spring of water which neither overflows its edges, nor recedes, even if water be drawn from it" (VIII,11).

Their conversation centers upon the cistern at first and then turns to the circumstances surrounding the trial due to their anxiety about the sage. Damis expresses his grief again and then asks if they will ever see him again [*ἆρ' ὀψόμεθά ποτε, ὦ θεοί, τὸν καλόν τε καὶ ἀγαθὸν ἑταῖρον;*]. Suddenly Apollonius who has heard their cry and is already present with them (unnoticed) replies: "Ye shall see him, nay, ye have already seen him" [*ὄψεσθε...μᾶλλον δὲ ἑωράκατε*, VIII,12]. Demetrius then asks: "alive" [*ζῶντα*]. . ."for if you are dead, we have anyhow never ceased to lament you" [*εἰ δὲ τεθνεῶτα, οὔπω πεπαύμεθα ἐπὶ σοὶ κλάοντες*, *ibid.*]. At this moment Apollonius stretches out his hand and invites him to take hold of him to assuage their fears and to convince themselves of his reality, for if he is a ghost [*εἴδωλον*] from the realm of Persephone he will evade them [*διαφύγωσε*] "such as the gods of the underworld reveal to those who are dejected with much mourning" [*οἷα φαίνουσιν οἱ χθόνιοι θεοὶ τοῖς ἀθυμοτέροις τὰ πένθη*], but if there is resistance to the touch then Demetrius can persuade Damis also that he is alive and has not abandoned his body [*εἰ δὲ ὑπομείναιμι ἀπτόμενον, πεῖθε καὶ Δάμιν ζῆν τέ με καὶ μὴ ἀποβεβληκέναι τὸ σῶμα*]. Thus they were able to disbelieve no longer, rose up and threw themselves on his neck, kissed him and asked him about his defense at the trial [*οὐκέθ' οἷοι ἀπιστεῖν ἦσαν, ἀλλ' ἀναστάντες ἐξεκρέμαντο τοῦ ἀνδρὸς καὶ ἠσπάζοντο, ὑπέρ τε τῆς ἀπολογίας ἠρώτων*]. There follows then a discourse on the trial by Apollonius during which he states that he had made his defense that very same day, a remark which causes amazement in Demetrius since that meant that Apollonius had accomplished so long a journey in the fraction of a day. Apollonius then tells him to imagine what he will: "flying ram or wings of wax excepted, so long as you ascribe it to the intervention of a divine escort!" [*πλὴν κριοῦ...καὶ πτερῶν κηροῦ ξυγκειμένων πάντα οἴου, θεὸν ἐπιγράφων τῇ πομπῇ ταύτῃ*, *ibid.*]. Further discourse follows and they depart for town. Of the events and remarks rounding out this account the following may prove important for the interpretation of the scene: In urging his friends to begin their journey back to town because of the late hour Apollonius adds: "and it is pleasant too to talk as ye go along the road, for conversation assists you on your way like an escort" [*...ἡδίους δ' οἱ καθ' ὁδὸν λόγοι παραπέμψαι βαδίζοντες*, *ibid.*]. "Let us then start and discuss your questions as we go along. . ." [*ἴωμεν οὖν διαλαλοῦντες ὑπὲρ ὧν ἐρωτᾶτε...*] and as their conversation is then related in brief summary form, once again reference is made to the *Iliad* quotation to which is then also appended: "and he told them exactly how he vanished from the seat of judgment" [*καὶ τὸ ἀπελθεῖν τῆς κρίσεως, ὡς ἀπῆλθε*, *ibid.*]. Finally, Demetrius is still worried about further dangers to Apollonius, but finds comfort in assurances of Apollonius and especially in the remarks of Damis in reference to an incident while he and Apollonius were in prison together before the trial–the latter had removed his leg from the iron without opening it and then put it back–that ". . .it was then for the first time that I understood our master to be a divine being, transcending all our poor wisdom and knowledge" [*τότε πρῶτον κατενόησα τοῦ ἀνδρός, θεσπέσιόν τε εἶναι αὐτὸν καὶ κρείσσω τῆς ἡμεδαπῆς σοφίας*, VIII,13]. After this exchange the scene slowly draws to a close with the two companions ministering to Apollonius and the latter retiring to catch up on some much needed sleep after offering a prayer to Apollo and the sun and uttering some lines from Homer as a hymn to sleep (*ibid.*).

Romulus

Another frequently referred to analogy is the account of the *apotheosis* of *Romulus* contained in a variety of ancient texts, but told in its Greek form by Plutarch († ca. A.D. 120) at the end of his biography of Romulus (*Parallel Lives of Famous Greeks and Romans*, Bk. I: *Theseus and Romulus*) and in a shorter form by Dionysius of Halicarnassus (end of the first century B.C.) in his *Antiquitates Romanae*, II, 63,3f.[633] Leading up to the actual account of the appearance of Romulus, Plutarch records that the people, the nobles and the king are gathered outside the city when suddenly:

"strange and unaccountable disorders with incredible changes filled the air; the light of the sun failed, and night came down upon them, not with peace and quiet, but with the awful peals of

633 Again traditions antedating these authors are to be presupposed, cf. analysis below pp. 230ff. The most recent work on the life of Romulus and traditions about him is by K. Lukan, *Romulus oder auf den Spuren der Gründer Roms* (Wien, 1970), who points to the tension between *apotheosis* and a known grave for Romulus, pp. 195ff. Cf. H.J. Rose, "Romulus and Remus," *OCD*, p. 780. Plutarch, *Lives*, I (*Thesus and Romulus, Lycurgus and Numa, Solon and Publicola*), trans. by B. Perrin, LCL (London, 1967). Dionysius of Halicarnassus, *The Roman Antiquities*, I, trans. by E. Cary, LCL (London, 1937).

thunder and furious blasts driving rain from every quarter, during which the multitude dispersed and fled, but the nobles gathered closely together; and when the storm had ceased, and the sun shone out, and the multitude, now gathered together again in the same place as before, anxiously sought for their king, the nobles would not suffer them to inquire into his disappearance nor busy themselves about it, but exhorted them all to honour and revere Romulus, since he had been *caught up into heaven*, and was to be a benevolent *god* for them instead of a good king [...ὡς ἀνηρπασμένον εἰς θεοὺς καὶ θεὸν εὐμενῆ γενησόμενον...]" XXVII,7.

Some accepted the account and rejoiced while others supposed foul play and the murder of Romulus by the patricians (XXVII,8). At this point in the narrative Plutarch introduces the appearance account itself:

"At this pass, then, it is said that one of the patricians, a man of noblest birth, and of the most reputable character, a trusted and intimate friend also of Romulus himself, and one of the colonists from Alba, Julius Proculus by name, went into the forum and solemnly swore by the most sacred emblems before all the people that, as he was travelling on the road, he had seen Romulus coming to meet him, fair and stately to the eye as never before, and arrayed in bright and shining armour [ὡς ὁδὸν αὐτῷ βαδίζοντι Ῥωμύλος ἐξ ἐναντίας προσιὼν φανείη, καλὸς μὲν ὀφθῆναι καὶ μέγας, ὡς οὔποτε πρόσθεν, ὅπλοις δὲ λαμπροῖς καὶ φλέγουσι κεκοσμένος]. He himself, then, affrighted at the sight [αὐτὸς μὲν οὖν ἐκπλαγεὶς πρὸς τὴν ὄψιν], had said: 'O King, what possessed thee, or what purpose hadst thou, that thou hast left us patricians a prey to unjust and wicked accusations, and the whole city sorrowing without end at the loss of its father? ' Whereupon Romulus had replied: 'It was the pleasure of the gods, O Proculus, from whom I came, that I should be with mankind only a short time, and that after founding a city destined to be the greatest on earth for empire and glory, I should dwell again in heaven. So farewell, and tell the Romans that if they practise self-restraint, and add to it valour, they will reach the utmost heights of human power. And I will be your propitious deity, Quirinus' [θεοῖς ἔδοξεν, ὦ Πρόκλε, τοσοῦτον ἡμᾶς γενέσθαι μετ' ἀνθρώπων χρόνον, ἐκεῖθεν ὄντας, καὶ πόλιν ἐπ' ἀρχῇ καὶ δόξῃ μεγίστῃ κτίσαντας αὖθις οἰκεῖν οὐρανόν. ἀλλὰ χαῖρε, καὶ φράζε Ῥωμαίοις ὅτι σωφροσύνην μετ' ἀνδρείας ἀσκοῦντες ἐπὶ πλεῖστον ἀνθρωπίνης ἀφίξονται δυνάμεως. ἐγὼ δὲ ὑμῖν εὐμενὴς ἔσομαι δαίμων Κυρῖνος]. These things seemed to the Romans worthy of belief, from the character of the man who related them, and from the oath which he had taken; moreover, some influence from heaven also, akin to inspiration, laid hold upon their emotions, for no man contradicted Proculus, but all put aside suspicion and calumny and prayed to Quirinus, and honoured him as a god." XXVIII,1-3

This account of Romulus' appearance is of further importance because of the remark following it introducing two other accounts of *apotheose:* "Now this is like the fables which the Greeks tell about Aristeas of Proconnesus and Cleomedes of Astypaleia" [Ἔοικε μὲν οὖν ταῦτα τοῖς ὑφ' Ἑλλήνων περί τε Ἀριστέου τοῦ Προκοννησίου καὶ Κλεομήδους τοῦ Ἀστυπαλαιέως μυθολογουμένοις, XXVIII,4].[634] Plutarch suggests that we have before us a story *Gattung* of not insignificant distribu-

634 The "mythology" question raised here by Plutarch continues to be of current interest in terms of the demythology program of R. Bultmann for NT hermeneutics. For his clearest statements on the scope and intention of the program of demythologization cf. "Neues Testament und Mythologie" (=*Kerygma und Mythos*, I [Ein theologisches Gespräch], ed. by H.-W. Bartsch [Hamburg, 1948], pp. 15-53) which was his 1941 publication that got the whole project rolling, his "Zum Problem der Entmythologisierung," *Kerygma und Mythos*, VI,1 (Entmythologisierung und existentielle Interpretation, 1963), pp. 19-27 (and now in Bultmann's *Glauben und Verstehen. Ges. Aufs.*, IV [Tüb., 1965], pp. 128-137) and his *Jesus Christ and Mythology* (N.Y., 1958, Ger. trans., *Jesus Christus und die Mythologie*, Stundenbuch, 47

tion in the world of Greek religious thought. We shall expand here on the brief summaries given by Plutarch himself (*ibid.*) by drawing upon earlier and more complete accounts of his two illustrations.

Aristeas of Proconnesus

The story of the *apotheosis* of *Aristeas of Proconnesus*[635] is told by Herodotus († ca. 440 B.C.) in his *Persian Wars*, IV,14,1f. and 15,1f.[636] The author says that he heard this story [λόγος 14,1] about Aristeas told in Proconnesus and Cyzicus. Aristeas had entered a textile shop and while there he died. The proprietor closed his place of business in order to inform the relatives of their misfortune. As word spreads about town, however, a man of Cyzicus having arrived from Artakes contradicts the story of the apparent death of Aristeas saying that they had met on the way to Cyzicus and had conversed with one another. Although the man was prepared to argue his point further the relatives continue on their course of preparations for burial and return to the textile shop to fetch the body. But when the shop is opened he is "neither dead nor alive nor anywhere within to be seen" (14,3). Yet, seven years later he appears in Proconnesus to write the poem called by the Greeks the Arimaspeia and then disappears a second time (*ibid.*). Word has it, according to

[Hamburg, 1964], pp. 7-101, and now *Glauben und Verstehen*, IV, pp. 141-189). As a joint publication with G. Bornkamm and F.K. Schumann cf. his "Die christliche Hoffnung und das Problem der Entmythologisierung" in the book bearing the same title (Stutt., 1954), pp. 21-32, and now in *Glauben und Verstehen*, III, pp. 81-90. It would exceed the scope of our line of questioning here to develop the demythology debate. This can be followed up in the ever-growing series of publications under the title, *Kerygma und Mythos* now containing some nine volumes and edited by H.-W. Bartsch, plus some nine other volumes on the debate published by the H. Reich Verlag in Hamburg (cf. *Evang. Zeitstimmen*, 59/60, pp. 77f.). Also G. Bornkamm, "Die Theologie Bultmanns in der neueren Diskussion. Literaturbericht zum Problem der Entmythologisierung und Hermeneutik," *Geschichte und Glaube. Ges. Aufs.*, III (Mü., 1968), pp. 173-275 (originally, *ThR*[NF], 29 [1963], pp. 33-141). With focus on the OT side, also J. Barr, "The Meaning of 'Mythology' in Relation to the Old Testament," *VT*, 9 (1959), pp. 1-10. As has become readily apparent the program stands on many philosophical presuppositions which have been subjected now in the developing discussion to scrutiny and critique by systematic theologians, philosophers, linguists, psychologists and others. In addition to the *Kerygma und Mythos* series. cf. Goppelt, "Osterkerygma," pp. 81ff. and his "Begründung des Glaubens durch Jesus," *Christologie und Ethik* (Gött., 1968), pp. 45ff. and Pannenberg, *Christentum, passim,* and a score of publications dealing with Christian symbolism, the function of language for faith, the meaning of "language event" and the drama and timeless potential of metaphor in biblical language and hermeneutics as a truly international exchange of opinions by E. Jüngel, E. Fuchs, G. Ebeling, G. Eichholz, A. Laeuchli, R.W. Funk, A. Wilder, D.O. Via *et al.* Cf. also the three volume series *New Frontiers in Theology*, ed. by J.M. Robinson and J.B. Cobb (N.Y.). Common knowledge is that the question of "typology" plays an important role as an aspect of this endeavor to probe into NT backgrounds, hereto L. Goppelt, *Typos. Die typologische Deutung des Alten Testaments im Neuen* (WB-Darmstadt, 1966[='39]), the response of Bultmann, "Ursprung und Sinn der Typologie als hermeneutischer Methode," *Pro Regno Pro Sanctuario. Fst. G. van der Leeuw* (Nijkerk,Holland, 1950), pp. 89-100 and *ThLZ*, 75 (1950), pp. 205-212 and now *Exegetica. Ges. Aufs.*, ed. by E. Dinkler (Tüb., 1967), pp. 369-380, also Pannenberg, *Christentum*, pp. 54ff. and esp. p. 58 and n. 129.

635 Cf. W.K.C. Guthrie, "Aristeas," *OCD*, p. 90.

636 *Herodoti Historiae*, ed. by C. Hude, OCT (Oxford, 1960[='27, 3rd ed.]).

another report from Herodotus, that Aristeas appeared again some 240 years later to the Metapontines of Italy (15,1). In fact, Herodotus claims to know that this actually happened [*τάδε δὲ οἶδα*, *ibid.*]. At this final appearance Aristeas tells the Metapontines to erect an altar to Apollo, and to himself a statue, saying that he had accompanied Apollo once to their country (and to none other of the Italians) not in his present form but as a crow! (15,2). The Metapontines send to Delphi asking what they should make of this strange figure [*τὸ φάσμα τοῦ ἀνθρώπου*] and the reply is to comply with his wishes [*πείθεσθαι τῷ φάσματι*] as it would thus be best for them (15,3). Thus, says Herodotus, there is to this day a statue near the image [*ἀγάλμα*] of Apollo in the market place with bay trees around it bearing the name of Aristeas (15,4).

Cleomedes of Astypaleia

The story surrounding the end of *Cleomedes of Astypaleia*[637] finds documentation in various texts and/or text fragments,[638] but its most well-known form is found in Pausanias' († ca. A.D. 150-200) *Descriptions of Greece*, VI [=*Elis* II], 9,6ff.[639] The story tells of the translation of Cleomedes like the heroes of old. During the Olympic festival Cleomedes kills a certain Iccus of Epidaurus during a boxing match and having been convicted by the judges of foul play he returned to Astypaleia without the prize and greatly grieved. In a fit of anger he pulls down the pillar supporting the roof of a school housing some sixty children. The parents want to stone him and so he takes refuge in the sanctuary of Athena. Once inside he climbs into a chest and closes the lid on top of himself. His pursuers struggle in vain to open the chest and at last they break it open, but find Cleomedes neither dead nor alive: he has disappeared. They then send envoys to Delphi to inquire into the meaning of this and the reply of the Pythian priestess ran as follows:

"Last of heroes is Cleomedes of Astypaleia; Honour him with sacrifices as being no longer a mortal" [*ὕστατος ἡρώων Κλεομήδης Ἀστυπαλαιεύς, ὅν θυσίαις τιμᾶ τε μηκέτι θνητὸν ἐόντα*]." 9,8

From that time forth then Cleomedes was honored as a hero among the Astypalaeans (9,8).

Alcmene

In returning to Plutarch we find him adding one more reference to the previous illustrations of—for him—"similar" stories: the disappearance of *Alcmene*.[640] "It

637 W. Kroll, "Kleomedes von Astypalaia," *PW*, 21 (Stutt., 1956[='21]), col. 694.

638 Cf. the interesting refs. in Origen, *Contra Celsum*, III, 33 (Origenes, *Werke*, I, pp. 229f.) and Eusebius, *Werke: Die Praeparatio Evangelica* (*Die griechisch christlichen Schriftsteller der ersten Jahrhunderte*, VIII, 1, ed. by K. Mras [Berlin, 1954]), pp. 284ff.

639 Pausanias, *Descriptions of Greece*, III, trans. by W.H.S. Jones, LCL (London, 1966), pp. 56f.

640 Cf. also F. Jacoby (ed.), *Fragmente der griechischen Historiker*, I,3 (Leiden, 1954-1969), C. Müller (ed.), *FHG*, I,70; IV,639b (Paris, 1841-1870, with Lat. trans. 1966-1967)=

is said also that the body of Alcmene disappeared, as they were carrying her forth for burial, and a stone was seen lying on the bier instead" [λέγεται δὲ καὶ τὸν Ἀλκμήνης ἐκκομιζομένης νεκρὸν ἄδηλον γενέσθαι λίθον δὲ φανῆναι κείμενον ἐπὶ τῆς κλίνης, XXVIII,6]. Then with a skepticism spanning all of the accounts, including the Romulus story, in keeping with his own religious views on the disparity between body and soul he says:

"In short, many such fables are told by writers who improbably ascribe divinity to the mortal features in human nature, as well as to the divine. At any rate, to reject entirely the divinity of human virtue, were impious and base; but to mix heaven with earth is foolish ['Απογνῶναι μὲν οὖν παντάπασι τὴν θειότητα τῆς ἀρετῆς ἀνόσιον καὶ ἀγεννές, οὐρανῷ δὲ μιγνύειν γῆν ἀβέλτερον XXVIII,6]. Let us therefore take the safe course and grant, with Pindar, that:

'Our bodies all must follow death's supreme behest, But something living still survives, an image of life, for this alone comes from the gods.'

Yes, it comes from them, and to them it returns, not with its body, but only when it is most completely separated and set free from the body, and becomes altogether pure, fleshless, and undefiled. For 'a dry soul is best,' according to Heracleitus, and it flies from the body as lightning flashes from a cloud. But the soul which is contaminated with body, and surfeited with body, like a damp and heavy exhalation, is slow to release itself and slow to rise towards its source. We must not, therefore, violate nature by sending the bodies of good men with their souls to heaven, but implicitly believe that their virtues and their souls, in accordance with nature and divine justice, ascend from men to heroes, from heroes to demi-gods, and from demi-gods, after they have been made pure and holy, as in the final rites of initiation, and have freed themselves from mortality and sense, to gods, not by civic law, but in very truth and according to right reason, thus achieving the fairest and most blessed consummation." XXVIII,6-8

This kind of skepticism towards *apotheosis* is far from singular in the Hellenistic world.

Peregrinus Proteus

Often referred to in this complex of parallels is the death, ascension and appearance of *Peregrinus Proteus*[641] recorded with a goodly measure of ridicule by Lucian of Samosata († ca. A.D. 180) in his *End of Peregrinus*, 36ff.[642] The account runs as follows:

"Peregrinus. . .laying aside the wallet, the cloak, and that notable Heracles-club, stood there in a shirt that was downright filthy. Then he requested incense to throw on the fire; when someone had proffered it, he threw it on, and gazing towards the south—even the south, too, had to

Pherecydes *ap. Ant.* 33,3 and H.J. Rose, "Alcmene," *OCD*, p. 32, R. Laqueur, "Pherekydes (Genealoge)," *PW*, 38, cols. 1991-2025, esp. 2024, Farnell, *op. cit.*, p. 409 and W.D. Ross, "Pherecydes of Athens," *OCD*, p. 676 and P. Kroh, *Lexikon der antiken Autoren* (Stutt., 1972), p. 462.

641 Cf. W.D. Ross, "Peregrinus," *OCD*, p. 663 and K.v. Fritz, "Peregrinus (Proteus)," *PW*, 19,1, cols. 656-663.

642 Lucian, *The Passing of Peregrinus*, V, trans. by A.M. Harmon, LCL (London, 1962[= '36]), pp. 1-51, esp. pp. 40f. and 44ff.

do with the show–he said: 'Spirits of my mother and my father, receive me with favour.' With that he leaped into the fire; he was not visible, however, but was encompassed by the flames, which had risen to a great height."[643]

Lucian then relates how he delighted in deceiving the gullible ones who had come late as follows:

"I would thicken the plot a bit on my own account, saying that when the pyre was kindled and Proteus flung himself bodily in, a great earthquake first took place, accompanied by a bellowing of the ground, and then a vulture, flying up out of the midst of the flames, went off to Heaven, saying, in human speech, with a loud voice: 'I am through with the earth; to Olympus I fare.' They were wonder-struck and blessed themselves with a shudder, and asked me whether the vulture sped eastwards or westwards; I made them whatever reply occurred to me."[644]

He then draws his account to a close with the following:

"On my return to the festival, I came upon a grey-haired man whose face, I assure you, inspired confidence in addition to his beard and his general air of consequence, telling all about Proteus, and how, since his cremation, he had beheld him in white raiment a little while ago, and had just now left him walking about cheerfully in the Portico of the Seven Voices, wearing a garland of wild olive [*καὶ ὡς μετὰ τὸ καυθῆναι θεάσαιτο αὐτὸν ἐν λευκῇ ἐσθῆτι μικρὸν ἔμπροσθεν, καὶ νῦν ἀπολίποι περιπατοῦντα φαιδρὸν ἐν τῇ ἑπταφώνῳ στοᾷ κοτίνῳ τε ἐστεμμένον*]. Then on top of it all he put the vulture, swearing that he himself had seen it flying up out of the pyre, when I myself had just previously let it fly to ridicule fools and dullards."[645]

Demainete

Another Lucian text, *Philopseudes*, 27f.,[646] records a noteworthy appearance of the deceased wife of Eukrates, *Demainete*, after her cremation. The account runs as follows:

"While we were exchanging these words the sons of Eucrates came in upon us from the palaestra, one already of age, the other about fifteen years old, and after greeting us sat down upon the couch beside their father. . . .Then, as if reminded by the sight of his sons, Eucrates said: '. . .everyone knows how I loved their mother, my wife of blessed memory; I made it plain by what I did for her not only while she was alive but even when she died, for I burned on the pyre with her all the ornaments and the clothing that she liked while she lived. On the seventh day after her death I was lying here on the couch, just as I am now, consoling my grief; for I was peacefully reading Plato's book about the soul. While I was thus engaged, Demaenete herself in person came in upon me and sat down beside me, just as Eucratides here is sitting now. . . [*ἑβδόμῃ δὲ μετὰ τὴν τελευτὴν ἡμέρᾳ ἐγὼ μὲν ἐνταῦθα ἐπὶ τῆς κλίνης ὥσπερ νῦν ἐκείμην παραμυθούμενος τὸ πένθος· ἀνεγίγνωσκον γὰρ τὸ περὶ ψυχῆς τοῦ Πλάτωνος βιβλίον ἐφ' ἡσυχίας· ἐπεισέρχεται δὲ μεταξὺ ἡ Δημαινέτη αὐτὴ ἐκείνη καὶ καθίζεται πλησίον ὥσπερ νῦν Εὐκρατίδης οὑτοσί*]. When I saw her. . .I caught her in my arms with a cry of grief and began to weep. She would not permit me to cry, however, but began to find fault with me because, although I had given her everything else, I had not burned one of her gilt sandals, which, she said,

643 *Ibid.*, 36 (=p. 41).
644 *Ibid.*, 39 (=p. 45).
645 *Ibid.*, 40 (=pp. 45f.).
646 Lucian, *op. cit.*, III, pp. 319-381, esp. 360ff.

was under the chest, where it had been thrown aside ['Εγὼ δὲ...ὡς εἶδον, περιπλακεὶς αὐτῇ ἐδάκρυον ἀνακωκύσας· ἡ δὲ οὐκ εἴα βοᾶν, ἀλλ' ᾐτιᾶτό με ὅτι τὰ ἀλλὰ πάντα χαρισάμενος αὐτῇ θάτερον τοῖν σανδάλοιν χρυσοῖν ὄντοιν οὐ κατακαύσαιμι, εἶναι δὲ αὐτὸ ἔφασκεν ὑπὸ τῇ κιβωτῷ παραπεσόν]. That was why we did not find it and burned only the one. We were continuing our conversation when a cursed toy [little] dog that was under the couch, a Maltese, barked, and she vanished at his barking [. . .ἔτι δὲ ἡμῶν διαλεγομένων κατάρατόν τι κυνίδιον ὑπὸ τῇ κλίνῃ ὄν Μελιταῖον ὑλάκτησεν, ἡ δὲ ἠφανίσθη πρὸς τὴν ὑλακήν]. The sandal, however, was found under the chest and was burned afterwards."[647]

(*Fragments*)

In fragmentary form there exist other accounts of appearances of the dead, but their very brevity makes a comparison most difficult. Two examples would be the inscriptions telling of the appearance of a dead son to his mother,[648] and another youth, a certain M. Lucceius Nepos, appearing to his father and offering comfort: "quid, o! me ad sidera caeli ablatum quereris? desine flere deum!"[649]

2. Analysis

One of the first major problems to be overcome in comparing the account of *Apollonius of Tyana* as an analogy is the obvious fact that in the representation itself Apollonius is not appearing after death. It could be argued that one of the *traditions* taken over by Philostratus *originally* served as the conclusion to an account of the sage's execution after being found guilty of the charges in the trial before Domitian, but the question of the trial and its outcome itself is a highly debated one in Apollonius research, and the Dicaearchia appearance as the conclussion to a death scene in any direct sense is fraught with many problems.[650] It could, however, be argued with a measure of certainty that the "apparent death" belonging to the style of the θεῖος ἀνήρ concept[651] was indeed the point behind Philostratus' representation of the trial and its outcome—the *Iliad* quotation did in fact play a role in neopythagorean thought in general—so that in an indirect sense the appearance before Damis and Demetrius was actually a kind of resurrection miracle story, i.e., the "divine man" has now exceeded the borders of human existence in such a way that he lives above the conditions of time and space in the divine sphere, the sphere into which he enters years later in an even more direct and outward sense.[652]

At least from a neopythagorean perspective, then, we may say that this is an appearance story and that it has a genuine possibility as analogy in terms of its motifs.

647 *Ibid.*, 27 (=pp. 361ff.).

648 I owe this ref. to Pax, "Epiphanie," col. 869. Cf. Cougny *Epigr.* 2,373.

649 I owe this ref. to Bickermann, *op. cit.*, pp. 281f. Cf. *CLEp.*, 1109 (*CIL*, VI (*Pars tertia*), 21521 = p. 2244).

650 Cf. Ehrhardt, "Romulus," pp. 95f., Reitzenstein, *Wundererzählungen*, pp. 46ff., Petzke, *op. cit.*, pp. 141, 184 and 186, Bieler, *op. cit.*, I, pp. 48f., Leipoldt, "Auferstehungs-Geschichten," cols. 741f., Haufe, "Volksfrömmigkeit," pp. 75f., and Esser, *op. cit.*, p. 94.

651 Cf. above, n. 626.

652 Ehrhardt, "Romulus," p. 97, Leipoldt, "Auferstehungs-Geschichten," col. 742, Haufe, "Volksfrömmigkeit," pp. 75f., and apparently also Braun, "Christologie," pp. 258f., n. 46.

That is, an examination of motif elements in the story increase the degree of potential since they bear a striking similarity not only to the motifs singled out above for the appearance *Gattung* of the gospel tradition in general, but also more directly for those of one appearance in particular, namely, the Emmaus story.[653] Similarities such as the number of persons, descriptions of their frame of mind, doubts and hopelessness, the location outside the town and finally the general description of the appearance as one of concealed identity and the centrality of renewed recognition are all considerable. Somewhat more remote because of placement, but nevertheless important for the basic motif similarity is the presence of the disappearance motif, the journey together and the concept of reunion. There are, of course, considerable dissimilarities too, but when one understands them as being elements essential only to the representation of an appearing ϑεῖος ἀνήρ for the Greek mind (e.g., nymph grotto, play on Homeric heritage and the references to the realm of Persephone and its counterpart the "living," etc.) the questions are obvious: how are the similarities to be accounted for and are similarity and identity synonymous? It would be an attractive thesis in regard to the first question to maintain that they arrived at this similarity independent of one another by sharing *Gattung* background and thereby coincidentally using the same grouping of motifs.[654] Put differently,

653 Among those who make a general comparison and note affinities are: Ehrhardt, "Romulus," pp. 97ff. (contra is Petzke, *op. cit.*, p. 186), Braun, "Christologie," pp. 258f., n. 46, Reitzenstein, *Wundererzählungen*, pp. 49 and 125, Bieler, *op. cit.*, I, pp. 48f., Leipoldt, "Auferstehungs-Geschichten," col. 742, C. Clemen, *Religionsgeschichtliche Erklärung des Neuen Testaments. Die Abhängigkeit des ältesten Christentums von Religionen und philosophischen Systemen* (Gießen, 1924, 2nd ed.), pp. 258f. (referring to Wettstein and Klostermann), Taeger, *op. cit.*, II, pp. 602ff., and by direct or indirect reference many of the proponents of *theios anêr* backgrounds in general (cf. n. 624). Cf. Esser, *op. cit.*, p. 156.

654 Such would be the conclusion in terms of the working hypothesis—with or without specific reference to the exact comparison here in question—of the last mentioned *theios anêr* proponents in the foregoing note. Cf. also Leipoldt, "Auferstehungs-Geschichten," col. 742, who tends in this direction, but leaves the question open, Taeger, *op. cit.*, II, pp. 602ff., and more distant E. Rohde, *Psyche*, I, pp. 178ff. and II, pp. 371ff. and his *Gr. Roman, passim.* In general the study of the *Vita Apollonii* and of the larger complex of similar literature in antiquity above and beyond the direct question of dependence upon the gospels and/or vice versa is to be welcomed; suffering under this concern in the history of research both areas have been forced upon one another illegitimately. Cf. Petzke, *op. cit.*, pp. 230ff. and Walter, "Petzke review," cols. 30f. But when Petzke says regarding the comparison here: "Der Vergleich ist allerdings deshalb hinfällig, weil—zumindest im jetzigen Kontext—die Szene VIII,10ff. keine Erscheinung nach dem Tode darstellt" (p. 141), he has underestimated the ramifications of the category "death" for Philostratus; moreover, his elimination of the legitimacy of comparison here becomes exceedingly important in the question of dependence when he goes on to say regarding the events at the beginning and end of the *Vita Apollonii*: "Eine Betrachtung der Einzelzüge läßt jedoch eine von Philostrat beabsichtigte Gleichsetzung des Apollonius mit Jesus oder gar eine bewußte Überbietung als völlig unwahrscheinlich gelten. Außergewöhnliche Umstände bei Geburt und Tod sind keine Besonderheiten; diese Vorstellungen sind gesamtantik" (p. 141). Where Petzke refers to the point of comparison with various gospel appearance accounts he considers them too general to detect direct dependence (pp. 186f.) and says then in general regarding a comparison of Apollonius traditions with those of Jesus "daß sich bei der Ausgestaltung des jeweiligen Personenbildes parallele Entwicklungen und ähnliche Phänomene nachweisen lassen" (p. 162). The question regarding the Puteoli "appearance," however, is whether or not this characterization of things goes far enough.

two storytellers/writers had a catalogue of motifs for a particular representation at their disposal and they came up with two stories so similar without the interpretive need for recourse to any kind of interdependence. It has been suggested and is very probable in the light of chronological and biographical factors that this was not the case, but that Philostratus in one sense or another is dependent upon the gospel accounts (especially Lk.) and maybe directly upon the Emmaus story.[655] In spite of interesting attempts to refute this claim by placing, for example, the Apollonius traditions into a broad stream of Hellenistic thought contemporaneous with the NT for which Apollonius is but one—yet particularly graphic—example among many sharing the consequent accounts of death, resurrection and appearance and into which Apollonius can be placed taking on, therefore, typical character, it appears probable that the particulars of this account in question bespeak a relationship of dependence. Herewith is not said, however, that elements of the narrative were, therefore, unknown to Philostratus outside of this relationship. To the contrary, that Philostratus could very well have been familiar with a Greek appearance story type is shown by an analysis of the other more or less contemporaneous sources in our anthology. With regard to the second question—similarity/identity—not only form, motifs and terminology are key, but also an implied essential relationship. Here a reply is pending.

That we are dealing with a genuinely Greek type of story in the *Romulus* account is shown by the little or no interest it generated among Roman authors writing about his life; it made no significant impression on them.[656] It is, therefore, a matter of no small significance that the most complete accounts which have come down to us are recorded by two Greek authors. The story in both shorter and longer forms has in and of itself apologetic character: with it the patricians are absolved of the accusation of murder and the ruling powers are given support.[657] In the eyes of

655 Formerly, the relationship between Philostratus here and the gospels and the dependence of the former upon the latter was formulated by and large as competition and polemic, though Reitzenstein, for example (*Wundererzählungen*, pp. 79 and 125), was inclined to speak of an influence of Christian faith rather than of literary dependence. For the background to this view of "polemic" reaching far back into the history of the early church cf. Ehrhardt, "Romulus," pp. 97ff., F.C. Conybeare (Philostratus, *op. cit.*, I, pp. viiff.), and the treatise of Eusebius, (Philostratus, *op. cit.*, II, pp. 484ff.); also F. Chr. Baur, *Apollonius von Tyana und Christus* (Hildesheim, 1966[=1876]), pp. 149f. and 156ff. Ehrhardt, "Romulus," p. 99 (claiming support in Mildenberger, *op. cit.*, pp. 266f.) concludes that the goal of Philostratus was not polemic, but rather that his "Schilderung der Erscheinung des Apollonius in Puteoli die älteste geglückte Entmythologisierung eines Auferstehungs-Berichts [Emmaus] enthält." Be that as it may, direct dependence is in fact the most likely explanation for the similarities no matter what Philostratus' motivation was.

656 Cf. Ehrhardt, "Romulus," p. 94, also H.J. Rose, *Handbook of Greek Mythology* (London, 1972[='58, 6th ed.]), p. 316, O. Weinreich, "De dis ignotis quaestiones selectae," *ARW*, 18 (1915), pp. 35f. n. 2 and 36f.

657 Ehrhardt, "Romulus," p. 94. The theme of *apotheosis* for Romulus here buttressed the concept of the diety of the ruler fundamentally in the cult of the Caesar since Romulus was looked upon as a prototype. Cf. Haufe, "Volksfrömmigkeit," p. 76, and *Zukunftserwartung*, p. 251, n. 105a, Leipoldt, "Auferstehungs-Geschichten," col. 740, Weinreich, "quaestiones selectae," p. 35, n. 1 and Kahrstedt, *op. cit.*, pp. 15f. *et al.*

Plutarch, however, the more important issue is the question of the choice of *Gattung* expression through which the author of this story finds a vehicle for his apologetic concerns, a vehicle which, for Plutarch, propagates deceit and impiety.[658] The critique of Plutarch is not unique, but was uttered by many throughout the life and development of the *θεῖος ἀνήρ* concept as a constant companion wherever philosophy and popular religion came into confrontation.[659] But of primary significance here is the matter of the exact determination of the *Gattung* of the story itself. This can be done 1) through an evaluation of the variations of this story in extant texts in comparison with the Plutarch version, and 2) through a further comparison of this earliest and most reliable form with Plutarch's own parallel references.

The Latin references[660] to the *apotheosis* of Romulus (Ennius[661] *Annals*, I, 113ff.; Livius[662] *Ab Urbe Condita*, I,40,3) are very brief and offer little assistance in determining the motifs of the story. The shorter form of Dionysius of Halicarnassus poses the question of which direction the redactional work proceeded: shorter to longer or vice versa? In contrast to Plutarch the account by Dionysius[663] gives the impression more of summary than narrative. Where the longer account describes the events leading up to the encounter with Julius Proculus, the shorter one merely

658 Cf. above p. 228. Regarding Plutarch's understanding of Myth as vehicle of expression while insisting on the supremacy of reason and common sense cf. J. Oakesmith, *The Religion of Plutarch* (London, 1961), pp. 152-171. Plutarch's opposition to the idea of *apotheosis* is also found in his *Demetr.* 30 and also *de Iside et Osiride* 24. Cf. Lösch, *op. cit.*, pp. 47f. and 125.

659 Cf. above, n. 625.

660 In addition to Ennius and Livius cf. Cicero *de re publica*, II,10,17 and 20, cf. also I,16,25, Ovidius *Metamorphoses*, XIV,805ff. (dependent on Ennius) and his *Fasti*, II,491ff., Horatius *Odes* (Carmina), III,3,9ff. and also Aelius Lampridius *Life of Commodus*, 2,2.

661 Ennius † 169 B.C. cf. E.H. Warmington, "Ennius," *OCD*, p. 316 and his translation of Ennius, *Annals* (*Remains of Old Latin*), LCL (London, 1935). The fragments run as follows: (Quotation from Servius *ad Aen* VI,777), "secundum Ennium, referetur (Romulus) inter deos cum Aenea" (*Annals*, I,113; also a quotation from Servius, VI,763). "Aevum, proprie aeternitas est quae non nisi in deos venit" (*Annals*, I,114); then, "Romulus in caelo cum dis genitalibus aevum degit" (*Annals*, I,115, cf. Cicero *Tusc. Disp.*, I,12,29 and *CIL*, IV,3135; and as quotation from *Nonius* 120,1 "'Hora' iuventutis dea. . .Teque Quirine pater veneror Horamque Quirini" (*Annals*, I,116).

662 Livius † A.D. 17. Cf. A.H. McDonald, "Livius," *OCD*, pp. 509ff.

663 The Dionysius account runs as follows: "For while the Romans were yet in doubt whether divine providence or human treachery had been the cause of his disappearance [*ἔτι γάρ ἀγνοούντων τὸν ἀφανισμὸν αὐτοῦ Ῥωμαίων εἴτε κατὰ δαίμονος πρόνοιαν ἔιτ' ἐξ ἐπιβουλῆς ἀνθρωπίνης ἐγένετο. . .*, II,63,3], a certain man, named Julius, descended from Ascanius, who was a husbandman [*γεωργικὸς ἀνήρ, ibid.*] and of such a blameless life that he would never have told an untruth for his private advantage [*καὶ τὸν βίον ἀνεπίληπτος, οἷος μηδὲν ἂν ψεύσασθαι κέρδους ἕνεκεν οἰκείου, ibid.*], arrived in the Forum [*εἰς τὴν ἀγορὰν, ibid.*] and said that, as he was coming in from the country, he saw Romulus departing from the city fully armed [*παραγιγνόμενος ἐξ ἀγροῦ Ῥωμύλον ἰδεῖν ἀπιόντα ἐκ τῆς πόλεως ἔχοντα τὰ ὅπλα, ibid.*] and that, as he drew near to him, he heard him say these words: 'Julius, announce to the Romans from me, that the genius to whom I was allotted at my birth is conducting me to the gods, now that I have finished my mortal life, and that I am Quirinus'[*καὶ ἐπειδὴ ἐγγὺς ἐγένετο ἀκοῦσαι ταῦτα αὐτοῦ λέγοντος· Ἄγγελλε Ῥωμαίοις, Ἰούλιε, τὰ παρ' ἐμοῦ, ὅτι με ὁ λαχὼν ὅτ' ἐγενόμην δαίμων εἰς θεοὺς ἄγεται τὸν θνητὸν ἐκπληρώσαντα αἰῶνα. εἰμὶ δὲ Κυρῖνος*, I,63,3 and 4]."

states that the disappearance [ἀφανισμός] of Romulus was attributed either to divine intervention or to human malice. Regarding the recipient of the appearance both accounts agree on the name Julius (Livius suppresses it), but the addition of Proculus is probably an enlargement of Plutarch just as the addition "of the family of Askanius, a farmer of impeccable character" is probably in part at least to be seen as a compliment paid to Caesar Augustus.[664] The credibility of the witness is present in characteristic emphasis for both accounts, since, after all, so much is dependent upon his integrity.[665] The place where Julius gives his witness is also identical: in the market place. The appearance itself for the shorter version demonstrates several differences: 1) Romulus is leaving the city, 2) no conversation is depicted, but after Julius draws near to him (instead of the reverse) a command is uttered: go to the Romans with the message that his protective spirit [με ὁ λαχών] is taking him after his death to the gods, since he has finished his sojourn [αἰών], and 3) Romulus identifies himself for the future as Quirinus,[666] but he does not call himself a deity. Roughly similar is the description of Romulus—though in far less detail—as clad in complete armour and the command in general to return to the Romans with a message. Although the rule of thumb, shorter versions are older than longer ones, is generally true, the style and terminology of the shorter account here along with elements which have been singled out for accent suggest that it is a condensed form of a longer account which in all probability compared roughly to that offered by Plutarch.

The following motifs then were apparently central for the narrative in its original form: 1) an explanation must be found for Romulus' mysterious disappearance, 2) a trustworthy man—probably identified as a certain Julius—relates a miraculous encounter with—not a vision of—the person in question: a) outside the city b) via the initiative of the appearing one c) who evokes consternation at his recognition d) because of his presence and e) his striking outward appearance f) who offers the explanation for his disappearance g) who affirms a future relationship to his subjects in a different form, and h) who then sends the recipient of the appearance back to relate (what has happened and) what was said. Under motif f)—explanation of his disappearance—the specific understanding of the author, in contrast to Plutarch's use of the story, about the nature of human fate, the question of death and the relationship of the human to the divine *for the θεῖος ἀνήρ figure,* is expressed. This is an important observation for the conceptual direction of the entire story in its type as Greek story, for it belongs indeed to this *Gattung.* In this respect the tone of the "appearance" of Apollonius of Tyana can legitimately be compared in terms of history-of-religion backgrounds without regard to the particulars of the latter's literary origins: both stories want to say something about the divine charac-

664 Ehrhardt, "Romulus," p. 94.

665 Perhaps the oath is a later accretion owing to the story's function in a Roman context. Cf. Leipoldt, "Auferstehungs-Geschichten," col. 740.

666 For the Sabine background of the deity Quirinus cf. H.J. Rose, "Quirinus," *OCD,* p. 755.

ter of the persons in question and to affirm their further existence beyond the borders of human mortality.

With regard to the *Gattung* question and Plutarch's association of this account of Romulus' *apotheosis* with the stories about *Aristeas* and *Cleomedes* certain unresolved problems arise. First of all, the Aristeas account does refer to appearances the motif elements of which—as recounted by Herodotus—do, in fact, bear in part striking similarities to the Romulus account; yet, only the first appearance is recounted and in extreme brevity by Plutarch (with variations to the Herodotus account), while the Cleomedes story did not apparently at any time in its circulation have the appearance aspect at all and this account is told by Plutarch in much greater detail and breadth—showing, moreover, contrasts to the Pausanias version—so that one must probably speak of independent variants to the same story. This would suggest that for Plutarch in any case the actual *Gattung* which he has in mind is that which relates *disappearance* rather than appearance. This is substantiated by his third reference, namely, the Alcmene burial account. The constant in the account is, therefore, for Plutarch the theme of disappearance and what may then be surmised for *θεῖος ἀνήρ* thought and the variable is the appearance element.

Secondly, therefore, this raises the question of the Aristeas tradition in general. Herodotus has placed together three appearance accounts, the first of which bears similar storyteller motifs to the prolegomena leading up to the Romulus appearance. Moreover, the appearance itself takes place before one person—a traveler from Cyzicus (in contrast to the Plutarch summary)—but its description is reduced to a bare minimum of detail retaining, nevertheless, the emphasis upon physical aspects—it is no vision—and vocal utterances. The traveler offers his witness as a more or less natural outcome and is not commissioned, as it were, to return with a message. The second "appearance" is extremely ambiguous and belongs to the Aristeas tradition only in a very questionable sense, because of its origin more probably as a later pseudepigraphical identification of this individual with a literary work.[667] The third appearance does bear greater similarity since it suggests the physical appearance of a human figure and emphasizes the verbal aspects of the encounter, but it is more probably to be identified with the history-of-religion theme of later persons coming on the scene and claiming to be a reincarnation of great men of the past, not unlike the claimants of Neronian reincarnation [*Ψευδονέρωνες*].[668]

The reference in the account itself to an earlier appearance of Aristeas in the form of a bird while in the company of Apollo cannot be understood exclusively within the heroic and *θεῖος ἀνήρ* traditions, but is clearly a mixed form used in accounts of the divine epiphanic appearances of the gods in the earliest period of (Homeric) Hellenic sagas.[669] Thus, the Aristeas tradition found expression in the gamut of "appearance" forms and of all three (or more precisely four) types only

667 Regarding the "epic" concerning the Arimaspeans, cf. W.K.C. Guthrie, "Arimaspeans," *OCD*, p. 88 and "Aristeas," p. 90.

668 Cf., e.g., E. Rohde, *Psyche*, II, p. 377, n. 1.

669 Cf. above, n. 621.

the first is of primary significance for the specific *Gattung* here under consideration (as Plutarch has correctly seen).

In contrast to the uncertainties fixing the death of the person in question for the Apollonius, Romulus and Cleomedes stories the Aristeas account relates such in the witness of the shop owner. Even here, however, as has often been pointed out, the ϑεῖος ἀνήρ must not actually die, but can also experience an apparent death,[670] and the narrative regarding Aristeas in this respect is fraught with a lack of clarity compared, for example, with the Alcmene reference of Plutarch where the issue has been settled and the body is on its way to the cemetery or with the fiery end of Peregrinus or Demainete. In any case, the story does want to be understood within the *Gattung*—certain difficulties with the acceptance of Aristeas and also Cleomedes and Alcmene within the ϑεῖος ἀνήρ concept as persons of wisdom and/or virtuous and mighty deeds notwithstanding—and the motif elements of disappearance and reappearance related in narrative form, however brief, with emphasis on the real, non-visionary and verbal exchange aspects bespeak a generic relationship to the *Gattung.*

On the other hand, as mentioned above, the Cleomedes story has limited value for comparison because it makes its point without an appearance account. It is important, however, for three reasons: 1) it confirms the supposition along with the Alcmene reference that the disappearance motif is key for Plutarch in his understanding of these so-called Greek μυϑολογούμενοι, 2) it substitutes an oracular utterance for the appearance motif whereby the Pythian priestess in Delphi and not the person in question himself delivers the solution to the disappearance question by way of confirmation of his translation from this human sphere to another, and 3) it links the event with a kind of culmination to the heroic past whereby the origin of the ϑεῖος ἀνήρ type is anchored in this tradition as the locus for its interpretation. Cleomedes has passed from the visible world and has been exalted to another without having to taste death.

The *Alcmene* account is also of limited value for the same reason as the Cleomedes story. The miraculous replacement of the supposedly resurrected and exalted body with a stone constitutes a special problem for the larger narrative and conceptual context of the Alcmene tradition of antiquity in general[671] and is of no particular significance for the motif determination of the appearance *Gattung,* unless it be proposed that the stone like the oracular utterance of the Cleomedes story is to have revelational, confirmatory character which seems unlikely; the body has not been turned into a stone, but has disappeared and the stone rather than having symbolic significance is probably there for effect only.

In turning finally to the accounts of *Peregrinus* and *Demainete* in Lucian we are confronted with similarities, but also with further differences in comparison with

670 Cf. above p. 221 and ns. 625 and 626.

671 Cf. above, n. 640. Alcmene is the mythological daughter of Electryon who while married to Amphitryon bears Heracles to Zeus—who had visited her in her husband's absence—and Iphicles to her husband and is involved in various episodes of ruin and revenge; she was honored in a cult in Thebes and elsewhere. Cf. Rose, "Alcmene," p. 32.

the foregoing. Peregrinus, in a way more graphically and conclusively than any of the others, dies violently and does not just disappear. Yet, something–a volatilized vapor soul[672]–ascends in the flames, as observers claim, conform to good Greek thought. A further and somewhat contradictory affirmation arises consequently in the report of the man who claims to have seen him walking about in white raiment. To be clarified is the function of the two forms affirming his victory over death and their relationship to one another: the essence seen ascending in the flames was sufficient to establish conformity with Greek standards of thought in general regarding the soul–especially for important persons–and the "appearance" episode confirms the *θεῖος ἀνήρ-Gattung* exit. Thus this ascending soul must be seen as an additional visual element introduced alongside the θεῖος ἀνήρ concept–probably by Lucian himself for purposes of ridicule[673]–which in fact pre-empts the appearance, as it were, since the "disappearance" is only a figurative one and which in the present form of things actually competes for visual preference. It is possible, therefore, that the appearance episode did exist in greater narrative detail and has been reduced to an affirmation by Lucian who is at odds with the entire concept anyway. A reconstruction is very difficult–yes, impossible–but one can at least underscore the motif elements in the summary which *in toto* agree with ones we have isolated up to this point for the other accounts: 1) the encounter is related by a reliable witness, 2) the appearance was not a vision, but (presumably) a physical encounter, 3) Peregrinus is said to have been on a journey ("walking about"?) and 4) he has a striking appearance (white raiment as symbol of holiness and/or deity? and wears the garland of victory); nothing is recounted of a verbal exchange. Outside the bizarre element of death by suicide and the probable later addition of the ascending soul, Peregrinus' appearance may then be taken–provided the qualifications above are correct–as a witness to the θεῖος ἀνήρ appearance concept.[674]

The *Demainete* account on the other hand is of dubious worth because although it is presented with telling vividness, its structure and development betray the model upon which it has been constructed: the concept of a visionary dream experience. The reading motif is probably artificial since in the style of a Hitchcock drama that "pointer" is focused upon–however briefly–which in the end turns out to be the key unravelling the entire riddle: the book, a Plato text on the immortality of the soul, is here in truth a *liber interpres.* By removing this motif as secondary the

672 R. Pack, "The 'Volatilization' of Peregrinus Proteus," *AJPhil,* 66 (1946), pp. 337f. Pack also points out affinities to Apollonius and Romulus (agreeing with Weinreich, "quaestiones selectae," pp. 35ff.) and chooses to understand the scheme of *apotheosis* here and there in terms of neopythagorean and neoplatonic teaching on the immortality of the soul (*passim.*) Proximity to the cult of the Caesar, e.g., Augustus' ascension (Suetonius, *Aug.,* 100), etc., also his p. 336, n. 8.

673 Cf. the conclusion to the narrative above, p. 229.

674 H.D. Betz, *Lukian,* pp. 102f., points out that the term *theios anēr* appears only once in Lucian's works, but there are many synonyms which establish the concept for him (pp. 101, n. 1 and 102f.). Moreover, *typische Züge* in the manner of presentation also confirm this assertion (p. 104). Among them are the elements under discussion here (pp. 124ff.) where he places emphasis upon their function for the establishment of cult worship.

vision/dream type fits this account very well: Eukrates awakens and the figure of his deceased wife disappears when his dog interrupts the dream with its barking. Whatever reasons Lucian may have had for using this story it is to be distinguished from his account of the θεῖος ἀνήρ appearance of Peregrinus.[675] The same is to be said–with a certain degree of caution because of the limited size of the texts–of the two *fragments* mentioned at the end of our anthology: they probably stem from the dream type of appearance account and demand consideration under the separate and distinct heading of that category.

3. Relationship to the Gospel Appearance Gattung

It has become clear in the foregoing analysis of texts containing certain similarities of structure and form to one another and to the appearance *Gattung* of the gospel tradition that the former owe their origin to a very specific problem of subject matter pertaining to the *Gattung* θεῖος ἀνήρ itself, namely, a reply to the question: where has he gone since he is no longer with us and no grave can be found as proof of his death? Exceptions to the rule may be found, e.g., Peregrinus and possibly Aristeas too, but especially in the case of the latter this is dubious. The "appearance" or its substitute gave the solution to a particular problem: the θεῖος ἀνήρ did not die, but has *disappeared,* he has been *translated* from this to another sphere, he *lives on* in a higher form of existence and continues in one way or another to function on behalf of or at least in connection with those dependent on him. Moreover, this is a necessity from the viewpoint of the *Gattung* because a θεῖος ἀνήρ cannot die like others, but in the light of his wisdom and virtuous, mighty deeds he must be exalted on high. This story *Gattung* is a Greek type and has its origins in the heroic epics of the Homeric period and was developed further in the transition from small literary units to larger ones–as in the background of ancient novels in general. Where similarities in these stories thoroughly overlap with those of the gospel accounts–as in the case of Apollonius–dependence of a direct nature, the latter upon the former, is probable, understood in part as a characteristic borrowing in the later stages of the literary development from "small literature" to larger mentioned above.

These points from our text analysis make the following observations on the relationship of these texts to the gospel appearance stories possible: 1) while the motif element of disappearance is present in the Emmaus story and perhaps can be postulated as existing behind some of the others as well, it does not assume the same dimensions as in those texts of the Hellenistic world, i.e., it is not the source for the story as an answer to the "where is he" question. It comes rather at the end of a recognition sequel and functions in a different manner for the conceptual

675 In the context of the *Philopseudes* it is clear that divided opinion on death, afterlife and the relationship of this life to both is under discussion and the *Demainete* account is but one illustration among many in the work of the other world's capacity to break in upon this one. Cf. above on parapsychology, n. 622, also H.D. Betz, *Lukian,* p. 162.

structure of the whole. That is to say, it has a different function in the dimension of subject matter, but formally it could have been taken over. 2) The ϑεῖος ἀνήρ appearance stories further intended to confirm in terms of their direction of statement the continued existence of the "hero," and was itself a variable in expressing this, since oracular words or sighted ascending souls, for example, could serve as an adequate substitute or enlargement, while for the gospel tradition the central concept is not mere confirmation of ongoing existence in some other sphere, and—importantly—the form could not be replaced by another form of "confirming words" as can be seen by the retention of its distinction and integrity over against the kerygma and empty tomb traditions in the formulation of narrative text. 3) In view of these inner tensions with which any attempt to apply the "analogy" category must reckon, a formal analogy via the presence of similar motifs, concepts and forms of expression may well be an option, but closer consideration of the statement intention of the ϑεῖος ἀνήρ appearance story makes it impossible to consider these accounts as analogous in an essential sense. That is to say, both complexes share motifs like that of the figure in question being seen, recognized as a bodily reality, alive, interrupting a state of sorrow, causing a shift to rejoicing and dispelling fears, moving about or traveling, and engaging the participants in conversation, as well as the already mentioned disappearance motif, which is so key to the ϑεῖος ἀνήρ type; as formal categories they show a certain parallelization and correspondence. But these similarities resist their fusion into categories of identity since their statement intention as a vehicle within a particular thought-world demonstrates distinctions which are not parallel to one another. To answer then our question posed at the beginning, we may say that a determination of the meaning of the term analogy has led to the differentiation between formal and essential categories, and that the relationship among the texts in question for analogy comparison may be understood in terms of formal correspondence. The ϑεῖος ἀνήρ appearance stories do express a certain conceptual and linguistic framework which was simply a given horizon of thought for the period and which is not entirely foreign to the gospel appearance stories, but sufficient differences between them have become apparent to necessitate a further probe into the backgrounds question.

B. The Old Testament/Jewish World

The far-reaching neglect in the history of research on the question of backgrounds is true not only for those of the Hellenistic world but also for those of the OT/Jewish one. In the main, where more or less passing references are not made to Hellenistic texts or concepts these are made to the OT—and in particular its *theophany stories*—and the intertestamental and early Jewish literature. A characteristic and often cited example is the statement of H. Gunkel about the Emmaus story:

"Christus erscheint hier unbekannt als Wanderer. . .und offenbart sein geheimnisvolles göttliches Wesen an einzelnen Zügen; aber sobald er erkannt wird, ist er verschwunden. Dieser

Aufriss der Geschichte ist ganz analog den ältesten Erzählungen vom Erscheinen der Gottheit; die Geschichte könnte ihrem Stil nach in der Genesis stehen!"[676]

As interesting and as suggestive as this reference may be and as often as it has been repeated in the history of research, it rarely, if ever, has been followed up with an analysis of the question: in what way can a relationship between these *Erzählungen* of Genesis (and elsewhere) and the gospel appearance stories (and not only the Emmaus story) be posited and what scope and significance exists in that relationship if such can be demonstrated?[677]

676 Gunkel, *Verständnis*, p. 71. Finding Gunkel's reference here unnecessary and objectionable where he uses the designation *Mystisches* (*ibid.*) is Clemen, *op. cit.*, p. 258. Also objecting to the Gunkel reference as the cause for some sixty years of neglect of the Emmaus story because of the myth category and reference to typical stories of gods wandering among men in disguise is Ehrhardt ("Romulus," p. 93). He thinks the identification of myth type should be rather "die Epiphanie vor Wanderern, nicht aber die Epiphanie des Wanderers. . ." (p. 94). Cf. also his "Disciples," pp. 185 and 194. Ehrhardt's objection of category is dubious since Jesus is also a traveler in the Emmaus story. Moreover, his opting for a comparison of the Romulus and Apollonius traditions only is too one-sided.

677 Seeing the particular significance of theophany backgrounds to the gospel appearance stories as *Gattung* is, for example, Goppelt, "Osterkerygma," p. 92, n. 34. Also W. Trilling, *Christusverkündigung in den synoptischen Evangelien. Beispiele gattungsgemäßer Auslegung*, BHB, IV (Mü., 1969), pp. 226ff. and Lohse, *Auferstehung*, pp. 31f., who refers to the Gen. 18 account and the story of the visit of Jupiter and (Minerva) to an old couple, Philemon and Baucis, in a village that is destroyed because of its lack of hospitality toward the divine pair (Ovid, *Metamorphoses*, VIII, 618-724), and says that a formal relationship between them and the Emmaus story cannot be denied. His description of that relationship both for the Emmaus pericope itself and for the two comparative examples one to another is far too brief and sketchy in nature. His acceptance of a somewhat undifferentiated designation of the term "legend" for all three as a category applied to the type of story, even if it is not a value judgment, is apparently the reason for a lack of interest in pursuing matters of detail. Similarly undifferentiated are the brief remarks of Evans, *Resurrection*, pp. 92ff. and 105. Koester, "One Jesus," pp. 193ff., singles out the Apocryphon of John as exhibiting features which are not derived from the canonical gospels, but rather as revelation discourse are derived from a theophany pattern independent of the canonical Easter stories, i.e., the latter are not dominated by that pattern in their present form although indications within Mt. 28 and the transfiguration story (Mk. 9:2ff.) as well as the GP [IX] 35ff. suggest that theophany elements did belong "to the original features of the resurrection stories" (p. 195, n. 129). The absence of an analysis and a comparison of OT theophany texts with the gospel appearance stories as well as the undifferentiated grouping of the "theophany type" together with texts such as Acts 9, Rev. 1, Ezek. 1ff. and Daniel 10 as "revelation" or "apocalyptic" genre make his approach too general. Differentiating between *post-mortem* appearances of a man and appearances of a deity in human form (with ref. to Gunkel) H.D. Betz, "Ursprung," p. 9, n. 8, refers to the latter in connection with the Emmaus story, but does not elaborate. Bultmann also makes reference to naive OT pictures of God wandering about on earth as being carried over in the gospel appearance stories in his, "Untersuchungen," selecting Lk. 24:36ff. and Jn. 21:1ff. as good examples, yet his assumption for the former that Jesus "mit ihnen ißt und trinkt" (p. 188) is not evident there at all. Moreover, he claims here that the visual aspects of these OT texts, as well as in the gospel stories, are of secondary importance in comparison with specific words "in denen der eigentliche Sinn der Erscheinungen beruht" (p. 188). This view would seem to reflect more the theological position of the author than exegetical conclusions as much as for the OT (cf. his reference to the rise and development of the Bath-Qol tradition, pp. 188f. and n. 160) as for the NT. Disclaiming OT theophany backgrounds at all for the gospel appearance stories is Leaney, "Theophany," because the latter have a "historical foundation" while the former do not (pp. 107 and 111f.). Similar is the view of H. Schlier, *Über die Auferstehung Jesu Christi* (Einsiedeln, 1968), who

We have taken as our comparative focal point the literary form of the gospel appearance stories with their pre-redactional motifs, structural elements and conceptual scope. A formal comparison then of these with the *theios anēr Gattung* of the Hellenistic world was concluded to be possible and legitimate, while essential considerations led to reservations on the category of analogy. These *theios anēr* texts had over against those to follow below the advantage of falling directly within the scope of the question of death and the "divine man's" survival thereafter on another plane of existence. The texts below do not enjoy this immediacy.[678] Nevertheless, a comparison of them suggests itself because 1) formal considerations bring the two into very close proximity, and 2) the gospel appearance stories themselves do not find their primary statement intention in the affirmation that the Lord is now alive again; other strata of the resurrection tradition may very well indeed have served this particular interest, but the appearance stories are personal encounters which display a rich constellation of complex theological interests. In view of these two considerations then the fact that the texts below are not directly related to the question of death does not preclude the legitimacy of comparison. Moreover, it will be seen below that a trend from a later period did in fact bring this form into very close proximity with the death question.

Additional clarification and precision is needed in determining just which appearance or theophany stories are to be drawn upon for comparison. In the area of OT studies itself the term "theophany" and/or "theophany *Gattung*" is a matter of debate because of the great variety of texts that have been subsumed under this heading and the general paucity of recent and exact form-critical and history-of-tradition research of them.[679] Yet, it must be made clear at this point that our

understands the term "seeing" as meaning essentially "experience" and, therefore, the relative value of any history-of-religion "analogy" (p. 35). He does say, however, "Der Emmausbericht ist beeinflußt von der Form der Theophanieerzählungen. . ." (p. 12). Cf. also G. Koch, *op. cit.*, pp. 227f.

678 Regarding death and resurrection in the OT/Jewish thought world, cf. K. Schubert, "Das Problem der Auferstehungshoffnung in den Qumrântexten und in der frührabbinischen Literatur," *WZKM*, 56 (1960), pp. 154-167 and his "Die Entwicklung der Auferstehungslehre von der nachexilischen bis zur frührabbinischen Zeit," *BZ*(NF), 6 (1962), pp. 177-214, G. Nickelsburg, *Resurrection, Immortality and Eternal Life in Judaism*, Diss. (Harvard, 1968) (Microfilm No. 674578), J. Buitkamp, *Die Auferstehungsvorstellungen in den Qumrantexten und ihr alttestamentlicher, apokryphischer, pseudepigraphischer und rabbinischer Hintergrund*, Diss. (Groningen, 1965), W.E. Davies, *The Origin and Development of Old Testament and Inter-Testamental Belief Regarding Life After Death*, Diss. (Boston Grad. School, 1957), G. Molin, "Entwicklung und Motive der Auferstehungshoffnung vom AT bis zur rabbinischen Zeit," *Judaica*, 9 (1953), pp. 225-239, J. Kammerer, *Die Auferstehung der Toten im Alten Testament als Element der eschatologischen Restauration des Bundesvolkes Israel*, Diss. (Wien, 1968), and N.J. Tromp, *Primitive Conceptions of Death and the Nether World in the Old Testament*, BeO, 21 (Rome, 1969).

679 As far as this writer was able to ascertain only four monographs and a handful of articles have appeared on the subject of OT theophanies in ca. the last decade. Of particular interest is the 1964 (Bonn) dissertation of Jörg Jeremias which appeared as book in 1965: *Theophanie*, and is soon to appear in a revised edition. Another dissertation written in 1963 at New York's Union Theological Seminary and published as book in 1967 is J. Kuntz, *The Self-Revelation of God* (Phil., 1967). A recent monograph, but one which is of limited value for our investigation because of its primary focus on J and E's contributions to OT redactional criticism,

comparison here is motivated by the history-of-religion context for NT rather than OT studies, an open recognition, therefore, that our development of comparison below leaves much OT interest in these texts untouched. Nevertheless, one may speak perhaps of a consensus of sorts that the so-called anthropomorph-theophanic texts of the OT are to be clearly differentiated from theophanies in nature on both formal and essential grounds.[680] Rather than to speak here of two separate *Gattungen*, however, it is perhaps more advisable to avoid the term *Gattung* altogether and to speak rather of forms or vehicles of expression with fixed motifs and a catalyzed structure, of representations and descriptions of theophanies, and of schematizations because of the broad spectrum of interests expressed in the stories which have found their expression in this form. I.e., we are less interested here in the complex questions of OT research regarding the application of the term *Gattung* with its interest in *Sitz im Leben* for the history of Israel as we are in the mode of expression and descriptive characteristics of these anthropomorphic theophanies.[681]

is: E. Zenger, *Die Sinaitheophanie. Untersuchungen zum jahwistischen und elohistischen Geschichtswerk* (Würzburg, 1972; cf. rev. by Jörg Jeremias, *ThLZ*, 98 [1973], cols. 582-584). The most recent monograph focuses upon the science of linguistics and literature for OT studies: H. Mölle, *Das "Erscheinen" Gottes im Pentateuch. Ein literaturwissenschaftlicher Beitrag zur alttestamentlichen Exegese*, EHS XXIII,18 (Frankfurt, 1973). Articles in learned journals of somewhat recent vintage are: J. Barr, "Theophany and Anthropomorphism in the Old Testament," *Suppl. VT*, 8 (1960), pp. 31-38, J.L. Crenshaw, "Amos and the Theophanic Tradition," *ZAW*, 80 (1968), pp. 203-215, H.E. von Waldow, "Theophanie" (rev. of Jeremias), *VF*, BhEvTh, 14/1 (1969), pp. 69-76, F. Schutenhaus, "Das Kommen und Erscheinen Gottes im Alten Testament," *ZAW*, 76 (1964), pp. 1-22, J. Lindblom, "Theophanies in Holy Places in Hebrew Religion," *HUCA*, 32 (1961), pp. 91-106 and his "Die Vorstellung vom Sprechen Jahwes zu den Menschen im Alten Testament," *ZAW*, 75 (1963), pp. 263-288, J. Muilenburg, "The Speech of Theophany," *HDSB*, 28 (1964), pp. 35-47 and J. Koenig, "Aux origines des théophanies iahvistes," *RHR*, 169 (1966), pp. 1-36. Older works and other literature dealing with the general theme of "revelation"–some of which deal more thoroughly with the "theophany" question than others–will be cited below where appropriate.

680 Jörg Jeremias, *Theophanie*, pp. 1f., who then focuses his analysis on the coming of Jahweh and the disruption of natural phenomena only. C. Westermann suggests "aus praktischen Gründen" calling those appearances of God "um sich zu offenbaren" *theophanies* and those "um seinem Volk zu helfen" *epiphanies* (*Das Loben Gottes in den Psalmen* [Gött., 1963, 3rd ed.], p. 74), but the imprecision of the terms in view of the variety of texts that are referred to under them in the secondary literature makes their usefulness dubious. Cf. Schutenhaus, *op. cit.*, p. 21. It is one of the chief weaknesses of the otherwise suggestive and interesting work of Kuntz, *op. cit.*, that he does not follow this differentiation, although he too acknowledges at one point that the patriarchal theophany narratives "seem to relate to a different element / within the total Israelite structure of faith than so many other Old Testament theophanic traditions. . ." (pp. 215f., n. 1).

681 In view of the present state of the science of linguistics and literature a clear and useful definition of the term *Gattung* has become increasingly complex and as indicated in a very helpful discussion on April 17, 1973 this will constitute one of the chief areas of revision for Prof. Jeremias' book *Theophanie*. Cf. J.A. Baird, "Genre Analysis as a Method of Historical Criticism," pp. 385-411 and W.G. Doty, "The Concept of Genre in Literary Analysis," pp. 413-448 both in *SBL Proceedings* (LA), II (1972), H.E. von Waldow, "Some Thoughts on Old Testament Form Criticism," *SBL Seminar Papers* (Atlanta, Ga.), II (1971), pp. 587-600, W. Richter, *Traditionsgeschichtliche Untersuchungen zum Richterbuch*, BBB, 18, ed. by F. Nötscher and K. Th. Schäfer (Bonn, 1963), pp. 344ff. and his *Exegese als Literaturwissenschaft. Entwurf einer alttestamentlichen Literaturtheorie und Methodologie* (Gött., 1971), pp. 125ff.

As was the case among the Hellenistic texts so too here a strict differentiation is to be made between theophanies cast in the dream, vision and/or oracular form, etc., and the anthropomorphic/disguise encounter type.[682] In these stories YHWH appears and speaks to men sometimes clearly in human form, other times presumably so.[683] They find their origin in the very earliest strata of OT traditions and take their setting in or in relatively close proximity to the patriarchal period.

Furthermore, the question of the chronological, theological relationship between these OT theophany texts and our NT appearance stories must be raised. It is necessary to compare the literature of the intertestamental period to determine if the anthropomorphic theophany form was still in use and if so whether or not it had undergone any significant changes. It would be an error to bridge these latter texts for whatever reason as though they did not exist since they represent developments of thought and setting which are of direct chronological consequence for NT times. The triangle, as it were—OT/"Apocrypha-Pseudepigrapha"/NT—and the relationship of the three corners to one another under our line of questioning must be examined.

1. Sources

In choosing texts for comparison we are forced by the nature of the task and texts themselves to be selective.[684] We cannot attempt an exhaustive survey nor can we treat the material, as mentioned above, from the perspective of OT studies, which it certainly otherwise deserves. One attempt, however, in OT research among

682 Lindblom, "Theophanies," pp. 91ff., agrees in general with such a differentiation although he chooses to designate the anthropomorphic or "real" theophany type as "visions in a waking state" (p. 93), a category which in itself is fraught with considerable difficulties (cf. above, n. 621); moreover, he equates "visions" with "hallucinatory experiences" (p. 106), a deviation from literarily formal categories. Cf. his "Vorstellung," pp. 264ff., 272f. and 287. Also differentiating between the anthropomorphic form from dreams, etc., is F. Nötscher, *'Das Angesicht Gottes schauen' nach biblischer und babylonischer Auffassung* (Würzburg, 1924), pp. 22ff.

683 Barr distinguishes between anthropomorphic expressions in general and the appearances of God in human form as narratives since the former do not really display an attempt to deal with the *morphe* of God, they are more metaphorical ("Theophany," p. 31). "In contrast with all this, it is the theophanies where God lets himself be seen that there is a real attempt to grapple with the form / of his appearance" (pp. 31f.); they form "a special class" (p. 32). Nötscher also points out that where the appearance form in a face to face encounter is mentioned it is characteristically one of a *Menschengestalt* (*Angesicht*, p. 20). Similar is W. Baudissin, "'Gott schauen' in der alttestamentlichen Religion," *ARW*, 18 (1915), p. 186.

684 This selection was arrived at only after perusal of the secondary literature and the text groupings offered there as well as an examination of the texts in their own right. It is maintained, therefore, that the anthology is not arbitrary, but truly representative of the form under consideration. As suggested by Prof. K. Baltzer in a conversation, March 7, 1974, one could include the Elijah/Elisha story of II Ki. 2 as a parallel from a certain perspective of subject matter, since here the commissioning/sending motif is key. Because, however, of radical formal dissimilarities (this is a translation story) and the fact that other motifs present in the NT *Gattung* are missing, this story has not been included among the major texts of comparison.

others to deal with basically the same texts of our anthology is deserving of mention because of its methodological approach: N. Habel, "The Form and Significance of the Call Narrative," *ZAW*, 77 (1965), pp. 297-323. Its goal understands itself to be the search for the underlying literary "structure" of the so-called pre-prophetic call stories which repeats itself through all accounts in spite of their contextual variations; in short, the author is looking for a pre-redactional "call story *Gattung.*" He also seeks to establish the relevance of this literary form for the prophetic message. In his own words, "The goal of the present investigation is to isolate the primary literary features of the 'call narrative,' to discuss their significance where pertinent, and to trace their development as closely as possible."[685] In his source examples (Jud. 6:11b-17 and Ex. 3:1-12) for initial investigation he claims to have found a specific pattern, i.e., 1) divine confrontation 2) introductory word 3) commission 4) objection 5) reassurance 6) sign, regarding which he concludes:

> "The formal sequence of parallels, common literary pattern, similar themes and identical expressions found in the call narratives of Moses and Gideon establish the probability of a common pre-literary (or literary) form or Gattung with associated traditions utilized by the authors of these two call accounts. This common heritage provided for these authors a form appropriate for the delineation of the call of Yahweh's messengers and mediators. The use of such a form or Gattung to delineate the traditions concerning the experience of an individual does not nullify the reality of a call experience as such, but it does color and modify the formulation of that experience as it is related to subsequent generations of Israel. . .the call Gattung is not confined to the prophets but has a significant pre-prophetic history."[686]

We must ask if Habel does not claim too much here for his sources and their analysis. He has indeed established the presence—if we may forget for a moment the six point pattern—of a "formal sequence of parallels," "similar themes" and even on occasion "identical expressions" which could be taken as indicators of a traditional form or, if one will, *Gattung*. But the key question is whether or not this form existed in the fixed categories of his six point pattern; in a word, did the "call *Gattung*" exist more or less as a literary skeleton "appropriate for the delineation of the call of Yahweh's messengers and mediators," which an author selected from a catalogue of other options and proceeded then to give it flesh, as it were. This does indeed appear to be Habel's view: the pattern dictates that first a divine confrontation is needed so the author constructs one in terms of the story he wishes to "delineate" and so on until the pattern is complete and the finished product is now the combination of prescribed pattern and desired content. Of course, Habel does not wish in any way to prejudice the historicity or actuality of the call, but he does claim most clearly that this call "experience" was pressed, as it were, into this pattern (or mold) to "color and modify the formulation." The assumption is therefore, that the call and the form were originally independent of one another and that their

685 N. Habel, "The Form and Significance of the Call Narratives," *ZAW*, 77 (1965), p. 297. His method and conclusions come very close to what was seen earlier for Dodd on the appearance stories.

686 *Ibid.*, p. 305.

union is literarily secondary. Yet, a close examination of the alleged pattern in its details shows up a significant number of variations, especially when he attempts to apply the pattern to the classical prophets which, he claims, they have consciously taken up to express a line of succession between their own calls and the earlier ones.[687] His explanation for these latter variations is the incorporation of ancillary traditions,[688] but in accord with his basic hypothesis the incorporation of specific traditions into the pattern should not alter the latter at all. He seeks finally to locate the origin of the "call *Gattung*" as pattern in the commissioning practice of ancient Israel (e.g., Gen. 24:34-48).[689]

It must be said that Habel has correctly seen a relationship in the so-called preprophetic call narratives in their far-reaching correspondence of form, theme and expression, but over against the stories in which it appears and the manner in which it ostensibly has been chosen and utilized by the authors of those stories his view appears to be too schematic and fixed in view of the processes of tradition formation.[690] Our method distinguishes itself, therefore, from that of Habel in that 1) we are not dealing with "call narratives" in search of a "call *Gattung,*" but rather "appearance narratives" in search of an appearance form and structure, and, therefore, 2) any use of the word "pattern" will not be synonymous with "stencil" (*Schablone*) or "stamp," because of its implications in Habel's overall concept, but rather it will be–where used–synonymous with the more neutral terms "progression" (*Reihenfolge*), "structure" or "shape," i.e., a certain scope is provided in a given story and within it one may note a distinct progression of occurrences. In the overall representation of the appearance stories we shall take note of the pattern in each as a loosely formed but definite scheme which takes into account variations and differences rather than superimposing a rigid "pattern" upon them in order to come out with the lowest common denominators and to reduce their particularities. Moreover, we emphasize again that we shall approach and analyze our anthology from the following line of questioning: how were these texts read and understood *in NT times* and did they–and if so how did they–exercise any influence upon the formation of the gospel appearance stories? This methodological decision brings with it two consequences: 1) the separation and analysis of layers of tradition so central for a study of the stories in OT research will go by and large untouched since we are not specifically interested in *their* history of tradition but rather in their end product, and 2) while a familiarity with these stories in their Hebrew form is to be presupposed in the primitive Christian community, a comparison of their LXX form recommends itself, since direct or indirect overlap of terminology and structure above all will be most readily apparent in that form. Where the LXX text varies from the Hebrew original we shall note the consequences of the departure for our analysis.

687 *Ibid.*, pp. 306ff. and 316ff.

688 *Ibid.*, pp. 309f.

689 *Ibid.*, pp. 320ff.

690 Cf. a more appropriate approach in the method of W. Richter, *Die sogenannten vorprophetischen Berufungsberichte. Eine literaturwissenschaftliche Studie zu 1 Sam 9,1-10,16, Ex 3f und Ri 6,11b-17,* FRLANT, 101 (Gött., 1970), *passim* and his *Untersuchungen, passim.*

Gen. 18

Abraham is sitting before his tent in Mamre and God appears to him [*Ὤφθη δὲ αὐτῷ ὁ θεὸς*, vs. 1]. He looks up and sees three men standing before him [*ἀναβλέψας δὲ τοῖς ὀφθαλμοῖς αὐτοῦ εἶδεν, καὶ ἰδοὺ τρεῖς ἄνδρες εἱστήκεισαν ἐπάνω αὐτοῦ*, vs. 2]. He runs out from the tent to greet them and offers them rest and refreshment in good semitic hospitality, but is obviously unaware that the Lord is herewith paying him a visit. The strangers consent to stay and accept his hospitality; he places food before them and they eat [*καὶ ἐφάγοσαν*, vs. 8]. During a conversation overheard by Sarah, Abraham is promised that his wife would bear a child in the same season the following year in spite of their age problem. Sarah expresses her doubts to herself, the promise is affirmed by way of an exchange between herself and the strangers and then they in the company of Abraham depart for Sodom. In a conversation along the way Abraham learns of their mission in Sodom and while the other two proceed on ahead Abraham remains before the Lord, draws near and raises questions about that mission [*καὶ ἀποστρέψαντες ἐκεῖθεν οἱ ἄνδρες ἦλθον εἰς Σοδομα, Αβρααμ δὲ ἦν ἑστηκὼς ἐναντίον κυρίου. Καὶ ἐγγίσας Αβρααμ εἶπεν*, vss. 22f.]. He asks if it would not be possible to spare the city if fifty righteous men could be found or forty-five or forty or thirty or twenty or even ten, to which the Lord consents in every instance. When the conversation ends the Lord departs from him and Abraham returns home [*ἀπῆλθεν δὲ κύριος ὡς ἐπαύσατο λαλῶν τῷ Αβρααμ, καὶ Αβρααμ ἀπέστρεψεν εἰς τὸν τόπον αὐτοῦ*, vs. 33].

Ex. 3f.

Moses is tending the flocks of his father-in-law, Jethro, near the mountain of God when the angel of the Lord appears to him in a burning bush [*ὤφθη δὲ αὐτῷ ἄγγελος κυρίου ἐν φλογὶ πυρὸς ἐκ τοῦ βάτου*, vs. 2]. When Moses draws near to behold the sight the Lord speaks to him saying that he should come no closer and should remove his shoes because the ground is holy [*ἐκάλεσεν αὐτὸν κύριος ἐκ τοῦ βάτου λέγων Μωυσῆ, Μωυσῆ...Μὴ ἐγγίσῃς ὧδε· λῦσαι τὸ ὑπόδημα ἐκ τῶν ποδῶν σου. ὁ γὰρ τόπος, ἐν ᾧ σὺ ἕστηκας, γῆ ἁγία ἐστίν*, vss. 4f.]. Then the Lord identifies himself as the God of Abraham, Isaac and Jacob [*εἶπεν αὐτῷ Ἐγώ εἰμι ὁ θεὸς τοῦ πατρός σου, θεὸς Αβρααμ καὶ θεὸς Ισαακ καὶ θεὸς Ιακωβ*, vs. 6]. Moses is told further that he is to deliver God's people from bondage in Egypt and in reply to Moses' sense of inadequacy to the task the Lord assures him that he would be with him [*Ἔσομαι μετὰ σοῦ. . .*, vs. 12]. Moses asks the Lord for his name so that the people will believe that he has indeed met with him and the Lord replies: I am who I am, he sends you [*Ἐγώ εἰμι ὁ ὤν·. . .Οὕτως ἐρεῖς τοῖς υἱοῖς Ισραηλ Ὁ ὢν ἀπέσταλκέν με πρὸς ὑμᾶς*, vs. 13f.]. Thereupon follows a rather extensive and familiar rehearsal of all that Moses shall do and say when he carries out his commission to return to Egypt and deliver those in bondage there; the encounter comes to an end simply with the words "and Moses returned to Jethro. . ." [Ἐπορεύθη δὲ Μωυσῆς καὶ ἀπέστρεψεν πρὸς Ιοθορ. . . . , 4:18, the beginning of a new subject matter].

Jud. 6

The angel of the Lord comes and sits beneath the terebinth at Ophrah and there appears to Gideon [*καὶ ἦλθεν ἄγγελος κυρίου καὶ ἐκάθισεν. . .καὶ ὤφθη αὐτῷ ἄγγελος κυρίου*, vss. 11f.]. The angel greets him and tells him that he is to go and do battle with the Midianites and that he would triumph because he himself has sent him and the Lord is with him [Κύριος *μετὰ σοῦ, δυνατὸς τῇ ἰσχύι. . .καὶ ἐπέβλεψεν πρὸς αὐτὸν ὁ ἄγγελος κυρίου* (יהוה) *καὶ εἶπεν αὐτῷ πορεύου. . .καὶ ἰδοὺ ἐξαπέστειλά σε. . .καὶ εἶπεν πρὸς αὐτὸν ὁ ἄγγελος κυρίου* (אהיה עמך ויאמר יהוה)*. . .κύριος ἔσται μετὰ σοῦ*, vss. 12bff.]. In spite of a sense of inadequacy Gideon finds assurance in these words. Gideon requests a sign, however, and asks the stranger to remain until he returns with a gift. The angel agrees to wait and when Gideon returns with an offering the angel has him place it on a rock before him. Thereupon the angel stretches forth his staff, fire springs forth from the rock, consumes the offering and the angel disappears [*καὶ ἐξέτεινεν ὁ ἄγγελος κυρίου τὸ ἄκρον τῆς ῥάβδου τῆς ἐν τῇ χειρὶ αὐτοῦ. . .καὶ ὁ ἄγγελος κυρίου ἀπῆλθεν ἐξ ὀφθαλμῶν αὐτοῦ*, vs. 21]. To this Gideon replies that he now knows of truth that it has been the angel of the Lord he has seen face to face; to this is added the Lord's assurance that he should be calm and not fearful and that he would not die [*καὶ εἶδεν* Γεδεων *ὅτι ἄγγελος κυρίου ἐστίν. . .*Ἆ ἆ, *κύριε, κύριε, ὅτι εἶδον τὸν ἄγγελον κυρίου πρόσωπον πρὸς πρόσωπον. καὶ εἶπεν αὐτῷ κύριος* Εἰρήνη *σοι, μὴ φοβοῦ μὴ ἀποθάνῃς*, vss. 22f.]. So Gideon builds an altar and names it YHWH-Shalom.

Jud. 13

Manoah and his wife are childless. But the angel of the Lord appears to her and promises her a child [*καὶ ὤφθη ἄγγελος κυρίου πρὸς τὴν γυναῖκα καὶ εἶπεν. . .*, vs. 3]. She relates the visit of the man of God to her husband, describes his appearance and says that she had not gotten his name [Ἄνθρωπος *τοῦ θεοῦ ἦλθεν πρός με, καὶ ἡ ὅρασις αὐτοῦ ὡς ὅρασις ἀγγέλου τοῦ θεοῦ ἐπιφανὴς σφόδρα. . .καὶ τὸ ὄνομα αὐτοῦ οὐκ ἀπήγγειλέν μοι*, vs. 6]. Then Manoah prays to the Lord for confirmation by way of another appearance of the same man of God [*καὶ ἐδεήθη* Μανωε *τοῦ κυρίου καὶ εἶπεν* Ἐν *ἐμοί, κύριε,*[691] *ἄνθρωπος τοῦ θεοῦ, ὃν ἀπέστειλας πρὸς ἡμᾶς, ἐλθέτω δὴ πρὸς ἡμᾶς καὶ φωτισάτω ἡμᾶς τί ποιήσωμεν τῷ παιδαρίῳ τῷ τικτο-*

691 Codex B reads: *κύριε* Αδωναιε, *τὸν ἄνθρωπον* and *συμβιβασάτω* (instruct, enlighten) instead of *φωτισάτω*.

μένῳ, vs. 8]. His request is granted and he comes again to Manoah's wife in the fields, but her husband is once again absent. She runs quickly and fetches her husband who then engages the man in conversation regarding his identity and the promise of the child. Convinced then Manoah bids him to take a meal and remain, but the man refuses the meal and urges Manoah rather to prepare an offering for the Lord. Manoah agrees and asks him for his name—for he did not know that it was the angel of the Lord [*ὅτι οὐκ ἔγνω Μανωε ὅτι ἄγγελος κυρίου ἐστίν*, vs. 16]—but the angel replies somewhat mysteriously: "how can you ask my name, it is one of wonder." The offering having then been prepared flames leap up from the altar towards heaven and the angel ascends out of sight in those flames [*καὶ ἐγένετο ἐν τῷ ἀναβῆναι τὴν φλόγα. . .καὶ ἀνέβη ὁ ἄγγελος κυρίου ἐν τῇ φλογί*, vs. 20]. Manoah and his wife fall on their faces and although the angel does not appear again Manoah knew that it had been the angel of the Lord [*καὶ οὐ προσέθηκεν ἔτι ὁ ἄγγελος κυρίου ὀφθῆναι. . .τότε ἔγνω Μανωε ὅτι ἄγγελος κυρίου ἐστίν*, vs. 21]. Fear comes upon Manoah for they would now surely die since they had seen God [*θανάτῳ ἀποθανούμεθα, ὅτι θεὸν ἑωράκαμεν*, vs. 22], but his wife contradicts with the words, if God had wanted them to die he would neither have accepted their offering nor would he have allowed them to see and hear all this [*Εἰ ἐβούλετο κύριος θανατῶσαι ἡμᾶς. . .καὶ οὐκ ἂν ἐφώτισεν*[692] *ἡμᾶς πάντα ταῦτα καὶ οὐκ ἂν ἀκουστὰ ἐποίησεν ἡμῖν ταῦτα*, vs. 23]. Finally she gives birth to Samson.

I Sam. 3

Samuel, but a youth, is living with Eli at the sanctuary at Shiloh. In those days the word of the Lord was seldom heard and no vision was granted [*καὶ ῥῆμα κυρίου ἦν τίμιον ἐν ταῖς ἡμέραις ἐκείναις, οὐκ ἦν ὅρασις διαστέλλουσα*, vs. 1]. One night Samuel hears a voice calling his name; not knowing that it was the Lord calling he assumes that it is the voice of Eli and goes to answer his bidding. Eli assuring the youth that he had not called sends him back to his chamber. This scene repeats itself three times. Just prior to the third time the clarifying words are added: up until this time Samuel did not know God nor had the word of the Lord been revealed to him [*καὶ Σαμουηλ πρὶν ἢ γνῶναι θεὸν καὶ ἀποκαλυφθῆναι αὐτῷ ῥῆμα κυρίου*, vs. 7]. Eli becomes aware of the origin of the voice and bids Samuel to return again to his chamber but if the voice should come again he should be prepared to answer: speak, Lord, your servant is listening. It occurs indeed as Eli has said and the Lord came and stood before him and spoke with him as man to man [*καὶ ἦλθεν κύριος καὶ κατέστη καὶ ἐκάλεσεν αὐτὸν ὡς ἅπαξ καὶ ἅπαξ*, vs. 10] and told Samuel that he was going to bring judgment upon the house of Eli and Samuel is to deliver the message. He does so, is recognized by Eli as having found favor with God and grows steadily hereafter in his commission as the Lord is with him [*καὶ ἐμεγαλύνθη Σαμουηλ, καὶ ἦν κύριος μετ' αὐτοῦ. . .πιστὸς Σαμουηλ εἰς προφήτην τῷ κυρίῳ*,vss.

692 Codex B reads: *ἔδειξεν* instead of *ἐφώτισεν*.

19f.]. And the Lord continued to appear at Shiloh because here he had revealed himself to Samuel [*καὶ προσέθετο κύριος δηλωθῆναι ἐν Σηλωμ, ὅτι ἀπεκαλύφθη κύριος πρὸς Σαμουηλ*, vs. 21].

The Anthropomorphic Theophanies in the Intertestamental Literature

Tobit 5 and 12

A loyal Jew of Galilee by the name of Tobit along with his wife and son, Tobias, are living under the volatile hardships of captivity in Nineveh during the reign of Shalmaneser and thereafter. While others of their people neglect the observance of the laws (especially dietary ones) in a foreign land their tenacity wins for them special honor. A change of circumstances, however, alters this situation so that a combination of ill-repute and misfortune–Tobit loses his sight in an accident–finally brings Tobit to the place of seeking death in prayer before God. A relative of his at Ecbatana in Media, Sarah, was praying a similar prayer at this time because she had been married seven times only to have each husband killed by a foul demon, Asmodeus, who was jealously in love with her. Into this dilemma God sends his angel Raphael to help. Tobit prepares to send his son, Tobias, to Media on business and has him seek out a travel companion. The lad finds a certain man named Azarius to accompany him and show him the way; Azarius is, however, the angel Raphael in disguise and Tobias does not recognize him [*καὶ ἐπορεύθη ζητῆσαι ἄνθρωπον καὶ εὗρεν τὸν Ραφαηλ, ὃς ἦν ἄγγελος, καὶ οὐκ ᾔδει,*[693] 5:4]. After interviewing Azarius and satisfying himself that he is a worthy travel companion for his son Tobit sends them on their way agreeing to a daily wage for his efforts and invoking God's blessing and guardian angel upon them both on their journey [*καὶ εἶπεν αὐτῷ ὁ πατὴρ αὐτοῦ Πορεύου μετὰ τοῦ ἀνθρώπου· ὁ δὲ ἐν τῷ οὐρανῷ οἰκῶν θεὸς εὐοδώσει τὴν ὁδὸν ὑμῶν, καὶ ὁ ἄγγελος αὐτοῦ συμπορευθήτω ὑμῖν*, 5:17]! Along the journey Azarius informs Tobias that he will marry Sarah and disarm the murderous demon in Media with the heart, liver and gall of a fish they have taken from a river. After succeeding in his struggle with the demon, taking care of business matters and celebrating his marriage to Sarah, the three set out for Tobit's home in Nineveh. Upon return Tobias is able to restore his father's sight with some leftover fish gall and they celebrate the marriage together there again. When the time comes for Azarius to be rewarded for his trouble he reveals his true identity; he is Raphael one of the seven angels who present the prayers of the saints and enter into the presence of the glory of the Holy One; he admonishes them to further prayer and alms and then disappears from sight. The discourse and scene run as follows:

693 Codex S reads: *τὸν ἄγγελον ἑστηκότα ἀπέναντι αὐτοῦ καὶ οὐκ ἔγνω ὅτι ἄγγελος τοῦ θεοῦ ἐστιν* calling to remembrance the "coming and standing" form used on occasion elsewhere above.

καὶ νῦν ἀπέστειλέν με ὁ θεὸς ἰάσασθαί σε καὶ τὴν νύμφην σου Σαρραν. ἐγώ εἰμι Ραφαηλ, εἷς ἐκ τῶν ἑπτὰ ἁγίων ἀγγέλων, οἳ προσαναφέρουσιν τὰς προσευχὰς τῶν ἁγίων καὶ εἰσπορεύονται ἐνώπιον τῆς δόξης τοῦ ἁγίου.[694] καὶ ἐταράχθησαν οἱ δύο καὶ ἔπεσον ἐπὶ πρόσωπον, ὅτι ἐφοβήθησαν. καὶ εἶπεν αὐτοῖς Μὴ φοβεῖσθε, εἰρήνη ὑμῖν ἔσται· τὸν δὲ θεὸν εὐλογεῖτε εἰς τὸν αἰῶνα. ὅτι οὐ τῇ ἐμαυτοῦ χάριτι, ἀλλὰ τῇ θελήσει τοῦ θεοῦ ἡμῶν ἦλθον. . .καὶ νῦν ἐξομολογεῖσθε τῷ θεῷ.[695] διότι ἀναβαίνω πρὸς τὸν ἀποστείλαντά με, καὶ γράψατε πάντα τὰ συντελεσθέντα εἰς βιβλίον καὶ ἀνέστησαν.[696] καὶ οὐκέτι εἶδον αὐτόν.[697] καὶ ἐξωμολογοῦντο[698] τὰ ἔργα τὰ μεγάλα καὶ θαυμαστὰ τοῦ θεοῦ καὶ ὡς ὤφθη αὐτοῖς ὁ ἄγγελος κυρίου (12:14ff.).

Thereafter comes a psalm of thanksgiving from Tobit.

Testament of Abraham[699]

Abraham has reached his appointed time of death and God sends his messenger Michael to inform the patriarch of his approaching departure. Michael goes out as told and comes to Abraham finding him sitting before his work animals [*καὶ ἐπορεύθη* Μιχαὴλ *καὶ ἦλθεν πρὸς* Ἀβραὰμ *καὶ εὗρεν αὐτὸν καθιζόμενον ἔμπροσθεν τῶν βοῶν αὐτοῦ*,[700] 2:1=James, p. 105]. When Abraham sees him he gets up to greet him, but does not know who he is [*ἰδὼν οὖν* Ἀβραὰμ *τὸν ἀρχάγγελον* Μιχαὴλ, *ἀναστὰς ἐκ τῆς γῆς ἠσπάσατο αὐτόν, μὴ εἰδὼς τίς ἐστιν*, 2:2 James, pp. 105f.]. Then Abraham goes on to extend to him courteous hospitality and after a brief exchange they journey on foot together to Abraham's dwelling. Along the way a tree tells Abraham that his visitor is holy and he stores the secret in his heart until later confirmation. Having arrived the stranger is then also welcomed by Sarah and Isaac; Abraham orders water to be fetched so that he may wash the stranger's feet. During a tearful scene involving Abraham, Isaac and Michael at this point due to Abraham's suspicion that this may be the last time he will be able to offer such hospitality the teardrops of the angel fall into a bowl and turn into precious stones. As sundown approaches Michael returns to heaven to tell the Lord that he cannot deliver the message because Abraham is God's friend, a righteous man and hospitable to strangers [*καὶ ἤγγισεν ὁ ἥλιος τοῦ δῦναι· καὶ ἐξῆλθεν* Μιχαὴλ *ἔξω τοῦ οἴκου, καὶ ἀνελήφθη εἰς τοὺς οὐρανοὺς προσκυνῆσαι ἐνώπιον τοῦ θεοῦ. . .κἀγὼ οὐ τολμῶ, κύριε, ἐμφανισθῆναι αὐτῷ, ὅτι φίλος σου ἐστὶν καὶ δίκαιος ἄνθρωπος, ξένους ὑποδεχόμενος*, 4:4, 10 James, pp. 108f.]. Michael is then sent back, told to partici-

694 Codex S reads: *τῆς δόξης κυρίου.*

695 Codex S reads: *εὐλογεῖτε ἐπὶ τῆς γῆς κύριον καὶ ἐξομολογεῖσθε τῷ θεῷ.*

696 Codex S reads: *καὶ ἀνέβη* before *καὶ ἀνέστησαν.*

697 Codex S reads: *ἠδύναντο ἰδεῖν.*

698 Codex S reads: *καὶ ηὐλόγουν καὶ ὕμνουν τὸν θεὸν καὶ ἐξομολογοῦντο...*

699 We follow here the B rec. edited by M.R. James (ed.), *The Testament of Abraham* (Greek text with introduction and notes), TSt, II, 2, ed. by J.A. Robinson (Nendeln, Liechtenstein, 1967[=Cambridge, 1892]), pp. 105ff., instead of rec. A because the former is freer of Christian interpolations and offers the closest approximation to the original wording of the earliest text (pp. 50f.).

700 It is of some interest to note that rec. A makes this into a distinctive group appearance by adding: *μετὰ τοὺς υἱοὺς Μασὲκ καὶ ἑτέροις παισὶν τὸν ἀριθμὸν δώδεκα* (James, p. 78; cf. his reference to the defective grammar here and to Gen. 15:2 on p. 121).

pate in the hospitality of the patriarch and is assured that Isaac would be told in a dream [κατ' ὄναρ] of the fate awaiting his father (4:14ff.). All goes as the Lord has said and when Isaac comes to his father and the guest in a state of turmoil over the dream once again all three weep tears of sorrow. Sarah comes in assuming that the stranger has brought ill-fated news about Abraham's brother Lot. Michael tells her that he is not the messenger of such news and she then questions Abraham's reaction since they should rejoice at the return of the man of God. To this Abraham inquires how she could know that he is a man of God and Sarah then relates that she recognized Michael as one of the three strangers who had visited them of old in Mamre [Πόθεν γινώσκεις ὅτι ἄνθρωπος τοῦ θεοῦ ἐστίν; ἀποκριθεὶς δὲ ἡ Σάρρα εἶπεν· Ὅτι παραφέρω καὶ λέγω ὅτι οὗτός ἐστιν τῶν τριῶν ἀνδρῶν εἷς, τῶν ἐν τῇ δρυΐ τῇ Μαμβρῇ ἐπιξενισθέντων ἡμῖν, 6:9f. James, p. 110]. Abraham congratulates her and confirms her discovery by saying that he too had recognized him while washing his feet [καλῶς ἐνόησας, ὦ γύναι· ὅτι κἀγὼ ὅτε τοὺς πόδας αὐτοῦ ἔπλυνα, ἔγνων ἐν τῇ καρδίᾳ μου ὅτι οὗτοι εἰσιν οἱ πόδες οὓς ἔπλυνα ἐν τῇ δρυΐ τῇ Μαμβρῇ, 6:12f.]. So, the man of God now recognized in his true identity confirms the content of Isaac's dream, but Abraham cannot accept the thought of the separation of his soul from his body and requests a bodily journey to heaven first to see the secrets of the other world, to learn the course of death, judgment and eternity and to stand before God. Michael is told by the Lord to grant the request and a bodily journey to heaven follows after which Abraham is returned to earth for his appointed day of final departure. He then meets the angel of death and only after something of a struggle does Abraham finally agree to the departure of his soul in heavenly ascension. His body is then buried beside Sarah who has also since died and great honor and glory is ascribed to God.

2. Analysis

We noted above (pp. 239ff.) that a comparison of the anthropomorphic theophany texts from the OT and intertestamental literature suggests itself on formal grounds and in view of theological considerations regarding the gospel appearances themselves. These observations ameliorate the situation that at least for the OT examples the questions of death and resurrection are not part of their direct context or scope (Ex. 33 and the death question poses a special problem). A further and related difficulty, however, seen from the side of the gospel appearance texts themselves is the fact that nowhere in any of them does a reference to these OT texts or later counterparts occur.[701] This means that with direct literary pointers entirely

701 The references in Acts 7 are distinct from the heavenly radiance as midrashic retelling not unlike the texts in n. 722 below. The only other possible direct play on this tradition for the NT seems to be Heb. 13:2 (cf. O. Michel, *Der Brief an die Hebräer*, Meyer, 13 [Gött., 1966, 12th ed.], pp. 480f.). More distant perhaps Mt. 25:38-40; 10:40; 20:26 and Rom. 12:13 and other references of paranetic scope and origin. Abraham as a man of faith in Paul is a different problem. Cf., e.g., F. Hahn, "Genesis 15,6 im Neuen Testament," *Probleme Biblischer Theologie. Fst. G. von Rad*, ed. by H.W. Wolff (Mü., 1971), pp. 90-107.

missing any relationship between these literary complexes must be established in turn once again on the same kind of formal and/or essential grounds. If a relationship can indeed be determined in this manner the degree of "overlap" will be something of an index perhaps of just how conscious a dependence level in fact actually existed.

Gen. 18

We have selected this account not only because of the frequent reference made to it in the secondary literature dealing with our theme, but also because it is the most complete and graphic account among the group of Genesis and other anthropomorphic theophany stories. It should not be assumed, however, that it stands isolated from them since they have many features in common,[702] perhaps sharing a common type of origin as well, namely, "holy place etiology."[703] Gen. 12, for example, shares terminological similarities such as the termini *ὤφθη κύριος* and *εἶπεν* (vss. 1 and 7), although all attempts at description of the appearance are missing. The same can be said basically for Gen. 15 also with some variations of both terminology and concept. Gen. 17 shares the termini *ὤφθη κύριος* and *εἶπεν* also, but makes one descriptive advancement over against Gen. 12 in that the appearance concludes with *συνετέλεσεν δὲ λαλῶν πρὸς αὐτὸν καὶ ἀνέβη ὁ θεὸς ἀπὸ Αβρααμ* (cf. vss. 1,9,15 leading up to the above quotation in 22). The story of Lot and Sodom in Gen. 19 is, in its present form, a continuation of the Abraham encounter; with

702 Among others also W. Richter, *Untersuchungen*, pp. 137ff.

703 Barr, "Theophany," agrees with this designation of origin in general, but expresses his reserve over Gen. 18 when he says: "Many of these stories will have been transmitted as sacred stories or foundation stories of holy places where these events were remembered. I do not think, however, they can all be explained in this way; for example, Gen. XVIII, in some ways the oldest and most characteristic of them all, is hardly the foundation story of Mamre and seems to me to belong to a longer and more personal story of Abraham" (p. 38). Similar reserve is expressed by Pax, ΕΠΙΦΑΝΕΙΑ, pp. 114ff. Cf. further, G. Mayer, "Aspekte des Abrahambildes in der hellenistisch-jüdischen Literatur," *EvTh*, 32/2 (1972), pp. 118ff. Most recently the question of etiological origins was examined by H.C. White, "The Divine Oath in Genesis," *JBL*, 92 (1973), pp. 165ff. He makes a form analysis of appearance scenes in Gen. 12, 26, 28, 35 and 17 ". . .to determine the life setting where that form originated and the extent to which it has been modified by later Israelite traditionists. This will make it possible to speak more precisely about the relation of nomadic, tribal religion and localized, Canaanite epiphany religion, as well as the extent of later Israelite influence upon the religion of the promise presented in these passages" (p. 168). On the form common to all he establishes: 1) the principal characters in each scene are God and man, 2) only God speaks in the actual encounter, 3) man either responds to the words of God with words and/or actions, or he is instructed as to what he should do as a response, and finally, 4) the content in all of them is the giving of a promise of God (p. 169). For White the self-identification and oath formulae are standard elements for the promise aspect, the former subordinate to the latter. In Canaanite cult centers such forms could have served etiological goals, but only in part, since their ultimate origins are to be sought in the "ritual basis of the act of altar-erection" (p. 176). He concludes, "These Genesis legends should then be identified as constituting the genre of a 'divine promissory oath' rather than a cult etiology or salvation oracle" (p. 178). Agreeing with the studies of Maag and Rendtorff, he adds, ". . .one is justified in speaking of the divine promise as a word-event in which the epiphany of the power of God occurs precisely in the giving of his promissory word" (p. 179).

certain minor variations of terminology the opening scenery is the same as in Gen. 18 while the middle section which develops the discourse between Lot and his visitors with the townspeople pounding at the door seems to differentiate between those visitors and the Lord who sent them (especially vs. 13, cf. 18:22). Nevertheless, there is a shift to the singular voice from vs. 18ff. which appears to identify what happens thereafter with the direct action of the Lord (especially vss. 27 and 29). The appearance to Isaac in Gen. 26 is also clad in the same terminology as the others, e.g., *ὤφθη. . .κύριος* and *εἶπεν* (vss. 2 and 24) with the exception that it takes place *ἐν τῇ νυκτὶ ἐκείνῃ* (vs. 24) which may or may not indicate that a dream is intended. A greater degree of descriptive breadth is achieved in the Jacob appearance in Gen. 28, but it would appear that the actual appearance and utterance of the Lord which comes in vss. 13ff. [*ὁ δὲ κύριος ἐπεστήρικτο ἐπ' αὐτῆς καὶ εἶπεν* Ἐγὼ *κύριος ὁ θεὸς* Αβρααμ *τοῦ πατρός σοῦ καὶ ὁ θεὸς* Ισαακ • Μὴ *φοβοῦ. . .καὶ ἰδοὺ ἐγὼ μετὰ σοῦ διαφυλάσσων σε. . .*] has been capsuled in the dream form (cf. vss. 12 and 16).[704] Another appearance seems to stand behind the Jacob story of Gen. 35 but while the opening verses do share certain terminological similarities to the other stories (cf. vss. 1,3 and 7) the form of telling is indirect discourse. With vss. 9ff., however, direct discourse begins with "*Ὤφθη δὲ ὁ θεὸς* [*καὶ ηὐλόγησεν αὐτὸν ὁ θεὸς*] *καὶ εἶπεν αὐτῷ ὁ θεός*, vs. 11 also has *εἶπεν δὲ αὐτῷ ὁ θεός* Ἐγὼ *ὁ θεός σου* and then as in Gen. 17:22 we read *ἀνέβη δὲ ὁ θεὸς ἀπ' αὐτοῦ ἐκ τοῦ τόπου, οὗ ἐλάλησεν μετ' αὐτοῦ. . .*(vs. 13).

In view of the above similarities it would appear a fair surmise that Gen. 18 would have been understood *in NT times* and *earlier* not in isolation from but in connection with the other anthropomorphic theophanies of that book and elsewhere. This appearance before Abraham at Mamre, however, goes to greater descriptive lengths than the others and focuses on several—for want of a better term—"realistic" features: it is an appearance of God in the form of a man (or three men?)[705] in a setting which is remarkably mundane, nomadic and typical for semitic hospitality. In vss. 4ff. references to objects such as trees, water, a meal, eating and the like along with those to conditions of tiredness and the need for rest, etc., all point up the natural setting and course of things. The story has gone about as far as it could go in bringing God from the remote regions beyond to the immediate

704 Lindblom, "Vorstellung," pp. 270f.

705 For the question of the identification of Jahweh with one or all three cf. G. von Rad, *Das erste Buch Mose. Genesis*, ATD, 2/4 (Gött., 1964, 7th ed.), pp. 173f., who also sees in the account a type quite singular in the entire OT and of probable Canaanite origin. He quotes Homer's *Odyssee*, XVII,485-487, and refers to the Hyrieus story with the visit of three gods and their promise of a child as story types related to this one (p. 174). For the Hyrieus reference cf. also Rose, *Greek Mythology*, pp. 115f. and n. 54, L. Radermacher, "Zur Charakteristik neutestamentlicher Erzählungen," *ARW*, 28 (1930), p. 36 and Gunkel, *Märchen*, p. 78, who adds regarding Gen. 18 and 19 and the compared history-of-religion texts, they are "Märchenstoffe internationaler Art" (p. 80). That Gen. 18 is quite singular for the OT was also the stress of Prof. K. Baltzer in conversations on the 4th and 13th of April, 1973. In the rabbinic literature the three men are identified with the angels Michael, Gabriel and Raphael; M. is to speak to Sarah, G. is to destroy Sodom and R. is to heal Abraham's circumcision wound (BM 86b) while elsewhere R. is also to deliver Lot (Targ J to Gen. 18:2) cf. Billerbeck, *op. cit.*, II, p. 96.

context of a man in a form that makes the otherwise unseen God visible. As is clear, however, from the distribution of visual and verbal terminology—from vss. 1-33 not counting other forms of the verb *to speak* the term *εἶπεν* appears 21 times of which 12 have the Lord or the three men as subject—an equally prominent interest of the text is the conversation and promise dimension; it does not display a one-sided infatuation, as it were, with sight.

Ex. 3f.

In comparing this appearance account we are confronted immediately with the question: does this story really stand parallel to the above and its cognates? Description is at a minimum; central emphasis is upon the verbal aspect. Moreover, the angel of the Lord appears here. Is the angel to be identified with God himself? This first obstacle is not a serious one since we noted above that for the other Gen. texts it was characteristic to emphasize the verbal communications and that even for Gen. 18 partiality to the visual at the cost of the verbal is not present; the emphasis lies on a graphic representation of a personal encounter. In its way Ex. 3 is just as graphic.[706] The other matter, i.e., the appearance of the angel of God, is no obstacle either since in this text—and on occasion elsewhere, as we shall see—the account in its context does in fact identify the angel with the Lord himself, not only through use of the terminus *ἄγγελος κυρίου*,[707] but also syntactically: *ὤφθη δὲ αὐτῷ ἄγγελος κυρίου ἐν φλογὶ πυρὸς ἐκ τοῦ βάτου*. . .and *ἐκάλεσεν αὐτὸν κύριος ἐκ τοῦ βάτου λέγων*. . . (vss. 2 and 4). The angel appears and the Lord speaks![708] It is to be acknowledged that the form of the appearing angel resides in an obscure reference to the flaming bush which is not consumed by the fire. Yet, other features

706 Says Lindblom: "In der Sinaiperikope wird niemals von Visionen, Träumen und dergleichen geredet. Der Verkehr zwischen Jahwe und Mose ist überall durchaus anthropomorph-realistisch und als ein unmittelbarer Umgang gedacht. Das gilt nicht am wenigsten vom Sprechen Jahwes zu Mose, wovon in diesen Erzählungen immer wieder die Rede ist" ("Vorstellung," p. 266). On the other hand, it is to be acknowledged that this text concentrates on the address aspect and offers only indirect indications of an appearance form. Yet, the vivid qualities of description pertaining to the encounter in all probability called to mind the same associations for the reader in NT times as in the other texts, if one can assume, for example, that such graphic treatment of this encounter portrayal as is found in the opening chapter of the Book of Jubilees was common knowledge for such readers at this time.

707 So among others Lindblom about the mal'ak: ". . .An vielen Stellen aber ist er einfach eine Erscheinungsform Jahwes, sachlich mit ihm identisch. Das ist der Fall, wenn in einer Rede die Worte des mal'ak und die Worte Gottes unterschiedslos abwechseln und für den Zuschauer der äußeren Erscheinung die Identität von beiden selbstverständlich ist. Es ist eine bisher kaum beobachtete Tatsache, daß in solchen Erzählungen mal'ak immer durch den vollen Ausdruck מלאך יהוה oder מי אלהים geradezu als ein erstarrter terminus technicus begegnet und mal'ak nicht mit dem bestimmten Artikel oder Suffix versehen wird, was in vielen Fällen das stilistisch natürlichste wäre" (*ibid.*, p. 268; cf. also his "Theophanies," p. 101f.). Kremer, *Osterbotschaft*, pp. 25ff. brings this kind of angel appearance together with the angel(s) in the tomb traditions.

708 As Barr says: "The voice and presence of the mal'ak alternate in a number of stories so much with the voice and appearing of Yahweh that it is hardly possible to understand his place as a substitute for the latter" ("Theophany," p. 33).

underscore the very direct, personal nature of the encounter: the Lord *sees* Moses approaching to observe the burning-bush phenomenon, he *calls* out his name twice and *warns* him from coming any closer, he *identifies* himself,[709] *informs* Moses of his intention to send him to Egypt to free his people and *assures* him that *he will be with him*, etc.[710] This personal aspect of God's appearance before Moses is emphasized once again in Ex. 33 similarly as in 3 but adds: *καὶ ἐλάλησεν κύριος πρὸς Μωυσῆν ἐνώπιος ἐνωπίῳ, ὡς εἴ τις λαλήσει πρὸς τὸν ἑαυτοῦ φίλον* and *'Αυτὸς προπορεύσομαί σου καὶ καταπαύσω σε* (vss. 11 and 14). The reason for the reserve in presenting any kind of visual image in the Moses appearance tradition also becomes apparent in this text where Moses asks to see God's glory: *Δεῖξόν μοι τὴν σεαυτοῦ δόξαν. καὶ εἶπεν 'Εγὼ παρελεύσομαι πρότερός σου τῇ δόξῃ μου καὶ καλέσω ἐπὶ τῷ ὀνόματι μου Κύριος ἐναντίον σου· καὶ ἐλεήσω ὃν ἂν ἐλεῶ, καὶ οἰκτιρήσω ὃν ἂν οἰκτίρω. καὶ εἶπεν Οὐ δυνήσῃ ἰδεῖν μου τὸν πρόσωπον· οὐ γὰρ μὴ ἴδῃ ἄνθρωπος τὸ πρόσωπόν μου καὶ ζήσεται* (vss. 18ff.). This article of faith, as it were, has not only influenced the Moses appearance tradition, but also apparently inner OT thought trends on revelation in general and that to a far-reaching degree.[711] Significant here, however, is that in spite of the seeing-prohibition an encounter is recorded in Ex. 3 as well as 33 which shares personal, realistic features comparable to the conceptual scope of the patriarchal appearance in every way, even if the pictorial motifs and structural elements are at variance.[712]

Jud. 6

As in the Ex. 3 text here too it is the angel of the Lord who appears, but this time not only is there an identification between the angel and the Lord[713] apparent in the terminus *ἄγγελος κυρίου* and the obvious reference to the "see-God-and-die"

709 W. Zimmerli refers here to a *Selbstvorstellungsformel* and sees in the form an emphasis on the personal nature of the encounter ("Ich bin Jahwe," *Geschichte und Altes Testament. Fst. A. Alt*, BHTh, 16, ed. by G. Ebeling [Tüb., 1953], pp. 182, 200ff. and *passim*). S. Mowinckel agreeing with Vriezen stresses that the emphasis lies on the verb and not the personal pronoun and that this means not an abstract statement of being, but rather a dynamic statement of acting, i.e., "I am the God who acts" ("The Name of the God of Moses," *HUCA*, 32 [1961], p. 127). Further, H. Hegermann, "Das griechischsprechende Judentum," *Literatur und Religion des Frühjudentums*, ed. by J. Maier and J. Schreiner (Würzburg, 1973), p. 340, cites this LXX example among others and says, "Trotz solcher Beispiele philosophierender Deutung des Bibeltexts wird die religiöse Grundstruktur der Texte nicht angetastet."

710 Habel sees in the "I am with you" promise a technical theological formula as divine affirmation of Jahweh's character; it should be translated "I am indeed with you" (*op. cit.*, pp. 300ff.).

711 Barr, "Theophany," p. 34. Taking this tension as his point of departure in OT traditions and then treating its origin and development is Baudissin, *op. cit.*, pp. 186ff.

712 Concerning Ex. 33 and the tensions here Barr says: "it is no doubt the most sophisticated and delicate discussion of the seeing of God by man in the OT" ("Theophany," p. 35). That varied and complex traditions have gone into the formation of this appearance account would appear self-evident, cf. W. Richter, *Berufungsberichte*, pp. 57ff. and 81ff., M. Noth, *Überlieferungsgeschichte des Pentateuch* (Stutt., 1948), pp. 172ff. Some reserve is expressed by Habel, *op. cit.*, pp. 300ff., regarding Noth's conclusions.

713 N.B. the Hebrew text of vss. 12bff. where יהוה speaks directly.

tradition of Ex. 33 (vs. 22f.), but also a greater attention to the form of the appearing One.[714] As in the patriarchal accounts there is a basic uncertainty in the narrative about the recognition of just who the stranger is. The story reveals an increasing crescendo of movement towards discovery by Gideon of the divine nature of his visitor, on the one hand, and on the other, the confirmation of the promise that he will conquer because this has been the Lord's commission.[715] The focal point of discovery and assurance comes in the miraculous disappearance of the angel from sight and the word of the Lord that he should be at peace and not fear that he would now die.

Jud. 13

What was said about the *ἄγγελος κυρίου* above is valid here as well, but this time a higher degree of anthropomorphic imagery and variety of expression is evident.[716] The appearing One is seen by the wife of Manoah first of all and then subsequently by Manoah himself as a "man of God" [*ἄνθρωπος τοῦ θεοῦ*], his appearance [*ὅρασις*] was *ὡς ὅρασις ἀγγέλου τοῦ θεοῦ ἐπιφανὴς σφόδρα* (vs. 6);[717] the request of Manoah to see the "man of God" again (vs. 8) is granted as God sends *τὸν ἄγγελον τοῦ θεοῦ* a second time (vs. 9) and Manoah's wife relates having met *τὸν ἄνδρα* again (vs. 10); Manoah meets *τὸν ἄνδρα* himself asking if he is indeed the same *ὁ ἀνήρ* (vs. 11); *ὁ ἄγγελος* replies yes Ἐγώ (vs. 11); *ὁ ἄγγελος κυρίου* speaks further (vs. 13) and then Manoah addresses *τὸν ἄγγελον κυρίου* (vs. 15); the same angel reference occurs twice more in vs. 16, once in vs. 17, once in vs. 18, once in vs. 20 and twice more in vs. 21. The degree of identification between the angel and the Lord as in the other texts is here heightened by the apparent connection between the name of angel *θαυμαστόν* and the dedication of Manoah's offering *τῷ κυρίῳ τῷ θαυμαστὰ ποιοῦντι κυρίῳ* (vss. 18f.) and by the same reference as Jud. 6:22f. to the "see-God-and-die" tradition of Ex. 33 (vs. 22): *ὅτι θεὸν ἑωράκ-*

714 Among others stressing the relationship, but not direct dependence between this and other accounts in our anthology are W. Richter, *Berufungsberichte*, pp. 40ff., 127ff., 181 *et passim*, and his *Untersuchungen*, pp. 137ff. and 142, P. Kübel, "Epiphanie und Altarbau," *ZAW*, 83 (1971), pp. 227ff., Kutsch, *op. cit.*, cols. 79ff., Nötscher, *Angesicht*, pp. 20ff., Lindblom, "Theophanies," p. 102. Habel goes a step further when he speaks of a pattern (*op. cit.*, p. 305, cf. above pp. 240f.).

715 It is worth noting here that in vss. 12bff. where the Masoretic text has the Lord himself speak, the subject shifts then back to the mal'ak thereafter, with the exception of vs. 23 where both M and LXX read "Lord."

716 W. Richter, *Untersuchungen*, pp. 140ff., Barr, "Theophany," p. 37 and above n. 702.

717 This is one of the relatively rare occasions where the terms *ὅρασις* and *ἐπιφανής* are used. While *ὅρασις* seems to have the technical function of repeating in nominal form the *ὤφθη* of vs. 3 [וירא, מראהו], *ἐπιφανής* translates here the same term translated *φοβερός* in the Jacob story in Gen. 28:17, so that a very nonliteral rendering of the Hebrew text is given: for the awesomeness of the נורא original is substituted the equivalent of "very plain," "clearly" or "manifestly." Thereby a premature departure from the anthropological stress to the recognition of the visitor's true identity after his miraculous ascension and accompanying fear is avoided–not to mention the contradiction to vs. 16. B reads *εἶδος* instead of *ὅρασις* and *φοβερόν* instead of *ἐπιφανής*.

αμεν. It must be granted, however, that the angel/man of God is sent by God in answer to prayer for the second time in vs. 9 so that a degree of uncertainty is apparently built into the story as well. Nevertheless, the above noted variety of expression indicates a heightened concentration upon graphic realism in comparison with the trends noted in the other texts; of all those compared up to this point this one comes closest to matching the anthropomorphic features of Gen. 18. Yet, here as there a balance between the visual and auditory is noteworthy (cf. also vs. 23!). The angel of the Lord appears to express the promise of a child to Manoah's wife and then to Manoah himself. The story has, as was similarly noted above regarding the Gideon appearance, a definite movement towards dénouement, building in suspense in good storyteller fashion. The primary theme of the story is the promise of Samson's birth and the kind of man (Nazirite) he is going to become; further, of central importance here as generally for this type of story is the name and identity of the appearing One.[718] Everything builds toward the discovery of this identity and name, i.e., just as in chapter 6 the goal is confirmation of his divine nature and thereby also the credibility of his words and the reliability of his promise. Here as there once again the moment of discovery comes in the angel's disappearance: here his ascension in the flames of the prepared offering. This time instead of a divine voice of assurance that they would not die it is the same message expressed in the faith of Manoah's wife.

I Sam. 3

Undoubtedly this appearance account combines features missing or only hinted at in the other accounts. As in Gen. 28 it seems to combine two kinds of appearances: a dream or vision coupled with a voice communication and a more visually realistic personal encounter. The latter is the conclusion to the sequence, as it were, with the Lord coming and standing before Samuel and speaking as one man to another (vs. 10)–terminology we have come across before.[719] Pictorial elements do not go beyond this–the rest of the focus is upon the immediate and long-range commissioning of Samuel–, but that which is described–meager as it may be–is probably sufficient to place the story *partem* in this group of anthropomorphic theophanies.[720] Terminologically the summary of this and succeeding appearances at Shiloh varies from the other accounts, but this is probably due to the combining of two different types of appearances and the need for terminology sufficient to describe both.[721] Be that as it may, the substance of vss. 10ff. is indisputably that

718 Cf. above n. 695.

719 Lindblom, "Theophanies," p. 101.

720 As in our analysis of the Ex. 3 account we can only base its inclusion on an assumed association here in the mind of the reader called up by the terminology and pattern. Cf. n. 706.

721 It is interesting to note once again that where the LXX translates the infinitival להראה of vs. 21 with δηλωθῆναι it uses ὅρασις in vs. 1 [translating however הזרן]; for נגלה of vs. 21 it renders ἀπεκαλύφθη a term which is not only found earlier in the text (vs. 7) for the revealing of God's word and in Gen. 35:7 [the LXX renders ἐπεφάνη however], but

of an anthropomorphic type: a personal confrontation between the Lord–presumably in some (human) form–and Samuel has taken place. Further, the term *ὅρασις* occurs in vss. 1 and 15 as descriptive noun in close proximity to the noun *ῥῆμα* in both instances making clear that we do not have to do here with voice communication alone.

The Intertestamental Literature

Where the texts analyzed above did not differentiate by and large between the Lord and the appearing form, e.g., that of the angel of the Lord, the intertestamental literature–where the retention of the anthropomorph-theophanic form is relatively uncommon[722]–makes a strict caesura, as it were; a significant internal

also in the later prophetic literature. As noted above, for Ex. 33 (cf. n. 717) here too a complex interweaving of various kinds of tradition is to be recognized, cf. Lindblom, "Theophanies," p. 101.

722 Even a cursory reading of the apocrypha and pseudepigrapha makes this clear. The *Testament of Isaac* follows our selection from the *Testament of Abraham* very closely and seems to depend on the latter for its use of the appearance form. In the *Testament of Job* (42) the Lord himself appears and speaks but through the medium of a storm and cloud. In the (Syrian) *Apocalypse of Baruch* (ch. 55) the seer sits under a tree and is met by the angel Ramiel sent by God to interpret the vision he has seen. In the *Paralipomena Jeremiae* (*The Texts of the Words of Baruch*) (ch. 3), angels descend at night with torches to destroy Jerusalem, Jeremiah and Baruch weep and plead with them to wait until Jeremiah can speak with the Lord himself (vs. 4) and thereupon the Lord orders them to interrupt their mission until Jeremiah has had his chance to speak. From this point on in the dialogue begins the appearance, but it is not clear in the text just how the encounter and dialogue are to be conceived of, but it could be possible that a repetition of the scene in Gen. 18:22ff. is intended. In any case, it would appear that a kind of anthropomorphic theophany has taken place since at its conclusion (vs. 17, *Paraleipomena Jeremiou* [TT, I], Pseudepigrapha Series, 1, ed. by R.A. Kraft and A.-E. Purintun [Missoula, Mont. (SBL)], p. 18) the Lord ascends *ταῦτα εἰπὼν ὁ κύριος ἀνέβη ἀπὸ Ἰερεμίου εἰς τὸν οὐρανόν*. *IV Ezra* speaks in terms of visions: the narrator speaks of being in bed, agitated in spirit (cf. also *Poimandres* I,1) and then comes a monologue to the Lord (ch. 1 [3]) to which comes a reply from the angel Uriel (ch. 2 [4]). The pattern repeats itself throughout with emphasis on the hour of the night, the angel, the agitation of spirit. The seventh "vision" then is a repetition of the voice from the bush in Ex. 3 (ch. 12 [14]) and distinguishes itself from the others referring to them as signs, visions and interpretations while this one actually resists such categories (ch. 12:8). The second half of this "vision" describes the command to write and publish a record of all that has been revealed, assurance that the Holy Spirit will assist and selection of five secretaries for the actual writing. Ezra is told by the voice to drink a special potion and immediately wisdom flows from his mouth (ecstatic or oracular utterance?) while the secretaries write it down–ninety-four books in all of which books 1-24 are to be published at first. The work having been completed Ezra is translated to heaven (vs. 50). In *Ezekiel, the Tragic Poet* (vss. 90ff.) the Ex. 3 appearance is put into the form of Greek drama, but the appearance form is of minimal and secondary importance. The theophanies of the *Ethiopian Book of Enoch* are visions of judgment: angels are the emissaries of destruction. The view of the Lord upon his throne recalls, moreover, the imagery of Isaiah's call (cf., e.g., chs. 14:14ff. and 15). Enoch sees a great deal, but most of the time they are things of awe and things to come (cf., e.g., ch. 83). In the *Slavic Book of Enoch* the motifs of agitation of spirit, sleep and dreams are a prelude to the seer's vision of two men who are described, however, as heavenly beings (ch. 1:1ff.). He is then taken on a heavenly journey while sitting on their wings (ch. 3).

alteration has been made. A further development of thought concerning angelology has taken place as well as the scope and nature of God's abode of residence and revelation: the scenery is initially the realm of human earthly experience, but the focus of attention shifts very quickly to the "above and beyond," the other world, the heavens and their opening on special occasions to seekers of higher and eternal

The same kind of heavenly radiance appearance (?) is part and parcel of the visit of the man from heaven, the messenger of God, the angel sent to Aseneth after her prayer in *Joseph and Aseneth* (ch. 14f.). Although attempts are made at describing a human form (cf., e.g., chs. 14:9 and 15:11) recurring references to light beaming from parts of his body make it difficult to see here the anthropomorphic theophany form. Philo, *Book of Biblical Antiquities* (ch. 8:3), more or less affirms that God appeared and spoke to Abraham, but places no emphasis on the anthropomorphic elements of such appearances. Similar is the treatment given to Ex. 3 (ch. 10:1), but on the visit of the angel to Gideon he dwells at length (ch. 35) bringing significant changes to bear on the biblical text: the consumption of the offering is here a changing of water into fire and blood (ch. 35:6f.). Philo also devotes elaborate attention to Jud. 13 (ch. 42) again, however, making significant alterations: Manoah's wife is told that she is to blame in her childless marriage, but God was going to end her fruitlessness, says the angel; the name of the angel is also found out to be Phadael (similar amplification of the story, e.g., the jealousy of Manoah, the seemly description of the angel's outward appearance and his appeal for Manoah's wife and her prayer that he might come again and speak with her husband, without any particularly independent development of the appearance form itself is found in Josephus, *Antiquities of the Jews*, V,8,1-3 cf. also his treatment of Gen. 18 where the three visitors are all angels distinct in identity from the Lord himself, I,11,2f.). Similar accretions are added to Philo's recounting of I Sam. 3 (ch. 53), but significantly the actual appearance terminology in vss. 10f. and 21 has been dropped (ch. 53:8). Philo (and Josephus it would appear) is clearly uncomfortable in ascribing anthropological terminology to Jahweh himself. The *Book of Jubilees* (or *Little Genesis*) can retell the anthropomorphic theophanies (e.g., chs. 15 or 32, etc.) and make similar enlargements to those of Philo and Josephus; in ch. 32:17ff., for example, the Jacob appearance/dream is retold with stress on the late hour, the name change and promise and the Ascension of the Lord which Jacob watches until he enters the heavens. Thereafter another encounter takes place: a vision at night of an angel with tablets telling the apocalyptic future of Israel (vss. 21ff.) and the plans for building a place of worship instead of a residence at Bethel and with the message that Jacob would die in Egypt; he is told to write all this down and his memory–he is assured–would be aided by divine assistance. Then the angel also ascends and Jacob wakes up from his sleep (vs. 26). The so-called *Treasure Cave* mentions briefly Gen. 12, but says nothing about Gen. 18 (cf. ch. 28). Regarding Ex. 3 it says that Moses was eighty years old when God spoke to him out of the bush (ch. 34:8), but no further interest is shown in the anthropomorphic theophany form. In the *Testament of the Twelve Patriarchs* there is a reference (Christian interpolation) to the God who takes on a body, eats with men and redeems them (*Test. Simeon,* 6,7), a kind of dream-vision ascension and viewing of heavenly things (*Test. Levi* 2:5ff., 5:1ff., 8:1ff. and the *Aram. Frag.* 7), an intermediary angel as go-between (*Test. Dan* 6,2), a visionary experience (*Test. Naphthali* from the Hebrew chronicle of *Jerachmeel* 2, 4 and 7) and the motif of God coming to earth (*ibid.*, 8,4) in the lifetime of Abraham, but the picture is of seventy servant angels–Michael their chief–who teach the inhabitants of the world their languages; only the house of Abraham learns the holy language, Hebrew (*ibid.*, chs. 9 and 10). In the *Testament of Solomon* (ch. 1:6f.) the angel Michael comes and gives a ring to Solomon who is praying in the temple and Michael speaks on God's behalf. The ring is then used on a demon who recognizes and dislikes its power against him. Finally, the *Qumran* literature shows an equally apparent distance to the use of the anthropomorphic theophany form, even though the presence and activity of angels, for example, are otherwise relatively well attested. Cf. J. Strugnell, "The Angelic Liturgy at Qumran-4Q Serek Šîrôt 'Ôlat Haššabbāt," *Suppl. NovTest*, 7 (Leiden, 1960), *passim* and his literature on pp. 318f. (cf. also in connection with the *Testament of Abraham* and as overview perspective below n. 729.

truth.[723] In a word, a kind of gnostic, apocalyptic view of the universe, life and time is in progress.[724]

Tobit 5 and 12[725]

The appearance here is of the angel Raphael sent by God, but he is disguised as Azarius and therefore taken to be a man. In a greater degree than heretofore was the case the anthropomorphic features are thrown open for view as Tobit puts Azarius to the test about his family background and familiarity with the territory through which the proposed journey was to go. A further note of irony, pointing up the non-recognition motif (cf. 5:4), is the blessing pronounced upon Tobit's son and Azarius: and may the angel of the Lord accompany you on your journey (cf. 5:7)![726] In the course of the narrative bizarre elements in comparison with the

723 W.C. van Unnik, "Die 'Geöffneten Himmel' in der Offenbarungsvision des Apokryphons des Johannes," *Apophoreta. Fst. E. Haenchen* (Berlin, 1964), pp. 275ff., Lentzen-Deis, *op. cit.*, pp. 320ff., D.S. Russel, *The Method and Message of Jewish Apocalyptic* (London, 1971[='64]), pp. 158-177 and 235-262 and J. Maier, *Geschichte der jüdischen Religion* (Berlin, 1972), pp. 162ff. and 193ff.

724 It would be a mistaken assumption here to maintain that this shift of perspective is in and of itself the product of a departure from the anthropomorph-theophanic form in this period. It is to be seen rather as the consequential development of the rise and growth of alternate expressions of revelation already present in the OT texts, manifest, for example, in the call visions of the classical prophets or in the use of the *kabod* concept with its universal implications. That is to say, where the anthropomorph-theophanic form is retained and an alteration becomes evident it is due to the far-reaching influence of these other traditions and especially—in all probability—the see-God-and-die tradition of Ex. 33 (cf. above, n. 624). The relationship between the anthropomorphic theophanies and other forms of revelation for the OT and subsequent Jewish literature is the focus of an ongoing dialogue between R. Rendtorff and W. Zimmerli, cf. Rendtorff, "Offenbarungsvorstellungen" and "Geschichte und Wort im Alten Testament," *EvTh*, 22 (1961), pp. 621-649 and W. Zimmerli, "'Offenbarung' im Alten Testament," *EvTh*, 22 (NF=17), pp. 15-31 (etc.). The differences between them take their focus in the place and meaning of the revelation of God's person ("I am Jahweh") and word in relationship to that of God's action in historical events. As is well known this discussion has direct implications for the NT and systematic reflections of the program publication edited by W. Pannenberg, *Offenbarung als Geschichte, KuD*, Beiheft 1 (Gött., 1970^4). An excellent overview of the conflicting methodologies and presuppositions is found in R. Knierim, "Offenbarung im Alten Testament," *Probleme Biblischer Theologie. Fst. G. von Rad*, ed. by H.W. Wolff (Mü., 1971). Cf. also J.M. Robinson, "Offenbarung als Wort und als Geschichte," *Neuland in der Theologie*, III. *Theologie als Geschichte*, ed. by J.M. Robinson and J.B. Cobb, Jr. (Zürich, 1967), pp. 63ff.

725 For an introduction to text tradition, analysis of general context and overview of secondary literature, cf. L. Rost, *Einleitung in die alttestamentlichen Apokryphen und Pseudepigraphen einschließlich der großen Qumran-Handschriften* (Heidelberg, 1971), pp. 44ff. and B.M. Metzger, *An Introduction to the Apocrypha* (N.Y., 1957), pp. 31ff., both of whom stress that its several recensions bear witness to its popularity in both Jewish and Christian circles from the time of its composition—ca. second century B.C.—down through the centuries.

726 The article on the Emmaus story by Schnider and Stenger ("Struktur"), takes up a brief analysis of this story as illustration of a text type which they consider to be comparable

OT canonical texts appear, e.g., the demon Asmodeus, his jealousy, defense methods through fish parts and the restoration of Tobit's sight through the same, etc. The story builds in its intensity, the reader waits for and anticipates the moment of recognition when Azarius reveals his true identity. When that moment comes the scene is by no means altogether different from our previous texts, although certain fundamental additions of concept and terminology are present. Raphael's identity strikes terror into the hearts of Tobit and Tobias, but he calms their fears and assures them of God's benevolence and action on their behalf; their loyalty has been rewarded with the helping, protective appearance of his messenger. Thereby the two-sided emphasis of the other appearances–visual and auditory communication–is retained. The nature of the message differs from our other texts, however, in that God *above* initiates help but remains *above* while the angel has come [ἦλθον, 12:19]; the instruction to bless is directed *above* (from the perspective of Tobit and son) and the angel is ascending back to the one *above* who sent him. All that has here transpired is then to be written down in a book, another variant feature to any previous account in our anthology–a typical motif for the literature of this period. The disappearance motif is added–an element we have encountered before [καὶ οὐκέτι εἶδον αὐτόν, 12:21]–and the recipients of the appearance bless God for his marvelous works as ὤφθη αὐτοῖς ὁ ἄγγελος κυρίου (vs. 22), a terminological parallel to the above, but in intention a variant.

The Testament of Abraham

This text is extremely interesting and useful for our comparison for the following reasons: 1) its shorter recension is in all probability pre-Christian[727] and makes use of the anthropomorphic theophany form, and 2) it gives us an example of later direct use of Gen. 18 demonstrating how this OT text was read and understood and employed in this period which is either slightly earlier than or roughly contempora-

to the Emmaus pericope in form (pp. 110ff.). Although this article does make reference to Jud. 6 and 13 (p. 111, n. 36), along with Homer's *Odyssee* I,320, as examples of those stories where the unrecognized appearing *himmlische Gestalt* reveals his true identity before disappearing "durch ein wunderbares Zeichen. . .durch eine Handlung. . ." (p. 111), it fails thereby and in general to distinguish clearly enough between the stories of Greek origin and concept and those we are examining in this section. Of course, its selection of Tobit is only as illustration of the nonrecognition motif apparently, but a further refining of categories as well as an extension of scope to include a larger grouping of anthropomorphic theophanies would be desirable. The article contends further that the central point of the story is the journey and the understanding that it has been accomplished under divine protection and guidance whereby the recognition scene merely confirms this fact and as such is then subordinate to the former (p. 111). In terms of the immediate structure of the Tobit story this is probably true, although it is to be asked if the very form utilized did not suggest to the reader/hearer certain associations that allowed for greater interest in the recognition scene itself for its own sake.

727 Cf. above, n. 699.

neous to Christian beginnings.[728] It is the only text in our anthology with this immediate perspective.[729]

The clear differentiation between the angel and the Lord in the Tobit text is also to be noted here: God sends his messenger Michael to Abraham at the appointed time of the patriarch's death. But similar to the Tobit text—and in this right to the OT canonical theophanies—this unexpected visitor is not recognized [*μὴ εἰδὼς τίς ἐστιν*, 2:2]. With some exceptions the opening exchange and Abraham's offer of hospitality corresponds closely to the motifs and structural elements of Gen. 18. This time, however, Isaac, the child of promise, is a grown man and participates in the welcome of the stranger. Furthermore, the footwashing plays a key role in the recognition motif. Other elements add color to the account which are only incidental to the use of the theophany form if not to the story itself, e.g., the voice from the tree, the weeping of the men and Michael's tears turning to precious stones, the return of the angel to heaven at sundown and his inability to deliver the message and the dream of Isaac, etc. The anticipated moment of recognition comes somewhat obliquely at the second weeping scene where the angel's denial of having brought ill-fated news is cause for Sarah to see in him the "man of God" [*ἄνθρωπος τοῦ θεοῦ*], one of the three of old come to them at Mamre. Equally oblique is Abraham's own insight of recognition of the feet he had washed being indeed those of one of those strangers (confirming in the main the message delivered by the voice from the tree). For all intents and purposes the anthropomorphic theophany form ends at this point for the angel Michael now recognized in his true identity does not disappear or go away, but remains 1) to confirm the content of Isaac's dream, and 2) to escort Abraham on a heavenly journey prior to the separation of his soul from his body at death. Moreover, the anthropomorphic form has merely served as a kind of dress leading up to this heavenly journey; the balance between the visual and

728 Concerning the origins of the text James is inclined to place it in the second century A.D. under Christian authorship (*Abraham*, p. 29), but this is disputed by K. Kohler who sees it as a Jewish work of high antiquity ("The Pre-Talmudic Haggada.II.C.—The Apocalypse of Abraham and its Kindred," *JQR*, 7 [1895], p. 581); similar is H.H. Rowley who places it in or around the first century A.D. (*Apokalyptik. Ihre Form und Bedeutung zur Biblischen Zeit*, trans. by I. and R. Pesch [Einsiedeln, 1965, 3rd ed.], p. 104). James does admit, however, that very old traditions do stand behind it and recognizes that Gen. 18 probably served as model for the appearance of Michael which has its closest parallel in the appearance of Raphael in the Book of Tobit (*Abraham*, pp. 29 and 55).

729 As was seen on occasion above (n. 722) it was not particularly unusual for texts from this period to retell the OT stories of theophanies and to embellish them in certain aspects of the narrative to make them even more interesting, but an independent application of that anthropomorphic form found in those OT stories and not merely alterations of motifs would seem to have been extremely rare. In the main the Gen. 18 story is used by the rabbis not to dwell on the appearance form, but to stress the importance of being a ready host (*Gastfreundschaft*), e.g., Schabbath 127[a] says that Rab. J[e]huda quotes another rabbi as having said: "Die Gastfreundschaft ist größer als die Begrüßung der Sch[e]khina" and points to the words of Gen. 18:3 which the Midrasch "deutet, als ob Abraham mit diesen Worten / Gott aufgefordert habe, zu warten, bis er die drei Männer als Gäste in sein Haus eingeführt habe" (=Billerbeck, *op. cit.*, I, pp. 588f.). This tendency can be seen further among other examples from these writings (cf. *ibid.* and p. 838 = Qidduschin 32[b], and excursus *Liebeswerke*, II,A.1f. in vol. IV,1, pp. 565ff.).

auditory has been retained only formally as the words of the angel prior to recognition contain little more than praise for Abraham's piety and hospitality to strangers. The verbal communication motif inherent to other accounts has been shifted basically to another dimension, namely the dream! Both the theophany and dream forms, moreover, serve as subordinate themes to the focus of the story: the heavenly journey and all that Abraham *sees* in the realm *above and beyond* this world. In a word, the theophany of Gen. 18 is used as an external vehicle to introduce a new theological concern and interest: an apocalyptic view.

3. Relationship to the Gospel Appearance Gattung

Our survey of selected anthropomorphic theophany texts of the OT has shown that while they are distinct from one another in their context and particular message they share a basic similarity and unity of form and intention. This form or schematic representation and direction of statement exist in recurrent terminology, motifs, structural elements and fundamental conceptual scope. And yet, these factors while apparently participating in a prescribed and given shape or pattern are not static so as not to allow for flexible variation. The foremost aspect of variation is the exact visual shape in which the Lord appears, a quite natural phenomenon in view of the fundamental problems connected with conceiving of an otherwise unseen God becoming visible and in view of the weight of the Ex. 33 tradition for OT theology. Yet, this appearance shape is, nevertheless, represented as always being concrete and visibly real–in contrast to other forms of divine communication. Gen. 18 is singularly definite in degree of identification of the Lord with an appearing human form, [730] but where other such theophanies allow for the form of an angel–as indistinguishable as it may be from the Lord himself–the non-recognition motif is still retained since even this form is seen in anthropomorphic categories. Another constant within the variation of detail of appearance is that the appearing One comes unexpectedly at the intervening initiative of the Lord.[731] Moreover, the visual aspects are not allowed to stand by themselves: a balance is achieved between these and auditory aspects. A sighting is not in and of itself important, but rather it shares an equality of emphasis with verbal communication. The appearing One is

730 It may indeed be the case that the origins of such a story are not to be sought in Hebrew religion, but rather in Canaanite backgrounds and the folklore of ancient people in general as has often been maintained (cf. above, n. 705), but it must be admitted that the story has been sufficiently edited to fit the anthropomorph-theophanic form and concept of the OT so as to make it a fundamentally distinct form from its original and to make it thoroughly compatible with the other examples adduced for comparison.

731 Addressing himself to this feature in the call narratives of the OT (and here specifically to Jud. 6) Habel says: "It is significant that the angel appears. . .to Gideon at a time of historical crisis and in the midst of his normal routine activities. . .The call, therefore, appears as a disruptive experience for which there has been no obvious preparation. The call marks the initial interruption of God in the life of the individual. Such a moment was related as a supernatural confrontation which could be comprehended with the senses and tested by rational dialogue. There are no traces of ecstasy here" (*op. cit.*, p. 298).

engaged in conversation with the initial topic more often than not being his identity and/or name. In connection with this topic an important message is related which takes the form of a promise regarding the future and in one form or another it involves the action of the one who has received the appearance, i.e., something of a commission is always present. Direct or assumed then the appearance form culminates with a disappearance or a departure of some sort, the appearance comes to an end[732] and the consequences for the person(s) involved are recorded.

These features point then to a basic conceptual foundation for these theophanies in their present form: 1) they are the immediate, personal encounter between the Lord and the person(s) singled out for the appearance, and 2) they are not at their core individualistic but focus on a larger circle, more precisely, God's chosen people: the appearance and the action of those commissioned are to have consequential effects upon the larger body. It may be said without trying to force a harmony in all aspects that on this level these texts demonstrate a basic unity with the other forms of God's self-revelation of himself in the OT in spite of the high degree of diversity in the modes of expression themselves. That is to say, for example, that the classical prophetic tradition in its call dimension is no less immediate and personal nor does it take its focus any less in the present (judgment) and future (hope) of the people of God. A generic relationship exists between these complexes of God's self-revelation.[733]

The intertestamental literature, of which we have selected only two examples, appears no longer able to tolerate the coming and appearing of YHWH himself and thereby follows a trend already begun in the OT itself. An intermediary angel/messenger—distinct from YHWH himself—takes over this function wherever the anthropomorphic theophany form is adopted at all, a phenomenon which is relatively rare for this literature. This is a significant alteration since it allows for continuing use of the form while placing that form in the service of a new theological concept: the loyal Jew in the context of suffering is assured that his loyalty and

732 G. Lohfink in his excellent study of the ascension problem points out that the concept of ascending into the heavens with or without the terminus ἀνέβη frequently comes at the end of a divine appearance (*Himmelfahrt,* pp. 70ff.). We have indeed seen the use of the terminus in Jud. 13 and in the otherwise scant descriptive terminology in Gen. 17 as well as in the two examples from the intertestamental literature, yet in view of the overall variety on this point in the theophanies this feature appears to be an alternate mode of expressing the departure aspect and is not one of the constants. Lohfink is correct in making a fundamental distinction between the appearance and the ascension story forms.

733 Habel, *op. cit., passim* sees in the early prophetic call narratives a literary pattern—the call *Gattung*—which was then adopted by the classical prophets to show that their own calls stood in direct relationship of succession to this early use of the *Gattung* (p. 306). Where he seems to have a more or less strong case for his analysis of the earlier texts his move to the classical prophets is fatal: he is forced to harmonize elements that simply belong to differing forms of representation. The conclusion would seem to suggest itself: their relationship is to be sought in the subject matter and not in the form. W. Richter, *Berufungsberichte,* speaks rather of a relationship of concept and horizon—a rich tradition to be looked back upon—i.e., *Schemata,* without forcing the dependence level between the *Schriftpropheten* and their precursors (p. 181 *et passim*), which seems preferable in view of the major differences (cf. also his *Untersuchungen,* p. 142).

perseverance in the law of God does not go unrewarded (Tobit)–a subtle but significant shift from the Gideon- or Samuel-appearance for example–, or the piety of a vanguard of the faith can be singled out and honored by an appearance as a literary device placed in the service of other forms of revelation and theological reflection, e.g., translation, heavenly journey with its throwing open of the economy and judgment of the realm above, and the ascension of the soul at the burial of the body (Testament of Abraham).

In returning to the question of the relationship between the complexes of literature here under examination–OT/"Apocrypha-Pseudepigrapha"/NT–this summary leads to some important and unavoidable conclusions: the gospel appearance stories share by and large the terminology, motifs, structural elements and conceptual scope of the form employed in the other two complexes, but demonstrate no substantial parallel to the intention of the intertestamental literature; they are not apocalyptic in essence and do not find in that corpus any analogy on internal grounds.[734] While a case might be made for the empty tomb tradition on this level perhaps–though even here the anthropomorphic terminology is characteristically absent–the same cannot be posed for the gospel appearance stories. The OT anthropomorphic theophanies, on the other hand, come essentially closer to this category. Here as there we find *not only* correspondence of terminology and structure–the reader is directed here to the Text-Synopsis below for an overview of the structure, motifs and terminology of the entire complex–, *but also* a far-reaching correspondence in the subject matter communicated: it is a very personal encounter where the resolution of non-recognition is important; it is an encounter through which the human partner(s) is addressed in promise and commission; it is an encounter through which the human partner(s) expresses a reaction mingling uncertainty, doubt and a feeling of inadequacy with both fear and worship at having been in the presence of the appearing One. All of these aspects are present so conspicuously in one form or another in the gospel appearance stories that the conclusion would seem to offer itself: *the OT anthropomorphic theophany stories did stand formally and essentially behind the conception of the gospel appearance stories–even though they are nowhere quoted directly–so that the formulation of the latter took place as a conscious reflex, a deliberate reaching back to this OT traditional complex, and that to the exclusion of other possibilities, to give them a definite form of expression and thereby also direction of statement.*

The questions yet to be answered are: how did such a relationship arise in the historical context of primitive Christianity, and what theological consequences did it have for resurrection faith? These questions pose the problem of integration on both the historical and theological level of our entire line of questioning up to this point and constitute the focus of our summary and conclusions.

734 It should be noted that our conclusions here about the resistance of these appearance stories to apocalyptic origins calls for a reappraisal of the relationship between these and the heavenly radiance type where the latter has heretofore dominated interest as though it alone were central to resurrection faith. It is not the purpose of our investigation to pursue the problems connected with this other category, but simply to establish the distinction and to lay claim to the integrity of the one over against the other.

V. Summary and Conclusions

We have seen in the introduction that the interpretation of the gospel appearance stories has a long and complex history. The variety of approaches has been surveyed according to methodological considerations, since a rehearsal of the immense quantity of secondary literature would otherwise have been prohibitive. We chose as our focus of attention a line of questioning which did not concentrate upon the question of the Easter event itself, but rather that of the literary form of the gospel appearance stories. Out of the overview and analysis of the literature with this general scope emerged a group of key questions which provided the issues of debate and contours of development for our investigation. Even as early as Celsus, for example, we noted the historical question being raised: did Jesus rise from the dead and appear as it is told in the gospels? and then its negation on grounds of both subject matter and history-of-religion analogy. Although we affirmed the importance of the question itself and noted that it has been posed in our sampling of the history of research with a high degree of differentiation and a variety of motivation, it seemed advisable, nonetheless, in view of the frequent mixing of the systematic and exegetical lines of questioning to set aside for the moment the historical question in order to pursue a history-of-tradition analysis of those gospel appearance stories.

Methodologically then, this decision brought us into a critical dialogue with the questions posed by the NT exegetical—above all form-critical—discussion. The skepticism of Graß, Evans, *et al.*, over against the potential of history-of-tradition research on these appearance stories we deemed unjustified. To the contrary, we concluded that there is much more to be done in an application of the method.

The primary question emerging from the exegetical discussion then is that of the *origin* of the gospel appearance stories. Aside from the obvious implications of the origins question for the matter of ultimate historical veracity, its chief expression in the methods discussion—regardless of how it is posed—points directly to the problem of resurrection traditions in their *variety* and *relationship* to one another. The group of questions around this aspect of the origins question provided the focus of chapter II. The initial problem to be settled there was the question of relationship over against the kerygma tradition. The most influential voice on that question was that of Dibelius, whose thesis that the gospel appearance stories are late missionary sermon paradigms or illustrations of the kerygma (as seen for example in I Cor. 15 and the sermons of Acts) has been widely accepted since its original formulation. The first task of our investigation, therefore, was to test the adequacy of this view. Calling into question its presuppositions we asked if a relationship of dependence can be based on either formal or internal grounds and came to the conclusion that on both counts the hypothesis is without support. A comparison, for instance, of the formal points of contact between them demonstrates that too many gaps of a substantial nature are left untouched by this view. Moreover, internally it was asked if the gospel stories can be assumed to have spoken adequately in the missionary environment of primitive Christianity at all and again we had to conclude that this alleged background is unsatisfactory and leaves too many unanswered questions in view of the complex nature of their specific theological statements. Some other *Sitz im Leben* must be found. In sum then, our confrontation with the Dibelius hypothesis led to its rejection: *the stories did not emerge as illustrations for the kerygma*. Where a direct relationship can be established it is at the redactional level (Lk. 24:34 and Acts 10 and 13).

A special problem in connection with the kerygma tradition in more recent research was pointed out to be the widely held view that an identity exists between that tradition's understanding of what post-resurrection appearances were originally and the experience of such by Paul. This understanding is generally subsumed under the designation *Lichtglanz* type and it is held to be the percursor and competitor of the "later" anthropomorphic, materialistic type of the gospel stories. Further, it is even claimed that the gospel stories were originally heavenly radiance appearances too and only changed later out of apologetic necessity. To this scheme of things we concluded that, while further research is necessary to clear up many uncertainties with regard to the specific nature and origins of this so-called heavenly radiance type, it cannot be argued satisfactorily that this tradition had anything to do with gospel traditions in general (other than perhaps some remote connections in the Mount of Transfiguration story) and by no means any influence on the formation of the gospel appearance stories. They are separate and distinct traditional strata.

Another key question in the exegetical discussion is the problem of the relationship between the *empty tomb* tradition(s) and the appearance stories since they are so closely bound together in our gospels. While a general consensus of opinion exists in NT research that they were originally independent of one another a certain degree of unrest is evident over the influence of the tomb tradition(s) and locale upon the appearance stories. We found it necessary, therefore, to unravel the complex interdependence at the redactional level to determine where the tomb accounts ended and original appearance stories began. We concluded that in one instance an appearance story (Mt. 28:9,10) had been constructed redactionally out of a tomb account and that in another instance (Jn. 20:14-18) such an account had played a not insignificant role.

Other aspects of the tomb tradition question became further cause for probing the relationship problem as well. It has been proposed, namely, that the *grave guard* story in Mt. goes back along with a similar account in GP to an original appearance story—probably to Peter—at the grave or some variation thereof. The proposal was seen, however, to rest on rather unlikely footing in comparison with the proposal that matthaean redactional creation is its source and that GP while enlarging on the theme of nonbelieving witness to the Resurrection itself is dependent upon it.

This issue of dependence and later enlargement raised the question of the possibility that other appearance story complexes associated with the gospel tradition both within the immediate context of Easter event representations and without might preserve additional early appearance traditions. We saw, however, that this whole sector is problematical. The *ascension story*, for instance, is cast in the form of a group appearance story but this context is secondary. The *summaries* of the unauthentic ending of *Mk*. cannot be granted a separate voice in the quest for the earliest gospel appearance story traditions—in spite of some vigorous attempts to prove otherwise—because they depend upon a knowledge of the canonical ones. Among the so-called *extra-canonical* sources we saw that they too presuppose familiarity with the canonical gospels and go beyond them (the Epistula Apostolorum, the Syriac Didaskalia and the gnostic gospels) on occasion by developing a new *Gattung* of lengthy post-resurrection dialogue scenes. The two possible exceptions are GP and the Gospel of the Hebrews, but the one breaks off where an appearance story could have come and the other is so embedded in themes known from the canonical sources (especially Mt.) and unfamiliar James traditions that their inclusion as separate voices is all too speculative. In this same connection the so-called "*displaced*" appearance stories are often adduced for consideration and, as we saw, the majority of them are so firmly embedded in Galilaean traditions of Jesus' earthly ministry and are so thoroughly clothed in motifs and themes other than those of the appearance stories that they resist comparison at all on form-critical grounds. The one possible exception was considered to be perhaps an early form of the Walking on the Water miracle story (Mk. 6:45ff. parr.) before it became anchored in its present location or perhaps an auxiliary form of that story.

In all then, the critical dialogue with the questions raised in the present state of research on specific issues of relationship in chapter II led to the conclusion that the appearance stories of the gospel tradition—with the exception of Mt. 28:9,10 and perhaps part of Jn. 20:14-18—do not owe their origin in any sense to dependence upon other traditional strata. *They build an independent stream of tradition next to those of the kerygma and tomb traditions*. Those stories are: the *Group*, *Emmaus*, *Galilaean* and *Magdalene* appearance stories.

In response to the need for a history-of-tradition analysis of these stories in their own right, which emerged out of the relationship question of chapter II, we found that the various attempts in the history of their research at answering the questions addressed to them could offer little assistance. The present state of research has been so widely influenced by the Dibelius approach on the relationship question and the general skepticism of Graß *et al.* over against the historical critical method and the ability of these stories to speak historically reliable information that an impasse of sorts has been reached. In a word, these stories have evoked widespread embarrassment over the years and have been relegated to a place of subordination as sermon illustrations and legends; a frontal confrontation with their form and content as story narrative in their traditional context by and large has been avoided. With certain justification one may say of the history of research, a *history-of-tradition analysis* of the gospel appearance stories has not existed.

We did find, however, that several attempts among form-critics offer some promising options. The studies of Albertz, Brun and Dodd raised questions in this regard with two primary foci: 1) can the gospel appearance stories be grouped and analyzed according to themes and motifs which can then shed light on their specific historical background in the situation of primitive Christianity (Albertz and Brun) and 2) can they be divided into particular story types literarily and analyzed on the merits of their internal characteristics (Dodd)? While we affirmed the orientation of these questions our critical dialogue with the general positions of these scholars led to the necessity of distancing ourselves from them on certain aspects and contending for further development on others. Regarding critique of the former, for example, it was seen to be inadequate to group the stories according to categories of single/group appearances because the schematization depends upon the assumption that the kerygma is the correct measure for the gospel stories and stands or falls on the viability of the Dibelius hypothesis. Any approximation thereto in the gospels is at the redactional level. Moreover, the close identification of particular themes and motifs with early ecclesiastical polemic and apologetic was based on an insufficient differentiation between tradition and redaction and tended by and large to overlook the motif chains that allow the stories to speak as a total form. Only Dodd began to work free of this pre-occupation with individual elements towards a more comprehensive grasp of the whole through his recognition of a pattern common to the literary categories of concise, intermediate and circumstantial stories. These categories and the proposed common pattern remained too schematized and restrictive for Dodd as well, however, since they remain–in much the same way as his study on the sermons of Acts–basically an outline or skeleton upon which the imaginative storyteller could drape the trappings of his particular story and never really arrives at an identifiable form as theological expression outside the formal strictures of the "sermon illustration" of Dibelius.

In turning then to a *history-of-tradition analysis* of the gospel appearance stories, therefore, we followed the general deliberations of these form-critics and especially the literary form analysis of Dodd but with a greater interest in their structure and motif elements as leading not just to an outline but rather to a form more closely identifiable with a *Gattung.* Thus, we began with the sometimes arduous task of demarcating tradition from redaction in order to lay bare the traditional matrix of the stories. Our conclusion to this stage of the analysis was that these stories in their pre-redactional form do, in fact, demonstrate a similar form of representation, which we then offered for cross section overview in the Text-Synopsis. We noted, moreover, that the similarities do not suggest that individual motifs were selected here and there to piece together a story form constructed more or less from an outline such as Dodd implies, but rather that they build a more comprehensive picture of particulars under subjection to an overriding, composite whole, whereby each aspect plays a role in the focal expression of the total narrative. Not isolated story elements gave rise to a more or less fixed pattern, but a unified story form with more or less constant motifs and themes appears to have been the warp and woof of this vehicle of expression from the very beginning. In short, they were *stories* and not story-constructs and as such they participated in a particular story *Gattung.*

These conclusions raised the questions: what origins can be determined for the *Gattung* and what can be said about its *Sitz im Leben*? To answer these questions we turned first to a history-of-religion comparison of the *Gattung.* After an investigation of appearance stories of deceased individuals elevated to the position of θεῖος ἀνήρ with a Hellenistic milieu we concluded that while formal parallels do indeed exist between this and the gospel appearance story form, essential, internal considerations led to the conclusion that contrary to popular opinion the Hellenistic backgrounds offer little help *in making precise* the actual origins of the gospel appearance story *Gattung.* We turned then to a consideration of the OT and Jewish backgrounds for possible analogies and came to the conclusion that such backgrounds do indeed provide a very fertile field of formal *and* essential parallels. We found that the OT knew of a separate "anthropomorphic" theophany representation–it appeared advisable under the present state of unrest in OT studies over the suitability of the term *Gattung* for the texts in question to avoid it–, which is to be distinguished from other forms of expressing Jahweh's self-revelation. In spite of the fact that the field was competitive this form of representation retained its integrity and tenacity throughout the OT history of transmission extending down to NT times in a handful of apocryphal and pseudepigraphal texts. Close scrutiny of the earlier OT form and that of the later form showed up certain basic alterations which led to the conclusion that while the outer form had been retained by those later texts they had in fact been placed in the service of a different statement intention. Through a comparison of these and those then in the Text-Synopsis to the gospel appearance story *Gattung* we came to the conclusion that the OT "anthropomorphic" stories came exceedingly close to the one in the gospels in both form and subject matter. These points of contact appeared in fact to be so evident that the conclusion became unavoidable that *some kind of direct relationship existed between them in the formation of the gospel appearance story Gattung.*

This observation about the intimate contact between them raises some final questions. How is one to conceive of the *Sitz im Leben,* its development against the historical and theological backdrop of primitive Christianity? And again, what can be said about the relationship between that which we have thus far been able to say from our analysis and the last step of a history-of-tradition analysis, even localization of ultimate origins? First of all, the recourse to a specific OT tradition must be made plausible, a matter which in general is of no great difficulty in the light of OT backgrounds evident so frequently in NT writings. Proof texts, play on various themes and indirect echoes out of the OT there reflect a familiarity with and life out of these backgrounds for the primitive Christian community in its earliest beginnings. The problem lies in lining up a specific dependence relationship between the two traditional strata. As was shown, no direct references in the one to the other are present so that the basis for the link must take place at correspondence on the conceptual level. What aspects of the thought worlds in those traditions could have united them? As was shown in general for *all* of the history-of-religion texts compared formal parallels were evident throughout; the formal expressions of an appearance of deity or divine man–frequently in connection with the problem of death–were common in the ancient world as a cross-cultural phenomenon. In this regard a formal use of an OT theophany representation would have had the advantage of being readily received and acknowledged in the context of primitive Christianity. The very ring of familiarity, however, in view of the great variety of subject matter communicated through the form would have made further qualification necessary before the specific intent of the form would have become precise. That the form would have been commented upon in both liturgical and homiletic circumstances is probable, but it is equally probable, however, that the particulars of the "anthropomorphic" form itself with their evident overlap with the OT theophany form would in part have been its own commentary. That is to say, the literary *Gattung* could speak a definitive word of its own on the intention behind its use.

This observation moves us perhaps a step closer to a plausible *Sitz im Leben* by raising the question of the direction of statement inherent to the gospel appearance story *Gattung*. We have noted on occasion above that an affirmation that the Lord was not dead but alive again does not cover the complexity of the theological intention of the appearance stories. Such is certainly resident there, as it is in the proclamation of the kerygmatic formula tradition as well, but this affirmation alone cannot supply the reason for the use of such a story form as this. The human situation of the primitive church must have been exceedingly difficult and complex: the task was to express an event without parallel in human history, understood as the eschatologically "New" in the Resurrection of Jesus. Moreover, in the light of the processes of gospel formation it was essential to anchor this expression in some form of continuity and identity with the appearance of the earthly Jesus fundamentally, above all in the particular aspect of the identity of the resurrected One with the crucified One. In other strata of resurrection traditions the necessity for graphic representation of this continuity was not as pre-eminent as here. In keeping then with a fundamental commitment to the belief that God through Jesus revealed himself in human form, which is anchored in the synoptic tradition of Jesus' earthly ministry, and in keeping with its christological implications which are variously bound up with faith in the God who revealed himself in the witness of the OT, a particular expression of the latter provided both the specific and personal encounter dimension of that revelation and the human form provided the fertile soil of analogy. That is to say, the OT "anthropomorphic" theophany stories combined graphic elements essential to the needs of an "anthropomorphic" expression of appearances of the risen Lord. That is not all, however. This much was readily available in a broad stream of contemporary religious thought. That *God* appears in this theophanic representation in human form is, as we saw in the Text-Synopsis, a key aspect of that representation, but in addition to the visual other aspects of the encounter, e.g., divine initiative in a crisis situation, the utter surprise and unpreparedness of the recipients, the comfort and assurances, the promises and the disclosures conveyed and the sending of consequence for the individual(s) and the larger body, the people of God, offered a comprehensive form ideal as vehicle of expression for the theological address of the *Gattung*. All of these factors made it possible, it would seem, for the primitive church to utilize this form of representation in its task of unprecedented scope and difficulty.

"Utilize" is a key expression here, because it would be an error to assume that OT texts were simply taken over, copied down. This is much too wooden and, as we saw above, variations within both complexes in relationship to one another as well as among themselves belie any such direct (artificial) view of outgrowth or accretion. That is to say, the impression the accounts convey is that they are both specific theological expressions and genuinely told and retold stories; they did not emerge as a construct from the desk of a scribe. Where a relationship is so fluid constant reflection upon the particular eschatological orientation of the gospel appearance stories must have been in the mind of the storyteller/writer. The gospel appearance stories emerge out of personal reflection as a direct synthesis of elements in tension with one another: a story form is readily available as conceptual possibility in the theophany accounts, but an encounter which resists telling in narrative, historical form tugs against the author's sense of propriety—just as in fact it had done for the authors of OT theophany stories as well. The form then becomes an approximation, which, however, in view of the need to express that Jesus "appeared," "reunited out of apparent tragedy," "turned his followers toward the world" and "put them in his service"—to suggest but a few of the directions of statement contained here which were constantly being reshaped and actualized in new contexts—was inevitable and a price paid willingly. This too, however, in the context of primitive Christianity, as for our own, is the nature of all theological statements.

This tension between the inadequacy of formal expression and the actual subject matter intended raises the final question of the relationship between the gospel appearance stories and the historicity of the Easter appearances themselves. This question must be raised and even though any conclusions here are purely tentative and must be the subject of further systematic reflection, we must state here in conclusion our perspective from impressions gathered through direct exegetical investigation of the texts.

The goal of our investigation was a history-of-tradition analysis with a focus on *Gattung* determination. That is, of course, a very limited line of questioning, but the potential of the method to participate in the discussion on the historicity question must not be underestimated. It has enabled us, for example, to see these stories more concretely and in greater depth perception as specific theological statements analogous to those of the OT "anthropomorphic" theophany representations. This observation in itself draws into question the adequacy of designations like "legend" and "myth" as accurate history-of-religion termini. As we have seen these designations are so heavily loaded in the history of research with historically negative connotations that their replacement with a more accurate history-of-religion category opens new possibilities by virtue of its comparable neutrality on the historical question as on others as well. Furthermore, critical dialogue with other perspectives on the relationship question within resurrection traditions led to the conclusion that the pre-redactional gospel appearance stories are dependent on none of them for their origin but constitute rather an independent stream of tradition. This means in regard to the historical question that they cannot be called late accretions without historical foundation. Even if their independence of other traditions cannot automatically be adduced as an argument in favor of their historicity, at least the question must be left open at that point. In all, one can be perhaps in view of these two factors more optimistic than has been heretofore the case so often that the solution to the historicity question lies inextricably united with the history-of-tradition question.

Our impressions on this question have been formed chiefly by our concentration upon *Gattung* determination and it is to be granted that further investigation of the traditional matrix of the appearance stories might yield further possibilities of contact with the human situation behind them. We have stressed, however, that these stories participate in a specific form as *theological statements* and the consequence of this radical tenacity in form seems to indicate that they are not primarily interested in or capable of delivering essentially historical information as eyewitness reports. They seem to resist probing inquiry into the "how did it happen question." This deals, of course, a severe blow to the parapsychological explanation of the appearance stories, because the vehicle of expression itself inherent to the *Gattung* closes the doors on all attempts to speculate about the frame of mind or general proclivity of the participants towards mental aberration. On the other hand, it must be asked if the determination of a specific form and stress upon the function of these stories as theological statements necessarily militate against any and all aspects of the historicity question. Although one can say that these stories give a confessional statement of meaning and witness on an experience or occurrence of revelation, the question is to be posed: can one gain access to the experience behind the confession in some form?

One could perhaps point to the occasional reference in our analysis to undercurrents and suggestions in both appearance and empty tomb accounts of the gospel tradition which might direct attention back to the personal recollection of persons allegedly involved as support for continuing a quest in this direction. Moreover, it could be argued that sheer literary compositions from an author's imagination, albeit even fabrications, are hardly thinkable in the historical context implied, and could be taken as further encouragement to follow up a search for the witnesses as persons. Yet, the witness appears to have been formulated in the tradition at no time in this way. From the very beginning of their formulation and transmission as tradition they were inseparably bound to the *diction* of the *Gattung* we have analyzed.

If this is indeed the case, what consequences does it have for the question of experience behind the confessional expression? Among the many suggestive possibilities one thing is clear: in comparison with the definite contours of address in the *Gattung* some other remnant of witness to the experience in the form of a report or the like was *for the tradition itself* of far less consequence and importance. In terms of a confrontation with the tradition then it would be a mistake to try to bypass the clear articulation of interest expressed in the *Gattung* with its placement of the appearances into this specific stream of witness to God's historical self-disclosure and to reach back gropingly into the shadows of uncertainty. As occurrences the appearances could not be retold in everyday language but only communicated as witness in a form of expression that approximated the nature of the encounter in the teller's meditative frame of reference. Accordingly, therefore, we would affirm that while the stories are not anti-historical as such, their choice of expression makes it impossible to understand them correctly outside the context of that choice. It would seem that the farthest point in the origins of the tradition to which we may reach back is to the *Gattung* itself which declared that the risen Lord encountered and re-established fellowship with his own and sent them out in his service. Affirming historicity of this kind, which is in keeping with the statement-intention of the *Gattung* itself, becomes both an exegetical conclusion and a statement of faith.

BIBLIOGRAPHY

A. Primary Sources

Achelis, H./J. Flemming, *Syrische Didaskalia* (TU, ed. W. Eltester and E. Klostermann, 25,2), Berlin, 1904.

Adlington, W. (trans.), *Apuleius, The Golden Ass. Being the Metamorphoses of Lucius Apuleius*, 1566, rev. by S. Gaselee (LCL), London, 1965.

Aland, K./E. Nestle (eds.), *Novum Testamentum Graece*, Stutt., 1963^{25}.

– /M. Black/B. Metzger/A. Wikgren/C.M. Martini (eds.), *The Greek New Testament*, Stutt., 1968^{2}.

– (ed.), *Synopsis Quattuor Evangeliorum*, Stutt., 1965^{3}.

Allen, T.W. (ed.), *Homeri, Ilias*, 3 vols., Oxford, 1931.

Barret, C.K. (ed.), *The New Testament Background: Selected Documents*, N.Y., 1961.

The Holy Bible (RSV), N.Y., 1946, 1952.

Cartlidge, D.R./D.L. Dungan (eds.), *Sourcebook of Texts for the Comparative Study of the Gospels*, Missoula, Mont., 1972^{2}.

Cary, E. (trans.), *Dionysius of Halicarnassus, The Roman Antiquities*, rev. by E. Spelman, vol. I (LCL), London, 1937.

Chadwick, H. (trans., intro. and notes), *Origen, Contra Celsum*, Cambridge, 1965^{2}.

Charles, R.H. (ed.), *The Apocrypha and Pseudepigrapha of the Old Testament*, 2 vols., Oxford, 1963(='13).

– (ed.), *The Greek Versions of the Testaments of the Twelve Patriarchs*, WB, Darmstadt, 1966^{3}.

Chrysostomi, Joannis, *Opera Omnia*, Tomi III and IX, Venetis, 1741.

Conybeare, F.C. (trans.), *Philostratus, The Life of Apollonius of Tyana*, 2 vols. (LCL), London, 1969(='12).

Delitzsch, F., *Hebrew New Testament*, London, 1889.

Delling, G. (ed.), *Antike Wundertexte* (KIT, 79), Berlin, 1960^{2}.

Feldman, L.H. (trans.), *Josephus, Antiquities of the Jews*, vol. IX (LCL), London, 1969.

Fiebig, P. (ed.), *Rabbinische Wundergeschichten des neutestamentlichen Zeitalters in vokalisiertem Text* (KIT, 78), Bonn, 1911.

Field, F. (*concinnavit, emendavit, et multis partibus auxit*), *Origenis Hexaplorum*, Tomus II, Oxford, 1875.

Gavorse, J. (trans.), *Suetonius, The Lives of the Twelve Caesars*, N.Y., 1931.

Gibson, M.D. (trans.), *The Didascalia Apostolorum*, London, 1903.

Harmon, A.M. (trans.), *Lucian, The Lover of Lies*, vol. III (LCL), London, 1960(='21), pp. 319-381.

– (trans.), *Lucian, The Passing of Peregrinus*, vol. V (LCL), London, 1962(='36), pp. 1-51.

Hennecke, E./W. Schneemelcher (eds.), *Neutestamentliche Apokryphen*, 2 vols., Tüb., (I) 1959^{3} and (II) 1964^{3}.

Henzen, G./I.B. de Rossi (eds.), *Corpus Inscriptionum Latinarum. Inscriptiones Urbis Romae Latinae*, vol. VI, 3, Berlin, 1886.

Hude, C. (ed.), *Herodoti, Historiae*, 2 vols. (OCT), Oxford, (I) 1960(='27) and (II) 1958(='27^{3}).

Jacoby, F. (ed.), *Fragmenta der griechischen Historiker*, 3 vols., Leiden, 1954-1969.

James, M.R. (ed.), *The Apocryphal New Testament*, Oxford, 1953.

– (ed.), *The Testament of Abraham*. Greek text with intro., notes; appendix of Extracts from the Arabic Version of the Testaments of Abraham, Isaac and Jacob by W.E. Barnes (TSt., II, 2), Cambridge, 1892 (repr. Nendeln, Liechtenstein, 1967).

Jones, W.H.S. (trans.), *Pausanias, Descriptions of Greece*, vol. III (LCL), London, 1966.

Kittel, R. (ed.), *Biblia Hebraica*, Stutt., 1961^{3}.

Koetschau, P. (ed.), *Origenis, Werke: Die Schrift vom Martyrium, I-IV: Gegen Celsus*, vol. I, Leipzig, 1899.

Kraft, R.A./A.E. Purintun (eds.), *Paraleipomena Jeremiou* (TT, 1, Pseudepigrapha Series, 1: SBL), Missoula, Mont., 1972.

de Lagarde, P. (ed.), *Didaskalia Apostolorum Syricae*, Gött., 1911.
Lake, K. (trans.), *The Apostolic Fathers*, 2 vols. (LCL), London, 1959(='12 and '13).
Leipoldt, J./W. Grundmann (eds.), *Umwelt des Urchristentums*, 3 vols., Berlin, 1967.
Lohse, E. (ed.), *Die Texte aus Qumran*, Darmstadt, 1964.
Miller, F.J. (trans.), *Ovid, Metamorphoses*, vol. III (LCL), London, 1971(='21[2]).
Mras, K., (ed.), *Eusebius, Werke: Die Praeparatio Evangelica* (*Die griechisch christlichen Schriftsteller der ersten Jahrhunderte*, VIII, 1), Berlin, 1954.
Müller, C. and Th. (eds.), *Fragmenta Historicorum Graecorum*, Paris, 1841-1870 (Lat. trans. 1966-67).
Murray, A.T. (trans.), *Homer, The Iliad*, 2 vols. (LCL), London, (I) 1971(='24) and (II) 1967 (='25).
Perrin, B. (trans.), *Plutarch, Parallel Lives of Famous Greeks and Romans, I: Theseus and Romulus, Lycurgus and Numa, Solon and Publicola*, vol. I (LCL), London, 1967.
Preuschen, E., *Antilegomena. Die Reste der außerkanonischen Evangelien und urchristlichen Überlieferung*, Gieszen, 1905[2].
Rießler, P. (trans.), *Altjüdisches Schrifttum außerhalb der Bibel*, WB, Darmstadt, 1966.
Seidensticker, P. (ed.), *Zeitgenössische Texte zur Osterbotschaft der Evangelien* (StBSt., 27), Stutt., 1967.
Thackery, H.S.J. (trans.), *Josephus, Antiquities of the Jews*, vol. V (LCL), London, 1966.
Warmington, E.H. (trans.), *Ennius, Annals* (*Remains of Old Latin*, LCL), London, 1935.
Wikgren, A./E.C. Colwell/R. Marcus (eds.), *Hellenistic Greek Texts*, Chicago, 1958(='47).
Whiston, W. (trans.), *Josephus, Antiquities of the Jews*, Phil., 1957.
Vaganay, L. (ed.), *L'évangile de Pierre*, Paris, 1930.

B. Reference Works

Baird, J.A. (ed.), *A Critical Concordance to the Synoptic Gospels* (The Computer Bible, eds. J.A. Baird and D.N. Freedman, 1), Wooster, Ohio, 1971.
Bauer, W., *Griechisch-Deutsches Wörterbuch zu den Schriften des Neuen Testaments und der urchristlichen Literatur*, Berlin, 1963[5].
Billerbeck, P. and Strack, H.L., *Kommentar zum Neuen Testament aus Talmud und Midrasch*, Bd. I-V, Mü., 1922-28 (Bd. V [Index], 1956 and Bd. VI [Index], 1961).
Blass, F. and Debrunner, A., *Grammatik des neutestamentlichen Griechisch*, Gött., 1954[9].
Dalman, G., *Grammatik des jüdisch-palästinischen Aramäisch und aramäische Dialektproben*, Darmstadt, 1960(='05[2]).
Gesenius, W., *Hebräisches und aramäisches Handwörterbuch über das Alte Testament*, Berlin, 1954(='15[17]).
Hatch, E. and Redpath, H.A., *A Concordance to the Septuagint and the Other Greek Versions of the Old Testament*, 2 vols., Graz, 1954.
Keep, R.P., *A Homeric Dictionary* (based on G. Autenrieth), N.Y., 1895.
Kroh, P., *Lexikon der antiken Autoren*, Stutt., 1972.
Kuhn, K.G. (ed.), *Konkordanz zu den Qumrantexten*, Gött., 1960.
Lewis, C.T. and Short, C., *A Latin Dictionary*, Oxford, 1962.
Liddell, H.J. and Scott, R., *Greek-English Lexicon*, new edition rev. and augmented by H.S. Jones to 1 vol., Oxford, 1958[9](='40). *Supplement*, ed. E.A. Barber, Oxford, 1968.
Lisowsky, G., *Konkordanz zum hebräischen Alten Testament*, Stutt., 1958.
Metzger, B.M., *A Textual Commentary on the Greek New Testament*, London, 1971.
Morgenthaler, R., *Statistik des neutestamentlichen Wortschatzes*, Frankfurt, 1958.
Moulton, J.H., *A Grammar of New Testament Greek*, vol. I (Prolegomena), Edinburgh, 1957 (='08[3]).
– and Howard, W.F., *A Grammar of New Testament Greek*, vol. II (Accidence and Word Formation with an appendix on Semitisms in the NT), Edinburgh, 1956(='29).
– and Turner, N., *A Grammar of New Testament Greek*, vol. III (Syntax), Edinburgh, 1963.
– and Milligan, G., *The Vocabulary of the Greek Testament*, London, 1957(='30).

Moulton, W.F. and Geden, A.S., *A Concordance to the Greek Testament*, Edinburgh, 1957 (='26[3]).
Powell, J.E., *A Lexicon to Herodotus* (Olms Paperbacks, 26), Hildesheim, 1966[2].
Robertson, A.T., *A Grammar of the Greek New Testament in the Light of Historical Research*, Nashville, Tenn., 1934.
Rose, H.J., *A Handbook of Greek Mythology*, London, 1972(='58[6]).
Rost, L., *Einleitung in die alttestamentlichen Apokryphen und Pseudepigraphen einschließlich der großen Qumran-Handschriften*, Heidelberg, 1971.

C. Monographs, Commentaries and Articles

Achtemeier, P.J., "Toward the Isolation of Pre-Markan Miracle Catenae," *JBL*, 89 (1970), pp. 265-291.
– "The Origin and Function of the Pre-Markan Miracle Catenae," *JBL*, 91 (1972), pp. 198-221.
– "Gospel Miracle Tradition and the Divine Man," *Int*, 26 (1972), pp. 174-197.
Aland, K., "Der wiedergefundene Markusschluß? Eine Bemerkung zur textkritischen Arbeit," *ZThK*, 67 (1970), pp. 3-13.
Albertz, M., "Zur Formgeschichte der Auferstehungsberichte," *ZNW*, 21 (1922), pp. 259-269.
Allen, E.L., "The Lost Kerygma," *NTS*, 3 (1957), pp. 349-353.
Allen, W.C., *A Critical and Exegetical Commentary on the Gospel According to St. Matthew* (ICC), Edinburgh, 1912[3].
Almquist, H., *Plutarch und das Neue Testament. Ein Beitrag zum Corpus Hellenisticum Novi Testamenti* (ASNU, ed. A. Fridrichsen, 15), Uppsala, 1946.
Anderson, H., "The Easter Witness of the Evangelists," *The New Testament in Historical and Contemporary Perspective* (Fst. G.H.C. MacGregor, eds. H. Anderson and W. Barclay), Oxford, 1965, pp. 35-55.
– *Jesus and Christian Origins*, N.Y., 1964.
Angus, S., *The Religious Quests of the Graeco-Roman World. A Study in the Historical Background of Early Christianity*, N.Y., 1967(='29).
Annand, R., "'He was seen of Cephas.' A Suggestion about the first Resurrection Appearance of Peter," *SJTh*, 11 (1958), pp. 180-187.
Auer, E.G., *Der dritte Tag*, Metzingen, Württ., 1970.
Bailey, J.A., *The Traditions Common to the Gospels of Luke and John* (Suppl. NovTest, 7), Leiden, 1963.
Baird, J.A., "Genre Analysis as a Method of Historical Criticism," *SBL Proceedings* (LA), II (1972), pp. 385-411.
Balz, H.R., "*τεσσεράκοντα*," *ThW*, VIII, pp. 134-139.
– "Furcht vor Gott?," *EvTh*, 29 (1969), pp. 626-644.
– *Methodische Probleme der neutestamentlichen Christologie* (WMANT, 25), Neukirchen, 1967.
Bammel, E., "Herkunft und Funktion der Traditionselemente in 1 Kor. 15,1-11," *ThZ*, 11 (1955), pp. 401-419.
Barr, J., "The Meaning of 'Mythology' in Relation to the Old Testament," *VT*, 9 (1959), pp. 1-10.
– "Theophany and Anthropomorphism in the Old Testament," *Suppl. VT*, 8 (1960), pp. 31-38.
– *The Semantics of Biblical Language*, Oxford, 1961.
Barrett, C.K., *The Gospel According to St. John. An Introduction with Commentary and Notes on the Greek Text*, London, 1960.
Barth, G., "Das Gesetzesverständnis des Evangelisten Matthäus," *Überlieferung und Auslegung im Matthäusevangelium* (G. Bornkamm, G. Barth and H.J. Held), Neukirchen, 1961[2], pp. 54-154.
Barth, M., *Der Augenzeuge. Eine Untersuchung über die Wahrnehmung des Menschensohnes durch die Apostel*, Zürich, 1946.
Bartsch, H.-W., "Parusieerwartung und Osterbotschaft," *EvTh*, 7 ('47/'48), pp. 115ff., now in *Entmythologisierende Auslegung. Ges. Aufs.* (Theol. Beiträge, 26), Hamburg-Bergstedt, 1962, pp. 61-69.

Bartsch, H.-W., "Die Passions- und Ostergeschichten bei Matthäus," *Basileia* (Fst. W. Freytag), Stutt., 1959, pp. 27ff., now in *Entmythologisierende Auslegung. Ges. Aufs.* (Theol. Beiträge, 26), Hamburg-Bergstedt, 1962, pp. 80-92.
– "Zum Problem der Parusieverzögerung bei den Synoptikern," *EvTh*, 19 (1959), pp. 116f., now in *Entmythologisierende Auslegung. Ges. Aufs.* (Theol. Beiträge, 26), Hamburg-Bergstedt, 1962, pp. 69-80.
– "Die Argumentation des Paulus in 1 Kor 15,3-11," *ZNW*, 55 (1964), pp. 261-274.
– "Der Schluß des Markusevangeliums. Ein überlieferungsgeschichtliches Problem," *ThZ*, 27 (1971), pp. 241-254.
– *Das Auferstehungszeugnis. Sein historisches und sein theologisches Problem* (ThF, 41), Hamburg-Bergstedt, 1965.
Bater, R.R., "Towards a More Biblical View of the Resurrection," *Int*, 23 (1969), pp. 47-65.
Baudissin, W.W., "'Gott schauen' in der alttestamentlichen Religion," *ARW*, 18 (1915), pp. 173-239.
Baur, F.Chr., *Apollonius von Tyana und Christus. Ein Beitrag zur Religionsgeschichte der ersten Jahrhunderte nach Christus*, Hildesheim, 1966(=1876).
Beare, F.W., "Sayings of the Risen Jesus in the Synoptic Tradition: an inquiry into their origin and significance," *Christian History and Interpretation* (Studies Presented to John Knox, ed. W.R. Farmer *et al.*), Cambridge, 1967, pp. 161-181.
– "Concerning Jesus of Nazareth," *JBL*, 87 (1968), pp. 125-135.
– *The Earliest Records of Jesus* (A Companion to the Huck-Lietzmann Synopsis), Oxford, 1964.
Benoit, P., O.P., "Marie-Magdeleine et les Disciples au Tombeau selon Joh 20,1-18," *Judentum, Urchristentum, Kirche* (Fst. J. Jeremias), Berlin, 1964, pp. 141-152.
– *The Passion and Resurrection of Jesus Christ*, trans. by B. Weatherhead, N.Y., 1969. (Originally, *Passion et Résurrection du Seigneur*, Paris, 1966.)
Benz, E., *Die Vision. Erfahrungsformen und Bilderwelt*, Stutt., 1969.
Bertram, G., "Die Himmelfahrt Jesu vom Kreuz aus und der Glaube an seine Auferstehung," *Fst. A. Deissmann*, Tüb., 1927, pp. 187-217.
Betz, H.D., "Jesus as Divine Man," *Jesus and the Historian* (Essays in Honor of E.C. Colwell, ed. T. Trotter), Phil., 1968 , pp. 114-133.
– "Eine Christus-Aretalogie bei Paulus (2 Kor 12,7-10)," *ZThK*, 66 (1969), pp. 288-305.
– "Ursprung und Wesen christlichen Glaubens nach der Emmauslegende (Lk 24,13-32)," *ZNW*, 66 (1969), pp. 7-21, also, "The Origin and Nature of Christian Faith According to the Emmaus Legend (Luke 24:13-32), *Int*, 23 (1969), pp. 32-46.
– *Lukian von Samosata und das Neue Testament. Religionsgeschichtliche und paränetische Parallelen. Ein Beitrag zum Corpus Hellenisticum Novi Testamenti* (TU, eds. W. Eltester and E. Klostermann, 76), Berlin, 1961.
– *Nachfolge und Nachahmung Jesu Christi im Neuen Testament* (BHTh, ed. G. Ebeling, 37), Tüb., 1967.
Betz, O., "Die Vision des Paulus im Tempel von Jerusalem. Apg 22,17-21 als Beitrag zur Deutung des Damaskuserlebnisses," *Verborum Veritas* (Fst. G. Stählin), Wuppertal, 1970, pp. 113-123.
– "The Concept of the so-called 'Divine Man' in Mark's Christology," *Studies in New Testament and Early Christian Literature* (Essays in Honor of A.P. Wikgren, ed. D.E. Aune), Leiden, 1972, pp. 229-240.
Bickermann, E., "Das leere Grab," *ZNW*, 23 (1924), pp. 281-292.
Bieler, L., ΘΕΙΟΣ ΑΝΗΡ. *Das Bild des "göttlichen Menschen" in Spätantike und Frühchristentum*, 2 vols., Wien, (I) 1935, (II) 1936.
Black, M., *An Aramaic Approach to the Gospels* (with an appendix on the Son of Man by G. Vermes), Oxford, 1967³.
Blank, J., *Paulus und Jesus. Eine theologische Grundlegung* (StANT, 18), Mü., 1968.
Bligh, J., S.J., "Scripture Reading. Matching Passages, 3: The Resurrection Narratives," *The Way, A Quarterly Review of Christian Spirituality*, 9 (1969), pp. 148-161.
Blinzler, J., *Johannes und die Synoptiker. Ein Forschungsbericht* (StBSt, 5), Stutt., 1965.
Bode, E.L., *The First Easter Morning. The Gospel Accounts of the Women's Visit to the Tomb of Jesus* (AnBibl, 45), Rome, 1970.
Böcher, O., *Dämonenfurcht und Dämonenabwehr. Ein Beitrag zur Vorgeschichte der christlichen Taufe* (BWANT, 90), Stutt., 1970.
– *Christus Exorcista. Dämonismus und Taufe im Neuen Testament* (BWANT, 96), Stutt., 1972.

Boismard, M.E., "Le chapître XXI de saint Jean. Essai de critique littéraire," *RB*, 54 (1947), pp. 473-501.
Boman, T., *Die Jesus-Überlieferung im Lichte der neueren Volkskunde*, Gött., 1967.
Bornkamm, G., "Die Sturmstillung im Matthäusevangelium," *Überlieferung und Auslegung im Matthäusevangelium* (G. Bornkamm, G. Barth, H.J. Held), Neukirchen, 1961², pp. 48-53.
– "Die Theologie Bultmanns in der neueren Diskussion. Literaturbericht zum Problem der Entmytholigisierung und Hermeneutik," *ThR*(NF), 29 (1963), pp. 33-141, now in *Geschichte und Glaube. Ges. Aufs.*, III, Mü., 1968, pp. 173-275.
– "Der Auferstandene und der Irdische. Mt 28,16-30," *Zeit und Geschichte* (Fst. R. Bultmann, ed. E. Dinkler), Tüb., 1964, pp. 171-191.
Bousset, W., *Kyrios Christos. Geschichte des Christusglaubens von den Anfängen des Christentums bis Irenaeus*, Gött., 1967⁶(='21²).
Bouwman, G., *Das dritte Evangelium, Einübung in die formgeschichtliche Methode*, Düss., 1968.
Bowra, C.M., "Simonides," *OCD*, London, 1961(='49), p. 840.
Branton, R., "Resurrection in the Early Church," *Early Christian Origins* (Studies in Honor of H.R. Willoughby, ed. A. Wikgren), Chicago, 1961, pp. 35-47.
Braun, H., "Zur Terminologie der Acta von der Auferstehung Jesu," *ThLZ*, 77 (1952), cols. 533-536.
– "Der Sinn der neutestamentlichen Christologie," *ZThK*, 54 (1957), pp. 341-377, now in *Gesammelte Studien zum NT und seiner Umwelt*, Tüb., 1962, pp. 243-282.
– "Die Bedeutung der Qumranfunde für die Frage nach dem Verhältnis des historischen Jesus zum kerygmatischen Christus," *Der historische Jesus und der kerygmatische Christus*, eds. H. Ristow and K. Matthiae, Berlin-Ost, 1964, pp. 142-148.
– "Vom Verstehen des Neuen Testaments," *Glauben heute. Ein Lesebuch zur evangelischen Theologie der Gegenwart* (Stundenbuch, ed. G. Otto, 48), Hamburg, 1965, pp. 153-174.
– *Jesus* (TTh, ed. J. Schultz, 1), Stutt., 1969².
Broer, I., "Zur heutigen Diskussion der Grabesgeschichte," *BuL*, 10 (1969), pp. 40-52.
– *Die Urgemeinde und das Grab Jesu: Eine Analyse der Grablegungsgeschichte im Neuen Testament* (StANT, 31), Mü., 1972.
Brown, R.E., *The Gospel According to John*, 2 vols. (Anchor, eds. W.F. Albright and D.N. Freedman), London, 1971.
Brun, L., "Zur Kompositionstecknik des Lukasevangeliums," *SO*, 9 (1930), pp. 38-50.
– "Die Berufung der ersten Jünger Jesu in der evangelischen Tradition," *SO*, 11 (1932), pp. 35-54.
– *Die Auferstehung Christi in der urchristlichen Ueberlieferung*, Oslo, 1925.
Buitkamp, J., *Die Auferstehungsvorstellungen in den Qumrantexten und ihr alttestamentlicher, apokryphischer, pseudepigraphischer und rabbinischer Hintergrund* (Diss.), Groningen, 1965.
Bultmann, R., "Karl Barth, 'Die Auferstehung der Toten,'" *ThBl*, 5 (1926), pp. 1-14, now in *Glauben und Verstehen. Ges. Aufs.*, I, Tüb., 1961⁴(='33), pp. 38-64.
– "Untersuchungen zum Johannesevangelium," *ZNW*, 27 (1928), pp. 113-163 and 29 (1930), pp. 169-192, now in *Exegetica, Ges. Aufs.*, Tüb., 1967, pp. 124-197.
– "Urchristentum und Religionsgeschichte," *ThR*(NF), 4 (1932), pp. 1-21.
– "L. Bieler, Theios Anēr I.II (Review)," *ZKG*, 56, III.F.7 (1937), pp. 640-643.
– "Neues Testament und Mythologie. Das Problem der Entmythologisierung der neutestamentlichen Verkündigung," *Kerygma und Mythos*, I (ed. H.-W. Bartsch), Hamburg, 1948, pp. 15-53 (originally "Offenbarung und Heilsgeschehen: II Neues Testament und Mythologie" [BEvTh, 7 (1941)]; Eng. trans. by R.H. Fuller, "New Testament and Mythology," *Kerygma and Myth*, N.Y., 1961['53], pp. 1-44).
– "Ursprung und Sinn der Typologie als hermeneutischer Methode," *Pro Regno Pro Sanctuario* (Fst. G. van der Leeuw), Nijkerk, Holland, 1950, pp. 89-100 and *ThLZ*, 75 (1950), cols. 205-212, and now in *Exegetica. Ges. Aufs.* ed. E. Dinkler, Tüb., 1967, pp. 369-380.
– "Die christliche Hoffnung und das Problem der Entmythologisierung," *Die christliche Hoffnung und das Problem der Entmythologisierung* (G. Bornkamm, R. Bultmann, F.K. Schumann), Stutt., 1954, now in *Glauben und Verstehen. Ges. Aufs.*, III, Tüb., 1960.
– "Das Verhältnis der urchristlichen Christusbotschaft zum historischen Jesus" (SAH, 3), 1960, now in *Exegetica. Ges. Aufs.*, ed. E. Dinkler, Tüb., 1967, pp. 445-469.
– "Die Erforschung der synoptischen Evangelien," *Aus der Welt der Religion* (NF), 1, Berlin, 1961⁴, pp. 7-51, now in *Glauben und Verstehen. Ges. Aufs.*, IV, Tüb., 1965, pp. 1-41.

Bultmann, R., "Zum Problem der Entmythologisierung," *Kerygma und Mythos*, VI, 1 (Entmythologisierung und existentiale Interpretation), Hamburg, 1963, pp. 19-27, now in *Glauben und Verstehen. Ges. Aufs.*, IV, Tüb., 1965, pp. 128-137.
– and D. Lührmann, "φαίνω (etc.)," *ThW*, IX, pp. 1-11.
– *Das Evangelium des Johannes* (Meyer, II), Gött., 1968[19](='41[10]), Ergänzungsheft, 1968.
– *Jesus Christ and Mythology* (Ger. trans., *Jesus Christus und die Mythologie* [Stundenbuch, ed. G. Otto, 47], Hamburg, 1964, now in *Glauben und Verstehen. Ges. Aufs.*, IV., Tüb., 1965, pp. 141-189), N.Y., 1958.
– *Theologie des Neuen Testaments*, Tüb., 1968[6].
– *Die Geschichte der synoptischen Tradition*, Gött., 1970[8](='31[2]), Ergänzungsheft, 1971[4].
Burkill, T.A., "Mark 3,7-12 and the Alleged Dualism in the Evangelist's Miracle Material," *JBL*, 87 (1968), pp. 409-417.
Cadbury, H.J., "Luke: Translator or Author?," *AJTh*, 24 (1920), pp. 436-455.
– "Lexical Notes on Luke - Acts. I," *JBL*, 44 (1925), pp. 214-227.
– "Lexical Notes on Luke - Acts. III. Luke's Interest in Lodging," *JBL*, 45 (1926), pp. 305-322.
– *The Making of Luke - Acts*, London, 1958.
von Campenhausen, H., *Tradition und Leben, Kräfte der Kirchengeschichte*, Tüb., 1960.
– *Der Ablauf der Osterereignisse und das leere Grab*, Heidelberg, 1966[3].
Carlston, C.E., "Transfiguration and Resurrection," *JBL*, 80 (1961), pp. 233-240.
Cary, M., *A History of the Greek World 323-146 B.C.* (Methuen, ed. M. Cary, 3), N.Y., 1932.
Cassian, B., "John XXI," *NTS*, 3 ('56/'57), pp. 132-136.
Chadwick, H., "Origen, Celsus, and the Resurrection of the Body," *HThR*, 41 (1948), pp. 83-102.
Charlot, J., *The Construction of the Formula in 1 Corinthians 15,3-15* (Diss.), Mü., 1968.
Clark, N., *Interpreting the Resurrection*, London, 1967.
Clemen, C., *Religionsgeschichtliche Erklärung des Neuen Testaments. Die Abhängigkeit des ältesten Christentums von nicht jüdischen Religionen und philosophischen Systemen*, Gießen, 1924[2].
Collison-Morley, L., *Greek and Roman Ghost Stories*, Chicago, 1967(='12).
Conzelmann, H., "Zur Analyse der Bekenntnisformel 1 Kor 15,3-5," *EvTh*, 25 (1965), pp. 1-11.
– "φῶς (etc.)," *ThW*, IX, pp. 302-349.
– *Grundriß der Theologie des Neuen Testaments* (Einführung in die evang. Theol., 2), Mü., 1968[2].
– *Geschichte des Urchristentums, Grundrisse zum Neuen Testament* (NTD, Ergänzungsreihe 5), Gött., 1969.
– *Die Apostelgeschichte* (HNT, ed. H. Lietzmann, 7), Tüb., 1972[2].
Cornelius, F., *Die Glaubwürdigkeit der Evangelien*, Mü., 1969.
Crenshaw, J.L., "Amos and the Theophanic Tradition," *ZAW*, 80 (1968), pp. 203-215.
Cribbs, F.L., "A Reassessment of the Date of Origin and the Destination of the Gospel of John," *JBL*, 89 (1970), pp. 38-55.
– "St. Luke and the Johannine Tradition," *JBL*, 90 (1971), pp. 422-450.
Cullmann, O., "The Breaking of the Bread and the Resurrection Appearances," *Essays on the Lord's Supper*, ed. by F.J. Leenhardt and O. Cullmann, trans. by J.G. Davies, Richmond, Va., 1958, pp. 8-16. (Originally "La signification de la Sainte-Cène dans le christianisme primitif," *RHPhR*, 16 (1936), pp. 1-22; Ger. in *Oscar Cullmann. Vorträge und Aufsätze 1925-1962* (ed. K. Fröhlich), Tüb., 1966, pp. 505-523.)
– *Urchristentum und Gottesdienst*, Zürich, 1950.
– *Die Christologie des Neuen Testaments*, Tüb., 1957 (Eng. ed., NT Library, Phil., 1963[2] [='59]).
– *Petrus. Jünger, Apostel, Märtyrer* (Siebenstern-Taschenbuch, 90/91), Mü., 1967(='60[2]).
Cumont, F., *The Oriental Religions in Roman Paganism*, N.Y., 1956(='11).
Curtis, K.P.G., "Three Points of Contact between Matthew and John in the Burial and Resurrection Narratives," *JThS*, 23 (1972), pp. 440-444.
Dahl, N.A., "The Story of Abraham in Luke-Acts," *Studies in Luke-Acts* (Essays presented in Honor of P. Schubert, eds. L.E. Keck and J.L. Martyn), London, 1968, pp. 139-158.
Davies, J.G., "Factors Leading to the Emergence of Belief in the Resurrection of the Flesh," *JThS*, 23 (1972), pp. 448-455.
Davies, W.E., *The Origin and Development of Old Testament and Inter-Testamental Belief Regarding Life after Death* (Diss.), Boston Grad. School, 1957.
Deissmann, A., *Licht vom Osten. Das Neue Testament und die neuentdeckten Texte der hellenistisch-römischen Welt*, Tüb., 1923[4].

Delorme, J., "Résurrection et Tombeau de Jésus: Marc 16,1-8 dans la tradition évangélique," *La Résurrection du Christ et L'Exégèse Moderne*, Paris, 1969, pp. 105-151.
– "Luc V.1-11: Analyse Structurale et Histoire de la Rédaction," *NTS*, 18 ('71/'72), pp. 331-350.
Dembowski, H., "Jesus Christus - Herr der Götter," *EvTh*, 29 (1969), pp. 572-588.
Descamps, A., "La structure des récits évangéliques de la résurrection," *Bb*, 40 (1959), pp. 726-741.
Deubner, L., *De incubatione*, Leipzig, 1900.
Dhanis, E., S.I., "L'ensevelissement de Jésus et la visite au tombeau dans l'évangile de saint Marc (Mc., XV, 40-XVI,8)," *Greg*, 39 (1958), pp. 367-410.
Dibelius, M., "Die alttestamentlichen Motive in der Leidensgeschichte des Petrus- und des Johannes-Evangeliums," *Abhandlungen zur semitischen Religionskunde und Sprachwissenschaft* (Fst. W.W. Grafen von Baudissin, eds. W. Frankenberg and F. Kücher, *ZAW*, Bh. 33), Gießen, 1918, pp. 125-150.
– *Die Formgeschichte des Evangeliums*, ed. G. Bornkamm, Tüb., 1961[4].
Dietrich, W., *Das Petrusbild der lukanischen Schriften* (BWANT [V.F], eds. K.H. Rengstorf and L. Rost, 14), Stutt., 1972.
Dodd, C.H., "Matthew and Paul," *New Testament Studies*, Manchester, 1953, pp. 53-66. (Originally *ET*, 58 [1947]).
– "The Appearances of the Risen Christ: An Essay in Form-Criticism of the Gospels," *Studies in the Gospels* (Essays in Memory of R.H. Lightfoot, ed. D.E. Nineham), Oxford, 1957, pp. 9-35, now in his *More New Testament Studies*, London, 1968, pp. 102-133.
– *The Apostolic Preaching and its Developments*, N.Y., 1962(='36).
– *Historical Tradition in the Fourth Gospel*, Cambridge, 1963.
Dölger, F.J., *Ichthys, II: Der Heilige Fisch in den antiken Religionen und im Christentum*, Münster, 1922.
Dornseiff, F., "Lukas der Schriftsteller," *ZNW*, 35 (1936), pp. 129-155.
Doty, W.G., "The Concept of Genre in Literary Analysis," *SBL Proceedings* (LA), 2 (1972), pp. 413-448.
Drews, A., *Die Christusmythe*, vol. I and II, Jena, 1910[3].
Dupont, J., O.S.B., "The Meal at Emmaus," *The Eucharist in the New Testament – A Symposium* (J. Delorme, P. Benoit O.P., M.E. Boismard O.P., J. Dupont O.S.B., D. Mollat S.J.) trans. by E.M. Stewart, London, 1965, pp. 105-121. (Originally, "Les pélerins d'Emmaüs [Luc, XXIV, 13-35]," *Miscellanea Biblica B. Ubach* [Scripta et Documenta, I] Montserrat, 1953, pp. 349-374.)
– "Ressuscité 'Le Troisième Jour'," *Bb*, 40 (1959), pp. 742-761.
– "ἀνελήμφθη (Act. I.2)," *NTS*, 8 ('61/'62), pp. 154-157.
– *The Sources of Acts – The Present Position*, trans. by K. Pond, London, 1964. (Originally, *Les Sources du Livre des Actes*, Belgium [Editions Desclée de Brouwer S.A., Bruges, n.d.]).
Ehrhardt, A., "The Disciples of Emmaus," *NTS*, 10 ('63/'64), pp. 182-201.
– "Emmaus, Romulus und Apollonius," *Mullus* (Fst. Th. Klauser, JbAC, ErgBd 1), Münster, 1964, pp. 93-99.
Ehrlich, E.L., *Der Traum im Alten Testament* (BZAW, 73), Berlin, 1953.
Eitrem, S., "Zur Apotheose," *SO*, 10 (1932), pp. 31-56, 11 (1932), pp. 11-34, 15/16 (1936), pp. 111-137.
Elliot, J.K., "The Text and Language of the Endings to Mark's Gospel," *ThZ*, 27 (1971), pp. 255-262.
Ellis, E.E., "Die Funktion der Eschatologie im Lukasevangelium," *ZThK*, 66 ('69/'70), pp. 387-402.
– "Midraschartige Züge in den Reden der Apostelgeschichte," *ZNW*, 62 (1971), pp. 94-104.
Ellis, I.P., "'But Some Doubted'," *NTS*, 14 ('67/'68), pp. 574-580.
Esser, D., *Formgeschichtliche Studien zur hellenistischen und zur frühchristlichen Literatur unter besonderer Berücksichtigung der vita Apollonii des Philostrat und der Evangelien* (Diss.), Bonn, 1969.
Evans, C.F., "'I Will Go Before You Into Galilee'," *JThS*(n.s.), 5 (1954), pp. 3-18.
– *Resurrection and the New Testament* (StBTh, 2nd Series, 12), London, 1970.
Farnell, L.R., *Greek Hero Cults and Ideas of Immortality*, Oxford, 1970(='21).
Fascher, E., "Anastasis-Resurrectio-Auferstehung. Eine programmatische Studie zum Thema 'Sprache und Offenbarung'," *ZNW*, 40 (1941), pp. 166-229.

Fascher, E., "Die Osterberichte und das Problem einer biblischen Hermeneutik," *Der historische Jesus und der kerygmatische Christus*, eds. H. Ristow and K. Matthiae, Berlin, 1960, pp. 200-207.
Ferrar, A.M., *A Study in St. Mark*, London, 1951.
Feuillet, A., P.S.S., "La Recherche du Christ dans la Nouvelle Alliance d'après la Christophanie de Jo. 20,11-18. Comparaison avec Cant. 3,1-4 l'épisode des Pélerins d'Emmaüs," *L'Homme Devant Dieu* (Mélanges offerts au père Henri de Lubac. Exégèse et Patristique, Théologie 56), Aubier, 1963, pp. 93-112.
Fiebig, P., *Jüdische Wundergeschichten des neutestamentlichen Zeitalters unter besonderer Berücksichtigung ihres Verhältnisses zum Neuen Testament bearbeitet. Ein Beitrag zum Streit um die "Christusmythe,"* Tüb., 1911.
– *Der Erzählungsstil der Evangelien im Lichte des rabbinischen Erzählungsstils untersucht, zugleich ein Beitrag zum Streit um die "Christusmythe"* (UNT, ed. H. Windisch, 11), Leipzig, 1925.
Field, F., *Notes on the Translation of the New Testament*, Cambridge, 1899.
Finegan, J., *Die Überlieferung der Leidens- und Auferstehungsgeschichte Jesu*, Gießen, 1934.
– *Mark of the Taw*, Richmond, Va., 1972.
Foakes-Jackson, F.J., *The Acts of the Apostles*, (Moffatt), London, 1931.
– and Lake, K., *The Beginnings of Christianity, Part I* (The Acts of the Apostles), vols. I-V (vol. III, J.H. Ropes, vols. IV and V, K. Lake and H.J. Cadbury), Grand Rapids, Mich., 1966. (originally London, 1920-33).
Foerster, W. and Quell, D.G., "κύριος," *ThW*, III, pp. 1038-1098.
Fortna, R.T., *The Gospel of Signs. A Reconstruction of the Narrative Source Underlying the Fourth Gospel* (SNTSMS, 11), Cambridge, 1970.
Foulkes, F., "Some Aspects on St. Paul's Treatment of the Resurrection of Christ in 1 Corinthians XV," *ABR*, 16 (1968), pp. 15-30.
Freed, E.D., "Variations in the Language and Thought of John," *ZNW*, 55 (1964), pp. 167-197.
Fridrichsen, A., "Zum Stil des paulinischen Peristasenkatalogs 2 Cor. 11,23ff," *SO*, 7 (1928), pp. 26-29.
– "Peristasenkatalog und Res Gestae. Nachtrag zu 2 Cor. 11,23ff," *SO*, 8 (1929), pp. 78-82.
– "Sprachliches und Stilistisches zum Neuen Testament," *Kungl. Humansitiska Vetenskaps-Samfundet* (I), Uppsala, 1943, pp. 24-36.
Friedrich, G., "Die Auferstehung Jesu, eine Tat Gottes oder ein Interpretament der Jünger?," *KuD*, 17 (1971), pp. 153-187.
– "Die Bedeutung der Auferweckung Jesu nach Aussagen des Neuen Testaments," *ThZ*, 27 (1971), pp. 305-324.
von Fritz, K., "Peregrinus (Proteus)," *PW*, 19, 1, cols. 656-663.
Fuchs, C. and Künneth, W., *Die Auferstehung Christi von den Toten (Dokumentation eines Streitgesprächs*, ed. Chr. Möller), Neukirchen, 1973.
Fuller, D.P., *Easter Faith and History*, Grand Rapids, Mich., 1965.
Fuller, R.H., *The Formation of the Resurrection Narratives*, London, 1972.
Gaechter, P., S.J., "Die Engelerscheinungen in den Auferstehungsberichten," *ZKTh*, 89 (1967), pp. 191-202.
– "Die 'Brüder' Jesu," *ZKTh*, 89 (1967), pp. 458-459.
Gardner-Smith, P., "The Gospel of Peter," *JThS*, 27 (1926), pp. 255-271.
– "The Date of the Gospel of Peter," *JThS*, 27 (1926), pp. 401-407.
– *The Narratives of the Resurrection*, London, 1926.
Gatzweiler, K., "La Résurrection de Jésus, Ses Répercussions dans L'Histoire," *REL*, 53 (1967), pp. 257-284.
Geense, A., *Auferstehung und Offenbarung. Über den Ort der Frage nach der Auferstehung Jesu Christi in der heutigen deutschen evangelischen Theologie*, Gött., 1971.
Geering, L., *Resurrection: A Symbol of Hope*, London, 1971.
Geffcken, J., *Der Ausgang des griechisch-römischen Heidentums*, WB Darmstadt, 1972(='29).
George, A., "Les récits d'apparitions aux onze à partir de Luc 24,26-53," *La Résurrection du Christ et L'Exégèse Moderne* (Les Editions du Cerf), Paris, 1969, pp. 75-104.
Georgi, D., "Bleibende Aufgaben, die uns Rudolf Bultmann stellt," *Weiter Aktuell. Die Theologie Rudolf Bultmanns als Vermächtnis* (Evang. Zeitstimmen, 59/60), Hamburg, 1971, pp. 65-76.

Georgi, D., "The Records of Jesus in the Light of Ancient Accounts of Revered Men," *SBL Proceedings* (LA), 2 (1972), pp. 527-542.

– *Die Gegner des Paulus im 2. Korintherbrief. Studien zur religiösen Propaganda in der Spätantike.* (WMANT, eds. G. Bornkamm and G. von Rad, 11), Neukirchen, 1964.

Gilmour, S.M., "The Christophany To More Than Five Hundred Brethren," *JBL*, 80 (1961), pp. 248-252.

– "Easter and Pentecost," *JBL*, 81 (1962), pp. 62-66.

Gils, F., C.S.Sp., "Pierre et la foi au Christ Ressucité," *EThL*, 38 (1962), pp. 5-43.

Gnilka, J., "Der Missionsauftrag des Herrn nach Mt 28 und Apg. 1," *BuL*, 9 (1968), pp. 1-9.

Goguel, M., *Introduction au Nouveau Testament*, vol. III (Le Livre des Actes), Paris, 1922.

– *La Foi à la résurrection de Jésus dans le christianisme primitif*, Paris, 1933.

Goppelt, L., "Am dritten Tage auferstanden von den Toten," *Das Wahrzeichen des Christenglaubens. Eine Besinnung auf das Apostolische Glaubensbekenntnis*, ed. H. Lamparter, Wuppertal-Barmen, 1956, pp. 131-142.

– "Tradition nach Paulus," *KuD*, 4 (1958), pp. 213-233.

– "Das Osterkerygma heute," *Christologie und Ethik. Ges. Aufs.*, Gött., 1968, pp. 79-101.

– "Die Begründung des Glaubens durch Jesus," *Christologie und Ethik. Ges. Aufs.*, Gött., 1968, pp. 44-65.

– "Die Herrschaft Christi und die Welt," *Christologie und Ethik. Ges. Aufs.*, Gött., 1968, pp. 102-136.

– "πίνω (etc.)," *ThW*, VI, pp. 135-160.

– "Die Auferstehung Jesu in der Kritik, ihr Sinn und ihre Glaubwürdigkeit," *Grundlagen des Glaubens* (Tutzinger Texte, eds. P. Rieger and J. Strauß, 8), Mü., 1970, pp. 55-74.

– "Die Auferstehung Jesu: Ihre Wirklichkeit und ihre Wirkung nach 1 Kor 15," *Der auferstandene Christus und das Heil der Welt.* (Das Kirchberger Gespräch über die Bedeutung der Auferstehung für das Heil der Welt zwischen Vertretern der Evangelischen Kirche in Deutschland und der Russischen Orthodoxen Kirche, Studienheft, Kirchliches Außenamt der EKD, 7), Witten, 1972, pp. 98-111.

– *Typos. Die typologische Deutung des Alten Testaments im Neuen*, WB Darmstadt, 1966(='39).

– *Christentum und Judentum im ersten und zweiten Jahrhundert* (BFChTh, 2, 55), Gütersloh, 1954.

– *Die apostolische und nachapostolische Zeit* (Die Kirche in ihrer Geschichte, eds. K.D. Schmidt and E. Wolf, 1, A), Gött., 1966.

Grant, F.C., *Hellenistic Religions*, N.Y., 1953.

Graß, H., *Ostergeschehen und Osterberichte*, Gött., 1970^{4}(='61^{2}).

Grech, P., "The 'Testimonia' and Modern Hermeneutics," *NTS*, 19 (1972/'73), pp. 318-324.

Green, H.B., "The Command to Baptize and Other Matthaean Interpolations," *StEv*, 4 (1968), pp. 60-63.

Grundmann, W., "Das Problem des hellenistischen Christentums innerhalb der Jerusalemer Urgemeinde," *ZNW*, 38 (1939), pp. 45-73.

– "Zur Rede Jesu vom Vater im Johannes-Evangelium. Eine redaktions- und bekenntnisgeschichtliche Untersuchung zu Joh 20,17 und seiner Vorbereitung," *ZNW*, 52 (1961), pp. 213-230.

– *Das Evangelium nach Matthäus*, ThHK, 1, Berlin-Ost, 1971^{2}.

– *Das Evangelium nach Markus*, ThHK, 2, Berlin-Ost, 1971^{5}.

– *Das Evangelium nach Lukas*, ThHK, 3, Berlin-Ost, 1971^{6}.

Güttgemanns, E., "'Text' und 'Geschichte' als Grundkategorien der Generativen Poetik. Thesen zur aktuellen Diskussion um die 'Wirklichkeit' der Auferstehungstexte," *LB*, 11/12 (1972), pp. 2-12.

– "Linguistische Analyse von Mk 16,1-8," *LB*, 11/12 (1972), pp. 13-53.

– "Einleitende Bemerkungen zur strukturalen Erzählforschung," *LB*, 23/24 (1973), pp. 2-47.

– *Offene Fragen zur Formgeschichte des Evangeliums*, Mü., 1970.

de Guglielmo, A., O.F.M., "Emmaus," *CBQ*, 3 (1941), pp. 293-301.

Gundry, R.H., *The Use of the Old Testament in St. Matthew's Gospel with Special Reference to the Messianic Hope* (Suppl. NovTest, 18), Leiden, 1967.

Gunkel, H., *Zum religionsgeschichtlichen Verständnis des Neuen Testaments* (FRLANT, eds. W. Bousset and H. Gunkel, 1), Gött., 1910^{2}.

Gunkel, H., *Genesis* (GHkAT, ed. W. Nowack, I, 1), Gött., 1910^{3}.
– *Das Märchen im Alten Testament* (Religionsgeschichtliche Volksbücher, begun by F.M. Schiele, II. Reihe: Die Religion des ATs, 23/26), Tüb., 1921.
Guthrie, W.K.C., "Arimaspeans," *OCD*, London, 1961(='49), pp. 88.
– "Aristeas," *OCD*, London, 1961(='49), p. 90.
Gutwenger, E., S.J., "Zur Geschichtlichkeit der Auferstehung Jesu," *ZKTh*, 88 (1966), pp. 257-282.
Haacker, K., "Bemerkungen zum Freer-Logion," *ZNW*, 63 (1972), pp. 125-129.
Haag, H., "'Offenbaren' in der hebräischen Bibel," *ThZ*, 16 (1960), pp. 251-258.
Habel, N., "The Form and Significance of the Call Narratives," *ZAW*, 77 (1965), pp. 297-323.
Haenchen, E., "Petrus-Probleme," *NTS*, 7 ('60/'61), pp. 187-197.
– "Quellenanalyse und Kompositionsanalyse in Act 15," *Judentum, Urchristentum, Kirche* (Fst. J. Jeremias, ed. W. Eltester), Berlin, 1964, pp. 153-164.
– *Die Apostelgeschichte* (Meyer, III), Gött., 1968^{15}.
– *Der Weg Jesu. Eine Erklärung des Markus-Evangeliums und der kanonischen Parallelen*, Berlin, 1968^{2}.
– and P. Weigandt, "The Original Text of Acts," *NTS*, 14 ('67/'68), pp. 469-481.
Hahn, F., "Das Problem 'Schrift und Tradition' im Urchristentum," *EvTh*, 30 (1970), pp. 449-468.
– "Genesis 15^{6} im Neuen Testament," *Probleme Biblischer Theologie* (Fst. G. von Rad, ed. H.W. Wolff), Mü., 1971, pp. 90-107.
– "Sehen und Glauben im Johannesevangelium," *Neues Testament und Geschichte* (Fst. O. Cullmann), Zürich, 1972, pp. 125-141.
– *Christologische Hoheitstitel. Ihre Geschichte im frühen Christentum*, Gött., 1966(='63).
Haller, E., "Märchen und Zeugnis. Auslegung der Erzählung 2 Könige 4,1-7," *Probleme Biblischer Theologie* (Fst. G. von Rad, ed. H.W. Wolff), Mü., 1971, pp. 108-115.
Hamilton, M., *Incubation or the Cure of Disease in Pagan Temples and Christian Churches*, London, 1906.
Hamilton, N.Q., "Resurrection Tradition and the Composition of Mark," *JBL*, 84 (1965), pp. 415-421.
Hansen, G., "Herrscherkult und Friedensidee," *Umwelt des Urchristentums*, I (*Darstellung des neutestamentlichen Zeitalters*), Berlin, 1967^{2}, pp. 127-142.
Harrison, E.F., "The Resurrection of Jesus Christ in the Book of Acts and in Early Christian Literature," *Understanding the Sacred Text* (Fst. M.S. Enslin, ed. J. Reumann), Valley Forge, Pa., 1972, pp. 217-231.
von Harnack, A., "Ein jüngst entdeckter Auferstehungsbericht," *Theologische Studien* (Fst. B. Weiß), Gött., 1897, pp. 1-8.
– *Die Apostelgeschichte* (*Beiträge zur Einleitung in das Neue Testament*, III), Leipzig, 1908.
Hartmann, G., "Die Vorlage der Osterberichte in Joh 20," *ZNW*, 55 (1964), pp. 197-220.
Haufe, G., "Hellenistische Volksfrömmigkeit," *Umwelt des Urchristentums*, I (*Darstellung des neutestamentlichen Zeitalters*), Berlin, 1967^{2}, pp. 68-100.
– "Die Mysterien," *Umwelt des Urchristentums*, I (*Darstellung des neutestamentlichen Zeitalters*), Berlin, 1967^{2}, pp. 101-126.
– *Jesu persönliche Zukunftserwartung und der Ursprung der ältesten christlichen Osterterminologie* (Diss.), Leipzig, 1959. Referat, *ThLZ*, 85 (1960), cols. 467-468.
Hebert, G., S.S.M., "The Resurrection-Narrative in St. Mark's Gospel," *SJTh*, 15 (1962), pp. 66-73.
Hegermann, H., "Das hellenistische Judentum," *Umwelt des Urchristentums*, I (*Darstellung des neutestamentlichen Zeitalters*), Berlin, 1967^{2}, pp. 292-345.
– "W. Kramer, Christos Kyrios Gottessohn (Review)," *ThLZ*, 92 (1967), cols. 589-593.
– "W. Marxsen, Die Auferstehung Jesu von Nazareth (Review)," *ThLZ*, 97 (1972), cols. 31-32.
– "Griechisch-jüdisches Schrifttum," *Literatur und Religion des Frühjudentums*, eds. J. Maier and J. Schreiner, Würzburg, 1973, pp. 163-180.
– "Das griechischsprechende Judentum," *Literatur und Religion des Frühjudentums*, eds. J. Maier and J. Schreiner, Würzburg, 1973, pp. 328-369.
– *Die Vorstellung vom Schöpfungsmittler im hellenistischen Judentum und Urchristentum* (TU, eds. W. Eltester and E. Klostermann, 82), Berlin, 1961. Referat, *ThLZ*, 85 (1960), cols. 468-469.

Heitmüller, W., "Zum Problem Paulus und Jesus," *ZNW*, 13 (1912), pp. 320-337.
– "Jesus und Paulus," *ZThK*, 25 (1915), pp. 156-179
Held, H.J., "Matthäus als Interpret der Wundergeschichten," *Überlieferung und Auslegung im Matthäusevangelium* (G. Bornkamm, G. Barth and H.J. Held), Neukirchen, 1961[2], pp. 155-287.
Helmbold, A.K., "Gnostic Elements in the 'Ascension of Isaiah'," *NTS*, 18 ('71/'72), pp. 222-227.
Helzle, E., *Der Schluß des Markusevangeliums (Mk 16,9-20) und das Freer-Logion (Mk 16,14 W), Ihre Tendenzen und ihr gegenseitiges Verhältnis. Eine wortexegetische Untersuchung* (Diss.), Tüb., 1959. Referat, *ThLZ*, 85 (1960), cols. 470-472.
Hengel, M., "Maria Magdalena und die Frauen als Zeugen," *Abraham unser Vater* (Fst. O. Michel, ed. O. Betz), Leiden, 1963, pp. 243-256.
– "Die Ursprünge der christlichen Mission," *NTS*, 18 ('71/'72), pp. 15-38.
Héring, J., *La première Épitre de saint Paul aux Corinthiens*, Neuchâtel (Suisse), 1959.
Hirsch, E., *Frühgeschichte des Evangeliums*, I (*Das Werden des Markusevangeliums*), Tüb., 1941.
Hodges, Z.C., "The Women and the Empty Tomb," *BS*, 123 (1966), pp. 301-309.
– "Form-Criticism and the Resurrection Accounts," *BS*, 124 (1967), pp. 339-348.
Hooke, S.H., *The Resurrection of Christ as History and Experience*, London, 1967.
Hornschuh, M., *Studien zur Epistula Apostolorum* (PTS, eds. K. Aland and W. Schneemelcher, 5), Berlin, 1965.
van der Horst, P.W., "Can a Book End with ΓΑΡ? A Note on Mark XVI.8," *JThS*(n.s.), 23 (1972), pp. 121-124.
Hoskyns, E.C., "Adversaria Exegetica (Mark 14[28])," *Th*, 7 (1923), pp. 147-155.
Huffman, N., "Emmaus Among the Resurrection Narratives," *JBL*, 64 (1945), pp. 205-226.
– "The Translation and Significance of hōsperei tō 'ektrōmati (I Cor. 15:8)," an address delivered at the Toronto annual meeting of SBL on Nov. 18, 1969, an unpublished carbon copy of which was graciously supplied by the author upon request on Jan. 15, 1970, pp. 1-11.
van Iersel, B.M.F., "Die wunderbare Speisung und das Abendmahl in der synoptischen Tradition," *NovTest*, 7 ('64/'65), pp. 167-195.
– "Jezus' Verrijzenis in het Nieuwe Testament," *VTh*, 38 (1968), pp. 131-143.
Ittel, G.W., *Ostern und das leere Grab*, Gütersloh, 1967.
Jeremias, J., "Untersuchungen zum Quellenproblem der Apostelgeschichte," *ZNW*, 36 (1937), pp. 205-221.
– "Die Drei-Tage-Worte der Evangelien," *Tradition und Glaube. Das frühe Christentum in seiner Umwelt*. (Fst. K.G. Kuhn, eds. G. Jeremias, H.W. Kuhn, H. Stegemann), Gött., 1971, pp. 221-229.
– *Jesu Verheißung für die Völker*, Stutt., 1959[2](='56).
– *Die Abendmahlsworte Jesu*, Gött., 1960[3]. (Eng. trans. by N. Perrin, *The Eucharistic Words of Jesus*, N.Y., 1966.)
– *Neutestamentliche Theologie*, I (*Die Verkündigung Jesu*), Gütersloh, 1971.
Jeremias, Jörg, *Theophanie. Die Geschichte einer alttestamentlichen Gattung* (WMANT, eds. G. Bornkamm and G. von Rad, 10), Neukirchen, 1965.
– "E. Zenger, Die Sinaitheophanie (Review)," *ThLZ*, 98 (1973), cols. 582-584.
Jeremias, Joh., *Wissen wir etwas Sicheres über Jesus?*, Leipzig, 1912.
Johnson, A., *The One and the Many in the Israelite Conception of God*, Cardiff, 1942.
Johnson, B.A., *The Empty Tomb Tradition in the Gospel of Peter Related to Mt. 28,1-7* (Diss.), Harvard, 1966, microfilm No. 65170. Summary also, *HThR*, 59 (1966), pp. 447-448.
Johnson, S.E., "The Davidic-Royal Motif in the Gospels," *JBL*, 87 (1968), pp. 136-150.
Kahlefeld, H., "Die Oster-Evangelien. Bericht und Verkündigung," *Paschatis Sollemnia. Studien zu Osterfeier und Osterfrömmigkeit* (Fst. J.A. Jungmann, eds. B. Fischer and J. Wagner), Basel, 1959, pp. 23-31.
Kahrstedt, U., *Kulturgeschichte der römischen Kaiserzeit*, Bern, 1958[2].
Kammerer, J., *Die Auferstehung der Toten im Alten Testament als Element der eschatologischen Restauration des Bundesvolkes Israel* (Diss.), Wien, 1968.
Karnetzki, M., "Die galiläische Redaktion im Markusevangelium," *ZNW*, 52 (1961), pp. 238-272.
Kassing, A., *Auferstanden für Uns*, Mainz, 1969.

Kaster, J., *The Literature and Mythology of Ancient Egypt*, London, 1970.
Keck, L., "Mark 3:7-12 and Mark's Christology," *JBL*, 84 (1965), pp. 341-351.
Kee, H.C., "The Terminology of Mark's Exorcism Stories," *NTS*, 14 ('67/'68), pp. 232-246.
– "The Transfiguration in Mark: Epiphany or Apocalyptic Vision?" *Understanding the Sacred Text* (Fst. M.S. Enslin, ed. J. Reumann), Valley Forge, Pa., 1972, pp. 135-152.
– "Aretalogy and Gospel," *JBL*, 92 (1973), pp. 402-422.
Kegel, G., *Auferstehung Jesu–Auferstehung der Toten*, Gütersloh, 1970.
Kerényi, K., *Die griechisch-orientalische Romanliteratur in religionsgeschichtlicher Beleuchtung. Ein Versuch mit Nachbetrachtungen*, WB, Darmstadt, 1962[2](='27).
Kertelge, K., "Zur Interpretation der Wunder Jesu. Ein Literaturbericht," *BuL*, 9 (1968), pp. 140-153.
– *Die Wunder Jesu im Markusevangelium* (StANT, 23), Mü., 1970.
Klappert, B., "Zur Frage des semitischen oder griechischen Urtextes von 1 Kor 15,3-5," *NTS*, 13 (1967), pp. 168-173.
– *Die Auferweckung des Gekreuzigten. Der Ansatz der Christologie K. Barths im Zusammenhang der Christologie der Gegenwart*, Neukirchen, 1971.
Klatt, W., *Hermann Gunkel. Zu seiner Theologie der Religionsgeschichte und zur Entstehung der formgeschichtlichen Methode* (FRLANT, 100), Gött., 1966.
Klein, G., "Die Verleugnung des Petrus. Eine traditionsgeschichtliche Untersuchung," *ZThK*, 58 (1961), pp. 285-328.
– "Die Berufung des Petrus," *ZNW*, 58 (1967), pp. 1-44.
– *Die zwölf Apostel. Ursprung und Gehalt einer Idee* (FRLANT, 77), Gött., 1961.
Knierim, R., "Offenbarung im Alten Testament," *Probleme Biblischer Theologie* (Fst. G. von Rad, ed. H.W. Wolff), Mü., 1971, pp. 206-235.
Knox, W., *The Acts of the Apostles*, Cambridge, 1948.
Koch, G., *Die Auferstehung Jesu Christi* (BHTh, ed. G. Ebeling, 27), Tüb., 1965[2](='59).
Koch, K., *Ratlos vor der Apokalyptik*, Gütersloh, 1970.
Koenig, J., "Aux origines des théophanies iahvistes," *RHR*, 169 (1966), pp. 1-36.
Koester, H., "One Jesus and Four Primitive Gospels," *Trajectories Through Early Christianity* (Essays by J.M. Robinson and H. Koester), Phil., 1971, pp. 158-204.
– "The Structure and Criteria of Early Christian Beliefs," *Trajectories Through Early Christianity* (Essays by J.M. Robinson and H. Koester), Phil., 1971, pp. 205-231.
– "The Intention and Scope of Trajectories," *Trajectories Through Early Christianity* (Essays by J.M. Robinson and H. Koester), Phil., 1971, pp. 269-279.
Kohler, K., "The Pre-Talmudic Haggada. II.C.–The Apocalypse of Abraham and its Kindred," *JQR*, 7 (1895), pp. 581-606.
Kragerud, A., *Der Lieblingsjünger im Johannesevangelium*, Hamburg, 1959.
Kramer, W., *Christos Kyrios Gottessohn. Untersuchungen zu Gebrauch und Bedeutung der christologischen Bezeichnungen bei Paulus und den vorpaulinischen Gemeinden*, Zürich, 1963.
Kratz, R., *Auferweckung als Befreiung. Eine Studie zur Passions- und Auferstehungstheologie des Matthäus* (StBSt, 65), Stutt., 1973.
Kremer, J., "Ist Jesus wirklich von den Toten auferstanden?," *StZ*, 183, 94/5 (1969), pp. 310-320.
– *Die Osterbotschaft der vier Evangelien*, Stutt., 1969[3].
– *Das älteste Zeugnis von der Auferstehung Christi* (StBSt, 17), Stutt., 1970[3].
– *. . .denn sie werden leben. Sechs Kapitel über Tod, Auferstehung, neues Leben*, Stutt., 1972.
Kroll, W., "Kleomedes von Astypalaia," *PW*, 21, col. 694.
Kübel, P., "Epiphanie und Altarbau," *ZAW*, 83 (1971), pp. 225-231.
Kümmel, W.G., "Lukas in der Anklage der heutigen Theologie," *ZNW*, 63 (1972), pp. 149-165.
– *Das Neue Testament im 20. Jahrhundert. Ein Forschungsbericht* (StBSt, 50), Stutt., 1970.
– *Das Neue Testament. Geschichte der Erforschung seiner Probleme*, Mü., 1970[2]. Eng. trans. 1973.
– *Einleitung in das Neue Testament*, Heidelberg, 1973[17].
Künneth, W., *Theologie der Auferstehung*, Mü., 1951[4].
Kuhn, K.G., "μαρανα θά," *ThW*, IV, pp. 470-475.
Kuntz, J.K., *The Self-Revelation of God*, Phil., 1967.

Kutsch, E., "Gideons Berufung und Altarbau Jdc 6,11-24," *ThLZ*, 81 (1956), cols. 75-84.
Kwiran, M., *The Resurrection of the Dead. Exegesis of 1. Cor. 15 in German Protestant Theology from F.C. Baur to W. Künneth.* (Theol. Diss., ed. Bo Reicke, 8), Bassel, 1972.
Lai, P.H., "Production du sens par la foi. Autorités religieuses contestées/fondées. Analyse structurale de Matthieu 27,57-28,20," *RSR*, 61 (1973), pp. 65-96.
Lake, K., *The Historical Evidence for the Resurrection of Jesus Christ*, N.Y., 1907.
Laqueur, R., "Pherekydes (Genealoge)," *PW*, 38, cols. 1991-2025.
Leaney, A.R.C., "Jesus and Peter: the Call and the Postresurrection Appearance (Lk V,1-11 and XXIV,34)," *ET*, 65 (1954), pp. 381-382.
– "The Resurrection Narratives in Luke (XXIV,12-53)," *NTS*, 2 ('55/'56), pp. 110-114.
– "Theophany, Resurrection and History," *StEv*, 5 (1968), pp. 101-113.
– *The Gospel According to Luke*, N.Y., 1958.
Legault, A., "Christophanies et Angelophanies dans les recrits évangeliques de la Résurrection," *Science et esprit*, 21 (1969), pp. 443-457.
Lehmann, K., *Auferweckt am dritten Tage nach der Schrift. Früheste Christologie, Bekenntnisbildung und Schriftauslegung im Lichte von 1 Kor. 15,3-5* (Quaestiones Disputatae, eds. K. Rahner and H. Schlier, 38), Freiburg, 1968.
Leipoldt, J., "Zu den Auferstehungs-Geschichten," *ThLZ*, 73 (1948), cols. 737-742.
– *Sterbende und auferstehende Götter. Ein Beitrag zum Streite um Arthur Drews' Christusmythe*, Leipzig, 1923.
– and S. Morenz, *Heilige Schriften*, Leipzig, 1953.
Lentzen-Deis, F., "Das Motiv der 'Himmelsöffnung' in verschiedenen Gattungen der Umweltliteratur des Neuen Testaments," *Bb*, 50 Fasc. 3 (1969), pp. 301-327.
Léon-Dufour, X., S.J., "Apparitions du ressuscité et herméneutique," *La Résurrection du Christ et L'Exégèse Moderne*, Paris, 1969, pp. 153-173.
Leroy, H., *Rätsel und Mißverständnis. Ein Beitrag zur Formgeschichte des Johannesevangeliums*, (BBB, 30), Bonn, 1968.
Lessing, G.E. (ed.), *Von dem Zwecke Jesu und seiner Jünger. Noch ein Fragment des Wolfenbüttelschen Ungenannten, 1778.* (and *Ein Mehreres aus den Papieren des Ungenannten*, Fünftes Fragment–"Über die Auferstehungsgeschichte"), *Lessings Werke*, Vollständige Ausgabe in 25 Teilen, eds. J. Petersen and W. von Olshausen, 22. Teil (vol. 18) ed. L. Zscharnack, Hildesheim, 1970(='25), pp. 207-326 (pp. 152-186).
Levine, B.A., "On the Presence of God in Biblical Religion," *Religions in Antiquity* (Essays in Memory of E.R. Goodenough, ed. J. Neusner, Studies in the History of Religions. Supplements to Numen XIV), Leiden, 1968, pp. 71-87.
Lewis, J.O., "Gen 32:23-33, Seeing a Hidden God," *SBL Proceedings* (LA), 2 (1972), pp. 449-457.
Lindars, B., "The Composition of John XX," *NTS*, 7 ('60/'61), pp. 142-147.
– *New Testament Apologetic. The Doctrinal Significance of the Old Testament Quotations*, London, 1961.
Lindblom, J., "Theophanies in Holy Places in Hebrew Religion," *HUCA* (Fst. J. Morgenstein), 32 (1961), pp. 29-106.
– "Die Vorstellung vom Sprechen Jahwes zu den Menschen im Alten Testament," *ZAW*, 75 (NF, 34, 1963), pp. 263-288.
Lindton, O., "Der vermißte Markusschluß," *ThBl*, 8 (1929), cols. 229-234.
Linnemann, E., "Der (wiedergefundene) Markusschluß," *ZThK*, 66 (1969), pp. 255-287.
Lipinski, E., "Les disciples d'Emmaüs," *REL*, 53 (1967), pp. 220-226.
Löning, K., *Die Saulustradition in der Apostelgeschichte* (NTA,NF 9), Münster, 1973.
Lösch, S., *Deitas Jesu und antike Apotheose. Ein Beitrag zur Exegese und Religionsgeschichte*, Rottenburg a. N., 1933.
Lohfink, G., "Eine alttestamentliche Darstellungsform für Gotteserscheinungen in den Damaskusberichten (Apg. 9;22;26)," *BZ*, 9 (1965), pp. 246-257.
– "Die Auferstehung Jesu und die historische Kritik," *BuL*, 9 (1968), pp. 37-53.
– *Paulus vor Damaskus* (StBSt, 4), Stutt., 1967[3](='66).
– *Die Himmelfahrt Jesu. Untersuchungen zu den Himmelfahrts- und Erhöhungstexten bei Lukas* (StANT, 26), Mü., 1971.
Lohmeyer, E., *Galiläa und Jerusalem*, Gött., 1956(='36).
– *Das Evangelium des Markus* (Meyer, I/2), Gött., 1967[17](='37[10]), Ergänzungsheft, 1967[3].

Lohse, E., "Die Bedeutung des Pfingstberichtes im Rahmen des lukanischen Geschichtswerkes," *EvTh*, 13 (1953), pp. 422-436.

– *Die Auferstehung Jesu Christi im Zeugnis des Lukasevangeliums* (BSt, eds. O. Weber, H. Gollwitzer and H.J. Kraus, 31), Neukirchen, 1961.

– *Grundrisse zum Neuen Testament: Umwelt des Neuen Testaments* (NTD, Erg. Heft 1), Gött., 1971.

Lorenzen, T., "Ist der Auferstandene in Galiläa erschienen? Bemerkungen zu einem Aufsatz von B. Steinseifer," *ZNW*, 64 (1973), pp. 209-221.

– *Johannes 21. Eine traditionsgeschichtliche Analyse; zugleich ein Beitrag zur Lieblingsjüngerfrage* (Diss.), Zürich, 1970, now also, *Der Lieblingsjünger im Johannesevangelium. Eine redaktionsgeschichtliche Studie* (StBSt, 55), Stutt., 1971.

Lührmann, D., "Epiphaneia. Zur Bedeutungsgeschichte eines griechischen Wortes," *Tradition und Glaube. Das frühe Christentum in seiner Umwelt* (Fst. K.G. Kuhn, eds. G. Jeremias, H.W. Kuhn, H. Stegemann), Gött., 1971, pp. 185-199.

Lukan, K., *Romulus oder auf den Spuren der Gründer Roms*, Wien, 1970.

Luzarraga, J., "Retraducción semitica de *φοβέομαι* en Mc 16,8," *Bb*, 50 (1969), pp. 497-510.

Maag, V., "Malkût Jhwh," *Suppl. VT*, III, Leiden, 1960, pp. 129-153.

Maier, J., *Geschichte der jüdischen Religion*, Berlin, 1972.

Malina, B.J., "The Literary Structure and Form of Matt. XXVIII.16-20," *NTS*, 17 ('70/'71), pp. 87-103.

Marin, L., "Die Frauen am Grabe. Versuch einer Strukturanalyse an einem Text des Evangeliums," *Erzählende Semiotik nach Berichten der Bibel*, trans. K.H. Neufeld S.J., eds. C. Chabrol and L. Marin, Mü., 1973, pp. 67-85.

Martyn, J.L., *History and Theology in the Fourth Gospel*, N.Y., 1968.

Marxsen, W., *Der Evangelist Markus. Studien zur Redaktionsgeschichte des Evangeliums* (FRLANT,NF, 49), Gött., 1959^{2}.

– *Anfangsprobleme der Christologie*, Gütersloh, 1960.

– *Die Auferstehung Jesu als historisches und als theologisches Problem*, Gütersloh, 1966^{4}, now in *Die Bedeutung der Auferstehungsbotschaft für den Glauben an Jesus Christus* (Schriftenreihe der Evangelischen Kirche der Union, ed. F. Viering), Gütersloh, 1968^{7}(= '66), pp. 9-39.

– *Die Auferstehung Jesu von Nazareth*, Gütersloh, 1968.

Masson, Ch., "Le Tombeau Vide. Essai sur la formation d'une tradition," *RThPh*(n.s.), 32 (1944), pp. 161-174.

Mayer, G., "Aspekte des Abrahambildes in der hellenistisch-jüdischen Literatur," *EvTh*, 32, 2 (1972), pp. 118-127.

McArthur, H.K., "On the Third Day (I Cor. 15:4)," an address delivered before the annual meeting of SBL in Toronto on Nov. 18, 1969, an unpublished carbon copy of the unrevised version was graciously supplied on request by the author on Dec. 29, 1969, pp. 1-8, now in *NTS*, 18 ('71/'72), pp. 81-86.

– *The Quest Through the Centuries. The Search for the Historical Jesus*, Phil., 1966.

McCasland, S.V., "Further Thought about the Resurrection of Jesus," *Search The Scriptures* (NT Studies in Honor of R.R. Stamm, eds. J.M. Meyers, O. Reimherr, H.N. Bream), Leiden, 1969, pp. 95-105.

McDonald, A.H., "Livius," *OCD*, London, 1961(='49), pp. 509-511.

McIndoe, J.H., "The Young Man at the Tomb," *ET*, 80, 4 (1969), p. 125.

Metzger, B.M., "A Suggestion Concerning the Meaning of I Cor. XV.4b," *JThS*(n.s.), 8 (1957), pp. 118-123.

– "The Meaning of Christ's Ascension," *Search The Scriptures* (Studies in Honor of R.T. Stamm, eds. J.M. Meyers, O. Reimherr, H.N. Bream), Leiden, 1969, pp. 118-128, and as "The Ascension of Jesus Christ," *Historical and Literary Studies. Pagan, Jewish and Christian* (NTTS, 8), Leiden, 1968, pp. 77-87.

– "The Ending of the Gospel According to Mark in the Ethiopic Manuscripts," *Understanding the Sacred Text* (Fst. M.S. Enslin, ed. J. Reumann), Valley Forge, Pa., 1972, pp. 165-180.

– *An Introduction to the Apocrypha*, N.Y., 1957.

– *Chapters in the History of New Testament Textual Criticism* (NTTS, 4), Leiden, 1963.

– *The Text of the New Testament*, N.Y., 1964.

Meyer, E., *Ursprung und Anfänge des Christentums*, I (*Die Evangelien*), Stutt., 1929.

Michaelis, W., "ὁράω, εἶδον, βλέπω (etc.)," *ThW*, V, pp. 315-381.
– *Die Erscheinungen des Auferstandenen*, Basel, 1944.
Michel, O., "Der Abschluß des Matthäusevangeliums," *EvTh*, 10 ('50/'51), pp. 16-26.
– "Ein johanneischer Osterbericht," *Studien zum NT und zur Patristik* (Fst. E. Klostermann), Berlin, 1961, pp. 35-42.
– *Der Brief an die Hebräer* (Meyer, XIII), Gött., 1966[12].
Micklem, N., *Behold the Man, a Study in the Fourth Gospel*, London, 1969.
Mildenberger, F., "Auferstanden am dritten Tage nach der Schrift," *EvTh*, 23 (1963), pp. 265-280.
Minear, P.S., "Luke's Use of the Birth Stories," *Studies in Luke-Acts* (Essays presented in Honor of P. Schubert, eds. L.E. Keck and J.L. Martyn), London, 1968, pp. 111-130.
Moe, O., "Hat Paulus den trinitarischen Taufbefehl Matth. 28,19 und ein trinitarisches Taufbekenntnis gekannt?" *Zur Theorie des Christentums* (Fst. R. Seeberg, ed. W. Koepp), Leipzig, 1929, pp. 179-196.
Mölle, H., *Das "Erscheinen" Gottes im Pentateuch. Ein literaturwissenschaftlicher Beitrag zur alttestamentlichen Exegese* (EHS,XXIII,18), Frankfurt, 1973.
Molin, G., "Entwicklung und Motiv der Auferstehungshoffnung vom AT bis zur rabbinischen Zeit," *Judaica*, 9 (1953), pp. 225-239.
Morgenthaler, R., *Die lukanische Geschichtsschreibung als Zeugnis. Gestalt und Gehalt der Kunst des Lukas*, 2 vols., Zürich, 1948.
Morlet, M., "La Résurrection du Christ. Où en est la recherche exégètique actuelle?" *Esprit et Vie. L'Ami du Clerge*, 79 (1969), pp. 601-606.
Morris, L., *The Gospel According to John* (NICNT, ed. F.F. Bruce), Grand Rapids, Mich., 1971.
Mosbech, H., "Apostolos in the New Testament," *StTh*, 2, Fasc. 2 (Lund, 1948), pp. 166-200.
Moule, C.F.D., "St Mark 16:8 Once More," *NTS*, 2 (1955), pp. 58-59.
– "The Post-Resurrection Appearances in the Light of Festival Pilgrimages," *NTS*, 4 ('57/'58), pp. 58-61.
Mouson, J., "Présence du Ressuscité. Les récits évangéliques d'apparitions," *Col. Mech.*, 54 (1969), pp. 178-220.
Mowinckel, S., "The Name of the God of Moses," *HUCA* (Fst. J. Morgenstein), 32 (1961), pp. 121-133.
Müller, U.B., "Die christologische Absicht des Markusevangeliums und die Verklärungsgeschichte," *ZNW*, 64 (1973), pp. 159-193.
Muilenburg, J., "The Speech of Theophany," *HDSB*, 28 (1964), pp. 35-47.
Munck, J., "Paulus Tanquam Abortivus (ICor. 15:8)," *New Testament Essays* (Studies in Memory of T.W. Manson (1893-1958), ed. A.J.B. Higgins), Manchester, 1959, pp. 180-193.
Mussies, G., *Dio Chrysostom and the New Testament* (SCHNT, eds. H.D. Betz, G. Delling and W.C. van Unnik, 2), Leiden, 1972.
Mußner, F., *Die Auferstehung Jesu* (BHB, 7), Mü., 1969.
Nauck, W., "Die Bedeutung des leeren Grabes für den Glauben an den Auferstandenen," *ZNW*, 47 (1956), pp. 243-267.
Neill, S., *The Interpretation of the New Testament 1861-1961*, N.Y., 1966.
Neirynck, F., "La rédaction Matthéenne et la structure du premier évangile," *EThL*, 43 (1967), pp. 41-73.
– "Les femmes au tombeau: Étude de la rédaction Matthéenne (Matt. XXVIII.1-10)," *NTS*, 15 ('68/'69), pp. 168-190.
Nickelsburg, G., *Resurrection, Immortality and Eternal Life in Judaism* (Diss.), Harvard, 1968, microfilm No. 674578, now: HThSt, 26 (Cambridge, Mass., 1973).
Niebuhr, R., *Resurrection and Historical Reason*, N.Y., 1957.
Niederwimmer, K., "Johannes Markus und die Frage nach dem Verfasser des zweiten Evangeliums," *ZNW*, 57 (1966), pp. 172-187.
– *Jesus*, Gött., 1968.
Nikolainen, A.T., *Der Auferstehungsglaube in der Bibel und ihrer Umwelt*, 2 vols. (AFAW, 49,3 and 59,3), Helsinki, (I) 1944 and (II) 1946.
Nilsson, M.P., *Griechischer Glaube*, Mü., 1950.
– *Geschichte der* griechischen *Religion*, vols. I and II (HAW, ed. W. Otto, 5,2, 1 and 2), Mü., (I) 1971 and (II) 1950.

Nötscher, F., "Zur Auferstehung nach drei Tagen," *Vom Alten zum Neuen Testament. Ges. Aufs.* (BBB, eds. F. Nötscher and K.Th. Schäfer, 17), Bonn, 1962, pp. 231-236. (Originally, *Bb*, 35 [1954], pp. 313-319.)
– *'Das Angesicht Gottes schauen' nach biblischer und babylonischer Auffassung*, Würzburg, 1924.
Norden, E., *Agnostos Theos*, WB Darmstadt, 1971⁵(='12).
– *Die Geburt des Kindes*, WB Darmstadt, 1969(='24).
Noth, M., *Überlieferungsgeschichte des Pentateuch*, Stutt., 1948.
– *Das Zweite Buch Mose* (ATD, 5), Gött., 1959.
Nützel, H., *Die Verklärungserzählung im Markusevangelium. Eine redaktionsgeschichtliche Untersuchung* (FB, 6), Würzburg, 1973.
Oakesmith, J., *The Religion of Plutarch. As expounded in his "Ethics,"* London, 1901.
Obrist, F., *Echtheitsfragen und Deutung der Primatsstelle Mt 16,18f in der Deutschen Protestantischen Theologie der letzten dreissig Jahre* (NTA, 21, 3/4), Münster, 1961.
Oepke, A., "Wie entsteht nach den Schriften des Neuen Testaments der Glaube an die Auferstehung Jesu?," *WZKMU*, 3 ('53/'54), pp. 77-80.
O'Neill, J.C., "The Silence of Jesus," *NTS*, 15 ('68/'69), pp. 153-167.
– "On the Resurrection as an Historical Question," *Christ Faith and History* (Cambridge Studies in Christology, eds. S.W. Sykes and J.P. Clayton), Cambridge, 1972.
Oppenheim, A.L., "The Interpretation of Dreams in the Ancient Near East. With a Translation of an Assyrian Dream-Book," *TAPhS*(n.s.), vol.46, part 3, Phil., 1956, pp. 177-373.
von der Osten-Sacken, P., "Die Apologie des paulinischen Apostolats in 1 Kor 15,1-11," *ZNW*, 64 (1973), pp. 245-262.
Otto, E., "Der Mensch als Geschöpf und Bild Gottes in Ägypten," *Probleme Biblischer Theologie* (Fst. G. von Rad, ed. H.W. Wolff), Mü., 1971, pp. 335-348.
Otto, W.F., *Theophania. Der Geist der altgriechischen Religion*, Hamburg, 1959(='56).
Pack, R., "The 'Volatilization' of Peregrinus Proteus," *AJPhil*, 67 (1946), pp. 334-345.
Pannenberg, W., "Die historische Problematik der Auferstehung Jesu," *Diskussion um Kreuz und Auferstehung*, ed. B. Klappert, Wuppertal, 1967, pp. 233-249.
– "Dogmatische Erwägungen zur Auferstehung Jesu," *KuD*, 14 (1968), pp. 105-118.
– "Dogmatische Thesen zur Lehre von der Offenbarung," *Offenbarung als Geschichte*, ed. W. Pannenberg (*KuD*, Bh 1), Gött., 1970⁴, pp. 91-114.
– *Grundzüge der Christologie*, Gütersloh, 1966²(='64).
– *Christentum und Mythos*, Gütersloh, 1972.
Patsch, H., *Abendmahl und historischer Jesus* (CThM: Bibelwissenschaft, eds. L. Goppelt and C. Westermann, 1), Stutt., 1972.
Pax, E., "Epiphanie," *RAC*, V, cols. 832-909.
– ΕΠΙΦΑΝΕΙΑ. *Ein religionsgeschichtlicher Beitrag zur biblischen Theologie*, Mü., 1955.
Pelletier, A., "Les apparitions du Ressuscité en termes de la Septante," *Bb*, 51 (1970), pp. 76-79.
Perlitt, L., "Die Verborgenheit Gottes," *Probleme Biblischer Theologie* (Fst. G. von Rad, ed. H.W. Wolff), Mü., 1971, pp. 367-382.
Perrin, N., "Towards an Interpretation of the Gospel of Mark," *Christology* (Fst. N. Perrin, ed. H.D. Betz), Claremont, Calif., 1971, pp. 1-78.
Pesch, R., "Eine alttestamentliche Ausführungsformel," *BZ*, 10 (1966), pp. 220-245 and *BZ*, 11 (1967), pp. 79-95.
– "Die Stellung und Bedeutung Petri in der Kirche des Neuen Testaments. Zur Situation der Forschung," *Conc*, 7 (1971), pp. 240-245.
– *Die Vision des Stephanus* (StBSt, 12), Stutt., 1966.
– *Der Reiche Fischfang, Lk 5,1-11/Jo 21,1-14* (KBANT), Düsseldorf, 1969.
Petzke, G., *Die Traditionen über Apollonius von Tyana und das Neue Testament* (SCHNT, eds. H.D. Betz, G. Delling and W.C. van Unnik, 1), Leiden, 1970.
Pfister, F., *Der Reliquienkult im Altertum*, 2 vols. (RVV,5), Gießen, 1909/12.
Pfister, R., "Epiphanie," *PW Suppl.*, IV, cols. 277-323.
Plümacher, E., *Lukas als hellenistischer Schriftsteller. Studien zur Apostelgeschichte*, Gött., 1972.
Plummer, A., *The Gospel According to Luke* (ICC), Edinburgh, 1960(='22⁵).

Porteous, N.W., "Magnalia Dei," *Probleme Biblischer Theologie* (Fst. G. von Rad, ed. H.W. Wolff), Mü., 1971, pp. 417-427.

Prümm, K., *Religionsgeschichtliches Handbuch für den Raum der altchristlichen Umwelt. Hellenistisch-römische Geistesströmungen und Kulte mit Beachtung des Eigenlebens der Provinzen*, Rome, 1954.

von Rad, G., *Das erste Buch Mose. Genesis* (ATD, 2/4), Gött., 1964^{7}.

Radermacher, L., "Zur Charakteristik neutestamentlicher Erzählungen," *ARW*, 28 (1930), pp. 31-41.

Rahnenführer, D., "Das Testament des Hiob und das Neue Testament," *ZNW*, 62 (1971), pp. 68-93.

Ramsay, W.M., "Luke the Physician," *Luke the Physician and other Studies in the History of Religion*, Grand Rapids, Mich., 1956(='08), pp. 1-68.

Ramsey, A.M., *The Glory of God and the Transfiguration of Christ*, London, 1949.

– *The Resurrection of Christ*, London, 1961.

Rehkopf, F., *Die lukanische Sonderquelle* (WUNT, 5), Tüb., 1959.

Reitzenstein, R., *Hellenistische Wundererzählungen*, WB Darmstadt, 1963^{2}(='06).

– *Die hellenistischen Mysterienreligionen nach ihren Grundgedanken und Wirkungen*, WB Darmstadt, 1966(='27^{3}).

Renan, E., *The Life of Jesus* (anonymous Eng. trans. of *Vie de Jésus*, Paris, 1863), N.Y., n.d.

Rendtorff, R., "Die Offenbarungsvorstellungen im Alten Israel," *Offenbarung als Geschichte*, ed W. Pannenberg (*KuD*, Bh 1), Gött., 1970^{4}, pp. 21-41.

– "Geschichte und Wort im Alten Testament," *EvTh*, 22 (1962), pp. 621-649.

Rengstorf, K.H., "Old and New Testament Traces of a Formula of the Judean Royal Ritual," *NovTest*, 5 (1962), pp. 229-244.

– "σημεῖον," *ThW*, VII, pp. 241-257.

– *Das Evangelium nach Lukas* (NTD, 3), Gött., 1968^{13}.

– *Die Auferstehung Jesu. Form, Art und Sinn der urchristlichen Osterbotschaft*, Witten/Ruhr, 1967^{5}.

Rese, M., *Alttestamentliche Motive in der Christologie des Lukas*, Gütersloh, 1969.

Richardson, A., *An Introduction to the Theology of the New Testament*, N.Y., 1958.

Richter, H.-F., *Auferstehung und Wirklichkeit. Eine exegetische, hermeneutische und ontologische Untersuchung zu 1. Korinther 15,1/11*, Berlin, 1969.

Richter, W., *Traditionsgeschichtliche Untersuchungen zum Richterbuch* (BBB, eds. F. Nötscher and K. Th. Schäfer, 18), Bonn, 1963.

– *Die sogenannten vorprophetischen Berufungsberichte. Eine literaturwissenschaftliche Studie zu 1 Sam 9,1-10,16, Ex 3f und Ri 6,11b-17* (FRLANT, 101), Gött., 1970.

– *Exegese als Literaturwissenschaft. Entwurf einer alttestamentlichen Literaturtheorie und Methodologie*, Gött., 1971.

Robert, C., *Die griechische Heldensage* (*Griechische Mythologie*, vol. II: *Die Heroen*, L. Preller, rev. by C. Robert, Landschaftliche Sagen, 1), Berlin, 1966^{5}(='20^{4}).

Robinson, J.M., "Offenbarung als Wort und als Geschichte," *Neuland in der Theologie*, III (*Theologie als Geschichte*, eds. J.M. Robinson and J.B. Cobb, Jr.), Zürich, 1967, pp. 11-134.

– "The Dismantling and Reassembling of the Categories of New Testament Scholarship," *Trajectories Through Early Christianity* (Essays by J.M. Robinson and H. Koester), Phil., 1971, pp. 1-19, and *Int*, 25 (1971), pp. 63-77.

– "Kerygma and History in the New Testament," *Trajectories Through Early Christianity* (Essays by J.M. Robinson and H. Koester), Phil., 1971, pp. 20-70.

– "Logoi Sophon. On the Gattung of Q," *Trajectories Through Early Christianity* (Essays by J.M. Robinson and H. Koester), Phil., 1971, pp. 71-113.

– "The Johannine Trajectory," *Trajectories Through Early Christianity* (Essays by J.M. Robinson and H. Koester), Phil., 1971, pp. 232-268.

– "On the Gattung of Mark (and John)," *Jesus and Man's Hope. A Perspective Book*, I, ed. D.G. Buttrick, Pittsburgh, 1970, pp. 99-129.

Rohde, E., *Psyche. Seelencult und Unsterblichkeitsglaube der Griechen*, vols. I and II, Tüb., 1925^{9} and ^{10}.

– *Der griechische Roman und seine Vorläufer*, Hildesheim, 1960^{4}(='14^{3}).

Rohde, J., *Die redaktionsgeschichtliche Methode*, Hamburg, 1966.

Roloff, J., "Der johanneische 'Lieblingsjünger' und der Lehrer der Gerechtigkeit," *NTS*, 15 ('68/'69), pp. 129-151.

– "Das Markusevangelium als Geschichtsdarstellung," *EvTh*, 29 (1969), pp. 73-93.

Roloff, J., "Heil als Gemeinschaft. Kommunikative Faktoren im urchristlichen Herrenmahl," *Gottesdienst und Öffentlichkeit. Zur Theorie und Didaktik neuer Kommunikation* (Fst. H.R. Müller-Schwefe, eds. P. Cornehl and H.E. Bahr, Konkretionen, 8), Hamburg, 1970, pp. 88-117.
– "Anfänge der soteriologischen Deutung des Todes Jesu (Mk. X.45 und Lk. XXII.27)," *NTS*, 19 (1972), pp. 38-64.
– *Apostolat–Verkündigung–Kirche*, Gütersloh, 1965.
– *Das Kerygma und der irdische Jesus. Historische Motive in den Jesus-Erzählungen der Evangelien*, Gött., 1970.
Rordorf, W., *Der Sonntag, Geschichte des Ruhe- und Gottesdiensttages im ältesten Christentum*, (AThANT, 43), Zürich, 1962.
Rose, H.J., "Alcmene," *OCD*, London, 1961(='49), p. 32.
– "Apollonius," *OCD*, London, 1961(='49), p. 72.
– "Quirinus," *OCD*, London, 1961(='49), p. 755.
– "Romulus and Remus," *OCD*, London, 1961(='49), p. 780.
Ross, W.D., "Peregrinus," *OCD*, London, 1961(='49), p. 663.
– "Pherecydes of Athens," *OCD*, London, 1961(='49), p. 676.
Rowley, H.H., *Apokalyptik. Ihre Form und Bedeutung zur biblischen Zeit*, trans. by I. and R. Pesch, Einsiedeln, 1965[3].
Ruckstuhl, E., "Die evangelischen Ostererzählungen," *Die Auferstehung Jesu Christi. Heilsgeschichtliche Tatsache und Brennpunkt des Glaubens* (Christ in der Zeit, eds. E. Ruckstuhl and J. Pfammatter, 17), Luzern, 1968, pp. 31-59.
Ruef, J.S., "The Resurrection Appearances: Theme and Variations," an address delivered at the 1966 annual meeting of SBL, an unpublished overview of which was graciously supplied by the author upon request on August 31, 1967.
Russel, D.S., *The Method and Message of Jewish Apocalyptic*, London, 1971(='64).
Sanders, E.P., *The Tendencies of the Synoptic Tradition*, Cambridge, 1969.
Sanders, J.N., "Those Whom Jesus Loved," *NTS*, 1 ('54/'55), pp. 29-41.
Schenke, L., *Auferstehungsverkündigung und leeres Grab. Eine traditionsgeschichtliche Untersuchung von Mk. 16,1-8* (StBSt, 33), Stutt., 1968.
Schille, G., *Anfänge der Kirche. Erwägungen zur apostolischen Frühgeschichte* (BEvTh, ed. C. Wolf, 43), Mü., 1966.
– *Osterglaube* (ATh, 51), Stutt., 1973.
Schlatter, A., *Das Evangelium des Lukas*, Stutt., 1931.
Schlier, H., *Über die Auferstehung Jesu Christi*, Einsiedeln, 1968.
Schmidt, C., *Gespräche Jesu mit seinen Jüngern nach der Auferstehung* (TU, eds. W. Eltester and E. Klostermann, 43), Leipzig, 1919.
Schmidt, K.L., "Die Stellung der Evangelien in der allgemeinen Literaturgeschichte," ΕΥΧΑΡΙΣΤΗΡΙΟΝ. *Studien zur Religion und Literatur des Alten und Neuen Testaments* (Fst. H. Gunkel, 2), Gött., 1923, pp. 51-134.
Schmithals, W., "Der Markusschluß, die Verklärungsgeschichte und die Aussendung der Zwölf," *ZThK*, 69 (1972), pp. 379-411.
Schmitt, J., "La résurrection du Christ: des formules kerygmatiques aux récits évangéliques," *Parole de Dieu et sacerdoce*, Paris, 1962, pp. 93-105.
– "Urkerygma und Evangelienberichte. Bestand und Wandel der neutestamentlichen Auferstehungstradition," *BuK*, 22 (1967), pp. 14-18.
Schnackenburg, R., "On the Origin of the Fourth Gospel," *Jesus and Man's Hope. A Perspective Book*, I, ed. D.G. Buttrick, Pittsburgh, Pa., 1970, pp. 223-246.
– "Der Jünger, den Jesus liebte," *EKK*, 2, Zürich, 1970, pp. 97-117.
Schneider, C., *Geistesgeschichte des antiken Christentums*, vol. II, Mü., 1954.
– *Kulturgeschichte des Hellenismus*, Mü., (I) 1967, (II) 1969.
Schnider, F. and Stenger, W., "Beobachtungen zur Struktur der Emmausperikope (Lk 24,13-35)," *BZ*(NF), 16/1 (1972), pp. 94-114.
– *Die Ostergeschichten der Evangelien* (Schriften zur Katechetik, ed. P. Neuenzeit, 13), Mü., 1970.
Schniewind, J., *Die Parallelperikopen bei Lukas und Johannes*, Hildesheim, 1958(='14).
Schreiber, J., "Die Christologie des Markusevangeliums," *ZThK*, 58 (1961), pp. 154-183.
Schubert, K., "Das Problem der Auferstehungshoffnung in den Qumrântexten und in der frührabbinischen Literatur," *WZKM*, 56 (1960, Fst. H.W. Duda), pp. 154-167.

Schubert, K., "Die Entwicklung der Auferstehungslehre von der nachexilischen bis zur frührabbinischen Zeit," *BZ*(NF), 6 (1962), pp. 177-214.
Schubert, P., "The Final Cycle of Speeches in the Book of Acts," *JBL*, 87 (1968), pp. 1-16.
– "The Structure and Significance of Luke 24," *Neutestamentliche Studien für Rudolf Bultmann*, Berlin, 1954, pp. 165-186.
Schürmann, H., "Die Dublettenvermeidungen im Lukasevangelium. Ein Beitrag zur Verdeutlichung des lukanischen Redaktionsverfahrens," *Traditionsgeschichtliche Untersuchungen zu den synoptischen Evangelien. Ges. Aufs.*, Düss., 1968, pp. 279-289.
– "Die Verheißung an Simon Petrus. Auslegung von Lk 5,1-11," *Ursprung und Gestalt. Ges. Aufs.*, Düss., 1970, pp. 268-276.
Schütz, J.H., "Apostolic Authority and the Control of Tradition: I Cor. XV," *NTS*, 15 (1969), pp. 439-457.
Schulz, S., "Maranatha und Kyrios Jesus," *ZNW*, 53 (1962), pp. 125-144.
– *Die Stunde der Botschaft. Einführung in die Theologie der vier Evangelien*, Hamburg, 1970[2].
– *"Q." Die Spruchquelle der Evangelisten*, Zürich, 1972.
Schutenhaus, F., "Das Kommen und Erscheinen Gottes im Alten Testament," *ZAW*, 76 (1964, NF 35), pp. 1-22.
Schwank, B., "Die Ostererscheinungen des Johannesevangeliums und die Post-mortem-Erscheinungen der Parapsychologie," *EuA*, 44 (1968), pp. 36-53.
Schwartz, E., "Johannes und Kerinthos," *ZNW*, 15 (1914), pp. 210-219.
Schweitzer, A., *The Quest of the Historical Jesus* (trans. by W. Montgomery from the first Ger. ed., *Von Reimarus zu Wrede*, Tüb., 1906), N.Y., 1962.
Schweizer, E., "Eine hebräisierende Sonderquelle des Lukas?," *ThZ*, 6 (1950), pp. 161-185.
– "Zur Frage des Messiasgeheimnisses bei Markus," *ZNW*, 56 (1965), pp. 1ff.,now in *Beiträge zur Theologie des Neuen Testaments*, Zürich, 1970, pp. 11-20.
– "Die Leiblichkeit des Menschen: Leben-Tod-Auferstehung," *EvTh*, 29 (1969), pp. 40-55.
– "Neuere Markus-Forschung in USA," *EvTh*, 33/5 (1973), pp. 533-537.
– *Gemeinde und Gemeindeordnung im Neuen Testament* (AThANT, 35), Zürich, 1962[2].
– *Erniedrigung und Erhöhung bei Jesus und seinen Nachfolgern*, Zürich, 1962.
– *Das Evangelium nach Markus* (NTD, 1), Gött., 1968[2].
– *Das Evangelium nach Matthäus* (NTD, 2), Gött., 1973.
Scroggs, R. and K.I. Groff, "Baptism in Mark: Dying and Rising with Christ," *JBL*, 92 (1973), pp. 531-548.
Seidensticker, P., "Das Antiochenische Glaubensbekenntnis 1 Kor 15,3-7 im Lichte seiner Traditionsgeschichte," *ThGl*, 57 (1967), pp. 286-323.
– *Die Auferstehung Jesu in der Botschaft der Evangelisten* (StBSt, 26), Stutt., 1967.
Shepherd, M.H., Jr., "Paul and the Double Resurrection Tradition," *JBL*, 64 (1945), pp. 227-240.
Siber, P., *Mit Christus leben. Eine Studie zur paulinischen Auferstehungshoffnung* (AThANT, 6), Zürich, 1972.
Smalley, S.S., The Sign in John XXI," *NTS*, 20 ('73/'74), pp. 275-288.
Smith, D.M., "J. Fortna, the Gospel of Signs (Review)," *JBL*, 89 (1970), p. 501.
Smith, M., "The Report about Peter of I Clement V.4," *NTS*, 7 ('60/'61), pp. 86-88.
– "Prolegomena to a Discussion of Aretalogies, Divine Men, the Gospels and Jesus," *JBL*, 90 (1971), pp. 174-199.
Sparks, H.F.D., "The Semitisms of the Acts," *JThS*(n.s.), 1 (1950), pp. 16-28.
Spörlein, B., *Die Leugnung der Auferstehung. Eine historisch-kritische Untersuchung zu 1 Kor 15* (BU, ed. O. Kuß, 7), Regensburg, 1972[3].
Stählin, G. (trans. W.P. Todd), "'On the Third Day.' The Easter Traditions of the Primitive Church," *Int*, 10 (1956), pp. 282-299.
Steinseifer, B., "Der Ort der Erscheinungen des Auferstandenen," *ZNW*, 62 (1971), p. 232-265.
Stier, F., *Gott und sein Engel im Alten Testament*, Münster, 1934.
Strauß, D.F., *Gesammelte Schriften*, Bonn, 1876.
– *Das Leben Jesu*, vols. I and II (Volks-Ausgabe), Bonn, 1904[14].
Strecker, G., *Der Weg der Gerechtigkeit–Untersuchung zur Theologie des Matthäus*, Gött., 1971[3].
Strobel, A., "Die Jüngerschaft im Lichte des österlichen Geschehens," *Anfänge der Kirche im Neuen Testament*, Gött., 1967, pp. 37-77.

Strobel, A., "Der Berg der Offenbarung (Mt 28,16; Apg. 1,12). Erwägungen zu einem urchristlichen Erwartungstopos," *Verborum Veritatis* (Fst. G. Stählin, eds. O. Böcher and K. Haacker), Wuppertal, 1970, pp. 133-146.
– *Kerygma und Apokalyptik*, Gött., 1967.
Strugnell, J., "The Angelic Liturgy at Qumran–4QSerek Šîrôt 'Ôlat Haššabbāt," *Suppl. VT*, 7, Leiden, 1960, pp. 318-345.
Stuhlmacher, P., "Das Bekenntnis zur Auferweckung Jesu von den Toten und die Biblische Theologie," *ZThK*, 70 (1973), pp. 365-403.
– *Das paulinische Evangelium*, I: *Vorgeschichte* (FRLANT, eds. E. Käsemann and E. Würthwein, 95), Gött., 1968.
Suggs, M.J., "The Passion and Resurrection Narratives," *Jesus and Man's Hope. A Perspective Book*, II, eds. D.G. Miller and D.Y. Hadidian, Pittsburgh, Pa., 1971, pp. 323-337.
Suhl, A., *Die Funktion der alttestamentlichen Zitate und Anspielungen im Markus-Evangelium*, Gütersloh, 1965.
Taeger, F., *Charisma. Studien zur Geschichte des antiken Herrscherkultes*, vols. I and II, Stutt., (I) 1957 and (II) 1960.
Talbert, C.H., "An Anti-Gnostic Tendency in Lucan Christology," *NTS*, 14 ('67/'68), pp. 259-271.
– and E.V. McKnight," Can the Griesbach Hypothesis Be Falsified?," *JBL*, 91 (1972), pp. 338-368.
Taylor, V., *The Gospel According to St Mark*, N.Y., 1966[2].
Teeple, H.M., "The Historical Beginnings of the Resurrection Faith," *Studies in New Testament and Early Christian Literature* (Essays in Honor of A.P. Wikgren, ed. D.A. Aune), Leiden, 1972, pp. 107-120.
Theißen, G., *Urchristliche Wundergeschichten. Ein Beitrag zur formgeschichtlichen Erforschung der synoptischen Evangelien* (StNT, 8), Gütersloh, 1974.
Thielicke, H., "The Resurrection Kerygma," *The Easter Message Today*, N.Y., 1964, pp. 59-116.
Thrall, M.E., "Elijah and Moses in Mark's Account of the Transfiguration," *NTS*, 16 (1970), pp. 305-317.
Thüsing, W., "Erhöhungsvorstellung und Parusieerwartung in der ältesten nachösterlichen Christologie," *BZ*, 11 (1967), pp. 95-108, 205-222 and *BZ*, 12 (1968), pp. 54-80, 223-240.
– *Die Erhöhung und Verherrlichung Jesu im Johannesevangelium* (NTA, 21, 1/2), Münster, 1960.
Tiede, D.L., *The Charismatic Figure as Miracle Worker* (SBL Dissertation Series, 1), Missoula, Mont., 1972.
– "G. Petzke, Die Traditionen über Apollonius von Tyana und das Neue Testament (Review)," *JBL*, 92 (1973), pp. 465-467.
Tödt, H.E., *Der Menschensohn in der synoptischen Überlieferung*, Gütersloh, 1963(='59).
Torrey, C.C., *The Composition and Date of Acts* (HThSt, 1), Cambridge, 1916.
Trilling, W., *Das wahre Israel–Studien zur Theologie des Matthäus-Evangeliums*, Mü., 1964[3].
– *Christusverkündigung in den synoptischen Evangelien. Beispiele gattungsgemäßer Auslegung*, (BHB, IV), Mü., 1969.
Tromp, N.J., *Primitive Conceptions of Death and the Nether World in the Old Testament* (BeO, 21), Rome, 1969.
Trompf, G.W., "The First Resurrection Appearance and the Ending of Mark's Gospel," *NTS*, 18 ('71/'72), pp. 308-330.
Trummer, P., *Anastasis. Ein Beitrag zur Auslegung und Auslegungsgeschichte von I Kor 15* (Diss.), Graz, 1966.
van Unnik, W.C., "Die 'Geöffneten Himmel' in der Offenbarungsvision des Apokryphons des Johannes," *Apophoreta* (Fst. E. Haenchen), Berlin, 1964, pp. 269-280.
– "Luke-Acts, a Storm Center in Contemporary Scholarship," *Studies in Luke-Acts* (Essays presented in honor of P. Schubert, eds. L.E. Keck and J.E. Martyn), Nashville, Tenn., 1966, pp. 15-32.
van Vliet, H., *No Single Testimony. A Study on the Adoption of the Law of Deut. 19,15 par. in the New Testament* (StTh, IV), Utrecht, 1958.
Vögtle, A., "Wie kam es zur Artikulierung des Osterglaubens?," *BuL*, 14/4 (1973), pp. 231-244.
Völter, D., "Petrusevangelium oder Ägypterevangelium," *ZNW*, 6 (1905), pp. 368-372.

de Vries, J., *Heldenlied und Heldensage* (Sammlung Dalp, 78), Bern, 1961.
Waetjen, H., "The Ending of Mark and the Gospel's Shift in Eschatology," *ASTI*, 4 (1965), pp. 114-131.
Wagner, G., *Das religionsgeschichtliche Problem von Römer 6,1-11* (AThANT, 39), Zürich, 1962.
von Waldow, H.E., "Some Thoughts on Old Testament Form Criticism," *SBL Seminar Papers* (Atlanta, Ga.), 2 (1971), pp. 587-600.
– "Theophanie," *VF* (BhEvTh), 14/1 (1969), pp. 69-76.
Walker, N., "After Three Days," *NovTest*, 4 (1960), pp. 261-262.
Walker, W.O., Jr., "Postcrucifixion Appearances and Christian Origins," *JBL*, 88 (1969), pp. 157-165.
– "Christian Origins and Resurrection Faith," *JRel*, 52 (1972), pp. 41-55. A copy of an address, bearing the same title and of which this article forms an expansion of the final section, given by the author at the Toronto annual meeting of SBL on Nov. 18, 1969 was graciously supplied upon request on Jan. 2, 1970 along with an offset print of his 1969 JBL article.
Walter, N., "G. Petzke, Die Traditionen über Apollonius von Tyana und das Neue Testament (Review)," *ThLZ*, 97 (1972), cols. 29-31.
– "Eine vormatthäische Schilderung der Auferstehung Jesu," *NTS*, 19 ('72/'73), pp. 415-429.
Warmington, E.H., "Ennius," *OCD*, London, 1961(='49), p. 316.
Weber, W., *Christusmystik. Eine religionsgeschichtliche Darstellung der paulinischen Christusfrömmigkeit*, Leipzig, 1924.
Weeden, Th.J., "The Heresy that Necessitated Mark's Gospel," *ZNW*, 59 (1968), pp. 145-158.
– *Mark–Traditions in Conflict*, Phil., 1971.
Weinreich, O., "De dis ignotis quaestiones selectae," *ARW*, 18 (1915), pp. 1-52.
– *Antike Heilungswunder. Untersuchungen zum Wunderglauben der Griechen und Römer* (RVV,8,1), Gießen, 1909.
– *Fabel, Aretalogie, Novelle. Beiträge zu Phädrus, Petron, Martial und Apuleius* (SAH, 7), Heidelberg, 1931.
Weiß, J., *Das Urchristentum*, Gött., 1917.
Wendland, P., *Die hellenistisch-römische Kultur in ihren Beziehungen zu Judentum und Christentum* (HNT, expanded from 1912 3rd ed. with bibliography by H. Dorrie), Tüb., 1972[4].
Wendt, H.H., "Die Hauptquelle der Apostelgeschichte," *ZNW*, 24 (1925), pp. 293-305.
Weniger, L., "Theophanien, altgriechische Götteradvente," *ARW*, 22 ('23/'24), pp. 16-57.
Westermann, C., "Arten der Erzählung in der Genesis," *Forschung am Alten Testament* (ThB, 24, AT), Mü., 1964, pp. 9-91.
– "Alttestamentliche Elemente in Lukas 2,1-20," *Tradition und Glaube* (Fst. K.G. Kuhn, ed. G. Jeremias *et al.*), Gött., 1971, pp. 317-327.
– *Das Loben Gottes in den Psalmen*, Gött., 1963[3].
White, H.C., "The Divine Oath in Genesis," *JBL*, 92 (1973), pp. 165-179.
Wichelhaus, M., "Am ersten Tage der Woche," *NovTest*, 11 (Fasc. I/2, 1969), pp. 45-66.
Wikenhauser, A., *Die Apostelgeschichte* (RNT, 4), Regensburg, 1956.
– *Das Evangelium nach Johannes* (RNT, 4), Regensburg, 1961[3].
Wilckens, U., "Das Offenbarungsverständnis in der Geschichte des Urchristentums," *Offenbarung als Geschichte*, ed. W. Pannenberg (*KuD*, Bh 1), Gött., 1970[4], pp. 42-90.
– "Der Ursprung der Überlieferung der Erscheinungen des Auferstandenen," *Dogma und Denkstrukturen* (Fst. E. Schlink, ed. W. Joest and W. Pannenberg), Gött., 1963, pp. 56-95.
– "Die Perikope vom leeren Grabe Jesu in der nachmarkinischen Traditionsgeschichte," *Fst. Friedrich Smend*, Berlin, 1963, pp. 30-41.
– "Jesusüberlieferung und Christuskerygma–Zwei Wege urchristlicher Überlieferungsgeschichte," *ThViat*, 10 ('65/'66), Berlin, 1966, pp. 310-339.
– "Die Überlieferungsgeschichte der Auferstehung Jesu," *Die Bedeutung der Auferstehungsbotschaft für den Glauben an Jesus Christus* (EKD Schriftreihe, ed. F. Viering), Gütersloh, 1968[7](='66), pp. 41-63.
– "Interpreting Luke-Acts in a period of Existentialist Theology," *Studies in Luke-Acts* (Essays presented in Honor of P. Schubert, eds. L.E. Keck and J.L. Martyn), London, 1968, pp. 60-83.
– *Die Missionsreden der Apostelgeschichte. Form- und traditionsgeschichtliche Untersuchungen*, Neukirchen, 1963[2].

Wilckens, U., *Auferstehung. Das biblische Auferstehungszeugnis historisch untersucht und erklärt* (TTh, ed. H.J. Schultz, 4), Berlin, 1970 (= also, Gütersloher Taschenbuch, 80, Gütersloh, 1974).
Wilcox, M., *The Semitisms of Acts*, Oxford, 1965.
Wilder, A.N., "Variant Traditions of the Resurrection in Acts," *JBL*, 62 (1943), pp. 307-318.
Wilhelm, R., *Die Märchen der Weltliteratur*, Jena, 1917.
Wilkens, W., *Die Entstehungsgeschichte des vierten Evangeliums*, Zollikon, 1958.
Williams, C.S.C., *A Commentary on the Acts of the Apostles* (BNTC), London, 1964.
Wilson, S.G., "The Ascension: A Critique and an Interpretation," *ZNW*, 59 (1968), pp. 269-281.
Windisch, H., *Johannes und die Synoptiker. Wollte der vierte Evangelist die älteren Evangelien ergänzen oder ersetzen?* (UNT, ed. H. Windisch, 12), Leipzig, 1926.
– *Paulus und Christus. Ein biblisch-religionsgeschichtlicher Vergleich* (UNT, ed. H. Windisch, 24), Leipzig, 1934.
Winter, P., "The Treatment of His Sources by the Third Evangelist in Luke XXI-XXIV," *Studia Theologia*, 8 (Fasc. II, 1954), pp. 138-172.
– "I Corinthians XV, 3b-7," *NovTest*, 2 (1958), pp. 142-150.
Witt, R.E., *Isis in the Graeco-Roman World* (*Aspects of Greek and Roman Life*, ed. H.H. Scullard), London, 1971.
Zahn, Th., *Das Evangelium des Lucas* (KNT, III), Leipzig, 1920[3] and [4].
– *Die Apostelgeschichte des Lucas* (KNT, V, 1), Leipzig, 1922[3].
Zenger, E., *Die Sinaitheophanie. Untersuchungen zum jahwistischen und elohistischen Geschichtswerk*, Würzburg, 1972.
Zimmerli, W., "Ich bin Jahwe," *Geschichte und Altes Testament* (Fst. A. Alt, BhTh, ed. G. Ebeling, 16), Tüb., 1953.
– "Sinaibund und Abrahambund. Ein Beitrag zum Verständnis der Priesterschrift," *ThZ*, 16 (1960), pp. 268-280.
– "'Offenbarung' im Alten Testament," *EvTh*, 22 (NF 17, 1962), pp. 15-31.
Zumstein, J., "Matthieu 28:16-20," *RThPh*, 22 (1972), pp. 14-33.

Index of Passages *

Old Testament

Extra-Canonical Sources

* all references to footnotes are preceded by "n." or "ns."

New Testament

Extra-Canonical Sources and Apostolic Fathers

Other Ancient Writers

Index of Modern Authors*

* all references to footnotes are preceded by "n." or "ns."

TEXT-SYNOPSIS

This Text-Synopsis of NT and OT appearance stories offers a rapid overview of structures and motifs in accord with the breakdown of categories in the left-hand columns. To avoid oversimplification and reduction to the lowest common denominator many of the particulars characteristic of the dynamic interplay of structure and motif for each story have been retained. Some features are clearly redactional, but in some cases they represent a re-formation of an already existing form of expression accessible now only through the later adaption. It is to be granted that the retention of such features makes the Text-Synopsis somewhat unwieldy, but since this was the only way to preserve the integrity of expression for each story in its own right, it was deemed necessary. Chains of expression in each verticle column can be followed by watching the progression of verse references.